Computational Biology: Concepts and Applications

Computational Biology: Concepts and Applications

Edited by **Daniel McGuire**

New York

Published by Callisto Reference,
106 Park Avenue, Suite 200,
New York, NY 10016, USA
www.callistoreference.com

Computational Biology: Concepts and Applications
Edited by Daniel McGuire

International Standard Book Number: 978-1-63239-118-6 (Hardback)

Printed in the United States of America.

Contents

Preface

With rapid advances in science and technology and continuous research and development in all academic fields, it is all but natural that they have grown much beyond their initial boundaries and scope. New subjects have opened new windows of possibilities for the entire mankind and have enabled to unlock various mysteries of nature.

One such subject is computational biology that is a dynamic application of mathematical modeling with computational techniques in the study of social, behavioral and biological systems. A part of this study is computational genomics. It is the study of genomes of cells and organisms. Under this a very unique project called the human genome project is being undertaken by researchers across the world. This project aims to sequence the entire human genome into a set of data to study, analyze and discover new facts and knowledge about every individual. The success of this project would lead to personalized medicine for an individual patient.

With the rapid progress in these sequencing technologies, latest and more effective transcriptomes can be sequenced at a lower cost. But then there is a demerit in the new technologies that being their length which is too short and that poses a stiff challenge to sequence assembly algorithms.

A very close connection with humanity happened when the researchers started using the tools of computational biology to discover the accurate tools for cancer detection and diagnosis. Multiple antigen miniarrays were the means to find the tools for cancer detection; these can be validated by examining their characteristics in classifying individuals as either cancer patients or normal.

Another highly advanced wing of computational biology is study of bistable behavior of phage lambda genetic switch.

This book is a profound study of highly advanced facets of computational biology and their far reaching consequences on the humanity and other living organisms. The authors must be congratulated and encouraged to go ahead and find newer ways and means of serving, protecting and strengthening the mankind.

Editor

Numerical Characterization of DNA Sequence Based on Dinucleotides

Xingqin Qi,[1] Edgar Fuller,[2] Qin Wu,[3] and Cun-Quan Zhang[2]

[1] School of Mathematics and Statistics, Shandong University at Weihai, Weihai 264209, China
[2] Department of Mathematics, West Virginia University, Morgantown, WV 26506, USA
[3] School of IOT Engineering, Jiangnan University, Wuxi 214122, China

Correspondence should be addressed to Xingqin Qi, qixingqin@163.com

Academic Editors: S. Cacchione and A. Pask

Sequence comparison is a primary technique for the analysis of DNA sequences. In order to make quantitative comparisons, one devises mathematical descriptors that capture the essence of the base composition and distribution of the sequence. Alignment methods and graphical techniques (where each sequence is represented by a curve in high-dimension Euclidean space) have been used popularly for a long time. In this contribution we will introduce a new nongraphical and nonalignment approach based on the frequencies of the dinucleotide XY in DNA sequences. The most important feature of this method is that it not only identifies adjacent XY pairs but also nonadjacent XY ones where X and Y are separated by some number of nucleotides. This methodology preserves information in DNA sequence that is ignored by other methods. We test our method on the coding regions of exon-1 of β–globin for 11 species, and the utility of this new method is demonstrated.

1. Introduction

The number of identifiable DNA sequences responsible for various physiological structures is rapidly increasing as more and more collected DNA sequences are added to scientific databases. It is, however, difficult to obtain information directly from sequences since the sheer volume of data is computational demanding. It is one of the challenges for biologists to analyze mathematically the large volume of genomic DNA sequence data. Many schemes have been proposed to numerically characterize DNA sequences.

Sequence alignment has been used as a very powerful tool for comparison of two closely related genomes at the base-by-base nucleotide sequence level. This method relies heavily on the orderings of nucleotides appearing in the sequence. With the divergence of species over time, though, genomic rearrangements and in particular genetic shuffling make sequence alignment unreliable or impossible.

Graphical techniques are another powerful tool for the analysis and visualization of DNA sequences. Using graphical approaches can provide intuitive pictures or useful insights that assist the analysis of complicated relations between DNA sequences. This methodology starts with a graphical representation of DNA sequence which could be based on 2D, 3D, 4D, 5D, and 6D spaces and represents DNA as matrices by associating with the selected geometrical objects, then vectors composed of the invariants of matrices will be used to compare DNA sequences, see [1–10]. Such schemes have an advantage in that they offer an instant, though, visual and qualitative summary of the lengthy DNA sequences. This approach also involves many unresolved questions. For example, how does one obtain suitable matrices to characterize DNA sequences and how are invariants selected suitable for sequence comparisons? In many cases, the calculation of the matrices or the invariants will become more and more difficult with the length of the sequence. There are also approaches which could arrive a mathematical representation of DNA sequences by nongraphical ways, see [11–13]. And more recently, a new representation based on symbolic dynamics [14] and a new representation based on digital signal method [15] are also illustrated.

In this contribution, we introduce a novel nongraphical and nonalignment approach for DNA sequence comparison. We use DNA sequence directly by considering the frequencies of dinucleotide. We represent each DNA sequence by a dinucleotide frequency matrix or by a dinucleotide frequency vector, based on which two distance measurements are defined, respectively. Then comparisons between DNA sequences could be carried out by calculating the distances between these mathematical descriptors. The most important feature of this method is that the mathematical descriptors not only take into consideration the frequencies of adjacent XY pairs but also of nonadjacent XY pairs. In this way, information contained in the relative spacing of nucleotides is preserved. The method is very simple and fast, and does not require sequence alignment or sequence graphical representation which would cause complex calculations. It can be used to analyze both short and long DNA sequences. As an application, this method is tested on the exon-1 coding sequences of β-globin for 11 species and the results are consistent with what have been reported previously [5, 9, 12, 14, 15], which prove the utility of this new method.

2. Dinucleotide Frequency Matrix and Dinucleotide Frequency Vector

Typically, DNA sequence data is represented as a string of letters A, C, G, and T, which signify the four nucleotides: adenine, cytosine, guanine, and thymine, respectively. There are 16 possible dinucleotides, that is, $\Omega = \{$AT, AA, AC, AG, TT, TA, TC, TG, GT, GA, GC, GG, CT, CA, CC, CG$\}$. In the following, we always use XY to represent dinucleotides, and note that dinucleotide XY is distinguished from.

Let s be a sequence of length n and denote the number of occurrences of adjacent XY in s by $Y^{(1)}$. Clearly, if s is a sequence of length, then $\sum_{XY \in \Omega} XY^{(1)} = n - 1$. The occurrence frequency for XY is defined as

$$f_{XY}^{(1)} = \frac{XY^{(1)}}{(n-1)}. \tag{1}$$

We get one 16-dimensional vector $\hat{f}^{(1)}$ associated with sequence s based on adjacent dinucleotides:

$$\hat{f}^{(1)} = \left(f_{AT}^{(1)}, f_{AA}^{(1)}, f_{AC}^{(1)}, \ldots, f_{CT}^{(1)}, f_{CA}^{(1)}, f_{CC}^{(1)}, f_{CG}^{(1)} \right). \tag{2}$$

Notice that there would be a loss of information when one condenses sequence s to a single 16-dimensional vector. A way to recover some of the lost information associated with a sequence s to a single 16-vector is to introduce additional 16 vectors to store the frequency information of pairs XY when X and Y are not adjacent but are separated at various distance. For example, if $s =$ ATCGATC, the *adjacent* dinucleotides are AT, TC, CG, GA with occurrence frequency 2/6, 2/6, 1/6, and 1/6, respectively. The dinucleotides *at distance* 2 (i.e., separated by one nucleotide) in s are AC, TG, CA, GT, AC with occurrence frequency 2/5, 1/5, 1/5, and 1/5, respectively. These two 16-dimensional vectors will contain additional information beyond that found in the initial dinucleotide vector.

Generally, let s be a sequence of length. Denote $XY^{(d)}$ as the number of occurrence of XY in s when X and Y are

separated by $d - 1$ nucleotides. Clearly, $\sum_{XY \in \Omega} XY^{(d)} = n - d$. Define

$$f_{XY}^{(d)} = \frac{XY^{(d)}}{(n-d)}, \tag{3}$$

as the occurrence frequency. For each given integer, we could get one 16-dimensional vector $\hat{f}^{(d)}$ associated with sequence s:

$$\hat{f}^{(d)} = \left(f_{AT}^{(d)}, f_{AA}^{(d)}, f_{AC}^{(d)}, \ldots, f_{CT}^{(d)}, f_{CA}^{(d)}, f_{CC}^{(d)}, f_{CG}^{(d)} \right). \tag{4}$$

The distance d between X and Y could be 1, 2 or even larger integers. When we scan sequence s to count the occurrence of dinucleotides XY at distance, the nucleotides of s from position 1 to $(n - d)$ are counted as "X", while the nucleotides of s from position $(d + 1)$ to n are counted as "Y". When $d \leq \lfloor (n - 1)/2 \rfloor$, there is an overlapping interval $[d+1, n-d]$ between the two intervals $[1, n-d]$ and $[d + 1, n]$, which means the nucleotides in the overlapping interval will counted as both X and Y; but if $d > \lceil (n-1)/2 \rceil$, the two intervals $[1, n-d]$ and $[d+1, n]$ will disjoint, and the information of these nucleotides in the interval $[n - d + 1, d]$ will be lost. So in the following, to avoid loss of information, d must not be larger than $\lceil (n-1)/2 \rceil$, that is, $d \leq \lceil (n-1)/2 \rceil$. Furthermore, to make the information in $\hat{f}^{(d)}$ more accurate, we hope that the overlapping interval $[d + 1, n - d]$ will be large enough. Based on this intuition, we would prefer to these d such that $(n - 2d)/n \geq 50\%$, which guarantees that more than half of the nucleotides in sequence s will be counted as both X and Y. So d is restricted to $d \leq \lfloor n/4 \rfloor$ for each DNA sequence s with length.

Let s be a DNA sequence of length, for a given $d \leq \lfloor n/4 \rfloor$, the *dinucleotide frequency matrix* associated with s is defined as

$$F(s) = \begin{pmatrix} \hat{f}^{(1)} \\ \hat{f}^{(2)} \\ \hat{f}^{(3)} \\ \vdots \\ \hat{f}^{(d)} \end{pmatrix}, \tag{5}$$

where $\hat{f}^{(i)}$ is the 16-dimensional occurrence frequency vector when X and Y are separated by $(i - 1)$ nucleotides. The size of matrix $F(s)$ is $d \times 16$.

We also present another mathematical descriptor associated with s named *dinucleotide frequency vector* which is defined as

$$\hat{F}(s) = \left(\hat{f}^{(1)}, \hat{f}^{(2)}, \hat{f}^{(3)}, \ldots, \hat{f}^{(d)} \right), \tag{6}$$

then $\hat{F}(s)$ is a $1 \times 16d$ row vector.

3. Two Distance Measurements Based on Dinucleotide Frequency

From Section 2, we get correspondences between one DNA sequence s and the dinucleotide frequency matrix $F(s)$ and the dinucleotide frequency vector $\hat{F}(s)$. Note that the sizes of $F(s)$ and $\hat{F}(s)$ all depend on. To make the comparisons for a set of DNA sequences meaningful, we should use an identical d for all these DNA sequences. Denote the set of DNA sequences by, by the discussion in Section 2, we define the identical d_0 as

$$d_0 = \min_{s \in S} \left\lfloor \frac{(|s|)}{4} \right\rfloor, \tag{7}$$

where $|s|$ is the length of s. The choice of d_0 will guarantee that either the frequency matrix or the frequency vector will involve enough accurate information, and the dinucleotide frequency matrices and dinucleotide frequency vectors associated with sequences in S all have the same size. DNA sequences comparisons could be completed by studying their corresponding matrices and vectors. In the following we will introduce two different distance measurements based on dinucleotide frequencies matrix and dinucleotide frequency vector, respectively.

3.1. City Block Distance for Dinucleotide Frequency Matrix. Given two DNA sequences s and h, then we get the dinucleotide frequency matrix $F(s)$ and $F(h)$ as in Section 2, comparison between s and h becomes comparison between $F(s)$ and $F(h)$. Using this, we define the city block distance $d_1(s, h)$ between s and h as

$$d_1(s, h) = \sum_{1 \leq i \leq d_0, \, 1 \leq j \leq 16} \left| F_{ij}(s) - F_{ij}(h) \right|. \tag{8}$$

3.2. Cosine Distance for Dinucleotide Frequency Vector. We also obtain a mapping from a DNA sequence s to a vector $\hat{F}(s)$ in the $16d_0$-dimensional linear space. Comparison between DNA sequences also could become comparison between these $16d_0$-dimensional vectors. This is based on the assumption that two DNA sequences are similar if the corresponding $16d_0$-dimensional vectors in the $16d_0$-dimensional space have similar directions. Given two DNA sequences s and h, the dinucleotide frequency vectors are $\hat{F}(s)$ and $\hat{F}(h)$, we define the cosine distance $d_2(s, h)$ between s and h as

$$d_2(s, h) = 1 - \cos\left(\hat{F}(s), \hat{F}(h)\right), \tag{9}$$

where $\cos(\hat{F}(s), \hat{F}(h))$ is the cosine value of the included angle between vectors $\hat{F}(s)$ and $\hat{F}(h)$.

4. Applications and Experimental Results

4.1. Experimental Results. A comparison between a pair of DNA sequences to judge their similarity or dissimilarity could be carried out by calculating the distance $d_1(s, h)$ or $d_2(s, h)$. The smaller is the distance, the much similar are the two DNA sequences (The code is available on request).

To test the utility of above method, we make a comparison for the coding regions of exon-1 of β-globin gene for 11 different species, which were also studied by Randić et al. in [12]. Table 1 presents their accession numbers in

TABLE 1: ID Information for Exon-1 of β-globin gene of 11 species.

Species	ID/Accession	Database	length
Human	U01317	NCBI	92
Chimpanzee	X02345	NCBI	105
Gorilla	X61109	NCBI	93
Lemur	M15734	NCBI	92
Rat	X06701	NCBI	92
Mouse	V00722	NCBI	93
Rabbit	V00882	NCBI	92
Goat	M15387	NCBI	86
Bovine	X00376	NCBI	86
Opossum	J03643	NCBI	92
Gallus	V00409	NCBI	92

NCBI database, while Table 2 lists these 11 coding sequences concretely.

At first, we present the similarity/dissimilarity matrix based on distance measurement d_1, see Table 3. When we examine this table, we notice that smallest entries are always associated with the pairs (human, chimpanzee) with $d_1 = 2.5567$, (human, gorilla) with $d_1 = 2.4026$, and (gorilla, chimpanzee) with $d_1 = 2.7338$. That means the more similar species pairs are human-gorilla, human-chimpanzee, and gorilla-chimpanzee. We also observe that the largest entry $d_1 = 9.0347$ is associated with gallus and lemur and the larger entries appear in the rows belonging to gallus and opossum, which is consistent with the facts that gallus is the only nonmammalian species among these 11 species and opossum is the most remote species from the remaining mammals. These observed facts are consistent with the results reported in previous studies [5, 9, 12] determined by matrix invariants techniques, and also consistent with the reported results from nongraphical means [14, 15]. More interesting, in Table 3, the distance between goat and bovine is $d_1 = 2.3438$, which is actually the smallest entry in Table 3. That implies goat and bovine are regarded to be much similar to each other by our method, which is consistent with their biology taxonomy that bovine and goat are both even-toed ungulates and belong to the family of "Bovidae".

Table 4 presents the similarity/dissimilarity matrix based on the distance measurement d_2. The smallest entries are also associated with the pairs (human, chimpanzee) with $d_2 = 0.0087$; (human, gorilla), with $d_2 = 0.0074$, and (gorilla, chimpanzee), and with $d_2 = 0.0112$. We find that the largest entry ($d_2 = 0.1139$) is associated with (gallus, lemur), and the rows corresponding to gallus and opossum have larger entries, which is also consistent with the facts that gallus is the only nonmammalian species among these 11 species and opossum is the most remote species from the remaining mammals. The observed facts in Table 4 are consistent with the previously reported results in [5, 9, 12, 14, 15] as well. And the distance between goat and bovine ($d_2 = 0.0109$) is also much smaller as we expect.

We can see that there is an overall qualitative agreement between Tables 3 and 4. To see it visually, we denote

TABLE 2: The coding sequence of exon-1 of β-globin gene for 11 species.

Species	DNA sequence
Human	ATGGTGCACCTGACTCCTGAGGAGAAGTCTGCCGTTACTGCCCTGTGGGGCAAGGTGAACGTGGAT-GAAGTTGGTGGTGAGGCCCTGGGCAG
Chimpanzee	ATGGTGCACCTGACTCCTGAGGAGAAGTCTGCCGTTACTGCCCTGTGGGGCAAGGTGAACGTGGAT-GAAGTTGGTGGTGAGGCCCTGGGCAGGTTGGTATCAAGG
Gorilla	ATGGTGCACCTGACTCCTGAGGAGAAGTCTGCCGTTACTGCCCTGTGGGGCAAGGTGAACGTGGAT-GAAGTTGGTGGTGAGGCCCTGGGCAGG
Lemur	ATGACTTTGCTGAGTGCTGAGGAGAATGCTCATGTCACCTCTCTGTGGGGCAAGGTGGATGTAGAG-AAAGTTGGTGGCGAGGCCTTGGGCAG
Rat	ATGGTGCACCTAACTGATGCTGAGAAGGCTACTGTTAGTGGCCTGTGGGGAAAGGTGAACCCTGAT-AATGTTGGCGCTGAGGCCCTGGGCAG
Mouse	ATGGTTGCACCTGACTGATGCTGAGAAGTCTGCTGTCTCTTGCCTGTGGGCAAAGGTGAACCCCGA-TGAAGTTGGTGGTGAGGCCCTGGGCAGG
Rabbit	ATGGTGCATCTGTCCAGTGAGGAGAAGTCTGCGGTCACTGCCCTGTGGGGCAAGGTGAATGTGGAA-GAAGTTGGTGGTGAGGCCCTGGGCAG
Goat	ATGCTGACTGCTGAGGAGAAGGCTGCCGTCACCGGCTTCTGGGGCAAGGTGAAAGTGGATGAAGTT-GGTGCTGAGGCCCTGGGCAG
Bovine	ATGCTGACTGCTGAGGAGAAGGCTGCCGTCACCGCCTTTTGGGGCAAGGTGAAAGTGGATGAAGTT-GGTGGTGAGGCCCTGGGCAG
Opossum	ATGGTGCACTTGACTTCTGAGGAGAAGAACTGCATCACTACCATCTGGTCTAAGGTGCAGGTTGAC-CAGACTGGTGGTGAGGCCCTTGGCAG
Gallus	ATGGTGCACTGGACTGCTGAGGAGAAGCAGCTCATCACCGGCCTCTGGGGCAAGGTCAATGTGGCC-GAATGTGGGGCCGAAGCCCTGGCCAG

TABLE 3: The upper triangular part of the dissimilarity/similarity matrix based on d_1.

Species	Human	Chimpanzee	Gorilla	Lemur	Rat	Mouse	Rabbit	Goat	Bovine	Opossum	Gallus
Human	0	2.5567	2.4026	6.4922	5.6622	4.9144	4.2904	5.3220	4.8306	6.8358	7.4959
Chimpanzee		0	2.7338	6.5340	5.9455	5.1613	4.9587	5.6525	4.9670	7.4568	7.9791
Gorilla			0	7.0466	6.2344	5.2819	5.0310	5.3353	4.9340	7.8956	8.0582
Lemur				0	6.9735	6.8419	5.6647	6.9332	6.0195	8.2293	9.0347
Rat					0	5.2540	6.8004	6.5847	6.2545	7.5359	8.2347
Mouse						0	6.5730	6.7863	6.4133	7.2900	7.8317
Rabbit							0	5.9265	5.2974	8.0743	8.3210
Goat								0	2.3438	8.0158	7.7129
Bovine									0	7.9847	8.2938
Opossum										0	8.0268
Gallus											0

TABLE 4: The upper triangular part of the dissimilarity/similarity matrix based on d_2.

Species	Human	Chimpanzee	Gorilla	Lemur	Rat	Mouse	Rabbit	Goat	Bovine	Opossum	Gallus
Human	0	0.0087	0.0074	0.0567	0.0464	0.0372	0.0253	0.0354	0.0287	0.0719	0.0819
Chimpanzee		0	0.0112	0.0564	0.0487	0.0383	0.0303	0.0403	0.0320	0.0793	0.0899
Gorilla			0	0.0619	0.0538	0.0398	0.0312	0.0357	0.0302	0.0887	0.0877
Lemur				0	0.0691	0.0635	0.0454	0.0616	0.0463	0.0939	0.1139
Rat					0	0.0417	0.0631	0.0592	0.0552	0.0832	0.1048
Mouse						0	0.0588	0.0573	0.0528	0.0765	0.0932
Rabbit							0	0.0444	0.0349	0.0998	0.0933
Goat								0	0.0109	0.0948	0.0792
Bovine									0	0.0923	0.0937
Opossum										0	0.0897
Gallus											0

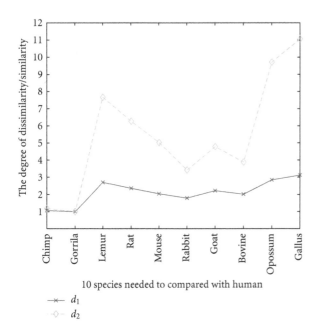

FIGURE 1: The degree of dissimilarity/similarity of the other 10 species with human, where the degree of dissimilarity/similarity of the pair human-gorilla is defined relatively as 1.

the degree of dissimilarity/similarity of the pair human-gorilla as 1 in each table, then the results of the examination of the degree of dissimilarity/similarity between human and other several species under the two distance measurements are shown in Figure 1. We can see that the curvilinear trend of these two curves are almost the same, which demonstrates the overall agreement among dissimilarity/similarities obtained by these two distance methods.

4.2. Discussion. For the above exon-1 coding data of 11 species, d_0 is chosen to be 21 followed by (7). A 336-dimensional vector is used to characterize each DNA sequence under the second distance measure. To confirm the efficacy of the vectors constructed in this high-dimensional data representation, we perform principal component analysis (PCA) on these 336 parameters. Figure 2(a) shows the projection of the 11 vectors on a 2D property space composed of the top two principal components PC1, PC2. We can see that in the 2D space, gallus (labeled by "⊙") and opossum (labeled by "∇") are furthest from the other 9 species, and human, chimpanzee, and gorilla are very close to each other. These result are consistent with what we have got from Table 4. Note that these top two principal components contribute 48% (see Figure 2(b)) to the total information. Some information is lost when we do the projection, for example, bovine seems much closer to rabbit than goat in the 2D projection, but we know this is not true in Table 4 when all 336 parameters are considered. However, this rough approximation confirms that our mathematical descriptor characterizes DNA sequence structure effectively.

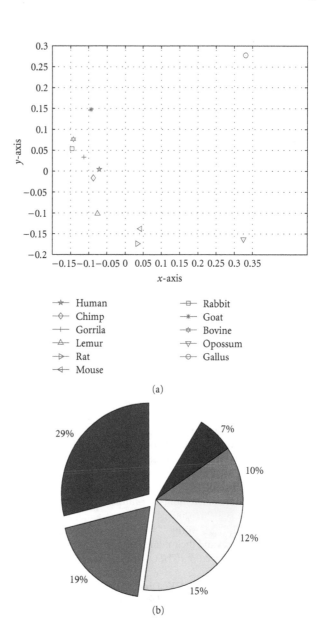

FIGURE 2: (a) The projection of the 336-dimensional vectors of 11 species on a 2D space composed of the top two principal components; (b) The contributions of the first 6 principal components.

5. Conclusion

In this paper, we have presented a new method based on dinucleotide frequencies for DNA sequence comparison. The dinucleotide frequency matrix and dinucleotide frequency vector are used to mathematically characterize a DNA sequence. The most important feature of this method is that the mathematical descriptors not only involve the frequencies of adjacent XY pairs but also nonadjacent XY pairs (i.e., when X and Y are separated by various number of nucleotides), such that a lot of important information is avoided to lose. This new method does not require sequence alignment or sequence graphical representation, which avoids the complex calculation found in either sequence alignment or sequence graphical representation.

The method is very simple and fast, and it can be used to analyze both short and long DNA sequences with high efficiencies.

Acknowledgments

This work is supported partly by Shandong Province Natural Science Foundation of China with no. ZR2010AQ018 and no. ZR2011FQ010 and partly by Independent Innovation Foundation of Shandong University with no. 2010ZRJQ005. This project also has been partially supported by a WV EPSCoR Grant and an NSA Grant H98230-12-1-0233.

References

[1] E. Hamori and J. Ruskin, "H curves, a novel method of representation of nucleotide series especially suited for long DNA sequences," *Journal of Biological Chemistry*, vol. 258, no. 2, pp. 1318–1327, 1983.

[2] A. Nandy, "A new graphical representation and analysis of DNA sequence structure: I. Methodology and Application to Globin Genes," *Current Science*, vol. 66, pp. 309–314, 1994.

[3] M. Randić, M. Vračko, A. Nandy, and S. C. Basak, "On 3-D graphical representation of DNA primary sequences and their numerical characterization," *Journal of Chemical Information and Computer Sciences*, vol. 40, no. 5, pp. 1235–1244, 2000.

[4] Y. Zhang, B. Liao, and K. Ding, "On 2D graphical representation of DNA sequence of nondegeneracy," *Chemical Physics Letters*, vol. 411, no. 1-3, pp. 28–32, 2005.

[5] M. Randić, M. Vračko, N. Lerš, and D. Plavšić, "Analysis of similarity/dissimilarity of DNA sequences based on novel 2-D graphical representation," *Chemical Physics Letters*, vol. 371, no. 1-2, pp. 202–207, 2003.

[6] B. Liao and T. M. Wang, "3-D graphical representation of DNA sequences and their numerical characterization," *Journal of Molecular Structure (THEOCHEM)*, vol. 681, no. 1–3, pp. 209–212, 2004.

[7] Y. Zhang, B. Liao, and K. Ding, "On 3DD-curves of DNA sequences," *Molecular Simulation*, vol. 32, no. 1, pp. 29–34, 2006.

[8] R. Chi and K. Ding, "Novel 4D numerical representation of DNA sequences," *Chemical Physics Letters*, vol. 407, no. 1–3, pp. 63–67, 2005.

[9] B. Liao, R. Li, W. Zhu, and X. Xiang, "On the similarity of DNA primary sequences based on 5-D representation," *Journal of Mathematical Chemistry*, vol. 42, no. 1, pp. 47–57, 2007.

[10] B. Liao and T. M. Wang, "Analysis of similarity/dissimilarity of DNA sequences based on nonoverlapping triplets of nucleotide bases," *Journal of Chemical Information and Computer Sciences*, vol. 44, no. 5, pp. 1666–1670, 2004.

[11] M. Randić, "Condensed representation of DNA primary sequences," *Journal of Chemical Information and Computer Sciences*, vol. 40, no. 1, pp. 50–56, 2000.

[12] M. Randić, X. Guo, and S. C. Basak, "On the characterization of DNA primary sequences by triplet of nucleic acid bases," *Journal of Chemical Information and Computer Sciences*, vol. 41, no. 3, pp. 619–626, 2001.

[13] Y. Zhang, "A simple method to construct the similarity matrices of DNA sequences," *Match*, vol. 60, no. 2, pp. 313–324, 2008.

[14] S. Wang, F. Tian, W. Feng, and X. Liu, "Applications of representation method for DNA sequences based on symbolic dynamics," *Journal of Molecular Structure: THEOCHEM*, vol. 909, no. 1–3, pp. 33–42, 2009.

[15] Z. H. Qi and X. Q. Qi, "Numerical characterization of DNA sequences based on digital signal method," *Computers in Biology and Medicine*, vol. 39, no. 4, pp. 388–391, 2009.

Transmission Model of Hepatitis B Virus with the Migration Effect

Muhammad Altaf Khan,[1] **Saeed Islam,**[1] **Muhammad Arif,**[1] **and Zahoor ul Haq**[2]

[1] *Department of Mathematics, Abdul Wali Khan University, Mardan, Khyber Pakhtunkhwa, Pakistan*
[2] *Department of Management Sciences, Abdul Wali Khan University, Mardan, Khyber Pakhtunkhwa, Pakistan*

Correspondence should be addressed to Muhammad Altaf Khan; altafdir@gmail.com

Academic Editor: Kanury Rao

Hepatitis B is a globally infectious disease. Mathematical modeling of HBV transmission is an interesting research area. In this paper, we present characteristics of HBV virus transmission in the form of a mathematical model. We analyzed the effect of immigrants in the model to study the effect of immigrants for the host population. We added the following flow parameters: "the transmission between migrated and exposed class" and "the transmission between migrated and acute class." With these new features, we obtained a compartment model of six differential equations. First, we find the basic threshold quantity Ro and then find the local asymptotic stability of disease-free equilibrium and endemic equilibrium. Furthermore, we find the global stability of the disease-free and endemic equilibria. Previous similar publications have not added the kind of information about the numerical results of the model. In our case, from numerical simulation, a detailed discussion of the parameters and their numerical results is presented. We claim that with these assumptions and by adding the migrated class, the model informs policy for governments, to be aware of the immigrants and subject them to tests about the disease status. Immigrants for short visits and students should be subjected to tests to reduce the number of immigrants with disease.

1. Introduction

According to World Health Organization, about 350 million people are infected with the hepatitis B virus (HBV)[1] and about 170 million people are chronically infected with the hepatitis C virus (HCV)[2]. The majority of those infected live in developing countries with few incidences in Western countries. Migration is one of the defining issues of our time. For example, more than 5 million Canadians migrate out of the country each year and over 250,000 new immigrants arrive in Canada each year. Countries of the world are increasingly connected through travel and migration, and thus, migration has health implications in one location for both local and global migrations, since infectious diseases do not remain isolated geographically. The UK Hepatitis Foundation estimated in 2007 that the number of hepatitis B cases in the UK doubled in the previous 6 years chiefly due to immigration of infected people, many from the new member states of the European Union where the prevalence of viral hepatitis is higher. The United Arab Emirates mandated that hepatitis C

testing is to be done at the time of residence visa renewals and added hepatitis C to the list of diseases such as HIV and hepatitis B as diseases warranting deportation [1]. In China, hepatitis B virus infection is a major public health problem. Hepatitis B is the first one among the diseases with legal management measures. In China, an estimated 93 million people have been infected with the hepatitis B virus [2]. The seroepidemiological survey on HBV infection conducted in 2006 showed that HBsAg carrier rate was 7.18 percent in the overall dynamics of HBV. In this paper, we consider a system of ordinary differential equations which describes the transmission of HBV transmission in China. Several mathematical models have been formulated on the HBV transmission in China. Medley and coauthors used a mathematical model and developed the strategies to eliminate the HBV in New Zealand in 2008 [3, 4]. Anderson and May [5] used a mathematical model which illustrated the effects of carriers on the transmission of HBV. An age structure model was proposed by Zhao et al. [6] to predict the dynamics of HBV transmission and evaluate the long-term effectiveness of the vaccination program in China. Wang et al. [7] proposed and analyzed the hepatitis B virus infection in a diffusion model confined to a finite domain. A hepatitis B virus (HBV) model with spatial diffusion and saturation response of the infection rate is investigated by Xu and Ma [8]. Also, Zou et al. [9] proposed a mathematical model to understand the transmission dynamics and prevalence of HBV in mainland China. A model to describe waning of immunity after sometime has been studied by a number of authors [10–16]. In the context of rapid global migration, there is a potential for any disease to be transferred faster than was previously possible. These implications concerning the movement of HBV and HCV merit far more attention by countries and the international community than they have given the problem to date. This is especially important given that the scope and speed of migration is expected to grow in coming years. In the context of rapid global migration, there is a potential for any disease to be transferred faster than was previously possible. These implications concerning the movement of HBV and HCV merit far more attention by countries and the international community than they have given the problem to date. This is especially important given that the scope and speed of migration is expected to grow in coming years.

In this paper, we construct the compartmental model of hepatitis B transmission. We have categorized the model into six compartments: Susceptible-$S(t)$, Exposed-$E(t)$, Acute-$A(t)$, Carrier-$C(t)$, Vaccinated-$V(t)$, and Migrated-$M(t)$ individuals. The migrated class of individuals comes from different parts of the world to the host country, and their interaction occurs in the form of sexual interactions, blood transportation, and transfusion. We modify the model from Pang et al. [10] by adding some new transmission dynamics and introduce the migrated class in the model. Furthermore, some authors [11, 13, 15, 17] show that acute hepatitis B could be found today in newborns of infected mothers. Pang et al. [10] added the vertical transmission term to exposed class from chronic carriers class on the basis of the characteristics of HBV transmission. In this paper, we improved the model of [10], with these new features, by adding the migrated class $M(t)$ and the following parameters:

(i) μ_1: the transmission rate from migrated class to exposed class,

(ii) μ_2: the transmission rate from migrated to acute class,

(iii) δ: the death rate at the migrated class.

The paper is organized as follows. Section 2 is devoted to the mathematical formation of the model. In Section 3 we find the Basic Reproduction Number, the disease-free equilibrium, and endemic equilibrium of the proposed model. Local asymptotic stability of the disease-free equilibrium and endemic equilibrium is discussed in Section 4. In Section 5, we study the global asymptotic stability of disease-free and endemic equilibria using the Lyapunov function. In Section 6, we study the numerical results of the proposed model and present the results in the form of plots for illustrations. The conclusion and references are presented in Section 7.

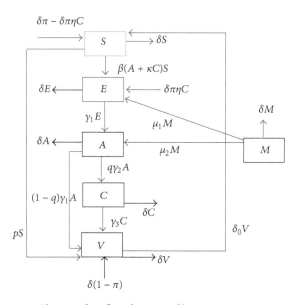

FIGURE 1: The complete flow diagram of hepatitis B virus transmission model.

2. Model Formulation

In this section, we present the mathematical formulation of the compartmental model of hepatitis B, which consists of a system of differential equations. The model is based on the characteristics of HBV transmission. We divide the total population into six compartments, that is, Susceptible individuals $S(t)$, exposed $E(t)$, Acute $A(t)$, Carrier $C(t)$, Immunity class $V(t)$, and Migrated $M(t)$. The flow diagram (Figure 1) and the system is given in the following:

$$\frac{dS(t)}{dt} = \delta\pi\left(1 - \eta C(t)\right) - \delta S(t) - \beta\left(A(t) + \kappa C(t)\right)S(t)$$
$$+ \delta_0 V(t) - pS(t),$$

$$\frac{dE(t)}{dt} = \beta\left(A(t) + \kappa C(t)\right)S(t) - \delta E(t) + \delta\pi\eta C(t)$$
$$- \gamma_1 E(t) + \mu_1 M(t),$$

$$\frac{dA(t)}{dt} = \gamma_1 E(t) - \delta A(t) - q\gamma_2 A(t) - (1-q)\gamma_1 A(t)$$
$$+ \mu_2 M(t),$$

$$\frac{dC(t)}{dt} = q\gamma_2 A(t) - \delta C(t) - \gamma_3 C(t),$$

$$\frac{dV(t)}{dt} = \gamma_3 C(t) + (1-q)\gamma_1 A(t) - \delta_0 V(t) - \delta V(t)$$
$$+ \delta(1-\pi) + pS(t),$$

$$\frac{dM(t)}{dt} = -\left(\mu_1 + \mu_2\right)M(t) - \delta M(t).$$

$$(1)$$

Subject to the initial conditions,

$$S(0) \geq 0, \quad E(0) \geq 0, \quad A(0) \geq 0,$$
$$C(0) \geq 0, \quad V(0) \geq 0, \quad M(0) \geq 0. \tag{2}$$

The proportion of failure immunization is shown by π. δ represent both the death and birth rate. At the γ_1 rate the exposed individuals become infectious and move to the Acute class. γ_2 is the rate at which the individuals move to the carrier class, γ_3 is the flow of carrier to vaccinated class, β shows the transmission coefficient, κ represents the carrier infectiousness to acute infection, q is the proportion of acute individuals that become carrier, δ_o represent the loss of immunity rate and the individual become the susceptible again, p represents the vaccination of susceptible individuals, μ_1 represents the rate of flow from migrated class to exposed class, and γ_2 is the rate of transmission from migrated class to acute class. η is the unimmunized children born to carrier mothers, $\delta(1 - \pi)$ measures the successful immunization of newborn babies, and the term $\delta\pi(1 - \eta C(t))$ shows that the newborns are unimmunized and become susceptible again.

We assume that the total population size is equal to 1, and just for simplifications, $S(t)$ is the susceptible, $E(t)$ the exposed, $A(t)$ the acute, $C(t)$ the carrier, $V(t)$ the immunity, and $M(t)$ is the migrated class representing the state variables in our proposed population model. The sum of the total population is $S(t) + E(t) + A(t) + C(t) + V(t) + M(t) = 1$, holds. We just add (1), and we can easily get. We ignore the fifth equation in system (1); so, the new models become

$$\frac{dS(t)}{dt} = \delta\pi(1 - \eta C(t)) - \delta S(t) - \beta(A(t) + \kappa C(t))S(t)$$
$$+ \delta_o(1 - (S(t) + E(t) + A(t) + C(t) + M(t))) - pS(t),$$

$$\frac{dE(t)}{dt} = \beta(A(t) + \kappa C(t))S(t) - \delta E(t) + \delta\pi\eta C(t)$$
$$- \gamma_1 E(t) + \mu_1 M(t),$$

$$\frac{dA(t)}{dt} = \gamma_1 E(t) - \delta A(t) - q\gamma_2 A(t) - (1 - q)\gamma_1 A(t)$$
$$+ \mu_2 M(t),$$

$$\frac{dC(t)}{dt} = q\gamma_2 A(t) - \delta C(t) - \gamma_3 C(t),$$

$$\frac{dM(t)}{dt} = -(\mu_1 + \mu_2)M(t) - \delta M(t). \tag{3}$$

Let

$$\Gamma = \left\{ (S, E, A, C, M) \in \mathfrak{R}_+^5, \mid S(t) \leq \frac{\delta\pi + \delta_o}{\delta + \delta_o + p}, \right.$$
$$\left. \left(S + E + A + C + M \leq \frac{\delta\pi + \delta_o}{\delta + \delta_o} \right) \right\}. \tag{4}$$

Here, Γ is a positively invariant set. All the solutions lie inside Γ which is our main focus.

3. Basic Reproduction Number/Threshold Quantity

The basic reproduction number or the threshold quantity $\mathfrak{R}_0$ for the proposed model gives an average number of secondary infection when an infection is introduced in a purely susceptible population. We use the idea developed by [18], and also for detail see [19]. We have

$$\mathscr{F} = \begin{bmatrix} 0 & \beta S^o & \beta\kappa S^o \\ 0 & 0 & 0 \\ 0 & 0 & 0 \end{bmatrix}, \quad V = \begin{bmatrix} \delta + \gamma_1 & 0 & -\delta\pi\eta \\ -\gamma_1 & \delta + q\gamma_2 + (1-q)\gamma_1 & 0 \\ 0 & -q\gamma_2 & \delta + \gamma_3 \end{bmatrix},$$

$$V^{-1} = \frac{\begin{bmatrix} (\delta+q\gamma_2+(1-q)\gamma_1)(\delta+\gamma_3) & q\gamma_2\delta\pi\eta & \delta\pi\eta(\delta+q\gamma_2+(1-q)\gamma_1) \\ \gamma_1(\delta+\gamma_3) & (\delta+\gamma_1)(\delta+\gamma_3) & \delta\pi\eta\gamma_1 \\ q\gamma_1\gamma_2 & q\gamma_2(\delta+\gamma_1) & (\delta+\gamma_1)(\delta+q\gamma_2+(1-q)\gamma_1) \end{bmatrix}}{(\delta + \gamma_1)(\delta + q\gamma_2 + (1-q)\gamma_1)(\delta + \gamma_3) - \delta\pi\eta q\gamma_1\gamma_2}, \tag{5}$$

where $Q_1 = (\delta + q\gamma_2 + (1-q)\gamma_1)$ and

$$FV^{-1} = \begin{bmatrix} 0 & \dfrac{\beta S^o \delta\pi\eta q\gamma_2}{(\delta + \gamma_1)(\delta + q\gamma_2 + (1-q)\gamma_1)(\delta + \gamma_3) - \delta\pi\eta qr_1r_2} & \dfrac{\kappa\beta S^o(\delta + \gamma_1(1-q) + q\gamma_2)}{(\delta + \gamma_1)(\delta + q\gamma_2 + (1-q)\gamma_1)(\delta + \gamma_3) - \delta\pi\eta qr_1r_2} \\ 0 & 0 & 0 \\ 0 & 0 & 0 \end{bmatrix}. \tag{6}$$

So, the reproduction number given by $\rho(FV^{-1})$ is

$$\mathfrak{R}_o = \frac{\kappa\beta S^o\left(\delta + \gamma_1\left(1 - q\right) + q\gamma_2\right) + \delta\pi\eta q r_1 r_2}{\left(\delta + \gamma_1\right)\left(\delta + q\gamma_2 + \left(1 - q\right)\gamma_1\right)\left(\delta + \gamma_3\right)}. \quad (7)$$

Here, S^o shows the disease-free equilibrium (DFE), and $D_o = (S^o, 0, 0, 0, 0)$, giving $S^o = (\delta\pi + \delta_o)/(\delta + \delta_o + p)$. The endemic equilibrium point $T^* = (S^*, E^*, A^*, C^*, M^*)$ for system (3), whose endemic equilibrium is given in the following subsection.

Endemic Equilibria. To find the endemic equilibria of the system (3), by setting $S = S^*, E = E^*, A = A^*, C = C^*$, and $M = M^*$, equating left side of the system (3) equal to zero, we obtained

$$S^* = \frac{Q_1\left(\delta + \gamma_1\right)\left(\delta + \gamma_3\right)\left(1 - R_0\right) + \kappa\beta S^o Q_1}{\gamma_1\beta\left(\left(\delta + \gamma_3\right) + \kappa q\gamma_2\right)}$$
$$- \frac{\left(\delta + \gamma_3\right)\left[\left(\delta + \gamma_1\right) + \mu_1\gamma_1\right]M^*}{\gamma_1\beta\left(\left(\delta + \gamma_3\right) + \kappa q\gamma_2\right)A^*},$$

$$J_o\left(\zeta\right) = \begin{pmatrix} -\delta - \delta_o - p & \delta_o & -\beta S^o - \delta_o & -\delta\pi\eta - \beta\kappa S^o - \delta_o & 0 \\ 0 & -\left(\delta + \gamma_1\right) & \beta S^o & \beta\kappa S^o + \delta\pi\eta & \mu_1 \\ 0 & \gamma_1 & -Q_1 & 0 & \mu_2 \\ 0 & 0 & q\gamma_2 & -\left(\delta + \gamma_3\right) & 0 \\ 0 & 0 & 0 & 0 & -\left(\mu_1 + \mu_2 + \delta\right) \end{pmatrix}. \quad (9)$$

$$E^* = \frac{Q_1 A^* - \mu_2 M^*}{\gamma_1},$$
$$C^* = \frac{q\gamma_2}{\left(\delta + \gamma_3\right)}A^*. \quad (8)$$

4. Local Stability Analysis

In this section, we find the local stability of disease-free and endemic equilibria. First, we show the local asymptotical stability of DFE equilibrium, and then we find the local asymptotical stability of endemic equilibrium. Now, we show the local stability of DFE about the point $D_o = (S^o, 0, 0, 0, 0)$ in the following theorem.

Theorem 1. For $R_0 \leq 1$, the disease-free equilibrium of the system (3) about an equilibrium point $D_o = (S^o, 0, 0, 0, 0)$ is locally asymptotically stable if $((Q_1(\delta + \delta_o + p)(\delta + \gamma_1) > \beta\gamma_1(\delta\pi + \delta_o)))$; otherwise, the disease-free equilibrium of the system (3) is unstable for $R_0 > 1$.

Proof. To show the local stability of the system (3), about the point D_o, we set the left-hand side of the system (3) equating to zero, and we obtain the following Jacobian matrix $J_o(\zeta)$:

By the elementary row operation, we get the following matrix:

$$J_o\left(\zeta\right) = \begin{pmatrix} -\left(\delta + \delta_o + p\right) & -\delta_o & -\beta S^o - \delta_o & -\delta\pi\eta - \beta\kappa S^o & 0 \\ 0 & -\left(\delta + \gamma_1\right) & \beta S^o & \beta\kappa S^o + \delta\pi\eta & \mu_1 \\ 0 & 0 & -Q_1\left(\delta + \gamma_1\right) + \gamma_1\beta S^o & \gamma_1\left(\beta\kappa S^o + \delta\pi\eta\right) & \left(\delta + \gamma_1\right)\mu_2 + \mu_1\gamma_1 \\ 0 & 0 & 0 & T_1 & 0 \\ 0 & 0 & 0 & 0 & -\left(\mu_1 + \mu_2 + \delta\right) \end{pmatrix}, \quad (10)$$

where $Q_1 = (\delta + q\gamma_2 + (1 - q)\gamma_1)$ and $T_1 = -(-Q_1(\delta + \gamma_1) + \gamma_1\beta S^o) - q\gamma_1\gamma_2(\beta\kappa S^o + \delta\pi\eta)$. The characteristic equation to the previous Jacobian matrix is given by

$$\left(\lambda + \delta + \delta_o + p\right)\left(\lambda + \mu_1 + \mu_2 + \delta\right)\left(\lambda^3 + a_1\lambda^2 + a_2\lambda + a_3\right) = 0. \quad (11)$$

The first two eigenvalues $-(\delta + \delta_o + p)$ and $-(\mu_1 + \mu_2 + \delta)$ have negative real parts. For the rest of the eigenvalues, we get

$$a_1 = \left(\delta + \delta_o + p\right)\left(Q_1\left(\delta + \gamma_3\right) + 1 + Q_1\right)\left(1 - R_0\right)$$
$$+ \beta\left(\delta\pi + \delta_o\right)\left(\left(\gamma_1\left(\delta + \gamma_3\right) + q\gamma_1\gamma_2\right) - \left(Q_1\kappa + \gamma_1\right)\right)$$
$$\times \left(\delta + \delta_o + p\right)^{-1},$$

$$a_2 = \left(Q_1\left(\delta + \gamma_1\right)\left(\delta + \delta_o + p\right) - \beta\gamma_1\left(\delta\pi + \delta_o\right)\right)$$
$$\times \left\{\left(\delta + \delta_o + p\right)\left[\left(\delta + \gamma_1\right) + \left(\delta + \gamma_1\right)^2\right]\right.$$
$$+ \left(\delta + \gamma_1\right)\left[Q_1\left(\delta + \gamma_1\right)\left(\delta + \delta_o + p\right) - \beta\gamma_1\left(\delta\pi + \delta_o\right)\right]$$
$$\left. + q\gamma_1\gamma_2\left(\delta + \gamma_1\right)\left[\beta\kappa\left(\delta\pi + \delta_o\right) + \delta\pi\eta\left(\delta + \delta + p\right)\right]\right\}$$
$$\times \left(\delta + \delta_o + p\right)^{-2}$$
$$+ \left\{q\gamma_1\gamma_2\left(\delta + \gamma_1\right)\left(\beta\kappa\left(\delta\pi + \delta_o\right) + \delta\pi\eta\left(\delta + \delta_o + p\right)\right)\right\}$$
$$\times \left(\delta + \delta_o + p\right)^{-1},$$

$$a_3 = \frac{(\delta + \gamma_1)}{(\delta + \delta_o + p)} \left(Q_1 \left(\delta + \delta_o + p \right) \left(\delta + \gamma_1 \right) - \beta \gamma_1 \left(\delta \pi + \delta_o \right) \right)$$

$$\times \left[q \gamma_1 \gamma_2 \left(\beta \kappa \left(\delta \pi + \delta_o \right) + \delta \pi \eta \right) \right.$$

$$\left. + \left(Q_1 \left(\delta + \gamma_1 \right) \left(\delta + \delta_o + p \right) - \beta \gamma_1 \left(\delta \pi + \delta_o \right) \right) \right].$$

$$(12)$$

By the Routh-Hurwitz criteria, $a_1 > 0$, $a_3 > 0$, and $a_1 a_2 > a_3$. Here, $a_1 > 0$ when $R_0 \leq 1$ and $((Q_1(\delta + \delta_o + p)(\delta + \gamma_1) > \beta \gamma_1 (\delta \pi + \delta_o))$. Also, $a_2 > 0$ and $a_3 > 0$, and then $a_1 a_2 > a_3$. So, according to the Routh-Hurwitz criteria, the Jacobian matrix has negative real parts if and only if $R_0 \leq 1$. Thus by Routh-Hurwitz criteria, the DFE of the system (3) is locally asymptotically stable about the point $D_o = (S^o, 0, 0, 0, 0)$. The proof is completed. □

The stability of the disease-free equilibrium for $R_0 \leq 1$ means that the disease dies out from the population. Next we show that the endemic equilibrium of the system (3) is locally asymptotically stable for $R_0 > 1$. When the disease-free equilibrium is locally asymptotically stable for $R_0 \leq 1$, then

$$J^*(\zeta) = \begin{pmatrix} -(\delta + \delta_o + p + \beta(A^* + \kappa C^*)) & \delta_o & -\beta S^* - \delta_o & -\delta \pi \eta - \beta \kappa S^* - \delta_o & -\delta_o \\ \beta(A^* + \kappa C^*) & -(\delta + \gamma_1) & \beta S^* & \beta \kappa S^* + \delta \pi \eta & \mu_1 \\ 0 & \gamma_1 & -Q_1 & 0 & \mu_2 \\ 0 & 0 & q \gamma_2 & -(\delta + \gamma_3) & 0 \\ 0 & 0 & 0 & 0 & -(\delta + \mu_1 + \mu_2) \end{pmatrix}. \quad (14)$$

where

$$Z_1 = \delta + \delta_o + p + \beta(A^* + \kappa C^*),$$

$$Z_2 = \beta(A^* + \kappa C^*),$$

$$Z_3 = -(\delta \pi \eta + \beta \kappa S^* + \delta_o),$$

$$Z_4 = (\beta \kappa S^* + \delta \pi \eta),$$

$$Z_5 = -Q_1 \left(-Z_1 (\delta + \gamma_1) - Z_2 \delta_o \right) \quad (16)$$

$$+ \gamma_1 \left(Z_4 \beta S^* - Z_2 (\beta S^* + \delta_o) \right),$$

$$Z_6 = -\mu_2 \left(-Z_1 (\delta + \gamma_1) - Z_2 \delta_o \right) + \gamma_1 \left(Z_1 \mu_1 - Z_2 \delta_o \right),$$

$$Z_7 = -Z_5 (\delta + \gamma_3) - Z_5 \gamma_1 \left(Z_1 Z_4 + Z_2 Z_3 \right).$$

the endemic equilibrium does not exist, but we are interested to know about the properties of an endemic equilibrium for $R_0 > 1$.

4.1. Stability of Endemic Equilibrium (EE). In this subsection, we find the local asymptotic stability of EE about $D^* = (S^*, E^*, A^*, C^*, M^*)$, and we prove the local stability of endemic equilibrium in the following.

Theorem 2. *For $R_0 > 1$, the endemic equilibrium D^* of system (3) is locally asymptotical stable, if the following conditions hold:*

$$\gamma_1 Z_2 \delta_o S^{*2} > \gamma_1 \beta^2 \kappa,$$

$$G_1 > G_2; \quad (13)$$

otherwise, the system is unstable.

Proof. Here, we prove the that the system (3) about the equilibrium point D^* is locally stable, and for this, we obtain the Jacobian matrix $J^*(\zeta)$ of the system (3), in the following:

By elementary row operation and after simplification, we get the following Jacobian matrix:

$$J^*(\zeta) = \begin{pmatrix} -Z_1 & -\delta_o & -\beta S^* - \delta_o & Z_3 & -\delta_o \\ 0 & -Z_1(\delta + \gamma_1) - Z_2 \delta_o & Z_1 \beta S^* - Z_2(\beta S^* + \delta_o) & Z_1 Z_4 + Z_2 Z_3 & Z_1 \mu_1 - Z_2 \delta_o \\ 0 & 0 & Z_5 & \gamma_1(Z_1 Z_4 + Z_2 Z_3) & Z_6 \\ 0 & 0 & 0 & Z_7 & 0 \\ 0 & 0 & 0 & 0 & -(\mu_1 + \mu_2 + \delta) \end{pmatrix}, \quad (15)$$

The eigenvalue $\lambda_1 = -(\mu_1 + \mu_2 + \delta) < 0$, $\lambda_2 = -Z_1$, and using the value of Z_1 and further C^*, we get $\lambda_2 = -(\delta + \delta_o + p + \beta((\delta + \gamma_3) + \kappa q \gamma_2)A^*) < 0$. $\lambda_3 = -(Z_1(\delta + \gamma_1) + Z_2 \delta_o) < 0$, as $Z_1 > 0$ and $Z_2 > 0$. $\lambda_4 = Z_5$, $\lambda_4 < 0$, if and only if $Z_5 < 0$. After the simplifications, we get

$$\beta^* A^* \left(\gamma_1 Z_2 \delta_o - \gamma_1 \beta^2 \kappa S^{*2} \right)$$

$$+ \{ \gamma_1 \beta \delta \pi \eta \beta^{***} M^*$$

$$- [(\gamma_1 \beta \delta \pi \eta \beta^{**} + \beta^* Q_1) Z_1 (\delta + \gamma_1) \quad (17)$$

$$+ Q_1 Z_2 \delta_o \beta^*] \} > 0,$$

where $\beta^* = \gamma_1 \beta((\delta + \gamma_3) + \kappa q \gamma_2)$, $\beta^{**} = Q_1(\delta + \gamma_1)(\delta + \gamma_3)(1 - R_0) + \kappa \beta S^o Q_1$, and $\{ \gamma_1 \beta \delta \pi \eta \beta^{***} M^* > [(\gamma_1 \beta \delta \pi \eta \beta^{**} + \beta^* Q_1) Z_1 (\delta + \gamma_1) + Q_1 Z_2 \delta_o \beta^*] \}$, say $G_1 = \gamma_1 \beta \delta \pi \eta \beta^{***} M^*$ and

$G_2 = [(\gamma_1\beta\delta\pi\eta\beta^{**} + \beta^*Q_1)Z_1(\delta+\gamma_1) + Q_1Z_2\delta_o\beta^*]\beta^{***} = (\delta + \gamma_3)[(\delta+\gamma_1) + \gamma_1\mu_1]$. So, λ_4 has negative real part if $(\gamma_1Z_2\delta_o > \gamma_1\beta^2\kappa S^{*2})$. For $\lambda_5 = Z_7$, we obtained negative real parts, and by using the Z_5 which is positive under the conditions described in λ_4, and $Z_1 > 0$, $Z_2 > 0$, we get the negative real parts. Thus, all the eigenvalues have negative real parts, so by the Routh-Hurwitz criteria the endemic equilibrium point D^* is locally asymptotically stable when $R_0 > 1$. The proof is completed.   □

5. Global Stability of DFE

In this section, we present the global stability of disease-free equilibrium DFE of the system (3). For different biological model, the Lyapunov function was used by [20, 21] for the global stability. For our model, we define and construct Lyapunov function in the following for the global stability of DFE. Further the global stability of endemic equilibrium we use the Lyapunov function and find its global asymptotical stability.

Theorem 3. *For $R_0 \leq 1$, the disease-free equilibrium of the system (3) is stable globally asymptotically, if $S = S^o$ and unstable for $R_0 > 1$.*

Proof. Here, we define the Lyapunov function for the global stability of disease-free equilibrium, given by

$$V(t) = [d_1(S - S^o) + d_2E + d_3A + d_4C + d_5M]. \quad (18)$$

Differentiating the previous function with respect to t and using the system (3),

$$V'(t) = d_1S' + d_2E' + d_3A' + d_4C' + d_5M',$$

$$
\begin{aligned}
V'(t) &= d_1[\delta\pi(1 - \eta C(t)) - \delta S(t) - \beta(A(t) + \kappa C(t))S(t) \\
&\quad + \delta_o(1 - (S(t) + E(t) + A(t) + C(t) + M(t))) - pS(t)] \\
&\quad + d_2[\beta(A(t) + \kappa C(t))S(t) - \delta E(t) + \delta\pi\eta C(t) \\
&\quad - \gamma_1 E(t) + \mu_1 M(t)] \\
&\quad + d_3[\gamma_1 E(t) - \delta A(t) - q\gamma_2 A(t) - (1-q)\gamma_1 A(t) \\
&\quad + \mu_2 M(t)] \\
&\quad + d_4[q\gamma_2 A(t) - \delta C(t) - \gamma_3 C(t)] \\
&\quad + d_5[-(\mu_1 + \mu_2)M(t) - \delta M(t)],
\end{aligned}
\quad (19)
$$

where d_i, $i = 1, 2, \dots 5$, are some positive constants to be chosen later.

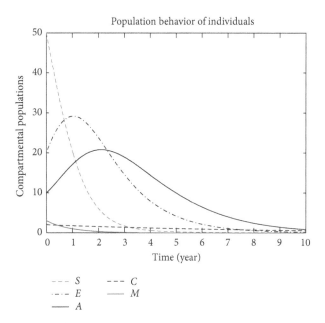

FIGURE 2: The plot shows the HBV transmission model of hepatitis B, with $\mu_1 = 0.90$ and $\mu_2 = 0.90$.

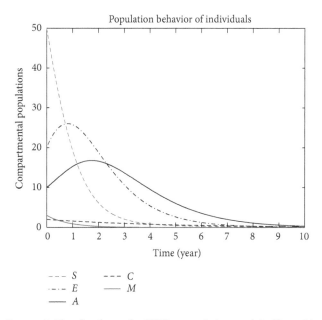

FIGURE 3: The plot shows the HBV transmission model of hepatitis B, with $\mu_1 = 0.80$ and $\mu_2 = 0.90$.

After the arrangement, we obtain

$$
\begin{aligned}
V'(t) &= [d_2 - d_1](\beta(A + \kappa C))S + [d_2 - d_1]\delta\pi\eta C \\
&\quad + [d_3\gamma_1 - d_2(\delta + \gamma_1)]E + [d_2\mu_1 - d_5\delta]M \\
&\quad + [d_4q\gamma_2 - d_3Q_1]A + d_1\delta\pi - d_1\delta S + d_1\delta_o \\
&\quad - d_1\delta_o(S + E + A + C + M) - d_1pS \\
&\quad - d_4(\delta + \gamma_3)C.
\end{aligned}
\quad (20)
$$

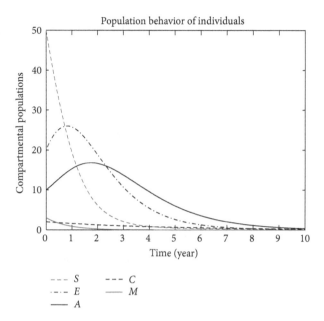

FIGURE 4: The plot shows the HBV transmission model of hepatitis B, with $\mu_1 = 0.70$ and $\mu_2 = 0.80$.

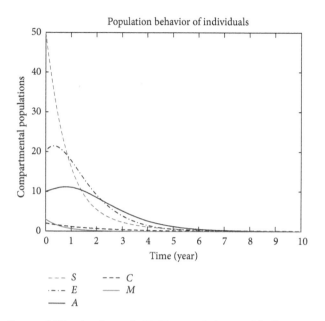

FIGURE 6: The plot shows the HBV transmission model of hepatitis B, with $\mu_1 = 0.20$ and $\mu_2 = 0.30$.

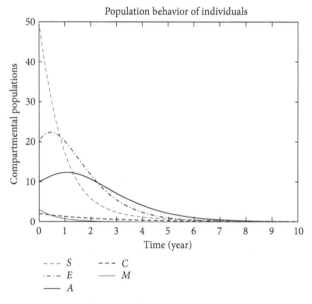

FIGURE 5: The plot shows the HBV transmission model of hepatitis B, with $\mu_1 = 0.50$ and $\mu_2 = 0.60$.

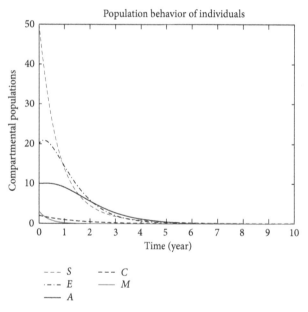

FIGURE 7: The plot shows the HBV transmission model of hepatitis B, with $\mu_1 = 0.20$ and $\mu_2 = 0.40$.

Choosing the constants, $d_1 = d_2 = \gamma_1$, $d_3 = (\delta + \gamma_1)$, $d_4 = Q_1(\delta + \gamma_1)/q\gamma_2$, and $d_5 = \gamma_1\mu_1/\delta$.

After the simplification, we get

$$V'(t) = -(S - S^o) - \gamma_1\delta_o E - \gamma_1\delta_o A$$
$$- \left(\gamma_1\delta_o + \frac{(\delta + \gamma_3)(\delta + \gamma_1)Q_1}{q\gamma_2}\right)C \quad (21)$$
$$- (\gamma_1\delta_o + (\delta_o + \gamma_1)\mu_2)M,$$

where $S^o = (\delta\pi + \delta_o)/(\delta + \delta_o + p)$. $V'(t) = 0$ if and only if $S = S^o$ and $E = A = C = M = 0$. Also, $V'(t)$ is negative for $(S > S^o)$. So, by [22], the DFE is globally asymptotically stable in Γ. The proof is completed. □

5.1. Global Stability of Endemic Equilibrium. In this subsection, we show the global asymptotical stability of the system (3). To do this, we state and prove the following theorem for the global stability of endemic equilibrium.

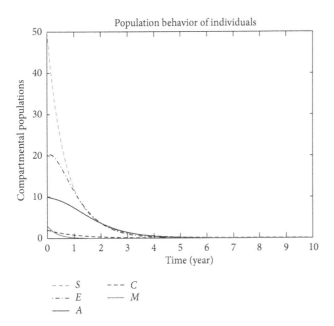

FIGURE 8: The plot shows the HBV transmission model of hepatitis B, with $\mu_1 = 0.10$ and $\mu_2 = 0.20$.

Theorem 4. For $R_0 > 1$, system (3) is globally asymptotically stable, if $S = S^*$ and $\delta_o > \mu_1$, and unstable for $R_0 \leq 1$.

Proof. To prove that system (3) is globally asymptotically stable, we define the Lyapunov in the following:

$$L(t) = \frac{(\mu_1 + \mu_2 + \mu_3)\gamma_1}{\gamma_1 + \delta}(S - S^*) + \frac{(\mu_1 + \mu_2 + \mu_3)\gamma_1}{\gamma_1 + \delta}E$$

$$+ (\mu_1 + \mu_2 + \mu_3)A + \frac{(\mu_1 + \mu_2 + \mu_3)Q_1}{q\gamma_2}C + \mu_2 M.$$

$$(22)$$

Taking the derivative with respect to time t, using the system (3),

$$L'(t) = \frac{(\mu_1 + \mu_2 + \mu_3)\gamma_1}{\gamma_1 + \delta}$$

$$\times [\delta\pi(1 - \eta C(t)) - \delta S(t) - \beta(A(t) + \kappa C(t))S(t)$$

$$+ \delta_o(1 - (S(t) + E(t) + A(t) + C(t) + M(t)))$$

$$- pS(t)]$$

$$+ \frac{(\mu_1 + \mu_2 + \mu_3)\gamma_1}{\gamma_1 + \delta}[\beta(A(t) + \kappa C(t))S(t) - \delta E(t)$$

$$+ \delta\pi\eta C(t) - \gamma_1 E(t) + \mu_1 M(t)]$$

$$+ (\mu_1 + \mu_2 + \mu_3)[\gamma_1 E(t) - \delta A(t) - q\gamma_2 A(t)$$

$$- (1 - q)\gamma_1 A(t) + \mu_2 M(t)]$$

$$+ \frac{(\mu_1 + \mu_2 + \mu_3)Q_1}{q\gamma_2}[q\gamma_2 A(t) - \delta C(t) - \gamma_3 C(t)]$$

$$+ \mu_2[-(\mu_1 + \mu_2 + \delta)M].$$

$$(23)$$

Simplifying, we obtained

$$L'(t) = -\frac{(\mu_1 + \mu_2 + \mu_3)\gamma_1}{(\gamma_1 + \delta)(\delta + \delta_o + p)}(S - S^*)$$

$$- \frac{(\mu_1 + \mu_2 + \mu_3)\gamma_1\delta_o}{(\gamma_1 + \delta)}[E + A + C] \quad (24)$$

$$- \frac{(\mu_1 + \mu_2 + \mu_3)\gamma_1}{(\gamma_1 + \delta)}[\delta_o - \mu_1]M.$$

The endemic equilibrium of the system (3) is globally asymptotically stable for $R_0 > 1$, if $S = S^*$ and $\delta_o > \mu_1$. So, the endemic equilibrium of the system (3) is globally asymptotically stable. The proof is completed. □

6. Numerical Simulations

In this section, we present the numerical simulation of the proposed model (3), by using the Runge-Kutta order four scheme. For different values of the parameters, the numerical results are presented in Figures 2, 3, 4, 5, 6, 7, and 8. The variation of migration parameters μ_1 and μ_2, with different values, is presented. In the numerical solution of the model, the parameters and their values are presented in Table 1. In our simulation, the susceptible individuals are shown by dashed line, the exposed individuals by dotted dashed, the acute individuals by bold line, the carrier by dashed line and the migrated individuals by red bold line. Figures 2 to 8 represent the compartmental population of hepatitis B individuals with migration effect. The values presented in Table 1 are fixed except for μ_1 and μ_2. In Figure 2, by the values for $\mu_1 = 0.9$ and $\mu_2 = 0.9$, we see that the population of exposed and acute individuals is increasing. In Figure 3, we set $\mu_1 = 0.8$ and $\mu_2 = 0.9$, and the population of exposed and acute individuals decreased. Decreasing the values of μ_1 and μ_2, we obtain different results; see Figures 2 to 8. When we decrease the population of immigrants who have the HBV virus, we see the decrease in the population of exposed and acute individuals. The parameters presented in Table 1 were used by different authors, for example, the natural death rate equally birth rate by [4], the rate at which the latent individuals become infectious by [3], the rate at which the individuals move to the carrier class by [3], the rate at which the individuals move to the carrier class [3], the transmission coefficient β by [24], δ_o the loss of immunity rate by [13], the value of η by [13], the value of κ by [10], and π and q from [23]. We assume the values for the parameters γ_3, p, μ_1, and μ_2 in our simulation.

7. Conclusion

A compartmental model of HBV transmission virus has been presented. A mathematical model has been obtained

TABLE 1: Parameter values used in numerical simulations.

Notation	Parameter description	Range	Source
δ	Natural death rate equally birth rate	0.0143	[4]
π	The failure immunization	0-1	[23]
γ_1	The rate at which the latent individuals become infectious	6	[3]
γ_2	The rate at which the individuals move to the carrier class	4	[3]
γ_3	The rate of flow from carrier to the vaccinated class	0.34	Assumed
β	The transmission coefficient	0.8	[24]
q	The proportion of individuals become carrier	0.005	[23]
δ_o	Represent the loss of immunity	0.06-0.03	[13]
p	Represent the vaccination of susceptible	0.3	Assumed
μ_1	The rate of flow from Migrated class to exposed class	0.23	Assumed
μ_2	The rate of flow from Migrated class to acute class	0.56	Assumed
η	Unimmunized children born to carrier mothers	0.7	[13]
κ	The infectiousness of carriers related to acute infection	0-1	[10]

by adding (1) the migrated class, (2) HBV transmission rate between migrated class and exposed class, (3) transmission rate between migrated class and acute class, and (4) death rate of individuals in the migrated class. By adding these new features, we have obtained a compartmental model of HBV with migration effect. First, we obtained the basic reproduction number for the proposed model. The disease-free equilibrium is locally as well as globally asymptotically stable for $R_0 \leq 1$. We obtained the local and global asymptotical stability for the endemic equilibrium. For the reproduction number $R_0 > 1$, the endemic equilibrium is, locally as well as globally, asymptotically stable. Furthermore, we have solved the compartment model numerically, and the results are presented in Figures 2 to 8. By changing the values of μ_1 and μ_2, different results have been obtained. It is concluded that when the value of μ_1 and μ_2 decreases, the population of (exposed, acute, and carrier) individuals also decrease. The proportion of infected individuals decreases when the proportion of migrated individuals (who have the HBV virus) decreases. So, the number of infected individuals is directly proportional to the number of migrated individuals.

Last yet not the least, the authors of this work have agreed to devise in a course of time a more advanced model on restraining HBV transmission through migration.

Acknowledgment

The authors would like to thank the Kanury V. S. Rao for their careful reading of the original manuscripts and their many valuable comments and suggestions that greatly improve the presentation of this work.

References

[1] F. Ahmed and G. R. Foster, "Global hepatitis, migration and its impact on Western healthcare," *Gut*, vol. 59, no. 8, pp. 1009–1011, 2010.

[2] "*Chinese center for disease control and prevention (CCDC)*," 2010, http://www.chinacdc.cn/n272442/n272530/n3479265/n3479303//37095.html.

[3] G. F. Medley, N. A. Lindop, W. J. Edmunds, and D. J. Nokes, "Hepatitis-B virus endemicity: heterogeneity, catastrophic dynamics and control," *Nature Medicine*, vol. 7, no. 5, pp. 619–624, 2001.

[4] S. Thornley, C. Bullen, and M. Roberts, "Hepatitis B in a high prevalence New Zealand population: a mathematical model applied to infection control policy," *Journal of Theoretical Biology*, vol. 254, no. 3, pp. 599–603, 2008.

[5] R. M. Anderson and R. M. May, *Infectious Disease of Humans: Dynamics and Control*, Oxford University Press, Oxford, UK, 1991.

[6] S. Zhao, Z. Xu, and Y. Lu, "A mathematical model of hepatitis B virus transmission and its application for vaccination strategy in China," *International Journal of Epidemiology*, vol. 29, no. 4, pp. 744–752, 2000.

[7] K. Wang, W. Wang, and S. Song, "Dynamics of an HBV model with diffusion and delay," *Journal of Theoretical Biology*, vol. 253, no. 1, pp. 36–44, 2008.

[8] R. Xu and Z. Ma, "An HBV model with diffusion and time delay," *Journal of Theoretical Biology*, vol. 257, no. 3, pp. 499–509, 2009.

[9] L. Zou, W. Zhang, and S. Ruan, "Modeling the transmission dynamics and control of hepatitis B virus in China," *Journal of Theoretical Biology*, vol. 262, no. 2, pp. 330–338, 2010.

[10] J. Pang, J. A. Cui, and X. Zhou, "Dynamical behavior of a hepatitis B virus transmission model with vaccination," *Journal of Theoretical Biology*, vol. 265, no. 4, pp. 572–578, 2010.

[11] K. P. Maier, *Hepatitis-Hepatitisfolgen*, Georg Thieme Verlag, Stuttgart, Germany, 2000.

[12] G. L. Mandell, R. G. Douglas, and J. E. Bennett, *Principles and Practice of Infectious Diseases*, A Wiley Medical Publication John Wiley and Sons, New York, NY, USA, 1979.

[13] C. W. Shepard, E. P. Simard, L. Finelli, A. E. Fiore, and B. P. Bell, "Hepatitis B virus infection: epidemiology and vaccination," *Epidemiologic Reviews*, vol. 28, no. 1, pp. 112–125, 2006.

[14] X. Weng and Y. Zhang, *Infectious Diseases*, Fudan University Press, Shanghai, China, 2003.

[15] J. Wu and Y. Luo, *Infectious Diseases*, Central South University Press, Changsha, China, 2004.

[16] J. B. Wyngaarden, L. H. Smith, and J. C. Bennett, *Cecil Text Book of Medicine*, WB Saunders, Philadelphia, Pa, USA, 19th edition, 1992.

[17] B. J. McMahon, W. L. M. Alward, and D. B. Hall, "Acute hepatitis B virus infection: relation of age to the clinical expression of disease and subsequent development of the carrier state," *Journal of Infectious Diseases*, vol. 151, no. 4, pp. 599–603, 1985.

[18] P. Van Den Driessche and J. Watmough, "Reproduction numbers and sub-threshold endemic equilibria for compartmental models of disease transmission," *Mathematical Biosciences*, vol. 180, pp. 29–48, 2002.

[19] O. Diekmann and J. A. P. Heesterbeek, *Mathematical Epidemiology of Infectious Diseases*, 2000.

[20] A. Mwasa and J. M. Tchuenche, "Mathematical analysis of a cholera model with public health interventions," *BioSystems*, vol. 105, no. 3, pp. 190–200, 2011.

[21] J. Li and Y. Yang, "SIR-SVS epidemic models with continuous and impulsive vaccination strategies," *Journal of Theoretical Biology*, vol. 280, no. 1, pp. 108–116, 2011.

[22] J. P. LaSalle, "Stability of nonautonomous systems," *Nonlinear Analysis*, vol. 1, no. 1, pp. 83–90, 1976.

[23] World Health Organization, "*Hepatitis B. WHO/CDS/CSR/LYO/2002.2: Hepatitis B*," http://www.who.int/csr/disease/hepatitis/whocdscsrlyo20022/en/.

[24] W. J. Edmunds, G. F. Medley, and D. J. Nokes, "The transmission dynamics and control of hepatitis B virus in the Gambia," *Statistics in Medicine*, vol. 15, pp. 2215–2233, 2002.

The Spinal Curvature of Three Different Sitting Positions Analysed in an Open MRI Scanner

Daniel Baumgartner,[1,2] **Roland Zemp,**[1] **Renate List,**[1] **Mirjam Stoop,**[1] **Jaroslav Naxera,**[3]
Jean Pierre Elsig,[4] **and Silvio Lorenzetti**[1]

[1] Institute for Biomechanics, ETH Zurich, Zurich, Switzerland
[2] School of Engineering, Winterthur, Switzerland
[3] Röntgeninstitut Zürich-Altstetten, Zurich, Switzerland
[4] Spine Surgery, 8700 Küsnacht, Switzerland

Correspondence should be addressed to Silvio Lorenzetti, slorenzetti@ethz.ch

Academic Editors: F. Galbusera and D. Gastaldi

Sitting is the most frequently performed posture of everyday life. Biomechanical interactions with office chairs have therefore a long-term effect on our musculoskeletal system and ultimately on our health and wellbeing. This paper highlights the kinematic effect of office chairs on the spinal column and its single segments. Novel chair concepts with multiple degrees of freedom provide enhanced spinal mobility. The angular changes of the spinal column in the sagittal plane in three different sitting positions (forward inclined, reclined, and upright) for six healthy subjects (aged 23 to 45 years) were determined using an open magnetic resonance imaging (MRI) scanner. An MRI-compatible and commercially available office chair was adapted for use in the scanner. The midpoint coordinates of the vertebral bodies, the wedge angles of the intervertebral discs, and the lumbar lordotic angle were analysed. The mean lordotic angles were $16.0 \pm 8.5°$ (mean $\pm$ standard deviation) in a forward inclined position, $24.7 \pm 8.3°$ in an upright position, and $28.7 \pm 8.1°$ in a reclined position. All segments from T10-T11 to L5-S1 were involved in movement during positional changes, whereas the range of motion in the lower lumbar segments was increased in comparison to the upper segments.

1. Introduction

During daily life, increasing amounts of time are spent in a sedentary position. In industrial countries, more than 75% of all office workers sit for periods of more than seven hours [1]. In contrast to walking and running, muscles are not actively used during sitting. The muscular function is replaced by the supporting effect of the seat. Muscular inactivation over a long period of time leads to a weakening of the corresponding muscles. Approximately half of all office workers are affected by back problems [2], and recent trends show an increase in this number. Current research is therefore focussed on sitting in relation to discomfort and pain [1]. Grimmer et al. [3] found that adolescents have high rates of back pain which are medically verifiable and follow into adulthood. Accelerated degeneration of the spine due to long-term sitting results in a higher number of

disc protrusions in the elderly [4]. Further negative effects such as muscle clenching, nerve irritation, reduced blood circulation due to compressed veins, or narrowing of the respiratory organs may appear [4–7]. Such diseases may potentially cause chronic health problems in the elderly. A study by Katzmarzyk et al. [8] showed a higher incidence of cardiovascular disease and a higher risk of mortality for office workers compared with physically active working people, independent of their physical activity level during leisure time. These data were confirmed in a similar study performed by Patel et al. [9]. A long-term sitting position therefore seems to be one of the highest risk factors for developing future health problems. This fact is also supported by a recent study of Dunstan et al. [10]. They established that short bouts of walking during sitting time lower postprandial glucose and insulin levels in overweight/obese adults. Dunstan et al. [10] finally concluded that this may improve glucose metabolism and potentially be an important public health and clinical intervention strategy for reducing cardiovascular risk.

Recent developments in the field of ergonomic office furniture allow different types of movements, such as forward and backward inclination as well as lateral tilting of the seat [11]. A less constrained seat system leads to an alternating load on the spine, particularly on the intervertebral discs. Active but controlled sitting is believed to activate muscles and supporting structures and therefore prevent static loads acting on joints, ligaments, and tendons. It has been shown that an alternating sitting position significantly enhances muscular activity [12].

Continuous upright sitting has been shown to be undesirable since the 1960s. Novel solutions with adjustable backrests or seats that alternate kyphosis and lordosis angles have been presented. The kneeling chair represented one of the first sitting concepts that significantly influenced spinal posture. For example, Bennett et al. [13] found an increased lumbar curvature when sitting in a Balans Multi-Chair (kneeling chair) compared to sitting upright in a straight-backed chair. Other concepts included applying very small active rotational seat movements using motor-driven actuation, which resulted in a twisting of the spine along the vertical axis within the natural range of movement of individual intervertebral discs [14]. These dynamic stimuli apparently influenced the length of the spine after sitting for a certain period of time. This continuous passive motion concept was previously published by Reinecke et al. [15] and was thoroughly investigated in later studies by Lengsfeld et al. [16] and van Deursen et al. [17]. Recently, this actively steered chair was the focus of a biomechanical investigation by van Dieën et al. [18].

The lordosis angle of different body postures and its effect on lumbar biomechanics have often been the focus of spinal research. Bridger et al. [19] concluded that the lordosis angle was smaller in a sitting position compared to a standing position. A forward tilted sitting position was therefore suggested in order to achieve similar lordosis angles as in standing. A reclined position reduces the load on the intervertebral discs and on the back muscles by an increased lordosis angle, which was shown by Colombini et al. [20]. Graf et al. [21] demonstrated a certain discomfort with a tilting seat angle of more than 15°. Apparently, the biomechanical analysis of the lordosis angle is of relevance when determining the influence on posture and wellbeing. A more accurate analysis of the behaviour of single functional spinal units instead of the lordosis angle could be of advantage.

Seat systems that allow several sitting positions have a significant influence on posture. The assessment of posture is hindered by the fact that the spine is positioned below soft tissue and the skin surface. The location of a single vertebra can only be assumed by the external shape of the thorax or by palpating the spinous processes on the skin surface. Hence, a reproducible analysis method to quantify the location of single vertebrae is needed. Magnetic resonance imaging (MRI) techniques are therefore valuable for displaying the exact vertebral position in sedentary positions [22, 23]. By use of an upright, open MRI scanner, acquisition of 3-D data in the standing or sitting position is possible. In this way, the spine of wheelchair users has been investigated in a study by Linder-Ganz et al. [23]. Savage et al. [24] and Videman et al. [4] correlated the clinical diagnosis displayed by MR images with the occurrence of symptomatic low back pain. Bertschinger et al. [22] compared sedentary patients in an open MRI scanner versus a traditional MRI scanner, in which patients have to lie down. In contrast to the standardised lying position in the closed-magnet unit, the spinal column is loaded by the gravitational weight of the thorax in the upright position. Thus, a sedentary position seems to be more clinically relevant in performing an accurate clinical diagnosis [25]. Consequently, the analysis of variable sedentary positions on office chairs and the influence of these positions on spinal biomechanics can be accurately analysed with an open, upright MRI scanner.

Dynamic or active sitting occurs when a chair enables the seated user to move in different planes. Flexibility and movement during sitting may be beneficial to wellbeing and allow different movement tasks to be performed. In our specific case, dynamic movement denotes a forward tilting mechanism of the seat pan. In particular, a higher degree of freedom for the hip flexural angle is provided which substantially influences the lumbopelvic mechanism and consequently the whole thoracolumbar region of the spine.

The aim of this study is to analyse the spinal shape and, in particular, the position of single intervertebral bodies in relation to the sitting posture. The results may help to evaluate novel designs of backrests from a physiological point of view.

2. Material and Methods

2.1. Subjects. Six subjects (three females and three males, average age: 32 years (range 23 years to 45 years), average height: 1.74 m (range 1.64 m to 1.78 m), average weight: 68 kg (range 60 kg to 77 kg)) were measured in the three different positions. The subjects needed to have a maximum trunk width of 48 cm (distance from left to right shoulder) to have enough space in the MRI scanner. Clinical and therapeutic interventions relating to back problems were exclusion criteria. These criteria included previous back surgeries, diagnosed postural deformities in the sagittal or frontal plane, and presence of ferromagnetic implants in the body. Before measurements were made, metallic objects such as necklaces or watches were removed.

No financial compensation was provided for participation in the study. A survey was filled out by every subject describing body parameters and history of back problems and clinical interventions. The study was approved by the ethics commission of the ETH Zurich (no. EK 2010-N-27).

2.2. Investigated Positions. The spinal posture and the position of the lumbar and lower thoracic vertebrae were analysed. Subjects were positioned on a specifically designed, MRI-compatible chair in the upright MRI scanner. The chair

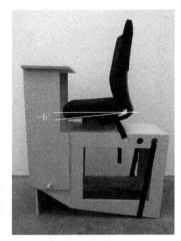

FIGURE 1: MRI-compatible chair in the three positions: upright (left), reclined (middle), and forward inclined (right).

did not contain any ferromagnetic assemblies to exclude image artefacts. The duration of the scanning period depended on the size of the subject and was approximately three to five minutes per position. During measuring, the subject had to maintain a static position as far as possible. Three different chair positions were analysed (Figure 1).

Upright (up). The lumbar spine was in contact with the backrest, but no force was transmitted. The hands were placed on the legs.

Reclined (re). The back had contact with the whole backrest of the chair, the hands were placed on the legs, and the head was kept looking straight ahead. The subject was able to choose the most individually appropriate position.

Forward Inclined (fi). The back had no contact with the backrest, and the upper body was supported by the arms lying on a table in front of the subject.

A randomised sequence of the positions for every patient was performed. While changing from one position to another, a recovery time of five to ten minutes was given. During that time, the subjects were requested to walk around and relax the musculoskeletal system.

2.3. Data Acquisition and Measuring Sequence. Measurements were taken in the Upright MRI Center, Zurich, with the FONAR Upright MRI scanner (0.6 Tesla). T2-weighted sagittal images were taken with a repetition time of 3435 ms, an echo time of 110 ms, and a layer thickness of 4 mm. The resolution was 240 × 240 pixels in an image plane of 380 × 380 mm.

In total, 15 sagittal sections were obtained for a vertebra with a 60 mm width. The scans were captured along the vertical axis of the spine in sagittal sections. In a lateral view, the cross-section of the single discs and their adjacent vertebrae are displayed. Discs and vertebrae can be easily separated due to the different contrasts, which is a result of the increased water content of the discs compared to the

vertebral bone. The vertebral end plates between the discs and the vertebrae are displayed in a dark colour (Figure 2(a)).

2.4. Data Analysis. The following parameters were evaluated based on the MR images of the most central section (median plane of the body).

Coordinates of the Midpoints of the Vertebrae. A coordinate system was placed corresponding to the main direction of the MR image with the origin through the lowest vertebra L5 (Figure 2(a)). The x- and y-coordinates were determined for all three sitting positions in the sagittal view for each vertebra (from L5 to Th10). The coordinates were determined based on the centre of a quadrangle built by the two endplates and the ventral and dorsal margins of the vertebral bodies.

Wedge Angles of the Intervertebral Discs. The wedge angles (from L5/S1 to Th10/Th11) were determined according to an established, clinical evaluation [26]. A tangent line was placed on the ventral and dorsal edges of each vertebra. The wedge angle was defined in between two lines of adjacent vertebral bodies (Figure 2(b)).

Lordotic Angle. The angle between the tangent line on the upper L1 endplate and the tangent line on the upper sacrum S1 endplate is defined as the lordotic angle α (Figure 2(b)).

Convention. A lordosis was defined as a positive angle and a kyphosis as a negative angle.

MegaCAD 2D software (Version 2011, MegaCAD-Center GmbH, Oberweningen, Switzerland) was used to examine the coordinates and angles.

2.5. Statistical Analysis. All statistics were determined using IBM SPSS Statistics (Version 19, SPSS Inc., Chicago, IL, USA). The statistical significance level was set at $P < 0.05$.

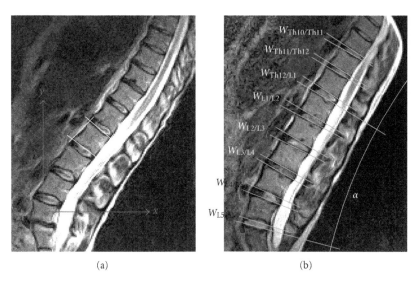

(a)   (b)

FIGURE 2: (a) The coordinate system (red arrows) and the quadrangle built by the two endplates and the ventral and dorsal margins of the vertebral body (yellow straight lines) to determine the coordinates of the vertebral midpoints (red stars). (b) The wedge angles of the intervertebral discs ($W_{L5/S1}$, $W_{L4/L5}$, ...) and the lordotic angle α.

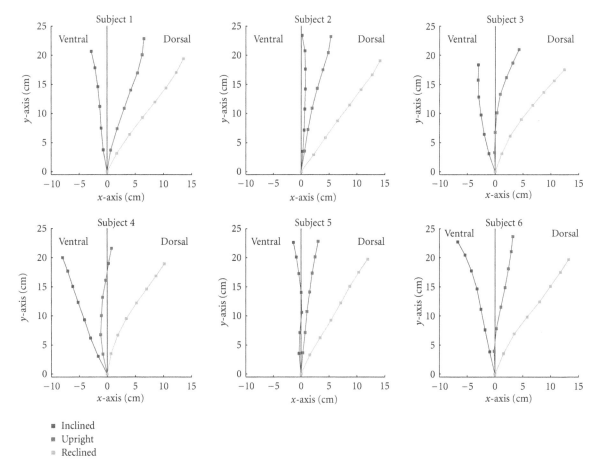

FIGURE 3: Coordinates of the midpoints for the vertebrae of the three positions. All curves are related to the same origin, represented by the midpoint of L5.

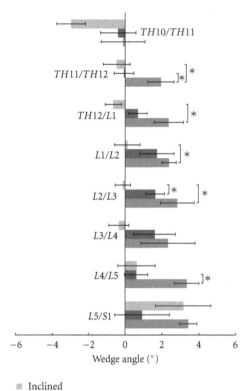

FIGURE 4: Mean wedge angles and their standard error of the intervertebral discs. *Significant differences between positions.

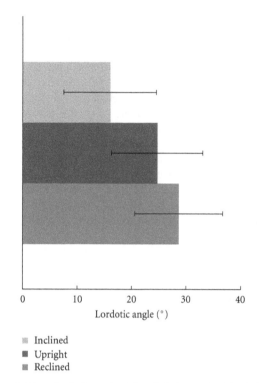

FIGURE 5: Mean lordotic angles (α) and their standard deviation for the three positions.

The averages of the wedge angles and the lordotic angle of the three positions (up, re, fi) were compared with the Wilcoxon tests in a crosswise manner.

3. Results

3.1. Coordinates of the Midpoints of the Vertebrae. Changes in the position and shape of the spine occurred during the three different sitting positions (Figure 3). The reclined sitting posture resulted in similar positions of the vertebrae for all subjects. In contrast, the largest differences in the position of the midpoints between the subjects occurred when patients were in the forward inclined sitting posture. In the upright sitting posture, five subjects had a slightly dorsally located spine. Only one subject (Subject 3) showed a ventral configuration of the vertebrae, especially in the lumbar region. For all subjects, the shape of the lumbar spine was similar during the upright and the inclined positions.

A line through the midpoints of the vertebrae, approximating the direction of the spine in the reclined position, was dorsally ascending with an angle between 30° and 40° relative to the vertical axis. The upright position was dorsally ascending with a large variability for all subjects.

3.2. Wedge Angles. The maximal measured mean wedge angle was 3.4 ± 1.2° (mean ± standard deviation) for the lowest lumbar segment in the reclined position. The maximal

mean changes within one segment were 3 ± 2° (mean ± standard deviation) from the forward to the reclined position for the wedge angle TH12/L1. Generally, a change in position was visible for all segmental heights, and some were significant (Figure 4). A general trend of a uniform movement pattern was not observed for the six subjects. Two subjects reached their maximum wedge angle in the upright position, while all others reached this angle in the reclined position.

3.3. Lordotic Angle. The mean lordotic angle α for the forward inclination was 16.0 ± 8.5° (mean ± standard deviation), for the upright position was 24.7 ± 8.3°, and for the reclined position was 28.7 ± 8.1° (Figure 5). High individual differences were observed for the lordotic angle. These large interindividual differences were also observed for the reclined position, although a standardised backrest was used. The lordotic angles were not significantly different between the three positions.

4. Discussion

All lumbar and lower thoracic intervertebral discs are involved in positional changes and contribute to the change in the spinal shape. These findings were revealed by applying the clinical evaluation method to determine the wedge angles. No specific segment can be identified in which the majority of the movement is performed. Slight trends in the absolute wedge angles of the intervertebral discs could be determined. The angles in the forward inclined and reclined positions seem to be higher for the lower lumbar vertebral discs and decrease towards the tenth thoracic vertebra. In contrast, individual differences between the subjects were much higher for the upright position compared with the other positions. No general movement pattern caused by changing positions was detected. High individual differences are visible, although the geometry of the test chair was standardised for all tested subjects.

The current study was performed with only 6 subjects, which represents the main limitation. Only some of the analysed spinal angles were significantly different. To provide more statistically significant data, more subjects would be required. However, some general statements about the behaviour of the vertebral discs of the lower back could be made.

In conclusion, the wedge angles and the position of the vertebral bodies change between the three described sitting positions. As a result, the load condition of the intervertebral discs changes. This is assumed to stimulate the metabolism of the intervertebral discs [27]. Even slight changes in the position cause a change in the disc loading. Positional changes from an upright to a reclined or forward inclined sitting position may therefore have a positive effect on the biological nutrition processes of the spine.

Ethical Approval

The mentioned study was approved by the ethics committee (EK 2010-N-27).

Funding

This study was supported by Vitra AG.

Conflict of Interests

All authors have no conflict of interests to declare.

Acknowledgments

The typescript was read and agreed upon by all authors. The authors would like to thank Nadja Mettler for the technical support at the Upright MRI Center Zurich.

References

[1] A. M. Lis, K. M. Black, H. Korn, and M. Nordin, "Association between sitting and occupational LBP," *European Spine Journal*, vol. 16, no. 2, pp. 283–298, 2007.

[2] M. H. Lloyd, S. Gauld, and C. A. Soutar, "Epidemiology study of back pain in miners and office workers," *Spine*, vol. 11, no. 2, pp. 136–140, 1986.

[3] K. Grimmer, L. Nyland, and S. Milanese, "Longitudinal investigation of low back pain in Australian adolescents: a five-year study.," *Physiotherapy Research International*, vol. 11, no. 3, pp. 161–172, 2006.

[4] T. Videman, M. C. Battié, L. E. Gibbons, K. Maravilla, H. Manninen, and J. Kaprio, "Associations between back pain history and lumbar MRI findings," *Spine*, vol. 28, no. 6, pp. 582–588, 2003.

[5] S. M. Chen, M. F. Liu, J. Cook, S. Bass, and S. K. Lo, "Sedentary lifestyle as a risk factor for low back pain: a systematic review," *International Archives of Occupational and Environmental Health*, vol. 82, no. 7, pp. 797–806, 2009.

[6] E. Stranden, "Dynamic leg volume changes when sitting in a locked and free floating tilt office chair," *Ergonomics*, vol. 43, no. 3, pp. 421–433, 2000.

[7] M. Harreby, B. Nygaard, T. Jessen et al., "Risk factors for low back pain in a cohort of 1389 Danish school children: an epidemiologic study," *European Spine Journal*, vol. 8, no. 6, pp. 444–450, 1999.

[8] P. T. Katzmarzyk, T. S. Church, C. L. Craig, and C. Bouchard, "Sitting time and mortality from all causes, cardiovascular disease, and cancer," *Medicine and Science in Sports and Exercise*, vol. 41, no. 5, pp. 998–1005, 2009.

[9] A. V. Patel, L. Bernstein, A. Deka et al., "Leisure time spent sitting in relation to total mortality in a prospective cohort of US adults," *American Journal of Epidemiology*, vol. 172, no. 4, pp. 419–429, 2010.

[10] D. W. Dunstan, B. A. Kingwell, R. Larsen et al., "Breaking up prolonged sitting reduces postprandial glucose and insulin responses," *Diabetes Care*, vol. 35, no. 5, pp. 976–983, 2012.

[11] L. Groenesteijn, P. Vink, M. de Looze, and F. Krause, "Effects of differences in office chair controls, seat and backrest angle design in relation to tasks," *Applied Ergonomics*, vol. 40, no. 3, pp. 362–370, 2009.

[12] S. J. Edmondston, M. Sharp, A. Symes, N. Alhabib, and G. T. Allison, "Changes in mechanical load and extensor muscle activity in the cervico-thoracic spine induced by sitting posture modification," *Ergonomics*, vol. 54, no. 2, pp. 179–186, 2011.

[13] D. L. Bennett, D. K. Gillis, L. Gross Portney, M. Romanow, and A. S. Sanchez, "Comparison of integrated electromyographic activity and lumbar curvature during standing and during sitting in three chairs," *Physical Therapy*, vol. 69, no. 11, pp. 902–913, 1989.

[14] M. Lengsfeld, I. R. König, J. Schmelter, and A. Ziegler, "Passive rotary dynamic sitting at the workplace by office-workers with lumbar pain: a randomized multicenter study," *Spine Journal*, vol. 7, no. 5, pp. 531–540, 2007.

[15] S. M. Reinecke, R. G. Hazard, and K. Coleman, "Continuous passive motion in seating: a new strategy against low back pain," *Journal of Spinal Disorders*, vol. 7, no. 1, pp. 29–35, 1994.

[16] M. Lengsfeld, D. L. Van Deursen, A. Rohlmann, L. L. J. M. Van Deursen, and P. Griss, "Spinal load changes during rotatory dynamic sitting," *Clinical Biomechanics*, vol. 15, no. 4, pp. 295–297, 2000.

[17] D. L. van Deursen, M. Lengsfeld, C. J. Snijders, J. J. M. Evers, and R. H. M. Goossens, "Mechanical effects of continuous passive motion on the lumbar spine in seating," *Journal of Biomechanics*, vol. 33, no. 6, pp. 695–699, 2000.

[18] J. H. van Dieën, M. P. De Looze, and V. Hermans, "Effects of dynamic office chairs on trunk kinematics, trunk extensor EMG and spinal shrinkage," *Ergonomics*, vol. 44, no. 7, pp. 739–750, 2001.

[19] R. S. Bridger, C. von Eisenhart-Rothe, and M. Henneberg, "Effects of seat slope and hip flexion on spinal angles in sitting," *Human Factors*, vol. 31, no. 6, pp. 679–688, 1989.

[20] D. Colombini, E. Occhipinti, A. Grieco, and M. Faccini, "Estimation of lumbar disc areas by means of anthropometric parameters," *Spine*, vol. 14, no. 1, pp. 51–55, 1989.

[21] M. Graf, U. Guggenbühl, and H. Krueger, "Investigations on the effects of seat shape and slope on posture, comfort and back muscle activity," *International Journal of Industrial Ergonomics*, vol. 12, no. 1-2, pp. 91–103, 1993.

[22] K. M. Bertschinger, F. H. Hetzer, J. E. Roos, K. Treiber, B. Marincek, and P. R. Hilfiker, "Dynamic MR imaging of the pelvic floor performed with patient sitting in an open-magnet unit versus with patient supine in a closed-magnet unit," *Radiology*, vol. 223, no. 2, pp. 501–508, 2002.

[23] E. Linder-Ganz, N. Shabshin, Y. Itzchak, and A. Gefen, "Assessment of mechanical conditions in sub-dermal tissues during sitting: a combined experimental-MRI and finite element approach," *Journal of Biomechanics*, vol. 40, no. 7, pp. 1443–1454, 2007.

[24] R. A. Savage, G. H. Whitehouse, and N. Roberts, "The relationship between the magnetic resonance imaging appearance of the lumbar spine and low back pain, age and occupation in males," *European Spine Journal*, vol. 6, no. 2, pp. 106–114, 1997.

[25] J. P. J. Elsig and D. L. Kaech, "Imaging-based planning for spine surgery," *Minimally Invasive Therapy and Allied Technologies*, vol. 15, no. 5, pp. 260–266, 2006.

[26] H. N. Modi, S. W. Suh, H. R. Song, J. H. Yang, H. J. Kim, and C. H. Modi, "Differential wedging of vertebral body and intervertebral disc in thoracic and lumbar spine in adolescent idiopathic scoliosis-a cross sectional study in 150 patients," *Scoliosis*, vol. 3, no. 1, p. 11, 2008.

[27] D. W. McMillan, G. Garbutt, and M. A. Adams, "Effect of sustained loading on the water content of intervertebral discs: implications for disc metabolism," *Annals of the Rheumatic Diseases*, vol. 55, no. 12, pp. 880–887, 1996.

4

Elucidation of Novel Structural Scaffold in Rohu TLR2 and Its Binding Site Analysis with Peptidoglycan, Lipoteichoic Acid and Zymosan Ligands, and Downstream MyD88 Adaptor Protein

Bikash Ranjan Sahoo,[1] Madhubanti Basu,[1] Banikalyan Swain,[1] Manas Ranjan Dikhit,[2] Pallipuram Jayasankar,[1] and Mrinal Samanta[1]

[1] Fish Health Management Division, Central Institute of Freshwater Aquaculture (CIFA), Kausalyaganga, Bhubaneswar, Odisha 751002, India
[2] Biomedical Informatics Centre, Rajendra Memorial Research Institute of Medical Sciences, Agamkuan, Patna, Bihar 800007, India

Correspondence should be addressed to Mrinal Samanta; msamanta1969@yahoo.com

Academic Editor: Claudio M. Soares

Toll-like receptors (TLRs) play key roles in sensing wide array of microbial signatures and induction of innate immunity. TLR2 in fish resembles higher eukaryotes by sensing peptidoglycan (PGN) and lipoteichoic acid (LTA) of bacterial cell wall and zymosan of yeasts. However, in fish TLR2, no study yet describes the ligand binding motifs in the leucine rich repeat regions (LRRs) of the extracellular domain (ECD) and important amino acids in TLR2-TIR (toll/interleukin-1 receptor) domain that could be engaged in transmitting downstream signaling. We predicted these in a commercially important freshwater fish species rohu (*Labeo rohita*) by constructing 3D models of TLR2-ECD, TLR2-TIR, and MyD88-TIR by comparative modeling followed by 40 ns (nanosecond) molecular dynamics simulation (MDS) for TLR2-ECD and 20 ns MDS for TLR2-TIR and MyD88-TIR. Protein (TLR2-ECD)–ligands (PGN, LTA, and zymosan) docking in rohu by AutoDock4.0, FlexX2.1, and GOLD4.1 anticipated LRR16–19, LRR12–14, and LRR20-CT as the most important ligand binding motifs. Protein (TLR2-TIR)—protein (MyD88-TIR) interaction by HADDOCK and ZDOCK predicted BB loop, αB-helix, αC-helix, and CD loop in TLR2-TIR and BB loop, αB-helix, and CD loop in MyD88-TIR as the critical binding domains. This study provides ligands recognition and downstream signaling.

1. Introduction

The innate immune response elicited by a variety of pattern recognition receptors (PRRs) is an immediate nonspecific and first line of defense of the host against invading various pathogens [1]. Toll-like receptors (TLRs) are a component of PRR and play a critical role by sensing organisms ranging from protozoa to bacteria and were involved in many infectious diseases [2]. They recognize a wide array of microbe associated molecular patterns (MAPMs) and activate downstream signaling to induce innate immunity [3]. The number of TLRs varied in different organisms and among these most TLRs are located on cell surface except for TLR3, TLR7, TLR8, and TLR9 [4, 5].

Toll-like receptor 2 (TLR2) was shown to be the principal mediator of macrophages activation. It functions as homodimer [6] or heterodimer with TLR1 or TLR6 [7] to recognize diverse bacterial products [8] and activation of MyD88-dependent signaling pathway. In this pathway, the TIR domain of MyD88 interacts with the TIR domain of TLR [9] and transmits downstream signals to induce innate immune genes expression.

PGN is a highly complex structural component and an important derivative of both Gram-positive and Gram-negative bacterial cell wall, and is the target of the innate immune system [10]. It is composed of alternating β-(1–4)-linked N-acetyl-glucosamine and N-acetyl-muramic acid residues cross-linked by peptide bridges [11]. It is recognized by various families of PRRs, including TLRs, nucleotide-binding oligomerization domain-containing proteins (NLRs), and peptidoglycan recognition proteins (PGRPs) [12]. In monocytes and macrophages, PGN binds to extracellular domain of TLR2 and activates signaling to induce inflammatory cytokines [13–15]. Structurally, PGN of most Gram-positive bacteria contains lysine at third position, and in Gram-negative and most rod-shaped Gram-positive bacteria lysine is replaced by DAP [16]. Nascent PGN of bacterial cell wall is poorly recognized by TLR2. However, after its autolysin the remodeled PGN binds TLR2 with high affinity [16]. LTA is an amphiphilic, negatively charged glycolipid [17] component of Gram-positive bacteria cell wall. TLR2 binds LTA and activates signaling cascade to induce TNF-α, IL-6, and IL-8 gene expression [18–20]. Zymosan is the cell wall derivative of *Saccharomyces cerevisiae*. It comprised mainly polysaccharides, of which β-glucan and mannan are the major constituents. It was widely used as a model to study fungus-mediated inflammation, phagocytosis, and the production of inflammatory cytokines and chemokines [21, 22]. TLR2 recognizes it directly or in coaction with CD14 and TLR6 [23, 24] to induce TNF-α gene expression [25]. TLR2 is the major pathway of proinflammatory signaling by zymosan interaction and is needed for the development of specific immune responses against pathogens [26].

Various studies on TLR2 have also been reported in zebrafish [27, 28], Japanese flounder [29], puffer fish [30], channel catfish [31], and in orange-spotted grouper [32, 33]. In European common carp, inductive over expression of TLR2 in macrophages was observed in response to PGN and LTA [34]. In the Indian major carps, modulation of TLR2 expression was reported in PGN, zymosan, and LTA treatment [35, 36].

India is the major supplier of fish in the world and ranks 3rd in freshwater fish production (FAO). Among various freshwater fishes, rohu (*Labeo rohita*) is the most commercially important and highly favored fish in the Indian subcontinent. TLR2 was characterized in rohu and the ligands that stimulate TLR2 signaling were also reported [35]. However, no studies have reported yet describing the structural characteristics of TLR2 in rohu and their key domains that binds to the specific ligands to stimulate cytokine expression. Furthermore, the key amino acids in the TLR2-TIR domains that interact with adapter molecule MyD88 to induce down-stream signaling were still unclear across the species.

To elucidate the structural scaffold in rohu TLR2, we report the 3D-model of extracellular domain of rohu TLR2 along with its key domains that are predicted to be involved in recognizing PGN, LTA and zymosan, and the critical region of interaction between TIR domains of TLR2 and MyD88. This is the first report across the fish species.

2. Materials and Methods

2.1. Domain Identification. Rohu TLR2 protein (GenBank ID: ADQ74644) with N-terminal extracellular domain (ECD), transmembrane domain, and C-terminal cytoplasmic TIR domain [35] was subjected to SignalP 4.1 server (http://www.cbs.dtu.dk/services/SignalP/) and NetNGlyc1.0 server (http://www.cbs.dtu.dk/services/NetNGlyc/) to predict the signal peptide and N-glycosylation sites respectively. The TIR domain in common carp MyD88 (GenBank ID: ADQ08685) was predicted by SMART (http://smart.embl-heidelberg.de/) and CD-search (http://www.ncbi.nlm.nih.gov/Structure/cdd/wrpsb.cgi) domain finding programs and was verified with published report of MyD88-TIR domains in zebrafish (Q5XJ85) and puffer fish (A8QMS7) in UniProt database (http://www.uniprot.org/).

2.2. Sequence Alignment, Template Identification, and Comparative Modeling of ECD and TIR Domain in Rohu TLR2, and MyD88-TIR Domain in Common Carp. Amino acid sequence of rohu TLR2 was aligned by MegAlign [37] in DNASTAR-Lasergene program with the amino acid sequences of TLR2 in other species derived from UniProtKB database. The TIR domains of rohu TLR2 and common carp MyD88 were aligned by MegAlign with amino acid sequences of TIR domains in other species deduced from UniProtKB database. The secondary structures of TLR2- and MyD88-TIR domains were predicted by PSIPRED program (http://bioinf.cs.ucl.ac.uk/psipred/).

Template search for TLR2-ECD (561 aa), TLR2-TIR (146 aa), and MyD88-TIR (137 aa) domains in PDB database identified mouse TLR1-TLR2 heterodimer (PDB ID: 2Z81), TIR domain of human TLR2 (PDB ID: 1O77), and TIR domain of human MyD88 (PDB ID: 2Z5V) as the best homologous structures with top identity score. To ascertain the sensitivity and accuracy of the selected templates, FUGUE [38] program was used to perform sequence-structure comparison between the target and the template and was represented by JOY annotation program [39]. For each three domains (TLR2-ECD, TLR2-TIR, and MyD88-TIR) a set of twenty 3D models were generated by Modeller9v10 program [40]. Among these 20 models (for each domain), the model with lowest discrete optimized protein energy (DOPE) score was considered for further studies. The lowest DOPE models of TLR2-ECD, TLR2-TIR, and MyD88-TIR were subjected for loop modeling and refinement in Accelrys DS 2.5 (San Diego, Accelrys) under CHARMM force field. The long BB loops and DD loops in TLR2-TIR and MyD88-TIR models after loop refinement were notably analyzed, and changes were marked by superimposing them with their respective templates. The refined models were subjected to energy minimization by DS 2.5.

2.3. Molecular Dynamics Simulation. Molecular dynamics (MD) simulations were carried out for the modeled systems using the GROMACS 4.5.5 program [41]. Homology models were set for MDS under GROMOS54a7 force field. The 3D models were placed in a cubic box maintaining a distance of 10 Å for TLR2-ECD, 9 Å for TLR2-TIR, and 9 Å for MyD88-TIR between the box edges and the protein surface. The systems were solvated in simple point charge (SPC) models and were neutralized by adding counter ions. In order to remove spurious contacts energy minimization of the solvated systems was done using the steepest descent integrator. The bond lengths and geometry of water molecules were constrained. All of the three restrained models were subjected to position-restrained MD under NPT conditions for 1 ns (nanosecond). Finally, 40 ns production MD run was carried out for TLR2-ECD and 20 ns for TLR2-TIR and MyD88-TIR models using particle mesh Ewald (PME) electrostatics method under NPT conditions. Snapshots of the trajectory were taken in every 0.5 picoseconds. GROMACS and VMD 1.9.1 (http://www.ks.uiuc.edu/Research/vmd/) routines were utilized to check trajectories and the quality of the simulations. The graphs of trajectory analysis were created using Xmgr 4.1.2 (http://plasma-gate.weizmann.ac.il/Xmgr/).

2.4. Model Validation. The final snapshot obtained at the end of each MDS was considered to represent the structures of the TLR2-ECD, TLR2-TIR, and MyD88-TIR models. These simulated models were set for validation by SAVES (http://nihserver.mbi.ucla.edu/SAVES/), WHAT IF [42], MolProbity [43], ProQ [44], ModFOLD [45], and MetaMQAP [46] servers. The simulated models were superimposed with their respective templates to examine the deflections by PyMOL (http://www.pymol.org/). Cross-check validation was carried out using model as template and the primary amino acids of the respective template as target.

2.5. Molecular Docking of PGN, LTA, and Zymosan with Rohu TLR2-ECD. Three different 2D structures of PGN [16], that is, (i) MurNac-L-Ala-*i*-D-Glu-L-Lys (PGN-I), (ii) MurNac-L-Ala-*i*-D-Glu-L-Lys-D-Ala-Gly (PGN-II), and (iii) MurNac-L-Ala-*i*-D-Glu-L-DAP-D-Ala (PGN-DAP), were generated by Chemsketch (http://www.acdlabs.com/resources/freeware/chemsketch/). The 2D structure of zymosan (CID: 11375554) was obtained from the NCBI PubChem database (http://pubchem.ncbi.nlm.nih.gov/) and LTA was from KEGG (KEGG: C06042) ligand database (http://www.genome.jp/ligand/). The 3D structures of all these compounds were generated using PRODRG2 server (http://davapc1.bioch.dundee.ac.uk/prodrg/) subjecting to chirality, full charges with energy minimization. The generated 3D structures were subjected to DS 2.5 for ligand minimization. The probable ligand binding pockets in TLR2-ECD were predicted by metaPocket finder [47] and Q-site finder [48]. The LTA binding site in mouse TLR2 (PDB ID: 3A7B) was also considered for docking. Molecular docking was carried out using AutoDock 4.0 [49], FlexX 2.1 [50], and GOLD 4.1 [51] following previously described methods [52] with receptor and ligand flexibility. In this, the important neighbouring residues at the predicted binding sites were set to flexible that covered all the active site residues and allowed for the flexible rotation of the ligand. Docking of previously reported PGN binding sites in other species [53] was also carried out. In AutoDock, the lowest-energy solution of the ligand all-atom RMSD cluster was taken to calculate the binding energy. The predicted interacting residues obtained by AutoDock were matched with the predicted binding pocket amino acids of metaPocket finder and Q-site finder,

and these binding pockets were referred for docking in FlexX and GOLD. The docking poses with H-bond forming amino acids were graphically represented by PyMOL and DS 2.5.

2.6. Protein-Protein Interaction. Rohu and common carp (*Cyprinus carpio*) belong to the Cyprinidae family and are very closely related. Till date, rohu MyD88 gene has not been cloned. Therefore, to understand the TLR2 and MyD88 interaction, we considered common carp MyD88 (GenBank ID: ADQ08685). The interface residues for TLR2-TIR and MyD88-TIR domains were predicted with reference to their template proteins structural and functional properties. Protein-Protein Interaction Site Predictor (cons-PPISP) (http://pipe.scs.fsu.edu/ppisp.html), Inter-ProSurf (http://curie.utmb.edu/prosurf.html), and Patch-Dock server (http://bioinfo3d.cs.tau.ac.il/PatchDock/) were used to find the interacting residues in TLR2-TIR and MyD88-TIR. Docking was performed using HADDOCK [54] and ZDOCK [55] web servers. Intermolecular contacts were analyzed with DIMPLOT, a part of LIG-PLOT software package (http://www.ebi.ac.uk/thornton-srv/software/LigPlus/) using default parameters.

2.7. Structural Refinement and Stability Evaluation of Complexes. The best protein-ligand complexes obtained from docking studies of PGN, LTA, and zymosan with TLR2-ECD were subjected to MDS using the previously defined parameters in GROMACS. To gain insight into the structural stability of the protein-ligand and protein-protein complexes, MD simulations were performed for PGN-I-TLR2-ECD, PGN-II-TLR2-ECD, PGN-DAP-TLR2-ECD, LTA-TLR2-ECD, zymosan-TLR2-ECD, and TLR2-TIR-MyD88-TIR complex for different time periods of MDS. A production MD run for 10 ns was carried out for TLR2-ECD ligand complexes and protein-protein complex. The existence of H-bonds in the complex in different periods of MDS was analyzed.

2.8. In Silico Site-Directed Mutagenesis. To identify the key amino acids among interacting amino acid residues in TLR2-ECD, TLR2-TIR, and MyD88-TIR domains, site-directed mutagenesis was carried out in DS 2.5 under build mutant protocol. Redocking was performed to calculate the fitness score in GOLD after mutation, and docking scores were cross-checked with previous fitness scores. Protein-protein interaction hot spots were predicted after mutagenesis by HADDOCK.

3. Results and Discussion

3.1. Domain Analysis. The full length TLR2 protein is constituted of 792 amino acids including a signal peptide of 30 amino acids (1–30 aa). The mature TLR2 protein ECD, trans-membrane (TM) and TIR domain constituted of 34–590, 595–612, and 645–790 amino acids respectively. The alignment of TLR2 amino acids with other species revealed their good conservation across the species (See Figure S1 in supplementary material available online at doi: http://dx.doi.org/10.1155/2013/185282). Among

Elucidation of Novel Structural Scaffold in Rohu TLR2 and Its Binding Site Analysis with Peptidoglycan, Lipoteichoic Acid and Zymosan Ligands, and Downstream MyD88 Adaptor Protein

27

TABLE 1: Sequence identities between rohu TLR2-ECD (target) and mouse TLR2-ECD (template).

LRR	Identity (%)	LRR	Identity (%)
1	47.82	12	27.77
2	29.16	13	20
3	63.63	14	33.33
4	52	15	37.93
5	34.46	16	34.78
6	35.57	17	50
7	9.52	18	52.38
8	15.38	19	50
9	28.57	20	40.9
10	26.31	21	29.16
11	28		

TABLE 2: Sequence identities between rohu TLR2-TIR (target) and human TLR2-TIR (template).

Position	Identity (%)	Position	Identity (%)
βA	100	CD loop	46.66
AA loop	66.67	βD	60
αA	58.33	DD loop	69.23
βB	42.85	αD	88.88
BB Loop	100	DE loop	50
αB	90.9	βE	100
βC	75	EE loop	50
αC	69.23	αE	50

TABLE 3: Sequence identities between common carp MyD88-TIR (target) and human MyD88-TIR (template).

Position	Identity (%)	Position	Identity (%)
βA	100	CC loop	66.66
AA loop	80	βD	60
αA	69.23	DD loop	70.58
βB	100	βE	100
BB Loop	86.66	EE loop	66.66
αB	100	αE	68.75
βC	85.71		

them, rohu TLR2 showed highest identity with common carp (88.1%) and lowest identity with mouse (40.5%). N-glycosylation site prediction server predicted 10 glycosylation sites, out of which 9 were in the ECD and 1 in the TIR domain. Among these 10 N-glycosylation sites, 8 were potential with a value greater than threshold value (0.5) and the remaining two were below the threshold. Single N-glycosylation site was present each at LRR1, 3, 8, 14, 16, 18, 21, and TIR domain, and the remaining two were at LRR6. The multiple sequence alignment of TLR2-TIR with other species (Figure 1(a)) and secondary structure analysis (Figure 1(b)) showed well-conserved α-helices, β-sheets, and biologically most important BB and DD loops [56]. In MyD88-TIR domain the multiple sequence alignment and secondary

TABLE 4: Validation report for TLR2-ECD, TLR2-TIR, and MyD88-TIR homology models.

(a) Validation by SAVES server

Ramachandran plot (PROCHECK)	TLR2-ECD Residue (%)	TLR2-TIR Residue (%)	MyD88-TIR Residue (%)
Most favored regions	66.7	78.7	73.2
Additionally allowed regions	30.0	20.6	24.4
Generously allowed regions	1.8	0.0	1.6
Disallowed regions	1.6	0.7	0.8
Verify3D score	95.37	97.28	87.6
ERRAT	61.059	86.364	86.325
PROVE (mean Z-score)	1.609	1.48	1.63

(b) Stereochemical quality of homology models by ProQ, ModFOLD, and MetaMQAP server

	TLR2-ECD	TLR2-TIR	MyD88-TIR
ProQ (LG/MX)	7.062/0.432	6.401/0.772	7.067/0.847
ModFOLD (Q/P)	0.6326/0.0065	0.7473/0.00038	0.5787/0.0022
MetaMQAP (GDT/RMSD)	68.93/2.137	78.767/1.523	72.628/2.319

*ProQ-LG: >1.5 fairly good; >2.5 very good; >4 extremely good. ProQ-MX: >0.1 fairly good; >0.5 very good; >0.8 extremely good. ModFOLD-Q: >0.5 medium confidence; >0.75 high confidence. ModFOLD-P: <0.05 medium confidence; <0.01 high confidence. MetaMQAP-GDT/RMSD: an ideal model has a GDT score over 59 and an RMSD around 2.0 Å.

structure prediction (Figures 2(a) and 2(b)) also revealed a good conservation among the phylogenetically divergent species.

3.2. Structural Analysis of TLR2-ECD, TLR2-TIR, and MyD88-TIR Domains. The BLAST search analysis showed that the ligand recognizing LRR regions in TLR2-ECD shared the close structural relationship with mouse TLR1-TLR2 heterodimer (PDB ID: 2Z81) having 35% and 52% sequence identities and similarities, respectively. The TLR2-TIR and MyD88-TIR domains shared 71% and 78% sequence identities with their respective templates (PDB ID: 1O77 and 2Z5V). The sequence-structure alignment by FUGUE revealed a good conservation of secondary structures (α-helices and β-sheets) between the target and template. The identity scores between the LRR regions of TLR2-ECD and 2Z81 were presented in Table 1. The sequence identities between the important biological regions as reported in human and mouse TIR domains with their respective templates were given in Tables 2 and 3. The structure-structure alignment between the lowest DOPE score models and their respective templates showed good structural conservation across the domains. The TLR2-ECD took a horseshoe shape with 23 LRR domains including LRRNT and LRRCT. Most of the LRR domains consisted of β-strands connected by long loop and some with α-helices. The β-strands faced towards the concave surface in TLR2-ECD model, and the α-helices were present

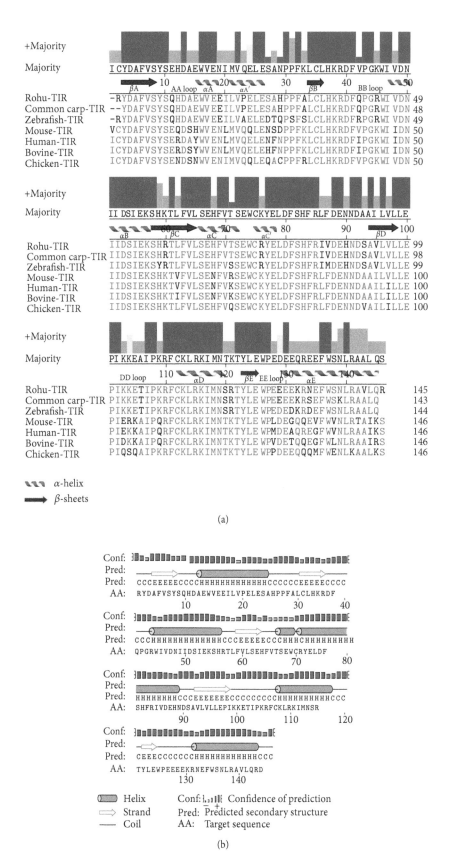

FIGURE 1: Multiple sequence alignment and secondary structure prediction of TLR2-TIR domain. (a) Multiple sequence alignment of TLR2-TIR domain of rohu with others by MegAlign program. Conserved residues were shown in yellow. Consensus residues are shown in the majority axis. (b) Secondary structure representation of TLR2-TIR domain by PSIPRED. Helices denoted as "H," beta strands as "E," and loops as "C."

Elucidation of Novel Structural Scaffold in Rohu TLR2 and Its Binding Site Analysis with Peptidoglycan, Lipoteichoic Acid and Zymosan Ligands, and Downstream MyD88 Adaptor Protein

29

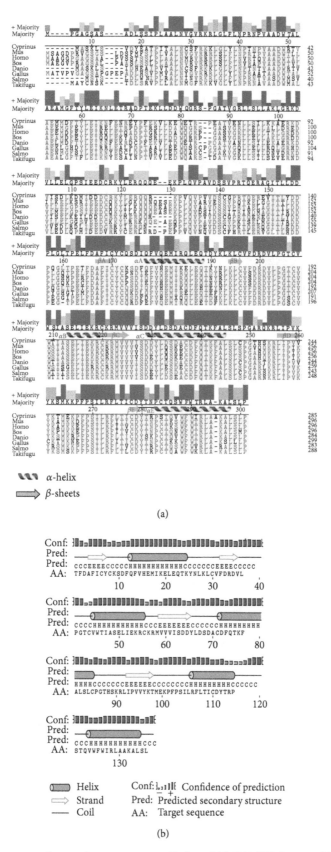

FIGURE 2: Multiple sequence alignment and secondary structure prediction of MyD88-TIR domain. (a) Multiple sequence alignment of MyD88-TIR domain of common carp with others by MegAlign program. Conserved residues were shown in yellow. Consensus residues are shown in the majority axis. (b) Secondary structure representation of MyD88-TIR domain by PSIPRED. Helices denoted as "H," beta strands as "E," and loops as "C."

TABLE 5: Molecular interaction of rohu TLR2-ECD with ligands.

(a) Docking analysis of TLR2-ECD with PGN, LTA, and zymosan by AutoDock 4.0

Grid centre and ligand	Interacting residues	Binding energy kcal/mol	No. of H-bonds[a]
PGN-I (B5)	Tyr366, Thr395, Asn397, Ser399, Tyr421, Asn423, Ser425, His426, Asn446, Ser448, Ser449, Asp467, Glu470, Thr497	−4.29	6
PGN-I (B6)	Ser259, Ser285, Tyr286, His312, Thr313, Arg342, Ser344, Tyr366	−4.33	6
PGN-DAP (B5)	Asp368, Leu369, Ser370, Gln371, Asn397, Ser399, Gln400, Tyr421, Asp423, Ser425, His426, Asn446, Ser448, Ser449, Asp467, Ser469, Glu470, Thr489	−3.19	11
PGN-DAP (B6)	Thr246, Glu254, Gly255, Lys258, Leu276, Thr277, Met279, Asp280, Gly281, Ser282, Ser283, Leu284, Ser304, Tyr305, Thr306, His307, Tyr308, Glu309	−3.38	7
LTA sites	Glu323, Phe324, Phe325, Glu326, Met330, Met331, Phe335, Thr349, Val350, Phe351, Val352, Ile353, Pro354, Pro355, Ile356, Leu360, Asn372, Leu373, Leu374, Pro381	−1.92	1
Zymosan	Leu473, Thr474, Val475, Phe476, Asn477, Thr495, Leu496, Pro497, His498, Gly499, Glu500, Leu501, Ser520, Ser521, Asp522, Arg525	−7.55	13

[a]Hydrogen bonds.

(b) Docking analysis of TLR2-ECD with PGN, LTA, and zymosan by FlexX 2.1

Ligands	Interacting residues	Binding energy kcal/mol	No. of H-Bonds[a]
PGN-I	Asn397, Ser399, Gln400, Asn401, His426, Ser428, Lys451, Glu470	−18.85	18
PGN-II	Ser428, Phe429, Val430, Ser448, Lys451, Arg453, Lys454, Asp472, Ser469, Gln470	−12.80	14
PGN-DAP	Gln400, Asn401, His426, Ser428, Ser449, Lys451	−15.47	15
LTA	Asn318, Leu319, Asp320, Ile321, Phe324, Asn347, Gly348, Thr349, Val350, Gln371	−6.92	13
Zymosan	Arg492, Leu493, Met494, Leu496, Arg516, Met517, Ser520, Asp522	−13.81	10

[a]Hydrogen bonds.

(c) Docking analysis of TLR2-ECD with PGN, LTA, and zymosan by GOLD 4.1

Ligands	Interacting residues	GOLD fitness score	No. of H-Bonds[a]
PGN-I (B5)	Ile394, Asn397, Ser399, Gln400, Tyr421, Asp423, Ser425, His426, Asn446, Ser448, Ser449, Asp467, Ser469, Glu470, Thr489, Gly490, Glu511, Arg512	42.38	17
PGN-II (B5)	Tyr366, Asp368, Ser370, Gln371, Asn397, Ser399, Gln400, Tyr421, Ser425, Asn446, Ser448, Val465, Asp467, Ser469, Glu470, Thr489, Gly490, Arg512	44.01	20
PGN-DAP (B5)	Asn446, Ser448, Ser449, Asp467, Ser469, Glu470, Ile487, Thr489, Gly490, Gln511, Arg512	40.55	13
PGN-II (B6)	Thr246, Glu247, Pro248, Phe249, Lys250, Thr252, Thr277, Asp280, Ser304, Tyr305, Thr306, His307, Tyr308,	23.00	8
LTA	Leu319, Asp320, Ile321, Phe324, Phe327, Met330, Met331, Phe335, Gly348, Thr349, Val350, Phe351, Glu380, Pro381	44.65	4
Zymosan	Arg492, Leu493, Met494, Thr495, Leu496, Ala514, Leu515, Arg516, Met517, Phe518, Asn519, Ser520, Ser521, Asp522, Arg525	39.71	8

[a]Hydrogen bonds.

at the convex surface. There were five α-helices and five β-sheets in TLR2-TIR domain and four α-helices and five β-sheets in MyD88-TIR domain.

3.3. Molecular Dynamics of Homology Models. The stability and MD properties were observed up to 40 ns for TLR2-ECD and up to 20 ns for TLR2-TIR and MyD88-TIR domains, and the RMSD values over time were shown in Figure 3. The MD analysis in TLR2-ECD showed that the RMSD trajectory rose from the beginning to 12 ns with an average RMSD of 4.23 Å. It attained an approximately stable plateau with an average RMSD of 4.673 Å till the end of simulation. The RMSD

trajectories of TLR2-TIR and MyD88-TIR were observed to be stable after 5 ns with an average RMSD of 2.74 Å and 3.68 Å, respectively. The RMSF of Cα atoms of each amino acid in TLR2-ECD identified LRR7-11 as the most flipped region (Figure 4(a)). These regions are constituted of six β-sheets, one α-helix, and long loops. In higher vertebrates, this region was reported as lipopeptide binding region [57]. The flexible long loops (BB and DD loops) in TLR2-TIR and MyD88-TIR domains showed major fluctuations in the RMSF graph and were expected to be engaged in protein-protein interaction (Figures 4(b) and 4(c)). Secondary structure analysis from the trajectory in TLR2-ECD showed little

Elucidation of Novel Structural Scaffold in Rohu TLR2 and Its Binding Site Analysis with Peptidoglycan, Lipoteichoic Acid and Zymosan Ligands, and Downstream MyD88 Adaptor Protein

31

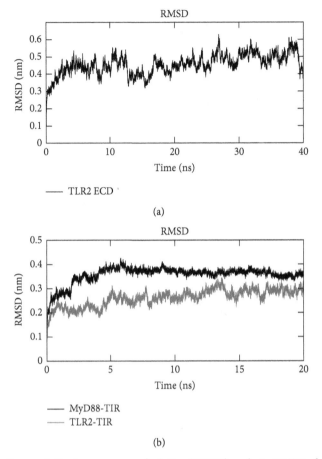

(a)

(b)

FIGURE 3: Root mean square deviation (RMSD) analysis. RMSD of (a) TLR2-ECD up to 40 ns and (b) MyD88-TIR and TLR2-TIR domains up to 20 ns MD simulation.

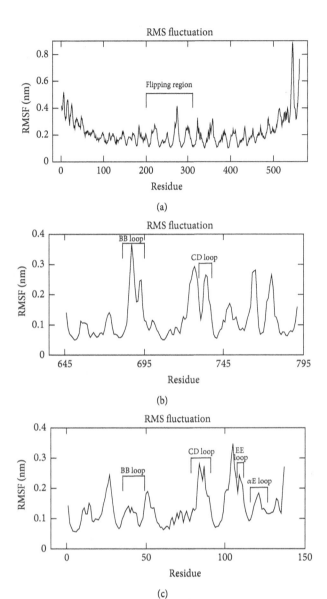

(a)

(b)

(c)

FIGURE 4: Root mean square fluctuation (RMSF) analysis for homology models. RMSF per residue over the dynamics was shown in graph. (a) TLR2-ECD; (b) TLR2-TIR; (c) MyD88-TIR.

variation of α-helices and β-sheets. However, the coil regions much varied with respect to simulation period. In TLR2-TIR, no major secondary structural changes were observed during MDS.

3.4. Validation of Homology Models.

The PROCHECK analysis at SAVES of three models (TLR2-ECD, TLR2-TIR, and MyD88-TIR) showed that the phi-psi angles of most of the residues were in the allowed regions of Ramachandran plot (Figure S2). The SAVES results (Table 4(a)) of all models were within the cut-off range suggesting the reliability of our proposed models. The protein stereochemical quality analysis by ProQ, ModFOLD, and MetaMQAP servers showed an acceptable score of all models (Table 4(b)). The average coarse packing quality, planarity, and the collision with symmetry axis, bond lengths, and bond angles obtained by the WHAT IF server of all models revealed the satisfactory acceptance of the models. The results of MolProbity server of all models were also within the range. The RMSD value for all atoms and Cα atoms by superimposing target models with their respective templates showed very low deviation along the significant biological domains. The low deviation between the target-template structures suggested the acceptance of

the proposed models. The cross-check validation report indicated acceptability between the experimental structures (PDB ID: 2Z81, 1O77, and 2Z5V) and their models. The RMSD values calculated by PyMOL superimposition program for Cα atoms between the PDB coordinates and the lowest DOPE score models of 2Z81, 1O77, and 2Z5V generated by Modeller were 1.13 Å, 0.518 Å, and 0.705 Å, respectively. The comparison of Ramachandran plot analysis of the homology models of 2Z81, 1O77, and 2Z5V showed similar results for both experimental and hypothetical models (Table S1). The cross-check validation fortified the acceptance of TLR2-ECD, TLR2-TIR, and MyD88-TIR models.

3.5. Binding Site Analysis of PGN, LTA, and Zymosan with TLR2-ECD.

For docking analysis, the predicted top seven (B1 to B7) probable ligand binding pockets in TLR2-ECD

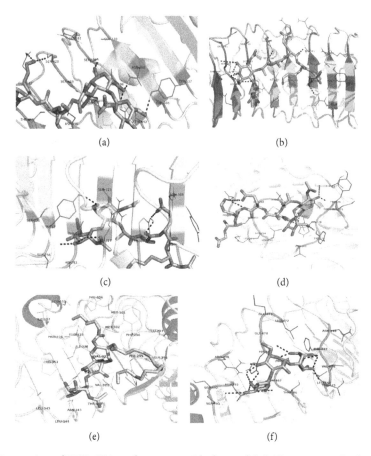

FIGURE 5: Illustration of the interaction of PGN, LTA, and zymosan with the modeled 3D structure of rohu TLR2-ECD by AutoDock 4.0 program. At B5 region, interaction of PGN-I with TLR2-ECD (a) and PGN-DAP with TLR2-ECD (b); at B6 region, interaction of PGN-I with TLR2-ECD (c) and PGN-DAP with TLR2-ECD (d); interaction of LTA with TLR2-ECD (e) and zymosan with TLR2-ECD (f). The TLR2-ECD was shown in ribbon and ligands (PGN, LTA, and zymosan) were shown in solid form. Amino acid number depicted in the figure was shown as per the matured protein (after removal of the signal peptide).

(close to the N-glycosylation sites) were considered (Table S2) including previously reported LTA binding site in mouse TLR2 [58]. Interaction of PGN with TLR2-ECD in AutoDock revealed PGN binding sites at B5, and it was in agreement with the previous observation [53]. Both PGN-I and PGN-DAP showed good interactions at B5 regions (Figures 5(a) and 5(b)). The lists of interacting amino acids were presented in Table 5(a). Docking at B6 site also presented good binding score for PGN ligands (Figures 5(c) and 5(d)). AutoDock identified B_{mouse} and B7 with highest binding affinities for LTA and zymosan, respectively (Figures 5(e) and 5(f)).

In FlexX docking, the binding sites B3 and B4 revealed high positive FlexX score for all ligands and, hence, excluded from further studies. The B5 site (LRR16–19) resulted in good FlexX score −18.85, −12.80, and −15.47 for PGN-I, PGN-II, and PGN-DAP, respectively. Docking at B6 site (LRR8-10) also resulted a satisfactory FlexX score for PGN-II (−13.23) and comparatively a low FlexX score was predicted for PGN-I and PGN-DAP. The rest of the binding pockets were found to be irrelevant for PGN interaction with very little positive and negative FlexX score. The interaction of LTA with TLR2-ECD with highest FlexX score (−6.92) was obtained at

B_{mouse} region (LRR12–14). Interaction of LTA at other binding sites yielded irrelevant FlexX score. Zymosan interacted with TLR2-ECD at B7 (LRR20-CT) region effectively with a FlexX score of (−13.81), and other binding sites were found to be very less interactive. The FlexX scores at different binding regions were presented in Table 5(b).

The GOLD scores for PGN-I, PGN-II, and PGN-DAP at B5 and B6 sites, for LTA at B_{mouse} and for zymosan at B7 site were given in Table 5(c). The GOLD fitness score was found to be highest in the proposed binding sites of FlexX program in comparison to other binding sites (Figures 6(a)–6(f)). The GOLD docking score of PGN-I, PGN-II, and PGN-DAP was predicted to be less at B6 site as compared to B5 site (Figures 6(a)–6(c)). Interaction of PGN-II at B6 site also showed a good GOLD fitness score (Figure 6(d)). Docking of zymosan (Figure 6(e)) and LTA (Figure 6(f)) in GOLD also ensured B7 and B_{mouse} as the potential binding sites.

3.6. TLR2-TIR and MyD88-TIR Interaction.
The MyD88 functions as an adaptor molecule that transmits signal to downstream molecules from ligand activated TLRs by interacting with the TIR domains. The predicted interface residues in

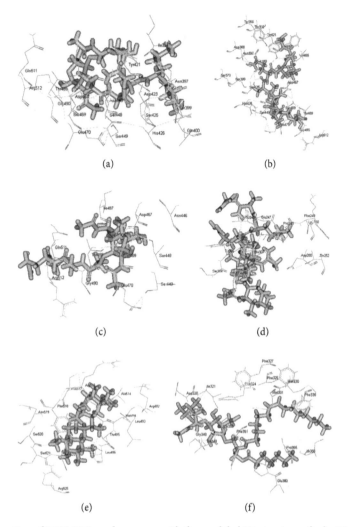

(a)

(b)

(c)

(d)

(e)

(f)

FIGURE 6: Illustration of the interaction of PGN, LTA, and zymosan with the modeled 3D structure of rohu TLR2-ECD by GOLD 4.1 program. Interaction of (a) PGN-I and TLR2-ECD at LRR16-19; (b) PGN-II and TLR2-ECD at LRR16-19; (c) PGN-DAP and TLR2-ECD at LRR16-19; (d) PGN-II and TLR2-ECD at LRR8-10; (e) zymosan and TLR2-ECD at LRR20-CT; (f) LTA and TLR2-ECD at LRR12-14. Rohu TLR2-ECD model was shown as line and ligands (PGN, LTA, and zymosan) are shown as stick.

cons-PPISP, InterProSurf, and PatchDock were observed to be present in the most flexible regions of TLR2-TIR and MyD88-TIR domains (Table S3). Majority of the interacting amino acids were distributed in BB loop, αB, αC, and CD loop in TLR2-TIR and BB loop, αB helix, and CD loop in MyD88-TIR (Table S3). The best cluster obtained in HADDOCK showed a very low RMSD (1.2 ± 0.7 Å) and intermolecular energy (−722.9 kcal mol-1) with a buried surface area of 2029.2 Å^2. The binding orientation and amino acid interactions generated by DS 2.5 were presented in Figure 7(a). The phylogenies of interacted amino acids identified the strongly bonded residues and were highlighted in Figure 7(b). DIMPLOT analysis of the complex showed that BB loop, αC, and αC′ helix residues of TLR2-TIR domain were mostly interacted with AA, BB loops and αB, αC helices of MyD88-TIR domain (Figure S3(a)). The protein-protein complex (Rank-1) in ZDOCK yielded approximately same interacting amino acids residues (as HADDOCK) for TLR2-TIR and

MyD88-TIR domains (Figure S3(b)). Amino acid residues in TLR2-TIR and MyD88-TIR domain involved in hydrogen bonding and hydrophobic interactions were presented in Table 6.

3.7. Stability Analysis of Protein Complexes by MDS. Previously it was reported that binding site B5 (LRR16–19) (corresponding to human) had the highest affinity for PGN recognition, and binding site B6 (LRR8–10) had a low potential for PGN recognition [53]. In this study, docking scores in B6 for PGN were comparatively lower than B5 region. However, the number of N-glycosylation sites closer to B6 was higher. This data may suggest the possibility of PGN interaction as it is comprised of N-acetylglucosamine. The H-bond analysis showed more number of H-bonds in B5 region (avg. 8 numbers) than B6 region (avg. 5 numbers) with highest binding affinity (Figures 8(a)–8(c)). The existence of H-bonds fluctuated at B6 region during different time periods

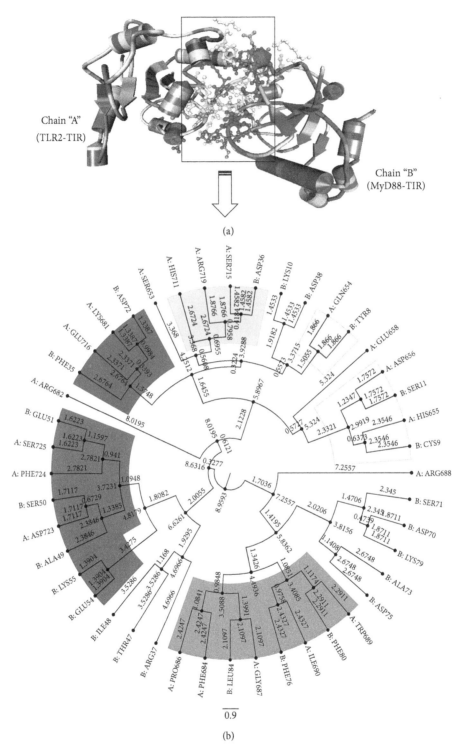

FIGURE 7: Interaction of TLR2-TIR and MyD88-TIR in Discovery Studio 2.5. (a) TLR2-TIR model is labeled as chain "A" and MyD88-TIR model is labeled as chain "B." Interface residues are shown inside a rectangle box in ball and stick representation. (b) Clustering of interface residues between TLR2-TIR and MyD88-TIR domain in tree format. Residues of TLR2-TIR are marked as chain "A" and MyD88-TIR as chain "B." Strongly interacting residues are highlighted with different colors.

of MD simulation (Figure 8(d)). Thus, both the docking analysis and MDS suggested B5 region (LRR16–19) as the possible PGN recognition site in rohu TLR2. H-bond analysis for LTA and zymosan at B_{mouse} (LRR12–14) and B7 (LRR20-CT)

region depicted a stable orientation with conserved number of H-bonds throughout the simulation (Figures 8(e) and 8(f)). The DIMPLOT analysis of TLR2-TIR and MyD88-TIR complex generated after 10 ns of MDS showed that

Elucidation of Novel Structural Scaffold in Rohu TLR2 and Its Binding Site Analysis with Peptidoglycan, Lipoteichoic Acid and Zymosan Ligands, and Downstream MyD88 Adaptor Protein

35

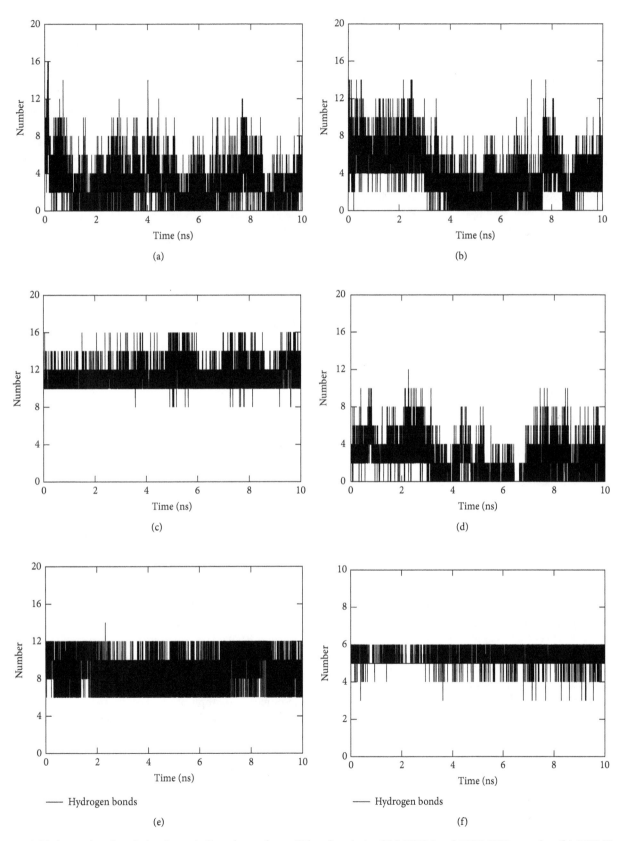

FIGURE 8: Hydrogen bond analysis of protein-ligand complexes. H-bond analysis of (a) PGN-I and TLR2-ECD complex, (b) PGN-II and TLR2-ECD complex, (c) PGN-DAP and TLR2-ECD complex, (d) PGN-II and TLR2-ECD complex at LRR8-10 region (B6), (e) LTA and TLR2-ECD complex at LRR20-CT, (f) and zymosan and TLR2-ECD complex at LRR12-14. X-axis represents time period of simulation and Y-axis represents number of hydrogen bonds.

TABLE 6: List of hydrogen bond forming and hydrophobic interacting residues between TLR2-TIR and MyD88-TIR domains.

Hydrogen bonds			Hydrophobic interactions	
Donor	Acceptor	Length (Å)	Donor	Acceptor
Trp689-NE1	Leu84-O	1.97	Ala73	Gln654
Ser715-O	Ser50-N	2.34	Gln77	His655
Ser715-O	Ile48-O	2.84	Tyr8	Asp656
Ser715-OG	Asp36-OD2	2.78	Ser71	His680
Asp723-OD2	Lys55-NZ	2.70	Asp72	Lys681
Thr714-N	Asp36-OD2	2.62	Cys9	Arg682
Thr714-O	Asp36-O	2.72	Phe76	Phe684
Ser83-OG	Gly687-N	2.94	Lys79	Pro686
Gln654-NE2	Asp38-OD2	2.72	Leu82	Gly687
Ser11-SG	Asp656-OD1	3.15	Ser83	Trp689
Cys9-NZ	Asp656-OD1	2.70	Phe80	Ile690
Asp72-N	Asp656-OD2	2.56	Leu84	Glu710
Cys9-NZ	His655-O	2.61	Cys85	His711
Cys9-NZ	His655-ND1	2.78	Pro86	Val713
Pro686-O	Ser50-OG	2.14	Asp36	Thr714
Arg688-NH2	Glu51-OE2	2.75	Ala73	Gln654
Asp692-OD1	Lys10-NZ	2.20	Gln77	His655
Lys681-NZ	Asp72-OD2	2.73	Tyr8	Asp656
His655-NE2	Asp75-OD2	1.91	Ser71	His680

the amino acid residues that were involved in protein-protein interaction were retained after the MDS (Figure S4). This suggested that the predicted interacting loops and helices in TLR2-TIR and MyD88-TIR domains were significant for protein-protein interaction.

3.8. Validation of Binding Domains by Site-Directed Mutagenesis. Alanine scanning of B5 regions of PGN binding domains showed loss of interaction due to absence of donors or acceptors in the active sites. But no single mutation of alanine for the interacting residues at this region showed a complete loss of docking. Proline and aspartic acid scanning of B5 region also ensued very low fitness score (9.6 and 12.8) in GOLD. Analysis of B5 region by mutating residues in pair, triplet, and quadruple combinations at a time indicated the viable importance of Asp394, Ser396, Asn397, and Ser399 as the fitness score attained a very minimum value in comparison to other GOLD runs.

Mutagenesis study at B7 residues in TLR2-ECD that formed H-bond with zymosan revealed a good fitness score for alanine scanning. However, proline scanning of all residues revealed loss of zymosan interaction with TLR2-ECD. Single proline mutation and acidic to basic mutation of different interacting residues followed by individual GOLD runs explored the importance of Ser520 and Asp522. A single mutation of Ser520-Pro520 and Asp522-Gln522 resulted in complete loss of zymosan interaction. Mutation of other residues altered the GOLD fitness score; however, in none of the cases docking loss was ensued. Alanine and proline scanning of LTA binding site resulted in low docking score

emphasizing the role of key residues Asp320 and Phe324 in LTA recognition.

4. Conclusion

The proposed 3D model of rohu TLR2 describes the protein features and its important domains. It also accentuates the importance of predicting key amino acids and LRR regions that are responsible for the specific ligand interaction and TLR2 signaling in fish and depicts a residue-detailed structural theoretical model. In the absence of crystal structure of TLR2 in any fish, this study provides structural insight into the TLR2 domains architecture. In rohu fish, the peptides at LRR16–19 (at B5), LRR12-14 (at B$_{mouse}$) and LRR20-CT (at B7) are predicted to be the most important interacting regions for PGN, LTA, and zymosan interactions, respectively. The structural organization of TIR domains in fish TLR2 and adapter molecule MyD88 have also been described. The interaction between TLR2-TIR and MyD88-TIR domain highlighted the contribution of BB loop, αB, αC, and CD loop in TLR2-TIR and BB loop, αB helix, and CD loop in MyD88-TIR domain. The data generated in this study are likely to be helpful to conduct further *in vivo* study to develop the strategy of innate immune activation and disease prevention in fish.

Acknowledgments

This work was financially supported by the grant of National Agricultural Innovation Project (NAIP), Indian Council of Agricultural Research (ICAR) (Project Code C4-C30018). The authors express their gratitude to Dr. A. Bandyopadhyay and Dr. S. Kochar, National Coordinator, NAIP-Comp-4, for their valuable suggestions and help. The authors would like to express their deepest gratitude to Dr. G. C. Sahoo, HOD, Bioinformatics Division, RMRIMS, Patna, India, for his valuable suggestion. Part of the work related to Discovery Studio, FlexX, and GOLD was carried out at RMRIMS, Patna. The authors would like to thank Mr. Roman Laskowski for providing the academic license of Ligplot. They thank Mr. Mahesh Patra (Research Associate) and Mr. Sukanta Kumar Pradhan, HOD, Department of Bioinformatics, Orissa University of Agriculture and Technology, Bhubaneswar, Odisha, India, for their support and constructive suggestions in data analysis. They gratefully acknowledge the Bioinformatics Resources and Applications Facility (BRAF) at the Center for Development of Advanced Computing (C-DAC), Pune, India.

References

[1] S. Akira, S. Uematsu, and O. Takeuchi, "Pathogen recognition and innate immunity," *Cell*, vol. 124, no. 4, pp. 783–801, 2006.

[2] S. de la Barrera, M. Alemán, and M. D. C. Sasiain, "Toll-like receptors in human infectious diseases," *Current Pharmaceutical Design*, vol. 12, no. 32, pp. 4173–4184, 2006.

[3] T. Kawai and S. Akira, "The role of pattern-recognition receptors in innate immunity: update on toll-like receptors," *Nature Immunology*, vol. 11, no. 5, pp. 373–384, 2010.

Elucidation of Novel Structural Scaffold in Rohu TLR2 and Its Binding Site Analysis with Peptidoglycan, Lipoteichoic Acid and Zymosan Ligands, and Downstream MyD88 Adaptor Protein

37

[4] R. Medzhitov, "Toll-like receptors and innate immunity," *Nature Reviews Immunology*, vol. 1, no. 2, pp. 135–145, 2001.

[5] B. A. Beutler, "TLRs and innate immunity," *Blood*, vol. 113, no. 7, pp. 1399–1407, 2009.

[6] U. Buwitt-Beckmann, H. Heine, K.-H. Wiesmüller et al., "TLR1- and TLR6-independent recognition of bacterial lipopeptides," *Journal of Biological Chemistry*, vol. 281, no. 14, pp. 9049–9057, 2006.

[7] O. Takeuchi, S. Sato, T. Horiuchi et al., "Cutting edge: role of Toll-like receptor 1 in mediating immune response to microbial lipoproteins," *Journal of Immunology*, vol. 169, no. 1, pp. 10–14, 2002.

[8] E. Lien, T. J. Sellati, A. Yoshimura et al., "Toll-like receptor 2 functions as a pattern recognition receptor for diverse bacterial products," *Journal of Biological Chemistry*, vol. 274, no. 47, pp. 33419–33425, 1999.

[9] R. Medzhitov, P. Preston-Hurlburt, E. Kopp et al., "MyD88 is an adaptor protein in the hToll/IL-1 receptor family signaling pathways," *Molecular Cell*, vol. 2, no. 2, pp. 253–258, 1998.

[10] R. Dziarski, "Recognition of bacterial peptidoglycan by the innate immune system," *Cellular and Molecular Life Sciences*, vol. 60, no. 9, pp. 1793–1804, 2003.

[11] K. H. Schleifer and O. Kandler, "Peptidoglycan types of bacterial cell walls and their taxonomic implications," *Bacteriological Reviews*, vol. 36, no. 4, pp. 407–477, 1972.

[12] R. Guan and R. A. Mariuzza, "Peptidoglycan recognition proteins of the innate immune system," *Trends in Microbiology*, vol. 15, no. 3, pp. 127–134, 2007.

[13] D. Iwaki, H. Mitsuzawa, S. Murakami et al., "The extracellular toll-like receptor 2 domain directly binds peptidoglycan derived from *Staphylococcus aureus*," *Journal of Biological Chemistry*, vol. 277, no. 27, pp. 24315–24320, 2002.

[14] H. Mitsuzawa, I. Wada, H. Sano et al., "Extracellular toll-like receptor 2 region containing Ser40-Ile64 but not Cys30-Ser39 is critical for the recognition of *Staphylococcus aureus* peptidoglycan," *Journal of Biological Chemistry*, vol. 276, no. 44, pp. 41350–41356, 2001.

[15] R. Schwandner, R. Dziarski, H. Wesche, M. Rothe, and C. J. Kirschning, "Peptidoglycan- and lipoteichoic acid-induced cell activation is mediated by Toll-like receptor 2," *Journal of Biological Chemistry*, vol. 274, no. 25, pp. 17406–17409, 1999.

[16] J. Asong, M. A. Wolfert, K. K. Maiti, D. Miller, and G.-J. Boons, "Binding and cellular activation studies reveal that toll-like receptor 2 can differentially recognize peptidoglycan from gram-positive and gram-negative bacteria," *Journal of Biological Chemistry*, vol. 284, no. 13, pp. 8643–8653, 2009.

[17] I. C. Sutcliffe and N. Shaw, "Atypical lipoteichoic acids of gram-positive bacteria," *Journal of Bacteriology*, vol. 173, no. 22, pp. 7065–7069, 1991.

[18] S. Deininger, S. Traub, D. Aichele et al., "Presentation of lipoteichoic acid potentiates its inflammatory activity," *Immunobiology*, vol. 213, no. 6, pp. 519–529, 2008.

[19] S. Von Aulock, S. Deininger, C. Draing, K. Gueinzius, O. Dehus, and C. Hermann, "Gender difference in cytokine secretion on immune stimulation with LPS and LTA," *Journal of Interferon and Cytokine Research*, vol. 26, no. 12, pp. 887–892, 2006.

[20] I.-T. Lee, S.-W. Wang, C.-W. Lee et al., "Lipoteichoic acid induces HO-1 expression via the TLR2/MyD88/c-Src/NADPH oxidase pathway and Nrf2 in human tracheal smooth muscle cells," *Journal of Immunology*, vol. 181, no. 7, pp. 5098–5110, 2008.

[21] B. N. Gantner, R. M. Simmons, S. J. Canavera, S. Akira, and D. M. Underhill, "Collaborative induction of inflammatory responses by dectin-1 and toll-like receptor 2," *Journal of Experimental Medicine*, vol. 197, no. 9, pp. 1107–1117, 2003.

[22] G. D. Brown, J. Herre, D. L. Williams, J. A. Willment, A. S. J. Marshall, and S. Gordon, "Dectin-1 mediates the biological effects of β-glucans," *Journal of Experimental Medicine*, vol. 197, no. 9, pp. 1119–1124, 2003.

[23] D. M. Underhill, A. Ozinsky, A. M. Hajjar et al., "The Toll-like receptor 2 is recruited to macrophage phagosomes and discriminates between pathogens," *Nature*, vol. 401, no. 6755, pp. 811–815, 1999.

[24] A. Ozinsky, D. M. Underhill, J. D. Fontenot et al., "The repertoire for pattern recognition of pathogens by the innate immune system is defined by cooperation between Toll-like receptors," *Proceedings of the National Academy of Sciences of the United States of America*, vol. 97, no. 25, pp. 13766–13771, 2000.

[25] M. Sato, H. Sano, D. Iwaki et al., "Direct binding of toll-like receptor 2 to Zymosan, and Zymosan-induced NF-κB activation and TNF-α secretion are down-regulated by lung collectin surfactant protein A," *Journal of Immunology*, vol. 171, no. 1, pp. 417–425, 2003.

[26] M. E. Frasnelli, D. Tarussio, V. Chobaz-Péclat, N. Busso, and A. So, "TLR2 modulates inflammation in zymosan-induced arthritis in mice," *Arthritis Research & Therapy*, vol. 7, no. 2, pp. R370–379, 2005.

[27] C. Jault, L. Pichon, and J. Chluba, "Toll-like receptor gene family and TIR-domain adapters in *Danio rerio*," *Molecular Immunology*, vol. 40, no. 11, pp. 759–771, 2004.

[28] A. H. Meijer, S. F. Gabby Krens, I. A. Medina Rodriguez et al., "Expression analysis of the Toll-like receptor and TIR domain adaptor families of zebrafish," *Molecular Immunology*, vol. 40, no. 11, pp. 773–783, 2004.

[29] I. Hirono, M. Takami, M. Miyata et al., "Characterization of gene structure and expression of two toll-like receptors from Japanese flounder *Paralichthys olivaceus*," *Immunogenetics*, vol. 56, no. 1, pp. 38–46, 2004.

[30] H. Oshiumi, T. Tsujita, K. Shida, M. Matsumoto, K. Ikeo, and T. Seya, "Prediction of the prototype of the human Toll-like receptor gene family from the pufferfish, *Fugu rubripes*, genome," *Immunogenetics*, vol. 54, no. 11, pp. 791–800, 2003.

[31] P. Baoprasertkul, E. Peatman, J. Abernathy, and Z. Liu, "Structural characterisation and expression analysis of Toll-like receptor 2 gene from catfish," *Fish and Shellfish Immunology*, vol. 22, no. 4, pp. 418–426, 2007.

[32] Y.-W. Li, X.-C. Luo, X.-M. Dan et al., "Orange-spotted grouper (*Epinephelus coioides*) TLR2, MyD88 and IL-1β involved in anti-*Cryptocaryon irritans* response," *Fish and Shellfish Immunology*, vol. 30, no. 6, pp. 1230–1240, 2011.

[33] Y. C. Wei, T. S. Pan, M. X. Chang et al., "Cloning and expression of Toll-like receptors 1 and 2 from a teleost fish, the orange-spotted grouper *Epinephelus coioides*," *Veterinary Immunology and Immunopathology*, vol. 141, no. 3-4, pp. 173–182, 2011.

[34] C. M. S. Ribeiro, T. Hermsen, A. J. Taverne-Thiele, H. F. J. Savelkoul, and G. F. Wiegertjes, "Evolution of recognition of ligands from gram-positive bacteria: similarities and differences in the TLR2-mediated response between mammalian vertebrates and teleost fish," *Journal of Immunology*, vol. 184, no. 5, pp. 2355–2368, 2010.

[35] M. Samanta, B. Swain, M. Basu et al., "Molecular characterization of toll-like receptor 2 (TLR2), analysis of its inductive

expression and associated down-stream signaling molecules following ligands exposure and bacterial infection in the Indian major carp, rohu (*Labeo rohita*)," *Fish and Shellfish Immunology*, vol. 32, no. 3, pp. 411–425, 2012.

[36] M. Basu, B. Swain, B. R. Sahoo, N. K. Maiti, and M. Samanta, "Induction of toll-like receptor (TLR) 2, and MyD88-dependent TLR- signaling in response to ligand stimulation and bacterial infections in the Indian major carp, mrigal (*Cirrhinus mrigala*)," *Molecular Biology Reports*, vol. 39, no. 5, pp. 6015–6028, 2012.

[37] J. P. Clewley and C. Arnold, "MEGALIGN. The multiple alignment module of LASERGENE," *Methods in Molecular Biology*, vol. 70, pp. 119–129, 1997.

[38] J. Shi, T. L. Blundell, and K. Mizuguchi, "FUGUE: sequence-structure homology recognition using environment-specific substitution tables and structure-dependent gap penalties," *Journal of Molecular Biology*, vol. 310, no. 1, pp. 243–257, 2001.

[39] K. Mizuguchi, C. M. Deane, T. L. Blundell, M. S. Johnson, and J. P. Overington, "JOY: protein sequence-structure representation and analysis," *Bioinformatics*, vol. 14, no. 7, pp. 617–623, 1998.

[40] A. Sali and T. L. Blundell, "Comparative protein modelling by satisfaction of spatial restraints," *Journal of Molecular Biology*, vol. 234, no. 3, pp. 779–815, 1993.

[41] D. Van Der Spoel, E. Lindahl, B. Hess, G. Groenhof, A. E. Mark, and H. J. C. Berendsen, "GROMACS: fast, flexible, and free," *Journal of Computational Chemistry*, vol. 26, no. 16, pp. 1701–1718, 2005.

[42] G. Vriend, "WHAT IF: a molecular modeling and drug design program," *Journal of Molecular Graphics*, vol. 8, no. 1, pp. 52–56, 1990.

[43] V. B. Chen, W. B. Arendall III, J. J. Headd et al., "MolProbity: all-atom structure validation for macromolecular crystallography," *Acta Crystallographica Section D*, vol. 66, no. 1, pp. 12–21, 2010.

[44] B. Wallner, H. Fang, and A. Elofsson, "Automatic consensus-based fold recognition using Pcons, ProQ, and Pmodeller," *Proteins*, vol. 53, no. 6, pp. 534–541, 2003.

[45] L. J. Mcguffin, "The ModFOLD server for the quality assessment of protein structural models," *Bioinformatics*, vol. 24, no. 4, pp. 586–587, 2008.

[46] M. Pawlowski, M. J. Gajda, R. Matlak, and J. M. Bujnicki, "MetaMQAP: a meta-server for the quality assessment of protein models," *BMC Bioinformatics*, vol. 9, article 403, 2008.

[47] B. Huang, "Metapocket: a meta approach to improve protein ligand binding site prediction," *OMICS A Journal of Integrative Biology*, vol. 13, no. 4, pp. 325–330, 2009.

[48] A. T. R. Laurie and R. M. Jackson, "Q-SiteFinder: an energy-based method for the prediction of protein-ligand binding sites," *Bioinformatics*, vol. 21, no. 9, pp. 1908–1916, 2005.

[49] R. Huey, G. M. Morris, A. J. Olson, and D. S. Goodsell, "A semi-empirical free energy force field with charge-based desolvation," *Journal of Computational Chemistry*, vol. 28, no. 6, pp. 1145–1152, 2007.

[50] M. Rarey, B. Kramer, T. Lengauer, and G. Klebe, "A fast flexible docking method using an incremental construction algorithm," *Journal of Molecular Biology*, vol. 261, no. 3, pp. 470–489, 1996.

[51] G. Jones, P. Willett, R. C. Glen, A. R. Leach, and R. Taylor, "Development and validation of a genetic algorithm for flexible docking," *Journal of Molecular Biology*, vol. 267, no. 3, pp. 727–748, 1997.

[52] B. R. Sahoo, M. Basu, B. Swain et al., "Structural insights of rohu TLR3, its binding site analysis with fish reovirus dsRNA, poly I:C and zebrafish TRIF," *International Journal of Biological Macromolecules*, vol. 51, no. 4, pp. 531–543, 2012.

[53] Y. Li, C. L. Efferson, R. Ramesh, G. E. Peoples, P. Hwu, and C. G. Ioannides, "A peptidoglycan monomer with the glutamine to serine change and basic peptides bind *in silico* to TLR-2 (403–455)," *Cancer Immunology, Immunotherapy*, vol. 60, no. 4, pp. 515–524, 2011.

[54] S. J. de Vries, M. van Dijk, and A. M. J. J. Bonvin, "The HADDOCK web server for data-driven biomolecular docking," *Nature Protocols*, vol. 5, no. 5, pp. 883–897, 2010.

[55] R. Chen, L. Li, and Z. Weng, "ZDOCK: an initial-stage protein-docking algorithm," *Proteins*, vol. 52, no. 1, pp. 80–87, 2003.

[56] S. Basith, B. Manavalan, R. G. Govindaraj, and S. Choi, "In silico approach to inhibition of signaling pathways of toll-like receptors 2 and 4 by ST2L," *PLoS ONE*, vol. 6, no. 8, Article ID e23989, 2011.

[57] M. S. Jin, S. E. Kim, J. Y. Heo et al., "Crystal structure of the TLR1-TLR2 heterodimer induced by binding of a tri-acylated lipopeptide," *Cell*, vol. 130, no. 6, pp. 1071–1082, 2007.

[58] J. Y. Kang, X. Nan, M. S. Jin et al., "Recognition of lipopeptide patterns by toll-like receptor 2-toll-like receptor 6 heterodimer," *Immunity*, vol. 31, no. 6, pp. 873–884, 2009.

5

A Local Genetic Algorithm for the Identification of Condition-Specific MicroRNA-Gene Modules

Wenbo Mu, Damian Roqueiro, and Yang Dai

Department of Bioengineering, University of Illinois at Chicago, Chicago, IL 60607, USA

Correspondence should be addressed to Yang Dai; yangdai@uic.edu

Academic Editors: R. Jiang, W. Tian, J. Wan, and X. Zhao

Transcription factor and microRNA are two types of key regulators of gene expression. Their regulatory mechanisms are highly complex. In this study, we propose a computational method to predict condition-specific regulatory modules that consist of microRNAs, transcription factors, and their commonly regulated genes. We used matched global expression profiles of mRNAs and microRNAs together with the predicted targets of transcription factors and microRNAs to construct an underlying regulatory network. Our method searches for highly scored modules from the network based on a two-step heuristic method that combines genetic and local search algorithms. Using two matched expression datasets, we demonstrate that our method can identify highly scored modules with statistical significance and biological relevance. The identified regulatory modules may provide useful insights on the mechanisms of transcription factors and microRNAs.

1. Introduction

Transcription factors (TFs) and microRNAs exert a widespread impact on gene expression. Most genes in genome are regulated by the TFs, which account for about 10% of the protein-coding genes in humans and mice [1]. TFs function by interacting with genomic cis-regulatory DNA elements. MicroRNAs primarily bind to regulatory elements located in the $3'$ untranslated region ($3'$UTR) of their target mRNAs. There are more than 1000 microRNAs, which target 60% of protein-encoding genes in the human genome, and each microRNA regulates about 200 transcripts (miRBase 2011 [2]). The identification of TF and microRNA targets is a key in understanding their roles in gene regulation. However, it is a laborious task. The availability of large amount of matched condition-specific microRNA and mRNA expression data for a specific cell or tissue type has provided a good resource for the prediction of microRNA functional target. Various methods using matched expression profiles coupled with sequence-based predictions of targets of microRNAs have been proposed [3]. On the other hand, the interplay between TFs and microRNAs was recently recognized [4]. However, there are only a limited number of integrated analysis tools [5–7]. Integrated analysis tools

for identifying functional regulatory modules involving microRNAs and TFs targets are still needed.

2. Materials and Methods

The proposed method starts with a matched global mRNA and microRNA expression dataset; that is, mRNA and microRNA expression levels were measured from the same sample. The method consists of four steps. (1) Perform differential expression analyses for microRNA and mRNA profiles. (2) Calculate correlations of expression for pairs of microRNAs, pairs of mRNAs, and pairs of microRNAs and mRNAs. (3) Predict TF and microRNA targets. (4) Predict microRNA-gene modules based on the information obtained from (1) to (3) by a heuristic method, which is the combination of a genetic algorithm and a local search. The framework of our proposed method is presented in Figure 1.

2.1. Datasets and Preprocessing. Two datasets were used in our study. The first dataset contains the expression profiles of 98 primary cancer, 13 metastatic cancer, and 28 normal prostate samples [8]. The mRNA expression profiles were measured using the Affymetrix Human Exon 1.0 ST

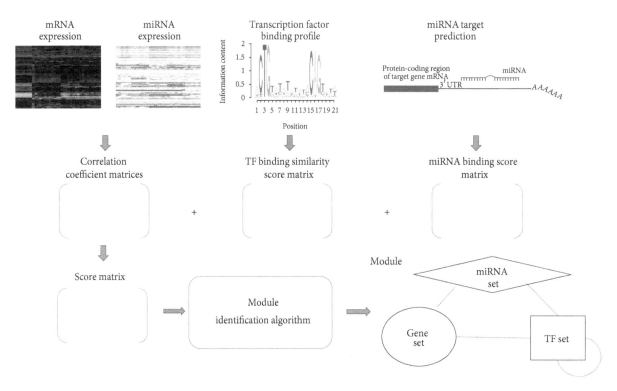

FIGURE 1: Method scheme.

Array which includes 26,447 mRNAs, and the microRNA expression profiles were measured by the Agilent Human microRNA Microarray 2.0 which includes 368 microRNAs. The normalized data were obtained from the NCBI Gene Expression Omnibus (GEO) [9] through GEO accession number GSE21032. The second dataset includes a wide variety of tumor and normal tissue types: 218 tumor samples of 14 common tumor types and 90 normal tissue types [10]. The mRNA expression profiles were measured with the Affymetrix Hu6800 and the Hu35KsubA Genechips and contained 16,063 genes. The corresponding microRNA expression profiles were measured with the bead-based flow cytometric microRNA expression profiling method on 217 mammalian microRNAs and 334 samples [11]. Among them, 68 cancer tissue samples on 11 tumor types and 21 normal samples have both mRNA expression profile and microRNA expression profile. These matched profiles were selected in our study. The normalized and log2-transformed data were obtained from the Broad Institute website (http://www.broad.mit.edu/cancer/pub/migcm/).

The differential expression analysis was performed on both mRNA and microRNA expression profiles. Prior to the analysis, 25% probes with the lowest variation (measured by coefficient of variation) for both mRNAs and microRNAs were discarded. The differential expression analysis was performed using *limma* package in Bioconductor, and the false discovery rate (FDR) was controlled by adjusting P values based on the Benjamini and Hochberg multiple testing procedure [12]. Since functional TFs are not necessarily differentially expressed, all genes whose protein products are TFs (TF genes) were kept in our analysis. For the rest of the

genes (nTF genes), a stringent cutoff of 0.001 for the adjusted P values was applied. Since a slight change of microRNA expresses can affect gene expression drastically, microRNAs with the adjusted P values less than 0.05 were defined as differentially expressed.

Pearson correlation coefficients (PCCs) were used to measure correlations of expression of (1) mRNA pairs, (2) microRNA pairs, and (3) mRNA-microRNA pairs. A permutation test on PCCs was employed for significance analysis. Specifically, random expression profiles were generated by shuffling the mRNA labels in the original datasets for 10,000 times, and the PCC was recalculated for each shuffled dataset. The P value was determined as the percentage of times that the PCC obtained from a shuffled dataset exceeded that obtained from the observed data.

Predicted microRNA targets were retrieved from the http://www.microRNA.org/ website, which provides access to the comprehensive database of predicted and experimentally validated microRNA targets [13–15]. The predicted targets for the conserved microRNAs with P value less than 0.05 were selected, resulting in a final set of 879,049 microRNA-gene pairs. The corresponding alignment scores associated with the microRNA targets were scaled to $(0, 1)$.

The predicted transcription factor binding sites (TFBSs) were obtained by mapping position weight matrices (PWMs) from TRANSFAC (ver. 2010.1) [16] of transcription factors to the promoter regions of genes using the MATCH algorithm [17]. We defined 10 KB upstream and 2 KB downstream of the transcription start site (TSS) as the promoter region of a gene. TFBSs were obtained from bindSDb [18], a database

```
Input:    Parameter list of the genetic algorithm
          Parameter list of local search
          Score matrix ScoreM.
          Number of Modules ModN
Output:   Module chromosomes M
Formal steps:
(1) Set m = 0
(2) while m != ModN do
(3)     Perform the genetic algorithm to identify co-expressed gene set and save to Gco
(4)     Apply the local search to Gco and save solution to M
(5)     Update PCC matrix
(6) end while
(7) Return M
```

ALGORITHM 1: Pseudocode for module identification.

developed to store both experimentally validated and predicted TFBSs based on the RefSeq gene information from the UCSC RefSeq track of the Human Genome Assembly (hg19) and the NCBI mRNA annotations. In case there are multiple PWMs for a TF, the maximum alignment score of all its PWMs to the predicted TFBSs was used to determine the unique relation between the TF and its multiple PWMs. The matching information between a TF and its gene symbol was obtained from TRANSFAC. Even with the stringent threshold for the alignment scores, the MATCH algorithm still produced a large number of TFBSs, among which many may be false positives. To reduce the number of false positives, we applied a cutoff value (described later) on the similarity scores to reduce the number of interactions significantly without losing too much information.

2.2. Proposed Algorithm. Our module identification method consists of two steps. (1) Identify coexpressed gene sets which include TF genes and nTF genes by the genetic algorithm (GA). This step located the highly plausible region of "good" solution in the searching space. (2) Search coregulators for the coexpressed gene sets obtained by the GA using the local search algorithm. All direct regulators of genes were candidates for the local search. In order to guarantee no duplicated modules to be considered in the future generations, after a module was identified from the local search, the correlation coefficient matrix of mRNAs was updated by removing the pairs involving the mRNAs in the current module. The pseudocode of our algorithm is given in Algorithm 1.

2.2.1. Design of the Genetic Algorithm. A binary string of fixed length was used to represent a chromosome, that is, a candidate of coexpressed gene sets in the GA. The value 1 stands for the gene included in the set and 0 for otherwise. Three setups with different percentages of genes included in the initial chromosomes were considered: 2%, 20%, and 80% of total genes. The roulette wheel selection was used for the selection of parent chromosomes for producing offspring. For the selected parents, the crossover was carried out separately for TF genes and nTF genes. The crossover probability P_{co} was in the range of (0.5–0.9) with an incremental size of 0.1. The

mutation probability P_{mu} was varied at four values: 0.00001, 0.0001, 0.001, and 0.01. In addition to these genetic operators, randomly generated chromosomes were introduced as new immigrants into the population pool to substitute the worst chromosome at each generation. Three immigration rates, 0.01, 0.001, and 0.0001, were considered.

The average of the absolute PCCs over all pairs of genes included in a chromosome was defined as the fitness score of the chromosome. Two termination conditions were considered: 5,000 generations limitation or the highest fitness score remains unchanged for 200 generations.

2.2.2. Design of Local Search Algorithm. After the best coexpressed gene set was obtained from the GA, the candidates for the local search were determined to be all regulators (microRNAs and TFs) that were either predicted to target the genes in the coexpressed gene set or had significant PCCs with them. The initial solution for the local search was constructed by the TF genes in coexpressed genes and the randomly added 1% microRNAs from the candidate pool of regulators. The fitness score of a local search solution, or module, was defined as follows.

Let M' and T' represent the set of microRNAs and TF genes in the module, respectively, G' the union of both TF genes and nTF genes, N the total number of interactions among the members in the module.

Define MGI as a score for the predicted targeting interactions between microRNAs and genes; MS_{ij} and Cor_{ij} as the binding score and the correlation coefficient between microRNA i and gene j, respectively:

$$MGI = \sum_{i \in M'} \sum_{j \in G'} \left(k_1 MS_{ij} + k_2 \left| Cor_{ij} \right| \right). \tag{1}$$

Here k_1 and k_2 are two parameters. In our study we used $k_2 = 1$ and $k_1 = 1, 2, 3$.

Define TGI as a score for the predicted target interactions between TF genes and all genes; TS_{ij} and Cor_{ij} as the binding score and correlation coefficient between TF-gene i and nTF-gene j, respectively:

$$\text{TGI} = \sum_{i \in T'} \sum_{j \in G'} \left(k_1 \text{TS}_{ij} + k_2 \left| \text{Cor}_{ij} \right| \right). \quad (2)$$

The total PCCs among microRNAs in M' were denoted by $\text{Cor}_{M'}$:

$$\text{Cor}_{M'} = \sum_{i,j \in M' i \neq j} \left| \text{Cor}_{ij} \right|. \quad (3)$$

To prevent the size of modules from unlimited increasing, the fitness score for a module was defined as the averaged value over the four sets of interaction scores described above:

$$F = \frac{\text{MGI} + \text{TGI} + \text{Cor}_{M'}}{N}. \quad (4)$$

The interaction scores of TF-gene and microRNA-gene and all absolute PCCs were further scaled in the range of (0.5–1). The local search was terminated either when it reached 1000 iterations or the fitness scores remained unchanged for 100 iterations.

At each iteration of the local search, a local change to either microRNAs or TFs was made. For the user's convenience, we added a user option that specifies a preferred size of regulators in local search, since in most circumstances a user may be only interested in several most important regulators. For study reported here, the numbers of microRNAs and TFs in the modules are controlled at less than 1% and 4% of candidate regulators, respectively. After microRNAs/TF genes were determined to change, a microRNA/TF-gene was chosen from all candidates if the restriction of size had not been reached. A chosen microRNA/TF-gene was removed from the solution if it was already in the solution. If the number of the current regulators in the solution had reached the limit, a microRNA/TF-gene in the candidate searching space but not belonging to the current solution was chosen to substitute one microRNA/TF-gene in the current solution.

2.3. Validation and Evaluation Criteria. In order to evaluate the overall quality of the identified modules, we defined a score by combining the fitness measurements used in the GA and local search. In addition to the fitness measurement used in local search, a term of total correlation coefficients among nTF genes in the module, $\text{Cor}_{R'}$, was added:

$$\text{Cor}_{R'} = \sum_{i,j \in R' i \neq j} \left| \text{Cor}_{ij} \right|. \quad (5)$$

The final score for an identified module was defined as below:

$$F = \frac{\text{MGI} + \text{TGI} + \text{Cor}_{M'} + \text{Cor}_{R'}}{N}, \quad (6)$$

where N is the total number of interactions among the members in the module.

In order to show our method can successfully identify modules with high fitness scores, we compared specific scores

of randomly generated modules with the identified modules. For each module, 1,000 randomized controls were generated and each control has the identical number of microRNAs, TF genes, and nTF genes with the identified modules. To evaluate the significance of our modules, we performed the permutation test for each module to determine P values. For each module at each permutation, a number of microRNAs/genes in module were substituted by the same number of randomly selected microRNAs/genes. The size of substitutions follows a discrete uniform distribution between 0 and the number of genes for each identified module. The P value was evaluated by the chance of obtaining a permutated module better than the original one. To evaluate the biological relevance of our modules, we performed the enrichment analyses for gene ontology (GO) terms and KEGG pathways for the identified modules using DAVID [19].

3. Results and Discussion

In this section, we first show how to determine the parameter values in our algorithm using Dataset I. Subsequently, we present the predicted modules based on the determined parameters for Dataset I. Most of the results were derived based on $k_1 = k_2 = 1$ unless otherwise is specified.

We identified 1,933 differentially expressed nTF genes and 144 differentially expressed microRNAs for Dataset I. These 1,933 nTF genes, 189 TF genes with mRNA measurements, and 144 microRNAs were used to calculate PCCs of their expression levels. Only those PCCs with P value less than 0.0001 were considered to be significant and were retained for the subsequence analysis (See Table S1 in Supplementary Material available online at http://dx.doi.org/10.1155/2013/197406.)

To determine the cutoff value on the TFBS similarity scores, we checked the effect of different thresholds on the predicted number of TF-gene pairs. A total of 16,292,671 alignments between PWMs and TFBSs were obtained from bindSDb based on the TRANSFAC threshold for the minimum false positives, and 3,469,371 TF-gene pairs were specified after determining the unique TFBS for a TF as described in Section 2. The different numbers of predicted TF-gene pairs and the numbers of involved TFs based on different thresholds for similarity scores were summarized in Table S2. We applied a cutoff 0.99 for the similarity scores, which significantly reduced the number of predicted pairs without drastically changing the numbers of TFs and target genes. Finally 1,705,837 predicted pairs between 260 TFs and 21,054 genes were retained for the module identification.

3.1. Determination of GA Parameters. We examined the average sizes of coexpressed gene sets obtained from the GA at three different sizes for the initial chromosomes setups, that is, inclusion of 2%, 20%, and 80% of genes. The average sizes of the coexpressed gene sets obtained from the GA were 54, 224, and 401, respectively. However, in the latter two cases, the fitness scores are far from converging at the termination. Therefore, we set the initial chromosomes with only 2% of randomly selected genes.

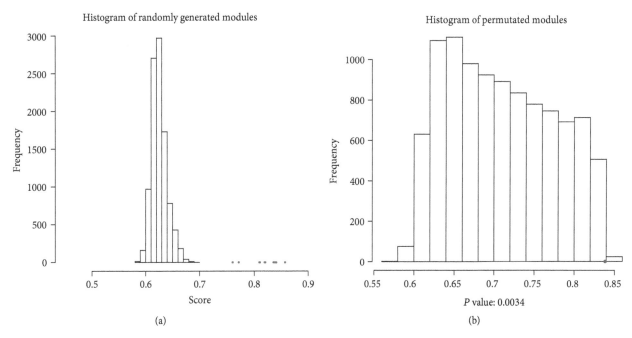

FIGURE 2: Histogram of control scores: (a) randomly generated modules; (b) permutated modules for module 1.

The proper choice of values for P_{co}, P_{mu}, and P_{new} is important to the performance of a GA. To find the good value for each genetic operator, we ran the GA by changing the value of one operator while keeping the other two fixed. For each value of a specific operator, we ran genetic algorithm for 10 times, 1000 generations each, and evaluated the performance by convergence rate. The convergence rate was defined as average incensement of fitness score per iteration. The GA performed better with P_{co} = 0.7, P_{mu} = 0.001, and P_{new} = 0.01 (Table S3). We used these values for the subsequent analysis.

3.2. Evaluation of Local Search. In order to demonstrate that the local search can find a local optimal solution, we recorded the start and end scores and calculated the convergence rate of the scores. The results for 10 modules (Figure S1) show that the local search did improve the fitness score and locate the local optimal solutions efficiently.

3.3. Module Evaluation. Figure 2(a) shows the histogram of fitness scores for 10,000 randomized modules and modules identified by our method (red dots). It suggests that our method was able to successfully identify modules with significantly higher scores. The identified modules, the corresponding scores, and the P values were listed in Table S4(a) (Supplementary file). All the modules were significant with P values less than 0.005 based on the permutation test. Figure 2(b) shows the distribution of scores for the 10,000 permuted modules of module 1. It indicates that the local optimal solution was found by our method.

Table 1 provides a summary of the 10 regulatory modules found by our method. The interactions were divided into

three categories based on the evidence of support: sequence-based binding prediction only, PCC only, and both. Most interactions predicted by sequence information also have significant PCCs, indicating the direct regulations. However, considerable fractions of interactions in the modules only have PCC support, implying indirect regulation between the regulators and targets.

The details of genes and microRNAs in the identified modules, enriched KEGG pathways and GO terms (adjusted P < 0.01) were included in Tables S4(b) and S4(c) (Supplementary File). The enriched GO terms that annotate at least 5 genes were summarized. Compared to the results of enrichment analysis for the modules identified with a lasso model for the same dataset [20], most of the common KEGG pathways related to cancers were found, including focal adhesion, MAPK signaling pathway, hypertrophic cardiomyopathy, vascular smooth muscle contraction, regulation of actin cytoskeleton, pathways in cancer, and Wnt signaling pathway.

3.4. Control of Interaction Types in the Predicted Modules. The definition of the fitness score is a key factor to control the type of interactions one wishes to include in the modules. In the previous section we reported the results when an equal weight, that is, $k_1 = k_2 = 1$, was imposed on the alignment scores of TFs/microRNAs and the correlation coefficients of expression in the fitness function. We examined if the increase of the weight on the alignment scores could lead to the increase of the number of interactions with support from both the predicted binding and significant PCC values. We performed the experiment using $k_2 = 2, 3$ and $k_1 = 1$. It can be observed that an increasing trend in the proportion of interactions was supported by the predicted binding and expression correlation between the regulators and targets

TABLE 1: Summary of regulatory interactions in the 10 predicted modules for Dataset I.

Module ID	# Nodes[a]	# Interactions[b]	# PCC and Binding[c]	# PCC[d]	# Binding[e]
1	3/7/22	264	53	197	14
2	3/3/36	704	33	665	6
3	3/7/39	823	60	751	12
4	3/15/21	384	135	228	21
5	3/7/17	233	74	149	10
6	3/3/49	1284	7	1273	4
7	3/4/46	1181	42	1127	12
8	3/7/42	988	99	877	12
9	3/7/49	1316	74	1232	10
10	3/7/53	1431	83	1339	9

[a]The numbers of miRNAs, TF-genes, and nTF-genes.

[b]The number of interactions.

[c]The number of interactions with support of both significant PCC and predicted binding.

[d]The number of interactions with support of only significant PCC.

[e]The number of interactions with support of only predicted binding.

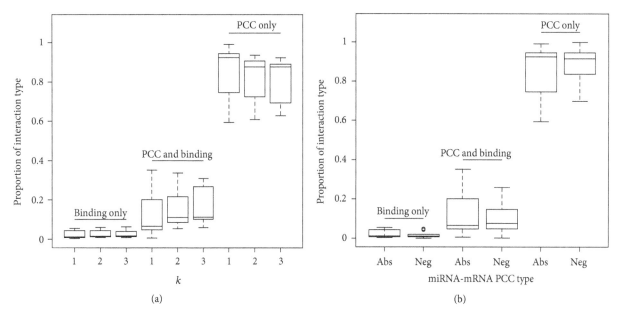

FIGURE 3: Boxplots of the proportion of three interaction types in the identified 10 modules with definitions for the fitness score. (a) The three boxplots in each type represent the results for $(k_1 = 1, k_2 = 1)$, $(k_1 = 2, k_2 = 1)$, and $(k_1 = 3, k_2 = 1)$, respectively. (b) The two boxplots in each type represent the results using (1) both positive and negative microRNA-mRNA PCCs and (2) negative microRNA-mRNA PCCs, respectively.

(Figure 3(a)) when k_2 increases. This result shows the flexibility of our method in finding regulatory modules according to user's preference on the interaction types.

We also examined the ability of our method in finding regulatory modules when only including microRNAs that were negatively correlated with the predicted genes in the coexpressed set in the local search step. Our algorithm was able to successfully identify significant modules (Supplementary File 1). Compared with the case where both negatively and positively expressed microRNA regulators were considered in a module, there was a slight increase in the proportion of the interaction type with support from both predicted binding and significant PCCs (Figure 3(b)).

3.5. Literature Validation. The interactions in the identified module 1 to module 10 were shown in Figure 4 and Figures S2 and S3. In module 1, no microRNAs genes become isolated, and the main network structure is not changed after removing those predicted by the PCC interactions. In module 10, however, the targets of MEIS1 become isolated, and many potential regulatory relationships between MEIS1 and target genes also disappear after removing the PCC predicted interactions. MEIS1, which encodes a homeobox protein belonging to the TALE "three amino acid loop extension" family of homeodomain-containing proteins, as well as MEIS2 and PBX1 are found to have a critical function to suppress prostate cancer initiation and progression [21].

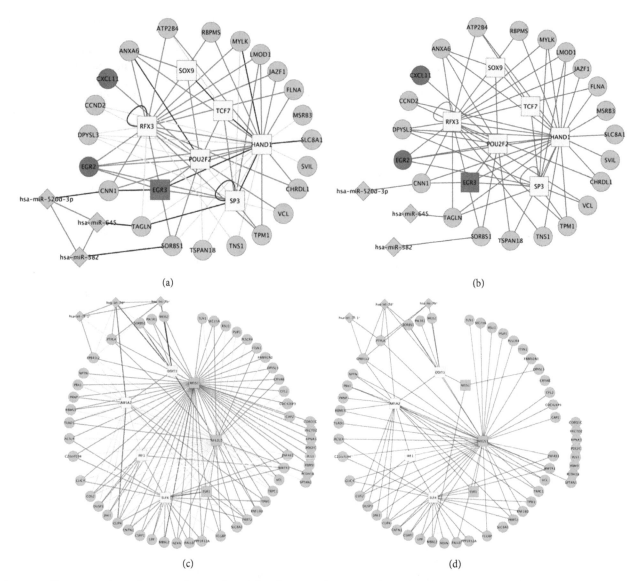

FIGURE 4: Two types of visualization of selected modules: (a) general representation of module 1; (b) sequence-based predictions only of module 1; (c) general representation of module 10; (d) sequence-based predictions only of module 10. Diamond, rectangle, and eclipse represent microRNA, TF genes, and nTF genes, respectively. Red nodes and green nodes represent overexpressed and underexpressed microRNAs/genes in tumor samples. Red lines and light green lines stand for positive correlations and negative correlations, respectively, while interactions that were predicted only by sequence information are drawn as black lines. For clear visualization, the links between nTF genes were not plotted.

The difference between Figures 4(c) and 4(d) suggests that MEIS1 may be a coactivator to regulate genes without directly binding to the promoters of the targets.

We also explored the literatures about other core regulators and regulatory relationships in identified modules. For example, hsa-miR-7f-1, which was identified as a core regulator in both modules 8 and 10, was found to be associated with lung cancer, breast cancer, colorectal cancer [22], pancreatic cancer [23], and pituitary adenomas [24]. Another microRNA, hsa-miR-328, identified in modules 1, 3, 7, and 9, was found to be dysregulated in both breast cancer [25] and colorectal cancer [26]. But their functional mechanisms to cancer development are still unknown. Our predicted

modules may be used to facilitate further experiments for functional study.

Our method also identified several important TFs and their regulatory relationships, such as EGR3, RFX3 and MYLK. EGR3 was found overexpressed in tumor cells and was identified as a core regulator in modules 1, 3, and 10. The protein encoded by EGR3 participates in the transcriptional regulation of genes in controlling biological rhythm and may also play a role in a wide variety of processes including muscle development, lymphocyte development, endothelial cell growth, and migration and neuronal development (Ref-Seq December 2010). EGR3 was found to be closely associated with the genesis and malignant progression of breast cancer by being involved in the estrogen-signaling pathway. Recently it was shown that EGR3 plays a pivot role in mechanism of prostate cancer initiation or early progression [27]. RFX3 is a transcriptional activator with highly conserved winged helix DNA-binding domain and can bind DNA as a monomer or as a heterodimer with other RFX family members. Its function in prostate cancer has not been well explored, but its regulation on the same set of genes together with MEIS1 in modules 7 and 9 suggests it may present as a coregulator with MEIS1 to be functional. MYLK was known to be involved in many biological processes including the inflammatory response (e.g., apoptosis, vascular permeability, and leukocyte diapedesis), cell motility and morphology and MARK signaling pathway. It was identified to be coregulated by MEIS1 and RFX3 in modules 7 and 9. It was involved in a total of 5 modules, suggesting its importance in cancer development, especially prostate cancer. A thorough literature search on all of the predicted interactions and core regulators for prostate cancer is not possible here. However, we demonstrated that our method is likely to be useful for identifying functional regulatory modules in specific diseases.

3.6. Prediction in Dataset II. Since Dataset II includes expression on a wide variety of tissue and normal samples, we applied our method to identify cancer-related common regulatory modules. Because of the multiple cell types and intrinsic complication of tumor cellular environment, we used the same procedure for differential expression analysis with a relatively loose cutoff for P values. The threshold of 0.05 for the adjusted P values was applied to the nTF genes and microRNAs. All TF genes were retained. This step resulted in 94 microRNAs, 162 TF genes, and 1,410 nTF genes. The sequence-based prediction for TF and microRNA targets led to a set of 74 microRNAs, 148 TF genes, and 1,194 nTF genes for module identification. We performed the same test to determine the optimal values for genetic operators. Crossover probability 0.7, mutation probability 0.001, and random immigrant probability 0.01 were obtained. These values were the same as those used for Dataset I, showing that the choice of parameters was not biased to a particular dataset.

All 10 modules achieved the significance level based on our permutation test. The numbers of interactions in the identified modules are showed in Table S5. All sequence-base predicted regulations were with significant PCC values between the regulators and regulated genes. The enriched GO terms and KEGG pathways include cancer relevant GO terms and KEGG pathways, such as positive regulation of RNA metabolic process and Wnt signaling pathway, suggesting the method also predicted microRNA-gene regulatory modules for Dataset II (Table S6(b), Supplementary File).

4. Discussion

Several related methods and databases for the identification of microRNA-TF-gene regulatory modules have been published. The method we proposed has a number of advantages over other module identification methods. For example, CircuitDB [7] and MIR@NT@N [5] utilized sequenced-based target predictions and protein-protein interactions to constrict microRNA-TF-gene module. But they are static databases and could not answer the question about alteration of gene expressions in a specific type of disease or lack of ability to incorporate the expression values into analysis. MAGIA2 [28] and miRGator 2.0 [29] provided tools for prediction of microRNA-gene modules by combining the sequence-based target prediction and user-supplied expression profiles, but they did not separate TF genes from the entire set of genes. In regulatory modules, many TF genes that are not differentially expressed could be as important as differentially expressed TF genes as coactivators. mir-ConnX [6] took both the sequence-based predictions and the specified TFs into consideration to construct condition-specific mRNA-microRNA networks. However, the resulting networks were often too large to pinpoint the most important functional modules in a disease. Our method bridged the gap between the above methods by utilizing both sequence-based predictions and expression profiles and emphasizing the transcription factor's effect for the detection of condition-specific regulatory modules.

Our method and other similar methods that identify microRNA-gene regulatory modules were based on the assumption that microRNAs are posttranscriptional regulators that regulate TFs' expressions. But several studies have proposed that TFs can regulate the transcription of microRNA directly [30, 31]. Currently those databases were built to predict the regulation of transcription factors on microRNA precursors. A possible extension of our method is to transfer it into relationships between transcription factors and mature microRNAs and to incorporate this knowledge into our module identification method.

As more information is incorporated, not all of them should be considered equally in evaluation; for example, experimentally validated regulation may be more valuable for the user. In addition, the microRNA's regulation on TF genes and nTF genes are measured equally in current method, but the microRNA's regulation on TF genes may be more interesting. We can improve our method by adding control parameters to emphasize specific types of relationships.

5. Conclusion

We proposed a computational method that combines the sequence-based target predictions and matched microRNA-gene expression profiles. Our method independently processes measurement of interactions, identification of coexpression gene sets, and regulatory modules. The major characteristics are (1) easy integration of other methods for identification of gene coexpression set, (2) easy refinement by including updated information of target prediction, and (3) easy setup of parameters to emphasize interest of research. It is a candidate tool for clinical researchers to use user-supplied data to perform further investigation and exploration.

Acknowledgment

The research was partially supported by the Chancellor's Discovery Fund, University of Illinois at Chicago.

References

[1] N. J. Martinez and A. J. M. Walhout, "The interplay between transcription factors and microRNAs in genome-scale regulatory networks," *BioEssays*, vol. 31, no. 4, pp. 435–445, 2009.

[2] miRBase, http://www.mirbase.org/.

[3] Y. Dai and X. Zhou, "Computational methods for the identification of microRNA targets," *Open Access Bioinformatics*, vol. 2010, no. 2, pp. 29–39, 2010.

[4] N. J. Martinez and A. J. M. Walhout, "The interplay between transcription factors and microRNAs in genome-scale regulatory networks," *BioEssays*, vol. 31, no. 4, pp. 435–445, 2009.

[5] A. Le Béchec, E. Portales-Casamar, G. Vetter et al., "MIR@NT@N: a framework integrating transcription factors, microRNAs and their targets to identify sub-network motifs in a meta-regulation network model," *BMC Bioinformatics*, vol. 12, no. 1, article 67, 2011.

[6] G. T. Huang, C. Athanassiou, and P. V. Benos, "mirConnX: condition-specific mRNA-microRNA network integrator," *Nucleic Acids Research*, vol. 39, supplement 2, pp. W416–W423, 2011.

[7] O. Friard, A. Re, D. Taverna, M. De Bortoli, and D. Corá, "CircuitsDB: a database of mixed microRNA/transcription factor feed-forward regulatory circuits in human and mouse," *BMC Bioinformatics*, vol. 11, no. 1, article 435, 2010.

[8] B. S. Taylor, N. Schultz, H. Hieronymus et al., "Integrative genomic profiling of human prostate cancer," *Cancer Cell*, vol. 18, no. 1, pp. 11–22, 2010.

[9] R. Edgar, M. Domrachev, and A. E. Lash, "Gene Expression Omnibus: NCBI gene expression and hybridization array data repository," *Nucleic Acids Research*, vol. 30, no. 1, pp. 207–210, 2002.

[10] S. Ramaswamy, P. Tamayo, R. Rifkin et al., "Multiclass cancer diagnosis using tumor gene expression signatures," *Proceedings of the National Academy of Sciences of the United States of America*, vol. 98, no. 26, pp. 15149–15154, 2001.

[11] J. Lu, G. Getz, E. A. Miska et al., "MicroRNA expression profiles classify human cancers," *Nature*, vol. 435, no. 7043, pp. 834–838, 2005.

[12] Y. Benjamini and Y. Hochberg, "Controlling the false discovery rate: a practical and powerful approach to multiple testing," *Journal of the Royal Statistical Society B*, vol. 57, no. 1, pp. 289–300, 1995.

[13] D. Betel, M. Wilson, A. Gabow, D. S. Marks, and C. Sander, "The microRNA.org resource: targets and expression," *Nucleic Acids Research*, vol. 36, supplement 1, pp. D149–D153, 2008.

[14] P. Landgraf, M. Rusu, R. Sheridan et al., "A mammalian microRNA expression atlas based on small RNA library sequencing," *Cell*, vol. 129, no. 7, pp. 1401–1414, 2007.

[15] B. John, A. J. Enright, A. Aravin, T. Tuschl, C. Sander, and D. S. Marks, "Human microRNA targets," *PLoS Biology*, vol. 2, no. 11, article e363, 2004.

[16] V. Matys, O. V. Kel-Margoulis, E. Fricke et al., "TRANSFAC and its module TRANSCompel: transcriptional gene regulation in eukaryotes," *Nucleic Acids Research*, vol. 34, pp. D108–D110, 2006.

[17] A. E. Kel, E. Gößling, I. Reuter, E. Cheremushkin, O. V. Kel-Margoulis, and E. Wingender, "MATCH: a tool for searching transcription factor binding sites in DNA sequences," *Nucleic Acids Research*, vol. 31, no. 13, pp. 3576–3579, 2003.

[18] D. Roqueiro, J. Frasor, and Y. Dai, "BindSDb: a binding-information spatial database," in *Proceedings of IEEE International Conference on Bioinformatics and Biomedicine Workshops (BIBMW '10)*, pp. 573–578, December 2010.

[19] D. W. Huang, B. T. Sherman, and R. A. Lempicki, "Systematic and integrative analysis of large gene lists using DAVID bioinformatics resources," *Nature Protocols*, vol. 4, no. 1, pp. 44–57, 2009.

[20] Y. Lu, Y. Zhou, W. Qu, M. Deng, and C. Zhang, "A lasso regression model for the construction of microRNA-target regulatory networks," *Bioinformatics*, vol. 27, no. 17, pp. 2406–2413, 2011.

[21] J. L. Chen, J. Li, K. J. Kiriluk et al., "Deregulation of a Hox protein regulatory network spanning prostate cancer initiation and progression," *Clinical Cancer Research*, vol. 18, no. 16, pp. 4291–4302, 2012.

[22] J. Jiang, E. J. Lee, Y. Gusev, and T. D. Schmittgen, "Real-time expression profiling of microRNA precursors in human cancer cell lines," *Nucleic Acids Research*, vol. 33, no. 17, pp. 5394–5403, 2005.

[23] E. J. Lee, Y. Gusev, J. Jiang et al., "Expression profiling identifies microRNA signature in pancreatic cancer," *International Journal of Cancer*, vol. 120, no. 5, pp. 1046–1054, 2007.

[24] G. A. Calin, A. Cimmino, M. Fabbri et al., "MiR-15a and miR-16-1 cluster functions in human leukemia," *Proceedings of the National Academy of Sciences of the United States of America*, vol. 105, no. 13, pp. 5166–5171, 2008.

[25] Y.-Z. Pan, M. E. Morris, and A.-M. Yu, "MicroRNA-328 negatively regulates the expression of breast cancer resistance protein (BCRP/ABCG2) in human cancer cells," *Molecular Pharmacology*, vol. 75, no. 6, pp. 1374–1379, 2009.

[26] E. Bandrés, E. Cubedo, X. Agirre et al., "Identification by real-time PCR of 13 mature microRNAs differentially expressed in colorectal cancer and non-tumoral tissues," *Molecular Cancer*, vol. 5, article 29, 2006.

[27] R. L. Pio, *The role of early growth response gene Egr3 in prostate cancer [Ph.D. thesis]*, University of California, Irvine, Calif, USA, 2012.

[28] A. Bisognin, G. Sales, A. Coppe, S. Bortoluzzi, and C. Romualdi, "MAGIA^2: from miRNA and genes expression data integrative analysis to microRNA-transcription factor mixed regulatory circuits (2012 update)," *Nucleic Acids Research*, vol. 40, no. 1, pp. W13–W21, 2012.

[29] J.-H. Cho, R. Gelinas, K. Wang et al., "Systems biology of interstitial lung diseases: integration of mRNA and microRNA expression changes," *BMC Medical Genomics*, vol. 4, no. 1, article 8, 2011.

[30] J. Wang, M. Lu, C. Qiu, and Q. Cui, "TransmiR: a transcription factor—microRNA regulation database," *Nucleic Acids Research*, vol. 38, supplement 1, pp. D119–D122, 2010.

[31] C. Qiu, J. Wang, P. Yao, E. Wang, and Q. Cui, "microRNA evolution in a human transcription factor and microRNA regulatory network," *BMC Systems Biology*, vol. 4, no. 1, article 90, 2010.

6

Pathway Detection from Protein Interaction Networks and Gene Expression Data Using Color-Coding Methods and Search Algorithms

Cheng-Yu Yeh,[1,2] Hsiang-Yuan Yeh,[1,2] Carlos Roberto Arias,[1,2] and Von-Wun Soo[1,2]

[1] *Department of Computer Science, National Tsing Hua University, Hsinchu 300, Taiwan*
[2] *Institute of Information Systems and Applications, National Tsing Hua University, Hsinchu 300, Taiwan*

Correspondence should be addressed to Hsiang-Yuan Yeh, d926708@oz.nthu.edu.tw and Von-Wun Soo, soo@cs.nthu.edu.tw

Academic Editor: Shanker Kalyana-Sundaram

With the large availability of protein interaction networks and microarray data supported, to identify the linear paths that have biological significance in search of a potential pathway is a challenge issue. We proposed a color-coding method based on the characteristics of biological network topology and applied heuristic search to speed up color-coding method. In the experiments, we tested our methods by applying to two datasets: yeast and human prostate cancer networks and gene expression data set. The comparisons of our method with other existing methods on known yeast MAPK pathways in terms of precision and recall show that we can find maximum number of the proteins and perform comparably well. On the other hand, our method is more efficient than previous ones and detects the paths of length 10 within 40 seconds using CPU Intel 1.73GHz and 1GB main memory running under windows operating system.

1. Background

With the large availability of protein-protein interaction data, to identify the corresponding networks such as functional enriched pathways is a big challenge. Protein interaction networks are the assembly of the protein signal cascades that transfer the biological function and information through the pathway, and the proteins in the cell react with the environment by transduction signals. We considered the protein interaction networks from available public databases as a graph in which nodes represent proteins and edges represent protein interactions, and we can apply search method to discover the significant paths which are identified with similar biological processes and functions. Therefore, protein-protein interactions provide important information in assembly of signaling pathways and have great potential for us to understand the cellular mechanism and functions. On the other hand, numerous biological studies used experimental data such as microarray data or GeneChip to identify the expression of the individual gene, and the expression values of genes have the over/underexpressions under some

conditions. Integrating both protein interaction network and gene expression data is a popular procedure in bioinformatics research area. Discovering the signaling pathways is to search the linear paths from cell-surface proteins to transcription factor proteins in nucleus. The previous research focused on extracting the specific network structure such as protein complexes from the gene expression data [1]. The definition of the pathway is not the same as uncovering/extracting the linear or tree-type pathways from the protein network. Biologists use the term "linear path" to denote a simple path in the protein interaction network where no node (protein) can occur more than once. Unfortunately, searching a linear path in the protein networks where each node occurs at most once is a NP-hard problem [2]. In the previous study, Steffen et al. applied an exhaustive search to identify the pathways in the protein networks that assumed all the weights of interactions be equal and reliable [3]. This method successfully detected some known pathways in yeast. However, only paths with short length could be detected while the exact search algorithm causes the exponential running time. Recent works estimated the weights of interactions

Pathway Detection from Protein Interaction Networks and Gene Expression Data Using Color-Coding
Methods and Search Algorithms

49

based on high-throughput microarray data, the number of times an interaction referenced in papers or experiments instead of using unweighted interaction in the networks. By assigning scores to protein interactions, Alon et al. proposed a randomized color-coding concept in search of a pathway as a minimum-weight paths searching problem [4]. The color-coding method can reduce the running time comparing with the exhaustive search for longer paths but it still has exponential runtime depending on the number of colors. The basic idea behind color coding is to randomly color each node from 1 and k kinds of colors and search for paths with distinct colors instead of searching for paths with distinct nodes. Shlomi et al. formalize pathway detection as pathway query problem that is the problem of finding a path in a labeled and weighted graph that best matches a prespecified query path [5].

Mayrose et al. used color-coding technique to detect the simple paths in a graph for mapping a peptide to the surface graph in protein 3D structure and applied branch-and-bound technique to decrease the search space in the dynamic programming, and it costs about 10-fold speedup of running time [6]. Scott et al. also provides a randomized color-coding and applied dynamic programming method to solve this problem limited to path length above 10 nodes but it requires several hours to execute [7]. They also applied some biological constraints to segment the pathways based on their cellular locations in Gene Ontology database to fit the biological meanings [8]. Hüffner et al. modified the color-coding method by increasing the number of colors and employed a fixed lower bound to find the candidate nodes in interest efficiently [9]. However, there is no way to know the true optimal cost-to-go using dynamic programming, and they still store a lot of space to get the optimal solution. Zhao et al. proposed an integer linear programming (ILP) model to find the signal pathways by utilizing both protein interactions and microarray data [10]. Comparing with previous color-coding methods, this method can recover signal pathways directly by running the program once instead of assembling the candidate pathways. PathFinder used the functional annotation to realize the characteristics of the known pathways and extracted the association rules from the known pathway based on the hierarchical of Gene Ontology (GO) annotation as template. They searched the candidate pathways which contain the characteristic similar to the template and filtered the protein-protein interaction network by integrating other biological knowledge [11]. GO terms include a brief description of the corresponding biological function of the genes, but only 60% of all human genes have associated GO terms, and these terms may be inconsistent due to differences in curators' judgment [12]. Due to the incomplete data, the approaches reduce the probability to extract the pathway.

The previous works show that the color-coding approach is capable of identifying biologically meaningful pathways. The central idea that underlies color-coding is to randomly color each node in the network using a small set of colors and to "hope" that the path becomes colorful. Random colorings need to be tried to ensure that the desired paths are not missed and to find a colorful path can be accomplished in $O(2^k m)$ time for an m-edge graph by dynamic programming

which is proved by Huffner's work [9]. The more important way to improve color-coding algorithms efficiently is to de-randomize it, and this kind of research was also mentioned in Huffner's paper [9]. However, there is no one focuses on this way to improve the color-coding approach, and that is also the reason we want to do. We presented a new and more efficient method for detecting the simple paths with biological constraints and heuristic function that differs from the above researches. We consider the topology characteristic of biological network such as high-degree nodes and articulation hubs into the color-coding method and applied heuristic method to prune the search space instead of exhaust searching for all the edges in the network. The paper is organized as follows: Section 2 describes the proposed methods in detail. Section 3 explains the experiments and discusses the results. Section 4 makes the conclusions.

2. Methods

Our methods consist of four modules: Module 1 integrated the public protein-protein interactions database and assigned weight values of interactions based on the Pearson correlation calculated from microarray data. Module 2 presented specific color-coding techniques based on the significance of biological network topology such as the degree of a node and an articulation hub. Module 3 applied a pruning strategy to speed up the color-coding methods. Module 4 used known pathways to validate the functional enrichment of pathways found by our methods.

2.1. Network Construction from Microarray Data and Protein-Protein Interactions Database. The microarray data implies gene expressions information in the biological experiments and characterize protein functions in vitro. The microarray dataset consists of N genes and M experiments, and it can be represented as $M*N$ matrix. It presents different gene expression levels X_{ij} ($i \in M$, $j \in N$) in this matrix. Gene expressions either overexpressed or underexpressed can be revealed in terms of two colored channel in the microarray data representing the intensity of the different developmental stage. The gene expression ratios were calculated as the median value of the pixels minus background pixel median value for one-color channel divided by the same for the other channel. We extracted the median value of the log base 2 of each gene among experimental dataset because the mean value of the normalized ratio is much easier to be affected by noise than the median value. Although microarray can be used to detect thousands of genes under a variety of conditions, there are still many missing values in microarray. The reasons for missing values include insufficient resolution, image corruption, and dust or scratches on the slide. If a gene contains many missing values in experiments, it is not easy to determine a precise expression value for each gene that causes a difficulty in the subsequent analysis of networks. However, we cannot simply remove all gene data that contains missing values because the number of remaining genes will become too small to predict the weight of interaction correctly. In order to get a better result, the genes that contain less than 20% entries missing in all experiment are picked. In order to get as complete data as possible, we use the K nearest neighbors (KNN) algorithm [13] to estimate the missing values. The gene expression levels of the genes might not always maintain the same expression in different microarray data. We choose a higher ratio between the overexpression and underexpression from microarray data to determine the expression level of the gene.

Current public protein-protein interaction (PPI) databases provide rich information, and they mostly differ on the way they acquire or validate their data. For example, human protein reference database (HPRD), Biomolecular Interaction Network Database (BIND), molecular INTeraction database (MINT), and mammalian protein-protein interaction database (MIPS) are manually curated; this means a team of biologists check the literature to find new interactions, and once an interaction is confirmed it is added to the database. On the other hand, database of interacting proteins (DIP) and European Bioinformatics Institute molecular interaction data (IntAct) are based on literature mining, and they achieve these using computational methods that retrieve the interaction knowledge automatically from published papers. Prieto and De Las Rivas have shown a limited intersection and overlap between the six major databases (BioGRID, BIND, MINT, HPRD, IntAct, DIP) [14]. The information contained in these databases is partly complementary, and the knowledge of the protein interactions can be increased and improved by combining multiple databases. Bio interaction resource (BioIR) integrates the major publicly available databases that contain protein-protein interaction information. The integrated PPI data warehouse included those databases we mentioned, and we successfully gathered 54283 available and nonredundant PPI pairs among 10710 proteins [15]. Notably, even the union of all databases is still incomplete with many unknown components and pathways of the human proteome. Then, we map genes in microarray data according to the BioIR database and extract their corresponding undirected protein interaction networks where the node set V represents protein v ($v \in V$) and edge set E represents the protein interactions e ($e \in E$) in the network.

In the randomized color-coding method, it requires a predefined pathway length. The length of the path is dependent on the execution time that they can run in practical use. In the scale-free properties of the biological network, there are minimum number of steps from a given genes to the other genes, and it means that a given gene grows rapidly which suffer from the "small world" effect [16]. According to the reason, we apply the heap-based Dijkstra's algorithm [17] for each node to get the longest shortest path of all pairs of nodes in the network. This information shows if any pair of nodes in the network can link to others at most this length. So, we use the number of the longest shortest path to be the maximum number of the length that we can search in the path. In our method, the fixed length of the path is not defined by the users and it is dependent on the topology of the protein network deposited in the protein interaction database.

We assume that a protein interaction participates in a signaling pathway and the genes producing the associated proteins should be coexpressed and might be coregulated.

Grigoriev showed that biologically relevant interacting proteins have high mRNA expression correlations [18] and the correlation of the expression genes provides some evidences and biological needs for the produced proteins in the coexpression network linked in PPI [19]. Previous works show that proteins in the same signaling network exist simultaneously at the time of their activation and the genes encoding these proteins may be transcribed approximately at the same time. The correlation coefficient can measure the strength of a linear relationship between two expression values of the gene in the microarray data. So, we applied Pearson correlation coefficient for every pairwise relation in the set of $(N^2 - N)/2$ pairs of N genes, and the range of the value would be $[-1, +1]$. In general statistical usage, the positive value in Pearson correlation indicates an increasing linear relationship, and negative value indicates a decreasing linear relationship. While the correlation is closer to $+1$ or -1, it denotes the perfect linear relationship between pair of genes. On the other hand, the correlation approaches to zero, and there would be little or no association among the pair of genes. We take the absolute value of correlation value to capture inhibitory activity (negative correlation) as well as activation activity (positive correlation). Then, we assign the interaction weight value of an edge as a negative logarithm of the value computed by the Pearson correlation from microarray data. Namely, we assign a weight $w(e)$ for each edge e from protein u to protein v and the weight is calculated as $w(e) = w(u, v) = -\log(corr(u, v))$. The negative logarithm makes the larger correlation score become of smaller weight and so on. We set the pathway identification problem is a minimum-weight linear path searching problem.

2.2. Color-Coding Methods Based on Characteristics of Network Topology. All possible paths in protein-protein interaction network should be ideally scanned to find the best path with the minimum weight. However, to enumerate and search a linear pathway with weights in the protein-protein interaction networks where each node occurs at most once a computationally intractable for realistic-size problems [6]. The idea of color-coding technique is to apply randomly k colors to proteins in the networks and search only those paths under some colored constrains in order to decrease the computational time in comparison with an exhaustive search. However, randomly chosen proteins with k colors may fail to detect pathways if any two neighbor nodes own the same color. Randomly colored method need to ensure that the desired or important proteins have different colors with its neighbors. Due to scale-free connectivity distribution of the biological network and "small world" effect that facilitates fast propagation to communicate with other genes, high degree proteins, called hubs, tend to connect with each other and may play an important role in regulatory events, and articulation points also play crucial roles in biological network since they tend to hold and maintain the functional communicating capabilities among proteins [16]. According to the characteristics of biological networks, we wish to detect the nodes with biological meaning using the following color-coding techniques.

Pathway Detection from Protein Interaction Networks and Gene Expression Data Using Color-Coding
Methods and Search Algorithms

51

(1) Scale-free networks have a few nodes with a very large number of links, and many nodes have only a few links [16]. The degree of a node in a graph is the number of edges adjacent to the node. Given limited colors, high-degree node should have a different color with its directed neighbor proteins. On the contrary, the node with single link called the leaf of a network can have the same color with its adjacent protein if unavoidable.

(2) Articulation points are critical vertices for communication in the network. The functional pathways should pass through the articulation point to transfer functional signals. The graph would fall into many connected components and become disconnected without articulation points. Therefore, for an articulation points should tend to have a different color with its directed neighbor proteins.

In the color-coding procedure, we assign every node v a color with the above characteristics, and the number of color is dependent on the length of longest shortest path we mentioned. First, we sorted the nodes in PPI networks by their degrees and sequentially based on their degrees to assign colors to a node that tend to have a different color with their neighbors dependent on the number of the colors we could use. If a node is already colored, we continue to search next higher degree of nodes until there is no non-color node in the graph. The node with degree 1 denotes the leaf in the network and cannot have any children below, so we can assign the same color with its neighbors. However, it is possible to have the same color for the common neighbors of high degree nodes using this method with a limited number of colors. Therefore, we must ensure that the common neighbor is an articulation node or not and give it different colors with its neighbors so that it can be detected. Algorithm 1 shows the pseudocode of our color-coding method.

Take an example as shown in Figure 1; it denotes the steps of color-coding method. Figure 1(a) shows randomly choose colors from white, grey, and black colors to draw the nodes with high degree based on step 4 in our color-coding method algorithm in Algorithm 1. Figure 1(b), if the node is with only one degree, can be the same color with its neighbor based on step 7. Take an example; nodes G, I, L (black), and C, E (grey) are assigned the same colors with each their hub neighbor node J and D. Figure 1(c) randomly assigns colors to the nodes that have not been colored and draw different color with hub based on step 9. Figure 1(d) check articulation hub has different color with its neighbors based on step 14–16. The articulation hubs such as node F colors white colors which is different with its neighbors, node D and J.

To extract a pathway that makes biological sense beside topology characteristic, we need to take into consideration biological knowledge as constraints in order to avoid extracting biologically insignificant pathways. Therefore, we assign each protein a number $L(p)$ of the unique cellular location based on the Gene Ontology database, and each protein can correspond to a location of intracellular, membrane, cytoplasm, or nucleus. According to the assigned location segment $L(p)$, we extract a path from p_1 to p_n so that the

path $(p_1, p_2, \ldots, p_n)$ for each p_i satisfies the partial ordering location constraints $L(p_1) \leq L(p_2) \leq \cdots \leq L(p_n)$. According to the characteristics of biological networks and nondecreasing cellular location, we can detect linear paths passing through articulation points or the high-degree nodes and also avoid extracting the paths in only one location of the cell. This restriction can reduce the complexity of the search process.

2.3. A* Algorithm as Heuristic Search. Based on the color coding method to extract a colorful pathway with k colors, it still cost exponential time to execute with parameter k. In search for paths using a traditional tree search method, it may expand a large collection of new nodes while traversing new level of tree. To speed up the search procedure, it needs to prune the unexplored new nodes heuristically. We use the idea of A* search to design a pruning strategy, and the heuristic function is to determine the weight of a pathway that reflects some biological feasibility and significance to some extent. First, we defined the weight of a path as the sum of weights of edges in the path. The formula is defined as follows (1):

$$w(p) = \sum_{e \in p} w(n), \qquad (1)$$

where $w(e)$ is the weight of a node n in the path.

In the preprocessing step, we determine the minimum weight of nodes in the network as $w_{\min}$. We calculate the weights of the simple paths with the same length l between different start and end proteins in the uncolored network. We ran the procedure 5000 times to determine the scores of all paths in the experiments formed a normal distribution. We extract an average weight of node as w_{avg} and the error rate based on the standard deviation w_{STD} to find the optimal pathway in estimating bound heuristic function of $h(x)$ for a node x. After searching a fix number of d in the paths, we calculate current weight of a path as function of $g(x)$, and the overall heuristic function of $f(x)$ is defined in (2) for finding a pathway with an optimal (minimum) weight

$$f(x) = g(x) + h(x) = w(P_d) + w_{\min} \times (l - d), \qquad (2)$$

where l means the total number of nodes in a path, d means the number of nodes from the starting point that we must traverse in the network, $w(P_d)$ means the weight accumulated up to the current node x with a length parameter d, and $w_{\min}$ means the minimum weight calculated in the preprocessing experiments.

Because the lower $f(x)$ a node is estimated, the more likely is it to be searched. So, we set a bound score for a path p with length l that is defined as follows (3) to control the quality of the path we could find:

$$\text{Bound\_Score}(p) = \left(w_{\text{avg}} + \alpha \times w_{\text{STD}} \right) \times l, \qquad (3)$$

α is a constant factor to control the bound, w_{avg} means the average weight calculated in the preprocessing experiments. w_{STD} means the standard deviation calculated in the preprocessing experiments.

```
Input: Network G (V,E), K colors
Output: colored network G'
(1) Sort all nodes v ∈ V by degree (from high degree to low degree) into Set S
(2) for each v ∈ S
(3)       If Colored(v) = true go to step 2 and search next node;
(4)       assign one color to node v from k colors;
(5)       Colored(v) = true;
(6)       For each v' ∈ neighbor(v) and Colored(v') = false;
(7)          If degree(v') = 1 then assign the same color with v;
(8)          else
(9)             assign color node v' that have a different color with hub v from other k-1 colors;
(10)         Colored(v') = true;
(11)      End for
(12) End for
(13) Extract articulation points u from network G;
(14) For each node u' ∈ u
(15)       check if u has the same color of any neighbor if so change it;
(16) End for
(17) Return colored network G'
```

ALGORITHM 1: The pseudocode of the color-coding method.

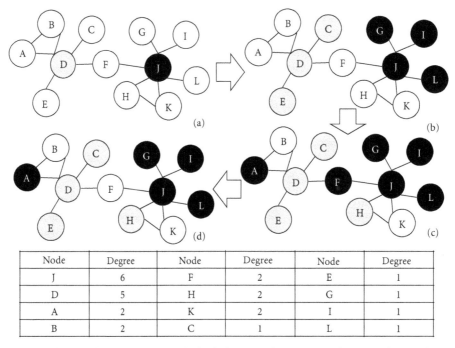

Node	Degree	Node	Degree	Node	Degree
J	6	F	2	E	1
D	5	H	2	G	1
A	2	K	2	I	1
B	2	C	1	L	1

FIGURE 1: The steps of color-coding method. (a) Coloring the high-degree nodes in step 4. (b) The node with degree 1 having same color with its neighbor in step 7. (c) Randomly color the uncolored nodes in step 9. (d) Check the articulation hubs such as node F with different color with its neighbors in step 15.

While we move to the next node through the edge in the each search process, we compute heuristic function $f(x)$ and compare it with the initially set bound score. If $f(x)$ exceeds the initially set bound score, we do not expand the node further. For the nodes that are allowed to expand, their children nodes are expanded, and their heuristic functions are computed and compared with the bound score again until the search reaches the end node. As the example in Figure 2, we consider finding a pathway with length $l = 7$ from the initial node A to the end node H.

First we explored a fix $d = 2$ from initial node A that lead us to node C; we start to estimate the weight of a path with an additional length of 5 that yields a total weight 11 from current node C. The estimated weight of the path is smaller than the bound score 12.95; therefore, we continue to traverse its children. The function of $f(x)$ of current node D is 13.2, and therefore we cannot search into its children. Signal transduction pathway discovery is to extract the linear or tree-like path in the protein-protein interaction. Our method guarantees to find optimal path from the colorful paths in real world complex biological networks; we prove the A* heuristic function straightforward to analyze if it is used to get the optimal colorful paths with Tree-Search using admissible and monotonicity (consistency) properties based on triangle inequality [20].

Pathway Detection from Protein Interaction Networks and Gene Expression Data Using Color-Coding
Methods and Search Algorithms

53

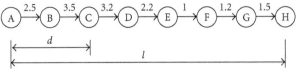

Initial variables:
$w_{avg} = 1.6; w_{STD} = 0.5; w_{min} = 1; \alpha = 0.5;$
Bound_score$(p) = (1.6 + 0.5 \times 0.5) \times 7 = 12.95;$

For node C:
$f(x) = 6 + 1 \times (7 - 2) = 11 <$ Bound_score(p)
$\rightarrow$continue to search node D

For node D:
$f(x) = 9.2 + 1 \times (7 - 3) = 13.2 >$ Bound_score(p)
$\rightarrow$stop searching

FIGURE 2: An example for A* searching method.

Lemma 1. *In (2), A* is optimal if $h(x)$ is an admissible heuristic, that means $h(x)$ never overestimates the weight of the interaction to reach the optimal path.*

Proof. Admissible heuristics are by nature optimistic because the cost of solving the problem is less than the cost actually is. Therefore, we assign the minimum weight w_{min} as $h(x)$ is always less or equal than the weight of interaction actually is. The $g(x)$ is the exact weight of the interaction we have already traversed; the $f(x)$ with estimated weight $h(x)$ never overestimates the true cost of an optimal path through the length l. □

Lemma 2. *A* is optimal if $h(x)$ is consistent which means protein x' is a mediator of protein x with the edge e and its weight is equal to the $w(x, x')$ in Figure 3. Triangle inequality in (4) stipulates that each side of the triangle cannot be longer than the sum of the other two sides. Therefore, the estimated cost of reaching the optimal path to x is no greater than the step cost of getting to x' plus the estimated cost of reaching the goal from x'*

$$f(x') = g(x') + h(x')$$
$$= g(x) + w(x, x') + h(x') \qquad (4)$$
$$\geq g(x) + h(x) = f(x).$$

Proof. We have

$$f(x') = g(x') + h(x') = g(x) + w(x, x') + h(x')$$
$$= w(P_d) + w(x, x') + w_{min} \times (l - d - 1)$$
$$= w(P_d) + (w(x, x') - w_{min}) + w_{min} \times (l - d) \quad (5)$$
$$\geq w(P_d) + w_{min} \times (l - d)$$
$$\geq g(x) + h(x) = f(x).$$

Our assignment of the minimum weight w_{min} as $h(x)$ is always less or equal than all the weights of the interactions $w(x, x')$ in the network; it shows the nondecreasing value of $f(x)$ along the path. □

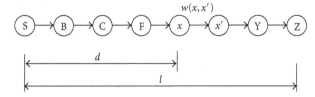

FIGURE 3: The example for consistent property of A* search.

2.4. Functional Evaluation on the Pathway Detection Results. Regardless of the efficiency improvement of pathway detection, its relevance of biological function is also important to validate the methods and results. Therefore, we evaluated the biological functional enrichment of the pathways that were found by our methods. We estimated the statistical significance of the detected pathways using the Ontologizer toolkit [21]. Ontologizer uses hypergeometrics distribution to measure the quality of a pathway by comparing it with a set of randomly pathways chosen from the whole networks. For each node in a given pathway, it is annotated with a GO term in Gene Ontology. In our experiments, we used the category under "biological processing" in GO database and "Parent-Child Interaction" and "Bonferroni option" of Ontologizer to evaluate our results. The P value denotes the statistical significant of our results, and we assume high functional enrich pathways as those with a P value below significant level 0.05. Generally speaking, the proteins involved in a biological pathway tend to have similar functions or processes. Gene Ontology database annotated function and process categories of genes that can be used to check if our predicted pathways belong to the similar function or processes. That is why we show our functional enrichment pathways with Gene Ontology annotation to enhance the understanding of the functions of genes involved in the pathways.

3. Experiments

We implemented our methods in java programming language in order to detect possible pathways in the biological networks. Then, we evaluated the methods using two sets of test data with CPU Intel 1.73 GHz and 1 GB main memory running under the windows operating system. The first test data is the network of yeast extracted from DIP [22] database, and it contains 3789 proteins and 14707 interactions. The gene expression data download from Mega Yeast gene expression data set which contains 6348 genes and 499 yeast microarray experiments [23]. We applied our method to search for the known pathways comparing with KEGG database and previous Steffen's Netsearch [3], Scott's color-coding [6], Zhao's ILP [10], and PathFinder [11] algorithms. As a second test data, we integrated microarray data extracted from [24] that consists of 62 primary tumors in Stanford microarray database (SMD) [25] and 4767 proteins having 21878 protein-protein interactions to search for the significant pathways in human prostate cancer. The length we search for in our method is based on the longest shortest paths in whole networks which are 11 in human protein interaction network and 9 in yeast network.

TABLE 1: The successful probability with varying lengths and fixed alpha = 0.5.

Path length	Our color-coding method	Randomized color-coding method
7	97%	82%
8	97%	89%
9	99%	92%
10	99%	93%

3.1. Global Results. After following our color-coding method, there are still some nodes need to be assigned colors by random, and it may make us fail to find the colorful path in the network. Therefore, we calculate the failure rate of our method to detect the colorful path. According to the weights of all paths in the experiments formed a normal distribution, we calculate our searching scope based on the standard deviation and alpha value. The number of possible permutation of the colorful path and the number of possible coloring of vertices in the path are shown in (6) [6]

$$\frac{P_L^K}{K^L} > e^{-K}. \tag{6}$$

Based on (6), we calculated the probability of the failure rate for pathway detection in (7) [6]

$$p(\text{failue}) = \left(1 - e^{-K}\right)^t. \tag{7}$$

In theory, if we let the probability of failure rate exceed the certain except value as 0.05, we should run more than 8900 of interactions of the program with length 8. Due to the failure rate of random color-coding method, the colorful paths cannot always be detected with color-coding method. We ran 10000 time to compute the paths that start between any node belonging to the membrane protein category (GO: 0005886 or GO: 0004872) and any node belong to the nucleus protein category (GO: 0005634) with varying lengths to calculate the probability of extracting colorful paths in yeast network. Table 1 shows the successful rate between our method and randomized color-coding method, and it shows that our method has higher probability to get colorful paths than randomized color-coding method. The maximum lengths of the paths among hubs and articulation points are 4 in human protein interaction network and 5 in yeast network. It denotes that our method can color the different colors among hubs and articulation points. It makes the search procedure can be explored and also help us to get the colorful paths in the network. On the other hand, we evaluated its functional enrichment for each path we detected in yeast network in Figure 4, and it denotes that 66% of them are functional enrichment with significant biological process (*P* value < 0.05) comparing random chosen.

3.2. Yeast Networks. We applied the previous state-of-art methods to compare with our method with yeast network and gene expression data and test to reconstruct the three known signal pathways: a pheromone response signaling

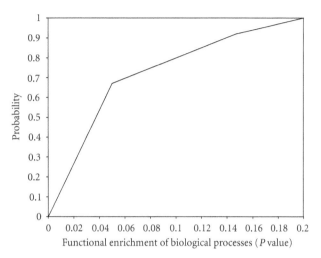

FIGURE 4: Cumulative distribution of *P* value in our detected paths. *x*-axis: *P* value, *y*-axis: percent of paths with corresponding *P* value or better.

pathway, a filamentous growth pathway, and cell wall integrity pathway. The signal pathways can be described as a main chain path that contains important protein cascades. The direct interactions in KEGG pathway may be actually undirected interactions through several proteins in the protein networks. For each pathway, we use one more than the number of nodes in the main chain path as the length of our color-coding method to search the colorful path. We first determined the degrees of proteins in the yeast networks and applied the program implemented by Hyung-Joon Kim to extract the articulation points whose time complexity is $O(n + m)$ in the worst case, where n and m is the number of nodes and edges in a network, respectively. The proportion of proteins with at least a degree 8 is 31.09% and 19.13% with degree 1 in yeast network. 482 articulation points are extracted from network, and the number of intersection of the articulation points and protein with a degree lower than 8 is 220.

The functional purpose of a pheromone response pathway is to address which mating type a yeast cell is. The main chain of a pheromone response pathway is from the membrane protein STE3 to transcription factor STE12 which is shown in Figure 5(a). Figure 5(b) shows the assembly networks for paths of lengths 6–10 using a random color-coding method by Scott's method. Figure 5(c) denotes an assembly pathway of length 9 detected by our method. Both methods assemble the pathways based on the nodes that have a hit with at least half of nodes in the main chain of the pheromone response pathway. Those two methods found KSS1 which is a MAP kinase and the negative regulator, AKR1, but our method detected STE20 which is missing in Scott's results. Scott's and our results both detected CDC24 which is not found by Netsearch and may form protein complexes with FAR1, and a heterotrimeric G-protein may mediate chemotropism that is essential for morphological changes in response to pheromone during mating processes [26]. It can be seen that all the proteins in the main chain are covered by our method. However, we failed to detect

Pathway Detection from Protein Interaction Networks and Gene Expression Data Using Color-Coding
Methods and Search Algorithms

55

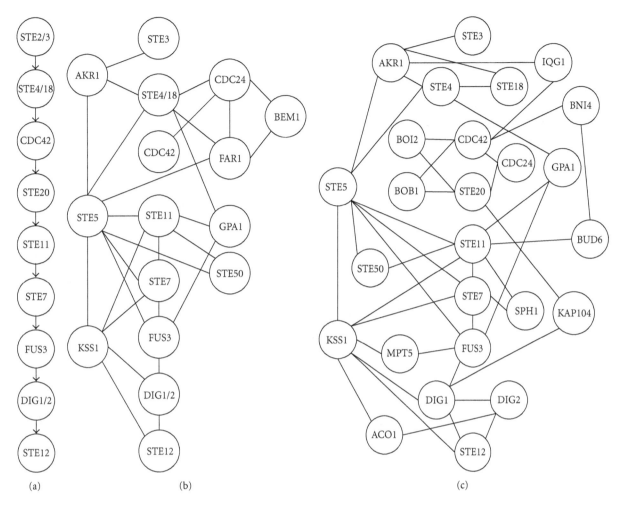

FIGURE 5: (a) The main chain path of pheromone response pathway (b) the assembly paths detected by Scott et al. method (c) the assembly paths detected by our method.

FAR1 and BEM1 comparing to Scott's method. The failure of detecting FAR1 because the paths are involved with those two proteins did not have a hit with at least half of nodes in the main chain of the pheromone response pathway. In our results, we detected BOI2 which appear in the same protein complexes with BEM1 founded by MIPS database [27]. MPT5 and SPH1 are also found by Steffen's Netsearch toolkits, and STE50 is detected by Zhao's ILP method. We also detected 7 new proteins (IQG1, BNI4, BUD6, BOB1, BOl2, KAP104, and ACO1) related to pheromone response. Most of them are sensitive to pheromone response and sexual differentiation. We found that BOI2 and BOB1 which can bind to SH3-2 domain of BEM1 are related to pheromone-responsive mitogen-activated protein kinase cascade [28]. KAP104 is critical for negative regulation of the pheromone response [29]. The previous research [30] denotes that the effects of CDC42 and IQG1 on the pheromone response pathway promote cytokinesis with AKR1. Although it is difficult to confirm in vivo that all proteins are exactly involved in the pathway, we use Gene Ontology to verify the proteins if they have the reasonable biological functions and processes in the pathways. As a final test to evaluate our results, the

paths we detected presented high statistical significance for the functional enrichment of "response to pheromone" category with P value below 0.05.

The main chain of the filamentous growth pathway from RAS2 to TEC1 is shown in Figure 6(a). The main chain detected by Scott's is shown in Figure 6(b), and the assembly paths detected by our method contain 26 proteins in Figure 6(c). Both methods can detect the path through CDC25 and HSP82 protein to form a main chain of the filamentous growth pathway due to the fact that there is no direct link between RAS2 and CDC24 in Figure 6(c). Then, we compared the network-generated previous works but we do not detect ABP1, COF1, LAS17, BUD6, and SRV2 which are found by Zhao's ILP method, because we extract protein BEM1 that are known to be involved in the function of actin filament organization and form the same protein complexes with those proteins [27]. RAS2 is regulated by GAPs IRA1 and activates to increase the cyclic AMP (cAMP) concentration. CDC15 kinase activates a protein kinase complex consisting of the kinases DBF2 [31]. BNI2 is the potential effectors of CDC42 in yeast [32]. The actin protein ACT1 displayed two-hybrid protein interactions with BNI1 and

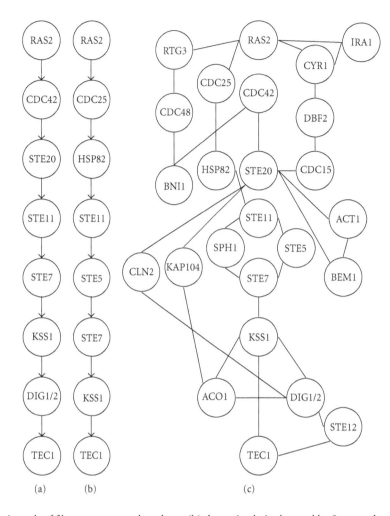

FIGURE 6: (a) The main chain path of filamentous growth pathway (b) the main chain detected by Scott et al. method (c) the assembly paths detected by our method.

repress filamentous differentiation in response to low nitrogen [33]. The expression of CLN2 also enhances the filamentous growth [33].

The cell wall integrity pathway from MID2 to RLM1 with path length 8 is shown in Figure 7(a), and this signaling pathway is critical for cell expansion during growth. The main chain detected by Scott's method is shown in Figure 7(b), and our method can identify the known pathway well as shown in Figure 7(c). It shows that cell wall signaling is controlled by the small G-proteins of GTPases, RHO1 that interacts with the action of guanosine nucleotide exchange factors such as ROM2 [31]. PKC1 interacts with the unit of oligosaccharyl transferase (OT) complex, OST1. SEC3 is a spatial landmark for the exocyst to the site of exocytosis independently of polarized secretion [34]. We found that our methods provide richer information consistent with current researches and also detect new related proteins. The proteins detected by previous and our methods in the yeast pheromone signaling, filamentous growth, and cell wall integrity pathways are shown in Supplemental Table S1 available online at doi: 10.1100/2012/315797. The results show that the number of proteins in the main chain we detected is higher than other

methods, and other new proteins are validated by published papers and experiments.

Due to the incomplete interactions there is no gold standard which means that the true signaling network is not available now. To see the performance of the different methods, we applied the same test set used in the previous works in terms of the precision, and recalls were employed in this work. The precision is defined as the percentage of the proteins detected by the computational methods that are also in the KEGG main chain pathway. The recall is the percentage of the proteins in the KEGG main chain pathway that are also detected by the computational methods. Due to the incomplete of knowledge of the signaling network, we also apply F-measure to evaluate the performance, and this value is not dependent on the absolute match value but only comparative measures. It is defined as $2 * $ precision $*$ recall/ (precision + recall). Table 2 compares our method and previous methods with respect to precision, recall, and F-measure. In the pheromone signaling pathways, PathFinder had 81.8% (9/11) recall and 56.3% (9/16) precision in recovering the pathways. Scott's color-coding method had 90.9% (10/11) recall and 55.6% (10/18) precision whereas the

Pathway Detection from Protein Interaction Networks and Gene Expression Data Using Color-Coding
Methods and Search Algorithms

57

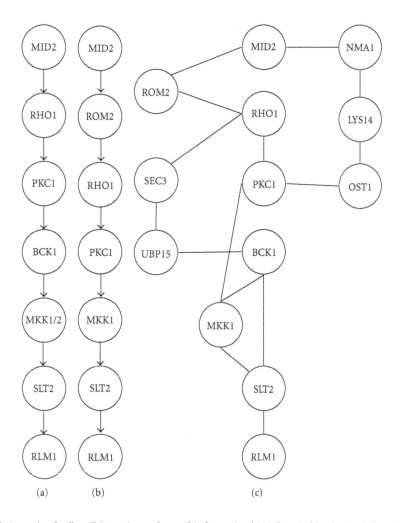

FIGURE 7: (a) The main chain path of cell wall integrity pathway (b) the main chain detected by Scott et al. method (c) the assembly paths detected by our method.

NetSearch prediction had 72.7% (8/11) recall and 42.1% (8/19) precision and ILP method had 100% (11/11) recall and 32.4% (11/34) precision. Our method had 100% (11/11) recall and 42.3% (11/26) precision. ILP and our proposed methods get the highest recall and we also have higher precision than ILP. It shows that we can detect all the proteins that have been known in the pathways without extracting more nonrelated proteins. In the filamentous growth pathways, Scott's color-coding method only detects 5 proteins in the main chain of the path. Pathfinder and our methods detect the maximum number of proteins involved in the main chain comparing with the other methods, but we get highest precision and F-measure. In the cell wall integrity pathways, we also get the higher precision and recall than the previous works. Since the true genes in the signaling networks are not actually known. Although it is difficult to know exactly correct genes in the signaling network, those genes may have casual relationships and are also reported in published papers. We can learn that our proposed method performs comparably well with previous existing methods in the yeast signaling pathways deposited in KEGG database.

3.3. The Significant Pathways of Prostate Cancer. Prostate cancer is a leading cancer and aggressive metastasis disease worldwide, and it is the second common cancer death among men [35]. Although numerous studies use microarray analysis to identify the individual genes during the disease processes, the important pathway remain unclear. In microarray data preprocessing, it consists 44,014 genes from microarray data after combining redundant gene. When we remove the genes that have more than 20% missing values in the microarray dataset, we extract 11,130 genes and imputed 7,588 number of data with KNN method. We evaluated the KNN method for imputing missing values in the microarray data. First, we deleted 1,750 origin values at random one by one to create test data sets and estimated the missing value to compare with the origin values. The accuracy of estimation values are calculated by root mean squared error (RMSE) which denote the different values between imputed values and original values, divided by the number of missing value we computed. The lower RMSE denotes higher accuracy for estimating the missing values. While setting the 11–15 nearest neighbors in KNN method, we could get the lowest error rate.

TABLE 2: Recall and precision of previous and our methods.

Pathways	Method	Recall (%)	Precision (%)	F-measure
Pheromone signaling pathway	Our method	100	42.3	0.59
	Pathfinder	81.8	56.3	0.67
	Color-coding	90.9	55.6	0.69
	ILP	100	32.4	0.49
	NetSearch	72.7	42.1	0.53
Filamentous growth pathway	Our method	100	34.6	0.51
	Pathfinder	100	27.3	0.43
	ILP	88.9	28.6	0.43
	NetSearch	77.8	31.8	0.45
Cell wall integrity pathway	Our method	87.5	53.8	0.67
	ILP	87.5	38.9	0.54
	NetSearch	87.5	36.8	0.52

According to the performance of KNN data impute algorithm in Supplemental Figure S1, we extract 15 neighbor genes which caused the lowest RMSE rate with 20% missing values in the microarray dataset.

The proportion of proteins with at least a degree 8 is 29.56% and 19.46% with 1 degree in the prostate cancer network. 639 articulation points are extracted from network, and the number of intersection of the articulation points and protein with a degree lower than 8 is 231. If we use the random color-coding method with limited color, it may get same color between articulation point and its neighbor using random color-coding method and lose a lot of biological meaning for pathway detection. That is the reason why we modify the traditional random color-coding method into the current one. Interestingly, several reports suggested that the degree of a node tends to be high in the networks if the protein represents a primary factor and protein mutation in the cancer cell, and the articulation points that cause a disruption in the network also tend to be related to cancer mutation [35]. The conclusion supported our color-coding methods based on the degree property of a network, and it provides an efficient way to search a pathway that contains those highly biologically significant proteins. We successfully reconstruct the paths from EGFR to BCL2 in KEGG pathway database in Figure 8 to validate our results. Figure 8(a) shows the one path in prostate cancer pathways, and Figure 8(b) shows the paths reconstructed from our method, and the dash line denotes the correspondence between the same genes between two paths. We can map genes in the prostate cancer signal pathway in KEGG database with more detail interactions except IKB that did not have a hit with at least a half of nodes.

As an example from membrane protein EGFR to BCL2 with length 15 in Supplemental Figures S2 and S3, we assembled network extracted from our method to explain the potential reaction pathway in human prostate cancer network. We evaluated our results related to prostate cancer with public Online Mendelian Inheritance in Man (OMIM) National Center for Biotechnology Information (NCBI) [36], KEGG pathway database [37], PGDB database [38], and published

papers. In particular, all paths we detected are 100% functional enrichment exceeding random expectation and belonging to the high significant cell cycle biological processes (P value = $5.668e-6$), and prostate cancer included the PIK3 pathway. The grey color nodes denote cancer-related genes annotated in databases and those genes belong to high-degree nodes or articulation hubs. For example, gene BRCA1 with degree 129 is strongly related to prostate cancer, and articulation hub of gene NCOA4 with only degree 8 is also the annotated cancer gene in prostate cancer. For a part of the network in Supplemental Figures S2 and S3, we discovered that protein AR is annotated in KEGG database as oncogene in the prostate cancer pathway, and papers [39, 40] also support the disease-related proteins in prostate cancer growth via TP53 mechanism. MYC, BRCA1, BRCA2, RNF14, CCND1, ATM, ESR1, NCOA4, SMARCA4, PCNA, SMAD2, CAV1, and RB1 are annotated the prostate cancer-related genes, and CDH1 is mark gene as tumor suppressors in PGDB database. The evidence for protein NR3C1 related to prostate cancer and MAPK proteins, member of the MAP kinase family, involved in the cellular processes such as apoptosis, cell proliferation, and it also leads to G1 cell cycle arrest in prostate cancer [41]. BRCA1 and BRCA2 proteins play important role in DNA repair in both S and G2 checkpoint phase of the cell cycle. Except the genes discovered by the public database, we list the genes that are extracted by our method in Supplemental Table S2 and those results we detected confirmed by present biological evidence from the literature.

3.4. Execution Time of Our Methods. We detect that the length of 11 is the longest shortest path in our prostate cancer network, so we try to detect the path with the length from 3 to 11 as our experiment testing. Based on the same protein-protein interactions and the weights of interactions, we ran the Scott and Huffner's work to compare with our method. We randomly choose the start protein that belongs to membrane protein category (GO: 0005886 or GO: 0004872) and end protein that belongs to the nucleus category (GO: 0005634). Comparing with the execution time, our method

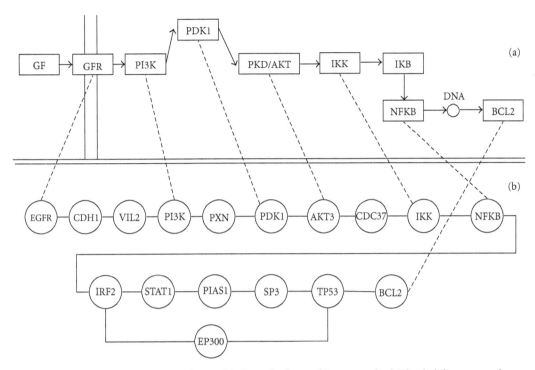

FIGURE 8: (a) One of the KEGG prostate cancer pathways (b) the paths detected by our method. The dash line means the mapping genes.

is faster than Scott color-coding method and we are able to detect the length of paths above 10 within 29 seconds while it took about 3 hours in Scott's method as shown in Figure 9. Scott's and Huffner's work applied dynamic programming in the color-coding method that still takes more time to execute in comparison with our method. Based on color-coding method to extract a colorful pathway of length k, it still costs exponential time to execute with parameter k. Our method with the pretraversed length $d = 3$ can detect the optimal colorful path under color-coding method. It may take a lot of time to detect paths only dependent on our color-coding method because we allow more candidate paths passing through the high degree and articulation hubs than previous random color-coding method. The user set parameter of alpha value let our method not only detects the optimal path but also can find the top paths that are still statistical and biologically significant.

The A* procedure with pretraversed length $d = 3$ presents an efficient way to extract longer lengths of paths. Therefore it is important to filter the higher weights of paths and keep looking for lower weights of paths in the search procedure. To consider the effect of parameter d, we implemented the experiments to discuss the runtime time between different path lengths from proteins HLA-B to YWHAZ against different pretraversed lengths d in A* searching procedure. The results are shown in Figure 10, and it denotes faster execution time with a shorter length of parameter d because it filtered out a large number of nodes to be expanded early.

4. Conclusion

We developed methods to detect pathways with a color-coding technique which takes into consideration the char-

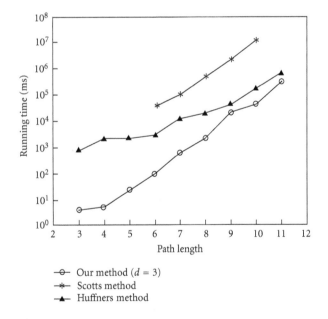

FIGURE 9: The comparison of runtime in human prostate cancer networks between Scott's, Huffner's method, and our methods.

acteristics of biological network topology and also speeds up the search with an A* heuristic method. We are able to reconstruct the yeast with the same known signaling pathway as previous studies but we also showed the potential to detect new functional related pathways as well. Based on the degree and articulation points, it ensures that those biological significant proteins can be found in the colorful path instead of merely random coloring. Purely A* search with traditional random color-coding method may extract paths

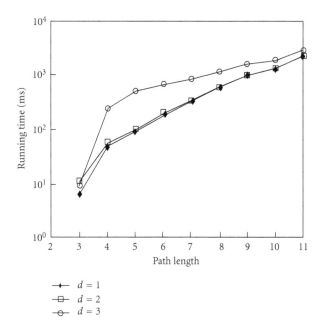

FIGURE 10: The comparison of runtime with different parameters d's for pathway detection from proteins HLA-B to YWHAZ.

without passing through articulation points or the high-degree nodes that might contain biological meanings. This approach is able to efficiently integrate microarray data and protein-protein interactions for the signal pathway detection of cancer. We are able to detect the proteins and their pathway related to prostate cancer by recent database and published papers. The merit of this research would help biologists to understand the cellular mechanism more easily. In the future, we can study the effects of other properties of network topology such as centroid and closeness with color-coding method. However, PPI database consists of interaction pairs under different physiological conditions that may not exist in all tissues, and it is also not complete such as phosphorylation interactions. In the future, we could use different microarray data about the cancers to test our methods and integrate further the protein-DNA interaction information to understand the reaction pathways of upstream and downstream biological interaction mechanisms response to various diseases. The edge orientation of the interaction of proteins may also be a problem in pathway detection. We can develop the computational analytic tools for detecting pathway that can provide more complete and in-depth information implied in the dataset for physicians so that they could either based on it conduct further clinical diagnosis or verification. It is also a useful idea to develop a pathway query system that allows users to set conditions on their interested proteins.

Authors' Contribution

Cheng-Yu Yeh and Hsiang-Yuan Yeh contributed equally to this work.

Acknowledgments

This paper is partially supported by the Bioresources Collection and Research Center of Linko Chang Gung Memorial Hospital and National Tsing Hua University of Taiwan under Grant no. CGTH96-T13 (CGMH-NTHU Joint Research no. 13).

References

[1] E. Segal, H. Wang, and D. Koller, "Discovering molecular pathways from protein interaction and gene expression data," *Bioinformatics*, vol. 19, no. 1, pp. i264–i272, 2003.

[2] R. G. Michael and S. J. David, *Computers and Intractability, A Guide to the Theory of NP-Completeness*, W. H. Freeman, New York, NY, USA, 1990.

[3] M. Steffen, A. Petti, J. Aach, P. D'haeseleer, and G. Church, "Automated modelling of signal transduction networks," *BMC Bioinformatics*, vol. 3, article 34, 2002.

[4] N. Alon, R. Yuster, and U. Zwick, "Color-coding," *Journal of ACM*, vol. 42, no. 4, pp. 844–856, 1995.

[5] T. Shlomi, D. Segal, E. Ruppin, and R. Sharan, "QPath: a method for querying pathways in a protein-protein interaction network," *BMC Bioinformatics*, vol. 7, article 199, 2006.

[6] I. Mayrose, T. Shlomi, and N. D. Rubinstein, "Epitope mapping using combinational phase-display libraries: a grpah-based algorithm," *Nucleic Acids Research*, vol. 35, no. 1, pp. 69–78, 2007.

[7] J. Scott, T. Ideker, R. M. Karp, and R. Sharan, "Efficient algorithms for detecting signaling pathways in protein interaction networks," in *Proceedings of the 9th Annual International Conference on Research in Computational Molecular Biology (RECOMB '05)*, vol. 3500 of *Lecture Notes in Bioinformatics*, pp. 1–13, Cambridge, Mass, USA, May 2005.

[8] M. Ashburner, C. A. Ball, J. A. Blake et al., "Gene ontology: tool for the unification of biology," *Nature Genetics*, vol. 25, no. 1, pp. 25–29, 2000.

[9] F. Hüffner, S. Wernicke, and T. Zichner, "Algorithm engineering for color-coding with applications to signaling pathway detection," *Algorithmica*, vol. 52, no. 2, pp. 114–132, 2008.

[10] X. Zhao, R. Wang, L. Chen, and K. Aihara, "Automatic modeling of signal pathways from protein-protein interaction networks," *Asia Pacific Bioinformatics Conference*, vol. 3, no. 42, pp. 287–296, 2007.

[11] G. Bebek and J. Yang, "PathFinder: mining signal transduction pathway segments from protein-protein interaction networks," *BMC Bioinformatics*, vol. 8, article 335, 2007.

[12] M. E. Dolan, L. Ni, E. Camon, and J. A. Blake, "A procedure for assessing GO annotation consistency," *Bioinformatics*, vol. 21, no. 1, pp. i136–i143, 2005.

[13] O. Troyanskaya, M. Cantor, G. Sherlock et al., "Missing value estimation methods for DNA microarrays," *Bioinformatics*, vol. 17, no. 6, pp. 520–525, 2001.

[14] C. Prieto and J. De Las Rivas, "APID: agile protein interaction DataAnalyzer," *Nucleic Acids Research*, vol. 34, pp. W298–W302, 2006.

[15] H. C. Liu, C. R. Arias, and V. W. Soo, "BioIR: an approach to public domain resource integration of human protein-protein interaction," in *Proceeding of the 7th Asia Pacific Bioinformatics Conference (APBC '9)*, 2009.

[16] A. L. Barabási and Z. N. Oltvai, "Network biology: understanding the cell's functional organization," *Nature Reviews Genetics*, vol. 5, no. 2, pp. 101–113, 2004.

Pathway Detection from Protein Interaction Networks and Gene Expression Data Using Color-Coding
Methods and Search Algorithms

61

[17] E. W. Dijkstra, "A note on two problems in connexion with graphs," *Numerische Mathematik*, vol. 1, no. 1, pp. 269–271, 1959.

[18] A. Grigoriev, "A relationship between gene expression and protein interactions on the proteome scale: analysis of the bacteriophage T7 and the yeast Saccharomyces cerevisiae," *Nucleic Acids Research*, vol. 29, no. 17, pp. 3513–3519, 2001.

[19] J. Zhu, B. Zhang, E. N. Smith et al., "Integrating large-scale functional genomic data to dissect the complexity of yeast regulatory networks," *Nature Genetics*, vol. 40, no. 7, pp. 854–861, 2008.

[20] S. Russell and P. Norvig, *Artificial Intelligence: A Modern Approach*, Prentice Hall, New York, NY, USA, 1995.

[21] S. Grossmann, S. Bauer, P. N. Robinson, and M. Vingron, "An improved statistic for detecting over-represented gene ontology annotations in gene sets," in *Proceedings of the 10th International Conference on Research in Computational Molecular Biology*, vol. 3909 of *Lecture Notes in Computer Science*, pp. 85–98, 2006.

[22] I. Xenarios, D. W. Rice, L. Salwinski, M. K. Baron, E. M. Marcotte, and D. Eisenberg, "DIP: the database of interacting proteins," *Nucleic Acids Research*, vol. 28, no. 1, pp. 289–291, 2000.

[23] Mega Yeast Gene Expression Data, http://gasch.genetics.wisc.edu/datasets.html.

[24] J. Lapointe, C. Li, J. P. Higgins et al., "Gene expression profiling identifies clinically relevant subtypes of prostate cancer," *Proceedings of the National Academy of Sciences of the United States of America*, vol. 101, no. 3, pp. 811–816, 2004.

[25] G. Sherlock, T. Hernandez-Boussard, A. Kasarskis et al., "The stanford microarray database," *Nucleic Acids Research*, vol. 29, no. 1, pp. 152–155, 2001.

[26] A. Nern and R. A. Arkowitz, "A Cdc24p-Far1p-Gβγ protein complex required for yeast orientation during mating," *Journal of Cell Biology*, vol. 144, no. 6, pp. 1187–1202, 1999.

[27] H. W. Mewes, C. Amid, R. Arnold et al., "MIPS: analysis and annotation of proteins from whole genomes," *Nucleic Acids Research*, vol. 32, pp. D41–D44, 2004.

[28] Y. Matsui, R. Matsui, R. Akada, and A. Toh-e, "Yeast src homology region 3 domain-binding proteins involved in bud formation," *Journal of Cell Biology*, vol. 133, no. 4, pp. 865–878, 1996.

[29] E. Blackwell, I. M. Halatek, H. J. N. Kim, A. T. Ellicott, A. A. Obukhov, and D. E. Stone, "Effect of the pheromone-responsive Gα and phosphatase proteins of Saccharomyces cerevisiae on the subcellular localization of the Fus3 mitogen-activated protein kinase," *Molecular and Cellular Biology*, vol. 23, no. 4, pp. 1135–1150, 2003.

[30] L. R. Kao, J. Peterson, R. Ji, L. Bender, and A. Bender, "Interactions between the ankyrin repeat-containing protein Akr1p and the pheromone response pathway in Saccharomyces cerevisiae," *Molecular and Cellular Biology*, vol. 16, no. 1, pp. 168–178, 1996.

[31] H. O. Park and E. Bi, "Central roles of small GTPases in the development of cell polarity in yeast and beyond," *Microbiology and Molecular Biology Reviews*, vol. 71, no. 1, pp. 48–96, 2007.

[32] D. I. Johnson, "Cdc42: an essential Rho-type GTPase controlling eukaryotic cell polarity," *Microbiology and Molecular Biology Reviews*, vol. 63, no. 1, pp. 54–105, 1999.

[33] S. P. Palecek, A. S. Parikh, and S. J. Kron, "Sensing, signalling and integrating physical processes during Saccharomyces cerevisiae invasive and filamentous growth," *Microbiology*, vol. 148, no. 4, pp. 893–907, 2002.

[34] D. E. Levin, "Cell wall integrity signaling in Saccharomyces cerevisiae," *Microbiology and Molecular Biology Reviews*, vol. 69, no. 2, pp. 262–291, 2005.

[35] H. Jeong, S. P. Mason, A. L. Barabási, and Z. N. Oltvai, "Lethality and centrality in protein networks," *Nature*, vol. 411, no. 6833, pp. 41–42, 2001.

[36] J. Amberger, C. A. Bocchini, A. F. Scott, and A. Hamosh, "McKusick's Online Mendelian Inheritance in Man (OMIM®)," *Nucleic Acids Research*, vol. 37, no. 1, pp. D793–D796, 2009.

[37] M. Kanehisa, S. Goto, S. Kawashima, Y. Okuno, and M. Hattori, "The KEGG resource for deciphering the genome," *Nucleic Acids Research*, vol. 32, pp. D277–D280, 2004.

[38] L. C. Li, H. Zhao, H. Shiina, C. J. Kane, and R. Dahiya, "PGDB: a curated and integrated database of genes related to the prostate," *Nucleic Acids Research*, vol. 31, no. 1, pp. 291–293, 2003.

[39] H. Wang, D. Yu, S. Agrawal, and R. Zhang, "Experimental therapy of human prostate cancer by inhibiting MDM2 expression with novel mixed-backbone antisense oligonucleotides: in vitro and in vivo activities and mechanisms," *Prostate*, vol. 54, no. 3, pp. 194–205, 2003.

[40] Z. Zhang, M. Li, H. Wang, S. Agrawal, and R. Zhang, "Antisense therapy targeting MDM2 oncogene in prostate cancer: effects on proliferation, apoptosis, multiple gene expression, and chemotherapy," *Proceedings of the National Academy of Sciences of the United States of America*, vol. 100, no. 20, pp. 11636–11641, 2003.

[41] S. Sarfaraz, F. Afaq, V. M. Adhami, A. Malik, and H. Mukhtar, "Cannabinoid receptor agonist-induced apoptosis of human prostate cancer cells LNCaP proceeds through sustained activation of ERK1/2 leading to G 1 cell cycle arrest," *The Journal of Biological Chemistry*, vol. 281, no. 51, pp. 39480–39491, 2006.

A Robust Hybrid Approach Based on Estimation of Distribution Algorithm and Support Vector Machine for Hunting Candidate Disease Genes

Li Li,[1,2] **Hongmei Chen,**[1] **Chang Liu,**[1] **Fang Wang,**[1] **Fangfang Zhang,**[1] **Lihua Bai,**[2] **Yihan Chen,**[2] **and Luying Peng**[1,2]

[1] *Division of Medical Genetics, Tongji University School of Medicine, Shanghai 200092, China*
[2] *Key Lab for Basic Research in Cardiology, Ministry of Education, Tongji University, Shanghai 200092, China*

Correspondence should be addressed to Yihan Chen; yihanchen@tongji.edu.cn and Luying Peng; luyingpeng@tongji.edu.cn

Academic Editors: R. Jiang, W. Tian, J. Wan, and X. Zhao

Microarray data are high dimension with high noise ratio and relatively small sample size, which makes it a challenge to use microarray data to identify candidate disease genes. Here, we have presented a hybrid method that combines estimation of distribution algorithm with support vector machine for selection of key feature genes. We have benchmarked the method using the microarray data of both diffuse B cell lymphoma and colon cancer to demonstrate its performance for identifying key features from the profile data of high-dimension gene expression. The method was compared with a probabilistic model based on genetic algorithm and another hybrid method based on both genetics algorithm and support vector machine. The results showed that the proposed method provides new computational strategy for hunting candidate disease genes from the profile data of disease gene expression. The selected candidate disease genes may help to improve the diagnosis and treatment for diseases.

1. Introduction

Complex diseases are frequently accompanied by changes in gene expression patterns which can serve as secondary endpoints or biomarkers [1]. Microarray technology, which allows researchers to simultaneously measure expression levels of thousands or tens of thousands of genes in a single experiment, has been widely used to explore the gene expression pattern of complex diseases [2]. Typically, there are only a small number of genes associated with diseases. Thus, the selection of feature genes that possess discriminatory power for disease phenotypes is a common task for mining microarray data that are usually high dimension (with thousands of genes) and have small sample size (with usually a few dozens of samples) [3].

The method of gene selection generally falls into one of the following three categories: the filter, wrapper, and embedded approaches. The filter approach collects the intrinsic characteristics of genes in discriminating the targeted phenotype class and usually employs statistical methods, such as mutual information, statistical tests (*t*-test, *F*-test), and Wilcoxon's rank test, to directly select feature genes [4, 5]. This approach is easily implemented, but ignores the complex interaction between genes. The "wrapper" approach [6] aims at selecting a subset of feature genes, typically with an induction algorithm to search for an initial gene subset which can then be used for further evaluating new feature gene subsets. The wrapper method is usually superior to the filter one since it involves intercorrelation of individual genes in a multivariate manner. The wrapper method can automatically determine the optimal number of feature genes for a particular classifier. The embedded method is similar to the wrapper method, while multiple algorithms can be combined in the embedded method to perform feature subset selection [6, 7]. In the embedded method, genetic algorithms (GAs) [8, 9] are generally used as the search engine for feature subset, while other classification methods, such as KNN/GA (K nearest neighbors/genetic algorithms) [10], GA-SVM (genetic algorithms-support vector machine) [11], and so forth, are used to select feature subset. Estimation of

A Robust Hybrid Approach Based on Estimation of Distribution Algorithm and Support Vector
Machine for Hunting Candidate Disease Genes

63

Step 1. M_0 ←Read gene expression profile matrix from database, m is the number of genes in M_0.
Step 2. D_0 ←Generate N individuals (the initial population) randomly. Each individual has an m-length vector of bits of either 1 or 0.
Step 3. For each individual j in D_0, determine:
   G_j ←a gene subset corresponding to individual j. If bit i equals to 1, include g_i in the subset.
   M_j ←gene expression profile submatrix.
   Fitness$_j$ ← eval(M_j).
Step 4. D_l^r ←retain $N/2$ individuals with the highest evaluations.
Step 5. $M \arg inal(z_i, l)$ ←calculate marginal distribution of variable z_i of bit i based on D_l^r by using the formula: $M \arg inal(z_i, l) = \left(\sum_{j=1}^{N/2} z_i^j \right) / (N/2)$, where z_i^j is the value of the variable z_i in individual j.
   $M_{weight}(z_i, l)$ ← calculate weight of z_i corresponding to feature i based on D_l^r.
   $M_{weight}(z_i, l) = \left\{ \sum_{j=1}^{N/2} \text{Pre}_{weight}(z_i^j) \right\} / (N/2)$, where $\text{Pre}_{weight}(z_i^j)$ is weight of bit i in individual j.
   $Prob(z_i, l + 1)$ ←compute probability distribution z_i of each bit i, which is written mathematically as:
   $Prob(z_i, l + 1) = lr\beta_i * Prob(z_i, l) + (1 - lr) * (1 - \beta_i) * M \arg inal(z_i, l) * M_{weight}(z_i, l)$.
   $lr \in (0, 1)$ is learning rate. $\beta_i \in (0, 1)$ is generated at random.
Step 6. D_{l+1}^{new} ←generate new $N/2$ individuals by sampling the probability distribution.
Step 7. $D_{l+1} \leftarrow D_l^r \cup D_{l+1}^{new}$.
Step 8. $D_0 \leftarrow D_{l+1}$.
Step 9. End←output the optimal individual based on the evaluation with: fitness$_j$ = eval(M_j).

ALGORITHM 1: The step-by-step recipe for the computational algorithm of the EDA-SVM approach.

distribution algorithm (EDA) [12] is a general framework of GA. Compared to traditional GA that employs crossover and mutation operators to create new population, EDA creates new populations by using a statistical approach to estimate the probability distribution of all promising individual solutions for the previous generation. EDA can also explicitly take into account specific interactions among the variables. When EDA is used to search for feature subsets, classification methods, such as Support vector machine (SVM) [13–19], which can deal with the high-dimension data in a limited sample space, can be used to select feature subsets.

In this study, we have developed a hybrid approach that combines both EDA and SVM (termed EDA-SVM) for selecting key feature genes. Here, EDA acts as the search engine, while SVM serves as the classifier, namely, the evaluator. We have applied EDA-SVM to two well-known microarray datasets: a colon data [20] and a diffuse large B cell lymphoma data [3]. Our results have shown that EDA-SVM can be used to identify a smaller number of informative genes with better accuracy in comparison to GA-SVM [11] and an estimation of distribution algorithm named PMBGA [21].

2. Materials and Methods

2.1. Description of DLBCL Datasets.
We have applied the EDA-SVM method to the two following data sets: the diffuse large B cell lymphoma (DLBCL) data [3], available at http://llmpp.nih.gov/lymphoma/data.shtml, and the colon data [20], available at http://microarray.princeton.edu/oncology/affydata/index.html. The colon data set consists of 62 tissue samples including 40 tumors and 22 normal tissues, which cover 2000 human gene expression.

The DLBCL data set harbors preprocessed expression profile of 4026 genes in tissues derived from 21 activated B-like DLBCL (AB-like DLBCL) samples and 21 germinal center B-like DLBCL (GCB-like DLBCL) samples.

2.2. Data Preprocessing.
In DLBCL dataset, among 4026 genes, 6% genes have missing values and are imputed by the KNN Impute algorithm [22] prior to the EDA-SVM analysis. The KNN Impute algorithm uses the expression profiles of K nearest neighbors (here $K = 5$) to impute the missing values for the target gene. Therefore, in colon data M_0 is a matrix with 62 rows and 2000 columns. In DLBCL data, M_0 is a matrix with 42 rows and 4026 columns.

2.3. EDA-SVM.
Figure 1 shows the main flowchart of the EDA-SVM. EDA acts as the search engine, while SVM serves as the classifier, namely, the evaluator. The computational procedures are described in Algorithm 1. The major elements of the EDA include feature subset coding, population initialization, fitness computation, estimation probability distribution, generation of offspring and control of parameter assignment. At the beginning, we randomly generated the N fixed-length binary strings (individuals) to build up the initial population. Then, we calculated the fitness for each feature subset. Classification accuracy acted as the fitness index (fitness) that was evaluated using a linear SVM. The algorithm is an iterative process in which each successive generation is produced by estimating the probability distribution model of the selected individuals (parents) in the current generation and sampling the probability distribution to generate new offsprings. In this manner, reasonable subsets are developed successively until the terminal condition is fulfilled. In two

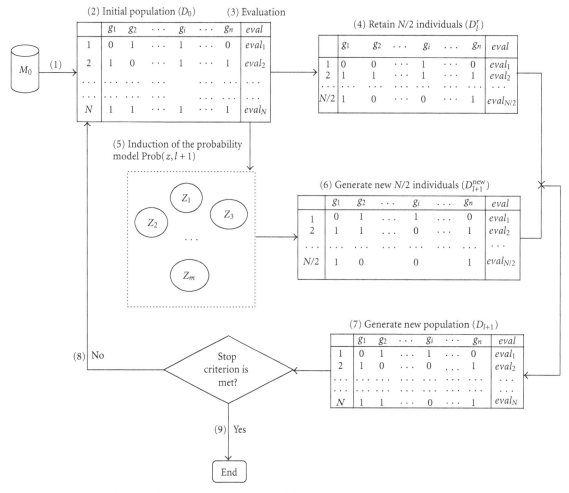

FIGURE 1: The main flow of EDA-SVM algorithm. M, D, G, and *eval* denote gene expression profile matrix, population, gene subset, and evaluation index, respectively.

data sets, lr is a learning rate and is assigned 0.08. Population size (N) is set as 40 and the maximal generations of 50 are determined, such that the solution space can be sufficiently searched while the best minimal subset can be obtained within the evolution time.

For each gene expression submatrix M_j, we classify the microarray samples with genes contained in individual j using a linear SVM. The classifier, [18], is

$$\widehat{y} = f(x) = \mathrm{sgn}\left(\sum_{i=1}^{L} a_i y_i K(x_i \cdot x) - b \right), \quad (1)$$

then, the accuracy of classification is

$$\mathrm{acc} = \frac{\left(\sum_{t=1}^{T} I(y_t, \widehat{y_t}) \right)}{T}, \quad (2)$$

where T is the number of test samples and

$$I(y_t, \widehat{y_t}) = \begin{cases} 1, & \text{if } y_t = \widehat{y_t}, \\ 0, & \text{otherwise}. \end{cases} \quad (3)$$

The weight of each feature i in individual j is

$$\mathrm{Pre}_{\mathrm{weight}}\left(z_i^j \right) = \begin{cases} 0, & \text{if } z_i^j = 0, \\ \left(\sum_{h=1}^{L} \alpha_h y_h x_h \right)^2, & \text{if } z_i^j \neq 0, \end{cases} \quad (4)$$

where x is a test sample vector and x_i is the learning sample vector. L is the number of learning samples. y_i is a class indicator (for a two-class application, $+1$ for the first class, -1 for the second class), and a_i is a nonnegative Lagrange multiplier associated with x_i and $a_i \neq 0$ for support vectors. sgn( ) is the sign function and $K(x_i \cdot x)$ is the kernel function: linear kernel ($K(x_i \cdot x) = x_i \cdot x$, i.e., their inner product).

In this study, a fivefold cross-validation (CV) resampling approach is used to construct the learning and test sets. First, the two-class samples are randomly divided into 5 nonoverlapping subsets of roughly equal size, respectively. A random combination of the subsets for the two classes constitutes a test set, and the rest of subsets is totally used as the learning set. The 5-fold CV resampling produces 25

A Robust Hybrid Approach Based on Estimation of Distribution Algorithm and Support Vector
Machine for Hunting Candidate Disease Genes

65

pairs of learning and test sets. Individual j is evaluated by the averaged value over the 25 pairs, that is,

$$\text{Fitness}_j = \frac{\left(\sum_{k=1}^{25} \text{acc}_k\right)}{25},$$

$$\text{weight}\left(z_i^j\right) = \frac{\left(\sum_{k=1}^{25} \text{Pre}_{\text{weight}k}\left(z_i^j\right)\right)}{25},$$

(5)

where k is the replicate number and acc_k is the classification accuracy for the kth replicate.

In the EDA-SVM algorithm, the optimization of the feature gene subset(s) is realized via survival competitions. For each generation, we retain 50% of the high-valued individuals that will directly enter next generation in order to keep these optimal solutions unchanged. On the other hand, in order to avoid the loss of the putative important feature genes, we initially contained about half of genes in each individual or preserving informative gene. Then, we adopt a stepwise data reduction procedure to minimize the feature subsets with more reliable classification accuracy. These gene expression matrices from the optimal individuals serve as the data on which the new round of iteration is performed. The data reduction process is completed once a stable gene subset is obtained.

2.4. GA-SVM. GA-SVM was previously developed [11] by us as a feature selection method. In GA-SVM, better feature subsets have a greater chance of being selected to form a new subset through crossover or mutation. Mutation changes some of the values (thus adding or deleting features) in a subset randomly. Crossover combines different features from a pair of subsets into a new subset. The algorithm is an iterative process in which each successive generation is produced by applying genetic operators to the members of the current generation. In this manner, good subsets are "evolved" over time until the stopping criteria are met. Thus, coding feature subset, population initialization, fitness computation, genetic operation, and control parameter assignment (population size, the maximal number of generations, and the selection probability) are the major elements of the GA-SVM method.

2.5. PMBGA. PMBGA can be applied for selection of a smaller size gene subset that would classify patient samples more accurately [21]. PMGBA generates initial population and builds a probability model and then selects individuals from the population. Probability distribution can be estimated based on the collection of selected individuals, and probability model can accordingly be amended so that a population is generated by sampling from the model. Instead of applying crossover and mutation operators in the process of generating new possible solutions (offspring), population can be updated in whole or in part relied on probability model.

3. Results

3.1. Benchmark EDA-SVM. The EDA-SVM method was applied firstly to the DLBCL data set. We started analysis with

all 4026 genes and progressively reduced the dimension of the feature genes successively for 8 iterations after convergence. The accuracy of EDA-SVM increased from 0.9339 initially to 0.9982 at convergence (Figure 2(a)), while the number of feature genes at the successive generations is 4026, 460, 66, 17, 11, 7, 6, and 6, respectively (Figure 2(b)). For the colon data set, EDA-SVM reached accuracy of 1.0 after 7 iterations, and the final gene subset includes only 5 genes (Figure 3).

We compared the performance of EDA-SVM with two alternative methods: GA-SVM and PMBGA (Figures 2 and 3). The convergence speed of EDA-SVM is the fastest among the three methods. EDA-SVM converged after 8 and 7 iterations for the DLBCL and colon datasets, respectively. In contrast, it took 13 and 10 iterations for GA-SVM to converge, and 10 and 10 iterations for PMBGA to converge. Moreover, both the accuracy and the stability of EDA-SVM also show advantages among the three methods. EDA-SVM quickly reaches high accuracy after only a couple of iterations, while both the other two methods took more iteration to reach high accuracy. In addition, the accuracy of the other two methods had large variation during the iteration, while the accuracy of EDA-SVM kept stable during the iteration after it reached the high accuracy.

3.2. Biological Analysis of the Selected Genes in the DLBCL Data. To understand the biological significance of the selected genes, we have analyzed the annotations of selected genes according to Gene Ontology (GO) (http://www.geneontology.org/) [23] and KEGG (http://www.genome.jp/kegg/kegg2.html) [24, 25] database. We selected six genes in the DLBCL data, which are SPIB, IRF8, NFKB2, LMO2, FCGRT, and BCL7B. The GO annotations of these six genes are shown in Table 1. Literature reviews of these six genes suggested that they are highly related to DLBCL. SPIB is an oncogene involved in the pathogenesis of AB-like DLBCL [26]. NFKB2 is a subunit of NF-κB whose signaling pathway might contribute to the biological and clinical differences between the GCB-like and the AB-like DLBCL [27]. LMO2 was found to be located in the most frequent regime of chromosomal translocation in childhood T cell acute lymphoblastic leukemia. It was reported that LMO2 expressed at high level in germinal center B cell lymphocytes and at low level in AB-like DLBCL, respectively [3]. LMO2 is also one of the six genes in a multivariate model previously developed for prolonged survival in the diffusive large b-cell lymphoma [28]. BCL7B was found to be directly involved in a three-way gene translocation together with Myc and IgH in a Burkitt lymphoma cell line, and the disruption of the N-terminal region of BCL7B was thought to be related to the pathogenesis of a subset of high-grade B cell non-Hodgkin lymphoma [29]. BCL2 contributes to the pathogenesis in AB-like DLBCL [10] and is the common target gene of miR-21 and miR-221, both of which are overexpressed in AB-like than GCB-like cell lines [30]. Based on the above evidences, EDA-SVM successfully identified genes that may play role in the pathogenesis of DLBCL.

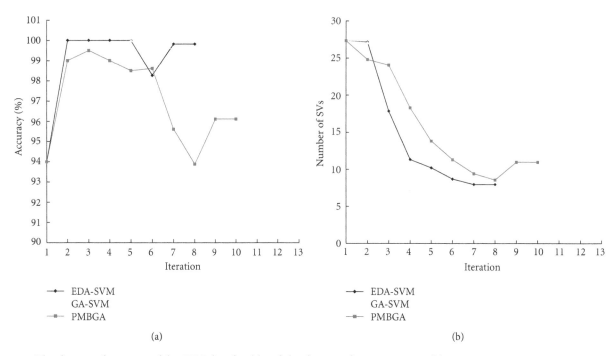

FIGURE 2: The changes of accuracy of the SVM classifier (a) and the changes of support vectors (b) over iterations in EDA-SVM, GA-SVM, and PMBGA based on DLBCL data set.

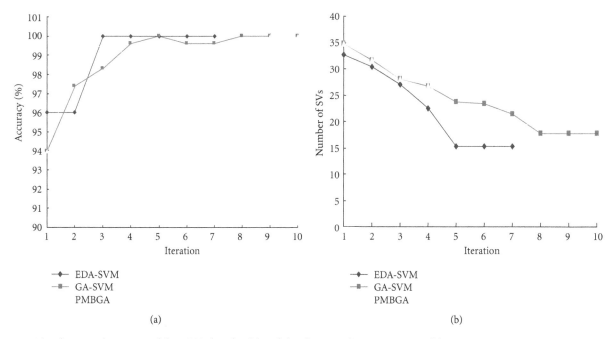

FIGURE 3: The changes of accuracy of the SVM classifier (a) and the changes of support vectors (b) over iterations in EDA-SVM, GA-SVM, and PMBGA based on colon data set.

4. Discussions and Conclusions

In this study, we have developed a hybrid method, EDA-SVM, which combines the estimation of distribution algorithms (EDA) with support vector machine (SVM) for selecting key feature genes from microarray data. Although similar combination strategies have been explored previously

[21], EDA-SVM shows unique advantages compared with the alternative methods, GA-SVM or PMBGA. For example, EDAV-SVM not only converged more quickly, but also achieved higher accuracy with stable performance than the other two methods did. Both EDA-SVM and PMBGA [21] use EDA as the search engine, and SVM acts as evaluation classifier in feature selection procedure. However, there are

A Robust Hybrid Approach Based on Estimation of Distribution Algorithm and Support Vector
Machine for Hunting Candidate Disease Genes

67

TABLE 1: The GO annotations of EDA-SVM feature genes.

Gene name Uigene ID	Biological process	Cellular component	Molecular function
SPIB (Hs.437905)	GO:0006350 Transcription GO:0006357 Regulation of transcription from RNA polymerase II promoter	GO:0005634 Nucleus GO:0005737 Cytoplasm	GO:0003700 Transcription factor activity GO:0003702: RNA polymerase II transcription factor activity
IRF8 (Hs.137427)	GO:0000122 Negative regulation of transcription from RNA polymerase II promoter GO:0006355 Regulation of transcription, DNA-dependent GO:0006350 Transcription GO:0006955 Immune response	GO:0005634 Nucleus	GO:0003705: RNA polymerase II transcription factor activity, enhancer binding
NFKB2 (Hs.73090)	Go:0006355 Regulation of transcription, DNA-dependent GO:0007165 Signal transduction	GO:0005634 Nucleus GO:0005737 Cytoplasm	GO:0005515 Protein binding GO:0003713 Transcription coactivator activity GO:0003700 Transcription factor activity
LMO2 (Hs.34560)	GO:0008270 Development	GO:0005634 Nucleus	GO:0008270 Zinc ion binding GO:0005515 Protein binding GO:0046872 Metal ion binding
FCGRT (Hs.111903)	GO:0019882 Antigen presentation GO:0007565 Pregnancy GO:0006955 Immune response	GO:0042612 MHC class I protein complex GO:0016021 Integral to membrane	GO:0019864 IgG binding GO:0004872 Receptor activity GO:0030106 MHC class I receptor activity
BCL7B (Hs.408219)	Unknown	Unknown	GO:0003779 Actin binding

several key differences between the two methods. First, EDA-SVM weights each feature using "M_{weight}", so that the contribution of each feature was fully considered during the update of each generation. In contrast, PMBGA assigns only a small random number to each feature. Second, for selecting minimal feature genes, EDA-SVM reduced the feature number step by step, while PMBGA did so by tuning the learning rate. Finally, the way to create the next generation in GA is also different between the two methods. As for the differences between EDA-SVM and GA-SVM, GA-SVM employs the traditional GA, while EDA-SVM generates new possible solutions (individuals) by sampling the probability distribution calculated from the selected solutions of previous generation.

The structure of genes in a microarray data can be described by a Bayesian network. However, microarray data usually contains the expression of thousands or tens thousands of genes, making it virtually impossible to build a Bayesian network with so many genes. In this study, we have shown with EDA-SVM that proper combination of machine learning algorithms can overcome the high-dimension problem, and quickly converge to a small set of feature genes strongly related to target phenotype. The success of EDA-SVM thus made it readily applicable for hunting disease genes in microarray data.

List of Abbreviations

DLBCL:	Diffuse large B-cell lymphoma
EDA-SVM:	Estimation for distribution algorithm-support vector machine
GO:	GeneOntology
KEGG:	Kyoto Encyclopedia of Genes and Genomes
GAs:	Genetic algorithms
EDA:	Estimation of distribution algorithm
AB-like DLBCL:	Activated B-like DLBCL
GCB-like DLBCL:	Germinal center B-like DLBCL
PMBGA:	Probabilistic Model Building Genetic Algorithm
GA-SVM:	Genetic algorithm-support vector machine.

Acknowledgments

This work is supported in part by National Natural Science Foundation of China (30971621, 81270231, and 31170791), the National Basic Research Program of China (973 Program) (2012CB9668003 and 2010CB945500), International Science and Technology Cooperation Program of China (2011DFB30010), the Fundamental Research Funds for the

Central Universities to L. Li, and Shanghai Municipal Health Bureau Project to L. Li. We thank Dr. Weidong Tian for critical review of the paper.

References

[1] W. Yang, D. Ying, and Y. L. Lau, "In-depth cDNA library sequencing provides quantitative gene expression profiling in cancer biomarker discovery," *Genomics, Proteomics and Bioinformatics*, vol. 7, no. 1-2, pp. 1–12, 2009.

[2] S. S. Shen-Orr, R. Tibshirani, P. Khatri et al., "Cell type-specific gene expression differences in complex tissues," *Nature Methods*, vol. 7, no. 4, pp. 287–289, 2010.

[3] A. A. Alizadeh, M. B. Elsen, R. E. Davis et al., "Distinct types of diffuse large B-cell lymphoma identified by gene expression profiling," *Nature*, vol. 403, no. 6769, pp. 503–511, 2000.

[4] P. J. Park, M. Pagano, and M. Bonetti, "A nonparametric scoring algorithm for identifying informative genes from microarray data," *Pacific Symposium on Biocomputing*, pp. 52–63, 2001.

[5] Y. Su, T. M. Murali, V. Pavlovic, M. Schaffer, and S. Kasif, "RankGene: Identification of diagnostic genes based on expression data," *Bioinformatics*, vol. 19, no. 12, pp. 1578–1579, 2003.

[6] R. Kahavi and G. H. John, "Wrapper for feature subset selection," *Artificial Intelligence*, vol. 97, pp. 273–324, 1997.

[7] X. Li, S. Rao, Y. Wang, and B. Gong, "Gene mining: a novel and powerful ensemble decision approach to hunting for disease genes using microarray expression profiling," *Nucleic Acids Research*, vol. 32, no. 9, pp. 2685–2694, 2004.

[8] S. J. Cho and M. A. Hermsmeier, "Genetic algorithm guided selection: variable selection and subset selection," *Journal of Chemical Information and Computer Sciences*, vol. 42, no. 4, pp. 927–936, 2002.

[9] X. M. Zhao, Y. M. Cheung, and D. S. Huang, "A novel approach to extracting features from motif content and protein composition for protein sequence classification," *Neural Networks*, vol. 18, no. 8, pp. 1019–1028, 2005.

[10] L. Li, T. A. Darden, C. R. Weinberg, A. J. Levine, and L. G. Pedersen, "Gene assessment and sample classification for gene expression data using a genetic algorithm/k-nearest neighbor method," *Combinatorial Chemistry and High Throughput Screening*, vol. 4, no. 8, pp. 727–739, 2001.

[11] L. Li, W. Jiang, X. Li et al., "A robust hybrid between genetic algorithm and support vector machine for extracting an optimal feature gene subset," *Genomics*, vol. 85, no. 1, pp. 16–23, 2005.

[12] Y. Saeys, S. Degroeve, D. Aeyels, P. Rouzé, and Y. Van de Peer, "Feature selection for splice site prediction: a new method using EDA-based feature ranking," *BMC Bioinformatics*, vol. 5, p. 64, 2004.

[13] M. P. S. Brown, W. N. Grundy, D. Lin et al., "Knowledge-based analysis of microarray gene expression data by using support vector machines," *Proceedings of the National Academy of Sciences of the United States of America*, vol. 97, no. 1, pp. 262–267, 2000.

[14] J. H. Oh and J. Gao, "A kernel-based approach for detecting outliers of high-dimensional biological data," *BMC Bioinformatics*, vol. 10, supplement 4, p. S7, 2009.

[15] S. Hua and Z. Sun, "A novel method of protein secondary structure prediction with high segment overlap measure: support vector machine approach," *Journal of Molecular Biology*, vol. 308, no. 2, pp. 397–407, 2001.

[16] Y. Zhu, X. Shen, and W. Pan, "Network-based support vector machine for classification of microarray samples," *BMC Bioinformatics*, vol. 10, supplement 1, p. S21, 2009.

[17] L. Evers and C. M. Messow, "Sparse kernel methods for high-dimensional survival data," *Bioinformatics*, vol. 24, no. 14, pp. 1632–1638, 2008.

[18] V. Vapnik, *Statistical Learning Theory*, Wiley, New York, NY, USA, 1998.

[19] C. J. C. Burges, "A tutorial on support vector machines for pattern recognition," *Data Mining and Knowledge Discovery*, vol. 2, no. 2, pp. 121–167, 1998.

[20] U. Alon, N. Barka, D. A. Notterman et al., "Broad patterns of gene expression revealed by clustering analysis of tumor and normal colon tissues probed by oligonucleotide arrays," *Proceedings of the National Academy of Sciences of the United States of America*, vol. 96, no. 12, pp. 6745–6750, 1999.

[21] T. K. Paul and H. Iba, "Gene selection for classification of cancers using probabilistic model building genetic algorithm," *BioSystems*, vol. 82, no. 3, pp. 208–225, 2005.

[22] O. Troyanskaya, M. Cantor, G. Sherlock et al., "Missing value estimation methods for DNA microarrays," *Bioinformatics*, vol. 17, no. 6, pp. 520–525, 2001.

[23] M. Ashburner, C. A. Ball, J. A. Blake et al., "Gene ontology: tool for the unification of biology. The Gene Ontology Consortium," *Nature Genetics*, vol. 25, no. 1, pp. 25–29, 2000.

[24] M. Kanehisa, S. Goto, S. Kawashima, Y. Okuno, and M. Hattori, "The KEGG resource for deciphering the genome," *Nucleic Acids Research*, vol. 32, pp. D277–D280, 2004.

[25] M. Kanehisa, S. Goto, S. Kawashima, and A. Nakaya, "Thed KEGG databases at GenomeNet," *Nucleic Acids Research*, vol. 30, no. 1, pp. 42–46, 2002.

[26] G. Lenz, G. W. Wright, N. C. T. Emre et al., "Molecular subtypes of diffuse large B-cell lymphoma arise by distinct genetic pathways," *Proceedings of the National Academy of Sciences of the United States of America*, vol. 105, no. 36, pp. 13520–13525, 2008.

[27] R. E. Davis, K. D. Brown, U. Siebenlist, and L. M. Staudt, "Constitutive nuclear factor kappaB activity is required for survival of activated B cell-like diffuse large B cell lymphoma cells," *The Journal of Experimental Medicine*, vol. 194, pp. 1861–1874, 2001.

[28] I. S. Lossos, D. K. Czerwinski, A. A. Alizadeh et al., "Prediction of survival in diffuse large-B-cell lymphoma based on the expression of six genes," *The New England Journal of Medicine*, vol. 350, no. 18, pp. 1828–1837, 2004.

[29] S. Amenta, M. Moschovi, C. Sofocleous, S. Kostaridou, A. Mavrou, and H. Fryssira, "Non-Hodgkin lymphoma in a child with Williams syndrome," *Cancer Genetics and Cytogenetics*, vol. 154, no. 1, pp. 86–88, 2004.

[30] C. H. Lawrie, S. Soneji, T. Marafioti et al., "MicroRNA expression distinguishes between germinal center B cell-like and activated B cell-like subtypes of diffuse large B cell lymphoma," *International Journal of Cancer*, vol. 121, no. 5, pp. 1156–1161, 2007.

8

A Review of Integration Strategies to Support Gene Regulatory Network Construction

Hailin Chen and Vincent VanBuren

Department of Medical Physiology, Texas A&M HSC College of Medicine, Temple, TX 76504, USA

Correspondence should be addressed to Vincent VanBuren, vanburen@tamu.edu

Academic Editors: R. Jiang, W. Tian, J. Wan, and X. Zhao

Gene regulatory network (GRN) construction is a central task of systems biology. Integration of different data sources to infer and construct GRNs is an important consideration for the success of this effort. In this paper, we will discuss distinctive strategies of data integration for GRN construction. Basically, the process of integration of different data sources is divided into two phases: the first phase is collection of the required data and the second phase is data processing with advanced algorithms to infer the GRNs. In this paper these two phases are called "structural integration" and "analytic integration," respectively. Compared with the nonintegration strategies, the integration strategies perform quite well and have better agreement with the experimental evidence.

1. Introduction

1.1. Conventional Strategies of Building GRNs. Biological functions comprise numerous reactions at all levels of biological organization, including cells, tissues, organs, and body, and interchange with the environment. Overall, every life phenomenon found in this multilevel system is supported through many reactions interconnecting with each other to compose the orchestra of life. It is, therefore, crucial to have a systematic perspective in biomedical research. To gain an overview of such a complex system, we can visualize it in the form of a network. For instance, protein-protein interactions, metabolic reactions, and genetic regulations correspond respectively to a protein-protein interaction network (PPI), metabolic network, and gene regulatory network (GRN), which are subnetworks of the complex multi-level system. In the representation of a network, nodes typically correspond to molecules, while edges represent the relationships between nodes. In the study of biological networks, GRNs are one of the most popular models, especially in the field of development. Developmental GRNs provide important clues to elucidate the temporal and spatial dynamics of gene expression during development. The use of sea urchin and *Drosophila* has led to some of the greatest successes in studying developmental GRNs to explain complex

developmental processes [1, 2]. Traditionally, the first step is to identify putative regulatory genes through genome-wide screening, such as expression microarrays, across distinct temporal and spatial states. Quantitative PCR is used afterwards to verify specific expression patterns [3]. Amazingly, the gene repertoire used in the control of development is relatively conserved across species, and thus regulatory genes can be identified by sequencing-based homology alignments [4]. As a central objective of modeling developmental GRNs is to identify the epistatic relations among these regulatory genes, the second step is to define experiments to perturb/activate the system and examine the responses via loss-of-function and gain-of-function experiments [3]. In a sea urchin GRN study, perturbation with morpholino-substituted antisense oligonucleotides (MASOs) was the main approach [5]. Rescue experiments are also an important part of this step. Finally, by assembling findings from many individual experiments, investigators may establish the developmental GRN. Validation of the established GRN can be accomplished precisely via mutagenesis of regulator binding sites for their target genes to observe the abolishment of the regulatory effect [6, 7].

Elucidation of gene regulation in the endomesoderm specification in the sea urchin and in the development of *Drosophila* embryos provides potent examples of the type of complexities revealed by the study of GRNs. In the sea urchin embryo, *blimp1* is autorepressive when its product accumulates to high levels. At the same time, it provides a required input for *Wnt8* expression, which produces a positive feedback effect for *blimp1* via inducing *Tcf* to activate *blimp1* expression. *Wnt8* can infect the adjacent cells/territories with this circular bioinformation flow via diffusion. This flow is terminated due to *blimp1* autorepression [8]. In the early development of the *Drosophila* embryo, *Snail* repressor activates the synthesis of *Delta* ligand in the ventral mesoderm via repressing the transcription of *Tom*, an inhibitor of the *Delta*, which is called a double-negative gate. *Delta* triggers *Notch* signaling in the adjacent cells via diffusion. However, transcription of the *Notch* signaling target genes is repressed by the intraterritorial *Snail* repression in the ventral mesoderm itself. An exactly parallel mechanism causing transcriptional alternation inter-territorially is also found in the sea urchin skeletogenic mesoderm [1, 2]. Despite such accomplishments, there is still a large portion of the overall GRN in animal models that has not been defined. The laborious approach to elucidating GRNs from experiments for every node and every edge produces reliable biological information as prior knowledge to support novel findings. However, due to the complications in GRNs as discussed above, elucidating the complete GRN of complex eukaryotic organisms with respect to the whole genome would be extremely difficult using this strategy, as much time and labor are required even for just one conditional state. The strategy described above is the bottom-up approach of network construction. Computational strategies offer a top-down approach to network construction that complements what is described above.

1.2. Computational Strategies for Building GRN

1.2.1. Nonintegration Strategies. During this blooming period of biomedical research, high-content experimental data is fuelling systems biology research, such as GRN construction at the genome-wide scope. For example, expression microarrays that can detect the relative abundance of gene transcripts by comparing two or more biological samples are commonly used for GRN construction. The new approaches provide a perspective on the global molecular interactions that bridge the gap between the external signal and internal response. There are several popular algorithms being used to construct GRNs from expression data (reviewed in [9]).

In the graphical representation of GRNs, nodes typically represent genes corresponding to the transcription factor proteins or target genes, while edges represent the regulations between the transcription factors and their targets. Boolean networks describe each element as a variable with the value 0 or 1 to represent the state of the element as "off" or "on," respectively. A Boolean network $G(V, F)$ is defined by a set of nodes corresponding to genes $V = \{x_1, \ldots, x_n\}$ and a list of Boolean functions $F = (f_1, \ldots, f_n)$ describes how genes in the network change their state (on or off) from one time point to the next. The future state of an element is completely determined by the states of other elements (regulators) by means of the underlying logical Boolean functions.

Second, Bayesian networks model the biomedical network with a *directed acyclic graph.* "*Directed*" means that there are arrows to indicate causal influences, and "*acyclic*" means that causal loops are prohibited. For each element, a conditional distribution $P(Xv \mid \text{parents}(Xv))$ is defined through the application of the conditional probability table (CPT), where parents(Xv) denotes the variables corresponding to the regulators of this element. Thereafter, an optimization approach is applied, with the Bayesian information Criteria (BIC) optimized to infer the best fitting network model among a finite set of models.

In a third alternative, differential equations extract the network from high-throughput experimental data through taking the instantaneous concentration of each element into consideration. The instantaneous concentration of each element is completely determined by the concentration (x_n) of other elements involving a regulation function.

Differential equation modeling:

$$\frac{dx_i}{dt} = f_i(x_1, \ldots, x_n, t). \tag{1}$$

In a fourth alternative, coexpression is used to model GRNs based on co-variance analysis. However, the comparison between the covariances from datasets having different scales would be difficult. The Pearson correlation coefficient addresses this difficulty. It measures the coexpression between any two elements across a series of states resulting in the value with the range from -1 to 1, which allows networks to be established based on a certain threshold for the magnitude of the correlation.

Finally, Mutual Information (MI) offers another approach to modeling GRNs based on the probability theory. The mutual dependence of any two elements in the network is measured using MI. It is reported that MI outperforms the correlation in some studies [10, 11]. Using a reasonable threshold, networks will be accurately constructed. Context likelihood of relatedness (CLR) [10, 12], MRNet (maximum relevance/minimum redundancy network) (R package), and ARACNE (algorithm for the reconstruction of accurate cellular networks) [11, 13] are the three representative strategies of network construction applying MI. Numerous approaches to GRN construction have been developed using various combinations of the five main approaches described above.

1.2.2. Motivations for an Integration Strategy. The most popular algorithms contributing to the construction of GRNs from genomic expression data were described above. However, each of them has certain drawbacks. The Boolean algorithm assigns each variable a binary value, which could omit important information of continuous variables. Bayesian network construction is promising for representing and inferring causal relationships, but this strategy is only effective for the construction of small GRNs, due to the superexponential increase in the algorithm running time for large networks. The differential equation algorithm requires knowledge of the equation of dynamics and parameter estimation to optimize the GRN model against real data. However, deriving an appropriate equation of dynamics remains a challenge. Furthermore, solving a differential equation system of any realistic complexity is difficult. As to the correlation and mutual information algorithms, manually setting appropriate thresholds without a principled reference poses difficulties. Strategies applying algorithms with these drawbacks are not satisfying; therefore, it motivates us to improve the computational strategies. New strategies continue to be developed against those difficulties. It is a great challenge to refurbish algorithms to improve GRN construction using genomic expression data. Improvements are difficult to obtain algorithmically; however, the integration of multiple types of genome-wide datasets with literature-based information of regulation as prior knowledge is a straightforward alternative to offer improvement. Generally, in the computational GRN construction methods mentioned above, only genomic expression data like microarray data is used to produce the desired network applying one of the algorithms described [10, 11]. Based on a straightforward intuition that more relevant information generates better confidence for making correct predictions, we are optimistic about the prospects of making improvement by data integration. We have increasing availability of genome-wide data with respect to every aspect of biology, genomic expression data, genome sequences, proteomic data, genome-wide protein-DNA binding site data [14], genomic SNPs, and high-content data collections created from various types of biological or pathological research objectives. Therefore, with reference to the literature-based information of regulation as the prior knowledge and the multiple types of genome-wide datasets available as analyzable data, an integration strategy can offer an excellent opportunity for elucidating complete GRNs.

2. Integration Strategies for Building GRNs

2.1. Sources for Integration. The past few decades were an age of rapid progress in the development of biomedical science. Numerous advanced technologies along with well-founded theories lead the way for new findings in industrial and academic biomedical research. For example, biomedical investigators have developed genomic expression by microarray, rapid genome and microbiome sequencing, proteome definition by mass spectrometry, genome-wide protein-DNA binding site definition by ChIP-seq, genomic SNP identification by SNP array, and high-content knowledge by literature mining. Overwhelmed with such impressive quantity of genome-wide achievements, we are encouraged to apply strategies to make good use of them intuitively, such as integrating them properly for GRN construction. First we need to take stock of the status of the biomedical sources that are available to us.

It is difficult to summarize all the biomedical sources as most sources are scattered in distinct research papers. We will focus our attention on databases, as they are an effective form of rearranging and storing sources for specific objectives. Nucleic Acids Research (NAR) summarizes the biomedical database status each year (Figure 1) (http://nar.oxfordjournals.org/). Here is a table (Table 1) summarizing some genome-wide databases popular in the research of systems biology.

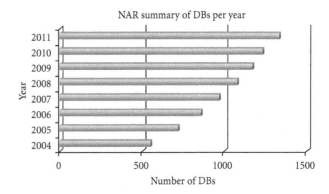

FIGURE 1: This is the database (DB) summary from NAR database issues. Each bar represents the total number of databases identified by NAR that year.

TABLE 1: Prominent databases.

Category	Databases
Metabolic pathways	KEGG, ENZYME
Signaling pathways	KEGG, WikiPathways
Protein-protein interactions	BIND, STRING
Transcription factor binding motifs	JASPAR, TRANSFAC
Genetic interaction networks	BIND, BioGRID
Gene expression	GEO, ArrayExpress
Sequences	UCSC Genome Browrer
Protein-compound interactions	DrugBank, STITCH, ResNet, CLiBE
Gene-disease associations	OMIM

2.2. Structural Integration. A large number of genome-wide sources are available that have not been fully leveraged to infer novel GRNs. Before entering into a discussion of the analytic algorithms for integrating multiple genome-wide datasets for GRNs construction, we must first address the challenge of extracting the desired datasets from the ocean of biomedical sources. Structural integration retrieves desired datasets from multiple heterogeneous sources to facilitate querying the data for further analytic integration. There are many sophisticated approaches being used for structurally integrating target datasets through programmatic extraction and recombination. Overall, these approaches to structural integration can be divided into three general categories: warehouse integration, mediator-based integration, and navigational integration [15].

Before discussing the approaches to structural integration in the following Sections 2.2.1–2.2.3, we will finish this section with a discussion of some key defining characteristics of structural integration.

Variety of Data. This describes the typical data that can be integrated and includes high-throughput datasets, molecular structures, molecular interactions, molecular pathways, Gene Ontology annotation, and disease characteristics, hence *vertical integration* is the aggregation of *semantically similar* data from multiple heterogeneous sources, while *horizontal integration* is the composition of *semantically complementary* data from multiple heterogeneous sources [15].

Heterogeneity of Descriptive Terms. Semantics is the study of the relation between form and meaning. Each source of data or knowledge may refer to the same semantic concept or field with its own descriptive term or identifier, which can lead to a semantic confusion between the many sources. Conversely, some sources may use the same term to refer to the different semantic concepts. Semantic mapping is indispensable in order to match descriptive terms or identifiers among multiple heterogeneous sources or between the sources and the objective integrated datasets.

Heterogeneity of Naming and Identity. One major hurdle in current data integration efforts is the issue of naming and identity such that a variety of aliases (e.g., synonyms for gene symbol) exist for many genes, proteins, and keywords. Alias mapping through lookups is critical for retrieving desired data from multiple heterogeneous sources.

2.2.1. Warehouse Integration. Warehouse integration arranges desired datasets from multiple sources into a local warehouse (e.g., a local database) before querying, through loading the required data from distinct sources and converting them into standard formats before being stored locally. Relying less on the Internet connectivity to access data limits the impact of various problems such as access restrictions, network bottlenecks, low response times, and the occasional unavailability of sources. Moreover, using local warehouses allows for improved accuracy, efficiency, and flexibility for the subsequent query as it is performed locally. However, this integration has an important drawback of the overall system maintenance. It is expensive to have the warehouse updated regularly to reflect those modifications of heterogeneous external sources [15, 16]. Furthermore, since the data retrieved and stored in the warehouse will eventually be converted into the warehouse-specific format every time the warehouse is updated, the semantic structure of the warehouse database may need to be reformatted often.

NCBI, the UCSC Genome Browser [17], and EMBL-EBI (http://www.ebi.ac.uk/) are three representative data warehouses. Given the appeal of these resources, efforts are increasingly made to improve the warehouse strategy against its drawbacks. The GeNS platform is one of the efforts to improve the efficiency of database maintenance. GeNS is a biological data integration platform for warehouse integration [18]. Representative databases were selected to cover a broad area of biomedical research when constructing the GeNS database. This warehouse accommodated the data from EMBL-EBI, UniPort (Swissport and TrEMBL), ExPASy (PROSITE and ENZYME), NCBI (Entrez, Taxonomy, Pubmed, RefSeq, GeneBank, and OMIM), Biomart, ArrayExpress, InterPro, Gene Ontology, KEGG (genes, pathways, orthology and drugs), and PharmGKB (genes, drugs, and diseases). A loader application responsible for converting the corresponding data from each source database into the format compatible with GeNS schema was designed to coordinate tasks such as alias mapping. In order to overcome the difficulty of maintenance, a general schema and a specific schema were both developed in GeNS. To physically store the data, a general model (general schema) that certified the framework of the database was used, while supporting this general model with a concrete meta model (specific schema) where all the entities and relations from a specific contributing database were specified locally [18]. Therefore, the addition/modification of databases into this warehouse needs modification in the meta model only, rather than in the general model.

2.2.2. Mediator-Based Integration. Mediator-based integration retrieves desired datasets from multiple heterogeneous sources at the time of querying through query translation, as opposed to the data translation that is manifested at the time of database creation in warehouse integration [15, 16]. The mediator, or core of the query translation, is an interface responsible for reformulating a query given by the user into the queries accommodating the local schemas of the underlying data sources via a single mediated schema defined by the mediator-based integration platform. Therefore, a mapping is required in the mediated schema to capture the semantic relation or the identity alias' relation between the sources and the given query, which thus allows the query made by a user to be translated via the mediator into the appropriate queries onto the individual sources. This correspondence mapping is a crucial step in creating the mediator, as it will influence the query reformulation and the addition of new sources to or the removal of the old sources from the integrated system.

There are two main approaches for establishing the mediator, global-as-view (GAV) and local-as-view (LAV) [15, 16]. The GAV has the mediator that translates the given queries directly into the formats of the source queries. The LAV has the format of query in every source defined into the common format of mediation, which is defined by the mediator via a wrapper. Therefore, each local source needs a wrapper component that exports a view of the local data into a common format of mediation via mediated schema. Since the mediator-based integration retrieves data at the run-time of querying, the problems such as access restriction, network bottlenecks, low response time, and the occasional unavailability of sources may occur. However, since the queries are performed in the real-time fashion, there is no special need of system maintenance via manually updating the databases. More specifically, LAV makes it very simple to add or to remove sources, while for GAV the addition or removal of sources is much more difficult, as it requires a modification of the mediated schema on the correspondence mapping.

The mediator approach is a very popular approach of data integration. Platforms like K2, TAMBIS, Discovery-Link, and BACIIS are all designed based on this approach. In the Discovery-Link platform (http://www.redbooks.ibm.com/abstracts/sg246290.html/), the source-specific wrapper symbolizes its data sources for further integration.

2.2.3. Navigational Integration. To extract the desired datasets, navigational integration follows the workflow in which the query outputs from a source are redirected as the query inputs to the next resource until the requested information is reached [15, 16]. It resembles the nature of the web in the context of increasing number of data sources, and it, therefore, frees users from manually browsing several web pages or data sources in order to obtain the desired datasets. However, the drawbacks of the navigational integration are similar to those of the mediator-based integration, such as access restrictions, network bottlenecks, low response times, and the occasional unavailability of sources. Additionally, the time and effort required to build the correspondence mapping are still costly.

Examples of this approach are Entrez and DiseaseCard databases. DiseaseCard [19] is a web-based collaborative service that aims to comprehensively integrate genetic and medical information, including the information of rare genetic diseases.

2.2.4. Choosing a Method for Structural Integration. Here is a brief comparison (Table 2) that summarizes the features of different structural integration approaches of extracting desired datasets from the ocean of biomedical sources.

The main purpose of the structural integration in most cases is to compile all available information for specific objectives to prepare for arbitrary analytic integration according to the user interest.

An ideal integration schema should have the following characteristics.

(1) Efficient. It can optimize the time that users need to finish the query. One of the recent ideas is to build semantic webs.

(2) Easy to maintain.

(3) Stable.

(4) System performance metrics. It is critical for an integration system to study source statistics in order to refine the query plans and improve the overall functionality and performance of the system. The essential statistics that should be learned are the coverage of sources, the average response time, the cost, and the overlap between sources [15].

(5) High quality. The data integrated are extracted from various heterogeneous sources, having different degrees of quality. For example, compared with the old data, new data from improved technologies may have better quality; also, compared with computationally predicted data, the experimental data is expected to have better quality. Quality varies within heterogeneous data sources, and some effort to account for these differences should be considered in the data integration strategies.

(6) Automated. the disciplines of operational optimization and machine learning should be applied for an effective automation program.

2.3. Analytic Integration. Along with the desired datasets extracted from multiple heterogeneous sources through structural integration, analytic integration is performed to infer GRNs via data integration algorithms applied to the desired datasets. The integration algorithm is, therefore, an essential ingredient for optimizing GRN construction. In contrast with the algorithms described in the above section, the integration algorithm needs to be capable of dealing with multiple types of data simultaneously. As a result, heterogeneous data should merge smoothly regardless of the differences in data types. As we discussed previously in Section 1, many types of genome-wide datasets could contribute to GRN construction. In the following discussion of the analytic integration for GRN construction from multiple types of genome-wide datasets or with reference to prior knowledge, there are three main schemas to consider: naïve Bayesian applications, supervised learning, and network topology applications. Each of these schemas represents a distinct approach to analytic integration, yet each can be applied to multiple categories of hypothesis inference, such as transcriptional regulation, protein-protein interaction, and gene-disease association.

2.3.1. Naïve Bayesian Applications. The Bayesian schema applying the naïve Bayesian is specified in the biological context: if association of two molecules occurs across multiple heterogeneous sources, there is an increased likelihood that they have a strong connection that may, for example, include a productive regulation or an indispensable physical interaction. Therefore, the functional importance of the pairwise connection is evaluated through its incidence across the multiple sources. And many types of genome-wide datasets, such as genomic expression and phylogenetic profiles, will contribute to the perceived functional importance of the pairwise connections in the genome-wide scope. Therefore, a scoring system is then applied to evaluate the functional importance of the pairwise connections in the genome-wide scope to gain insight about the confidence of the inferred GRNs or PPIs. Two successful examples with naïve Bayesian applications are described below.

The STRING web application was designed to infer the PPI via integrating multiple types of genome-wide datasets. It was primarily constructed from the integration of three genome-wide datasets, including phylogenetic profiles, a database of transcription units, and a database of gene-fusion events [20–24]. Phylogenetic profiles are derived from the evolutionary tree. During evolution, functionally linked proteins tend to be either preserved or eliminated in new species simultaneously. This property of correlated evolution is leveraged in the STRING database by characterizing each protein via its phylogenetic profile that records the presence or absence of an orthologous protein in every known genome. Those proteins having matching profiles have a strong tendency to be functionally linked. Transcriptional units (operons) are extracted from a number of genomes through identifying the conserved gene clusters. The protein products of the genes in transcriptional units are hypothesized to be functionally linked with each other. Gene-fusion

TABLE 2: Properties of distinctive structural integration approaches.

Approach	Maintenance	System stability	Effectiveness
Warehouse	Difficult, costly	Stable	Poor
Mediator-based	Easy for LAV	Depends on source availability, accessibility, traffic	Fair
Navigational	Easy	Depends on source availability, accessibility, traffic	Good

events can be interpreted by the example that the interacting proteins GyrA and GyrB subunits of *E. coli* DNA gyrase are orthologs of a single fused chain (topoisomerase II) in yeast; thus, the similarities of GyrA and GyrB to some segment of topoisomerase II might be used to predict their functional interaction in *E. coli*. STRING was developed as a multi-dimensional integration interface by combining its three original components (phylogenetic profiles, transcription units, and gene fusions) together with genomic expression and genome-wide dataset of protein-protein interaction discovered via text mining from PubMed abstract, and so forth. Putative protein-protein interaction of the PPI can be evaluated with the confidence score of functional association between two proteins across those genome-wide datasets. Different datasets are weighted differently for their respective contribution to the confidence score. In the STRING project, a weight was assigned to each dataset by benchmarking the performance of the prediction in this dataset against a common reference set of trusted knowledge. The developers chose the functional grouping of proteins maintained at KEGG (Kyoto Encyclopedia of Genes and Genomes) as the common reference set. The benchmark weight of each dataset in STRING corresponded to the probability of finding the linked proteins that were predicted in this dataset within the same KEGG pathway. In the equation of the confidence score, the confidence score is taken as S, the weight of each dataset is taken as S_i, and i is the number of qualfied datasets with incidence of the pairwise connection. Therefore, the confidence score of the putative protein-protein interaction is evaluated through qualifying the naive Bayesian probability of the incidence of the corresponding protein connection across those multiple datasets under the assumption of independence of the various datasets. Larger confidence scores indicate higher confidence in a functional protein-protein association:

$$S = 1 - \prod_i (1 - S_i), \tag{2}$$

where S_i is the weight assigned to each dataset over the common reference set.

Figure 2 shows an example result of a STRING query (http://STRING-db.org/) of the protein-protein interactions seeded by Gata4, a well-known transcription factor in cardiac development.

The confidence score for each putative protein-protein interaction is, therefore, a Bayesian-probability-like score supported by several types of genome-wide datasets. Putative PPI thus follows the evaluation in the genome-wide scope to gain confidence.

Another approach applies the Bayesian schema to rationally extend the ribosome biogenesis pathway in yeast

[25]. Li et al. constructed a computational predictor for inferring the ribosome biogenesis genes by integrating multiple heterogeneous datasets into a probabilistic model. This model employed a naive Bayesian probabilistic scoring system to integrate the multiple genome-wide datasets, including genomic expression, a genome-wide dataset of protein-protein interactions derived from literature curation, a genome-wide dataset of high-throughput yeast two-hybrid assays, a genome-wide dataset of affinity purification coupled with mass spectrometry, a genomic interaction dataset, and *in silico* genome-wide interaction datasets into a network (Figure 3). The plausibility that a putative yeast gene belongs to the ribosome biogenesis pathway was evaluated by calculating the naive Bayesian probability of the incidence of its association with the known ribosome biogenesis genes in the pathway. The ROC plot from cross-validation was employed to check the effectiveness of this schema (Figure 3). The top-scoring 212 genes were manually selected for the further experimental validation.

Bayesian schemas that apply the naive Bayesian probability are a powerful approach for analytic integration. Their application in the improves network construction in the examples given by evaluating the putative network with multiple genome-wide datasets integrated to calculate the confidence score. This schema always outperforms non-integration strategies. For example, the application of the Bayesian schema in an algorithm called MAGIC, as compared with the expression-based clustering methods, predicted more true positives than clustering methods did relative to the number of false positives [26].

2.3.2. Supervised Learning.

Supervised learning assumes that partial information is known for predictor variables and outcomes, and this partial information is leveraged to make deeper inferences of the target hypothesis. The known information is taken as the prior knowledge. Supervised approaches in statistics have been developed to make new inferences with the prior knowledge of the study objective to be integrated with the other relevant datasets. The accuracy of inferences regarding network topology is positively correlated with the amount of accurate prior knowledge. In contrast, unsupervised approaches have the problem that they are more likely to predict associations that are unreliable. The supervised learning schema can make inferences less error-prone. One analytic integration approach uses supervised learning to integrate the prior knowledge of the PPI with the other relevant genome-wide datasets to improve the effectiveness of PPI construction.

Kato et al. developed a schema for supervised learning of yeast PPI using known protein-protein interactions as a prior

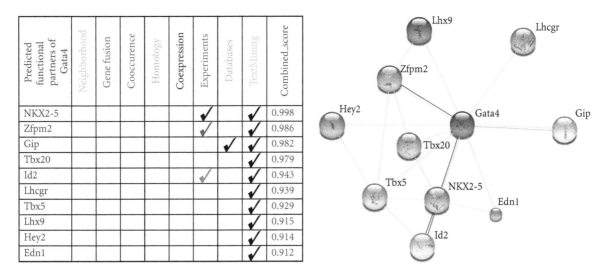

Predicted functional partners of Gata4	Neighborhood	Gene fusion	Cooccurence	Homology	Coexpression	Experiments	Databases	TextMining	Combined_score
NKX2-5						✓		✓	0.998
Zfpm2						✓		✓	0.986
Gip							✓	✓	0.982
Tbx20								✓	0.979
Id2						✓		✓	0.943
Lhcgr								✓	0.939
Tbx5								✓	0.929
Lhx9								✓	0.915
Hey2								✓	0.914
Edn1								✓	0.912

FIGURE 2: STRING search results for Gata4 from different sources. The network figure is the protein-protein interaction image from the search results (*Mus musculus*). Higher scores indicate greater confidence in the putative interaction. Here the highest confidence is given to NKX2-5 as an interactive partner of Gata4, as this is supported with experimental evidence.

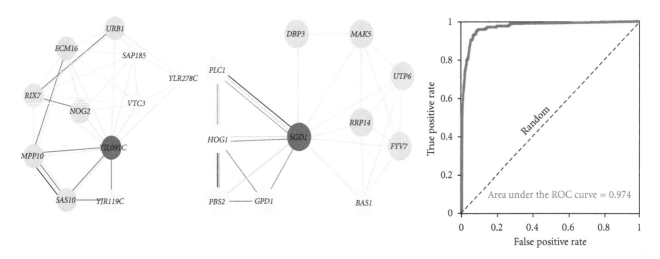

FIGURE 3: Predicted ribosome biogenesis genes are labeled as red nodes. Green nodes are the known ribosome biogenesis genes, and yellow nodes are genes that are not related to the ribosome biogenesis. Edge color indicates coexpression (light blue), affinity purification (red), yeast two-hybrid assay (green), genetic interaction (yellow), cocitation (gray), and literature curation (black). The ROC curve shows cross-validated recovery of the known ribosome biogenesis genes based on their network connectivity to one another. (This open-access figure was reproduced from Li et al., [25].)

knowledge to be integrated with the other relevant genome-wide datasets [27]. In this supervised network construction, a kernel matrix is applied as the basis of the integration. A kernel matrix is a matrix of similarity, and edges in the kernel-based network are assigned to the connected nodes whose kernel values (similarity) are above a certain threshold δ. The kernel matrix representation is an appropriate method for supervised PPI construction, as the network construction problem boils down to the problem of inferring an integrated kernel matrix of pairwise protein connections from combining the known yeast protein-protein interactions with the other relevant genome-wide datasets. Here, Kato et al.

generated 3 main steps of the yeast PPI construction applying supervised learning.

Step 1. They translated the prior knowledge (known part of yeast PPI) into the kernel matrix by diffusion kernels. Diffusion kernels are functions for processing the network structure to mine the underlying relationships between nodes in the kernel matrix. However, this resulted in a regional kernel matrix of pairwise protein connections given a genome-wide scope because only the pairwise kernel values (the intensity of pairwise protein associations) of the proteins that were in the known part of PPI could be reconstructed.

The regional kernel matrix could approximately recover the known PPI when the appropriate threshold δ of the kernel value was applied.

Step 2. A genome-wide dataset (e.g., genomic expression) with the same objective can be used to establish a new kernel matrix. Kato et al. took multiple types of genome-wide datasets into consideration for the PPI construction. They combined these new generated kernel matrices, each of which was calculated from a particular genome-wide dataset, such as genomic expression and genome-wide phylogenetic profiles, into a combined kernel matrix of pairwise protein associations in yeast.

Step 3. They integrated the combined kernel matrix with the regional kernel matrix of the known part of yeast PPI to infer the integrated kernel matrix of pairwise protein connections that offered the pairwise kernel values in the genome-wide scope to be able to qualify the PPI edges via comparing the kernel values against the threshold δ.

Accuracy of edge prediction was measured by a 10-fold cross-validation. With setting the parameter of the degree of kernel diffusion to 3.0 when translating the known PPI into the kernel matrix by diffusion kernels, the ROC score was 0.929 for the inferred yeast PPI.

The supervised learning improves the PPI construction via integrating the experimentally-proven evidence of the study objective as the supervisor into the analysis of the other relevant genome-wide datasets. Thus the GRNs construction can also apply the schema of the supervised learning via having the known transcription factor-target gene regulations as the prior knowledge to be integrated with the other expression-relevant genome-wide datasets. One study compared supervised methods with unsupervised methods for GRN construction and found that the supervised methods are more reliable than the unsupervised ones [28].

2.3.3. Network Topology Applications. In recent decades, a large amount of experimental evidence about biological networks has been collected, and this was coupled with progress in elucidating the network topological features. Approaches that have contributed to these strides in network biology include scale-free networks, small world networks, adaptive motifs, feed-back motifs, "AND" and "OR" logic motifs, and modular networks. Therefore, a systematic effort utilizing the network topological features will be required and will benefit the effectiveness of network construction. Modularity is one of the most accepted network topological features of GRNs. The modularity of GRNs can be represented by gene module members that are co-regulated via shared transcription factors combinatorially binding their promoters. Therefore, members in such gene modules manifest coexpression. Genomic expression and the genome-wide transcription factor-DNA binding sites are thus, integrated into GRN construction by identifying coexpressed genes with conserved TF binding sites in their promoters [29, 30]. Two examples applying this integration schema to the inference of GRNs are discussed below.

GRAM is an algorithm for discovering GRNs by incorporating information from transcription factor (TF) binding motifs, genome sequence, and genomic expression [31]. Regulatory relationships are effectively identified by genome-wide location analysis of DNA-binding TFs via blasting the corresponding TF binding motifs against promoter sequences to infer the binding sites at the genome-wide scope. However, location analysis may infer potential physical interactions between TFs and DNA at the genome-wide scope but may not necessarily identify functional bindings. Integrating the location analysis with genomic expression, GRAM employs an effective and exhaustive strategy for GRN construction. It searches over all the possible combinations of TFs indicated by location analysis. When the binding sites are in close proximity, the corresponding TFs are defined to be in combination. A TF's combinations are used to identify its regulating gene set members that have common combinations of TFs binding their promoters as defined by location analysis. From the complete gene set, a subset is generated by members that have highly correlated expression in the expression dataset. The subset is taken as the "seed" of a gene module. Then GRAM revisits the genomic expression to add more genes having relatively high correlated expression with the "seed" into the gene module using less strict criteria (Figure 4). GRAM allows genes to belong to more than one module. Regulation is, therefore, inferred between the co-expression module and its TFs combination to foster GRN construction.

In the GRAM project, this schema was applied to the TF binding motif data of 106 TFs and over 500 microarray expression experiments in *Saccharomyces cerevisiae*. The GRN was reconstructed via identification of modules. Gene modules were also identified as groups of genes annotated with similar pathways. Identified gene modules were controlled by more than one TF, which was the evidence for inferring the TFs' interactions (protein-protein interactions). GRAM can assign different regulators to genes with similar expression patterns, which cannot be accomplished using the expression clustering methods alone. Moreover, by applying the enrichment test of specific DNA binding motifs, genes in the discovered modules are more likely to be coregulated when compared with the set of genes obtained using genomic location analysis alone.

Another application of this integration schema in GRNs construction was developed by Segal et al. [32]. Those authors designed an algorithm integrating a *Saccharomyces cerevisiae* genomic expression dataset with the genome-wide TF binding sites that were inferred via searching the corresponding TF binding motifs in the genome-wide scope. In their framework, a regulatory module was a set of genes that were regulated in concert by a shared regulation program. A regulation program specified the expression of the genes in the module as a function of the expression of a small set of regulators (Figure 5). After the enrichment test of TF binding motifs to the regulatory module, novel regulations were predicted between the TFs corresponding to the overrepresented binding motifs and the regulatory module to foster the GRN construction. Segal et al. found in many regulatory modules that the TFs corresponding to

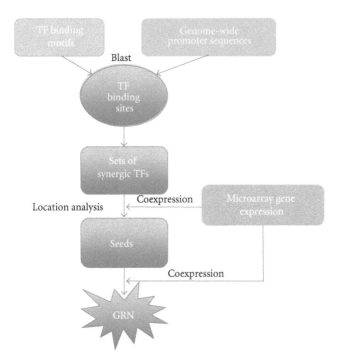

FIGURE 4: Workflow of the GRAM algorithm. Known TF binding motifs are blasted against the promoter sequences in the genome-wide scope to infer the corresponding TF binding sites. A set of synergic TFs is identified when the TFs' binding sites are close to each other. Regulated gene sets are defined by the corresponding sets of synergic TFs through location analysis. A "seed" of a gene module is selected from the regulated gene set based on the highly correlated expression. Then GRAM revisits the genomic expression to add more genes with closely correlated expression with the "seed" into the gene module of the "seed." The GRN construction is fostered by the established regulations between the coexpression gene modules and their corresponding sets of synergic TFs.

the overrepresented binding motifs of the module matched the known regulators of the genes in that module quite well.

Applying the modularity feature in GRNs construction via integrating genomic expression with genome-wide TF binding sites improves the quality of network construction. However, only limited information has been elucidated about the GRN topological features. The schema with GRN topology applied is expected to perform more compellingly with increasing knowledge of those features in GRN.

2.3.4. Choosing a Method of Analytic Integration. The Bayesian application schema for the naive Bayesian probability theorem is well accepted in most scientific fields. The naive Bayesian integrates multiple types of relevant genome-wide datasets into a scoring system that produces a confidence score for the inferred network (e.g., PPI and GRN). However, there is an important caveat with this approach: it is rational to apply the naive Bayesian theorem only when the situation satisfies the basic assumption that each type of source dataset is independent of any other. Therefore, under this assumption, there is no dependency between any two types. However, in reality some datasets have known

dependencies. For example, in the case of STRING, the datasets of experiments, databases, and text mining are not completely independent of each other. The method of evaluating individual weight is also a controversial part of this schema. In the case of STRING, KEGG is used as the standard for calculating the weights. However, KEGG is an incomplete database in the genome-wide scope, and it is actually constructed from various experiments, databases, and text-mining resources, so it is necessarily dependent on those resources. It is, therefore, not a good standard, as it is biased—giving high weights to its own resources while giving low weights to the others. This may promote its accuracy but limit its predictive power. Hence, naïve Bayesian applications in GRN construction may be affected by those limitations.

Supervised learning integrates prior knowledge of the study objective with the other relevant genome-wide datasets to learn the networks (e.g., PPI, GRN). However, the quality of its prediction varies with the quantity of the prior knowledge. Also, when multiple datasets are involved, weighting each dataset properly is still problematic. If we employ the nonweighting integration approach to make the primary prediction of the unknown part before it is trained by the prior knowledge, we may have better quality on the overall prediction even when the quantity of the prior knowledge is relatively small.

The schema of network topology is a compelling strategy of GRN construction via integrating genomic expression with genome-wide TF binding sites. It associates the two sources through the modularity feature to connect the gene co-expression with the conserved TF binding sites on their promoters. However, as mentioned in the two examples, the TF binding sites are inferred from the corresponding TF binding motifs via a genome-wide blast. It will be improved when the CHIP-seq datasets regarding different TFs are employed instead to generate the genome-wide TF binding sites. It is a developing schema that keeps step with the development of our knowledge of network topological features.

The schemas of supervised learning and network topology application may be described as advanced forms of the schema of Bayesian application, progressing from the naive to evidence-based logic. These approaches use principled and logical integration of datasets rather than integration only. Along with the increased experimentally proven knowledge about regulatory relationships, the schema of network topology application can be combined with supervised learning to gain increased confidence in the inferred GRNs. Overall, a positive-feedback effect that contributes to better GRNs helps to develop our knowledge of additional GRN topological features, while the more topological features provide more or better clues for GRNs' construction. The PPI could be embedded into the GRN to assess the TFs' combinatory regulations.

3. Summary and Future Directions

GRN construction via integration of multiple types of genome-wide datasets or via literature-based information

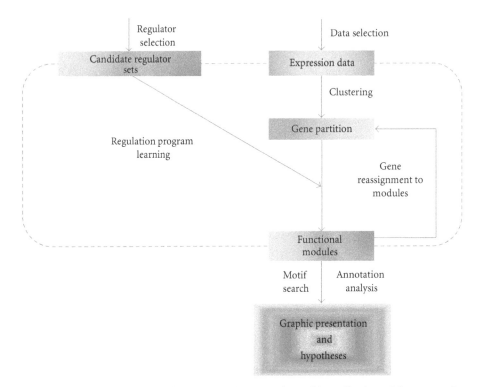

FIGURE 5: Workflow of the algorithm by Segal et al. This is an iterative procedure with application of the expectation maximization (EM) algorithm. In the maximization step (M step), genes are partitioned into modules that result from previous clustering upon genomic expression data and the best regulation program is learned for each module. In the E step, the best regulation programs corresponding are compared with each gene module to determine the optimal predictor (the optimal predictive regulation program). The module corresponding to the best predictor is selected and genes are reassigned to this module. The regulatory program learning stops on convergence. Secondly, TFs are associated with the regulatory module via an enrichment test of their corresponding binding motifs to the module.

about regulation as the prior knowledge partly avoids or overcomes the drawbacks of the nonintegration strategies. Along with the continuous increase in the availability of new data sources, new opportunities emerge for us to use integration strategies to construct GRNs. There are two main categories of integration strategies: *structural integrations* for extracting and recombining the required datasets and *analytic integrations* for processing the queried datasets to infer GRNs. There are three main types of structural integration: *warehouse integration* naively aggregates the required datasets into local storage before data querying, *mediator-based integration* establishes a mediator application to retrieve the required datasets via reformatting the user's query into the formats of queries in local data sources at the time of data processing, and the *navigational integration* follows the chain of data querying at the time of data processing via using the query outputs of one step in the process as query inputs in a next step. In a subsequent analytic integration, the schema of Bayesian applications use the naive Bayesian probability to integrate multiple types of genome-wide datasets into a scoring system to compute a confidence score for inferred GRNs. Supervised learning integrates the prior knowledge of the study objective with the other relevant genome-wide datasets to learn the GRNs. And the schema of network topology applications integrate genomic expression with genome-wide TF binding

sites through the modularity feature to connect gene co-expression with conserved TF binding sites in their promoters to foster the GRNs construction. Overall, the integration strategies perform well and reliably as compared to the non-integration strategies. Structural integration and analytic integration take central roles in the overall integration strategy of GRN construction.

Recently, cooperation of traditional experimental approaches with computational approaches has energized biomedical research. These new approaches offer the ability to computationally infer novel hypotheses from prior knowledge and relevant datasets to guide experimentation by setting research priorities. A salient example of this successful cooperation defines how to rationally extend the ribosome biogenesis pathway in yeast [25]. After revealing 212 candidates from the Bayesian applied integration analysis of multiple relevant genome-wide datasets, experiments were employed to validate their findings. Li et al. identified 15 previously unreported ribosome biogenesis genes (TIF4631, SUN66, YDL063C, JIL5, TOP1, SGD1, BCP1, YOR287C, BUD22, YIL091C, YOR006C/TSR3, YOL022C/TSR4, SAC3, NEW1, and FUN1). Segal et al. used a similar workflow to validate the GRN construction [32]. Therefore, GRNs inferred from the analysis with multiple types of integrated datasets offer a sophisticated atlas for setting research priorities.

Abbreviations

BIC: Bayesian Information Criteria
EMBL: European Molecular Biology Laboratory
GO: Gene ontology
GRN: Gene regulatory network
KEGG: Kyoto Encyclopedia of Genes and Genomes
NAR: Nucleic Acids Research
NCBI: National Center for Biotechnology Information
PCR: Polymerase chain reaction
PPI: Protein-protein interaction
SNP: Single-nucleotide polymorphism.

Glossary

Bayesian information criterion (BIC):	In statistics, it is a criterion for model selection among a finite set of models
Cis-regulatory motif:	A nucleotide pattern that is widespread and has a biological significance for regulatory factor binding
ChIP-seq:	A technology that combines chromotin immunoprecipitation (ChIP) with massive sequencing to identify the binding sites of DNA-associated proteins on a genomic scale
Cross-validation:	A technique for assessing how the results of a statistical analysis will generalize to an independent data set
Epistatic:	In genetics, it is the phenomenon where the effects of one gene are modified by one or several other genes
Gene ontology:	A controlled vocabulary for annotating genes and gene products
Gene regulatory network:	A network that summarizes gene regulatory influences in a biological process
In silico:	ALatin expression used to mean "performed on computer" or "computer simulation"
Mesoderm:	In all bilaterian animals, the mesoderm is one of the three primary germ cell layers in the early embryo
Operon:	In genetics, an operon is a functioning unit of genomic DNA containing a cluster of genes under the control of a single regulatory signal or promoter
Phylogenetic profile:	Also called phylogenetic tree, is a branching diagram or "tree" showing the inferred evolutionary relationships among various biological species or other entities based upon similarities and differences in their physical and/or genetic characteristics
Schema:	A representation of a plan, theory, or data structure, normally expressed as an outline or model
Semantic:	Relating to meaning language or logic; in a biological context, this usually refers to the meaning of specifically defined annotations, concepts, or logical relationships between biological entities
Wrapper:	A computer program that translates one format of data to another or a computer program that simplifies user interactions with a more complex program.

Acknowledgments

The authors thank David C. Zawieja, Jerry Trzeciakowski, and Xu Peng for their thoughtful comments on the paper.

References

[1] E. H. Davidson and M. S. Levine, "Properties of developmental gene regulatory networks," *Proceedings of the National Academy of Sciences of the United States of America*, vol. 105, no. 51, pp. 20063–20066, 2008.

[2] M. Levine and E. H. Davidson, "Gene regulatory networks for development," *Proceedings of the National Academy of Sciences of the United States of America*, vol. 102, no. 14, pp. 4936–4942, 2005.

[3] E. Li and E. H. Davidson, "Building developmental gene regulatory networks," *Birth Defects Research Part C*, vol. 87, no. 2, pp. 123–130, 2009.

[4] D. H. Erwin and E. H. Davidson, "The last common bilaterian ancestor," *Development*, vol. 129, no. 13, pp. 3021–3032, 2002.

[5] E. H. Davidson, J. P. Rast, P. Oliveri et al., "A genomic regulatory network for development," *Science*, vol. 295, no. 5560, pp. 1669–1678, 2002.

[6] D. Calva, F. S. Dahdaleh, G. Woodfield et al., "Discovery of SMAD4 promoters, transcription factor binding sites and deletions in juvenile polyposis patients," *Nucleic Acids Research*, vol. 39, no. 13, pp. 5369–5378, 2011.

[7] K. S. Zaret, J. K. Liu, and C. M. DiPersio, "Site-directed mutagenesis reveals a liver transcription factor essential for the albumin transcriptional enhancer," *Proceedings of the National Academy of Sciences of the United States of America*, vol. 87, no. 14, pp. 5469–5473, 1990.

[8] J. Smith, C. Theodoris, and E. H. Davidson, "A gene regulatory network subcircuit drives a dynamic pattern of gene expression," *Science*, vol. 318, no. 5851, pp. 794–797, 2007.

[9] H. de Jong, "Modeling and simulation of genetic regulatory systems: a literature review," *Journal of Computational Biology*, vol. 9, no. 1, pp. 67–103, 2002.

[10] J. J. Faith, B. Hayete, J. T. Thaden et al., "Large-scale mapping and validation of Escherichia coli transcriptional regulation from a compendium of expression profiles," *PLoS Biology*, vol. 5, no. 1, article e8, 2007.

[11] A. A. Margolin, I. Nemenman, K. Basso et al., "ARACNE: an algorithm for the reconstruction of gene regulatory networks in a mammalian cellular context," *BMC Bioinformatics*, vol. 7, supplement 1, article S7, 2006.

[12] A. Madar, A. Greenfield, E. Vanden-Eijnden, and R. Bonneau, "DREAM3: network inference using dynamic context likelihood of relatedness and the inferelator," *PloS One*, vol. 5, no. 3, article e9803, 2010.

[13] P. Zoppoli, S. Morganella, and M. Ceccarelli, "TimeDelay-ARACNE: reverse engineering of gene networks from time-course data by an information theoretic approach," *BMC Bioinformatics*, vol. 11, article 154, 2010.

[14] M. B. Gerstein, A. Kundaje, M. Hariharan et al., "Architecture of the human regulatory network derived from ENCODE data," *Nature*, vol. 489, no. 7414, pp. 91–100, 2012.

[15] T. Hernandez and S. Kambhampati, "Integration of biological sources: current systems and challenges ahead," *Sigmod Record*, vol. 33, no. 3, pp. 51–60, 2004.

[16] L. D. Stein, "Integrating biological databases," *Nature Reviews Genetics*, vol. 4, no. 5, pp. 337–345, 2003.

[17] P. A. Fujita, B. Rhead, A. S. Zweig et al., "The UCSC Genome Browser database: update 2011," *Nucleic Acids Research*, vol. 39, database issue, pp. D876–D882, 2011.

[18] J. Arrais, J. E. Pereira, J. Fernandes, and J. L. Oliveira, "GeNS: a biological data integration platform," *Proceedings of World Academy of Science, Engineering and Technology*, vol. 58, pp. 850–855, 2009.

[19] G. S. Dias, J. L. Oliveira, J. Vicente, and F. Martin-Sanchez, "Integrating medical and genomic data: a successful example for rare diseases," *Studies in Health Technology and Informatics*, vol. 124, pp. 125–130, 2006.

[20] L. J. Jensen, M. Kuhn, M. Stark et al., "STRING 8—a global view on proteins and their functional interactions in 630 organisms," *Nucleic Acids Research*, vol. 37, database issue, pp. D412–D416, 2009.

[21] B. Snel, G. Lehmann, P. Bork, and M. A. Huynen, "STRING: a web-server to retrieve and display the repeatedly occurring neighbourhood of a gene," *Nucleic Acids Research*, vol. 28, no. 18, pp. 3442–3444, 2000.

[22] C. von Mering, M. Huynen, D. Jaeggi, S. Schmidt, P. Bork, and B. Snel, "STRING: a database of predicted functional associations between proteins," *Nucleic Acids Research*, vol. 31, no. 1, pp. 258–261, 2003.

[23] C. von Mering, L. J. Jensen, M. Kuhn et al., "STRING 7—recent developments in the integration and prediction of protein interactions," *Nucleic Acids Research*, vol. 35, database issue, pp. D358–D362, 2007.

[24] C. von Mering, L. J. Jensen, B. Snel et al., "STRING: known and predicted protein-protein associations, integrated and transferred across organisms," *Nucleic Acids Research*, vol. 33, database issue, pp. D433–D437, 2005.

[25] Z. Li, I. Lee, E. Moradi, N. J. Hung, A. W. Johnson, and E. M. Marcotte, "Rational extension of the ribosome biogenesis pathway using network-guided genetics," *PLoS Biology*, vol. 7, no. 10, article e1000213, 2009.

[26] O. G. Troyanskaya, K. Dolinski, A. B. Owen, R. B. Altman, and D. Botstein, "A Bayesian framework for combining heterogeneous data sources for gene function prediction (in Saccharomyces cerevisiae)," *Proceedings of the National Academy of Sciences of the United States of America*, vol. 100, no. 14, pp. 8348–8353, 2003.

[27] T. Kato, K. Tsuda, and K. Asai, "Selective integration of multiple biological data for supervised network inference," *Bioinformatics*, vol. 21, no. 10, pp. 2488–2495, 2005.

[28] L. Cerulo, C. Elkan, and M. Ceccarelli, "Learning gene regulatory networks from only positive and unlabeled data," *BMC Bioinformatics*, vol. 11, article 228, 2010.

[29] G. Pavesi, P. Mereghetti, G. Mauri, and G. Pesole, "Weeder Web: discovery of transcription factor binding sites in a set of sequences from co-regulated genes," *Nucleic Acids Research*, vol. 32, web server issue, pp. W199–W203, 2004.

[30] G. Pavesi and G. Pesole, "Using Weeder for the discovery of conserved transcription factor binding sites," *Current Protocols in Bioinformatics*, chapter 2:unit 2.11, 2006.

[31] Z. Bar-Joseph, G. K. Gerber, T. I. Lee et al., "Computational discovery of gene modules and regulatory networks," *Nature Biotechnology*, vol. 21, no. 11, pp. 1337–1342, 2003.

[32] E. Segal, M. Shapira, A. Regev et al., "Module networks: identifying regulatory modules and their condition-specific regulators from gene expression data," *Nature Genetics*, vol. 34, no. 2, pp. 166–176, 2003.

9

Hierarchical Modular Structure Identification with Its Applications in Gene Coexpression Networks

Shuqin Zhang

Center for Computational Systems Biology, School of Mathematical Sciences, Fudan University, Shanghai 200433, China

Correspondence should be addressed to Shuqin Zhang, zhangs@fudan.edu.cn

Academic Editors: R. Jiang, W. Tian, J. Wan, and X. Zhao

Network module (community) structure has been a hot research topic in recent years. Many methods have been proposed for module detection and identification. Hierarchical structure of modules is shown to exist in many networks such as biological networks and social networks. Compared to the partitional module identification methods, less research is done on the inference of hierarchical modular structure. In this paper, we propose a method for constructing the hierarchical modular structure based on the stochastic block model. Statistical tests are applied to test the hierarchical relations between different modules. We give both artificial networks and real data examples to illustrate the performance of our approach. Application of the proposed method to yeast gene coexpression network shows that it does have a hierarchical modular structure with the modules on different levels corresponding to different gene functions.

1. Introduction

Networks are widely applied to model complex systems, including biological systems, social organizations, World-Wide-Webs, and so on. In a network, the nodes (vertices) represent the members in the system, while the edges represent the interactions among the members. If two nodes have interactions in a network, there will be an edge connecting them. With such a representation, the complex systems can be analyzed by computational methods.

Module (community) structure is a common property of many different types of networks. Modules are the dense subgroups of a network, where the nodes in the same module are more likely to connect each other than the nodes in other modules. In general, the members in the same module share some common properties or play similar roles. For example, in a gene coexpression network, the genes in the same module may belong to the same functional category such as lipid metabolism and acute-phase response [1]. Since the paper published by [2], module detection and identification becomes a hot research topic in several different areas such as computer science, physics, and statistics. A large number of related works have been published with the physicists making the most contributions [3–12]. Several recent review papers provide details and comparisons of the module identification methods [6, 9, 13]. Reference [13] compares the performance of several existing methods for both computation time and output. Reference0020[6] is a thorough, more recent discussion. Reference [9] contrasts different perspectives of the methods and sheds light on some important similarities of several methods. A recent comparison of some popular methods is shown in [14]. Among the compared methods, the method by maximizing the average degree within modules and minimizing the average connections between different modules outperforms other methods in identification accuracy. Its computational speed is also competitive [14]. Besides these computational methods, theoretical analysis on module identifications is presented very recently. Bickel and Chen gave the first statistical analysis on the properties of modules [15]. There based on the stochastic block model, they gave the sufficient conditions for a modularity to be a consistent estimator of modules and presented a new consistent modularity. However, the computation of maximizing this modularity is very time consuming.

Although so many related works are published, how to choose an appropriate number of modules keeps being an open problem. Different methods output different solutions when they are applied to the same network. In reality, all

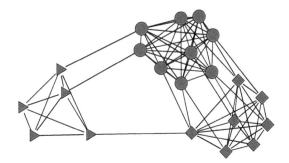

Figure 1: Example of hierarchical modular network structure.

of the different choices may be reasonable because different choices of this number may correspond to the modules on different levels. As explained in [16], some modular networks may have hierarchical structure. For example, in a friendship network, on the large scale, the modules may correspond to people from different countries. On the smaller scales, people in the same module may graduate from the same university, grow up in the same community, or even be born in the same family. Such hierarchical modular structure appears in different kinds of networks. For example, Meunier and colleagues gave an example on hierarchical modular structures in human brains [17]. Figure 1 shows an example of hierarchical modular network. There are two levels of the modules. We can identify three modules corresponding to different shapes of nodes on the lowest level or two modules with nodes represented by cubes and circles being combined together on the higher level.

Compared to the module identification in a partitional way (all the modules are on the same level), there are much fewer works on computational methods for hierarchical modular structure analysis [18–20]. Although these papers present some methods to construct the hierarchical modular structure, they do not give a clear picture on how these modules are organized and what the relationship among the modules is. In this paper, we mainly consider the problem of hierarchical modular structure in unweighted networks. Based on the module identification method presented in [14], we give the method on how to construct the hierarchical structure from all the possible modules in Section 2. Numerical experiments for both simulated networks and real data networks are presented to show the performance of our proposed method in Section 3. The application of the proposed method to yeast gene coexpression network shows that it does have a hierarchical structure, which corresponds to the different levels of gene functions. Conclusion remarks are given finally. By constructing the hierarchical structure, we aim to explore the functions of modules on different levels and explain why the number of modules may differ for different identification methods.

2. Methodology

Before going to the details on how to construct the hierarchical structure, we give its definition first. We consider a network $G(V, E)$ with n nodes, where V denotes the set of

nodes and E denotes the set of edges. The adjacency matrix is denoted as A with each entry being 0 or 1. The hierarchical structure of a network is defined based on the stochastic block model, which is a direct extension of the Erdös-Rényi random graph model [21]. The network is obtained by starting with a set of n nodes and adding edges between them in a probabilistic fashion. The presence of an edge between any two nodes is a Bernoulli event where the probability may be vertex-pair dependent. At the beginning, we assume there are K modules in the network. The network is generated in two steps. First, any node is assigned to a module M_i with a probability μ_i, where $\mu = (\mu_1, \mu_2, \ldots, \mu_K)$ satisfies $\sum_{i=1}^{K} \mu_i = 1$. Then any two nodes $u, v \in V$ and $u \in M_i, v \in M_j$ are connected with probability $P_{i,j}$ depending on M_i, M_j, and P is symmetric. If there is the modular structure in the network, then $P_{i,j} < \min\{P_{i,i}, P_{j,j}\}$. With this model, the hierarchical structure of a network can be defined recursively. For any three modules M_i, M_j, and M_k, if $P_{i,j} > \max\{P_{i,k}, P_{j,k}\}$, we say there is hierarchical structure among these three modules and M_i, M_j can be combined to a new module parallel to M_k.

To construct the hierarchical structure, we use the bottom-up strategy. We first find all the possible modules on the lowest level and then build the hierarchical structure. We use the method presented in [14] to find all the possible modules. Suppose K is given first. We let N_k denote the number of nodes in subnetwork V_k, L_{kk} denote twice the total number of edges in subnetwork V_k, and L_{kl} denote the total number of connections between the subnetworks V_k and V_l, where $k, l = 1, 2, \ldots, K$. The module identification problem is formulated as

$$\max_{\mathbf{P}} \Phi(\mathbf{P}) = \sum_{k=1}^{K} \frac{L_{kk}}{N_k} - \sum_{k=1}^{K} \sum_{l \neq k} \frac{L_{kl}}{N_k}, \tag{1}$$

where $\mathbf{P}$ is a partition of the network.

In matrix form, if we let

$$S_{ik} = \begin{cases} 1, & \text{if node } i \in V_k \\ 0, & \text{otherwise} \end{cases} \quad i = 1, 2, \ldots, n, \tag{2}$$

the problem is formulated as

$$\max \Psi(S) = \sum_{k=1}^{K} \frac{S_{\cdot,k}^T A S_{\cdot,k}}{S_{\cdot,k}^T S_{\cdot,k}} - \sum_{k=1}^{K} \sum_{l \neq k} \frac{S_{\cdot,k}^T A S_{\cdot,l}}{S_{\cdot,k}^T S_{\cdot,k}}$$

$$= \sum_{k=1}^{K} \frac{S_{\cdot,k}^T (2A - D) S_{\cdot,k}}{S_{\cdot,k}^T S_{\cdot,k}} \tag{3}$$

$$\text{s.t.} \quad S_{i,j} \in \{0, 1\} \quad \text{for } i, j = 1, 2, \ldots, K,$$

$$\sum_{k=1}^{K} S_{\cdot,k} = \mathbf{1}.$$

Here $\mathbf{1}$ is a vector with all elements being 1.

The objective function aims to both maximize the average degree within each module and minimize the average connections between different modules. We expect to achieve a good balance of the module size and make correct inference on the modules. The problem (3) is solved with an approximate method similar to the spectral clustering. We first compute the K eigenvectors of the matrix $2A - D$. By clustering these K eigenvectors as a matrix of n objects with K dimensions, we get the assignment of the n nodes into K modules.

Now, we discuss how to determine the lowest level of all the possible modules K. For any node $i \in V$, the degree can be written as

$$d_i = \sum_{k=1}^{K} d_i(V_k), \tag{4}$$

where

$$d_i(V_k) = \sum_{j \in V_k} A_{ij}, \tag{5}$$

which defines the connections that node i has in the subnetwork V_k. To determine the number of possible modules, we compare the average connectivity within a subnetwork and the average connectivity between it and any other subnetwork. If the average connectivity within a subnetwork is greater, we take it as a module, that is,

$$\frac{\sum_{i \in V_k} d_i(V_k)}{N_k} > \frac{\sum_{i \in V_k} d_i(V_l)}{N_k}, \quad l \neq k. \tag{6}$$

Alternatively, it can also be written as

$$L_{kk} > L_{kl}, \tag{7}$$

if we multiply both sides with N_k. This condition is very weak, thus with it, we hope we find all the modules as on the lowest level. We do the clustering for K increasing from two until the condition (6) does not hold and get all the possible modules. The efficiency of the above algorithm can be seen in [14].

Based on the above results, we construct the hierarchical structure in an agglomerative way (bottom-to-up). We directly use connection probability, which is computed from the clustering results through maximum likelihood estimation, to measure the distance between different modules. This connection probability matrix is denoted as $\hat{P}^0$. First the maximum connection probability between different modules is found, and we assume it is $\hat{P}^0_{i_0,j_0}$ with the corresponding two modules i_0, j_0 being recorded. The second largest connection probability for these two modules i_0, j_0 are also found, and we assume they are $\hat{P}^0_{i_0,k_0}$ and $\hat{P}^0_{j_0,l_0}$ with the corresponding modules being k_0 and l_0. To determine whether there is a hierarchical structure for these modules, we use Fisher exact test to see whether the connection probabilities $\hat{P}^0_{i_0,k_0}$ and $\hat{P}^0_{j_0,l_0}$ are the same as $\hat{P}^0_{i_0,j_0}$. That is, we need to test $\hat{P}^0_{i_0,j_0} = \hat{P}^0_{i_0,k_0}$ and $\hat{P}^0_{i_0,j_0} = \hat{P}^0_{j_0,l_0}$. Here we take a P value threshold to be 0.05. Three different cases may occur for these two relations. (1) Both of these two null hypotheses are rejected. In this case, there is hierarchical structure and the modules i_0, j_0 are on the lower level than k_0 and l_0. We combine the two modules i_0 and j_0 and take them as one module. (2) Only one of $\hat{P}^0_{i_0,j_0} = \hat{P}^0_{i_0,k_0}$ and $\hat{P}^0_{i_0,j_0} = \hat{P}^0_{j_0,l_0}$ is accepted. The

corresponding modules having the same connection probability are combined together. We look for the next largest connection probability for these three modules and test the relationship again. If two modules are tested to have the same connection probability, they are combined into one group, and the same step is implemented again. (3) Both of these two null hypotheses are accepted. These modules are taken as on the same level and combine together. We search the next largest connection probability to these four modules and do the statistical test until the hierarchical structure occurs or all the modules are combined together. After the above steps are finished, the connection probability between different modules is recalculated and recorded as $\hat{P}^1$. The above search and test steps are repeated for $\hat{P}^1$. Such steps are implemented recursively until all the modules are combined into one big module/network. For the statistical tests, we can also use t-test to test the relations between the connection probabilities if the distribution of the connections between different modules can be approximated by normal distribution. With this method, we can efficiently combine the modules with the same connection probability into the same level.

3. Numerical Experiments

In this section, we evaluate the performance of our proposed method through its application to several examples. We first start with two artificial networks having comparatively clear module structures. We then apply our method to two real networks to evaluate its performance. The first real network is the well-known karate club network and the second one is a yeast gene coexpression network.

3.1. Artificial Networks

3.1.1. A Network Composed of Cliques. We consider a network with 200 nodes, which is composed of 4 cliques. The sizes of the cliques are 90, 30, 40, and 40. The connections between different cliques are randomly generated with the following probability:

$$P = \begin{pmatrix} 1.000 & 0.200 & 0.002 & 0.003 \\ 0.200 & 1.000 & 0.005 & 0.010 \\ 0.002 & 0.005 & 1.000 & 0.030 \\ 0.003 & 0.010 & 0.030 & 1.000 \end{pmatrix}. \tag{8}$$

The pattern of the adjacency matrix is shown in Figure 2(a). From upper-left to lower-right, we denote the four modules as M_1, M_2, M_3, and M_4, which correspond to the position in the connection probability matrix. We can see the hierarchical structure of the network from the adjacency matrix. We apply our proposed method to this network. The condition (6) is satisfied until $K = 4$. The estimated connection probability matrix is

$$\hat{P} = \begin{pmatrix} 1.000 & 0.205 & 0.003 & 0.003 \\ 0.205 & 1.000 & 0.006 & 0.009 \\ 0.003 & 0.006 & 1.000 & 0.029 \\ 0.003 & 0.009 & 0.029 & 1.000 \end{pmatrix}. \tag{9}$$

We apply statistical tests to the corresponding modules, and finally we get the hierarchical structure as shown in

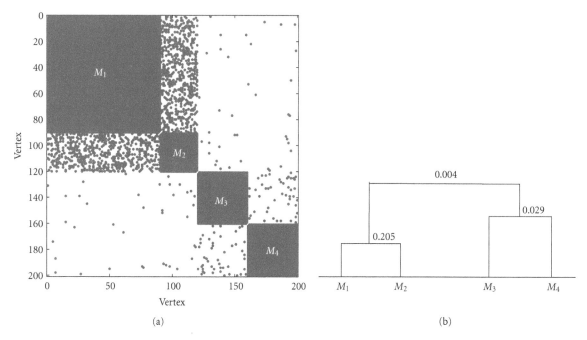

FIGURE 2: Example of hierarchical modular network structure. (a) Pattern of the adjacency matrix; (b) the hierarchical structure of the network.

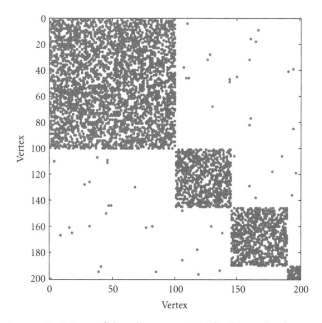

FIGURE 3: Pattern of the adjacency matrix for the randomly generated network.

Figure 2(b). The values on the hierarchical tree is the estimated connection probability of the corresponding modules. On the lowest level, there are four modules. If the tree is cut between 0.205 and 0.029, there are three modules while if the cutoff is greater than 0.029, there are only two modules. These results are consistent with the network generation strategy.

3.1.2. A Randomly Generated Network. In this example, we also consider a network with 200 nodes and 4 modules.

The size of each module is 10, 45, 45, and 100. We set the degree of each node within its module to be 6, 15, 15, and 30. Then the connections between different nodes are randomly generated. We keep all the edges generated for each node. So finally the average degree within each module is greater than the prespecified number. The connection probability between different modules is 0.002. The pattern of the adjacency matrix is shown in Figure 3. From upper-left to lower-right, the four modules are M_1, M_2, M_3, and M_4, respectively. With our proposed method, the network is partitioned into four modules correctly on the lowest level and the estimated connection probability is

$$\hat{P} = \begin{pmatrix} 0.298 & 0.002 & 0.002 & 0.003 \\ 0.002 & 0.328 & 0.002 & 0.004 \\ 0.002 & 0.002 & 0.321 & 0.000 \\ 0.003 & 0.004 & 0.000 & 0.560 \end{pmatrix}. \tag{10}$$

By using the statistical tests, these four modules are determined as parallel modules, which is the same as that in our network generation strategy.

3.2. Karate Club Network. We consider the Zachary's network of karate club members [22] in this example. There are 34 nodes in this network corresponding to the members in a karate club. This dataset has been applied as a benchmark to test many module identification algorithms since the true modules are known in this network. The people in the club were observed for a period of three years. The edges represent connections of the individuals outside the activities of the club. At some point, the administrator and the instructor of the club broke up due to a conflict between them. The club was separated into two groups supporting the administrator and the instructor. Figure 4 shows the network. Originally, there are two modules, which have 16 nodes (squares and

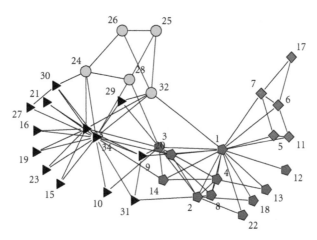

FIGURE 4: Zachary's karate club network. Different shapes show the modules. M_1: pentagon, M_2: square, M_3: triangle, M_4: circle.

pentagons in the figure) and 18 nodes (circles and triangles in the figure), respectively.

We apply our proposed method to this network. The criterion (6) is satisfied until $K = 4$. The result is shown in Figure 4, with different shapes of the nodes denoting different modules. The estimated connection probability matrix is

$$\hat{P} = \begin{pmatrix} 0.364 & 0.073 & 0.056 & 0.036 \\ 0.073 & 0.480 & 0.000 & 0.000 \\ 0.056 & 0.000 & 0.237 & 0.108 \\ 0.036 & 0.000 & 0.108 & 0.480 \end{pmatrix}. \quad (11)$$

From this matrix, it is easy to see that M_3 and M_4 are more likely to connect each other. With statistical tests, we can get that the connection probability among M_3, M_4, and M_1 is the same. Although M_2 has no connections to M_3 and M_4, it has a larger connection probability to M_1 than M_3, M_4 to M_1. Thus these four modules are on the same level. In [19], the authors considered constructing the hierarchical modular structure of this network too. At first, they also found four modules on the lowest level. Then they found that this network has two modules with some nodes (3, 9, 10, 14, 31) belonging to both of them. We did not consider the overlapping nodes in this article. However, we can see that because these overlapping nodes belong to both M_1 and M_3, and they connect both parts closely, our method detect M_1 and M_3, M_3 and M_4 as having the same connectivity.

3.3. Hierarchical Modular Structure in Yeast Gene Coexpression Network. In this section, we apply our proposed approach to analyze a gene coexpression network of yeast. The data set we use was generated by Brem and Kruglyak from a cross between two distinct isogenic strains BY and RM [23]. As described in [23], a total of 5740 ORFs were obtained after data preprocessing. In our analysis, we only use the 1,800 most differentially expressed genes as input to construct coexpression network and derive modules. When constructing the adjacency matrix of the network, we use the hard thresholding, that is: if the absolute value of Pearson correlation coefficient between two genes is greater than some given value, we assign an edge between them; otherwise, there is no edge. We compute the linear regression

coefficient between the frequency of degree d ($\log 10(f(d))$) and the $\log 10$ transformed degree d ($\log 10(d)$), and choose the threshold that leads to approximately scale free property of the network as described in [24]. Finally, the threshold is set to be 0.705, $\hat{R}$ is about 0.75. By such a setting, this gene coexpression network is divided into 690 unconnected parts with the largest part of size 788. Here, we only analyze the hierarchical modular structure of the largest connected network.

Starting from $K = 2$, we apply the method in [14] to this network, and the condition (6) holds until $K = 10$. To make the solution more accurate, we do a global maximization by changing the module index of boundary nodes starting from the approximate solution. Since the approximate solution is already good, this step is very fast. The structure of the network is shown in Figure 5(a), with different colors and shapes denoting different modules as described in Table 1. Then we construct the hierarchical modular structure as shown in Figure 5(b). On the lowest level, there are ten modules, while on the highest level, there are four modules.

Since coexpressed genes tend to be coregulated and possibly have similar functions, genes in the same module are expected to be enriched for some function categories. In order to understand the biological basis of the network modules, we consider each identified module for enrichment of annotations from gene ontology (GO) [25]. In our analysis, the enrichment analysis was performed by GO stats from Bioconductor. For each module, the statistically most significant GO categories are analyzed. Table 1 shows the enrichment results for the ten modules. "M-size" and "G-size" are the size of both the modules and the GO categories, respectively. "Overlap" is the overlap size of the module and the GO category. Table 2 shows the enrichment results for the modules on different levels. From the tables, it is easy to see that different gene function categories are enriched most on different levels. For example, module M_2 enriches the GO category "translation" most significantly, while the combined module M_2, M_8 enriches "Ribonucleoprotein complex biogenesis" most significantly, with M_2 containing 42 genes having this function. The combined module M_2, M_8, M_4, and M_1 also enriches this function, while M_4 itself enriches

TABLE 1: GO enrichment analysis results of the gene modules on the lowest level.

Module	Color, shape	M-size	Enriched GO category	P value	G-size	Overlap
M_1	White, square	190	Cellular carbohydrate metabolic process	3.23×10^{-9}	60	35
M_2	White, circle	126	Translation	4.70×10^{-59}	101	80
M_3	Grey, triangle	135	Organic acid biosynthetic process	5.41×10^{-35}	89	64
M_4	Grey, pentagon	62	Cellular respiration	4.13×10^{-27}	36	28
M_5	Black, circle	12	Amino acid catabolic process to alcohol via Ehrlich pathway	1.76×10^{-7}	5	4
M_6	Black, circle	13	Steroid biosynthetic process	2.20×10^{-15}	13	9
M_7	White, pentagon	19	Branched chain family amino acid metabolic process	4.37×10^{-8}	11	6
M_8	Grey, triangle	209	Ribonucleoprotein complex biogenesis	5.94×10^{-39}	149	106
M_9	Grey, square	11	Protein targeting to membrane	8.91×10^{-6}	4	3
M_{10}	White, square	11	Regulation of translational termination	1.55×10^{-4}	2	2

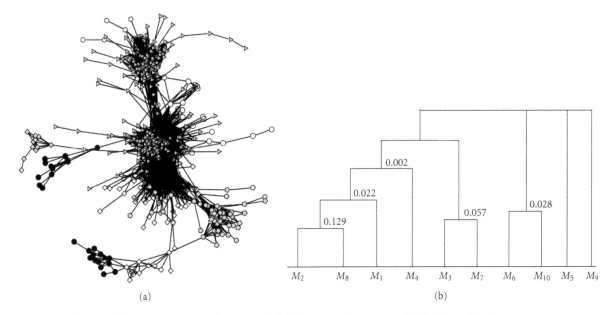

(a)   (b)

FIGURE 5: Yeast gene coexpression network. (a) The network structure, (b) the hierarchical structure.

"cellular respiration" significantly. On the uppermost level, the module composed of M_2, M_8, M_1, M_4, M_3, and M_7 enriches four GO function categories most significantly, and all the genes are overlapped. Three ("cellular component biogenesis," "cellular component biogenesis at cellular level," and "ribosome biogenesis") of them are different from the most enriched gene functions for each of these six modules. All these results indicate that hierarchical modular structure does exist in gene coexpression networks and different gene functions are enriched most on different levels.

We use the software REViGO to check the hierarchical structure of the enriched GO categories [26]. We consider the enriched GO categories in Tables 1 and 2 except the category "regulation of translational termination" because its G-size is very small and the P value is comparatively large. Figure 6 shows the tree map of the most enriched GO categories. The subgraph that we do not mark with the module corresponds to the combined module M_1, M_2, M_3, M_4, M_7, M_8. Here the modules M_6, M_9 and other modules are parallel to each other, which is consistent with our results. M_3 and M_7 belong to a large category, which is "branched chain family amino

acid metabolic process". This large category is different from the most enriched category for the combined module M_3 and M_7. This may come from the fact that since M_7 is very small, it does not cover a large part of its enriched category. M_1 and M_4 are parallel to each other which is also consistent with our analysis. All these results show that our proposed method can explain some of the hierarchical structure of the GO categories. Due to the network size, we did not handle all the genes of yeast. This may be a reason why some of our computational results are not consistent with the GO function tree map.

4. Conclusion

Module identification problem has attracted much attention from different fields and it continues being a hot research topic. How to determine the number of modules in a modular network has been an open problem during the study of module identification methods. This problem may come from the hierarchical structure of modular networks. The different numbers correspond to the different levels of

TABLE 2: GO enrichment analysis results of gene modules on the upper level.

Module	M-size	Enriched GO category	P value	G-size	Overlap
M_2, M_8	335	Ribonucleoprotein complex biogenesis	4.02×10^{-66}	149	148
M_1, M_2, M_8	525	Ribonucleoprotein complex biogenesis	1.33×10^{-29}	149	148
M_1, M_2, M_4, M_8	587	Ribonucleoprotein complex biogenesis	6.04×10^{-23}	149	149
M_3, M_7	154	Organic acid biosynthetic process	9.22×10^{-40}	89	71
M_1, M_2, M_3, M_4	741	Cellular component biogenesis	4.01×10^{-6}	175	175
M_7, M_8		Cellular component biogenesis at cellular level	1.84×10^{-5}	156	156
		Ribonucleoprotein complex biogenesis	3.19×10^{-5}	149	149
		Ribosome biogenesis	3.44×10^{-5}	148	148
M_6, M_{10}	24	Steroid biosynthetic process	2.36×10^{-19}	13	12

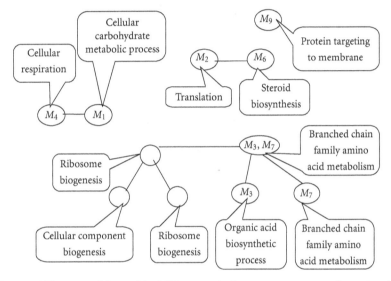

FIGURE 6: Tree map of the enriched GO categories in yeast gene coexpression network.

the hierarchical structure and they may be all reasonable. In this paper, we proposed a method for constructing the hierarchical modular structure of networks. With statistical tests, we can identify both the parallel modules and the hierarchical structure. According to different cutoffs of the hierarchical tree, different numbers of modules can be identified. This may solve the problem of the number of network modules to some extent. Several examples are given to demonstrate the efficiency of our method. Application of this method to gene coexpression networks shows that there are hierarchical modules in yeast gene coexpression network. On different levels of such networks, the genes in the module belong to different gene functions most. Thus studying the gene function through constructing the hierarchical modular structure instead of specifying the number of modules should perform better. Application of such algorithms to other kinds of networks may also contribute to other research fields.

Acknowledgments

This work was supported in part by NSFC Grants 10901042, 10971075, and 91130032. The primary version of this paper has appeared in IEEE ISB 2012.

References

[1] R. Guimerà and L. A. N. Amaral, "Functional cartography of complex metabolic networks," *Nature*, vol. 433, no. 7028, pp. 895–900, 2005.

[2] M. Girvan and M. E. J. Newman, "Community structure in social and biological networks," *Proceedings of the National Academy of Sciences of the United States of America*, vol. 99, no. 12, pp. 7821–7826, 2002.

[3] A. Arenas, J. Borge-Holthoefer, S. Gómez, and G. Zamora-López, "Optimal map of the modular structure of complex networks," *New Journal of Physics*, vol. 12, Article ID 053009, 2010.

[4] J. Dong and S. Horvath, "Understanding network concepts in modules," *BMC Systems Biology*, vol. 1, article 24, 2007.

[5] E. Estrada and N. Hatano, "Communicability in complex networks," *Physical Review E*, vol. 77, no. 3, Article ID 036111, 2008.

[6] S. Fortunato, "Community detection in graphs," *Physics Reports*, vol. 486, no. 3–5, pp. 75–174, 2010.

[7] M. E. J. Newman, "Finding community structure in networks using the eigenvectors of matrices," *Physical Review E*, vol. 74, no. 3, Article ID 036104, 2006.

[8] M. E. J. Newman, "Modularity and community structure in networks," *Proceedings of the National Academy of Sciences of the United States of America*, vol. 103, no. 23, pp. 8577–8582, 2006.

[9] M. A. Porter, J. P. Onnela, and P. J. Mucha., "Communities in networks," *Notices of the American Mathematical Society*, vol. 56, no. 9, pp. 1082–1102, 2010.

[10] F. Radicchi, C. Castellano, F. Cecconi, V. Loreto, and D. Paris, "Defining and identifying communities in networks," *Proceedings of the National Academy of Sciences of the United States of America*, vol. 101, no. 9, pp. 2658–2663, 2004.

[11] Z. Li, S. Zhang, R.-S. Wang, X.-S. Zhang, and L. Chen, "Quantitative function for community detection," *Physical Review E*, vol. 77, no. 3, Article ID 036109, 2008.

[12] M. Rosvall and C. T. Bergstrom, "An information-theoretic framework for resolving community structure in complex networks," *Proceedings of the National Academy of Sciences of the United States of America*, vol. 104, no. 18, pp. 7327–7331, 2007.

[13] L. Danon, A. Díaz-Guilera, J. Duch, and A. Arenas, "Comparing community structure identification," *Journal of Statistical Mechanics*, no. 9, Article ID 09008, pp. 219–228, 2005.

[14] S. Zhang and H. Zhao, "Community identification in networks with unbalanced structure," *Physical Review E*, vol. 85, no. 6, Article ID 066114, 2012.

[15] P. J. Bickel and A. Chen, "A nonparametric view of network models and Newman-Girvan and other modularities," *Proceedings of the National Academy of Sciences of the United States of America*, vol. 106, no. 50, pp. 21068–21073, 2009.

[16] A. Arenas, A. Díaz-Guilera, and C. J. Pérez-Vicente, "Synchronization reveals topological scales in complex networks," *Physical Review Letters*, vol. 96, no. 11, Article ID 114102, 2006.

[17] D. Meunier, R. Lambiotte, and E. T. Bullmore, "Modular and hierarchically modular organization of brain networks," *Frontiers Neuroscience*, vol. 4, no. 200, 2010.

[18] H. Shen, X. Cheng, K. Cai, and M.-B. Hu, "Detect overlapping and hierarchical community structure in networks," *Physica A*, vol. 388, no. 8, pp. 1706–1712, 2009.

[19] A. Lancichinetti, S. Fortunato, and J. Kertész, "Detecting the overlapping and hierarchical community structure in complex networks," *New Journal of Physics*, vol. 11, Article ID 033015, 2009.

[20] E. Ravasz, "Detecting hierarchical modularity in biological networks," *Computational Systems Biology*, vol. 54, pp. 145–160, 2009.

[21] P. Erdős and A. R. Rényi, "On random graphs. I," *Publicationes Mathematicae*, vol. 6, pp. 290–297, 1959.

[22] W. W. Zachary, "An information flow model for conflict and fission in small groups," *Journal of Anthropological Research*, vol. 33, pp. 452–473, 1977.

[23] R. B. Brem and L. Kruglyak, "The landscape of genetic complexity across 5,700 gene expression traits in yeast," *Proceedings of the National Academy of Sciences of the United States of America*, vol. 102, no. 5, pp. 1572–1577, 2005.

[24] B. Zhang and S. Horvath, "A general framework for weighted gene co-expression network analysis," *Statistical Applications in Genetics and Molecular Biology*, vol. 4, no. 1, article 17, 2005.

[25] M. Ashburner, C. A. Ball, J. A. Blake et al., "Gene ontology: tool for the unification of biology, the gene ontology consortium," *Nature Genetics*, vol. 25, no. 1, pp. 25–29, 2000.

[26] F. Supek, M. Bošnjak, N. Škunca, and T. Šmuc, "REVIGO summarizes and visualizes long lists of gene ontology terms," *PLoS ONE*, vol. 6, no. 7, Article ID 21800, 2011.

10

Diffusion Tensor Imaging-Based Research on Human White Matter Anatomy

Ming-guo Qiu,[1] Jing-na Zhang,[1] Ye Zhang,[1] Qi-yu Li,[2] Bing Xie,[3] and Jian Wang[3]

[1] *Department of Medical Informatics and Medical Image, College of Biomedical Engineering and Medical Imaging,*
Third Military Medical University, Chongqing 400038, China
[2] *Department of Anatomy, Third Military Medical University, Chongqing 400038, China*
[3] *Department of Radiology, Southwest Hospital, Third Military Medical University, Chongqing 400038, China*

Correspondence should be addressed to Ming-guo Qiu, qiumingguo@yahoo.com

Academic Editors: F. Galbusera and D. Gastaldi

The aim of this study is to investigate the white matter by the diffusion tensor imaging and the Chinese visible human dataset and to provide the 3D anatomical data of the corticospinal tract for the neurosurgical planning by studying the probabilistic maps and the reproducibility of the corticospinal tract. Diffusion tensor images and high-resolution T1-weighted images of 15 healthy volunteers were acquired; the DTI data were processed using DtiStudio and FSL software. The FA and color FA maps were compared with the sectional images of the Chinese visible human dataset. The probability maps of the corticospinal tract were generated as a quantitative measure of reproducibility for each voxel of the stereotaxic space. The fibers displayed by the diffusion tensor imaging were well consistent with the sectional images of the Chinese visible human dataset and the existing anatomical knowledge. The three-dimensional architecture of the white matter fibers could be clearly visualized on the diffusion tensor tractography. The diffusion tensor tractography can establish the 3D probability maps of the corticospinal tract, in which the degree of intersubject reproducibility of the corticospinal tract is consistent with the previous architectonic report. DTI is a reliable method of studying the fiber connectivity in human brain, but it is difficult to identify the tiny fibers. The probability maps are useful for evaluating and identifying the corticospinal tract in the DTI, providing anatomical information for the preoperative planning and improving the accuracy of surgical risk assessments preoperatively.

1. Introduction

The study of the brain white matter is an important and also a difficult part of the research on the human brain function and structure; the invasional fiber tracking methods used in the animals cannot be used in the human beings [1–3]. It is difficult to display the three-dimensional structure of the brain white matter by gross anatomy or sectional anatomy, and so it is to segment the white matter in the Chinese Visible Human dataset [4].

Diffusion tensor magnetic resonance imaging (DT-MRI) is a valuable tool for studying the microstructure of the brain in vivo and has the ability to reveal microstructural properties of the white matter [5–7]. It has been shown that, in the brain, ordered axonal structure, cell membrane, and myelin sheath strongly influence water diffusion and that

there is a direct link between water diffusion and axonal orientation and integrity. In fact, when diffusion tensor imaging (DTI) is performed within a compact tract with parallel running axonal trajectories like the corticospinal tract, the DT is strongly anisotropic and its principal eigenvector corresponds to the direction of the fiber tract [8, 9]. DTI has been used extensively in the study of the brain white matter; it can display the three-dimensional structure of the brain white matter and can quantitatively analyze the special fiber [10–12].

DTI has opened up new opportunities for analyzing the position and extent of individual fiber tracts in vivo using diffusion tensor tractography [13, 14]. The aim of the present study was to investigate the reliability of the diffusion tensor imaging by comparing it with the Chinese visible human dataset, to display the three-dimensional architecture of the white matter fibers in human brain by using diffusion tensor tractography, and to provide the 3D anatomical data of the corticospinal tract for the neurosurgical planning by studying the probabilistic maps and the reproducibility of the corticospinal tract.

2. Methods

2.1. Subjects. Fifteen healthy volunteers (aged 22–39, 9 males and 6 females) were recruited as the subjects of an ongoing functional MR imaging study. Volunteers had no history of a psychiatric disease or a neurological injury. An informed consent from all subjects was obtained in accordance with institutional guidelines.

2.2. Image Acquisition. DTI data were acquired using dual spin-echo, single shot echo-planar imaging sequence on a 3.0T Siemens Sonata scanner with 3-mm slice thickness, no interslice gap, TR = 6400 ms, TE = 88 ms, FOV = 220 × 220 mm, 12 noncollinear diffusion-sensitizing gradient directions with diffusion sensitivity b = 1000 s/mm^2, 6 averages, matrix = 128 × 128, and 40 contiguous slices yielding full brain coverage. Slices were positioned along the anterior commissure-posterior commissure line. A normalizing T2 image without diffusion weighting was also acquired. Immediately after the EPI scan, a whole-brain high-resolution T1-weighted anatomical image was acquired with 3D magnetization-prepared rapid acquisition gradient echo (MPRAGE) sequence, TR/TE/FA = 2300 ms/3.93 ms/8°, matrix = 256 × 256, and 1 mm slice thickness.

2.3. Image Processing and Analysis. Firstly, DTI data were processed with DtiStudio software [15] to reconstruct the FA, and the color FA maps. From the sectional images of the CVH dataset [4], the transversal, coronal, and sagittal images of the head (thickness = 0.1 mm) were selected. The reconstructed FA and color FA maps were compared with the sectional images of the CVH dataset, to define the position and the contour of the fiber tract.

Secondly, the white matter fibers in the brain were reconstructed using DtiStudio tractography, in order to visualize anatomical connections in the form of separate identifiable tracts or bundles. In a deterministic framework [15, 16], we defined a region of interest (ROI) as a volume that selects fibres. The placement of the ROI was chosen according to the structure that was investigated and guided by the knowledge coming from postmortem anatomical studies and the CVH dataset. If necessary, a second (and even a third) ROI would be selected, in order to separate the tract of interest from others. The different tracts selected were identified by confrontation with the postmortem studies.

Then the DTI data were analyzed using FSL 4.1 (FMRIB Software Library, Oxford, UK). Preprocessing of DTI data included eddy current correction and computations of the diffusion tensor elements and FA maps [6]. The masks were outlined with blue color at the peduncle and the posterior limb of the internal capsule in the FA color maps using FSLView. In the color FA maps, red, green, and blue colors were assigned to the right-left, anterior-posterior, and superior-inferior orientations, respectively. T1 images were registered to the ICBM152-T1 template, and then the diffusion space was transferred to the standard space, with the masks serving as the seeds and the waypoints for probabilistic tractography. The probability maps were generated as a quantitative measure of reproducibility for each voxel of the stereotaxic space.

3. Results

3.1. Comparing the FA and Color FA Maps with the Sections of CVH. The major fibers of the white matter can be identified on the FA maps and the color FA maps. In the color FA maps, the red, green, and blue colors were assigned to the right-left, anterior-posterior, and superior-inferior orientations, respectively. Comparing the FA maps and the color FA maps with the sections of CVH, we found that the white matter displayed by the FA maps and the color FA maps were well consistent with the sectional images of the CVH dataset and the known anatomy, but it is difficult to identify the tiny fibers in the FA maps and the color FA maps.

On the transversal FA map, color FA map, and sectional image of visible human at basal nuclei, the genu of corpus callosum and the splenium of corpus callosum were red, the anterior limb of internal capsule was green, and the posterior limb of internal capsule was blue. The external capsule and extreme capsule were mixed and could not be differentiated on the FA map or the color FA map, but were clear in the sectional image of the CVH (Figure 1).

The coronal FA map, color FA map, and sectional image of visible human at the posterior limb of internal capsule displayed clearly the body of corpus callosum, the pyramidal tract, and the external capsule and the extreme capsule, but the fibers in the temporal lobe cannot be displayed clearly in the coronal FA map or the color FA map (Figure 2). In the sagittal FA map, color tensor map, and sectional image of a visible human at the fornix, we can see the cingulate fasciculus, the corpus callosum, the fornix, and the superior cerebellar peduncle (Figure 3).

3.2. Tractography of the White Matter. We adopted the above-mentioned methodology in order to perform a virtual dissection of several well-known anatomical systems and displayed the tract of interest on 3D views. The fibers displayed by diffusion tensor tractography were well consistent with the known anatomy.

The 3D architecture of white matter fibers could be clearly visualized by diffusion tensor tractography, including the projection fibers of the pyramidal tract, the visual radiation, and the medial lemniscuses (Figures 4 and 5). The corticospinal tract is a large, well-characterized, and highly anisotropic tract. The ROI was placed more laterally in the ventrolateral part of the cerebral peduncle, and the selected fibres corresponded to the pyramidal tract, originating mainly from the region of the central sulcus and travelling down the brain stem (Figure 4). Looking at the color FA map at the level of the pons, we could easily identify the medial

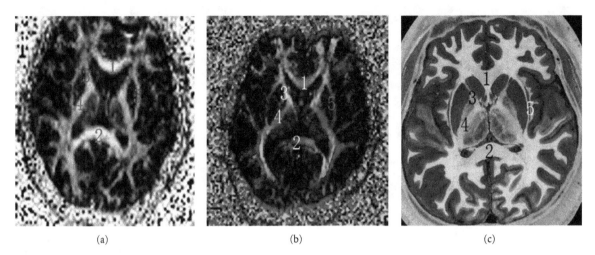

FIGURE 1: Transversal FA map, color tensor map, and sectional image of visible human at basal nuclei. (1) Genu of corpus callosum, (2) splenium of corpus callosum, (3) anterior limb of internal capsule, (4) posterior limb of internal capsule, and (5) external capsule and extreme capsule.

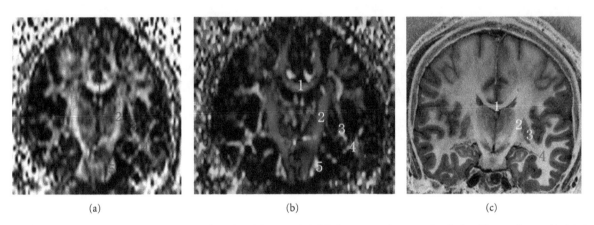

FIGURE 2: Coronal FA map, color tensor map, and sectional image of visible human at the posterior limb of internal capsule. (1) Body of corpus callosum, (2) pyramidal tract, (3) external capsule and extreme capsule, (4) inferior longitudinal fasciculus, and (5) middle cerebellar peduncle.

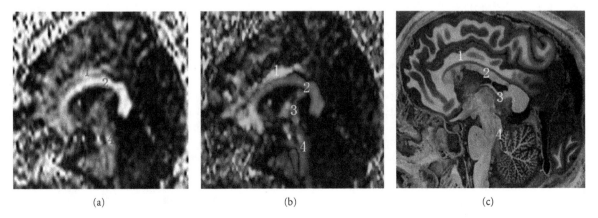

FIGURE 3: Sagittal FA map, color tensor map, and sectional image of visible human at the fornix. (1) Cingulate fasciculus, (2) corpus callosum, (3) fornix, and (4) superior cerebellar peduncle.

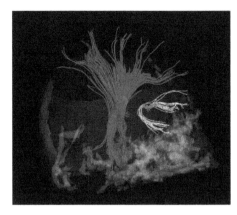

FIGURE 4: Spatial relation of the pyramidal tract (red), the medial lemniscus (blue), and the uncinate fasciculus (yellow).

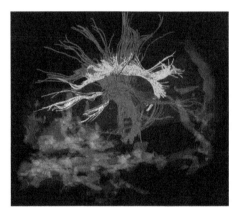

FIGURE 5: Spatial relation of the cingulated fasciculus (green), the fornix (purple), the uncinate fasciculus (yellow), the medial lemniscus (blue), and the pyramidal tract (red).

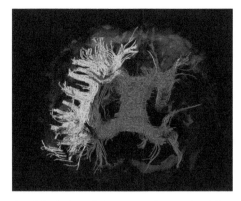

FIGURE 6: Spatial relation of the superior longitudinal fasciculus and the U-shaped fibers (green) to the corpus callosum (red).

FIGURE 7: Spatial relation of the superior longitudinal fasciculus (green), the inferior longitudinal fasciculus (cyan), the optic radiation (purple), the uncinate fasciculus (yellow), and the inferior frontooccipital fasciculus (blue).

lemniscus and select the first ROI. Another ROI was placed in the anterior limb of the internal capsule (Figures 4 and 5).

The commissural fibers include the corpus callosum and the fornix (Figures 5 and 6). In order to identify the fibres passing through the corpus callosum, we placed a large ROI encompassing the whole corpus callosum at the midsagittal plane (Figure 6). Some of the major pathways constituting the limbic system are known to be the fornix and the cingulate bundle. The horizontal portion of the fornix was isolated by placing an ROI in a frontal plane parasagittally beneath the body of the corpus callosum.

The association fibers include the uncinate fascicules, the cingulum and the superior and inferior longitudinal fasciculi (Figures 4 and 7). To identify the uncinate fascicle, we placed the first ROI in the anterior part of the temporal lobe and the second one in the frontal lobe (Figure 4). The cingulum was identified by using two ROIs placed in a frontal plane, 2 cm apart within the white matter of the cingulate gyrus (Figure 5). Corticocortical connection U-shaped fibers were widespread and formed only loose association bundles that are variable in size and shape (Figure 6). Figures 6 and 7 show the spatial relation of the superior longitudinal fasciculus and the U-shaped fibers to the corpus callosum; Figure 7

shows the inferior frontooccipital fasciculus as it was isolated by the two ROIs. The first was placed in the posterior parietal and the second in the frontal lobe. The superior longitudinal fascicle was selected by two ROIs placed below the motor and the posterior parietal cortices in frontal planes. In order to isolate the inferior longitudinal fascicle, we also used two selection ROIs. The posterior was, as for the inferior occipitofrontal fascicle, in the posterior parietal lobe, whereas the second was in the temporal lobe.

3.3. Probability Maps of the Corticospinal Tract. In the probability maps of the corticospinal tract showing the axial sections and the coronal sections in the ICBM152-T1 template, the color bars indicate the relative frequency of voxels containing the corticospinal tract from 0 to 100% (yellow) at the 20% step (Figure 8). The coordinates of the corticospinal tract in the anatomical MNI space (orientation according to the AC-PC line) showed that x was from -58 to 1 in the left and from 2 to 54 in the right, y was from 20 to -56 in the left and from 12 to -51 in the right, and z was from -20 to 80 in the left and from -20 to 76 in the right. The mean volume of the left corticospinal tract was (57416.67 ± 1944.56) mm^3 and that of the right corticospinal

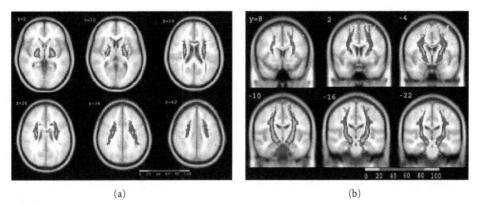

(a) (b)

FIGURE 8: The corticospinal tract overlapped in axial sections (a) and coronal sections (b). The color bars indicate the relative frequency of voxels containing the corticospinal tract from 0 to 100% (yellow) at the 20% step.

tract was $(54421.58 \pm 1232.43)\,\text{mm}^3$. The degree of the intersubject reproducibility shifted along its course with the highest reproducibility in the internal capsule, and the reproducibility of the corticospinal tract was higher in the right hemisphere than that in the left hemisphere.

4. Discussion

The white matter displayed by the FA maps and the color FA maps were well consistent with that in the sectional images of the CVH dataset and the existing anatomical knowledge [1, 2, 4]. But the DTI is insufficient to display the tiny white matter fiber such as the external capsule and the extreme capsule and the fibers in the temporal lobe. On the other hand, it is very difficult to identify and segment the white matter fibers in the CVH dataset [4]. With the different fibers crossing together, how to identify, segment, and reconstruct each fiber? It is difficult to solve the problem using the current CVH dataset and the image postprocessing technique. However, we can acquire the DTI data of the healthy subjects; the major fibers of the white matter can be identified in the FA maps. And in the color FA maps, the red, green, and blue colors were assigned to right-left, anterior-posterior, and superior-inferior orientations, respectively. These cannot be achieved by the previous imaging technique. Thus, the DTI provides more information than the conventional MRI. By fusing the DTI data with the CVH dataset, we can make up for each other's deficiencies so as to enrich the content and enhance the function of the current CVH dataset, to observe directly the relationship between the anatomical structure and the white matter fibers, and to extend the application of the CVH dataset in the clinic.

The three-dimensional architecture of the white matter fibers could be clearly visualized with the diffusion tensor tractography, including the projection fibers, the commissural fibers, and the association fibers. The results showed striking similarity with the existing anatomical knowledge; the position and the extent of the fibers were consistent with the previous studies [2, 17]. Our results suggest that the fibre tracking is a valuable way for mapping the brain

white matter. But it is necessary to note that, only the largest and the most homogeneous fibre bundles, which are not smaller than a voxel in diameter, can be followed [6, 7]. Using knowledge-based ROI for tract selection is not an ideal solution. A risk of biasing the results remains if the windows are not placed fairly. On the other hand, it is very important to master the anatomy of the white matter fiber, especially the sectional anatomy of the fiber, with the purpose of identifying the fiber on FA and color FA maps, and placing the ROI accurately.

Another remaining problem for fibre tracking is the limited resolution of the imaging scanner and the incapacity of a tensor to model properly multiple fibre tracts in one voxel [13, 18]. Current deterministic streamlining algorithms follow the main eigenvector of the diffusion tensor, reducing the available information. Thus, only the largest and the most homogeneous fibre bundles, which are not smaller than a voxel in diameter, can be followed. This fibre tracking method has the following limitations: firstly, the diffusion tensor maybe is the mixture of multiple fiber diffusion. In some areas, such as the stem of the largest and the most homogeneous fiber bundles or the fibers bigger than a voxel in diameter, the main eigenvector of the diffusion tensor can be thought as the direction of the local fiber tracking. But in areas where the fibers cross, converge, or depart from each other, the main eigenvector of the voxel is the mean diffusion tensor of the different mixed fibers, it is obviously wrong to take the direction of the local fiber tracking as the main eigenvector [13, 19]. If the eigenvector that has the biggest diffusion tensor replaces the mean eigenvector of the voxel, the reconstruction of the other fibers will be restricted. Secondly, the noise and the regional volume effect will induce the fiber tracking error. Because of the limited resolution of the diffusion imaging, the effect of the imaging scanner, and the other noise during the images acquiring, it will induce an unreal result and add the fiber tracking error. The streamlining algorithm can only display the largest and the most homogeneous fibre bundles and is difficult to display the crossing fiber and those in subcortex or near cortex, so it will underestimate the volume of the fiber, even miscalculate the direction of the fiber.

The variety of the brain white matter can provide the very important anatomical information, providing valuable morphological information for the study of the disease in the nervous system and the neurosurgical planning [14, 20, 21]. The DTI probabilistic tractography has opened up new opportunities for analyzing the position and the extent of individual fiber tracts in vivo. The probabilistic tractography is to analyze the direction in each voxel [6]. Behrens studied the connectivity of the brain by using probabilistic tractography firstly, which can analyze the fiber in the subcortical or near the cortex, including the thalamus and the language function area [6, 22]. Our results showed that the volume of corticospinal tract is bigger than that of previous results, that is maybe because of the more accurate probabilistic tractography [14, 20, 21]. The diffusion tensor probabilistic tractography can establish the 3D probability maps of the corticospinal tract, and the degree of intersubject reproducibility of the corticospinal tract is consistent with previous architectonic report [1, 2]. The maps are useful for evaluating and identifying the corticospinal tract in DTI, providing anatomical information for preoperative planning and improving the accuracy of surgical risk assessments preoperatively. It is valuable to establish the probabilistic maps of the major fiber tracts by diffusion tensor probabilistic tractography.

Acknowledgments

This study was sponsored by the National Natural Science Foundation of China (Grant number 30870696, 81171866), the starting funds of the Third Military University (TMMU2009XHG01), and the Natural Science Foundation of Chongqing (CSTC2009BB5019).

References

[1] U. Bürgel, I. Mecklenburg, U. Blohm, and K. Zilles, "Histological visualization of long fiber tracts in the white matter of adult human brains," *Journal of Brain Research*, vol. 38, no. 3, pp. 397–404, 1997.

[2] U. Bürgel, K. Amunts, L. Hoemke, H. Mohlberg, J. M. Gilsbach, and K. Zilles, "White matter fiber tracts of the human brain: three-dimensional mapping at microscopic resolution, topography and intersubject variability," *NeuroImage*, vol. 29, no. 4, pp. 1092–1105, 2006.

[3] J. Rademacher, U. Bürgel, S. Geyer et al., "Variability and asymmetry in the human precentral motor system: a cytoarchitectonic and myeloarchitectonic brain mapping study," *Brain*, vol. 124, no. 11, pp. 2232–2258, 2001.

[4] S. X. Zhang, P. A. Heng, and Z. J. Liu, "Chinese visible human project," *Clinical Anatomy*, vol. 19, no. 3, pp. 204–215, 2006.

[5] P. J. Basser, S. Pajevic, C. Pierpaoli, J. Duda, and A. Aldroubi, "In vivo fiber tractography using DT-MRI data," *Magnetic Resonance in Medicine*, vol. 44, pp. 625–632, 2000.

[6] T. E. J. Behrens, H. Johansen-Berg, M. W. Woolrich et al., "Non-invasive mapping of connections between human thalamus and cortex using diffusion imaging," *Nature Neuroscience*, vol. 6, no. 7, pp. 750–757, 2003.

[7] D. L. Bihan, J. F. Mangin, C. Poupon et al., "Diffusion tensor imaging: concepts and applications," *Journal of Magnetic Resonance Imaging*, vol. 13, no. 4, pp. 534–546, 2001.

[8] C. Beaulieu, "The basis of anisotropic water diffusion in the nervous system—a technical review," *NMR in Biomedicine*, vol. 15, no. 7-8, pp. 435–455, 2002.

[9] C. R. Tench, P. S. Morgan, M. Wilson, and L. D. Blumhardt, "White matter mapping using diffusion tensor MRI," *Magnetic Resonance Tomography*, vol. 47, pp. 967–970, 2002.

[10] C. Pierpaoli, P. Jezzard, P. J. Basser, A. Barnett, and G. di Chiro, "Diffusion tensor MR imaging of the human brain," *Radiology*, vol. 201, no. 3, pp. 637–648, 1996.

[11] O. Ciccarelli, T. E. Behrens, D. R. Altmann et al., "Probabilistic diffusion tractography: a potential tool to assess the rate of disease progression in amyotrophic lateral sclerosis," *Brain*, vol. 129, no. 7, pp. 1859–1871, 2006.

[12] V. A. Coenen, T. Krings, L. Mayfrank et al., "Three-dimensional visualization of the pyramidal tract in a neuronavigation system during brain tumor surgery: first experiences and technical note," *Neurosurgery*, vol. 49, no. 1, pp. 86–93, 2001.

[13] P. J. Hagmann, J. P. Thiran, L. Jonasson et al., "DTI mapping of human brain connectivity: statistical fibre tracking and virtual dissection," *NeuroImage*, vol. 19, no. 3, pp. 545–554, 2003.

[14] T. Krings, V. A. Coenen, H. Axer et al., "In vivo 3D visualization of normal pyramidal tracts in human subjects using diffusion weighted magnetic resonance imaging and a neuronavigation system," *Neuroscience Letters*, vol. 307, no. 3, pp. 192–196, 2001.

[15] S. Mori and P. C. M. van Zijl, "Fiber tracking: principles and strategies—a technical review," *NMR in Biomedicine*, vol. 15, no. 7-8, pp. 468–480, 2002.

[16] S. Wakana, H. Jiang, L. M. Nagae-Poetscher, P. C. M. van Zijl, and S. Mori, "Fiber tract-based atlas of human white matter anatomy," *Radiology*, vol. 230, no. 1, pp. 77–87, 2004.

[17] S. Mori, S. Wakana, P. C. M. van Zijl, and L. M. Nagae-Poetscher, *MRI Atlas of the Human White Matter*, Elsevier, Amsterdam, The Netherlands, 2005.

[18] N. Ramnani, T. E. J. Behrens, W. Penny, and P. M. Matthews, "New approaches for exploring anatomical and functional connectivity in the human brain," *Biological Psychiatry*, vol. 56, no. 9, pp. 613–619, 2004.

[19] S. Mori, B. J. Crain, V. P. Chacko, and P. C. M. van Zijl, "Three-dimensional tracking of axonal projections in the brain by magnetic resonance imaging," *Annals of Neurology*, vol. 45, no. 2, pp. 265–269, 1999.

[20] C. M. Ellis, J. Suckling, E. Amaro Jr. et al., "Volumetric analysis reveals corticospinal tract degeneration and extramotor involvement in ALS," *Neurology*, vol. 57, no. 9, pp. 1571–1578, 2001.

[21] S. Wang, H. Poptani, M. Bilello et al., "Diffusion tensor imaging in amyotrophic lateral sclerosis: volumetric analysis of the corticospinal tract," *American Journal of Neuroradiology*, vol. 27, no. 6, pp. 1234–1238, 2006.

[22] A. Anwander, M. Tittgemeyer, D. Y. von Cramon, A. D. Friederici, and T. R. Knösche, "Connectivity-based parcellation of Broca's area," *Cerebral Cortex*, vol. 17, no. 4, pp. 816–825, 2007.

11

Molecular Mechanisms and Function Prediction of Long Noncoding RNA

Handong Ma, Yun Hao, Xinran Dong, Qingtian Gong, Jingqi Chen, Jifeng Zhang, and Weidong Tian

Institute of Biostatistics, School of Life Science, Fudan University, 220 Handan Road, Shanghai 2004333, China

Correspondence should be addressed to Weidong Tian, weidong.tian@fudan.edu.cn

Academic Editors: G. P. Chrousos and T. Kino

The central dogma of gene expression considers RNA as the carrier of genetic information from DNA to protein. However, it has become more and more clear that RNA plays more important roles than simply being the information carrier. Recently, whole genome transcriptomic analyses have identified large numbers of dynamically expressed long noncoding RNAs (lncRNAs), many of which are involved in a variety of biological functions. Even so, the functions and molecular mechanisms of most lncRNAs still remain elusive. Therefore, it is necessary to develop computational methods to predict the function of lncRNAs in order to accelerate the study of lncRNAs. Here, we review the recent progress in the identification of lncRNAs, the molecular functions and mechanisms of lncRNAs, and the computational methods for predicting the function of lncRNAs.

1. Introduction

Proteins and related protein-coding genes have been the main subject of biological studies for years. However, with the development of RNA sequencing technology and computational methods for assembling the transcriptome, it has become clear that besides protein-coding genes much of the mammalian genome is transcribed, and many noncoding RNA (ncRNA) transcripts tend to play important roles in a variety of biological processes. Understanding the function of ncRNAs has become one of the most important goals of modern biological studies [1–3]. ncRNAs can be classified into several distinct subclasses, including processed small RNAs [4], promoter-associated RNAs [5], and functional long noncoding RNAs (lncRNAs) [6]. The term of lncRNA was introduced to distinguish the special class of ncRNA from well-known small regulatory RNAs (i.e. miRNAs and siRNAs). lncRNAs are generally longer than 200 nucleotides [3, 7, 8]. Recent studies have shown that lncRNAs may act as important *cis*- or *trans*-regulators in various biological processes. Mutations in lncRNAs are related with a wide range of diseases, especially cancers and neurodegenerative diseases. Even so, the functions and molecular mechanisms of most lncRNAs are unknown. Though several computational methods have been developed to predict the functions of lncRNAs, it still remains a challenging task, partly owing to the lack of conservation in both the sequence and secondary structures of lncRNAs [9–11]. In this paper, we will summarize the recent progresses and challenges in the identification, molecular mechanism, and function prediction of lncRNAs.

2. Definition and Classification of lncRNA

The definition of lncRNA is based on two criteria, the size and the lack of protein-coding potential. In this paper, lncRNA refers to nonprotein-coding RNA longer than 200 nt [7, 10–12], which distinguishes it them from mRNA and small regulatory RNA in a relatively satisfying way [11, 13]. Depending on their relationships with the nearest protein-coding genes, lncRNAs can be classified in three different ways [12, 14, 15]: (1) *sense or antisense*: lncRNAs that are located on the same strand or the opposite strand of the nearest protein-coding genes [16]; (2) *divergent or convergent*: lncRNAs that are transcribed in the divergent or convergent orientation compared to that of the nearest protein-coding genes [12]; (3) *intronic or intergenic*: lncRNAs that locate inside the introns of a protein-coding gene, or in the interval regions between two protein-coding genes [12, 17].

3. Identification of lncRNA

To identify lncRNAs, the first step is to obtain all transcripts including ncRNAs and mRNAs in cells, and then to distinguish lncRNAs from mRNAs and other types of ncRNAs. Traditional technologies, such as microarray, focus on the identification of protein-coding RNA transcripts. New technologies, such as RNA-Seq, are not limited to the identification of protein-coding RNA transcripts, and have led to the discovery of many novel ncRNA transcripts. The discrimination between lncRNAs and other small regulatory ncRNAs depends on their length. However, the length information alone is not enough to separate lncRNAs from mRNAs, and other criteria are needed for this purpose. Below, we will first briefly introduce new technologies in identifying RNA transcripts, especially ncRNA transcripts. Then, we will review current methods to distinguish lncRNAs from mRNAs.

3.1. Experimental Methods in Identifying lncRNA

Microarray. Traditional microarray technologies use predefined probes to determine the expression level of mRNA transcripts and are not appropriate to identify lncRNAs. However, it has been found that a few previously defined mRNAs or some probe sequences actually are lncRNAs; thus, former microarray datasets can be reannotated to study the expression of lncRNAs [60]. With more and more lncRNAs discovered, new probes specific for lncRNAs can be designed. For example, Babak et al. designed probes from conserved intergenic and intragenic region to identify potential ncRNA transcripts [61]. However, microarray is not sensitive enough to detect RNA transcripts with low-expression level. Thus the use of microarray to identify lncRNAs is limited due to the low expression level of many lncRNAs.

SAGE and EST. SAGE (serial analysis of gene expression) technology produces large numbers of short sequence tags and is capable of identifying both known and unknown transcripts. SAGE has been used and proved to be an efficient approach in studying lncRNAs. For example, Gibb et al. compiled 272 human SAGE libraries. By passing over 24 million tags they were able to generate lncRNA expression profiles in human normal and cancer tissues [62]. Lee et al. also used SAGE to identify potential lncRNA candidates in male germ cell [63]. However, SAGE is much more expensive than microarray, therefore is not widely employed in large-scale studies. EST (expressed sequence tag) is a short subsequence of cDNA, and is generated from one-shot sequencing of cDNA clone. The public database now contains over 72.6 million EST (GeneBank 2011), making it possible to discover novel transcripts. For example, Furuno et al. clustered EST to find functional and novel lncRNAs in mammalian [64]. Huang et al. used the public bovine-specific EST database to reconstruct transcript assemblies, and find transcripts in intergenic regions that are likely putative lncRNAs [65].

RNA-Seq. With the development of next generation sequencing (NGS) technologies, RNA-Seq (also named whole transcriptome shotgun sequencing) has been widely used for novel transcripts discovery and gene expression analysis. Compared to traditional microarray technology, RNA-Seq has many advantages in studying gene expression. It is more sensitive in detecting less-abundant transcripts, and identifying novel alternative splicing isoforms and novel ncRNA transcripts. The basic workflow for lncRNA identification using RNA-Seq is shown in Figure 1. RNA-Seq is currently the most widely used technology in identifying lncRNAs. For example, Li et al. applied RNA-Seq to identify lncRNAs during chicken muscle development [66]. Nam and Bartel integrated RNA-Seq, poly (A)-site, and ribosome mapping information to obtain lncRNAs in *C. elegans* [16]. Pauli et al. performed RNA-Seq experiments at eight stages during zebrafish early development, and identified 1133 noncoding multiexonic transcripts [67]. Prensner et al. used RNA-Seq to study lncRNA in human prostate cancer from 102 prostate tissues and cell lines, and concluded that lncRNAs may be used for cancer subtype classification [68].

RNA-IP. RNA-IP (RNA-immunoprecipitation) is a new method developed to identify lncRNA that interacts with specific protein. Antibodies of the protein are first used to isolate lncRNA-protein complexes. Then, cDNA library is constructed followed by deep sequencing of interacting lncRNAs. Using RNA-IP, Zhao et al. discovered a 1.6-kb lncRNA within Xist that interacts with PRC2 [69].

Chromatin Signature-Based Approach. The above-mentioned methods target on RNA transcripts directly. In contrast, chromatin signature-based approach uses chromatin signatures, such as H3K4me3 (the marker of active promoters) and H3K36me3 (the marker of transcribed region), to study actively transcribed genes including lncRNAs. In this approach, ChIP-Seq is used to generate genome-wide profiles of chromatin signatures [70], and the transcribed regions are mapped in the genome, where lncRNAs are determined and studied. For example, Guttman et al. identified 1,600 large multiexonic lncRNAs that are regulated by key transcription factors such as p53 and NFkB [71]. The advantage of this approach is its directness in investigating the mechanisms that regulate lncRNA expression.

3.2. Computational Methods in Identifying lncRNA

ORF Length Strategy. Unlike protein-coding genes, the start codons and termination codons in lncRNAs tend to distribute randomly. As a result, the ORF length of lncRNAs can hardly extend to over 100 from a probabilistic point of view. Based on this principle, one way to discriminate lncRNAs from mRNAs is by ORF length. For example, the FANTOM project used a maximum ORF length cutoff of 100 codons to differentiate noncoding RNAs from mRNAs [72]. However, some lncRNAs are known to have ORFs longer than 100 codons, while some protein coding genes have fewer than 100 amino acids, such as RCI2A gene in *Arabidopsis* which encodes a protein of 54 amino acids

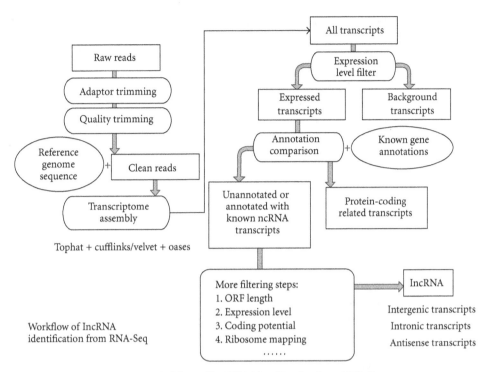

FIGURE 1: Workflow of lncRNA identification from RNA-Seq.

[73]. Thus, this approach may cause misclassification. To overcome the drawbacks of methods based on ORF length, Jia et al. utilize a comparative genomics method to refine ncRNA candidates. They defined the RNA sequences as ncRNAs only if the cDNAs have no homologous proteins longer than 30 amino acids across the mammalian genomes [7]. However, this method relies largely on the completeness of the databases. Therefore, deficiency in protein coding annotation may cause misclassification of lncRNAs as well.

Sequence and Secondary Structure Conservation Strategy. Compared to protein coding genes, noncoding genes are generally less conservative, meaning they are more inclined to mutate [21, 67]. Thus, measuring the coding potential is considered a way of identifying lncRNAs. Codon Substitution Frequency (CSF) is one of the criteria. For example, Guttman et al. used the maximum CSF score to assess the coding potential of a RNA sequence [71]. Clamp et al. and Lin et al. further combined CSF with reading frame conservation (RFC) to discriminate lncRNAs from mRNAs [74, 75]. Other similar methods include PhyloCSF use a phylogenetic framework to build two phylogenetic codon models that can distinguish coding from noncoding regions [76]. RNAcode combines amino acid substitution with gap patterns to assess the coding potential [77]. There are also methods that explore the conservation of RNA secondary structures to identify lncRNAs, including programs QRNA [78], RNAz [79], and EvoFOLD [80]. However, this approach is limited by lack of common conserved secondary structures specific for lncRNAs.

Machine Learning Strategies. Owing to the complex identities of lncRNAs, recently an increasing number of machine learning-based methods have been developed to integrate various sources of data to distinguish lncRNAs from mRNAs. Table 1 summarizes the machine learning methods and the features used to train the model for identifying lncRNAs. For instance, CONC utilizes a series of protein features such as amino acid composition, secondary structure, and peptide length, to train a SVM model that distinguishes lncRNAs from mRNAs [18]. CPC (Coding Potential Calculator) also uses SVM for modeling and extracting sequence features and the comparative genomics features to assess the coding potential of transcripts [19, 20]. Lu et al. developed a machine learning method that integrates GC content, DNA conservation, and expression information to predict lncRNAs in *C. elegans* [21].

Although the above-described methods have shown their effectiveness in identifying lncRNAs, exceptional cases still remain. For instance, whether an RNA transcript is translated or not may be changeable during the course of evolution. As an example, *Xist*, a well-known lncRNA, evolves from a protein-coding gene [81]. Besides, some genes are bifunctional, and both the coding and noncoding isoforms exist. The steroid receptor RNA activator (SRA) was characterized as a noncoding RNA previously but the coding product was detected later [82]. Such ambiguity will be clarified when more about lncRNAs are known.

4. lncRNA Function

lncRNAs have once been thought as the "dark matter" of the genome, because of our limited knowledge about their functions [83]. With more studies about lncRNAs conducted, it has become clear that lncRNAs have many specific functional features, and are likely to be involved in many diverse

TABLE 1: Machine-learning methods for identifying lncRNAs.

Method	Features	Algorithm	References
CONC	Peptide length	SVM	[18]
	Amino acid composition		
	Hydrophobicity		
	Secondary structure content		
	Percentage of residues exposed to solvent		
	Sequence compositional entropy		
	Number of homologs obtained by PSI-BLAST		
	Alignment entropy		
CPC	ORF prediction quality	SVM	[19, 20]
	Number of homologs obtained by BLASTX		
	Alignment quality		
	Segment distribution		
Lu et al.	RNA-seq experiments	Naïve Bayes Bayes Net Decision Tree Random Forest Logistic Regression SVM	[21]
	Tilling arrays		
	poly-A + RNA-seq experiments		
	poly-A + tilling arrays		
	GC content		
	DNA conservation		
	Predicted protein sequence conservation		
	Predicted secondary structure free energy		
	Predicted secondary structure conservation		

biological processes in cells. Rather than "dark matter," they may act as necessary functional parts in the genome. These functional features include but are not limited to (i) lncRNAs have conserved splice junctions and introns [84]; (ii) the expression patterns of lncRNAs are tissue- and cell-specific [12, 67]; (iii) the altered expression of lncRNAs can be found in neurodegeneration, cancer, and other diseases [9, 10]; (iv) lncRNAs are associated with particular chromatin signatures that are indicative of actively transcribed genes [11, 85]. Below, we will briefly summarize the cellular functions of lncRNAs and molecular mechanisms of their functions.

4.1. Cellular Functions of lncRNA. With thousands of lncR-NAs identified in mammals and other vertebrates [16], a few lncRNAs have been extensively studied, which have shed light on their possible functions. Firstly, lncRNAs are involved in various epigenetic regulations through recruitment of chromatin remodeling complexes to specific genomic loci, such as Xist, Air, and Kcnq1ot1 [22, 43]. Secondly, lncRNAs can regulate gene expression by interacting with protein partners in biological processes like protein synthesis, imprinting (Kcnq1ot1, Air), cell cycle control (TERRA), alternative splicing (MALAT1), and chromatin structure regulation (DNMT3b, PANDA) [9, 10, 38, 71, 85–89]. Thirdly, lncRNAs are involved in enhancer-regulating gene activation (eRNAs), in which cases they may interact directly with distal genomic

regions [90]. Fourthly, some lncRNAs serve as interacting partners or precursors for short regulatory ncRNAs [91]. For example, microRNAs (miRNAs) can be generated through sequential cleavage of lncRNAs, while Piwi-interacting RNAs (piRNAs) can be produced by processing a single lncRNA transcript [88].

Recent studies have shown the expression of lncRNA is tissue specific. Loewer et al. studied the expression of lncRNA in global remodeling of the epigenome and during repro-gramming of somatic cells to induce pluripotent stem cells (iPSCs). They found some lncRNAs have cell-type specific expression pattern [26, 92]. Loss-of-function studies on most intergenic lncRNAs expressed in mouse embryonic stem (ES) cells revealed that knockdown of intergenic lncRNAs has major consequences on gene expression patterns, which are comparable to the effects of knockdown of well-known ES cell regulators [93]. This indicated that lncRNAs might play important roles in regulating developmental process. The ENCODE project analyzed the tissue-specific expression of lncRNAs in 31 cell types, and found that many lncRNAs have brain-specific expression pattern [9, 12]. There are increasing lines of evidences that link dysregulations of lncRNAs to diverse human diseases ranging from neuron diseases to cancer [9, 10], suggesting that the involvement of lncRNAs in human diseases can be far more prevalent than previously thought [94].

4.2. Molecular Mechanisms of lncRNA. The precise mechanism of how lncRNAs function still remains largely unknown. Currently, there are several hypothesis about it, including (1) RNA:DNA:DNA triplex (*trans-*); (2) RNA:DNA hybrid; (3) RNA:RNA hybrid of lncRNA with a nascent transcript; (4) RNA-protein interaction (*cis-/trans-*). Although only (1), (2), and (4) have been experimentally demonstrated so far [14], it is generally thought that lncRNAs may function through the interaction with its partners, such as DNA, RNA, or protein, and serve the following roles: signal, decoy, scaffold, and guide [11, 14]. Table 2 lists lncRNAs that use different mechanisms when carrying out their functions. Below, we give examples for the above-mentioned mechanisms.

Signal. Some lncRNAs have been reported to respond to diverse stimuli, hinting they may act as molecular signals [12, 24, 25, 27, 35]. For example, lncRNAs can act as markers for imprinting (Air and Kcnq1ot1), X inactivation (Xist), and silencing (COOLAIR). ChIP-Seq studies showed that the gene-activating enhancers produce lncRNA transcripts (eRNAs) [29, 95], and their expression level positively correlates with that of nearby genes, indicating a possible role in regulating mRNA synthesis. This is supported by a recent Loss-of-Function study that found the knockdown of 7 out of 12 lncRNAs affects expression of their cognate neighboring genes [8].

Decoy. lncRNA can function as molecular decoy to negatively regulate an effector. Gas5 contains a hairpin sequence motif that resembles the DNA-binding site of the glucocorticoid receptor [31]. It can serve as a decoy to release the receptor from DNA to prevent transcription of metabolic genes [14]. Another example is the telomeric repeat-containing RNA (TERRA). It interacts with the telomerase protein through a repeat sequence complementary to the template sequence of telomerase RNA [11, 34].

Guide. Upon interaction with the target molecular, lncRNA may have the ability to guide it into the proper position either in *cis* (on neighboring genes) or in *trans* (on distantly located genes). The newly found eRNAs appear to exert their effects in *cis* by binding to specific enhancers and actively engaged in regulating mRNA synthesis [11, 29]. HOTAIR and HOTTIP are transcribed within the human *HOX* clusters, and serve as signals of anatomic positions by expressing in cells that have distal and posterior positional identities; they both require the interacting partners to be properly localized to the site of action [6]. In this process, chromosomal looping of the 5′ end of *HOXA* brings HOTTIP into the spatial proximity of multiple *HOXA* genes, enforcing the maintenance of H3K4me3 and gene activation [14]. This long-range gene activation mechanism suggests that chromosome looping plays a central role in delivering lncRNA to its site of action [11, 45].

Scaffold. Recent studies found that several lncRNAs have the capacity to bind more than two protein partners, where the lncRNAs serve as adaptors to form the functional protein complexes. The telomerase RNA TERC (TERRA) is a classic example of RNA scaffold, and is essential for telomerase function. *HOTAIR* binds the polycomb complex PRC2 to exert its "signal" function. A recent study found that the 3,700 nt of HOTAIR also interact with a second complex consisting of LSD1, CoREST, and REST to antagonize gene activation, further emphasizing its important role as the scaffold of the functional complex [11, 51].

Cis- and Trans-Action of lncRNAs. lncRNAs can be classified as *cis-* or *trans-*regulators depending on whether it exerts its function on a neighboring gene on the same allele from which it is transcribed [96]. It was considered that many lncRNAs act as *cis-*regulators, as the expression of lncRNA is significantly correlated with their neighboring protein-coding genes [97, 98]. However, recent studies have questioned that the positive correlation between lncRNAs and their neighboring genes may be due to shared upstream regulation (such as, lincRNA-*p21* [24] and lincRNA-*Sox2* [6]), positional correlation (such as, HOTAIR [6]), transcriptional "ripple effects" [98], and indirect regulation of neighboring genes, instead of the effects of *cis-*regulation. This was supported by the fact that knock down of different number of lncRNAs had little effect on the expression of neighboring genes [96]. In general, it has been accepted that some lncRNAs are *cis-*regulators [99, 100], while the vast majority may function as *trans-*regulators [6, 11, 93]. Recently, some *cis-*regulating lncRNAs were found to have the capacity to act in *trans* [33, 101, 102], highlighting the complexity of lncRNAs.

Although substantial research progresses have been made since the discovery of lncRNAs, it still remains a challenge to understand the functions of lncRNAs. One reason is, unlike protein-coding genes whose mutations may result in severely obvious phenotypes, mutations in lncRNAs often do not cause significant phenotypes [85]. It is likely that lncRNAs may function at specific stage of development process or under specific conditions, and thus condition-specific studies of lncRNAs' phenotypes may be necessary. With more omics data about lncRNAs accumulating, computational prediction of the function of lncRNAs can help to design experiments to accelerate the understanding of lncRNAs.

5. lncRNA Database

The current lncRNA databases are summarized in Table 3. lncRNAdb is an integrated database specific for lncRNAs, including annotation, sequence, structural, species, and function categories of lncRNAs [55]. NONCODE is a database about ncRNAs that have been experimentally confirmed. It covers almost all published 73,272 lncRNAs in human and mouse; it also includes expression profiles of lncRNAs and their potential functions predicted from Coding-Noncoding coexpression network (see below) [56]. LNCipedia is another integrated lncRNA database, which includes 21,488 annotated human lncRNAs. It contains lncRNAs information about the coding potential, secondary structure, and microRNA binding sites [57]. fRNAdb and NRED are databases for ncRNAs including lncRNAs [58, 59].

TABLE 2: Function classification of lncRNAs.

Archetype	lncRNA name	Length	Target	Function	cis-/trans-	References
Signal	KCNQ1ot1, Air, Xist	91 kb, 108 kb, ~17 kb	G9a, PRC, YY1	Transcriptional silencing of multiple genes; X inactivation (XCI)	cis-	[11, 14, 22, 23]
	HOTAIR, Frigidair, HOTTIP,	2.2 kb, N.A., 3.7 kb	LSD1-CoREST	Signals of anatomic position,	trans-	[6, 11, 14]
	lincRNA-p21, PANDA	3 kb; 1.5 kb	hnRNP-K	p53 targets in response to DNA damage	trans-	[14, 24, 25]
	lincRNA-RoR	2.6 kb	Oct4, Sox2, Nanog	Pluripotency-associated	N.A.[b]	[11, 26]
	COOLAIR, COLDAIR	Multiple spliced: 400 bp/750 bp; ~1.1 kb	FLC, PRC2	Combinatorial transcriptional regulation	N.A.	[27, 28]
Decoys	eRNA	Various sizes	MLL-WDR5, TFs[a]	Promotes mRNA synthesis	cis-	[29, 30]
	Gas5	~7 kb	Glucocorticoid receptor	Represses the glucocorticoid receptor	N.A.	[31]
	1/2-sbsRNAs	N.A.[c]	SMD	Formation of STAU1 binding sites	N.A.	[32]
	DHFR-Minor	7.3, 5.0, 1.4, and 0.8 kb	TFIIB	Inhibits assembly of the preinitiation complex	N.A.	[33]
	TERRA	Various sizes	Telomerase	Regulation and protection of chromosome ends	N.A.	[34]
	PANDA	1.5 kb	NF-YA	Inhibits expression of apoptotic genes	trans-	[35]
	PTENP1	~3.9 kb	PTEN	Sequestration of miRNAs	N.A.	[36, 37]
	MALAT1	~7 kb	SR splicing factors	Alters pattern of alternative splicing	N.A.	[38, 39]
Guides	Xist	~17 kb	PRC2, YY1	Inactives X chromosome	cis-	[14, 40–42]
	Air, COLDAIR	108 kb,	G9a, PRC2	Silences transcription, affects histone acetylation and methylation states	cis-	[28, 43, 44]
	HOTTIP	~3.8 kb	MLL-WDR5	Chromosomal looping, chromatin modifications	cis- (looping)	[11, 45]
	HOTAIR	2.2 kb	LSD1-CoREST	Alters and regulates epigenetic states	trans-	[14, 46, 47]
	Jpx	Multiple isoforms 3 kb	polycomb complex[a]	Activation of Xist RNA on the inactive X	trans-	[11, 48]
	lincRNA-p21		hnRNP-K[a]	p53 targets in response to DNA damage	trans-	[11, 24]
Scaffold	TERC	Various sizes	TERT	Telomerase catalytic activity	trans-	[49, 50]
	HOTAIR	2.2 kb	PRC2, LSD1, CoREST, REST	Demethylates histone H3 on K4 to antagonize gene activation	trans-	[46, 51]
	ANRIL	Multiple spliced: 3.9 kb/34.8 kb	PRC1, PRC2	Contributes to the functions of both PRC1 and PRC2 proteins	trans-	[52, 53]
	Alpha Satellite Repeat LncRNA	N.A.	SUMO-HP1	Molecular scaffold for the targeting and local accumulation of HP1	N.A.	[11, 54]

[a] Not yet understood.
[b] Not clearly referred as cis-action.
[c] No length data available in all six databases listed in Table 3.

Table 3: List of lncRNA databases.

Tools	Source	Description	Reference
lncRNAdb	http://www.lncrnadb.org/	Contain comprehensive list of lncRNAs in eukaryotes, and mRNAs with regulatory roles	[55]
NONCODE	http://noncode.org/	Integrative annotation of noncoding RNA (73,372 lncRNAs)	[56]
LNCipedia	http://www.lncipedia.org/	21 488 annotated human lncRNA transcripts with secondary structure information, protein coding potential, and microRNA binding sites	[57]
fRNAdb	http://www.ncrna.org/frnadb/	A large collection of noncoding transcripts including annotated/unannotated sequences from H-inv database, NONCODE, and RNAdb	[58]
NRED	http://jsm-research.imb.uq.edu.au/nred/cgi-bin/ncrnadb.pl/	Noncoding RNA Expression Database	[59]

The above databases provide great convenience for further analysis and applications of lncRNAs.

6. Function Prediction of lncRNA

Computational prediction of lncRNA functions is still at its early development stage. Unlike protein-coding genes whose sequence motifs are indicative of their function, lncRNA sequences are usually not conserved and do not contain conserved sequence motifs [103, 104]. The secondary structures of lncRNA are also not conserved [105]. Thus, it is difficult to infer the function of lncRNAs based on their sequences or secondary structures alone. Since current knowledge suggests that lncRNAs function by regulating or interacting with its partner molecular, current methods focus on exploring the relationships between lncRNAs and protein-coding genes or miRNAs. Below, we will describe several current approaches for predicting the functions of lncRNAs.

6.1. Comparative Genomics Approach. Although most lncRNAs are not conserved, there are lncRNAs that are conserved across species, indicating their essential functions. Amit et al. identified 78 lncRNAs transcripts conserved in both human and mouse, and found 70 are either located within or close (<1000 nt distance) to a coding gene that is also conserved in the two genomes [106]. They assumed these lncRNAs might have close functional relationships with the nearby coding genes. However, this approach is limited because of the poor conservation of lncRNAs and cannot be applied at genome scale.

6.2. Coexpression with Coding Genes Approach. Many studied lncRNAs play important regulatory roles, and it is likely that lncRNAs regulating a specific biological process may be coexpressed with the genes involved in the same process. Thus, identifying coding genes that are coexpressed with lncRNAs may help to infer the function of lncRNAs. Based on this assumption, Guttman et al. developed a coexpression based method to predict lncRNAs functions at genome scale [71]. For each lncRNA, they ranked coding genes based on their coexpression level with the lncRNAs, and then performed a Gene Set Enrichment Analysis (GSEA) for the top-ranked genes to identify enriched functional terms corresponding to the lncRNAs. Out of 150 lncRNAs subjected for experimental validation, 85 exhibited the predicted functions, proving the effectiveness of using the coexpressed coding genes to infer the function of lncRNAs from their coexpressed coding genes. According to their predictions, lncRNAs participate in a rather wide range of biological processes such as cell proliferation, development, and immune surveillance. Andrea et al. employed a similar approach to predict the function of lncRNAs during zebrafish embryogenesis [67].

Liao et al. furthered the coexpression idea by constructing a coding-noncoding (CNC) gene coexpression network [107]. In contrast to the GSEA method that collects coding genes coexpressed for each lncRNA, the CNC method considers not only the coexpression between lncRNAs and coding genes, but also within lncRNAs group and coding gene group. When predicting the function of lncRNAs, the CNC method employs two different approaches: the hub-based and the network-module-based. In the hub-based approach, functions are assigned to each lncRNA according to the functional enrichment of its neighboring genes. In the network-module-based approach, Markov cluster algorithm (MCL) is used to identify coexpressed functional module in the CNC network; then functions of the module are transferred to the lncRNAs inside the module. Liao et al. applied the CNC method to annotate the functions of 340 mouse lncRNAs, and found these lncRNAs function mainly in organ or tissue development, cellular transport, and metabolic processes.

6.3. Interaction with miRNAs and Proteins Approach. Recent analysis found that lncRNAs share a synergism with miRNA in the regulatory network [108, 109]. It is likely that some lncRNAs function by binding miRNA. Therefore, identifying well-established miRNAs that bind lncRNAs may help to infer the function of lncRNAs. Jeggari et al. developed an algorithm named miRcode that predicts putative microRNA binding sites in lncRNAs using criteria such as seed complementarity and evolutionary conservation [110]. Jalali et al. constructed a genome-wide network of validated RNA mediated interactions, and uncovered previously unknown mediatory roles of lncRNA between miRNA and mRNA (Saakshi Jalali, arXiv preprint). Besides the interaction with miRNA, the interaction of lncRNAs with proteins can also be explored to predict their functions. Bellucci et al. developed a method called "catRAPID" that correlates lncR-NAs with proteins by evaluating their interaction potential using physicochemical characteristics, including secondary structure, hydrogen bonding, van der Waals, and so forth [111]. However, unlike the coexpression based approach, the above two approaches were successful in only a number of lncRNAs, partly because the mechanism of how lncRNAs interact with miRNAs and proteins still remains unclear.

6.4. Challenges. Computational prediction of lncRNA functions is still at its primary stage. As the sequence and secondary structure of lncRNAs are generally not conserved, function prediction of lncRNAs mainly relies on their relationships with other moleculars, such as protein coding genes, miRNAs, and proteins. However, the molecular mechanism of how lncRNA function by interacting with other molecular remains largely unknown, making it difficult to develop computational methods to precisely predict the functions of lncRNAs. On the other hand, there are currently only a small number of lncRNAs whose functions are well understood, which makes it difficult to validate and optimize computational algorithms for predicting lncRNA functions. Finally, unlike protein-coding genes that have systematic functional annotation systems, there lacks an annotation system for lncRNA functions, making it difficult to evaluate computational algorithms for function prediction. Nevertheless, the success of predicting lncRNAs using the coexpression based approach has shown promises. With more functional genomics data about lncRNAs available in the near future, more powerful and accurate methods will be developed to help decipher the functions of lncRNAs.

7. Perspectives

It has been widely accepted that lncRNAs play important functional roles in cell, though the molecular mechanism of how lncRNAs function remains to be unraveled. In this paper, we have described several currently proposed models about the molecular mechanism of lncRNA functions. One commonality about these models is that lncRNAs function through the interaction with other molecular, including DNA, RNA, and proteins. Given the abundance of lncRNAs in genome, it is likely that the interaction between lncRNAs and other moleculars may be specific. This thus raises the possibility of developing novel methods to target certain lncRNA for gene-specific regulation. However, phenotypic studies of lncRNAs suggested that knockdown of many lncRNAs does not result in obvious phenotypes, making it difficult to understand their functions. Computational prediction of lncRNAs can provide hypothesis about the functions of lncRNAs, and help to design experiments to test them under specific conditions. Yet, it remains a significant challenge to develop effective methods to accurately infer the lncRNA functions, owing to the lack of detailed information about the molecular mechanisms of lncRNAs. In order

to develop powerful computational methods, more studies about the derivation of lncRNAs, the molecular mechanism of lncRNAs and tissue-specific, or development-specific expression about lncRNAs are necessary.

Acknowledgment

This work was supported by the National Natural Science Foundation of China (Grant no. 31071113).

References

[1] P. Carninci, T. Kasukawa, S. Katayama et al., "The transcriptional landscape of the mammalian genome," *Science*, vol. 309, pp. 1559–1563, 2005.

[2] E. Birney, J. A. Stamatoyannopoulos, A. Dutta et al., "Identification and analysis of functional elements in 1% of the human genome by the ENCODE pilot project," *Nature*, vol. 447, pp. 799–816, 2007.

[3] P. Kapranov, J. Cheng, S. Dike et al., "RNA maps reveal new RNA classes and a possible function for pervasive transcription," *Science*, vol. 316, no. 5830, pp. 1484–1488, 2007.

[4] J. E. Wilusz, S. M. Freier, and D. L. Spector, "3′ end processing of a long nuclear-retained noncoding RNA yields a tRNA-like cytoplasmic RNA," *Cell*, vol. 135, no. 5, pp. 919–932, 2008.

[5] A. C. Seila, J. M. Calabrese, S. S. Levine et al., "Divergent transcription from active promoters," *Science*, vol. 322, no. 5909, pp. 1849–1851, 2008.

[6] J. L. Rinn, M. Kertesz, J. K. Wang et al., "Functional demarcation of active and silent chromatin domains in human HOX loci by noncoding RNAs," *Cell*, vol. 129, no. 7, pp. 1311–1323, 2007.

[7] H. Jia, M. Osak, G. K. Bogu, L. W. Stanton, R. Johnson, and L. Lipovich, "Genome-wide computational identification and manual annotation of human long noncoding RNA genes," *RNA*, vol. 16, no. 8, pp. 1478–1487, 2010.

[8] U. A. Ørom, T. Derrien, M. Beringer et al., "Long noncoding RNAs with enhancer-like function in human cells," *Cell*, vol. 143, no. 1, pp. 46–58, 2010.

[9] I. A. Qureshi, J. S. Mattick, and M. F. Mehler, "Long noncoding RNAs in nervous system function and disease," *Brain Research*, vol. 1338, no. C, pp. 20–35, 2010.

[10] O. Wapinski and H. Y. Chang, "Long noncoding RNAs and human disease," *Trends in Cell Biology*, vol. 21, no. 6, pp. 354–361, 2011.

[11] K. C. Wang and H. Y. Chang, "Molecular mechanisms of long noncoding RNAs," *Molecular Cell*, vol. 43, pp. 904–914, 2011.

[12] T. Derrien, R. Johnson, G. Bussotti, A. Tanzer, S. Djebali et al., "The GENCODE v7 catalog of human long noncoding RNAs: analysis of their gene structure, evolution, and expression," *Genome Research*, vol. 22, pp. 1775–1789, 2012.

[13] M. E. Dinger, K. C. Pang, T. R. Mercer, and J. S. Mattick, "Differentiating protein-coding and noncoding RNA: challenges and ambiguities," *PLoS Computational Biology*, vol. 4, no. 11, Article ID e1000176, 2008.

[14] J. L. Rinn and H. Y. Chang, "Genome regulation by long noncoding RNAs," *Annual Review of Biochemistry*, vol. 81, pp. 145–166, 2012.

[15] C. P. Ponting, P. L. Oliver, and W. Reik, "Evolution and functions of long noncoding RNAs," *Cell*, vol. 136, no. 4, pp. 629–641, 2009.

[16] J.-W. Nam and D. P. Bartel, "Long noncoding RNAs in *C. elegans*," *Genome Research*, vol. 22, no. 12, pp. 2529–2540, 2012.

[17] M. C. Tsai, R. C. Spitale, and H. Y. Chang, "Long intergenic noncoding RNAs: new links in cancer progression," *Cancer Research*, vol. 71, no. 1, pp. 3–7, 2011.

[18] J. Liu, J. Gough, and B. Rost, "Distinguishing protein-coding from non-coding RNAs through support vector machines," *PLoS genetics*, vol. 2, no. 4, article no. e29, 2006.

[19] S. F. Altschul, T. L. Madden, A. A. Schäffer et al., "Gapped BLAST and PSI-BLAST: a new generation of protein database search programs," *Nucleic Acids Research*, vol. 25, no. 17, pp. 3389–3402, 1997.

[20] L. Kong, Y. Zhang, Z. Q. Ye et al., "CPC: assess the protein-coding potential of transcripts using sequence features and support vector machine," *Nucleic Acids Research*, vol. 35, pp. W345–W349, 2007.

[21] Z. J. Lu, K. Y. Yip, G. Wang et al., "Prediction and characterization of noncoding RNAs in *C. elegans* by integrating conservation, secondary structure, and high-throughput sequencing and array data," *Genome Research*, vol. 21, no. 5, pp. 276–285, 2011.

[22] R. R. Pandey, T. Mondal, F. Mohammad et al., "Kcnq1ot1 antisense noncoding RNA mediates lineage-specific transcriptional silencing through chromatin-level regulation," *Molecular Cell*, vol. 32, no. 2, pp. 232–246, 2008.

[23] F. Mohammad, T. Mondal, and C. Kanduri, "Epigenetics of imprinted long noncoding RNAs," *Epigenetics*, vol. 4, no. 5, pp. 277–286, 2009.

[24] M. Huarte, M. Guttman, D. Feldser et al., "A large intergenic noncoding RNA induced by p53 mediates global gene repression in the p53 response," *Cell*, vol. 142, no. 3, pp. 409–419, 2010.

[25] T. Hung, Y. Wang, M. F. Lin et al., "Extensive and coordinated transcription of noncoding RNAs within cell-cycle promoters," *Nature Genetics*, vol. 43, no. 7, pp. 621–629, 2011.

[26] S. Loewer, M. N. Cabili, M. Guttman et al., "Large intergenic non-coding RNA-RoR modulates reprogramming of human induced pluripotent stem cells," *Nature Genetics*, vol. 42, no. 12, pp. 1113–1117, 2010.

[27] S. Swiezewski, F. Liu, A. Magusin, and C. Dean, "Cold-induced silencing by long antisense transcripts of an *Arabidopsis* Polycomb target," *Nature*, vol. 462, no. 7274, pp. 799–802, 2009.

[28] J. B. Heo and S. Sung, "Vernalization-mediated epigenetic silencing by a long intronic noncoding RNA," *Science*, vol. 331, no. 6013, pp. 76–79, 2011.

[29] T. K. Kim, M. Hemberg, J. M. Gray et al., "Widespread transcription at neuronal activity-regulated enhancers," *Nature*, vol. 465, no. 7295, pp. 182–187, 2010.

[30] D. Wang, I. Garcia-Bassets, C. Benner et al., "Reprogramming transcription by distinct classes of enhancers functionally defined by eRNA," *Nature*, vol. 474, no. 7351, pp. 390–397, 2011.

[31] T. Kino, D. E. Hurt, T. Ichijo, N. Nader, and G. P. Chrousos, "Noncoding RNA Gas5 is a growth arrest- and starvation-associated repressor of the glucocorticoid receptor," *Science Signaling*, vol. 3, no. 107, article no. ra8, 2010.

[32] C. Gong and L. E. Maquat, "LncRNAs transactivate STAU1-mediated mRNA decay by duplexing with 39 UTRs via Alu eleme," *Nature*, vol. 470, no. 7333, pp. 284–288, 2011.

[33] I. Martianov, A. Ramadass, A. Serra Barros, N. Chow, and A. Akoulitchev, "Repression of the human dihydrofolate reductase gene by a non-coding interfering transcript," *Nature*, vol. 445, no. 7128, pp. 666–670, 2007.

[34] S. Redon, P. Reichenbach, and J. Lingner, "The non-coding RNA TERRA is a natural ligand and direct inhibitor of human telomerase," *Nucleic Acids Research*, vol. 38, no. 17, Article ID gkq296, pp. 5797–5806, 2010.

[35] T. Hung and H. Y. Chang, "Long noncoding RNA in genome regulation: prospects and mechanisms," *RNA Biology*, vol. 7, no. 5, pp. 582–585, 2010.

[36] L. Poliseno, L. Salmena, J. Zhang, B. Carver, W. J. Haveman, and P. P. Pandolfi, "A coding-independent function of gene and pseudogene mRNAs regulates tumour biology," *Nature*, vol. 465, no. 7301, pp. 1033–1038, 2010.

[37] M. S. Song, A. Carracedo, L. Salmena et al., "Nuclear PTEN regulates the APC-CDH1 tumor-suppressive complex in a phosphatase-independent manner," *Cell*, vol. 144, no. 2, pp. 187–199, 2011.

[38] V. Tripathi, J. D. Ellis, Z. Shen et al., "The nuclear-retained noncoding RNA MALAT1 regulates alternative splicing by modulating SR splicing factor phosphorylation," *Molecular Cell*, vol. 39, no. 6, pp. 925–938, 2010.

[39] D. Bernard, K. V. Prasanth, V. Tripathi et al., "A long nuclear-retained non-coding RNA regulates synaptogenesis by modulating gene expression," *EMBO Journal*, vol. 29, no. 18, pp. 3082–3093, 2010.

[40] K. Plath, S. Mlynarczyk-Evans, D. A. Nusinow, and B. Panning, "Xist RNA and the mechanism of X chromosome inactivation," *Annual Review of Genetics*, vol. 36, pp. 233–278, 2002.

[41] J. T. Lee, "The X as model for RNA's niche in epigenomic regulation," *Cold Spring Harbor Perspectives in Biology*, vol. 2, no. 9, Article ID a003749, 2010.

[42] B. K. Sun, A. M. Deaton, and J. T. Lee, "A transient heterochromatic state in Xist preempts X inactivation choice without RNA stabilization," *Molecular Cell*, vol. 21, no. 5, pp. 617–628, 2006.

[43] T. Nagano, J. A. Mitchell, L. A. Sanz et al., "The Air noncoding RNA epigenetically silences transcription by targeting G9a to chromatin," *Science*, vol. 322, no. 5908, pp. 1717–1720, 2008.

[44] J. Camblong, N. Iglesias, C. Fickentscher, G. Dieppois, and F. Stutz, "Antisense RNA stabilization induces transcriptional gene silencing via histone seacetylation in *S. cerevisiae*," *Cell*, vol. 131, no. 4, pp. 706–717, 2007.

[45] K. C. Wang, Y. W. Yang, B. Liu et al., "A long noncoding RNA maintains active chromatin to coordinate homeotic gene expression," *Nature*, vol. 472, no. 7341, pp. 120–126, 2011.

[46] A. M. Khalil, M. Guttman, M. Huarte et al., "Many human large intergenic noncoding RNAs associate with chromatin-modifying complexes and affect gene expression," *Proceedings of the National Academy of Sciences of the United States of America*, vol. 106, no. 28, pp. 11667–11672, 2009.

[47] J. Zhao, T. K. Ohsumi, J. T. Kung et al., "Genome-wide identification of polycomb-associated RNAs by RIP-seq," *Molecular Cell*, vol. 40, no. 6, pp. 939–953, 2010.

[48] D. Tian, S. Sun, and J. T. Lee, "The long noncoding RNA, Jpx, Is a molecular switch for X chromosome inactivation," *Cell*, vol. 143, no. 3, pp. 390–403, 2010.

[49] K. Collins, "Physiological assembly and activity of human telomerase complexes," *Mechanisms of Ageing and Development*, vol. 129, no. 1-2, pp. 91–98, 2008.

[50] D. C. Zappulla and T. R. Cech, "Yeast telomerase RNA: a flexible scaffold for protein subunits," *Proceedings of the National Academy of Sciences of the United States of America*, vol. 101, no. 27, pp. 10024–10029, 2004.

[51] M. C. Tsai, O. Manor, Y. Wan et al., "Long noncoding RNA as modular scaffold of histone modification complexes," *Science*, vol. 329, no. 5992, pp. 689–693, 2010.

[52] Y. Kotake, T. Nakagawa, K. Kitagawa et al., "Long non-coding RNA ANRIL is required for the PRC2 recruitment to and silencing of p15^{INK4B} tumor suppressor gene," *Oncogene*, vol. 30, no. 16, pp. 1956–1962, 2011.

[53] K. L. Yap, S. Li, A. M. Muñoz-Cabello et al., "Molecular interplay of the noncoding RNA *ANRIL* and methylated histone H3 lysine 27 by polycomb CBX7 in transcriptional silencing of *INK4a*," *Molecular Cell*, vol. 38, no. 5, pp. 662–674, 2010.

[54] C. Maison, D. Bailly, D. Roche et al., "SUMOylation promotes de novo targeting of HP1alpha to pericentric heterochromatin," *Nature Genetics*, vol. 43, no. 3, pp. 220–227, 2011.

[55] P. P. Amaral, M. B. Clark, D. K. Gascoigne, M. E. Dinger, and J. S. Mattick, "LncRNAdb: a reference database for long xoncoding RNAs," *Nucleic Acids Research*, vol. 39, no. 1, pp. D146–D151, 2011.

[56] D. Bu, K. Yu, S. Sun, C. Xie, G. Skogerbo et al., "NONCODE v3. 0: integrative annotation of long noncoding RNAs," *Nucleic Acids Research*, vol. 40, pp. D210–D215, 2012.

[57] P. J. Volders, K. Helsens, X. Wang, B. Menten, L. Martens et al., "LNCipedia: a database for annotated human lncRNA transcript sequences and structures," *Nucleic Acids Research*. In press.

[58] T. Kin, K. Yamada, G. Terai et al., "fRNAdb: a platform for mining/annotating functional RNA candidates from noncoding RNA sequences," *Nucleic Acids Research*, vol. 35, no. 1, pp. D145–D148, 2007.

[59] M. E. Dinger, K. C. Pang, T. R. Mercer, M. L. Crowe, S. M. Grimmond, and J. S. Mattick, "NRED: a database of long noncoding RNA expression," *Nucleic Acids Research*, vol. 37, no. 1, pp. D122–D126, 2009.

[60] S. K. Michelhaugh, L. Lipovich, J. Blythe, H. Jia, G. Kapatos, and M. J. Bannon, "Mining Affymetrix microarray data for long non-coding RNAs: altered expression in the nucleus accumbens of heroin abusers," *Journal of Neurochemistry*, vol. 116, no. 3, pp. 459–466, 2011.

[61] T. Babak, B. J. Blencowe, and T. R. Hughes, "A systematic search for new mammalian noncoding RNAs indicates little conserved intergenic transcription," *BMC Genomics*, vol. 6, article no. 14, 2005.

[62] E. A. Gibb, E. A. Vucic, K. S. Enfield, G. L. Stewart, K. M. Lonergan et al., "Human cancer long non-coding RNA transcriptomes," *PLoS One*, vol. 6, Article ID e25915, 2011.

[63] T. L. Lee, A. Xiao, and O. M. Rennert, "Identification of novel long noncoding RNA transcripts in male germ cells," *Methods in Molecular Biology*, vol. 825, pp. 105–114, 2012.

[64] M. Furuno, K. C. Pang, N. Ninomiya et al., "Clusters of internally primed transcripts reveal novel long noncoding RNAs," *PLoS Genetics*, vol. 2, no. 4, article no. e37, 2006.

[65] W. Huang, N. Long, and H. Khatib, "Genome-wide identification and initial characterization of bovine long non-coding RNAs from EST data," *Animal Genetics*, vol. 43, pp. 674–682, 2012.

[66] T. Li, S. Wang, R. Wu, X. Zhou, D. Zhu et al., "Identification of long non-protein coding RNAs in chicken skeletal muscle using next generation sequencing," *Genomics*, vol. 99, pp. 292–298, 2012.

[67] A. Pauli, E. Valen, M. F. Lin, M. Garber, N. L. Vastenhouw et al., "Systematic identification of long noncoding RNAs expressed during zebrafish embryogenesis," *Genome Research*, vol. 22, pp. 577–591, 2012.

[68] J. R. Prensner, M. K. Iyer, O. A. Balbin et al., "Transcriptome sequencing across a prostate cancer cohort identifies PCAT-1, an unannotated lincRNA implicated in disease progression," *Nature Biotechnology*, vol. 29, no. 8, pp. 742–749, 2011.

[69] J. Zhao, B. K. Sun, J. A. Erwin, J. J. Song, and J. T. Lee, "Polycomb proteins targeted by a short repeat RNA to the mouse X chromosome," *Science*, vol. 322, no. 5902, pp. 750–756, 2008.

[70] P. J. Park, "ChIP-seq: advantages and challenges of a maturing technology," *Nature Reviews Genetics*, vol. 10, no. 10, pp. 669–680, 2009.

[71] M. Guttman, I. Amit, M. Garber et al., "Chromatin signature reveals over a thousand highly conserved large non-coding RNAs in mammals," *Nature*, vol. 458, no. 7235, pp. 223–227, 2009.

[72] Y. Okazaki, M. Furuno, T. Kasukawa et al., "Analysis of the mouse transcriptome based on functional annotation of 60,770 full-length cDNAs," *Nature*, vol. 420, no. 6915, pp. 563–573, 2002.

[73] X. Yang, T. J. Tschaplinski, G. B. Hurst et al., "Discovery and annotation of small proteins using genomics, proteomics, and computational approaches," *Genome Research*, vol. 21, no. 4, pp. 634–641, 2011.

[74] M. F. Lin, J. W. Carlson, M. A. Crosby et al., "Revisiting the protein-coding gene catalog of *Drosophila melanogaster* using 12 fly genomes," *Genome Research*, vol. 17, no. 12, pp. 1823–1836, 2007.

[75] M. Clamp, B. Fry, M. Kamal et al., "Distinguishing protein-coding and noncoding genes in the human genome," *Proceedings of the National Academy of Sciences of the United States of America*, vol. 104, no. 49, pp. 19428–19433, 2007.

[76] M. F. Lin, I. Jungreis, and M. Kellis, "PhyloCSF: a comparative genomics method to distinguish protein coding and noncoding regions," *Bioinformatics*, vol. 27, no. 13, Article ID btr209, pp. i275–i282, 2011.

[77] S. Washietl, S. Findeiß, S. A. Müller et al., "RNAcode: robust discrimination of coding and noncoding regions in comparative sequence data," *RNA*, vol. 17, no. 4, pp. 578–594, 2011.

[78] E. Rivas and S. R. Eddy, "Noncoding RNA gene detection using comparative sequence analysis," *BMC Bioinformatics*, vol. 2, article no. 8, 2001.

[79] S. Washietl, I. L. Hofacker, and P. F. Stadler, "Fast and reliable prediction of noncoding RNAs," *Proceedings of the National Academy of Sciences of the United States of America*, vol. 102, no. 7, pp. 2454–2459, 2005.

[80] J. S. Pedersen, G. Bejerano, A. Siepel et al., "Identification and classification of conserved RNA secondary structures in the human genome," *PLoS Computational Biology*, vol. 2, no. 4, article no. e33, pp. 251–262, 2006.

[81] L. Duret, C. Chureau, S. Samain, J. Weissanbach, and P. Avner, "The Xist RNA gene evolved in eutherians by pseudogenization of a protein-coding gene," *Science*, vol. 312, no. 5780, pp. 1653–1655, 2006.

[82] S. Chooniedass-Kothari, E. Emberley, M. K. Hamedani et al., "The steroid receptor RNA activator is the first functional RNA encoding a protein," *FEBS Letters*, vol. 566, no. 1-3, pp. 43–47, 2004.

[83] E. D. Kim and S. Sung, "Long noncoding RNA: unveiling hidden layer of gene regulatory networks," *Trends in Plant Science*, vol. 17, pp. 16–21, 2012.

[84] M. Hiller, S. Findeiß, S. Lein et al., "Conserved introns reveal novel transcripts in *Drosophila melanogaster*," *Genome Research*, vol. 19, no. 7, pp. 1289–1300, 2009.

[85] J. S. Mattick, "The genetic signatures of noncoding RNAs," *PLoS Genetics*, vol. 5, no. 4, Article ID e1000459, 2009.

[86] E. Bernstein and C. D. Allis, "RNA meets chromatin," *Genes and Development*, vol. 19, no. 14, pp. 1635–1655, 2005.

[87] J. Whitehead, G. K. Pandey, and C. Kanduri, "Regulation of the mammalian epigenome by long noncoding RNAs," *Biochimica et Biophysica Acta*, vol. 1790, no. 9, pp. 936–947, 2009.

[88] J. E. Wilusz, H. Sunwoo, and D. L. Spector, "Long noncoding RNAs: functional surprises from the RNA world," *Genes and Development*, vol. 23, no. 13, pp. 1494–1504, 2009.

[89] M. Beltran, I. Puig, C. Peña et al., "A natural antisense transcript regulates Zeb2/Sip1 gene expression during Snail1-induced epithelial-mesenchymal transition," *Genes and Development*, vol. 22, no. 6, pp. 756–769, 2008.

[90] U. A. Ørom and R. Shiekhattar, "Noncoding RNAs and enhancers: complications of a long-distance relationship," *Trends in Genetics*, vol. 27, pp. 433–439, 2011.

[91] J. S. Mattick and I. V. Makunin, "Small regulatory RNAs in mammals," *Human Molecular Genetics*, vol. 14, no. 1, pp. R121–R132, 2005.

[92] T. Nagano and P. Fraser, "No-nonsense functions for long noncoding RNAs," *Cell*, vol. 145, no. 2, pp. 178–181, 2011.

[93] M. Guttman, J. Donaghey, B. W. Carey, M. Garber, J. K. Grenier et al., "lincRNAs act in the circuitry controlling pluripotency and differentiation," *Nature*, vol. 477, pp. 295–300, 2011.

[94] R. Johnson, "Long non-coding RNAs in Huntington's disease neurodegeneration," *Neurobiology of Disease*, vol. 46, pp. 245–254, 2012.

[95] F. De Santa, I. Barozzi, F. Mietton et al., "A large fraction of extragenic RNA Pol II transcription sites overlap enhancers," *PLoS Biology*, vol. 8, no. 5, Article ID e1000384, 2010.

[96] Z. H. Li and T. M. Rana, "Molecular mechanisms of RNA-triggered gene silencing machineries," *Accounts of Chemical Research*, vol. 45, pp. 1122–1131, 2012.

[97] J. Ponjavic, P. L. Oliver, G. Lunter, and C. P. Ponting, "Genomic and transcriptional co-localization of protein-coding and long non-coding RNA pairs in the developing brain," *PLoS Genetics*, vol. 5, no. 8, Article ID e1000617, 2009.

[98] M. Ebisuya, T. Yamamoto, M. Nakajima, and E. Nishida, "Ripples from neighbouring transcription," *Nature Cell Biology*, vol. 10, no. 9, pp. 1106–1113, 2008.

[99] C. J. Brown, A. Ballabio, J. L. Rupert et al., "A gene from the region of the human X inactivation centre is expressed exclusively from the inactive X chromosome," *Nature*, vol. 349, no. 6304, pp. 38–44, 1991.

[100] F. Sleutels, R. Zwart, and D. P. Barlow, "The non-coding Air RNA is required for silencing autosomal imprinted genes," *Nature*, vol. 415, no. 6873, pp. 810–813, 2002.

[101] J. T. Lee, "Lessons from X-chromosome inactivation: long ncRNA as guides and tethers to the epigenome," *Genes and Development*, vol. 23, no. 16, pp. 1831–1842, 2009.

[102] K. M. Schmitz, C. Mayer, A. Postepska, and I. Grummt, "Interaction of noncoding RNA with the rDNA promoter mediates recruitment of DNMT3b and silencing of rRNA genes," *Genes and Development*, vol. 24, no. 20, pp. 2264–2269, 2010.

[103] A. T. Willingham, A. P. Orth, S. Batalov et al., "Molecular biology: a strategy for probing the function of noncoding RNAs finds a repressor of NFAT," *Science*, vol. 309, no. 5740, pp. 1570–1573, 2005.

[104] T. R. Mercer, M. E. Dinger, and J. S. Mattick, "Long noncoding RNAs: insights into functions," *Nature Reviews Genetics*, vol. 10, no. 3, pp. 155–159, 2009.

[105] K. C. Pang, M. E. Dinger, T. R. Mercer et al., "Genome-wide identification of long noncoding RNAs in CD8+ T cells," *Journal of Immunology*, vol. 182, no. 12, pp. 7738–7748, 2009.

[106] A. N. Khachane and P. M. Harrison, "Mining mammalian transcript data for functional long non-coding RNAs," *PLoS One*, vol. 5, no. 4, Article ID e10316, 2010.

[107] Q. Liao, C. Liu, X. Yuan et al., "Large-scale prediction of long non-coding RNA functions in a coding-non-coding gene co-expression network," *Nucleic Acids Research*, vol. 39, no. 9, pp. 3864–3878, 2011.

[108] C. Braconi, T. Kogure, N. Valeri et al., "microRNA-29 can regulate expression of the long non-coding RNA gene MEG3 in hepatocellular cancer," *Oncogene*, vol. 30, pp. 4750–4756, 2011.

[109] M. S. Ebert and P. A. Sharp, "Emerging roles for natural microRNA sponges," *Current Biology*, vol. 20, no. 19, pp. R858–R861, 2010.

[110] A. Jeggari, D. S. Marks, and E. Larsson, "miRcode: a map of putative microRNA target sites in the long non-coding transcriptome," *Bioinformatics*, vol. 28, pp. 2062–2063, 2012.

[111] M. Bellucci, F. Agostini, M. Masin, and G. G. Tartaglia, "Predicting protein associations with long noncoding RNAs," *Nature Methods*, vol. 8, no. 6, pp. 444–445, 2011.

12

Mathematical Characterization of Protein Transmembrane Regions

Amrita Roy Choudhury,[1] Nikolay Zhukov,[2] and Marjana Novič[1]

[1] *Laboratory of Chemometrics, National Institute of Chemistry, Hajdrihova 19, 1001 Ljubljana, Slovenia*
[2] *Faculty of Mathematics, Informatics, and Mechanics, University of Warsaw, Banacha 2, 02-097 Warszawa, Poland*

Correspondence should be addressed to Marjana Novič; marjana.novic@ki.si

Academic Editors: Y. Cai and J. Wang

Graphical bioinformatics has paved a unique way of mathematical characterization of proteins and proteomic maps. The graphics representations and the corresponding mathematical descriptors have proved to be useful and have provided unique solutions to problems related to identification, comparisons, and analyses of protein sequences and proteomics maps. Based on sequence information alone, these descriptors are independent from physiochemical properties of amino acids and evolutionary information. In this work, we have presented invariants from amino acid adjacency matrix and decagonal isometries matrix as potential descriptors of protein sequences. Encoding protein sequences into amino acid adjacency matrix is already well established. We have shown its application in classification of transmembrane and nontransmembrane regions of membrane protein sequences. We have introduced the dodecagonal isometries matrix, which is a novel method of encoding protein sequences based on decagonal isometries group.

1. Introduction

With the advent of modern and faster experimental technologies, a large amount of sequences and proteomics data are produced every day. Combined with the genomic data, this forms a vast and ever-growing repository of information. However, to utilize this data in order to get an insightful knowledge of the biological systems and develop better pharmaceutical facilities, one needs to perform a detailed analysis of the data generated. The new age computational methods provide fast, accurate, precise analysis of the genomics and proteomics data. Therefore, there is a need to characterize biological sequences and data in mathematical formats that can be easily manipulated using the computational methods.

Mathematical graphs and matrices have been successfully utilized in representing, characterizing, and analyzing biological sequences. Even though the graphical representation of DNA was initiated around 25 years ago, graphical methods to represent protein sequences and proteomics maps emerged only recently [1, 2]. The delay is owed to the increase in complexity and associated arbitrariness in assigning and representing the 20 natural amino acids, which can be done in 20 factorial ways. The initial methods proposed to graphically represent the protein sequences are Magic Circle [3] and Starlike graphs [4]. Both representations are associated with no loss of information and offer novel local alignment methods using Euclidean distances between corresponding amino acids in the graphical representation. To characterize protein sequences numerically, structural matrices like D/D matrix and Line Distance matrix are developed from 2D graphs of proteins [3]. Invariants of such matrices, for example, eigenvalues, matrix diagonals, row sums, and so forth, further serve as numerical representation of the proteins.

Amino acid adjacency matrix (AA matrix) [5] is a matrix representation of protein sequences leading to mathematical characterizations. The protein sequence, in this case, is directly translated into the matrix form without the intermediate graphical representation. To represent a protein sequence mathematically, any invariant of its amino acid adjacency matrix can be used. Here, we have considered the row sum invariant of the amino acid adjacency matrix to numerically characterize protein sequences.

We have also introduced the encoding of transmembrane regions from the perspective of decagonal isometries group (D_{10}) into decagonal isometries matrix (DIM). The DIM is then transformed into 20-dimensional vector, which is then used to represent and numerically characterize the protein sequences.

It is important that the code of amino acid sequence is of uniform dimension, regardless of the length of the protein segment. We have adopted this criterion for both representations applied in transmembrane segments classification study. The amino acid sequence was the only information source for AA matrix and DIM representations developed or applied in this work. Conversely, other features associated with amino acids and proteins are often used in protein structure-property studies, such as secondary structure propensity, hydrophobicity, polarizability, solvent accessibility, normalized van der Waals volume, and polarity enrichment scores in case of the analysis and prediction of the metabolic stability of proteins [6]. The criterion of uniform dimensionality has been followed also in the study of single amino acid polymorphisms (SAPs), which is accounted for the majority of human inherited diseases. Each SAP is represented by 472 features including sequential, structural, and network features, the latter being the most influential [7]. However, in our study we have shown that the protein sequence alone if encoded into a suitable uniform representation vector enables us to build a successful classification model that separates transmembrane regions of a protein from nontransmembrane ones.

Transmembrane proteins pass through the complete biological membrane and perform vital functions to maintain the normal cell physiology. They are also very important as drug targets. These proteins are therefore of immense interest from both the academic and pharmaceutical point of views [8]. Despite the importance and interest, the vast majority of the transmembrane protein space remains unexplored due to experimental difficulties. Not all the transmembrane proteins, hypothesized to be present, are yet reported and sequenced. Only few of the known transmembrane proteins have their structures resolved to atomic details. In this work, we have focused on representing the transmembrane protein sequences numerically in order to develop novel transmembrane protein sequence analysis methods. Both the amino acid adjacency matrix and decagonal isometries matrix, explained in this work, are applied towards characterizing protein transmembrane regions and distinguishing them from the nontransmembrane regions.

2. Materials and Methods

2.1. Amino Acid Adjacency Matrix. The amino acid adjacency matrix (AA matrix) is a nonsymmetric matrix that presents the adjacency information of the 20 natural amino acids in the given protein sequence [5]. It is a 20 × 20 matrix with the rows and columns labeled with the 20 amino acids (Figure 1). Each position in the matrix represents the number of times the corresponding amino acids are adjacent in the given sequence; that is, value of matrix element (i, j) depends on the

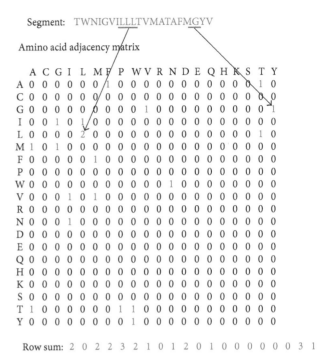

Segment: TWNIGVILLLTVMATAFMGYV

Amino acid adjacency matrix

	A	C	G	I	L	M	F	P	W	V	R	N	D	E	Q	H	K	S	T	Y
A	0	0	0	0	0	0	1	0	0	0	0	0	0	0	0	0	0	0	1	0
C	0	0	0	0	0	0	0	0	0	0	0	0	0	0	0	0	0	0	0	0
G	0	0	0	0	0	0	0	0	0	1	0	0	0	0	0	0	0	0	0	1
I	0	0	1	0	1	0	0	0	0	0	0	0	0	0	0	0	0	0	0	0
L	0	0	0	0	2	0	0	0	0	0	0	0	0	0	0	0	0	0	1	0
M	1	0	1	0	0	0	0	0	0	0	0	0	0	0	0	0	0	0	0	0
F	0	0	0	0	0	1	0	0	0	0	0	0	0	0	0	0	0	0	0	0
P	0	0	0	0	0	0	0	0	0	0	0	0	0	0	0	0	0	0	0	0
W	0	0	0	0	0	0	0	0	0	0	1	0	0	0	0	0	0	0	0	0
V	0	0	0	1	0	1	0	0	0	0	0	0	0	0	0	0	0	0	0	0
R	0	0	0	0	0	0	0	0	0	0	0	0	0	0	0	0	0	0	0	0
N	0	0	0	1	0	0	0	0	0	0	0	0	0	0	0	0	0	0	0	0
D	0	0	0	0	0	0	0	0	0	0	0	0	0	0	0	0	0	0	0	0
E	0	0	0	0	0	0	0	0	0	0	0	0	0	0	0	0	0	0	0	0
Q	0	0	0	0	0	0	0	0	0	0	0	0	0	0	0	0	0	0	0	0
H	0	0	0	0	0	0	0	0	0	0	0	0	0	0	0	0	0	0	0	0
K	0	0	0	0	0	0	0	0	0	0	0	0	0	0	0	0	0	0	0	0
S	0	0	0	0	0	0	0	0	0	0	0	0	0	0	0	0	0	0	0	0
T	1	0	0	0	0	0	0	1	1	0	0	0	0	0	0	0	0	0	0	0
Y	0	0	0	0	0	0	0	0	1	0	0	0	0	0	0	0	0	0	0	0

Row sum: 2 0 2 2 3 2 1 0 1 2 0 1 0 0 0 0 0 0 3 1

FIGURE 1: Amino acid adjacency matrix. The 20 × 20 matrix presenting the amino acid adjacency and abundance information in the given sequence. The nonzero elements show the number of times that corresponding amino acids are present adjacent to each other. The 20-dimensional row sum vector is used as a descriptor to numerically characterize the protein sequence.

number of times amino acid in row i is followed by amino acid in column j in the given sequence. For example, in Figure 1, amino acids G and Y are adjacent to each other only once, and hence the value of element (G, Y) is 1. Similarly the value of (L, L) is 2 as L occurs as its own first neighbor twice. The 400 matrix elements thus record the adjacencies of amino acids and their abundance in a given protein sequence.

As the matrix invariants do not depend on the labeling of the matrix, an arbitrary ordering of the amino acids is sufficient when one is interested in bringing out the characteristic features of a given sequence and in differentiating between sequences. In our work, we arbitrarily choose the amino acid to be in the following order: A, C, G, I, L, M, F, P, W, V, R, N, D, E, Q, H, K, S, T, Y.

It must be noted that the amino acid adjacency matrix is essentially different from both the GRANTHAM matrix [9] and the neighbor-dependent amino acid propensity [10]. The GRANTHAM matrix predicts the effect of amino acid substitution based on chemical properties. In our case, the matrix is independent of amino acid properties and does not reflect substitution effects. The matrix records the adjacency and not the propensity of the amino acid to be present at a particular structural location. In this study, we have considered only the first neighbor of a particular amino acid position. We have implemented the AA matrix representation of the transmembrane segments of membrane proteins in building transmembrane region prediction model. It must be noted that the transmembrane segments are around

20 residues in length. The short segments therefore result in sparse AA matrices. The matrix elements with zero values denote the absence of the corresponding amino acid pairs in the sequence. If a particular amino acid is not present in the given sequence, the corresponding row and column have all entries zero. In the given example (Figure 1), the amino acids C, P, R, D, E, Q, H, K, S are not present. One must also note that the last residue of the sequence is not shown in the adjacency matrix, as it has no adjacent residue to its right.

The important aspect of using matrix presentation of amino acid adjacencies is that it enables a concise numerical characterization of a protein segment by matrix invariants. The simplest characterization of protein can be presented as a 20-dimensional row sum vector that lists the abundance of the 20 amino acids except for the last residue of the protein segment, as explained in the previous paragraph.

2.2. Decagonal Isometries Matrix. This novel method introduces encoding of amino acid sequences from the perspective of the decagonal isometries group (D_{10}). The D_{10} has 20 elements—10 rotations O_n (by $n\pi/5$ degrees) and 10 symmetries S_n. A one-to-one correspondence can therefore be established between the elements of the group and the 20 amino acids. Our first step is arbitrarily assigning each element of D_{10} to an amino acid. Figure 2(a) presents the assignment of the amino acids to the elements of D_{10}. Next, we identify an arbitrary edge of a decagon with the number 0 and subsequently put numbers 1 to 9 on consecutive edges.

Before we start coding our protein sequence, the initial position of the decagon is set such that the edge labeled 0 is at the bottom. The sequence is then inductively encoded by applying the transformations indicated by the group elements that correspond to consecutive amino acids in the sequence (Figure 2(c)). At each step, we look at the edge n that lies at the bottom of the decagon. For example, encoding WW $\rightarrow$ WWN requires the S_1 symmetry transformation bringing the edge 5 of the decagon at the bottom (Figure 2(c)). The exact formulas of the said transformations are as follows:

$$O_n(X) = (X + n) \mod 10, \quad \text{for } n\text{th rotation},$$

$$S_n(X) = (10 + n - X) \mod 10, \quad \text{for } n\text{th symmetry}.$$
$$\text{(1)}$$

In theory, the number of times each edge lies at the bottom can be represented in a 10-dimensional vector to characterize the protein sequence. However, it would result in overcondensation of data. In order to reduce the loss of information, instead of considering just the bottom edge, at each step we also consider the edge to the right of the obtained bottom edge. A 10×10 decagonal isometries matrix (DIM) is thus constructed with the value $a_{i,j}$ being the number of times that "i"-edge appears at the bottom of the decagon with "j"-edge at its right while applying transformations to the decagon considering a given sequence. Notice that DIM can have nonzero values only right above or right below the diagonal (with the exception of $a_{9,0}$ and $a_{0,9}$ entries). This allows us to transform DIM into 20-dimensional vector by putting all potentially non-zero values in a fixed order.

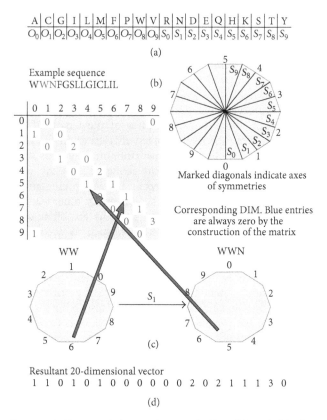

FIGURE 2: Decagonal isometries matrix D_{10}. (a) and (b) show correspondance between group elements and amino acids and indicate the initial step of coding. Decagons below show the explicit transformation for the given step (WW $\rightarrow$ WWN) and the resultant DIM (c). The 20-dimensional vector constructed from the matrix is used as a descriptor to numerically characterize the protein sequence (d).

The 20-dimensional vector finally acts as descriptors for the transmembrane protein segments encoded.

2.3. Representing Transmembrane Regions. The amino acid adjacency matrix and decagonal isometries matrix are used independently to encode the transmembrane and nontransmembrane protein segments. The associated matrix invariants mathematically characterize each of the membrane protein segments. Both representations are implemented independently and are used to distinguish between the transmembrane and non-transmembrane segments of membrane spanning proteins.

For this purpose, the transmembrane protein sequences are segmented into the transmembrane and non-transmembrane regions. The non-transmembrane regions are further divided into polypeptide segments of length 20 residues. It is essential to have the length of the non-transmembrane similar to that of the transmembrane segments in order to ensure better training of the classification models. All the transmembrane and non-transmembrane regions are then independently encoded using AA matrix and DIM. The encoded segments are divided into training and test sets. Table 1 lists the number of particular segments in each set.

TABLE 1: Training and test sets.

| Sets | Number of segments | | |
	Total segments	Transmembrane	Nontransmembrane
Training	4204	1867	2337
Test	450	200	250

We perform principal component analysis (PCA) with the descriptors derived from AA matrix to check if the numerical descriptors are able to discriminate the transmembrane segments from the non-transmembrane ones. As PCA is projection of multidimensional data onto a coordinate system defined by the principal components, it gives an initial validation regarding choice of descriptors. Next, two independent counter propagation neural network (CPNN) models are developed using the invariants from both the matrices to distinguish between the transmembrane and non-transmembrane segments of the protein sequences.

3. Results and Discussion

3.1. Amino Acid Adjacency Matrix. To check if the row sum vector derived from the AA matrix well characterizes the transmembrane segments numerically, we perform the principal component analysis (PCA) and develop a CPNN model.

Figure 3 shows the results from PCA analysis, where the transmembrane and non-transmembrane data are projected on 2D space defined by their first two principal components. PC1 contains 56.05% of the total variance, whereas PC2 contains 5.52% of the remaining variance. In total, the first two principal components contain 61.57% of the total variance present in the data. As we can see, the transmembrane and non-transmembrane segments, represented by the black and blue circles, respectively, are well separated over the first and second principal components. The region of overlap between the two clusters is very small with an overall distinction between the two groups. The PCA analysis is performed as a preliminary test. We have validated that the mathematical descriptors chosen are important to bring out the characteristic features of the protein segments. The descriptors are able to represent and distinguish the sequence characteristics of the two types of protein segments and group them successfully.

Next, we have developed a CPNN model to classify the protein segments as transmembrane or non-transmembrane ones. The model is optimized for both the training and the test sets simultaneously varying different network parameters. The goal is to obtain the optimal network parameters that minimize misclassification. In the final step, the optimized network is tested for its recall and prediction ability.

The following network parameters are found to be optimal: network size—40 × 40, number of epochs—500, and maximum correction factor—0.9. Figure 4 shows the top map of the optimized network with the transmembrane and non-transmembrane segments in two distinct clusters. The network shows only 4.33% error in recall ability; that is, it is able to correctly classify 95.67% of the segments in the

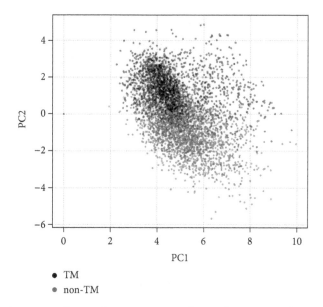

• TM
• non-TM

FIGURE 3: Principal component analysis. The transmembrane (black) and nontransmembrane (blue) segments form two different clusters.

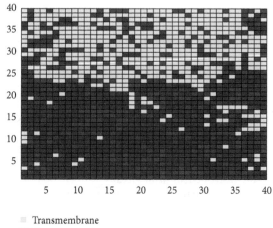

▫ Transmembrane
■ Nontransmembrane
■ Empty

FIGURE 4: Top map of the optimized network. The transmembrane (green) and nontransmembrane (brown) segments form two different clusters. Empty neurons are dark blue.

training set. For the test set, the error is 8.67%. Table 2 presents the detailed results of CPNN network.

3.2. Decagonal Isometries Matrix. The 20-dimensional vectors, derived from the decagonal isometries matrix, represent the transmembrane and non-transmembrane segments. The mathematically encoded protein segments in the training and test sets are then used to train and optimize a CPNN network. The goal is to optimize the network such that it is able to classify the two different types of protein segments based on the DIM invariant.

TABLE 2: Classification model using amino acid adjacency matrix.

Sets	Network results		
	Total segments	Segments correctly classified	% error
Training	4204	4022	4.33
Test	450	411	8.67

TABLE 3: Classification model using decagonal isometries matrix.

Sets	Network results	
	Correlation coefficient ($r * r$)	% error
Training	0.61	14.3
Test	0.255	27.1

The optimized network has the following configuration: network size—40 × 40, number of epochs—500, and maximum correction factor—0.5. The network shows 14.3% error in recall ability and 27.1% error in prediction ability, with error threshold at 0.501. The detailed results are given in Table 3.

3.3. Advantage of Mathematical Characterization. Analyzing the protein sequence is the first step towards determining its structure and function. With the growing number of proteins sequenced, there is a necessity of novel techniques to characterize the sequences. Presently, most commonly used protein sequence descriptors are based on evolutionary information and physiochemical properties. Even though these methods have proved to be efficient in most cases, in certain special cases like that of transmembrane proteins, they may fall short. As the vast field of transmembrane proteins largely remains unexplored with many transmembrane proteins yet to be sequenced, it is possible to obtain new protein sequences without any known homologs. In such case, traditional sequence analysis methods based on alignment profiles would not be sufficient to analyze the novel sequences. The evolutionary information-based descriptors are therefore inadequate. As several indices of the same physiochemical property exist, such descriptors can cause ambiguity. Therefore, there is a need of developing novel methods based on sequence information alone to represent protein sequences.

The two matrix representations, amino acid adjacency matrix and decagonal isometries matrix, of the protein segments are derived from the sequence information. The physiochemical properties of the amino acids and the evolutionary information of the sequence based on alignment profiles are not utilized for characterizing. Moreover, the matrices are labeled with the amino acids arbitrarily. The mathematical descriptors are dependent on the sequence information alone and successfully reveal underlying characteristics and patterns of a given sequence. Such descriptors are useful in representing novel sequences independently. Their numerical nature also makes them easier to be incorporated into a mathematical model. In addition, one can derive different invariants to be used as descriptors from the same

matrix representations depending on the problem to be addressed.

4. Conclusion

In this work, we have successfully used mathematical descriptors to characterize transmembrane regions of proteins. Amino acid adjacency matrix and decagonal isometries matrix are independently used to encode the protein segments. Both the representations are successful in revealing the sequence characteristics particular to a specific group of protein segments and in classifying them accordingly as transmembrane and non-transmembrane. The accuracy of the former method was better, which challenges the potential optimization and further development of the latter one. Depending only on the sequence information, the mathematical representations described here can prove to be powerful tool in developing novel sequence analysis methods, especially for less explored protein classes like transmembrane proteins.

Acknowledgment

This work is supported by the Ministry of Higher Education, Science and Technology of the Republic of Slovenia (P1-017 and J1-2151).

References

[1] M. Randić, "2-D graphical representation of proteins based on virtual genetic code," *SAR and QSAR in Environmental Research*, vol. 15, no. 3, pp. 147–157, 2004.

[2] M. Randić, J. Zupan, A. T. Balaban, D. Vikić-Topić, and D. Plavšić, "Graphical representation of proteins," *Chemical Reviews*, vol. 111, no. 2, pp. 790–862, 2011.

[3] M. Randić, D. Butina, and J. Zupan, "Novel 2-D graphical representation of proteins," *Chemical Physics Letters*, vol. 419, no. 4-6, pp. 528–532, 2006.

[4] M. Randić, J. Zupan, and D. Vikić-Topić, "On representations of proteins by star-like graph," *Journal of Molecular Graphics and Modelling*, vol. 26, pp. 290–305, 2007.

[5] M. Randić, M. Novič, and M. Vračko, "On novel representation of proteins based on amino acid adjacency matrix," *SAR and QSAR in Environmental Research*, vol. 19, no. 3-4, pp. 339–349, 2008.

[6] T. Huang, X. H. Shi, P. Wang et al., "Analysis and prediction of the metabolic stability of proteins based on their sequential features, subcellular locations and interaction networks," *PLoS ONE*, vol. 5, no. 6, Article ID e10972, 2010.

[7] T. Huang, P. Wang, Z. Ye et al., "Prediction of deleterious non-synonymous SNPs based on protein interaction network and hybrid properties," *PLoS ONE*, vol. 5, no. 7, Article ID e11900, 2010.

[8] A. Elofsson and G. von Heijne, "Membrane protein structure: prediction versus reality," *Annual Review of Biochemistry*, vol. 76, pp. 125–140, 2007.

[9] R. Grantham, "Amino acid difference formula to help explain protein evolution," *Science*, vol. 185, no. 4154, pp. 862–864, 1974.

[10] J. Wang and J. A. Feng, "Exploring the sequence patterns in the α-helices of proteins," *Protein Engineering*, vol. 16, no. 11, pp. 799–807, 2003.

13

Computational Elucidation of Structural Basis for Ligand Binding with *Leishmania donovani* Adenosine Kinase

Rajiv K. Kar,[1,2] **Md. Yousuf Ansari,**[1,2] **Priyanka Suryadevara,**[1,2] **Bikash R. Sahoo,**[1] **Ganesh C. Sahoo,**[1] **Manas R. Dikhit,**[1] **and Pradeep Das**[1,2]

[1] *Biomedical Informatics Centre, Rajendra Memorial Research Institute of Medical Science, Patna 800007, India*
[2] *Department of Pharmacoinformatics, National Institute of Pharmaceutical Education and Research (NIPER), Hajipur 844102, India*

Correspondence should be addressed to Manas R. Dikhit; mrdikhit@icmr.org.in

Academic Editor: Ali Ouaissi

Enzyme adenosine kinase is responsible for phosphorylation of adenosine to AMP and is crucial for parasites which are purine auxotrophs. The present study describes development of robust homology model of *Leishmania donovani* adenosine kinase to forecast interaction phenomenon with inhibitory molecules using structure-based drug designing strategy. Docking calculation using reported organic small molecules and natural products revealed key active site residues such as Arg131 and Asp16 for ligand binding, which is consistent with previous studies. Molecular dynamics simulation of ligand protein complex revealed the importance of hydrogen bonding with active site residues and solvent molecules, which may be crucial for successful development of drug candidates. Precise role of Phe168 residue in the active site was elucidated in this report that provided stability to ligand-protein complex via aromatic-π contacts. Overall, the present study is believed to provide valuable information to design a new compound with improved activity for antileishmanial therapeutics development.

1. Introduction

Leishmaniasis is a group of vector-borne diseases caused by obligate intramacrophage protozoan parasite of genus *Leishmania*. The global estimates for incidence and prevalence of leishmaniasis cases per year are about 0.5 and 2.5 million, respectively [1]. In India, visceral leishmaniasis (VL) has been reported in parts of West Bengal, Uttar Pradesh, and Bihar. It poses as a major health problem in the state of Bihar, accounting for almost 200,000 deaths occurring solely due to visceral leishmaniasis, which is nearly 90% of the total cases in India (reported since 1977) [2]. Despite the rise in toll for mortality and the deteriorated health conditions, there is no effective treatment available for the cure of this disease. The primary measure for control of leishmaniasis is early diagnosis and its accurate treatment [3]. The available marketed drugs contain many adverse effects and are effective in form of combination chemotherapy only [4]. Thus, it is one of the prime urgency to have an effective and promising therapeutics for this neglected tropical disease [5].

Adenosine kinase (ATP: adenosine $5'$-phosphotransferase, EC 2.7.1.20), an enzyme of purine salvage pathway catalyzing the transfer of terminal phosphate from ATP to adenosine, has been shown to possess broad substrate specificity [6]. *Leishmania donovani* lacks the ability to synthesize purines *de novo* and thus is well known to be purine auxotroph [7, 8]. Reports from different authors have revealed the importance of this enzyme in most eukaryotic cells and especially in the purine-auxotrophic parasitic protozoa. Looker and coworkers have reported that the activity profile got provoked almost 50-fold during the transformation of promastigote to amastigote, thereby indicating that adenosine kinase is one of the crucial enzyme targets important for parasite survival [9]. In the year 1987 Datta et al. have reported the isolation and characterization of enzyme in *L. donovani* owing to the importance in parasitology study [10]. Understanding the mechanism of action for this enzyme from *L. donovani* thus can be advantageous in a hope that it may provide relevant information necessary towards designing a novel and specific inhibitor as a therapeutic for leishmaniasis.

Adenosine analogs have advantages for development into antitrypanosomal drugs as reported in a recent study, as many of them, including Ara-A and cordycepin, experimentally proved to pass the blood-brain barrier that is a prerequisite to treat late stage African sleeping sickness [11]. Thus it gives an idea that adenosine analogues can be promising candidates for antitrypanosomal drugs and can be tested against similar targets in other protozoan parasites. A study by Vodnala et al., investigating the trypanosomal adenosine salvage activity by its functional expression in yeast, report a convenient means of testing adenosine antimetabolites for their import and activation [12]. The unique catalytic characteristics of *L. donovani* adenosine kinase (*Ld*Adk) and its stage-specific differential activity pattern have made this enzyme a prospective target for chemotherapeutic manipulation in the purine-auxotrophic parasitic protozoan such as *L. donovani* [13]. Our approach in this study is to find interaction basis of agents that can inhibit *Ld*Adk by *in silico* methods.

The present work aimed at elucidating *Ld*Adk inhibitors by means of computer-aided drug designing, which can guide the rational synthesis of novel inhibitors and may be helpful for developing newer therapeutics. In this report we have prepared a molecular dataset using the reported adenosine kinase (Adk) inhibitors [14–18] and natural products from Nigerian medicinal plants [17]. Since the crystal structure of *Ld*Adk is not reported till date, we proceed with homology modeling. Molecular dynamics (MD) simulation is a well-known technique which has been used here to derive the optimum flexibility of modeled protein structure—*Ld*Adk in solvent medium. Docking calculation has been performed in order to predict inhibitors for *Ld*Adk using different algorithms which is further being validated using MD simulation.

2. Methods

2.1. Homology Modeling. Full-length amino acid sequence of *Ld*Adk (accession number: O96439) was retrieved from Universal Protein Resource database (http://www.uniprot.org/) with a predicted molecular mass of 37.14 kDa. The primary amino acid sequence was used to search for a suitable template in Protein Data Bank (PDB) to generate 3D coordinates of *Ld*Adk. NCBI *BLASTp* search was performed against nonredundant database (PDB) with default parameter values [19]. Among the retrieved structural hits, adenosine kinase of *Trypanosoma brucei* (*Tb*Adk) (PDB ID: 3OTX) [20] was found to be the best hit based on maximum sequence identity (53%) and was considered as template for homology modeling. Selectivity of the proposed template in BLAST search was also cross-checked using SWISS-MODEL, RaptorX, CPH-models *v3.0*, and HHpred [21–24]. Initially ten homology models were generated using Modeller *v9.0* [23] and one model was generated using SWISS-MODEL web server [19]. The generated models were checked using Discovery Studio *v2.5* from which four models were selected with lowest DOPE score [25]. The models were confirmed using the Verify3D profile analysis method [26]. Stereochemical properties of the models were investigated in Ramachandran plot using PROCHECK analysis [27]. Homology model with maximum number of residues in the favored regions and additional

allowed regions in Ramachandran plot was selected for further investigations. The selected model was then refined by loop modeling and side chain refinement to increase the Profile3D score and to make the model reliable [28].

2.2. Structure Validation. Structural validation after each loop refinement step was done using ERRAT plot which gives a measure of the structural error for each residue in the protein [29]. The process was iterated until most of the amino acid residues were below 95% cutoff value in ERRAT plot. The refined model was further validated by Verify-3D [28]. ProSA was used to evaluate the generated 3D structure model of protein for potential errors [30]. The root mean square deviations (RMSD) between the main chain atoms of the models and templates were calculated by structural superimposition. Reliability of the models was assessed using Superpose program [31].

For further validation regarding accuracy of homology model and methods used to generate the three-dimensional model, a cross-check validation approach was used. In this strategy, the modeled adenosine kinase *Ld*Adk was chosen as template and adenosine kinase of *Tb*Adk sequence was considered query. Modeller (*v9.0*) program was used, and three-dimensional coordinates were generated for *Tb*Adk. The modeled *Tb*Adk structure was superimposed and comparison of the structures was done by means of all-atom RMSD.

2.3. Molecular Dataset. In order to elucidate structural and functional relevance in terms of ligand binding and specificity, docking studies were carried out using different programs. Adenosine kinase inhibitors (organic compounds and natural inhibitors) reported in the literature were generated by ChemSketch [14–18]. The generated structures were subjected to DS 2.5 for ligand minimization. We also blindly docked kinase inhibitors available in PubChem database (http://www.ncbi.nlm.nih.gov/pccompound). The molecules that are sourced from natural medicinal plants [32] were docked and analyzed separately. The molecular dataset prepared for the present study was categorized into (a) organic molecules reported as adenosine kinase inhibitors (dataset O) and (b) natural products (dataset N). Ligand preparations as required by various docking programs were executed separately.

2.4. MD Simulation and Active Site Prediction of LdAdk. MD simulations were conducted for the homology model of *Ld*Adk in explicit solvent using the GROMACS *v4.0.3* (the Groningen Machine for Chemical Simulations) package with Gromos43a1 force field parameters [33]. The model was solvated with 13, 597 water molecules (SPC/E water models) [34] in an octahedron box having edges at a distance of 0.9 nm from the molecular periphery. To obtain the neutrality of the system, six Na^+ ions were added (charge +6.00) to the system. The solvated system was subjected to energy minimization to remove the steric conflicts between atoms of protein and water molecules having a maximum step of 2000 with steepest descent integrator, that converge the energy when the maximum force was smaller than $1000\,kJ \cdot mol^{-1} \cdot nm^{-1}$.

Energy minimized model was subjected to position-restrained MD with NPT ensemble keeping number of particles (N), system pressure (P), and temperature (T) as constant parameters. This was carried out for 50,000 steps—a total of 100 ps time period. The reference temperature for coupling was 300 K by Berendsen temperature coupling [35], and 1 atm pressure was maintained by Parrinello-Rahman algorithm [36]. SHAKE algorithm [37] was used to restrain the hydrogen bonds with integration step of 2 fs, and the trajectory snapshots were saved at every 1 ps. The final MD was carried out for 3000 ps (3 ns) under Particle Mesh Ewald (PME) [38] electrostatistics in NPT condition. The probable ligand-binding pockets in the refined model of LdAdk were predicted by Q-Site Finder [39].

2.5. Docking Calculation

2.5.1. Docking Using Glide v9.10. The protein model was processed using the preparation wizard [40–42] and was optimized for hydrogen-bonding network by reorienting the hydroxyl groups as well as amide groups of Asn, Gln and choosing appropriate states of imidazole ring of His residue. Remaining parameters and steps for receptor grid generation and ligand preparation were similar to the methodology of our previous study [43]. A grid for the docking calculation was prepared after selecting the active site residues. The prepared molecular dataset was subjected to virtual screening protocol where an initial screening was done by high throughput virtual screening (HTVS). Resulted top scoring molecules (10%) were subjected to next round of standard precision (SP) docking. The final top 10% hits from SP docking were subjected to extra precision (XP) mode of docking which were analyzed later. Excellent pieces of literature [44, 45] are available describing the relevance of various mode, of docking using Glide and thus are not discussed in detail here. The molecules that are sourced from natural medicinal plants were docked and analyzed separately. The compounds having docking score below the threshold value (−9.0) were selected. The hits as retrieved from SP docking were used for a cross-check docking calculation using other docking programs like FlexX v1.13.5 and GOLD v5.1. It was suggested that consensus docking/scoring could be valuable to identify a new lead molecule [46].

2.5.2. Docking Using FlexX. All the default parameters as present in FlexX v1.13.5 [47] were used for carrying out the docking calculation. Resulting top-scoring 6 molecules (O1 to O6) and top 2 (N1 and N2) molecules from datasets O and N, respectively, are reported here. The receptor description file was defined using the nonhydrogen coordinates of the active site. The molecules used for docking were kept in mol2 file format for carrying out the docking studies.

2.5.3. Docking Using GOLD. The active site was defined to encompass all the atoms within a 10 Å radius sphere centered over the active site residues, so as to keep the grid axis the same as that of Glide. GOLD v5.1 [48] was used for performing the docking studies. For each of 10 independent genetic algorithm (GA) runs, a maximum number of 1000 GA

operations were performed. The parameters like: operators for crossover, mutation and migration were set to as 100, 100 and 0 respectively. All other parameters were kept as default.

2.6. MD Simulation of Protein-Ligand Complex. The coordinates of the top hit molecule with LdAdk as obtained from docking were used for MD simulation. Two protein-ligand complexes were taken, one containing the O1 molecule and another containing N1 with protein. The parameters and simulation conditions were similar to the conditions used for modeled LdAdk. Parameterization for the small molecules was done using PRODRG server (http://davapc1.bioch.dundee.ac.uk/prodrg/) [49]. The simulation was continued for a time scale of 3 ns, and the trajectories were saved at 1 ps interval which was later processed for analysis.

3. Results and Discussion

3.1. Model Structure of LdAdk. The absence of the crystal structure for LdAdk prompted us to generate a 3D model for docking studies. A high degree of sequence matching (template) is essential for the success of homology modeling. Template search was carried out based on query coverage and sequence identity concept. The BLASTp results for LdAdk showed 53% and 43% sequence identity with the Adenosine kinases of *T. brucei* rhodesiense (3OTX|A) and *A. gambiae* (3LOO|A), respectively. The template search carried out using various web servers and stand-alone tools also suggested that the crystal structure of TbAdk is the best template: ~53% sequence identity and 73% positives. Different models of LdAdk were built using Modeller and SWISS-MODEL using the best template. Discrete optimized protein energy (DOPE) suggested that the first model generated by Modeller (M1) revealed the lowest energy (−40008.88). The model generated by SWISS-MODEL (S1) also revealed a comparative lower DOPE score (−40003.27) (Figure 1(a)). The other two models, that is, Modeller 3 (M3) and Modeller 4 (M4), also revealed good DOPE scores of −39946.58 and −39946.66, respectively, but are comparatively less than M1 and S1. Upon calculation of Φ/Ψ distribution for backbone conformation, M1 model revealed the highest: 99% residues fell in most favored regions and additional allowed regions and 0.3% residues in generously allowed region, whereas only 0.7% (Ser196 and Asp257) fell in disallowed region (Figure 1(d)). Final structure with lowest energy (M1) was checked by Profile3D (DS v2.5). The self-compatibility score for the model appeared to be 162.92, which was much higher than the verify expected high score (157.16) and verify expected lowest score (70.72). All these results suggested the reliability of the proposed model.

3.2. Model Validation. Computer-aided drug design is one of the most efficient tools in the present time, empowering an ease to search novel lead molecules within less span of time with accuracy. In order to proceed for an accurate prediction of novel inhibitors and their interaction profile against LdAdk, it is indeed necessary to have a robust 3D model of the protein structure. Figure 1 showed the various validation results which help in conferring the rationality of the prepared homology model. Precision of the model was

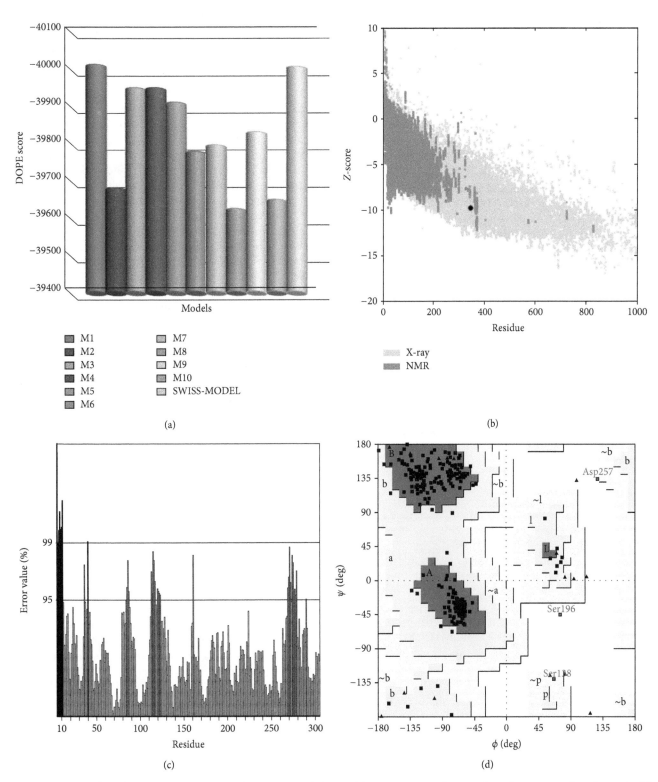

FIGURE 1: Figures describing various parameters for structure validation. (a) DOPE scores of various homology prepared in the study. (b) Z-score plot obtained from ProSA web server. (c) ERRAT plot for residue-wise analysis of homology model. (d) Ramachandran map of the homology model.

checked using the ProSA server, where the Z-score (-9.75) depicted (Figure 1(b)) the model to be within the domicile of reported X-ray crystal structures till date. ProSA web analysis also showed the protein model quality by plotting energies as a function of amino acid sequence position. It demonstrated that the energy remains negative for almost all amino acid residues indicating the acceptability of the predicted model. Similar assumptions were achieved using the ERRAT plot (Figure 1(c)), where the error value of almost all residues for the protein (87.53%) was found below the cutoff limits. Superimposition of LdAdk model with its closest homologue *T. brucei* resulted in a root mean square deviation (RMSD) of 0.467 Å (Figure 2). The overall structure of LdAdk contained a mixed fold and consisted of 12 α-helices and 14 β-strands with two distinct domains (Figure 2(a)). The smaller lid domain appears as α/β two-layer structure formed by five β-sheets ($\beta2$, $\beta3$, $\beta4$, $\beta7$, and $\beta8$) and two solvent-exposed α-helices ($\alpha1$ and $\alpha2$) located on top. The large domain was α/β domain composed of nine β-sheets ($\beta1$, $\beta5$, $\beta6$, and $\beta9$–$\beta14$), of which $\beta13$ was antiparallel. The β-sheets were surrounded by 10 α-helices ($\alpha3$–$\alpha12$) exposed to the solvent. A good structural overlapping was noticed between the model and the template, especially in α-helices and β-sheets regions (Figure 2(c)). The conservation of this sequence and the structural superimposition suggested that the LdAdk model is robust and accurate. In another validation approach the energy-minimized and loop-refined model of LdAdk was used as a template to build the model of TbAdk. This model was used to superimpose with the crystal structure (3OTX). Interestingly we have observed an all-atom RMSD of 0.568 Å, which suggested that our homology model was far more accurate.

3.3. MD Simulation of LdAdk Model Structure.

MD simulation is one of the well-known theoretical techniques, popularly used for assessing the stability of any predicted three-dimensional model. The prepared three-dimensional homology model of LdAdk was processed for MD simulation for a 3 ns time scale in the explicit solvent condition. Figure 3(a) showed all-atom RMSD of the modeled system against the time scale. An initial jump in the RMSD at 0 ps time depicts the minute adjustment of the protein model in the solvent condition. In general, the RMSD of any system, within 1 Å (10^{-10}), can be regarded as stable, and the deviation was found to occur within a range of 0.15–0.25 nm (10^{-9}) for the proposed model and suggested that the system was having a customary behavior in explicit condition under the effect of force field. Apparently, we also tried to get a depth for dynamicity of each residue by means of root mean square fluctuation (RMSF) (Figure 3(b)). The rmsf plot for the model system depicted similar stability and was well correlated with the RMSD plot. Interestingly, it showed much flexibility of resides in the range of 50–60 and 260–300 regions. According to the active site prediction as discussed in the earlier section, we found the same residues in these regions. Thus, MD simulation data of the model LdAdk illustrated that the active site residues were precisely dynamic as compared to the other residues of the model. As a general observation, for any

enzyme, either the active site or the loop facilitating the opening and closing of the active site channels is found to be dynamic, so as to facilitate the catalysis activity. The range of dynamicity of these active site residues fell within a range of 0.1–0.2 nm, suggesting the side chains of these amino acids were flexible.

3.4. Docking Calculation.

Theoretical validation of the LdAdk model confirmed the accuracy of the three-dimensional structure which can be used for prediction of suitable chemical inhibitory agents. The prepared molecular datasets O and N were used for our docking studies with modeled LdAdk. The predicted active site as discussed in the methodology section was used to dock all the molecules. The initial docking experiment was exercised using Glide module. The obtained molecules from SP mode of docking (part of virtual screening protocol) were used for comparative docking analysis using FlexX and GOLD. The final molecules as conferred from the XP results which were in good agreement with the results of FlexX and GOLD docking were adopted for visual analysis. Table 1 showed the various docking scores of the top six molecules from dataset O belonging to series of pyrrolo[2,3-d]pyrimidine nucleoside as reported by Ugarkar et al. [15] and top two molecules form dataset N. It was found that molecules O6, O2, and O3 were having Glide score > -11, whereas molecule N1 was having much higher Glide score of -14.5. Such results are much motivating as they generate interest to seek the insight of structural feature which provokes the difference in docking studies.

Figure 4 showed docked pose of six molecules (O1–O6) which showed almost similar kind of docking results with different algorithm as implemented in software. The detailed interactions of the top-scoring molecule were given in Table 2. Hydroxyl groups attached to the 3 and 4 position of tetrahydrofuran were found to form strong hydrogen bonds (H-bond) in all the cases with the side chains of Arg131 and Asp16. The positively charged side chain of Arg131 was making H-bond contact with the electron-rich oxygen atoms of diols whereas to the hydrogen atoms, the negatively charged side chain of Asp16 makes H-bond. It was also evidenced from the docked pose that the amino acids Gly61, Gly62, and Ser63 were interacting with the chemical moieties in all the cases. Asp299 was found to form polar contacts in few cases only (Figures 4(a), 4(b), 4(c), and 4(f)). The interaction with Asp299 can be considered because of larger functional groups attached, such as $-CH_2OH$ or $-C_2H_2NH_2$. Interestingly, the energetically most favored contact was found with Phe168 in all the cases which were governed by virtue of π-π stacking interaction. The fused heterocycle ring pyrrolo[2,3-d]pyrimidine was found to be stacked with the π-electron clouds of phenyl ring of Phe168 residue which was believed to provide energetic favor to the molecular conformation. Since the docking protocol utilizes the rigidity in the protein conformation, it is thus essential to get account of the dynamicity for active site residues in association with the flexibility of chemical moieties.

Docking results for N1 and N2 from dataset N were presented in Figure 5. Top-scoring hit N1 (1,6-digalloylglucose)

TABLE 1: Docking scores of top-hit ligands predicted from different structures.

Hits	Structure[a]	Glide score	GOLD score	FlexX score
O1		−10.92	45.24	−32.42
O2		−11.12	42.36	−31.83
O3		−11.18	45.90	−32.81
O4		−10.55	49.53	−33.43
O5		−10.04	47.43	−28.99
O6		−11.76	49.98	−32.01
N1		−14.5	58.81	−32.01

TABLE 1: Continued.

Hits	Structure[a]	Glide score	GOLD score	FlexX score
N2		−9.2	60.36	−23.63

[a]The structures have been generated using ACD/ChemSketch (http://www.acdlabs.com/).

TABLE 2: Polar contacts information from docking calculation between ligands and protein.

Hits	Residue	Atoms	Distance (Å)
O1	Asp 16	O(H)···(O), O(H)···(O)	1.8, 2.0
	Gly 62	(O)H···N(H)	1.7
	Ser 63	(N)···N(H)	1.7
	Arg 131	(O)H···N(H), (O)H···N(H)	1.9, 2.1
	Asp 299	O(H)···(O)	2.1
O2	Asp 16	O(H)···(O), O(H)···(O), O(H)···(O)	1.9, 2.3, 2.1
	Gly 62	(O)H···N(H)	1.9
	Ser 63	(N)···N(H)	2.0
	Arg 131	(O)H···N(H)	2.1
	Asp 299	(O)H···N(H), O(H)···(O)	2.4, 1.6
O3	Asp 16	O(H)···(O), O(H)···(O)	1.8, 1.9
	Gly 62	(O)H···N(H)	1.7
	Ser 63	(N)···N(H)	1.8
	Arg 131	N(H)···(O)H, N(H)···(O)H	1.7, 2.2
	Asp 299	H(O)···(O)	2.0
O4	Asp 16	O(H)···(O), O(H)···(O)	2.0, 1.8
	Gly 62	(O)H···N(H)	1.8
	Ser 63	(N)···N(H)	1.8
	Arg 131	(O)H···N(H), (O)H···N(H)	1.9, 2.0
O5	Asp 16	O(H)···(O), O(H)···(O)	1.8, 1.6
	Gly 62	(O)H···N(H)	1.6
	Ser 63	(N)···N(H)	1.8
	Arg 131	(O)H···N(H), (O)H···N(H)	2.0, 1.7
O6	Asp 16	O(H)···(O), O(H)···(O)	2.0, 1.9
	Gly 62	(O)H···N(H)	1.9
	Ser 63	(N)···N(H)	1.9
	Arg 131	(O)H···N(H)	2.1
	Asp 299	N(H)···(O)	2.1
N1	Asp 16	O(H)···(O)	1.9
	Thy 34	O(H)···(O), O(H)···(O)	2.0, 1.9
	Cys 37	O(H)···(O)	2.3
	Ser 63	(O)···N(H), (O)···N(H)	2.7, 1.9
	Arg 131	(O)···N(H), (O)H···N(H)	2.4, 2.2
	Ser 196	O(H)···(O)	2.2
	Asp 299	O(H)···(O)	1.7
N2	Asn 12	(O)···N(H)	1.8

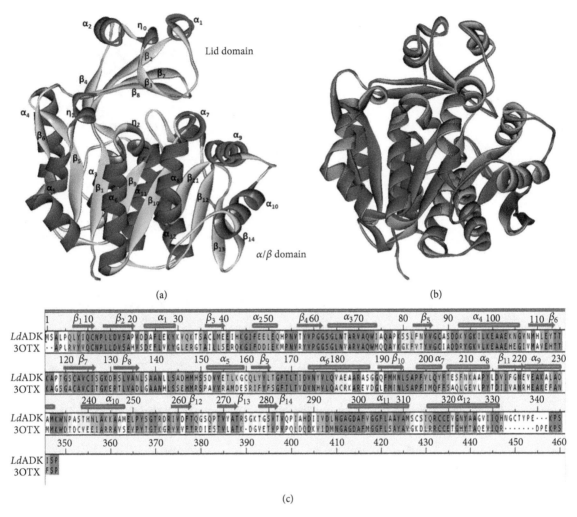

FIGURE 2: (a) Homology model structure of *Ld*Adk, with the α-helix, β-sheet, and turn regions shown with different colors. (b) Overlap of model homology structure (red) and crystal structure (green). (c) Sequence alignment window for template (3OTX) and query sequence (*Ld*Adk).

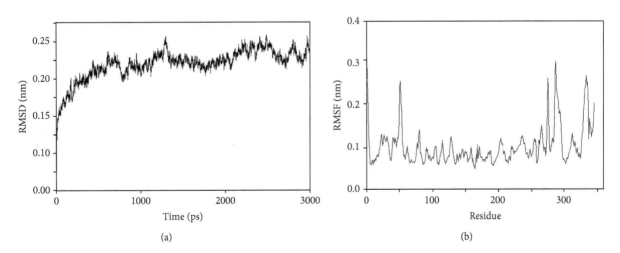

FIGURE 3: MD simulation results for *Ld*Adk protein model. (a) RMSD plot for the model system. (b) RMSF plot for the model system.

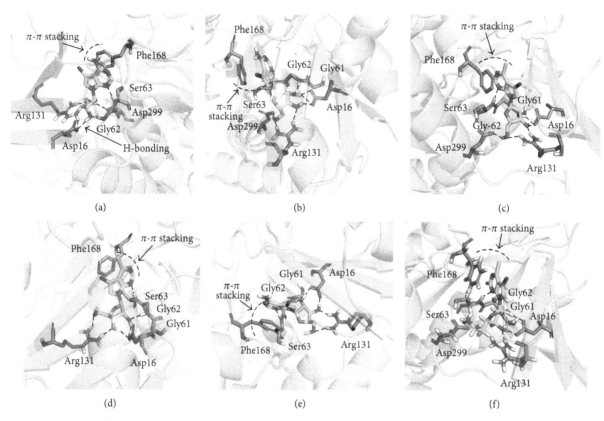

FIGURE 4: Interaction profile for the organic molecules, from docking studies for molecules (a) O1, (b) O2, (c) O3, (d) O4, (e) O5, and (f) O6.

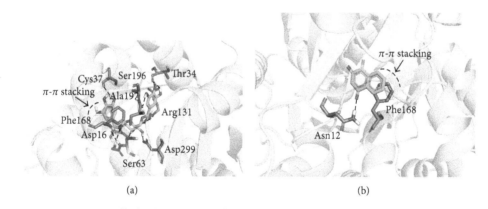

FIGURE 5: Interaction profile for the natural products, from docking studies for molecules (a) N1 and (b) N2.

was from source *Acacia nilotica*. A similar kind of interaction profile was found in this case which is comparable to the docking results found for O1 to O6 molecules. Active site residues Asp16, Ser63, Asp299, and Arg131 were found to form strong hydrogen bonds with the sugar moiety of N1. Out of these, Asp16 and Asp299 were found to behave as H-bond acceptors, whereas Ser63 and Arg131 were found to behave as H-bond donors while interacting with the sugar moiety. The hydroxyl groups attached to the aromatic ring parts of the molecule were found to be stabilized by virtue of polar contacts with the residues like Ala19, Thr34, Cys37, and Ser197, behaving as H-bond acceptors. The results seemed to be in agreement where the rich π-electron cloud of aromatic

system, having a pronounced electron-donating effect over the hydroxyl groups, and thus the H-bond formed by the system with the active site residues can be thought to be much stronger. Interestingly, the π-π stacking interaction was also found to be dominant in this case where the aromatic ring of the molecule was involved in aromatic stacking with the side chain of phenyl ring of residue Phe168.

Molecule N2 (lawsone), which was considered for analysis in our study based on the docking calculations, was sourced from *Lawsonia inermis*. N2 (chemical name: 2-hydroxynaphthalene-1,4-dione) has a core naphthalene group. The reason for considering this small phytochemical in our study is its structure, which is easy to adopt for synthesis

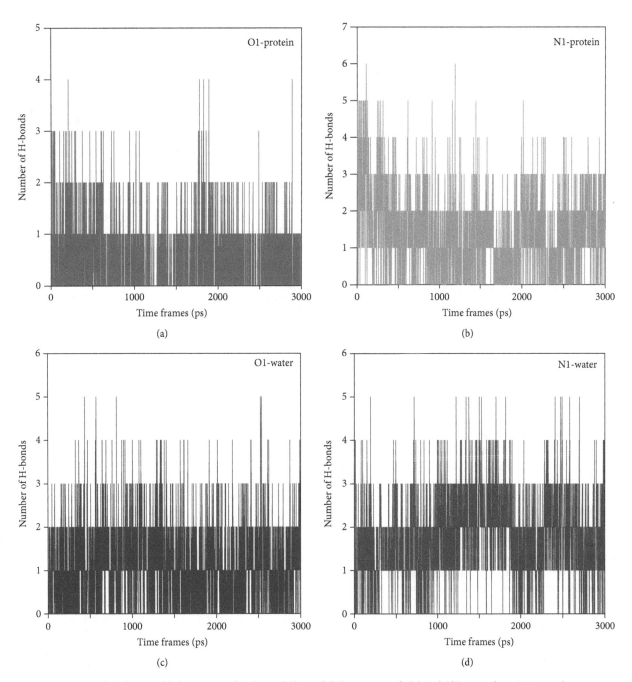

FIGURE 6: H-bonding profile between molecules and ((a) and (b)) protein and ((c) and (d)) water from MD simulation.

of series of molecules and can be tested for activity in the future. The docking study of N2 did not provide any remarkable interaction with the amino acids, except the carbonyl group attached to the naphthalene ring at position 4, and was found to make one H-bond with the amine group of Asn12. However, the π-π stacking interaction was prominent in this case with Phe168, which can be regarded as the key interaction facilitating a stable molecular conformation within the receptor macromolecule.

3.5. MD Simulation of Ligand Molecules with Protein. From the results of MD of the modeled protein, we observed that

the active site residues were indeed dynamic as compared to the other atoms in the model, whereas docking studies suggested many polar contacts in the active sites which facilitate binding based on the docking scores. Ever since, the protein model considered for the docking calculation was a rigid macromolecule; thus to validate the results we used all-atom MD simulation for ligand-protein complex. As conferred from Figure 3, the RMSD of the protein was much stable; thus we have not assessed the RMSD for the ligand-protein complex. Polar interactions of the system were considered with number of H-bonds formed between protein and ligand in the simulation time course. Figure 6 depicted

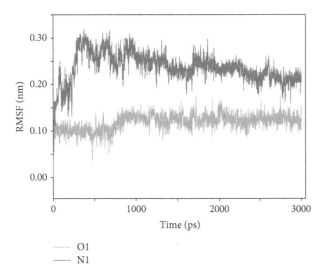

FIGURE 7: Root mean square fluctuation for the ligand atom plotted against time from MD simulation.

the quantitative H-bonding profile for both the O1 as well as the N1. For O1, two H-bonds seemed to provide much stronger contact with the protein (Figure 6(a)), whereas in N1, the same contact was being stabilized by 2-3 strong H-bonds. This gives an assumption that despite the dynamicity of active site residues, the ligand molecules were still intact within the active sites. To further confirm our observation, we checked the polar contacts formed within the ligand and solvent molecules. Since docking calculations have the dielectric effect of the water models as an implicit effect to add up in the scoring scheme, the quantitative measurement of such interaction profile had been taken into account by virtue of MD simulation. In both the cases, we observed almost similar H-bonding profile between the ligand molecules and water models, which ranges from 2 to 3 strong polar contacts. Thus, RMSF fluctuation of model LdAdk and the H-bonding profile of ligand-water suggested possible explanation, what factors make ligands intact within active site. Ever since the flexibility of active site residue is essential for the catalytic activity of any enzyme; this is indeed facilitated by the solvent perturbation inside the physiological condition. Thus, water molecules always show H-bonding network within the active site with the substrate. Similar observation was found in this study where the water molecules formed strong H-bond with the ligand.

To confer such results, rmsf of the ligand molecules with the active site in the simulation time period was assessed (Figure 7). An initial fluctuation of the molecules at the starting time scale of simulation conferred to the conformation adjustment due to energy minimization and equilibration prior to the production run. O1 showed no major fluctuations while interacting with the protein macromolecule and thus can be concluded to be much stable. In case of the N1, a shift in the rmsf was found corresponding to the first 500 ps. N1 seemed to be stabilized in the later part of simulation, as the rmsf did not fluctuate till the end.

Another interesting feature observed from the MD simulation and was cross-checked with the docking studies for O1 is the stability of halogen group in ligand. Figure 8(a) showed the van der Waals region for the halide atoms attached to the pyrrolo[2,3-d]pyrimidine ring with the nearest aminoacids from the docking calculations (interacting atoms areshown in ball and stick representation). Halide atoms were electronegative in nature, and stability of such functional moiety cannot be achieved from the hydrophobic side chains of residues such as Ala36, Leu133, and Ala135. Analyzing the frames of trajectory, a suitable explanation was found for what interaction could accompany electronegative π-clouds of halide atoms. MD simulation snapshots taken at an interval of 500 ps revealed that the π-cloud of aromatic phenyl ring of Phe168 not only interact with the aromatic π electrons of pyrrolo[2,3-d]pyrimidine ring but also accommodates the lone pair π-electrons of halide ion to provide stability of the ligand molecule in the active site. These results can explain the initial conformation fluctuation as evidenced in initial timeframe (Figure 8(b)). Thus, the overall MD results suggested a stable interaction between the ligand molecules and the LdAdk protein.

3.6. Correlation with Previous Studies. Ghosh and Datta have elucidated presence of arginine residue in active site of LdAdk which is crucial for enzyme activity. Treatment of LdAdk with arginine-specific reagents such as phenylglyoxal, butane-2,3-dione, and cyclohexane-1,2-dione has shown irreversible inactivation of the enzyme [50]. A similar assumption was adopted by Costa and coworkers in which they made an attempt to find out active conformation of chemical moiety neolignan sourced from plant family Myristicaceae, which exhibited prominent interaction in the active site of LdAdk [51]. It was assumed that active neolignans interact with arginine residue. Interestingly, all the six molecules form dataset O (namely, O1 to O6) and N1 showed prominent polar contact with Arg131 as conferred from our docking studies. In another report Datta et al. have shown that mutation of Arg131 causes significant reduction in catalytic activity of LdAdk [52]. Moreover they also concluded that Asp299 and Arg131 both are key catalytic residues in the protein; similar inference has been highlighted from our docking studies (Figure 4). The diglycyl motif (formed by consecutive glycine residues: Gly61 and Gly62) present in the active site are responsible for maintaining conformation flexibility [52] and thus was thereason the rmsf data from modeled LdAdk showed high fluctuation as compared to other residues of the protein. In other reports from the same laboratory, they also established that Asp16 is also one of the crucial residues in the active site and is found in our study also where Asp16 is actively involved in forming H-bonds with the ligands. Thus, it clearly explains that these residues are important to be considered from synthetic and experimental drug design point of view [53]. Remarkably, the importance of Phe168 was explored in our study, which is believed to provide significant contribution in ligand binding to LdAdk. These structural insights from aromatic-π interaction may be regarded as one of the key factors in lead design.

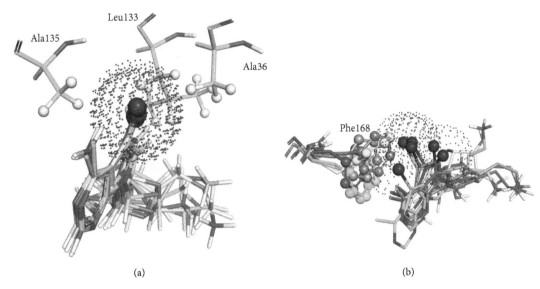

(a)   (b)

FIGURE 8: Van der waals and π-stacking interactions between halide atoms from organic molecule. (a) Structures from docking studies of all ligands with the nearby amino acid residues. (b) Structures from MD snapshots.

4. Conclusion

Construction of a robust homology model of *Ld*Adk in combination with docking and molecular dynamics simulation results in valuable structural insights for ligand binding. Importance of arginine and aspartic acid residues for a stable ligand binding was well correlated with the previous of literature. Specific role of phenylalanine residue is highlighted in the present study, which is crucial for designed ligand molecules having aromatic pharmacophores. The said contact is believed to be favorable via aromatic-π interaction and can be useful for designing selective inhibitors against *Ld*Adk. Molecular dynamic studies of ligand-protein complex also elucidated that the role of water molecules was also important for stability of ligand moieties in the active site by providing polar contacts. All these pieces of information are believed to be useful for rational design prospective of novel antileishmanial compounds.

References

[1] The World Health Report on leishmaniasis, http://www.who.int/leishmaniasis/en/.

[2] P. K. Sinha, S. Bimal, S. K. Singh, K. Pandey, D. N. Gangopadhyay, and S. K. Bhattacharya, "Pre- & post-treatment evaluation of immunological features in Indian visceral leishmaniasis (VL) patients with HIV co-infection," *Indian Journal of Medical Research*, vol. 123, no. 3, pp. 197–202, 2006.

[3] F. Chappuis, S. Sundar, A. Hailu et al., "Visceral leishmaniasis: what are the needs for diagnosis, treatment and control?" *Nature Reviews Microbiology*, vol. 5, no. 11, pp. 873–882, 2007.

[4] S. L. Croft, M. P. Barrett, and J. A. Urbina, "Chemotherapy of trypanosomiases and leishmaniasis," *Trends in Parasitology*, vol. 21, no. 11, pp. 508–512, 2005.

[5] S. Singh and R. Sivakumar, "Challenges and new discoveries in the treatment of leishmaniasis," *Journal of Infection and Chemotherapy*, vol. 10, no. 6, pp. 307–315, 2004.

[6] J. Park and R. S. Gupta, "Adenosine kinase and ribokinase—the RK family of proteins," *Cellular and Molecular Life Sciences*, vol. 65, no. 18, pp. 2875–2896, 2008.

[7] J. V. Tuttle and T. A. Krenitsky, "Purine phosphoribosyltransferases from *Leishmania donovani*," *Journal of Biological Chemistry*, vol. 255, no. 3, pp. 909–916, 1980.

[8] A. K. Datta, R. Datta, and B. Sen, "Antiparasitic chemotherapy: tinkering with the purine salvage pathway," *Advances in Experimental Medicine and Biology*, vol. 625, pp. 116–132, 2008.

[9] D. L. Looker, R. L. Berens, and J. J. Marr, "Purine metabolism in *Leishmania donovani* amastigotes and promastigotes," *Molecular and Biochemical Parasitology*, vol. 9, no. 1, pp. 15–28, 1983.

[10] A. K. Datta, D. Bhaumik, and R. Chatterjee, "Isolation and characterization of adenosine kinase from *Leishmania donovani*," *Journal of Biological Chemistry*, vol. 262, no. 12, pp. 5515–5521, 1987.

[11] M. Berg, P. van der Veken, A. Goeminne, A. Haemers, and K. Augustyns, "Inhibitors of the purine salvage pathway: a valuable approach for antiprotozoal chemotherapy?" *Current Medicinal Chemistry*, vol. 17, no. 23, pp. 2456–2481, 2010.

[12] M. Vodnala, A. Fijolek, R. Rofougaran, M. Mosimann, P. Mäser, and A. Hofer, "Adenosine kinase mediates high affinity adenosine salvage in *Trypanosoma brucei*," *Journal of Biological Chemistry*, vol. 283, no. 9, pp. 5380–5388, 2008.

[13] K. M. Sinha, M. Ghosh, I. Das, and A. K. Datta, "Molecular cloning and expression of adenosine kinase from *Leishmania donovani*: identification of unconventional P-loop motif," *Biochemical Journal*, vol. 339, no. 3, pp. 667–673, 1999.

[14] M. A. Matulenko, E. S. Paight, R. R. Frey et al., "4-Amino-5-aryl-6-arylethynylpyrimidines: structure-activity relationships of non-nucleoside adenosine kinase inhibitors," *Bioorganic and Medicinal Chemistry*, vol. 15, no. 4, pp. 1586–1605, 2007.

[15] B. G. Ugarkar, J. M. DaRe, J. J. Kopcho et al., "Adenosine kinase inhibitors. 1. Synthesis, enzyme inhibition, and antiseizure activity of 5-iodotubercidin analogues," *Journal of Medicinal Chemistry*, vol. 43, no. 15, pp. 2883–2893, 2000.

[16] M. A. Matulenko, C.-H. Lee, M. Jiang et al., "5-(3-Bromophenyl)-7-(6-morpholin-4-ylpyridin-3-yl)pyrido[2,3-d]

pyrimidin-4-ylamine: structure-activity relationships of 7-substituted heteroaryl analogs as non-nucleoside adenosine kinase inhibitors," *Bioorganic and Medicinal Chemistry*, vol. 13, no. 11, pp. 3705–3720, 2005.

[17] J. Caballero, M. Fernández, and F. D. González-Nilo, "A CoMSIA study on the adenosine kinase inhibition of pyrrolo[2,3-d]pyrimidine nucleoside analogues," *Bioorganic and Medicinal Chemistry*, vol. 16, no. 9, pp. 5103–5108, 2008.

[18] E. F. F. da Cunha, D. T. Mancini, and T. C. Ramalho, "Molecular modeling of the *Toxoplasma gondii* adenosine kinase inhibitors," *Medicinal Chemistry Research*, vol. 21, no. 5, pp. 590–600, 2011.

[19] S. F. Altschul, T. L. Madden, A. A. Schäffer et al., "Gapped BLAST and PSI-BLAST: a new generation of protein database search programs," *Nucleic Acids Research*, vol. 25, no. 17, pp. 3389–3402, 1997.

[20] S. Kuettel, J. Greenwald, D. Kostrewa, S. Ahmed, L. Scapozza, and R. Perozzo, "Crystal structures of *T. b. rhodesiense* adenosine kinase complexed with inhibitor and activator: implications for catalysis and hyperactivation," *PLoS Neglected Tropical Diseases*, vol. 5, no. 5, Article ID e1164, 2011.

[21] K. Arnold, L. Bordoli, J. Kopp, and T. Schwede, "The SWISS-MODEL workspace: a web-based environment for protein structure homology modelling," *Bioinformatics*, vol. 22, no. 2, pp. 195–201, 2006.

[22] J. Peng and J. Xu, "Raptorx: exploiting structure information for protein alignment by statistical inference," *Proteins*, vol. 79, no. 10, pp. 161–171, 2011.

[23] M. Nielsen, C. Lundegaard, O. Lund, and T. N. Petersen, "CPHmodels-3.0-remote homology modeling using structure-guided sequence profiles," *Nucleic Acids Research*, vol. 38, no. 2, pp. W576–W581, 2010.

[24] J. Söding, A. Biegert, and A. N. Lupas, "The HHpred interactive server for protein homology detection and structure prediction," *Nucleic Acids Research*, vol. 33, no. 2, pp. W244–W248, 2005.

[25] N. Eswar, B. Webb, M. A. Marti-Renom et al., "Comparative protein structure modeling using MODELLER," *Current Protocols in Protein Science*, chapter 2, unit 2.9, 2007.

[26] R. Luthy, J. U. Bowie, and D. Eisenberg, "Assesment of protein models with three-dimensional profiles," *Nature*, vol. 356, no. 6364, pp. 83–85, 1992.

[27] R. A. Laskowski, M. W. MacArthur, D. S. Moss, and J. M. Thornton, "PROCHECK: a program to check the stereochemical quality of protein structures," *Journal of Applied Crystallography*, vol. 26, pp. 283–291, 1993.

[28] V. Z. Spassov, P. K. Flook, and L. Yan, "LOOPER: a molecular mechanics-based algorithm for protein loop prediction," *Protein Engineering, Design and Selection*, vol. 21, no. 2, pp. 91–100, 2008.

[29] C. Colovos and T. O. Yeates, "Verification of protein structures: patterns of nonbonded atomic interactions," *Protein Science*, vol. 2, no. 9, pp. 1511–1519, 1993.

[30] M. Wiederstein and M. J. Sippl, "ProSA-web: interactive web service for the recognition of errors in three-dimensional structures of proteins," *Nucleic Acids Research*, vol. 35, pp. W407–W410, 2007.

[31] R. Maiti, G. H. Van Domselaar, H. Zhang, and D. S. Wishart, "SuperPose: a simple server for sophisticated structural superposition," *Nucleic Acids Research*, vol. 32, pp. W590–W594, 2004.

[32] W. N. Setzer and I. V. Ogungbe, "In-silico investigation of antitrypanosomal Phytochemicals from Nigerian medicinal plants," *Plos Neglected Tropical Diseases*, vol. 6, no. 7, Article ID e1727, 2012.

[33] D. Van Der Spoel, E. Lindahl, B. Hess, G. Groenhof, A. E. Mark, and H. J. C. Berendsen, "GROMACS: fast, flexible, and free," *Journal of Computational Chemistry*, vol. 26, no. 16, pp. 1701–1718, 2005.

[34] H. J. C. Berendsen, J. R. Grigera, and T. P. Straatsma, "The missing term in effective pair potentials," *Journal of Physical Chemistry*, vol. 91, no. 24, pp. 6269–6271, 1987.

[35] H. J. C. Berendsen, J. P. M. Postma, W. F. van Gunsteren, A. Dinola, and J. R. Haak, "Molecular dynamics with coupling to an external bath," *The Journal of Chemical Physics*, vol. 81, no. 8, pp. 3684–3690, 1984.

[36] R. Martoňák, A. Laio, and M. Parrinello, "Predicting crystal structures: the Parrinello-Rahman method revisited," *Physical Review Letters*, vol. 90, no. 7, Article ID 75503, 4 pages, 2003.

[37] J.-P. Ryckaert, G. Ciccotti, and H. J. C. Berendsen, "Numerical integration of the cartesian equations of motion of a system with constraints: molecular dynamics of n-alkanes," *Journal of Computational Physics*, vol. 23, no. 3, pp. 327–341, 1977.

[38] P. P. Ewald, "Die Berechnung optischer und elektrostatischer Gitterpotentiale," *Annals of Physics*, vol. 369, pp. 253–287, 1921.

[39] A. T. R. Laurie and R. M. Jackson, "Q-SiteFinder: an energy-based method for the prediction of protein-ligand binding sites," *Bioinformatics*, vol. 21, no. 9, pp. 1908–1916, 2005.

[40] Schrödinger Suite 2012 Schridinger Suite, *Epik Version 2.2*, Schridinger, LLC, New York, NY, USA, 2012.

[41] Schrödinger Suite 2012 Schridinger Suite, *Impact Version 5.7*, Schridinger, LLC, New York, NY, USA, 2012.

[42] Schrödinger Suite 2012 Schridinger Suite, *Prime Version 2.3*, Schridinger, LLC, New York, NY, USA, 2012.

[43] R. K. Kar, P. Suryadevara, B. R. Sahoo, G. C. Sahoo, M. R. Dikhit, and P. Das, "Exploring novel KDR inhibitors based on pharmaco-informatics methodology," *SAR and QSAR in Environmental Research*, vol. 24, no. 3, pp. 215–234, 2013.

[44] R. A. Friesner, R. B. Murphy, M. P. Repasky et al., "Extra precision glide: docking and scoring incorporating a model of hydrophobic enclosure for protein-ligand complexes," *Journal of Medicinal Chemistry*, vol. 49, no. 21, pp. 6177–6196, 2006.

[45] M. P. Repasky, M. Shelley, and R. A. Friesner, "Flexible ligand docking with Glide," *Current Protocols in Bioinformatics*, chapter 8, unit 8, 2007.

[46] M. A. Miteva, W. H. Lee, M. O. Montes, and B. O. Villoutreix, "Fast structure-based virtual ligand screening combining FRED, DOCK, and surflex," *Journal of Medicinal Chemistry*, vol. 48, no. 19, pp. 6012–6022, 2005.

[47] B. Kramer, M. Rarey, and T. Lengauer, "Evaluation of the FLEXX incremental construction algorithm for protein-ligand docking," *Proteins-Structure Function and Genetics*, vol. 37, pp. 228–241, 1999.

[48] G. Jones, P. Willett, R. C. Glen, A. R. Leach, and R. Taylor, "Development and validation of a genetic algorithm for flexible docking," *Journal of Molecular Biology*, vol. 267, no. 3, pp. 727–748, 1997.

[49] A. W. Schüttelkopf and D. M. F. Van Aalten, "PRODRG: a tool for high-throughput crystallography of protein-ligand complexes," *Acta Crystallographica D*, vol. 60, no. 8, pp. 1355–1363, 2004.

[50] M. Ghosh and A. K. Datta, "Probing the function(s) of active-site arginine residue in *Leishmania donovani* adenosine kinase," *Biochemical Journal*, vol. 298, no. 2, pp. 295–301, 1994.

[51] M. C. A. Costa, L. E. S. Barata, and Y. Takahata, "Conformation of neolignans that bind to the arginine residue in adenosine-kinase from *Leishmania donovani*," *Journal of Molecular Structure*, vol. 464, no. 1–3, pp. 281–287, 1999.

[52] R. Datta, I. Das, B. Sen et al., "Mutational analysis of the active-site residues crucial for catalytic activity of adenosine kinase from *Leishmania donovani*," *Biochemical Journal*, vol. 387, no. 3, pp. 591–600, 2005.

[53] R. Datta, I. Das, B. Sen et al., "Homology-model-guided site-specific mutagenesis reveals the mechanisms of substrate binding and product-regulation of adenosine kinase from *Leishmania donovani*," *Biochemical Journal*, vol. 394, no. 1, pp. 35–42, 2006.

14

Prediction of Deleterious Nonsynonymous Single-Nucleotide Polymorphism for Human Diseases

Jiaxin Wu and Rui Jiang

MOE Key Laboratory of Bioinformatics and Bioinformatics Division, TNLIST/Department of Automation, Tsinghua University, Beijing 100084, China

Correspondence should be addressed to Rui Jiang; ruijiang@tsinghua.edu.cn

Academic Editors: C. Proctor and R. Rivas

The identification of genetic variants that are responsible for human inherited diseases is a fundamental problem in human and medical genetics. As a typical type of genetic variation, nonsynonymous single-nucleotide polymorphisms (nsSNPs) occurring in protein coding regions may alter the encoded amino acid, potentially affect protein structure and function, and further result in human inherited diseases. Therefore, it is of great importance to develop computational approaches to facilitate the discrimination of deleterious nsSNPs from neutral ones. In this paper, we review databases that collect nsSNPs and summarize computational methods for the identification of deleterious nsSNPs. We classify the existing methods for characterizing nsSNPs into three categories (sequence based, structure based, and annotation based), and we introduce machine learning models for the prediction of deleterious nsSNPs. We further discuss methods for identifying deleterious nsSNPs in noncoding variants and those for dealing with rare variants.

1. Introduction

Understanding the relationship between phenotype and genotype is a fundamental problem in genetics. Of particular interest, the identification of genetic risk factors underlying human inherited diseases has long been a goal in human and medical genetics. Since genetic variation is believed to be the major factor that stimulates the diversity between individuals [1], considerable efforts have been taken to understand associations between human genetic variants and their phenotypic effects [2]. A number of successful stories have shown that such efforts are helpful in capturing the causative variants which affect human inherited diseases, providing important information for grasping genetic bases of complex diseases, and further promoting the prevention, diagnosis, and treatment of these diseases [3]. Nevertheless, recent studies have shown that the number of genetic variants is huge, more than 3.5 million variants in the whole genome for a single individual, roughly corresponding to 1,000 variants per megabase pair [4, 5], making the identification of causative variants a task of finding needles in stacks of needles. Furthermore, it has also been shown that although most genetic variants exist common in a population, there also exists a nonnegligible number of variants that occur in very low frequency, making established statistical methods for identifying such rare variants ineffective. Hence, the development of novel computational methods to identify causative variants now receives more and more attentions.

Genetic variants can typically be classified into several categories, including single-nucleotide polymorphisms (SNPs), small insertions and deletions, and structural variants [4]. Among these types of variants, single-nucleotide polymorphisms (SNPs) that occur in single bases of DNA sequences account for a majority of all genetic variants. It has been estimated that there exist nearly 10 million SNPs in the human genome, nearly one SNP for every 290 base-pairs. The vast number of SNPs along with growing functional annotations of the human genome sequence may provide plenty of knowledge to grasp links between genetic and phenotypic variations [6]. Particularly, as an important type of SNP, a nonsynonymous single-nucleotide polymorphism (nsSNP) occurring in a protein coding region alters the encoded amino acid sequence, potentially affects protein structure and function, and further causes human inherited diseases. It has been reported that nsSNPs constitute more than 50% of the mutations known to be involved in human inherited diseases [7] and each person may hold 24,000–40,000 nsSNPs [8]. It is also believed that although most of the susceptible deleterious nsSNPs are related to individual Mendelian diseases, functional changes aroused by nsSNPs will be of importance for complex diseases [8]. Therefore, more effort should be paid for studying the candidate deleterious nsSNPs [9].

The identification of genetic variants that are associated with human diseases is often undertaken using either a family-based linkage analysis or a population-based association study. In a linkage analysis, susceptible disease-causing loci (usually between 1 and 5 million bp in length) are mapped by identifying genetic markers that are coinherited with a query phenotype. Linkage analysis has poor prediction power for difficultly collecting family-based sequence data and poor performance for complex diseases which are caused by the combination of effects of several susceptible genetic variants and their interactions with environmental factors [10]. An association study compares frequencies of occurrence of genetic variants between a case population and a control population to detect associations between genetic variants and phenotypes [11]. With recent advances in high-throughput experimental techniques, association studies are now often conducted in genomewide scale, often referred to as genomewide association (GWA) studies. Although such a GWA study has shown some success in the past few years, it suffers from serious multiple testing problem when applied to a number of markers in a large population, and its basic hypothesis of Common Disease Common Variant (CDCV) has been challenged by the fact that both common variants and rare variants may be involved in the pathogenesis of common diseases.

To overcome these limitations and serve as a complementary category of these traditional statistical methods, computational approaches that rely on properties of variants instead of experimental data of patients have been designed for the detection of deleterious variants, with the growing functional annotations of the human genome sequence. Although such methods may never be accurate enough to replace wet-lab experiments, they may help in identifying and prioritizing a small number of susceptible and tractable candidate nsSNPs from pools of available data [1]. Recent studies [9–21] have shown that computational methods are capable of well estimating the functional effects of nsSNPs. These approaches may take advantage of structure information, sequence information, and annotations as classification features, as well as logistic regression [21], neural networks [1], Bayesian models [5], and other statistical approaches [18] as classifiers.

In this paper, we first summarize the databases for collecting nsSNP data and provide a framework of nsSNP function prediction methodology. We survey existing deleterious nsSNPs prediction methods and summarize the prediction features conducted in prediction models and the prediction algorithms to distinguish the deleterious nsSNPs. Then, we discuss computational methods that use comparative genomics to predict deleteriousness of nsSNPs in both coding and noncoding regions. We also look at prioritization

methods for disease-specific nsSNPs detection and discuss deleterious nsSNPs prediction methods for rare variants detection. Finally, we suggest using multiple prediction algorithms to enhance the prediction power and discuss challenges and likely future improvements of such methods.

2. Databases for nsSNPs

Many popular databases present useful information of nsSNPs. Particularly, as shown in Table 1, deleterious nsSNPs are mainly collected in four databases: the Online Mendelian Inheritance in Man (OMIM) database [22], the Human Gene Mutation Database (HGMD) [12], the UniProt/Swiss-Prot database [13], and the Human Genome Variation database (HGVbase) [14]. Other popular databases like the single-nucleotide polymorphism database (dbSNP) [15], the Protein Mutant Database (PMD) [16], and the database for nonsynonymous SNP's function prediction (dbNSFP) [9] are also important for collecting nsSNP data (also shown in Table 1).

The Online Mendelian Inheritance in Man (OMIM) is a powerful, comprehensive, and widely used database for collecting molecular relations between genetic variations and phenotypes. OMIM contains information of all known Mendelian disorders and their associated genes. Updated to October 23, 2012, OMIM has collected 21,458 entries of possible links between 4,753 phenotypes and over 12,000 genes, and 2,883 genes with phenotype-causing mutations.

The Human Gene Mutation Database (HGMD) records all germ-line disease-causing mutations and deleterious polymorphisms published in the literature. HGMD provides two versions of databases, one is for academic or nonprofit users, and the other is for professional usage. Updated to March 2012, the total mutation data collected in HGMD nonprofit version is 92,715, while the total mutation data in HGMD Professional version is 130,522.

The UniPROT/SWISS-PROT database is a high quality, manually curated, comprehensive protein sequence database, integrating information from the scientific literature and computational analysis. SWISS-PROT provides convincing protein sequences and annotations, such as protein function descriptions and domain structures. Updated to September 2012, UniProtKB/Swiss-Prot contains 538,010 sequence entries and 190,998,508 amino acids abstracted from 213,490 documents, including more than 67,000 nsSNPs.

The Human Genome Variation database (HGVbase) is an accurate, high-quality, and nonredundant database for comprehensive catalog of normal human gene and genome variation, especially SNPs. HGVbase provides both neutral polymorphisms and disease-related mutations. Updated to July 2005 (released 16.0), HGVbase contains 8,924,237 entries, including more than 20,000 coding SNPs and about 11,000 nsSNPs.

The single-nucleotide polymorphism database (dbSNP) is a comprehensive repository for single-nucleotide substitutions, short deletion, and insertion polymorphisms. Data in dbSNP can be combined with other available NCBI genomic data and freely downloaded in a variety of forms. Updated to February 2010, dbSNP has collected over 184 million

TABLE 1: Database for collecting nsSNP data.

Database	Website	Reference ID
Online Mendelian Inheritance in Man (OMIM)	http://www.omim.org/	[22]
Human Gene Mutation Database (HGMD)	http://www.hgmd.cf.ac.uk/ac/index.php	[12]
UniPROT/SWISS-PROT database	http://www.uniprot.org/	[13]
Human Genome Variation database (HGVbase)	http://hgvbase.cgb.ki.se	[14]
Single-nucleotide polymorphism database (dbSNP)	http://www.ncbi.nlm.nih.gov/snp	[15]
Protein Mutant Database (PMD)	http://pmd.ddbj.nig.ac.jp	[16]
Database for nonsynonymous SNPs' functional predictions (dbNSFP)	http://sites.google.com/site/jpopgen/dbNSFP	[9]

submissions representing more than 64 million distinct variants for 55 organisms, including more than 70,000 SNPs.

The Protein Mutant Database (PMD) [16] is a literature-based database for protein mutants, providing information of amino acid mutations at specific positions of proteins and the structural alterations. Each entry in the database corresponds to one article which may describe one or several protein mutants. Updated to 26 Mar 2007, PMD collects 45,239 entries and 218,873 mutants, including 54,975 nsSNPs occurring in 4,675 proteins.

The database for nonsynonymous SNPs' functional predictions (dbNSFP) [9] is a newly published database, providing both the information about nsSNPs and prediction scores from four popular algorithms (SIFT [17], PolyPhen-2 [18], LRT [19], and MutationTaster [5]) along with a conservation score (PhyloP) [10]. The dbNSFP is the first known integrated database of functional predictions from multiple algorithms for broad collection of human nsSNPs. Updated to March 27, 2009, dbNSFP includes a total of 75,931,005 entries, which covers 64,646,969 nsSNPs in the human genome.

3. Software Tools for Predicting Functional Implication of nsSNPs

With the accelerating advancement of high-throughput experimental techniques, annotations about functional elements in the human genome now become widely available; accordingly a variety of information can be used to study the deleteriousness of an nsSNP. A number of methods have been proposed for the prediction of deleterious nsSNPs, along with friendly web-based interactive software for users to facilitate their own research. In Table 2, we list eleven widely used tools, including SIFT [17], PolyPhen [2], SNAP [1], MSRV [11], LRT [19], PolyPhen-2 [18], MutationTaster [5], KGGSeq [23], SInBaD [21], GERP [24], and PhyloP [10]. The input data for a prediction tool usually requires the protein sequence or protein ID, the amino acid substitution, position of the substitution, chromosome, and/or sequence alignment. After providing all the required input data in the right format, the tools can run automatically and return the predication results, which are usually predictive scores ranging from 0 to 1.

Taking MSRV as an example, the input data for predicting a single amino acid substitution that results from a single base alternation in protein coding sequence includes the protein name, the amino acid substitution, and position of

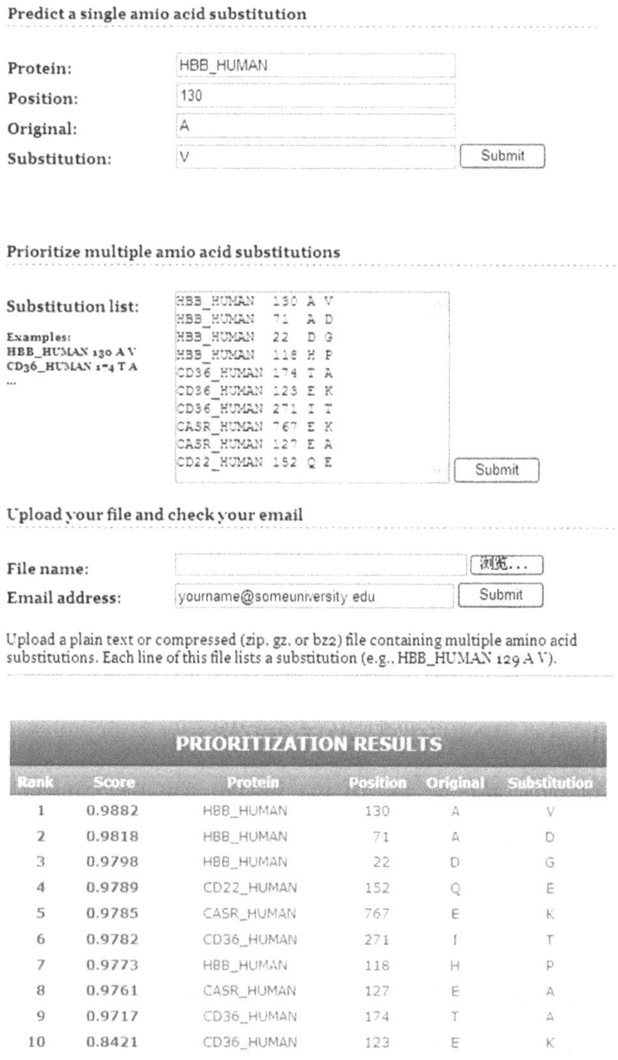

FIGURE 1: Web interface of MSRV.

the substitution in protein sequence, and the output data includes the prediction score ranging from 0 to 1, where 0 stands for neutral nsSNP and 1 means deleterious nsSNP. For prioritizing multiple amino acid substitutions, users can directly paste their substation lists in the required format to the website or upload their data from local computer. The outputs are the ranking list containing all the attached substitution and their scores (as shown in Figure 1).

TABLE 2: Tools for deleterious variant detection.

Method	Website	Features	Method description	Reference ID
SIFT	http://sift.bii.a-star.edu.sg/	Sequence based	Statistical method using PSSM with Dirichlet priors	[17]
PolyPhen	http://genetics.bwh.harvard.edu/pph/index.html	Sequence based, structure based, annotation	Rule-based model	[2]
SNAP	http://www.rostlab.org/services/SNAP/	Sequence based, annotation	Standard feed-forward neural networks with momentum term	[1]
MSRV	http://bioinfo.au.tsinghua.edu.cn/member/ruijiang/english/software.html	Sequence based	Multiple selection rule voting strategy using random forest	[11]
LRT	http://www.genetics.wustl.edu/jflab/lrt_query.html	Sequence based	Log ratio test	[19]
PolyPhen-2	http://genetics.bwh.harvard.edu/pph2/index.shtml	Sequence based, structure based	Naïve Bayes approach coupled with entropy-based discretization	[18]
MutationTaster	http://www.mutationtaster.org/	Sequence based, annotation	Naïve bayes model based on integrated data source	[5]
KGGSeq	http://statgenpro.psychiatry.hku.hk/limx/kggseq/	Sequence based, annotation	A three-level framework to combine a number of filtration and prioritization functions	[23]
SInBaD	http://tingchenlab.cmb.usc.edu/sinbad/	Sequence based	Separate mathematical models for promoters, exons, and introns, using logistic regression algorithm	[21]
GERP (score)	http://mendel.stanford.edu/sidowlab/downloads/gerp/index.html	Sequence based	A "Rejected Substitutions" score computation to infer the constrained region	[24]
PhyloP (score)	http://hgdownload.cse.ucsc.edu/goldenPath/hg18/phyloP44way	Sequence based	An exact P value computation under a continuous Markov substitution model	[10]

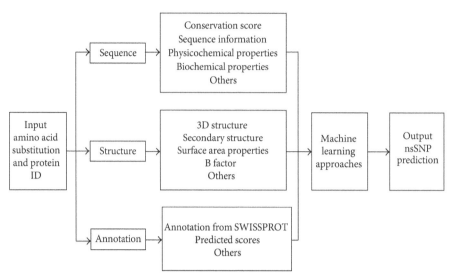

FIGURE 2: Typical procedure for deleterious nsSNPs detection.

Typically, the deleterious nsSNPs prediction problem is formulated as a binary classification model using diverse genomic data as features to compare the deleterious nsSNP with neutral nsSNP. The typical procedure is shown in Figure 2. Users should provide the information about protein ID or sequence, amino acid substitution, and/or multiple sequence alignment. After inputing all the required information, the classification tools can be implemented by extracting their own features and setting up the new classification model automatically. Finally, the deleterious score or the classification result may output by the tools. Classification features are collected and computed using sequence information, protein structural information, and/or annotations from known databases or prediction results. Sequence-based deleterious nsSNPs prediction methods usually take advantage of biochemical properties, physiochemical properties, sequence information, the evolutionary information of proteins, and the predicted 1D or 2D structure of proteins. Structure-based prediction methods may search a protein structure database and get some structural features for further classification. Annotation-based methods may take annotations from SWISS-PROT database [13] or use some published tools to get the preliminary scores for the query nsSNPs. In the next section, we focus on the eleven computational tools to analyze the deleterious nsSNPs prediction problem from the view of extracted features and classification methods.

4. Features for Characterizing nsSNPs

To fully capture diverse potential properties of deleterious nsSNPs, existing prediction tools take advantage of different types of features including sequencing-based information, structure-based information, and/or annotations to wholesomely carry out the classification of the deleterious nsSNPs from the neutral ones.

4.1. Sequencing-Based Information Provides the Strongest Signal for the Prediction Problem. Once a protein sequence containing the query nsSNP is provided, sequence-based deleterious nsSNP prediction methods calculate some specific features according to the sequence of the gene that contains the nsSNP and the location of the nsSNP in the DNA sequence, and/or look up in some databases to collect biochemical properties or physicochemical properties of the nsSNP or resulting single amino acid polymorphism. The most commonly utilized feature based on protein sequence for the query nsSNP is the conservation information calculated in different ways. Usually, people search the protein sequence against a sequence database to find sequences of homologous proteins. A multiple sequence alignment of the homologous sequences reveals what positions have been conserved throughout evolutionary time, and these positions are inferred to be important for function [8]. There are also many other ways to extract the classification features for nsSNPs according to the protein sequence where the nsSNPs locate [5, 25].

4.1.1. Conservation Scores. As an important feature for studying the deleteriousness of an nsSNP, the conservation score is used by most of prediction methods with their own way of calculation. The estimation of the deleteriousness of an nsSNP is based on the fact that sequences observed among living organisms are those that have not been removed by natural selection. In addition, comparative sequence analysis based on phylogenetic information by quantifying evolutionary changes in genes or genomes to find out the conserved positions that have evolved too slowly to be neutral can be identified [4]. Although evolutionary models may not identify all deleterious mutations, they provide a probabilistic framework in which the subset of deleterious mutations that disrupt highly conserved amino acid positions can be accurately identified [19].

Genome sequencing of a large number of closely related species makes it possible to develop better parameterized evolutionary models that more accurately predict human deleterious mutations [19]. Therefore, given a protein sequence as input, a sequence database is needed to find homologous sequences for the protein. A multiple sequence alignment of the homologous sequences reveals what positions have been conserved throughout evolutionary time, and these positions are inferred to be important for function [8]. The conservation-based prediction method then scores each nsSNP based on the amino acid appearing in the multiple alignment and the severity of the amino acid change. An amino acid that is not present at the substitution site in the multiple alignment can still be predicted to be neutral if there are amino acids with similar physiochemical properties present in the alignment [8].

There are many ways to compute the conservation score for every query nsSNP. PolyPhen identifies homologues of the input sequences via a BLAST [26] search of the NRDB database and uses the new version of the PSIC (position-specific independent counts) software [27] to calculate the profile matrix, whose elements of the matrix (profile scores) are logarithmic ratios of the likelihood of a given amino acid occurring at a particular site to the likelihood of this amino acid occurring at any site (background frequency). PolyPhen computes the absolute value of the difference between profile scores of both allelic variants in the polymorphic position. Besides the PSIC score, PolyPhen-2 also uses the sequence identity to the closest homologue carrying any amino acid that differs from the wild-type allele at the site of the mutation, congruency of the mutant allele to the multiple alignment, and alignment depth (excluding gaps) at the site of the mutation. PhyloP performs an exact P value computation under a continuous Markov substitution model to compute the conservation score that measures interspecies conservation at each SNP position. MSRV provides an easy and effective way to calculate the conservation scores for the original and substitute amino acid, which are the frequencies of occurrences of the amino acids in the corresponding position of the Pfam multiple sequence alignment. The same features are also used by the MutationTaster algorithm and the SNAP algorithm. The LRT method utilizes the log likelihood ratio of the conserved relative to neutral model to measure the deleteriousness of an nsSNP, with the null model that each codon is evolving neutrally with no difference in the rate of nonsynonymous to synonymous substitution and the alternative model that the codon has evolved under negative selection with a free parameter for the nonsynonymous to synonymous ratio [19].

4.1.2. Sequence Information.

Pure sequence information of the protein containing the nsSNP may offer useful indications that helped to identify the deleterious nsSNPs. Different methods adopt different ways to exhibit the usage of protein sequence. PolyPhen uses the characterization of the substitution site as a feature, while PolyPhen-2 employs CpG context of transition mutations. MutationTaster also computes a large number of features to grasp the potential difference between the deleterious nsSNPs and the nondeleterious nsSNPs, one of them is the length of protein, which checks if the resulting protein will be elongated, truncated, or whether nonsense-mediated mRNA decay is likely to occur, another is splice site analysis, which analyzes potential splice site changes.

4.1.3. Physicochemical Properties.

It is believed that the physicochemical properties of proteins, especially the changes of physicochemical properties before and after amino acid changes, may present valuable information about how an amino acid substitution may lead to structural or functional changes of a protein. MSRV adopts six physicochemical properties of amino acids, including molecular weight, pI value, hydrophobicity scale, and relative frequencies for the occurrences of amino acids in the secondary structures (helices, strands, and turns) of proteins with known secondary structural information. Six properties are calculated under four situations that are the properties of the original amino acids, properties of the substituted amino acids, properties calculated in a window-sized situation that includes the neighbors of the original amino acids in the query protein sequence, and properties calculated in a column-weighted circumstance in which the query protein sequence is aligned with its homologous proteins. The authors also exploit three more situations which consider the property changes of the substitute amino acid from the original amino acid in a later published paper [20]. Results have shown that the changes of the physicochemical properties are more important than themselves when dealing with the deleterious nsSNP detection problem [20].

4.1.4. Biochemical Properties.

Recent studies [28–31] have shown that deleterious substitutions are likely to affect protein structure; therefore, a better understanding about the protein biochemical properties of protein structure changes may accelerate the detection of deleterious nsSNPs. SNAP computes a series of biochemical properties and uses them as important features to construct classification models [1]. The properties contain several binary features, such as whether there is an inflexible proline into an alpha-helix, and some continuous features, such as mass of wild-type and mutant residues.

4.2. Structure-Based Information Facilitates the Prediction of Deleterious nsSNPs.

Given a protein sequence data, structure-based deleterious nsSNPs prediction methods find the best match against a protein structure database. Some structural features are extracted using the information surrounding the site of substitution instead of detailed information at the atomic level; therefore, if there is not a perfect match for a query protein in the protein structure database, the structure of a homologous protein can be used.

Mapping of an nsSNP to a known 3D structure reveals whether the replacement is likely to destroy the hydrophobic property of a protein, electrostatic interactions, interactions with ligands, or other important features of a protein [2]. Structural features performed by PolyPhen are based on the use of several structural parameters suggested previously [32–34]. PolyPhen uses the Dictionary of Protein Secondary Structure (DSSP) database [35] to obtain some structural parameters for the mapped amino acid residues, such as secondary structure, solvent accessible surface area absolute value. The solvent accessible surface area (SASA) is the surface area of a molecule which is accessible to a solvent and used to improve prediction of protein secondary structure [36, 37]. PolyPhen-2 refines the structural parameters using a feature selection mechanism and chooses three important structural features among thirteen candidate structural features. The selected features are normalized accessible surface area of amino acid residue, crystallographic beta-factor reflecting conformational mobility of the wild-type amino acid residue, and change in accessible surface area propensity for buried residues [18].

Methods solely based on protein structure features provide fewer predictions than methods using sequence-based features because there are far fewer protein structures than sequences for which homology can be found [8]. It is reported that the ratio of methods using sequence-based features to all the existing methods is as high as 81%, while the ratio for methods using only structure-based features is only 14% [8]. Independently consideration of isolated protein structure sometimes may lead to misleading prediction, because the proteins often interacted with others. Thus, new methods tend to use sequence-based information as the main features and structure-based information as the supporting features to operate the deleterious nsSNP detection problem.

4.3. Annotations Can Enhance the Prediction Power for Identifying Deleterious nsSNPs. Annotations can be used as supplementary features to enhance the prediction power for identifying deleterious nsSNPs. The SwissProt database annotates the positions of a protein that are located in the active site, involved in ligand binding, part of a disulfide bridge, or involved in other protein-protein interactions. Annotations can enhance the prediction power when incorporating with other features, such as sequence-based predictions of secondary structure and solvent accessibility [38, 39]. PolyPhen adds the SwissProt feature table terms to the final prediction rules, and MutationTaster and SNAP also utilize the SwissProt annotations as features to predict the deleteriousness of the query nsSNPs.

Besides annotations from published databases, the predicted deleterious score given by existing wide-accepted prediction tools can be treated as preliminary annotation for the prediction. For example, SNAP algorithm makes use of SIFT and PolyPhen prediction scores as classification features to enhance the prediction power. SNAP also determines whether the correct predictions made by their method overlapped with those covered by PolyPhen and SIFT [1].

5. Machine Learning Models for Classifying nsSNPs

Most predicting methods treat the identification of deleterious nsSNPs as a binary classification problem and adopt some popular binary classification machine learning algorithms, such as rule-based prediction model [2, 17], naïve Bayes classifier [5, 18], random forest [11], neural networks [1], and many others. After selecting suitable features, these prediction methods usually train and test on two types of datasets: a deleterious nsSNP set, which contains substitutions assumed to affect protein function, and a neutral set, which contains

substitutions assumed to have no effect. During the training procedure, machine learning approaches are adopted to construct a classification and give a prediction score measuring the deleteriousness of an nsSNP. A prediction method should predict the substitutions in the deleterious nsSNP set to be damaging to protein function and predict the substitutions in the neutral set to be not related to protein function. Sometimes, a confident score is also provided to explain how confident the prediction result is. A bigger confident score means that the prediction is more approximate to the truth. Criteria to evaluate the prediction methods are mainly accuracy (ACC), false negative error rate (FN), and false positive rate (FP). False negative error rate is the percentage of nsSNP substitutions incorrectly predicted to be neutral, and false positive error is the percentage of neutral substitutions incorrectly predicted to affect protein function [8].

SIFT incorporates position-specific information by using sequence alignment and is intended specifically for predicting whether an amino acid substitution affects protein function. SIFT starts with a query protein sequence. Relying on the observation that proteins in the same subfamily have high conservation in conserved regions, SIFT selects sequences that are similar to the query sequence by adding the most similar sequence extracted from the PSI-BLAST results iteratively to the growing collection until conservation in the conserved regions decreases [17]. After the collection of similar sequences from multiple sequence alignment by PSI-BLAST, SIFT converts the alignment into a position-specific scoring matrix (PSSM) and calculates the probability of an amino acid appearing at a specified position. Using the position-specific probability estimation, SIFT assigns a decision rule to make the classification model. SIFT also provides a measure of confidence in the prediction. To assess confidence in the prediction, SIFT calculates a conservation value at each position in the alignment. PolyPhen also uses a rule-based decision mechanism to make the prediction for candidate nsSNPs. The rule is based on the analysis of the ability of various structural parameters and profile scores to discriminate between disease mutations and substitutions [2]. The rule-based prediction can be treated as prediction using decision trees, which belongs to the binary classification.

Quite different from PolyPhen, PolyPhen-2 adopts a naïve Bayes approach coupled with entropy-based discretization. The naïve Bayes approach can work as well as some machine learning approaches and contains only one parameter, which is Laplace estimators used for representing factored probabilities and smoothing [18]. MutationTaster also uses a naïve Bayes classifier, which predicts the potential candidate disease-associated nsSNPs. Different from other algorithms, MutationTaster chooses between three different prediction models, which are either aimed at "silent" synonymous or intronic alterations, at alterations affecting a single amino acid, or at alterations causing complex changes in the amino acid sequence.

MSRV provides a more realistic solution for identifying disease-associated nsSNPs. MSRV prioritizes mutations occurring in genetic regions to find those that are most likely to cause diseases. MSRV first partitions the training set to 20 subsets according to different type of amino acid and utilizes a sequential forward feature selection method to choose the valuable features for each subset among extracted 26 physiochemical and conservation features. Then, MSRV trains a decision tree for each subset and takes advantage of random forest algorithm for the multiple selection strategy.

SNAP could potentially classify all nsSNPs in all proteins into deleterious (effect on function) and neutral (no effect) using sequence-based computationally acquired information alone. For each instance SNAP provides a reliability index, which is a well-calibrated measure reflecting the level of confidence of a particular prediction. SNAP uses an approximation of the rule of thumb for feature selection, and a standard feed-forward neural network with momentum term to build a classification model. SNAP also applies support vector machines (SVMs) for the prediction problem but receives a worse performance than a comparable neural network-based method.

6. Beyond Classification of nsSNPs

6.1. From Coding Mutations to Noncoding Mutations. Methods for predict deleteriousness of nsSNPs mainly focus on protein coding regions and conveniently use the properties derived from protein sequence or structure as classification features. Although nsSNPs in protein coding regions are important for studying the potential causative relationship between genetic variants and human inherited diseases, variants in intergenic regions, promoter regions, and intron regions can also strongly influence the phenotypic outcome [21]. In a recently published paper, Kjong-Van and Ting construct a new model named SInBaD (sequence-information-based decision-model) to evaluate any annotated human variant in all known exons, introns, splice junctions, and promoter regions. SInBaD uses nucleotide sequence conservation across multiple vertebrate species as features to find functional variants in regions other than just the coding regions. SinBaD builds three separate mathematical models for promoters, exons, and introns, using the human disease mutations annotated in human gene mutation database as the training dataset for functional variants. The authors perform deleterious variant analysis on four of the currently available individual human genomes and find out that there is considerable amount of predicted deleterious variants in promoter and intron region, especially the number of predicted deleterious variants in promoter region is almost 40% of the number of predicted deleterious variants in all regions.

Besides SinBaD, GERP also tries to overcome the limitation for noncoding mutation prediction. GERP identifies constrained elements in multiple alignments by quantifying substitution deficits, which represent that substitutions may occur if the element is neutral DNA and do not occur if the element is under functional constraint. These deficits, referred to as "Rejected Substitutions," are a natural measure of constraint that reflects the strength of past purifying selection on the element [24]. Although GERP is an algorithm to infer the constrained region, it gives each location a

substitution rejection score which can be further used as a conservation score for identifying deleterious variants.

6.2. From Deleterious Classification to Disease-Specific Prioritization. The nsSNP deleterious prediction becomes more and more wholesome when using valuable feature information, sequence information, and annotations from known database. Though effective, all these methods formulate the identification of nsSNPs that are associated with diseases as a classification problem and give no information about what specific disease the nsSNP is associated with. Therefore, the classification results of these methods can only provide limited information to practical applications. For example, an nsSNP *i* with the highest deleterious prediction score may totally change the function of the corresponding protein and have a strong relation with disease *A*. However, it is impossible that the nsSNP *i* is strongly related to all the other diseases. Therefore, disease-specific prediction models are constructed according to the features of variants, information of diseases, known disease-related variants, or other available disease-specific information. Wu et al. use ensemble learning methods to construct a prediction mechanism for disease-specific nsSNPs identification [40] and demonstrate high accuracy of their method. A biological knowledge-based mining platform for genomic and genetic studies using sequence data (KGGSeq) is also a disease-specific prioritization method which makes effort to find the causal mutations for a particular Mendelian disease among millions of variants.

6.3. From Common Variant Detection to Rare Variant Detection. Recently, the popular common-disease common-variant (CDCV) hypothesis that assumes the etiology of common diseases is intervened by commonly occurring genetic variants with small to modest effects has been challenged by the fact that both common variants and rare mutations may be involved in the pathogenesis of common diseases. In fact, studies have already revealed that the presence of multiple rare variants may augment the risk of some diseases. Corresponding to these findings, a common-disease rare-variant (CDVR) hypothesis that indicates that multiple rare variants can also serve as the main factor to influence some common diseases has been proposed. Therefore, deleterious rare variant prediction becomes a new challenge.

KGGSeq is modeled to a comprehensive three-level framework to combine a number of filtrations and prioritization functions into one analysis procedure for exome sequencing-based discovery of human Mendelian disease genes. The framework is composed by several rules to filter and prioritize variants at three different levels: genetic level, variant-gene level, and knowledge level. KGGSeq can implement rare variant detection for Mendelian disease. During a rare variant detection, KGGSeq uses some genetic information and rules to filter the candidate variants, as well as a mechanism to delete common variants deposited in public databases (including the 1000 Genomes Project and NCBI dbSNP) as well as existing in the in-house datasets according to an adjustable allele frequency threshold. KGGSeq also incorporates PPI, pathway, and literature information to narrow down the candidate rare variants.

6.4. From Single Prediction Score to Integration of Multiple Prediction Scores. More and more deleterious variant prediction methods are developed using different types of features and different training set. As each method has its own strength and weakness, it has been suggested that the combination of some of the prediction scores may enhance the accuracy for predicting a variant. Database for nonsynonymous SNPs' functional predictions (dbNSFP) follows this idea to first build an integrated database of functional predictions from multiple algorithms for the comprehensive collection of human nsSNPs. KGGSeq adopts the prediction scores from four popular algorithms (SIFT, PolyPhen-2, LRT, and MutationTaster) along with a conservation score (PhyloP) published by dbNSFP. KGGSeq uses these five scores as prediction features to train a logistic regression model and find these scores are in weak or moderate correlation. When individually operating the algorithm, MutationTaster outperforms than the other four prediction algorithms. In addition, the combination of predictions by all the five deleterious scores can provide better performance than individual scores as well as combined prediction by part of the deleteriousness scores.

7. Conclusions and Discussion

Deleterious variants detection becomes a more and more popular issue for research and guiding real experiment. In this paper we summarize the database for collecting nsSNP data, existing deleterious nsSNPs prediction methods, prediction features conducted in prediction model, and prediction algorithms to distinguish the deleterious nsSNPs. We discuss computational methods that use comparative genomics to predict deleteriousness in both coding and noncoding DNA, methods for disease-specific nsSNP detection, and methods for rare variant detection. We suggest using multiple prediction algorithms, as well as more available molecule level information may help to enhance the prediction power.

Although the prediction of deleterious nsSNPs seems to be more and more accurate when integrating more valuable information of nsSNPs, there still exist some challenges to deal with. Conservation scores are used by most of the prediction methods as main features to predict the functional effects of a candidate variant. However, not all the deleterious variants are in the constraint region or conserved among multiple sequence alignment. As a result, the nonconserved variants are difficult to identify using existing methods. Accuracy assessment is another problem. During the prediction, deleterious variants and neutral variants are collected from published database, such as OMIM and SWISSPROT. However, whether the so-called deleterious variants are really deleterious or not and whether the so-called neutral variants are really neutral or not may strongly affect the construction of predict model and the final accuracy measurement of the model. In addition, even if a variant is predicted to be deleterious with a strong confidence, the information about

which disease the variant is related to and which disease the variant has a casual relation with is still missing. Facts show that variants in noncoding region can strongly influence the phenotypic outcome, and more algorithms for noncoding region deleterious variant detection using more available features besides conservation scores should be designed for further studying the casual relationship between noncoding variants and diseases. Furthermore, standard evaluation rules should be proposed for better comparing the existing deleterious variant prediction methods.

As a suggestion, more molecule level protein information or gene information should be merged with existing features to further strengthen the prediction power. As the protein products of genes responsible for the same or phenotypically similar disorders tend to physically interact with each other so as to carry out certain biological functions [23], PPI data could be considered. Genes sharing similar GO terms trend to have similar functions; thus, gene-gene similarity calculated using GO terms could provide another choice. Moreover, pathway information can be included based on the fact that causative genes of the same (or phenotypically similar) diseases are inclined to distribute within the same pathways.

Acknowledgments

This research was partially supported by the National Basic Research Program of China (2012CB316504), the National High Technology Research and Development Program of China (2012AA020401), the National Natural Science Foundation of China (61175002 and 60805010), the Tsinghua University Initiative Scientific Research Program, and the Tsinghua National Laboratory for Information Science and Technology (TNList) Academic Exchange Foundation, and the Open Research Fund of State Key Laboratory of Bioelectronics, Southeast University.

References

[1] Y. Bromberg and B. Rost, "SNAP: predict effect of non-synonymous polymorphisms on function," *Nucleic Acids Research*, vol. 35, no. 11, pp. 3823–3835, 2007.

[2] V. Ramensky, P. Bork, and S. Sunyaev, "Human non-synonymous SNPs: server and survey," *Nucleic Acids Research*, vol. 30, no. 17, pp. 3894–3900, 2002.

[3] J. Wu, M. Gan, and R. Jiang, "Prioritisation of candidate single amino acid polymorphisms using one-class learning machines," *International Journal of Computational Biology and Drug Design*, vol. 4, no. 4, pp. 316–331, 2011.

[4] G. M. Cooper and J. Shendure, "Needles in stacks of needles: finding disease-causal variants in a wealth of genomic data," *Nature Reviews Genetics*, vol. 12, pp. 628–640, 2011.

[5] J. M. Schwarz, C. Rödelsperger, M. Schuelke, and D. Seelow, "MutationTaster evaluates disease-causing potential of sequence alterations," *Nature Methods*, vol. 7, no. 8, pp. 575–576, 2010.

[6] S. Nakken, I. Alseth, and T. Rognes, "Computational prediction of the effects of non-synonymous single nucleotide polymorphisms in human DNA repair genes," *Neuroscience*, vol. 145, no. 4, pp. 1273–1279, 2007.

[7] M. Krawczak, E. V. Ball, I. Fenton et al., "Human gene mutation database—a biomedical information and research resource," *Human Mutation*, vol. 15, no. 1, pp. 45–51, 2000.

[8] P. C. Ng and S. Henikoff, "Predicting the effects of amino acid substitutions on protein function," *Annual Review of Genomics and Human Genetics*, vol. 7, pp. 61–80, 2006.

[9] X. Liu, X. Jian, and E. Boerwinkle, "dbNSFP: a lightweight database of human nonsynonymous SNPs and their functional predictions," *Human Mutation*, vol. 32, no. 8, pp. 894–899, 2011.

[10] A. Siepel, K. Pollard, and D. Haussler, "New methods for detecting lineage-specific selection," in *Proceedings of the 10th International Conference on Research in Computational Molecular Biology (RECOMB '06)*, pp. 190–205, Venice, Italy, 2006.

[11] R. Jiang, H. Yang, L. Zhou, C. C. J. Kuo, F. Sun, and T. Chen, "Sequence-based prioritization of nonsynonymous single-nucleotide polymorphisms for the study of disease mutations," *American Journal of Human Genetics*, vol. 81, no. 2, pp. 346–360, 2007.

[12] P. D. Stenson, E. V. Ball, M. Mort et al., "Human Gene Mutation Database (HGMD): 2003 update," *Human Mutation*, vol. 21, no. 6, pp. 577–581, 2003.

[13] T. U. Consortium, "The universal protein resource (UniProt) in 2010," *Nucleic Acids Research*, vol. 38, pp. D142–D148, 2010.

[14] D. Fredman, M. Siegfried, Y. P. Yuan, P. Bork, H. Lehväslaiho, and A. J. Brookes, "HGVbase: a human sequence variation database emphasizing data quality and a broad spectrum of data sources," *Nucleic Acids Research*, vol. 30, no. 1, pp. 387–391, 2002.

[15] S. T. Sherry, M. H. Ward, M. Kholodov et al., "DbSNP: the NCBI database of genetic variation," *Nucleic Acids Research*, vol. 29, no. 1, pp. 308–311, 2001.

[16] T. Kawabata, M. Ota, and K. Nishikawa, "The protein mutant database," *Nucleic Acids Research*, vol. 27, no. 1, pp. 355–357, 1999.

[17] P. Kumar, S. Henikoff, and P. C. Ng, "Predicting the effects of coding non-synonymous variants on protein function using the SIFT algorithm," *Nature Protocols*, vol. 4, no. 7, pp. 1073–1081, 2009.

[18] I. A. Adzhubei, S. Schmidt, L. Peshkin et al., "A method and server for predicting damaging missense mutations," *Nature Methods*, vol. 7, no. 4, pp. 248–249, 2010.

[19] S. Chun and J. C. Fay, "Identification of deleterious mutations within three human genomes," *Genome Research*, vol. 19, no. 9, pp. 1553–1561, 2009.

[20] W. Jiaxin, G. Mingxin, Z. Wangshu, and J. Rui, "Prediction of disease-associated single amino acid polymorphisms based on physiochemical features," *International Journal of Bioscience, Biochemistry and Bioinformatics*, vol. 1, no. 2, pp. 102–108, 2011.

[21] L. Kjong-Van and C. Ting, "Exploring functional variant discovery in non-coding regions with SInBaD," *Nucleic Acids Research*, vol. 41, no. 1, p. e7, 2013.

[22] A. Hamosh, A. F. Scott, J. S. Amberger, C. A. Bocchini, and V. A. McKusick, "Online Mendelian Inheritance in Man (OMIM), a knowledgebase of human genes and genetic disorders," *Nucleic Acids Research*, vol. 33, pp. D514–D517, 2005.

[23] M. X. Li, H. S. Gui, J. S. H. Kwan et al., "A comprehensive framework for prioritizing variants in exome sequencing studies of Mendelian diseases," *Nucleic Acids Research*, vol. 40, no. 7, p. e53, 2012.

[24] G. M. Cooper, D. L. Goode, S. B. Ng et al., "Single-nucleotide evolutionary constraint scores highlight disease-causing mutations," *Nature Methods*, vol. 7, no. 4, pp. 250–251, 2010.

[25] A. Schlessinger, G. Yachdav, and B. Rost, "PROFbval: predict flexible and rigid residues in proteins," *Bioinformatics*, vol. 22, no. 7, pp. 891–893, 2006.

[26] S. F. Altschul, W. Gish, W. Miller, E. W. Myers, and D. J. Lipman, "Basic local alignment search tool," *Journal of Molecular Biology*, vol. 215, no. 3, pp. 403–410, 1990.

[27] S. R. Sunyaev, F. Eisenhaber, I. V. Rodchenkov, B. Eisenhaber, V. G. Tumanyan, and E. N. Kuznetsov, "PSIC: profile extraction from sequence alignments with position-specific counts of independent observations," *Protein Engineering*, vol. 12, no. 5, pp. 387–394, 1999.

[28] D. Chasman and R. M. Adams, "Predicting the functional consequences of non-synonymous single nucleotide polymorphisms: structure-based assessment of amino acid variation," *Journal of Molecular Biology*, vol. 307, no. 2, pp. 683–706, 2001.

[29] P. C. Ng and S. Henikoff, "Predicting deleterious amino acid substitutions," *Genome Research*, vol. 11, pp. 863–874, 2001.

[30] P. Yue, Z. Li, and J. Moult, "Loss of protein structure stability as a major causative factor in monogenic disease," *Journal of Molecular Biology*, vol. 353, no. 2, pp. 459–473, 2005.

[31] S. R. Sunyaev, V. Ramensky, I. Koch, W. I. Lathe, A. S. Kondrashov, and P. Bork, "Prediction of deleterious human alleles," *Human Molecular Genetics*, vol. 10, no. 6, pp. 591–597, 2001.

[32] S. Sunyaev, V. Ramensky, I. Koch, W. Lathe III, A. S. Kondrashov, and P. Bork, "Prediction of deleterious human alleles," *Human Molecular Genetics*, vol. 10, no. 6, pp. 591–597, 2001.

[33] Z. Wang and J. Moult, "SNPs, protein structure, and disease," *Human Mutation*, vol. 17, no. 4, pp. 263–270, 2001.

[34] D. Chasman and R. M. Adams, "Predicting the functional consequences of non-synonymous single nucleotide polymorphisms: structure-based assessment of amino acid variation," *Journal of Molecular Biology*, vol. 307, no. 2, pp. 683–706, 2001.

[35] W. Kabsch and C. Sander, "Dictionary of protein secondary structure: pattern recognition of hydrogen-bonded and geometrical features," *Biopolymers*, vol. 22, no. 12, pp. 2577–2637, 1983.

[36] A. Momen-Roknabadi, M. Sadeghi, H. Pezeshk, and S. A. Marashi, "Impact of residue accessible surface area on the prediction of protein secondary structures," *BMC Bioinformatics*, vol. 9, article 357, 2008.

[37] R. Adamczak, A. Porollo, and J. Meller, "Combining prediction of secondary structure and solvent accessibility in proteins," *Proteins*, vol. 59, no. 3, pp. 467–475, 2005.

[38] C. Ferrer-Costa, M. Orozco, and X. de la Cruz, "Sequence-based prediction of pathological mutations," *Proteins*, vol. 57, no. 4, pp. 811–819, 2004.

[39] F. Cambien, O. Poirier, V. Nicaud et al., "Sequence diversity in 36 candidate genes for cardiovascular disorders," *American Journal of Human Genetics*, vol. 65, no. 1, pp. 183–191, 1999.

[40] J. Wu, W. Zhang, and R. Jiang, "Comparative study of ensemble learning approaches in the identification of disease mutations," in *Proceedings of the 3rd International Conference on Biomedical Engineering and Informatics (BMEI '10)*, vol. 6, pp. 2306–2310, Yantai, China, October 2010.

15

Global Stability of Vector-Host Disease with Variable Population Size

Muhammad Altaf Khan,[1] Saeed Islam,[1] Sher Afzal Khan,[2] and Gul Zaman[3]

[1] Department of Mathematics, Abdul Wali Khan University, Mardan, Khyber Pakhtunkhwa, Pakistan
[2] Department of Computer Sciences, Abdul Wali Khan University, Mardan, Khyber Pakhtunkhwa, Pakistan
[3] Department of Mathematics, University of Malakand, Dir, Pakistan

Correspondence should be addressed to Muhammad Altaf Khan; altafdir@gmail.com

Academic Editor: Ali Khraibi

The paper presents the vector-host disease with a variability in population. We assume, the disease is fatal and for some cases the infected individuals become susceptible. We first show the local and global stability of the disease-free equilibrium, for the case when $R_0 < 1$. We also show that for $R_0 < 1$, the disease free-equilibrium of the model is both locally as well as globally stable. For $R_0 > 1$, there exists a unique positive endemic equilibrium. For $R_0 > 1$, the disease persistence occurs. The endemic equilibrium is locally as well as globally asymptotically stable for $R_0 > 1$. Numerical results are presented for the justifications of theoratical results.

1. Introduction

Mathematical modeling for disease transmission in host population is of great practical value in predicting and controlling disease spread (West Nile virus in North America in the 1990s, Avian influenza worldwide in the 2000s, SARS in Asia in 2003, etc.). The battle between infectious diseases and humans was heavily lopsided for much of the history. Since the pioneering work of Edward Jenner (a doctor, who worked in Gloucestershire, UK, noticed that individuals who had contracted cowpox rarely caught smallpox) on smallpox [1], the process of protecting individuals from infection by vaccination has become a routine, with substantial historical success in reducing both morbidity and mortality (see [2, 3] and references cited therein). Typically, after the initial infection, the host remains in a latent stage for a period of time before becoming infectious. For some diseases, the latent period is neither short nor negligible compared with the infectious period (scarlet fever: 1-2 days versus 14–21 days [4]; measles: 4–12 days versus 17–31 days [5]), leptospirosis, 2–12 days.

In this paper, we consider an epidemic model of vector-host population. The disease spread due to vector, for example, leptospirosis, dengue, malaria, west Nile virus, and so forth, is considered. We assume that the individuals after some time become susceptible again. Therefore, the term λ_h is added in the model. The model consists of the interaction of human and vector. The human population is divided in three subclasses, that is, susceptible human $S_h(t)$, infected human $I_h(t)$, and recovered human $R_h(t)$. The total population size of human is shown by N_1 and $N_1 = S_h(t) + I_h(t) + R_h(t)$. The vector population is divided in two subclasses, susceptible vector $S_v(t)$ and $I_v(t)$. The total size of the vector population is denoted by N_2, with $N_2 = S_v(t) + I_v(t)$. The disease spread from vector, like leptospirosis, effects humans as well as cattle [9]. The human are infected by means of drinking water contaminated by dead rats or by infectious cattle while drinking water. This infection can also spread through the urine of infected human. Those who work in the fields, like marshy places, rice planters, going in dirty water, those who swimming in water are mostly infected. Weil's first time describes leptospirosis as a unique disease process in 1886, while 30 years before Inada and his colleagues identified the causal organism. The symptoms of leptospirosis are high fever, headache, chills, muscle aches, conjunctivitis (red eyes), diarrhea, vomiting, and kidney or liver problems (which may also include jaundice), anemia, and, sometimes, rash. Symptoms may last from a few days and up to several weeks.

Deaths from this disease may occur but they are rare. For some cases, the infections can be mild and without obvious symptoms [10–14].

Many works have been done on vector-host models, as in [15–17]. Reference [15] presented a mathematical model of vector host in which the population dynamics of an SIR vector transmitted disease with two pathogen strains. They discussed the stability of the vector-host model and also presented the numerical simulation of their model. Reference [16], they presented the vector-host model of dengue disease; they analyzed the dengue model and presented their stability and numerical results for vector host dengue model. Reference [17], they presented a mathematical model in the form of demographic stochasticity and heterogeneity in transmission of infection dynamics of host-vector disease systems. Mathematical and theoretical discussion is presented in the paper. For more discussion, we refer the readers to the previously mentioned articles. In our models, we have presented the vector-host model with their stability analysis. We obtain, if $R_0 \leq 1$, it recover the community. However, for $R_0 > 1$ the disease remains in the community. We present the global stability of the model and also we present in a good way the numerical simulation of the proposed model, choosing the different values for the parameters.

Many models have been proposed to represent the dynamics of both human and vector population [18–20]. Pongsuumpun et al. [21] developed mathematical models to study the behavior of leptospirosis disease. They represent the rate of change for both rats and human population. The human population are further divided into two main groups juveniles and adults. Triampo et al. [7] considered a deterministic model for the transmission of leptospirosis disease [7]. In their work, they considered a number of leptospirosis infections in Thailand and shown the numerical simulations. Zaman [6] considered the real data presented in [7] to study the dynamical behavior and role of optimal control theory. The dynamical interaction including local and global stability of leptospirosis infected vector and human population which can be found in Zaman et al. [22]. In their work they also presented the bifurcation analysis and presented the numerical simulations for different values of infection rate.

The structure of the paper is organized as follows. Section 2 is devoted to the formulation of the mathematic model and reducing it to the normalized model. In Section 3, we present the infection-free equilibrium, the basic reproduction and the local and global stability of infection equilibrium. In Section 4, we present the disease persistence and existence of the endemic equilibrium. In Section 5, we show the local as well as the global stability of the endemic equilibrium for the reproduction number $R_0 > 1$. The numerical results, conclusion and references are presented in Section 6.

2. Mathematical Model

In this section, a vector-host epidemic model with direct transmission is presented. The host population at time t is divided into susceptible $S_h(t)$, $I_h(t)$ infected, and recovered $R_h(t)$ individuals. The vector population at time t is divided into susceptible $S_v(t)$ and infected vector population $I_v(t)$. The total population of humans is denoted by N_1, and the total population of the vector is denoted by N_2. Thus, $N_1(t) = S_h(t) + I_h(t) + R_h(t)$ and $N_2(t) = S_v(t) + I_v(t)$. The mathematical representation of the model which consists of the system of nonlinear differential equations with five state variables is given by

$$\frac{dS_h}{dt} = \Lambda_h N_1 - \mu_h S_h - \frac{\beta_2 S_h I_v}{N_2} - \frac{\beta_1 S_h I_h}{N_1} + \lambda_h R_h,$$

$$\frac{dI_h}{dt} = \frac{\beta_2 S_h I_v}{N_2} + \frac{\beta_1 S_h I_h}{N_1} - \mu_h I_h - \delta_h I_h - \gamma_h I_h,$$

$$\frac{dR_h}{dt} = \gamma_h I_h - \mu_h R_h - \lambda_h R_h, \tag{1}$$

$$\frac{dS_v}{dt} = \Lambda_v N_2 - \gamma_v S_v - \frac{\beta_3 S_v I_h}{N_1},$$

$$\frac{dI_v}{dt} = \frac{\beta_3 S_v I_h}{N_1} - \gamma_v I_v.$$

Here, Λ_h is the recruitment rate of human population; susceptible human can be infected by two ways of transmission, that is, directly, or through infected individuals; β_1, β_2 are the mediate transmission coefficients. μ_h is the natural mortality rate for humans; γ_h is the recovery rate for humans from the infections. We assumed that the disease may be fatal to some infectious hosts, so disease-related death rate from infected class occurs at human populations at δ_h. The immune human once again susceptible at constant rate λ_h, for some disease like dengue, the chances for susceptibility are less compared to dengue, West Nile virus, malaria, and so forth. Λ_v is the recruitment rate for vector population. The death rate of vector γ_v, β_3 is the disease carrying the vector to the host per unit time:

$$\frac{dN_1}{dt} = \Lambda_h N_1 - \mu_h N_1 - \delta_h I_h. \tag{2}$$

2.1. Normalized Model. For the normalization of the model, we let $\widehat{S}_h = \widehat{S}_h/N_1$, $\widehat{I}_h = I_h/N_1$, $\widehat{R}_h = R_h/N_1$, $\widehat{S}_v = S_v/N_2$, and $\widehat{I}_v = \widehat{I}_v/N_2$. It is easy to verify that $\widehat{S}_h$, $\widehat{I}_h$, $\widehat{R}_h$, $\widehat{S}_v$, and $\widehat{I}_v$ satisfy the following system of differential equations:

$$\frac{d\widehat{S}_h}{dt} = \Lambda_h \left(1 - \widehat{S}_h\right) + \delta_h \widehat{S}_h \widehat{I}_h - \beta_2 \widehat{S}_h \widehat{I}_v - \beta_1 \widehat{S}_h \widehat{I}_h$$
$$\qquad + \lambda_h \left(1 - \widehat{S}_h - \widehat{I}_h\right),$$

$$\frac{d\widehat{I}_h}{dt} = \beta_2 \widehat{S}_h \widehat{I}_v + \beta_1 \widehat{S}_h \widehat{I}_h - \left(\Lambda_h + \delta_h + \gamma_h\right) \widehat{I}_h + \delta_h \widehat{I}_h^2,$$

$$\frac{d\widehat{R}_h}{dt} = \gamma_h \widehat{I}_h - \left(\Lambda_h + \lambda_h\right) \widehat{R}_h + \delta_h \widehat{R}_h \widehat{I}_h, \tag{3}$$

$$\frac{d\widehat{S}_v}{dt} = \Lambda_v \left(1 - \widehat{S}_v\right) - \beta_3 \widehat{S}_v \widehat{I}_h,$$

$$\frac{dI_v}{dt} = \beta_3 \widehat{S}_v \widehat{I}_h - \gamma_v \widehat{I}_v.$$

With restriction, $\hat{S}_h + \hat{I}_h + \hat{R}_h = N_1 = 1$, $\hat{S}_v + \hat{I}_v = N_2 = 1$ and $\hat{I}_v = 1 - \hat{S}_v$. In the first equation of the normalized model, we substituted $\hat{R}_h = 1 - \hat{S}_h - \hat{I}_h$. So in the normalized system the $\hat{R}_h$ does not appear. We reduced to the normalized model (3), and we will study the reduced model:

$$\frac{d\hat{S}_h}{dt} = \Lambda_h \left(1 - \hat{S}_h\right) - \beta_2 \hat{S}_h \hat{I}_v + \delta_h \hat{S}_h \hat{I}_h - \beta_1 \hat{S}_h \hat{I}_h$$
$$+ \lambda_h \left(1 - \hat{S}_h - \hat{I}_h\right),$$

$$\frac{d\hat{I}_h}{dt} = \beta_2 \hat{S}_h \hat{I}_v + \beta_1 \hat{S}_h \hat{I}_h - \left(\Lambda_h + \delta_h + \gamma_h\right) \hat{I}_h + \delta_h \hat{I}_h^2$$

$$\frac{dI_v}{dt} = \beta_3 \left(1 - \hat{I}_v\right) \hat{I}_h - \gamma_v \hat{I}_v. \tag{4}$$

We determine $\hat{S}_v$ and $\hat{R}_h$ from $\hat{S}_v = 1 - \hat{I}_v$ and $\hat{R}_h = 1 - \hat{S}_h - \hat{I}_h$, respectively. For reduced system (4), the feasible region is

$$\Omega := \left\{ \left(\hat{S}_h, \hat{I}_h, \hat{I}_v\right) \in \mathbf{R}_+^3 \mid 0 \le \hat{S}_h + \hat{I}_h + \hat{I}_v \le 1 \right\}. \tag{5}$$

With the nonnegative initial conditions values of Ω, the system is positively invariant, and the proof is easy.

3. Infection-Free Equilibrium and Basic Reproduction Number

The basic reproduction for the reduced system (4) is given by

$$R_0 = \frac{\beta_1}{\left(\Lambda_h + \delta_h + \gamma_h\right)} + \frac{\beta_2 \beta_3}{\gamma_v \left(\Lambda_h + \delta_h + \gamma_h\right)}. \tag{6}$$

The disease eradicated from the population by two ways, first with the varying size in population and $\hat{I}_h \to 0$, and the second one is $I_h \to 0$, for detail see [23, 24]. We are thus inspired to seek the conditions for infection-free and endemic equilibrium. The infection-free equilibrium point for model (4) is $E_o = (\hat{S}_h = \hat{S}_h^0, 0, 0)$ and for endemic equilibrium $E^* = (\hat{S}_h^*, \hat{I}_h^*, \hat{S}_v^*)$. The infection-free equilibrium is obtained by setting the left side of the reduced model (4), we obtain $\hat{S}_h^0 = 1$. Obviously the infection-free equilibrium $E_o = (\hat{S}_h = \hat{S}_h^0 = 1, 0, 0)$ belongs to Ω of reduced model (4), which exists for all positive parameters. Next, we prove the infection-free local asymptotical stability of model (4) at the arbitrary point $E_1 = (\hat{S}_h, \hat{I}_h, \hat{I}_v)$.

Theorem 1. *The infection-free equilibrium of reduced model (4) is stable locally asymptotically stable for $R_0 < 1$ when $\gamma_v + C_1 > \beta_1$ and unstable for $R_0 \ge 1$.*

Proof. The Jacobean matrix of the reduced model about the equilibrium point E_0 is given by

$$J\left(E^0\right)$$

$$= \begin{pmatrix} -\beta_2 \hat{I}_v - \beta_1 \hat{I}_h - \Lambda_h + \delta \hat{I}_h & \left(\delta_h - \beta_1\right) \hat{S}_h - \lambda_h & -\beta_2 \hat{S}_h \\ \beta_2 \hat{I}_v + \beta_1 \hat{I}_h & \beta_1 \hat{S}_h - C_1 + 2\delta_h \hat{I}_h & \beta_2 \hat{S}_h \\ 0 & \beta_3 \left(1 - \hat{I}_v\right) & -\beta_3 \hat{I}_h - \gamma_v \end{pmatrix}, \tag{7}$$

where $C_1 = \Lambda_h + \gamma_h + \delta_h$.

The characteristics equation of the Jacobian matrix $J(E^0)$ is obtained by

$$\left(-\Lambda_h - \lambda\right) \left(\left(\left(\beta_1 - C_1\right) - \lambda\right) \left(\gamma_v - \lambda\right) - \beta_2 \beta_3\right) = 0. \tag{8}$$

The eigenvalue $-\lambda_h$ has a negative real part, and the rest of the two eigenvalues is calculated by Routh-Harwitz-Criteria. We write

$$\lambda^2 + \lambda \left(\gamma_v + C_1 - \beta_1\right) + \gamma_v C_1 \left(1 - R_0\right) = 0, \tag{9}$$

when $R_0 < 1$, then Routh-Hurtwiz Criteria are satisfied if $\gamma_v + C_1 > \beta_1$. The infection-free equilibrium is locally asymptotically stable. $\square$

Next, we show the global asymptotical stability of infection-free equilibrium, by defining the Lyapunove function.

Theorem 2. *If the threshold quantity $R_0 \le 1$, the infection-free equilibrium of the reduced model (4) is globally asymptotically stable and is an unstable infection-free equilibrium for system (4), when $R_0 > 1$.*

Proof. To show the global stability of infection-free equilibrium of reduced model (4), we define the Lyapunove function in the following:

$$P(t) = \gamma_v \hat{I}_h + \beta_2 \hat{I}_v. \tag{10}$$

Taking the time derivative of (10), along the solution of system (4), we obtain

$$P'(t) = \gamma_v \left[\beta_2 \hat{S}_h \hat{I}_v + \beta_1 \hat{S}_h \hat{I}_h - \left(\Lambda_h + \delta_h + \gamma_h\right) \hat{I}_h + \delta_h \hat{I}_h^2\right]$$
$$+ \beta_2 \left[\beta_3 \left(1 - \hat{I}_v\right) \hat{I}_h - \gamma_v \hat{I}_v\right]. \tag{11}$$

Using $\hat{S}_h = 1 - \hat{I}_h$ and simplifying, we get

$$P'(t) = -\gamma_v \beta_2 \hat{I}_v \hat{I}_h - \gamma_v \left(\beta_1 - \delta_h\right) \hat{I}_h^2 - \beta_2 \beta_3 \hat{I}_h \hat{I}_v$$
$$- \gamma_v \left(\Lambda_h + \gamma_h + \delta_h\right) \left(1 - R_0\right) \hat{I}_h. \tag{12}$$

When $R_0 \le 1$, the infection free-equilibrium is globally asymptotically stable, and $P'(t)$ is negative. $P'(t)$ becomes zero when $\hat{I}_h$ is zero and vice versa. By the Lasalle invariant principle [25], which implies that the infection-free equilibrium at the point E_0 is globally asymptotically stable in Ω. $\square$

4. Disease Persistence

In this section, we study the uniform persistence of the reduced system (4). The disease persistence occurs for the case when the threshold parameter $R_0 > 1$, by applying the acyclicity Theorem [26].

Definition 3. The reduced model (4) is called uniformly persistence if there exists a constant $c \in (0, 1)$ such that any solution $(\hat{S}_h, \hat{I}_h, \hat{I}_v)$ with $(\hat{S}_h(0), \hat{I}_h(0), \hat{I}_v(0)) \in \Omega$ satisfies

$$\min \left\{ \liminf_{t \to \infty} \hat{S}_h(t), \liminf_{t \to \infty} \hat{I}_h(t), \liminf_{t \to \infty} \hat{I}_v(t) \right\} \ge c. \tag{13}$$

Let X be a locally compact metric space with metric d, and let C be a closed nonempty subset of X with boundary $\partial\Omega$ and interior of Ω^o. Obviously, $\partial\Omega$ is the closed subset of Ω. Suppose that $\phi_t(x)$ be a dynamical system defined on Ω. A subset B in X is said to be invariant if $\phi(B,t) = B$. Define $T_\partial := \{x \in \partial\Omega : \phi_t(x) \in \partial\Omega, \text{ for all } t \geq 0\}$.

Lemma 4. *Assume that*

(H_1) *$\phi(t)$ has a global attractor;*

(H_2) *there exists an $N = N_1, \ldots, N_k$ of pair-wise disjoint, compact, and isolated invariant set on $\partial\Omega$ such that;*

(a_1) *$V_{x\in\partial\Omega} \subset V_{j=1}^k N_j$;*

(a_2) *no subset of N forming a cycle on $\partial\Omega$;*

(a_3) *each of N_j is also isolated in $\partial\Omega$;*

(a_4) *$W^s(N_j) \cap \Omega^o = \hat{\phi}$ for every $1 \leq j \leq k$, where $W^s(N_j)$ is the stable manifold of N_j. Then $\phi(t)$ is uniformly persistent with respect to Ω^o [26].*

By the application of Lemma 4 to our model, suppose that

$$\Omega := \left\{ (\widehat{S}_h, \widehat{I}_h, \widehat{I}_v) \in \mathbf{R}_+^3 \mid 0 \leq \widehat{S}_h + \widehat{I}_h + \widehat{I}_v \leq 1 \right\}, \quad (14)$$

from (5),

$$\Omega^o := \left\{ \widehat{S}_h, \widehat{I}_h, \widehat{I}_v \in E, \widehat{I}_h, \widehat{I}_v > 0 \right\}, \qquad \partial\Omega = \frac{\Omega}{\Omega^o}. \quad (15)$$

Clearly, $N_\partial = \partial\Omega$.

Hypotheisis (a_1) and (a_2) hold, for (4), reducing to $\widehat{S}_h' = (\Lambda_h + \lambda_h) - (\Lambda_h + \lambda_h)\widehat{S}_h$, when t_∞, then $\widehat{S}_h'(t) = 1$. When $R_o > 1$, the infection-free equilibrium is unstable. Also, $W^s(N) = \partial\Omega$. (a_3) and (a_4) are satisfied. Due to the boundedness the reduced system (4) always admits a global attractor, so H_1 is satisfied. We now state the above discussion in the form of the following result.

Theorem 5. *For $R_0 > 1$, the reduced system (4), is uniformly persistent.*

4.1. Existence of the Endemic Equilibrium. We have proved in Section 4 the local asymptotical stability of infection-free equilibrium when $R_0 < 1$. In such case, when the infection-free equilibrium is locally asymptotically stable for is $R_0 < 1$, the disease dies out and no endemic equilibrium exists. From epidemiological point of view, it is important to show the existence of endemic equilibrium when $R_0 > 1$.

Let $E^* = (\widehat{S}_h^*, \widehat{I}_h^*, \widehat{I}_v^*)$ belong to Ω which is an endemic equilibrium. From reduced system (4), its coordinates should satisfy

$$\Lambda_h \left(1 - \widehat{S}_h^*\right) - \beta_2 \widehat{S}_h^* \widehat{I}_v^* + \delta_h \widehat{S}_h^* \widehat{I}_h^* - \beta_1 \widehat{S}_h^* \widehat{I}_h^*$$

$$+ \lambda_h \left(1 - \widehat{S}_h^* - \widehat{I}_h^*\right) = 0,$$

$$\beta_2 \widehat{S}_h^* \widehat{I}_v^* + \beta_1 \widehat{S}_h^* \widehat{I}_h^* - \left(\Lambda_h + \delta_h + \gamma_h\right) \widehat{I}_h^* + \delta_h \widehat{I}_h^{*2} = 0,$$

$$\beta_3 \left(1 - \widehat{I}_v^*\right) \widehat{I}_h^* - \gamma_v \widehat{I}_v^* = 0, \quad (16)$$

with $\widehat{S}_h^* > 0$, $\widehat{I}_h^* > 0$, and $\widehat{I}_v^* > 0$. By adding the system (16), and solve for $\widehat{I}_h^*$, we obtain

$$\left(\left(\Lambda_h + \lambda_h\right) - \delta_h \widehat{I}_h^*\right)\left(1 - \widehat{S}_h^* - \widehat{I}_h^*\right)$$

$$= -\left(\gamma_v + \gamma_h\right) + \left(\beta_3 \widehat{I}_h^* - \gamma_v\right)\left(1 - \widehat{I}_v^*\right). \quad (17)$$

This gives the range for $\widehat{I}_h^*$ in the following:

$$0 < \widehat{I}_h^* < \left(\left\{ 1, \min \frac{(\Lambda_h + \lambda_h)}{\delta_h} \right\}, \left\{ 1, \min \left\{ \frac{\beta_3}{\gamma_v} \right\} \right\} \right). \quad (18)$$

From (18), note that the disease-related death δ, less than the $(\Lambda_h + \lambda_h)$, the birth rate Λ, the rate at which the human become susceptible λ_h, the sum of $(\Lambda_h + \lambda_h)$, and the contact rate coefficient β_3, and the less value of γ_v (natural death rate of vector) will lie in the interval $(0, 1)$. Now, further eliminate $\widehat{S}_h^*$ and $\widehat{I}_v^*$ from (10), then $\widehat{I}_h^*$ satisfies

$$\left(\left(\Lambda_h + \lambda_h\right) - \gamma_h \widehat{I}_h^*\right) - \left[\left(\lambda_h + \delta_h + \gamma_h\right) - \delta_h \widehat{I}_h^*\right] \widehat{I}_h^*$$

$$= \left(\Lambda_h + \lambda_h - \delta_h \widehat{I}_h^*\right) \left\{ \frac{\left(\Lambda_h + \delta_h + \gamma_h\right) - \delta_h \widehat{I}_h^*}{\beta_2 \beta_3 + \beta_1 \left(\gamma_v + \beta_3 \widehat{I}_h^*\right)} \left(\gamma_v + \beta_3 \widehat{I}_h^*\right) \right\}. \quad (19)$$

Further simplification gives

$$f\left(\widehat{I}_h^*\right) = \widehat{I}_h^{*3} + B_1 \widehat{I}_h^{*2} + B_2 \widehat{I}_h^* + B_3, \quad (20)$$

where

$$B_1 = \beta_1 \gamma_v \delta_h + \beta_3 \delta_h \left(\beta_2 + \Lambda_h + \gamma_h\right)$$

$$+ \frac{\beta_3 \left[\beta_1 \left(2\gamma_h + \lambda_h + \delta_h\right) - \left(\Lambda_h + \lambda_h\right)\left(\Lambda_h + \gamma_h\right)\right]}{\beta_1 \beta_3 \delta_h},$$

$$B_2 = \beta_1 \gamma_v \left(2\gamma_h + \lambda - h + \delta_h\right) + \beta_1 \beta_3 \left(\Lambda_h + \lambda_h\right)$$

$$+ \frac{\left(\Lambda_h + \lambda_h - \delta_h\right)\left[\delta_h \gamma_v + \gamma_v \left(\Lambda_h + \delta_h + \gamma_h\right)\right]}{\beta_1 \beta_3 \delta_h},$$

$$B_3 = \frac{\left(\Lambda_h + \gamma_h + \delta_h\right)\left(\Lambda_h + \lambda_h\right)\gamma_v \left(R_0 - 1\right)}{\beta_1 \beta_3 \delta_h}, \quad (21)$$

and the equilibria of the reduced system (4) is given by

$$S_h^* = \frac{\left(\left(\Lambda_h + \lambda_h\right) - \lambda_h \widehat{I}_h^*\right)\left(\beta_3 \widehat{I}_h^* + \gamma_v\right)}{\left(\beta_2 \beta_3 \widehat{I}_h^* + \left[\left(\Lambda_h + \lambda_h\right) + \widehat{I}_h^* \left(\beta_1 - \delta_h\right)\right]\left(\beta_3 I_h + \gamma_v\right)\right)},$$

$$I_v^* = \frac{\beta_3 I_h}{\beta_3 I_h + \gamma_v}. \quad (22)$$

The positive endemic equilibrium depends upon $(\Lambda_h + \lambda_h) > \lambda_h \widehat{I}_h^*$ and $\beta_1 \geq \delta_h$ when $R_0 > 1$ we get a positive endemic equilibrium point. We now state the above in the following result.

Theorem 6. *When $R_0 > 1$, a unique positive endemic equilibrium exists for reduced system (4), In other case the existence of disease-free equilibrium.*

$$
J^*(E^*) = \begin{pmatrix}
-\Lambda_h - \beta_2 \widehat{I}_v + \delta_h \widehat{I}_h - \beta_1 \widehat{I}_h - \lambda_h & \delta_h \widehat{S}_h - \beta_1 \widehat{S}_h - \lambda_h & -\beta_2 \widehat{S}_h \\
\beta_2 \widehat{I}_v + \beta_1 \widehat{I}_h & \beta_1 \widehat{S}_h - (\Lambda_h + \delta_h + \gamma_h) + 2\delta_h \widehat{I}_h & \beta_2 \widehat{S}_h \\
0 & \beta_3 \left(1 - \widehat{I}_v\right) & -\beta_3 \widehat{I}_h - \gamma_v
\end{pmatrix}. \tag{23}
$$

The second additive compound matrix for $J^*(E^*)$ is given in the following. Also see, the Appendix for the second additive compound matrix.

$$
J^{[2]}(E^*)
$$
$$
= \begin{pmatrix}
A_{11} & \beta_2 \widehat{S}_h & \beta_2 \widehat{S}_h \\
\beta_3 \left(1 - \widehat{I}_v\right) & A_{22} & -\beta_1 \widehat{S}_h + \delta_h \widehat{S}_h - \lambda_h \\
0 & \beta_2 \widehat{I}_v + \beta_1 \widehat{I}_h & A_{33}
\end{pmatrix}, \tag{24}
$$

where

$$
A_{11} = -\Lambda_h - \beta_2 \widehat{I}_v + \delta_h \widehat{I}_h - \beta_1 \widehat{I}_h - \lambda_h + \beta_1 \widehat{S}_h
$$
$$
- (\Lambda_h + \delta_h + \gamma_h) + 2\delta_h \widehat{I}_h,
$$
$$
A_{22} = -\Lambda_h - \beta_2 \widehat{I}_v + \delta_h \widehat{I}_h - \beta_1 \widehat{I}_h - \lambda_h - \beta_3 \widehat{I}_h - \gamma_v, \tag{25}
$$
$$
A_{33} = \beta_1 \widehat{S}_h - (\Lambda_h + \delta_h + \gamma_h) + 2\delta_h \widehat{I}_h - \beta_3 \widehat{I}_h - \gamma_v,
$$
$$
P = P\left(\widehat{S}_h, \widehat{I}_h, \widehat{I}_v\right) = \text{diag}\left(1, \frac{\widehat{I}_v}{\widehat{I}_h}, \frac{\widehat{I}_v}{\widehat{I}_h}\right).
$$

where

$$
P^{-1} = \text{diag}\left(1, \frac{\widehat{I}_h}{\widehat{I}_v}, \frac{\widehat{I}_h}{\widehat{I}_v}\right),
$$
$$
P_f = \text{diag}\left(0, \frac{\widehat{I}_v \widehat{I}_h' - \widehat{I}_v' \widehat{I}_h}{\widehat{I}_h^2}, \frac{\widehat{I}_v \widehat{I}_h' - \widehat{I}_v' \widehat{I}_h}{\widehat{I}_h^2}\right). \tag{26}
$$

And $P_f P^{-1}$ is

$$
P_f P^{-1} = \text{diag}\left(0, \frac{\widehat{I}_h'}{\widehat{I}_h} - \frac{\widehat{I}_v'}{\widehat{I}_v}, \frac{\widehat{I}_h'}{\widehat{I}_h} - \frac{\widehat{I}_v'}{\widehat{I}_v}\right). \tag{27}
$$

5. Global Stability of Endemic Equilibrium

Theorem 7. *For $R_0 > 1$, the reduced model (4), about the endemic equilibrium point E^*, is globally asymptotically stable, and unstable for $R_0 > 1$.*

Proof. To prove that the reduced model (4) is globally asymptotically stable, we obtain the Jacobian matrix J^* about E^* which is given by

And $P_f J^{[2]} P^{-1}$ is

$$
P_f J^{[2]} P^{-1}
$$
$$
= J^{[2]}
$$
$$
= \begin{pmatrix}
A_{11} & \beta_2 \widehat{S}_h & \beta_2 \widehat{S}_h \\
\beta_3 \left(1 - \widehat{I}_v\right) & A_{22} & -\beta_1 \widehat{S}_h + \delta_h \widehat{S}_h - \lambda_h \\
0 & \beta_2 \widehat{I}_v + \beta_1 \widehat{I}_h & A_{33}
\end{pmatrix}. \tag{28}
$$

So we write

$$
\widehat{B} = P_f P^{-1} + P_f J^{[2]} P^{-1} = \begin{pmatrix} \widehat{B}_{11} & \widehat{B}_{12} \\ \widehat{B}_{21} & \widehat{B}_{22} \end{pmatrix}, \tag{29}
$$

where

$$
\widehat{B}_{11} = -\Lambda_h - \beta_2 \widehat{I}_v + \delta_h \widehat{I}_h - \beta_1 \widehat{I}_h - \lambda_h
$$
$$
+ \beta_1 \widehat{S}_h - (\Lambda_h + \delta_h + \gamma_h) + 2\delta_h \widehat{I}_h,
$$
$$
\widehat{B}_{12} = \left(\beta_2 \widehat{S}_h, \beta_2 \widehat{S}_h\right), \qquad \widehat{B}_{21} = \left(\beta_3 \left(1 - \widehat{I}_v\right), 0\right)^T, \tag{30}
$$
$$
\widehat{B}_{22} = \begin{pmatrix}
A_{22} + \frac{\widehat{I}_h'}{\widehat{I}_h} - \frac{\widehat{I}_v'}{\widehat{I}_v} & -\beta_1 \widehat{S}_h + \delta_h \widehat{S}_h - \lambda_h \\
0 & \frac{\widehat{I}_h'}{\widehat{I}_h} - \frac{\widehat{I}_v'}{\widehat{I}_v} + A_{33}
\end{pmatrix}.
$$

Suppose that the vector $(\widehat{u}, \widehat{v}, \widehat{w})$ in R^3 and its norm $\| \cdot \|$ will be defined as

$$
\|(\widehat{u}, \widehat{v}, \widehat{w})\| = \max\left\{|\widehat{u}|, |\widehat{v}| + |\widehat{w}|\right\}. \tag{31}
$$

Suppose that $\mu \widehat{B}$ represents Lozinski measure with the previously defined norm. So, as described in [27], we choose

$$
\mu\left(\widehat{B}\right) \leq \sup\left(g_1, g_2\right), \tag{32}
$$

where

$$g_1 = \mu_1\left(\widehat{B}_{11}\right) + \left|\widehat{B}_{12}\right|, \qquad g_2 = \left|\widehat{B}_{21}\right| + \mu_2\left(\widehat{B}_{22}\right). \quad (33)$$

$|\widehat{B}_{21}|$ and $|\widehat{B}_{12}|$ are the matrix norm with respect to vector ℓ, and μ_1 represents the Lozinski measure with respect to this ℓ norm, then

$$\mu_1\left(\widehat{B}_{11}\right) = -\Lambda_h - \beta_2\widehat{I}_v + \delta_h\widehat{I}_h - \beta_1\widehat{I}_h - \lambda_h$$
$$+ \beta_1\widehat{S}_h - \left(\Lambda_h + \delta_h + \gamma_h\right) + 2\delta_h\widehat{I}_h,$$
$$\left|\widehat{B}_{21}\right| = \left|\beta_3\left(1 - \widehat{I}_v\right)\right|,$$
$$\left|\widehat{B}_{12}\right| = \max\left\{\beta_2\widehat{S}_h, \beta_2\widehat{S}_h\right\} = \beta_2\widehat{S}_h,$$
$$\mu_1\left(\widehat{B}_{22}\right) = \max\left\{\frac{\widehat{I}_h'}{\widehat{I}_h} - \frac{\widehat{I}_v'}{\widehat{I}_v} + A_{22}, \frac{\widehat{I}_h'}{\widehat{I}_h} - \frac{\widehat{I}_v'}{\widehat{I}_v} + A_{33}\right\}$$

$$\quad (34)$$

$$\therefore g_1 = \mu_1\left(\widehat{B}_{11}\right) + \left|\widehat{B}_{12}\right|$$
$$= -\left(\Lambda_h + \lambda_h\right) - \beta_2\widehat{I}_v - \beta_1\widehat{I}_h + \delta_h\widehat{I}_h$$
$$+ \delta_h\widehat{I}_h + \beta_2\widehat{S}_h + 2\delta_h\widehat{I}_h - \left(\Lambda_h + \gamma_h + \gamma_h\right)$$
$$= -\left(\Lambda_h + \lambda_h\right) - \beta_2\widehat{I}_v - \beta_1\widehat{I}_h + \beta_2\widehat{S}_h$$
$$+ 2\delta_h\widehat{I}_h + \frac{\widehat{I}_h'}{\widehat{I}_h} - \beta_2\widehat{S}_h\frac{\widehat{I}_v}{\widehat{I}_h} - \beta_1\widehat{S}_h.$$

Use

$$\frac{\widehat{I}_h'}{\widehat{I}_h} - \beta_2\widehat{S}_h\frac{\widehat{I}_v}{\widehat{I}_h} - \beta_1\widehat{S}_h = -\left(\Lambda_h + \gamma_h + \gamma_h\right) + \delta_h\widehat{I}_h. \quad (35)$$

From system (4) and equation (2),

$$g_1 \leq \frac{\widehat{I}_h'}{\widehat{I}_h} - \left(\Lambda_h + \lambda_h\right) - \widehat{I}_h\left(\beta_1 - 2\delta_h\right),$$

$$g_2 = \left|\widehat{B}_{21}\right| + \mu_1\left(\widehat{B}_{22}\right),$$
$$= \beta_3\left(1 - \widehat{I}_v\right) + \frac{\widehat{I}_h'}{\widehat{I}_h} - \frac{\widehat{I}_v'}{\widehat{I}_v} + A_{22} + A_{33} \quad (36)$$
$$= \beta_3\left(1 - \widehat{I}_v\right) + \frac{\widehat{I}_h'}{\widehat{I}_h} - \frac{\widehat{I}_v'}{\widehat{I}_v} - \Lambda_h - \beta_2\widehat{I}_v + \delta_h\widehat{I}_h - \beta_1\widehat{I}_h$$
$$- \lambda_h - \beta_3\widehat{I}_h + \beta_1\widehat{S}_h - \left(\Lambda_h + \delta_h + \gamma_h\right) + 2\delta_h\widehat{I}_h$$
$$- \beta_3\widehat{I}_h - \gamma_v.$$

Using

$$\frac{\widehat{I}_v'}{\widehat{I}_v} = \beta_3\widehat{S}_h\frac{\widehat{I}_h}{\widehat{I}_v} - \gamma_v. \quad (37)$$

From the third equation of system (4),

$$g_2 \leq \frac{\widehat{I}_h'}{\widehat{I}_h} - \left(\Lambda_h + \lambda_h\right) - \left(\beta_1 - 2\delta_h\right)\widehat{I}_h. \quad (38)$$

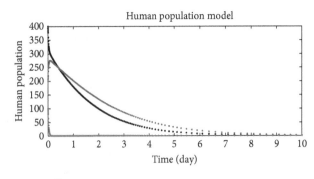

FIGURE 1: The plot shows the human population.

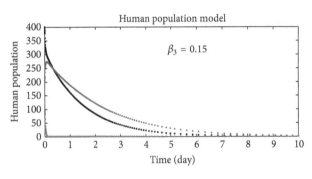

FIGURE 2: The plot shows the human population.

So,

$$\mu_1\widehat{B} \leq \sup\left(g_1, g_2\right) \leq \frac{\widehat{I}_h'}{\widehat{I}_h} - \beta, \quad \text{where } \beta = \left(\beta_1 - 2\delta_h\right), \quad (39)$$

then

$$\frac{1}{t}\int_0^t \mu_1\widehat{B}ds \leq \frac{1}{t}\int_0^t\left(\frac{\widehat{I}_h'}{\widehat{I}_h} - \beta\right)ds = \frac{1}{t}\ln\frac{\widehat{I}_h'(t)}{\widehat{I}_h'(0)} - \beta \quad (40)$$

implies that $q \leq -\beta/2 < 0$. Thus, the result [28] implies that the positive equilibrium point of E^* is globally asymptotically stable. □

6. Numerical Simulations and Conclusion

In this section, we discuss the numerical simulation of the reduced model (4), by using Runge-Kutta order four scheme. The model for different parameters and their numerical results are presented in Figures 1, 2, 3, 4, 5, 6, 7, and 8. The parameters and their values are presented in Table 1. Figure 1 represents the population dynamics of model (4). Varying the parameters in Figures 2 to 6, we obtained different results.

TABLE 1: Parameter values used in the numerical simulations of the model.

Notation	Parameter description	Value	Reference
Λ_h	Recruitment rate for human	1.6	[6]
λ_h	Proportionality constant	0.066	[7]
μ_h	Natural death rate of human	4.6×10^{-5}	[6]
γ_v	Natural death rate of vector	1.8×10^{-3}	[6]
δ_h	Death rate due to disease at human class	1.0×10^{-5}	[8]
γ_h	Recovery rate of the infection	2.7×10^{-3}	[8]
Λ_v	Birth rate of vector	1.9×10^{-3}	Assumed
β_2	Transmission between S_h and I_v	0.0089	Assumed
β_3	Transmission between S_v and I_h	0.0079	Assumed
β_1	Transmission coefficient between S_h and I_h	0.00013	Assumed
γ_v	Natural death rate of vector	0.0027	[6]

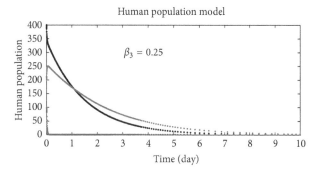

 S_h
I_h
I_v

FIGURE 3: The plot shows the human population.

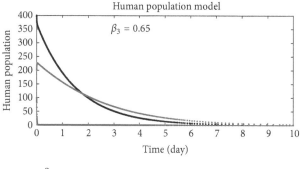

S_h
I_h
I_v

FIGURE 5: The plot shows the human population.

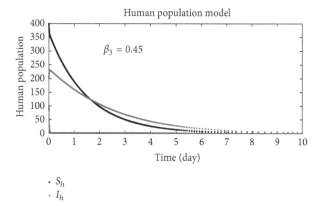

S_h
I_h
I_v

FIGURE 4: The plot shows the human population.

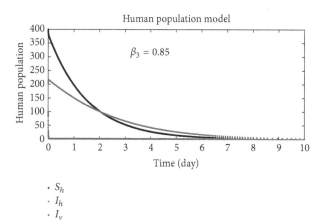

S_h
I_h
I_v

FIGURE 6: The plot shows the human population.

Increasing β_3, the number of infected human increases. The variability of the population effects the individuals numbers (infected individuals). For changing the value of β_1, we get different results in Figures 7 and 8. In this work, we have presented a mathematical model of vector-host disease like (leptospirosis, West Nile virus, dengue, etc.), which spreads through the vector, has been presented. The system is stable

locally as well as globally about the disease-free equilibrium $\widehat{S}_h^o = 1, 0, 0$, when reproduction number $R_0 < 1$, and the unstable equilibrium occurs for $R_0 \geq 1$. When the reproduction number $R_0 > 1$, there exists persistence. The disease permanently exists in the community if $R_0 > 1$. Then, we obtained the global stability of endemic equilibrium. The

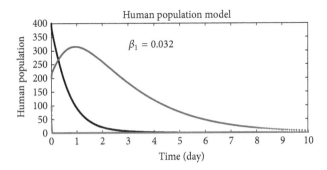

FIGURE 7: The plot shows the human population.

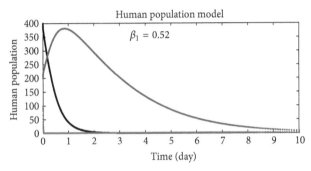

FIGURE 8: The plot shows the human population.

numerical simulations were presented for the illustration of theoretical results.

Appendix

Consider the following:

$$J^{[2]} = \begin{bmatrix} a_{11} + a_{22} & a_{23} & -a_{13} \\ a_{32} & a_{11} + a_{33} & a_{12} \\ -a_{31} & a_{21} & a_{22} + a_{33} \end{bmatrix}. \quad (A.1)$$

Acknowledgment

The authors would like to thank the handling Editor Ali Khraibi and reviewers for their careful reading of the manuscripts and for their valuable comments and suggestions which improved our work.

References

[1] F. Fenner, D. A. Henderson, I. Arita, Z. Jezek, and I. D. Ladnyi, *Smallpox and Its Eradication*, WHO, 1998.

[2] R. M. Anderson and R. M. May, *Infectious Diseases of Humans, Dynamics and Control*, Oxford University Press, Oxford, UK, 1991.

[3] M. A. Garly and P. Aaby, "The challenge of improving the efficacy of measles vaccine," *Acta Tropica*, vol. 85, no. 1, pp. 1–17, 2003.

[4] R. M. Anderson and R. M. May, "Population biology of infectious diseases," *Nature*, vol. 180, pp. 361–367, 1979.

[5] http://en.wikipedia.org/wiki/Measles.

[6] G. Zaman, "Dynamical behavior of leptospirosis disease and role of optimal control theory," *International Journal of Mathematics and Computation*, vol. 7, no. 10, 2010.

[7] W. Triampo, D. Baowan, I. M. Tang, N. Nuttavut, J. Wong-Ekkabut, and G. Doungchawee, "A simple deterministic model for the spread of leptospirosis in Thailand," *International Journal of Biomedical Science*, vol. 2, pp. 22–26, 2007.

[8] W. Tangkanakul, H. L. Smits, S. Jatanasen, and D. A. Ashford, "Leptospirosis: an emerging health problem in Thailand," *Southeast Asian Journal of Tropical Medicine and Public Health*, vol. 36, no. 2, pp. 281–288, 2005.

[9] R. U. M. Palaniappan, S. Ramanujam, and Y. Chang, "Leptospirosis: pathogenesis, immunity, and diagnosis," *Current Opinion in Infectious Diseases*, vol. 20, no. 3, pp. 284–292, 2007.

[10] R. Inada and Y. Ido, "Etiology mode of infection and specific therapy of Weil's disease," *The Journal of Experimental Medicine*, vol. 23, pp. 377–402, 1916.

[11] R. C. Abdulkader, A. C. Seguro, P. S. Malheiro, E. A. Burdmann, and M. Marcondes, "Peculiar electrolytic and hormonal abnormalities in acute renal failure due to leptospirosis," *American Journal of Tropical Medicine and Hygiene*, vol. 54, no. 1, pp. 1–6, 1996.

[12] V. M. Arean, G. Sarasin, and J. H. Green, "The pathogenesis of leptospirosis: toxin production by leptospira icterohaemorrhagiae," *American Journal of Veterinary Research*, vol. 28, pp. 836–843, 1964.

[13] V. M. Arean, "Studies on the pathogenesis of leptospirosis. II. A clinicopathologic evaluation of hepatic and renal function in experimental leptospiral infections," *Laboratory Investigation*, vol. 11, pp. 273–288, 1962.

[14] S. Barkay and H. Garzozi, "Leptospirosis and uveitis," *Annals of Ophthalmology*, vol. 16, no. 2, pp. 164–168, 1984.

[15] Z. Feng and J. X. Velasco-Hernández, "Competitive exclusion in a vector-host model for the dengue fever," *Journal of Mathematical Biology*, vol. 35, no. 5, pp. 523–544, 1997.

[16] L. Esteva and C. Vargas, "Coexistence of different serotypes of dengue virus," *Journal of Mathematical Biology*, vol. 46, no. 1, pp. 31–47, 2003.

[17] A. L. Lloyd, J. Zhang, and A. M. Root, "Stochasticity and heterogeneity in host-vector models," *Journal of the Royal Society Interface*, vol. 4, no. 16, pp. 851–863, 2007.

[18] N. Chitnis, T. Smith, and R. Steketee, "A mathematical model for the dynamics of malaria in mosquitoes feeding on a heterogeneous host population," *Journal of Biological Dynamics*, vol. 2, no. 3, pp. 259–285, 2008.

[19] M. Derouich and A. Boutayeb, "Dengue fever: mathematical modelling and computer simulation," *Applied Mathematics and Computation*, vol. 177, no. 2, pp. 528–544, 2006.

[20] L. Esteva and C. Vargas, "A model for dengue disease with variable human population," *Journal of Mathematical Biology*, vol. 38, no. 3, pp. 220–240, 1999.

[21] P. Pongsuumpun, T. Miami, and R. Kongnuy, "Age structural transmission model for leptospirosis," in *Proceedings of the 3rd International Symposium on Biomedical Engineering*, pp. 411–416, 2008.

[22] G. Zaman, M. Altaf Khan, S. Islam, M. I. Chohan, and I. H. Jung, "Modeling Dynamical Interactions between Leptospirosis Infected Vector and Human Population," *Applied Mathematical Sciences*, vol. 6, no. 25–28, pp. 1287–1302, 2012.

[23] S. Busenberg, K. L. Cooke, and H. Thieme, "Demographic change and persistence of HIV/AIDS in a heterogeneous population," *SIAM Journal on Applied Mathematics*, vol. 51, no. 4, pp. 1030–1052, 1991.

[24] C. Sun and Y. Hsieh, "Global analysis of an SEIR model with varying population size and vaccination," *Applied Mathematical Modelling*, vol. 34, no. 10, pp. 2685–2697, 2010.

[25] J. P. LaSalle, *The Stability of Dynamical Systems*, SIAM, Philadelphia, Pa, USA, 1976.

[26] X. Zhao, *Dynamical Systems in Population Biology*, CMS Books in Mathematics, Canadian Mathematical Society; Springer, 2003.

[27] R. H. Martin Jr., "Logarithmic norms and projections applied to linear differential systems," *Journal of Mathematical Analysis and Applications*, vol. 45, no. 2, pp. 432–454, 1974.

[28] M. Y. Li and J. S. Muldowney, "A geometric approach to global-stability problems," *SIAM Journal on Mathematical Analysis*, vol. 27, no. 4, pp. 1070–1083, 1996.

16

Computational and Bioinformatics Frameworks for Next-Generation Whole Exome and Genome Sequencing

Marisa P. Dolled-Filhart, Michael Lee Jr., Chih-wen Ou-yang, Rajini Rani Haraksingh, and Jimmy Cheng-Ho Lin

Rare Genomics Institute, 4100 Forest Park Avenue, Suite 204, St. Louis, MO 63108, USA

Correspondence should be addressed to Jimmy Cheng-Ho Lin; jimmy.lin@raregenomics.org

Academic Editors: R. Jiang, W. Tian, J. Wan, and X. Zhao

It has become increasingly apparent that one of the major hurdles in the genomic age will be the bioinformatics challenges of next-generation sequencing. We provide an overview of a general framework of bioinformatics analysis. For each of the three stages of (1) alignment, (2) variant calling, and (3) filtering and annotation, we describe the analysis required and survey the different software packages that are used. Furthermore, we discuss possible future developments as data sources grow and highlight opportunities for new bioinformatics tools to be developed.

1. Introduction

Without doubt, the development of next-generation sequencing has transformed biomedical research. Multiple second generation sequencing platforms, such as Roche/454, Illumina/Solexa, AB/SOLiD, and LIFE/Ion Torrent, have made high-throughput genetic analysis more readily accessible to researchers and even clinicians [1]. On the horizon, third generation sequencing technologies, such as Oxford Nanopore, Genia, NABsys, and GnuBio, will continue to increase throughput capabilities and decrease the cost of sequencing. With each new generation of sequencing technology, there is an exponential increase in the flood of data. The true challenges of high throughput sequencing will be bioinformatics. As ever larger datasets become more affordable, computational analysis rather than sequencing will be the rate-limiting factor in genomics research. In this paper, we provide an overview of the current computational framework and options for genomic analysis and provide some outlook on future developments and upcoming needs.

In this paper, we will discuss some of the options in each of the steps and provide a global outlook on the software "pipelines" currently in development (Figure 1).

2. Overview

While different sequencing technologies may use different initial raw data (e.g., imaging files or fluctuations in current), the eventual outputs are nucleotide base calls. Short strings of these bases, varying from dozens to hundreds of base pairs for each fragment, are combined together, often in a form of a FASTQ file. From here, bioinformatics analysis of the sequence falls into three general steps: (1) alignment, (2) variant calling, (3) filtering and annotation.

The first step is alignment—matching each of the short reads to positions on a reference genome (for the purposes of this paper, the human genome). The resulting sequence alignment is stored in a SAM (sequence alignment/map) or BAM (binary alignment/map) file [2]. The second step is variant calling—comparing the aligned sequences with known sequences to determine which positions deviate from the reference position. The produces a list of positions or calls recorded in a VCF (variant call format) file [3]. The third step includes both filtering as well as annotation. Filtering takes the tens of thousands of variants and reduces them to a smaller set. For cancers, this involves comparing cancerous cell genomes to normal genomes. For family data,

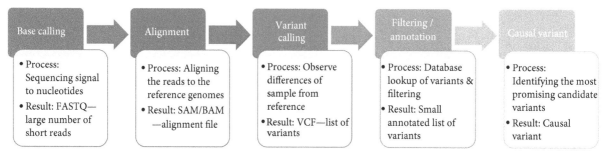

FIGURE 1: Next-generation sequencing bioinformatics workflow.

it involves selecting variants that conform to a specific genetic inheritance pattern. Annotation involves querying known information about each variant that is detected. Annotation may reveal, for example, that a variant is an already-known single nucleotide polymorphism, that a functional effect has already been predicted, that the function or activity of the gene in question is already known, or even that an associated disease has been identified.

Ultimately, the optimal result from the analysis is a small number of well-annotated variants that can explain a biological phenomenon. For example, for a Mendelian disease, analysis could identify the causative variant or gene. For cancer, analysis may point to driver mutations or targetable genes. Starting from base calls and ending with biologically important genetic variants, each step of analysis may be performed using one of many pieces of software. This paper discusses several of the bioinformatics options for each of these three steps.

3. Alignment

Alignment is the process of mapping short nucleotide reads to a reference genome. Because each of the millions of short reads must be compared to the 3 billion possible positions within the human genome, this computational step is not trivial. Software must assess the likely starting point of each read within the reference genome, and the task is complicated by the volume of short reads, unique versus non-unique mapping, and variation in base quality. This step is thus computationally intense and time consuming [4]. It is also a critical step, as any errors in alignment to the reference genome will be carried through to the rest of the analysis.

The Sequence Alignment/Map (SAM) and Binary Alignment/Map (BAM) formats are the standard file formats for storing NGS read alignments [2]. There are various software programs, some commercially available and others freely available to the scientific community, that can be used to perform sequencing read alignment. Various programs differ in speed and accuracy. Most alignment algorithms use an indexing method in order to more rapidly narrow down potential alignment locations within the reference genome with ungapped alignment, although other algorithms allow for gapped alignment. Different approaches to alignment involve hash tables, spaced seeds, and/or contiguous seeds. This method also enables comparison of differing output

structures (single versus multiple possible alignment outputs) [5].

Short reads generated from NGS may either be single-end reads or paired-end reads from the sample, and may range from dozens to hundreds of base pairs [5]; these reads need to be aligned correctly to their appropriate location within the reference genome. Algorithms typically utilize a hash-based index (e.g., MAQ, ELAND), BWT-based index (e.g., BWA, Bowtie, SOAP2), genome-based hash (e.g., Novoalign, SOAP), or a spaced-seed approach (e.g., SHRiMP). Some algorithms report the "best" match using heuristic approaches (e.g., BWA, Bowtie, MAQ), while others allow for all possible matches (e.g., SOAP3, SHRiMP). Algorithms differ in whether they can handle both single-end and paired-end reads, or just one type (e.g., SARUMAN for single-end reads), and whether they can perform gapped alignment (e.g., BWA, Bowtie2) in addition to ungapped alignment (e.g., MAQ, Bowtie). Some algorithms focus on speed (e.g., BWA, Bowtie), some on sensitivity (e.g., Novoalign), and some algorithms aim to the two (e.g., Stampy). Table 1 provides a listing of relevant algorithms for alignment of short reads to the reference genome. While there has been previous comparisons about these algorithms [6], we describe some of the newer programs, such as Bowtie and Bowtie 2, or SOAP/SOAP2/SOAP3, and others below.

3.1. Bowtie/Bowtie 2. The Bowtie algorithm is both ultrafast and memory efficient [7] due to its use of a refinement of the FM Index, which itself utilizes the Burrows-Wheeler transformation for ultrafast and memory-efficient alignment of reads to a reference genome. Bowtie improves upon BWT with a novel quality-aware backtracking algorithm that permits mismatches. However, there may be some tradeoffs between speed and alignment quality using this algorithm [5]. Bowtie2 allows for analysis of gapped reads, which may result either from true insertions or deletions, or from sequencing errors. The newer adaptions utilize full-text minute indices and hardware-accelerated dynamic programming algorithms to optimize both speed and accuracy [8].

3.2. BWA/BWA-SW. The BWA approach, based on BWT, provides efficient alignment of short reads against the reference genome [9]. This is the most commonly used approach for sequence alignment, and followed the development of the first-generation hash-table based alignment algorithm MAQ

TABLE 1

Program	Source type	Description	Website
Bowtie	Open source	Ungapped alignment Refined use of FM Index using the BWT Fast and memory-efficient alignment Quality value output	http://bowtie.cbcb.umd.edu/
Bowtie2	Open source	Extends Bowtie approach to be useful for gapped alignment	http://bowtie-bio.sourceforge.net/bowtie2/index.shtml
SEAL	Open source	Comparison of alignment algorithms using simulated short read sequencing runs	http://compbio.case.edu/seal/
SOAP3	Open source	Gapped and ungapped alignment Specialized for detecting and genotyping SNPs Hash table accelerates searching using BWT-based index Reports multiple possibilities rather than single best match Increased speed using GPU	http://www.cs.hku.hk/2bwt-tools/soap3/; http://soap.genomics.org.cn/soap3.html
BWA, BWA-SW	Open source	Most common/standard method used Index with BWT that is faster than the hash-based index used for MAQ Quality score reported	http://maq.sourceforge.net/
mrFAST, mrsFAST	Open source	Seed-and-extend alignment method with hash table inex for reference genome Reports all read mappings instead of single best mapping Useful for CNVs, structural variants	—
Novoalign	Commercially available	Novocraft's proprietary software with hashing strategy High accuracy for single end mapping Focused on sensitivity	http://www.novocraft.com/
SHRiMP/SHRiMP2	Open source	Specialized for SOLiD color-space reads using spaced seeds and SWA Also applicable for regular letter-space reads Handles higher level of polymorphisms	http://compbio.cs.toronto.edu/shrimp/
MAQ	Open source	Ungapped alignment Hash-based index with quality score for mapping	http://maq.sourceforget.net/
Stampy	Open source	Hybrid mapping algorithm and statistical model, complementary to BWA	http://www.well.ox.ac.uk/project-stampy/
ELAND	Commercially available	Hash-based alignment program	http://www.illumina.com/
LAST aligner	Open source	Probablistic alignment quality scores as well as usual score matrix Useful for preprocessing for SNP/indel calling	http://last.cbrc.jp/
SARUMAN	Open Source	Mapping approach for single-end reads that returns all possible alignments with given error threshold with high speed using GPUs	http://www.cebitec.uni-bielefeld.de/brf/saruman/saruman.html

[10]. BWA improved upon MAQ by allowing for gapped alignment of single end reads, which is important for longer reads that may contain indels, and allowed for increased speed. BWA-SW allows for matches without heuristics and alignment of longer sequences [11].

3.3. mrFAST/mrsFAST.

In contrast to algorithms focused on "unique" alignment of regions of the genome and selection of the "best" match, mrFAST [12] and mrsFAST [13] allow for rapid assessment of copy-number variation and assignment of sequences into both unique and the more complex duplicated regions of the genome [14, 15]. The methodology of these algorithms is a seed-and-extend approach similar to BLAST, which uses hash tables to index the reference genome. These algorithms can handle smaller structural variants (e.g., indels) and larger structural variants such as insertions, deletions, inversions, CNVs, and segmental duplications in a cache-oblivious manner.

3.4. SHRiMP/SHRiMP2.

Developed to handle a greater number of polymorphisms by utilizing a statistical model to screen out false positive hits, SHRiMP [16] can be utilized for color-spaced reads from AB SOLiD sequencers and can also be used for regular letter-space reads. SHRiMP2 [17] enables direct alignment for paired-reads and uses multiple spaced seeds, but instead of using indexed reads like SHRiMP, SHRiMP2 switched to an indexing method like Bowtie and BWA.

3.5. SOAP/SOAPv2/SOAPv3.

SOAP was developed for use in gapped and ungapped alignment of short reads using a seed strategy for either single-read or pair-end reads, and can also be applied to small RNA and mRNA tag sequences [18]. SOAP2 reduced memory usage and increased speed using BWT for hash-based indexing instead of the seed algorithm, and also includes SNP detection [19]. SOAP3 is a GPU (graphics processing unit) version of the compressed full-text index-based SOAP2, which allows for a speed improvement [20].

4. Variant Calling

After alignment of the short reads to the reference genome, the next step in the bioinformatics process is variant calling. Since the short reads are already aligned, the sample genome can be compared to the reference genome and variants can then be identified. These variants may be responsible for disease, or they may simply be genomic noise without any functional effect. Variant call format (VCF) is the standardized generic format for storing sequence variation including SNPs, indels, larger structural variants and annotations [3]. The computational challenges in SNP (variant) calling are due to the issues in identifying "true" variants versus alignment and/or sequencing errors. Yet the ability to detect SNPs with both high sensitivity and specificity is a key step in identifying sequence variants associated with disease, detection of rare variants, and assessment of allele frequencies in populations.

The difficulty of variant calling is complicated by three factors: (1) the presence of indels, which represent a major source of false positive SNV identifications, especially if alignment algorithms do not perform gapped alignments; (2) errors from library preparation due to PCR artifacts and variable GC content in the short reads unless paired-end sequencing is utilized; and (3) variable quality scores, with higher error rates generally found at bases at the ends of reads [4]. Therefore, the rate of false positive and false negative calls of SNVs and indels is a concern. A detailed review of SNP-calling algorithms and challenges recommends recalibration of per-base quality scores (e.g., GATK, SOAPsnp), use of an alignment algorithm with high sensitivity (e.g., Novoalign, Stampy), and SNP calling using Bayesian procedures or likelihood ratio tests and incorporation of linkage disequilibrium to improve SNP call accuracy [21]. We provide an overview of some of the software packages for variant calling below.

4.1. The Genome Analysis ToolKit (GATK).

Developed by the Broad Institute, the Genome Analysis ToolKit (GATK) is one of the most popular methods for variant calling using aligned reads. It is designed in a modular way and is based on the MapReduce functional programming approach [22]. The package has been used for projects such as The Cancer Genome Atlas [23] and the 1000 Genomes Project [24] that have covered analyses of HLA typing, multiple-sequence realignment, quality score recalibration, multiple-sample SNP genotyping and indel discovery and genotyping [22].

4.2. SOAPsnp.

Developed by the Beijing Genome Institute, SOAPsnp is an open source algorithm (http://soap .genomics.org.cn/) that requires access to a high-quality variant database using SOAP alignment results as an input [18]. It can be used for consensus calling and SNP detection for the Illumina Genome Analyzer platform and utilizes the phred-like quality score to calculate the likelihood of each genotype based on the alignment results and sequencing quality scores. Building upon the speed of the alignment algorithm Bowtie [7] and using SOAPsnp for SNP calling, an open source cloud-computing tool called Crossbow [7] was developed to perform both alignment and SNP calling.

4.3. VarScan/VarScan2.

Developed by the Genome Institute at Washington University in St. Louis, VarScan (http:// genome.wustl.edu/tools/cancer-genomics/) is an open source tool for short read variant detection of SNPs and indels that is compatible with multiple sequencing platforms and aligner algorithms such as Bowtie and Novoalign [25]. It can detect variants at 1% frequency, which can be useful for pooled samples; VarScan permits analysis of individual samples as well. VarScan2 [26] includes some improvements upon VarScan, such as the ability to analysis tumor-normal sample pairs for somatic mutations, LOH (loss of heterozygosity) and CNAs (copy number alterations). This program reads tumor and normal sample Samtools pileup or mpileup output simultaneously for pairwise comparisons of base calling and normalized sequence depth at each position.

4.4. ATLAS 2. Developed by the Baylor Genome Center, Atlas 2 can be used for variant calling of aligned data from multiple NGS platforms on a range of computing platforms [27]. Atlas 2 can also be implemented via a web resource called Genboree Workbench (http://www.genboree.org/). A few other web-based analysis tools are available such as DNANexus (http://www.dnanexus.com) and Galaxy [28]. Details of Atlas 2 in comparison to other variant calling algorithms such as SAMtools mpileup and GATK are included in Challis et al. [27], and reviewed by Ji [29].

5. Insertions and Deletions

While the majority of research has focused on diseases associated with SNPs, indel (insertion and deletion) mutations are a common polymorphism that can also demonstrate to biological effects. Studies have shown that small indels might be highly associated with neuropsychiatric diseases such as schizophrenia, autism, mental retardation, and Alzheimer's disease [30].

In addition, the presence of certain indels is associated with the disease progression of HBV-induced hepatocellular carcinoma (HCC) in the Korean population [31]. Indels are also used as genetic markers in natural populations [32]. With the advance of sequencing platforms and analysis tools, detection of indels through NGS has become more common. However, accurate mapping of indels to the reference genome is challenging, because it requires approaches that involve complicated gapped alignment and paired-end sequence inference [9]. Moreover, the occurrence rate of indels is approximately 8-fold lower than that of SNPs [33]. An optimal combination of both alignment and indel-calling algorithms is essential for identifying indels with high sensitivity and specificity. One review evaluated the performance of various alignment tools on microindel detection, and recommended single-end reads gapped alignment mapping tools such as BWA and Novoalign [34]. Various software approaches have been developed to identify indels, including a pattern growth approach (e.g., Pindel) and a Bayesian procedure (e.g., Dindel). A detailed review by Neuman et al. evaluated the performance of several difference indel-calling programs in the presence of varying parameters (read depth, read length, indel size, and frequency). By using both simulated and real data that included the *Caenorhabditis elegans* genome, they observed that Dindel has the highest sensitivity (indels found) at low coverage, although Dindel is only suitable for Illumina data analysis. VarScan and GATK require additional parameter adjustments, such as high coverage for VarScan, to reach their best performance. This review provides information for appropriate tool selection and parameter optimization to assist successful experimental designs and recommends Dindel as a suitable tool for low coverage experiments. Below, we survey the tools that have been commonly used for indel calling.

5.1. Pindel. Pindel is a software program which implements a pattern growth approach to detect breakpoints of large deletions (1–10 kb) and medium sized insertions (1 bp–20 bp)

from paired-end short reads in NGS data [35]. A recent, more advanced, version, Pindel2, has been introduced which includes the ability to identify insertions of any size, inversions and tandem duplications [35]. Pindel has been used for the 1000 Genomes Project (http://www.1000genomes.org/) [36], the Genome of the Netherlands project, and the Cancer Genome Atlas [23].

5.2. Dindel. Developed by the Welcome Trust Sanger Institute, Dindel is an open-source program that utilizes a Bayesian approach for calling small (<50 bp) insertions and deletions (http://www.sanger.ac.uk/resources/ software/dindel/) [37]. Principally, this algorithm realigns sequence reads mapped to a variety of candidate haplotypes that represent alternative sequences to the reference. Dindel has been used in the 1000 Genomes Project call sets and can only analyze data from Illumina.

5.3. GATK. As described in the variant calling section, the Genome Analysis ToolKit (GATK), which provides a collection of data analysis tools, can also allow indel calling based on the MapReduce programming approach [22]. Details of GATK in comparison to other indel calling methods including Dindel (VarScan, SAMtools mpileup) are evaluated in Neuman et al. [38].

6. Filtering and Annotation

After alignment and variant calling, a list of thousands of potential differences between the genome under study and the reference genome is generated. The next step is to determine which of these variants are likely to contribute to the pathological process under study. The third step involves a combination of both filtering (removing variants that fit specific genetic models or are not present in normal tissue) as well as annotation (looking up information about variants and identifying ones that fit the biological process).

Filtering can be done with a genetic pedigree or with cancer and normal samples from the same individual. In the instance of cancer, a common method is removing variants that are present in both the cancer sample and the normal sample, leaving only somatic variants, which have mutated from the germline sequence. In the instance of a pedigree, filtering can be done based on the different inheritance patterns. For example, if the inheritance pattern is autosomal recessive, the variants that are heterozygous in the parents and homozygous in the child can be chosen. Similar methods can be done with larger pedigrees based on the inheritance pattern.

In addition to filtering, further selection of causal variants can be based on existing annotation or predicted functional effect. Many tools exist to examine relevant variants by referencing previously known information about their biological functions and inferring potential effects based on their genomic context. In addition, many tools have been developed to identify genetic variants that cause disease pathogenesis or phenotypic variance [39]. Rare nonsynonymous SNPs are SNPs that cause amino acid substitution

(AAS) in the coding region, which potentially affect the function of the protein coded and could contribute to disease.

The advance of exome and genomic sequencing is yielding an extensive number of human genetic variants, and a number of disease-associated SNVs can be identified following alignment and variant calling. Unlike nonsense and frameshift mutations, which often result in a loss of protein function, pinpointing disease-causal variants among numerous SNVs has become one of the major challenges due to the lack of genetic information. For instance, ~1,300 loci are shown to be associated with ~200 diseases by GWASs but only a few of these loci have been identified as disease-causing variants [40]. Exome sequencing enables the identification of more novel genetic variants than previously possible, but it still requires computational and experimental approaches to predict whether a variant is deleterious. To this end, several approaches have been developed to identify rare nonsynonymous SNPs that cause amino acid substitution (AAS) in the coding region. The major principle of the protein-sequence-based methods to predict deleteriousness in the coding sequence is based on comparative genomics and functional genomics. Comparative sequencing analysis assumes that amino acid residues that are critical for protein function should be conserved among species and homologous proteins; therefore, mutations in highly conserved sites are more likely to result in more deleterious effect. Other modalities to predict disease-causing variants include protein biochemistry, such as amino acid charge, the presence of a binding site, and structure information of protein. SNVs that are predicted to alter protein feature (such as polarity and hydropathy) and structure (binding ability and alteration of secondary/tertiary structure) have a higher probability of being deleterious.

Although the majority of research has focused on protein-altering variants, noncoding variants constitute a large portion of human genetic variation. Results obtained from GWAS indicate that ~88% of trait-associated weak effect variants are found in noncoding regions, demonstrating the importance of functional annotation of both coding and noncoding variants [41]. Computational tools for protein-sequence-based prediction of deleteriousness fall into two categories: constraint-based predictors such as MAPP and SIFT, and trained classifiers such as MutationTaster and polyPhen. In addition to protein-sequence-based methods, another way to prioritize disease-casual SNVs is through nucleotide-sequence-based prediction in noncoding and coding DNA. This process also utilizes comparative genomics to predict deleteriousness, and is used by programs such as phastCons, GERP, and Gumby. In one detailed review of disease-causing variant identification, the authors introduced the concepts and tools that allow genetic annotation of both coding and noncoding variants [39]. They also compared the relative utility of nucleotide- and protein-based approaches using exome data, finding that nucleotide-based constraint scores defined by Genomic Evolutionary Rate Profiling (GERP) and protein-based deleterious impact scores provided by PolyPhen were similar for two Mendelian diseases, suggesting that nucleotide-based prediction can be as powerful as protein-based metrics [39]. Below, we survey tools that are helpful identifying disease-causal variants among numerous candidates.

6.1. Sorting Intolerant from Tolerant (SIFT). Sorting Intolerant From Tolerant (SIFT) (http://sift.jcvi.org/) prediction is based on conserved amino acid residues through different species using comparative sequencing analysis through PSI-BLAST [42]. This relies on the presumption that amino acid residues that are essential for protein function should be evolutionarily conserved by natural selection. Therefore, SNPs resulting in AAS on the conservative residues are more likely to be deleterious.

6.2. PolyPhen. PolyPhen/PolyPhen2 (http://genetics.bwh.harvard.edu/pph2/) algorithm predicts the potential impact of AAS on the structure and function of human protein based on protein sequence, phylogenetic and structural information [43]. An amino acid replacement might occur at a specific site where binding to other molecules or the formation of a secondary/tertiary structure is disrupted. Therefore, PolyPhen determines if the AAS is found at a site which is annotated as a disulfide bond, an active site, a binding site, or a specific motif such as transmembrane domain. Another function of PolyPhen is to compare the sequence and polymorphic regions of homologous proteins in the same family to identify AASs that are rare or never observed in the family. In addition, PolyPhen also maps of the substitution site to the known 3-dimensional protein structure to assess if an AAS has the potential to destroy protein structure via an alteration of, for example, the hydrophobic core of a protein, electrostatic interactions, or interactions with ligands or other molecules.

6.3. VariBench. VariBench (http://structure.bmc.lu.se/VariBench/) is the first benchmark database that provides testing and training tools for computational variation effect prediction [44]. It comprises experimentally validated variation datasets collected from the literature and relevant databases. The datasets housed in VariBench enable identification of variants that affect protein tolerance, protein stability, transcription factor binding sites, and splice sites. Additionally, VariBench maps variant positions to the DNA, RNA, and protein sequences at RefSeq, and to the 3-dimensional protein structures at Protein Data Bank (PDB).

6.4. snpEFF. snpEFF is an open source, Java-based program that rapidly categorizes SNP, indel, and MNP variants in genomic sequences as having either high, medium, low or modifier functional effects [45]. Variant annotation is based on genomic location (intron, exon, untranslated region, upstream, downstream, splice site, intergenic region) and predicted coding effect (synonymous/nonsynonymous amino acid replacement, gain/loss of start/stop site, frameshift mutations). The program may find several different functions for a single variant due to competing predictions based on alternative transcripts. snpEFF uses a VCF input and output style. Currently snpEFF does not support structural variants but there are plans to incorporate such support soon. snpEFF is compatible with GATK and Galaxy, which are popular variant-calling toolkits. The program currently supports 260 genome versions and can be used with custom genomes and annotations.

6.5. The SNPeffect Database. The SNPeffect Annotation database (http://snpeffect.switchlab.org/) uses sequence and structure information to predict the effect of protein-coding SNVs on the structural phenotype of proteins [46]. It is primarily focused on disease-causing and polymorphic variants in the human proteome. This program compares variant protein predictions to wild type protein information from the UniProtKB database, which currently contains more than 60,000 variant proteins. Variant characterization is achieved by integrating aggregation, amyloid prediction, chaperone-binding prediction, and protein stability analysis information by applying several algorithms to each wild type and mutant protein. The first algorithm, TANGO, detects regions that are prone to aggregation and calculates a score difference between the mutant and wild type protein. The WALTZ algorithm is applied to predict amyloid-forming regions in protein sequences using a position-specific scoring matrix to deduce amyloid-forming propensity. LIMBO is an algorithm that predicts chaperone binding sites for the Hsp70 chaperones. In cases where structural information is available, the FoldX algorithm is used to calculate the difference in free energy between the mutated protein and the wild type and determine whether the mutation stabilizes or destabilizes the structure. Mutations are also characterized as falling into catalytic sites according to information in the Catalytic Site Atlas or not, and falling into known domains or not. Subcellular information is predicted using PSORT.

6.6. SeattleSeq. SeattleSeq (http://snp.gs.washington.edu/ SeattleSeqAnnotation/) annotates known and novel SNPs with biological functions, protein positions and amino-acid changes, conservation scores, HapMap frequencies, PolyPhen predictions, and clinical associations based on an integrated database. Most of the annotation information is derived from the Genome Variation Server (http://gvs.gs.washington.edu/GVS134/), which includes information from dbSNP as well as other sources. The algorithm accepts input files in a number of formats including GATK and VCF output styles. Currently, annotation of indels is limited.

6.7. ANNOVAR. The ANNOVAR software tool (http:// www.openbioinformatics.org/annovar/) utilizes up-to date information to rapidly functionally annotate genetic variants called from sequencing data [47]. ANNOVAR works on a number of diverse genomes including hg18, hg19, mouse, worm, fly, and yeast. The annotation system allows the user flexibility in the set of genomic regions that are queried. Annotations can be gene-based (users can select the gene definition system; RefSeq, UCSC, ENSEMBL, GENCODE, etc.), region-based (transcription factor binding sites, DNAse I hypersensitivity sites, ENCODEmethylation sites, segmental duplication sites, DGV sites, etc.), filter-based (e.g., using only variants reported in dbSNP, or only variants with MAF > 1%), or based on any of many other user-driven functionalities.

6.8. The Variant Annotation, Analysis and Search Tool (VAAST). The Variant Annotation, Analysis and Search Tool (VAAST) identifies damaged genes and deleterious variants in personal genome sequences using a probabilistic search method [48]. The tool utilizes both existing amino acid substitution and aggregative approaches to variant prioritization and combines them into a single unified likelihood-framework. This method increases the accuracy with which disease causing variants are identified. VAAST scores both coding and noncoding, and both rare and common, variants simultaneously and aggregates this information to identify disease causing variants.

6.9. The Variant Analysis Tool (VAT). The Variant Analysis Tool, VAT, (http://vat.gersteinlab.org/) functionally annotates variants called from personal genomes at the transcript level and provides summary statistics across genes and individuals [49]. VAT is a computational framework that can be implemented through a command-line interface, a web application, or a virtual machine in a cloud-computing environment. This tool has been utilized extensively to annotate loss-of-function variants obtained as part of the 1000 Genomes Project [50]. The VAT modules *snpMapper*, *indelMapper and svMapper* relate SNPs, indels and SVs to protein-coding genes while the *genericMapper* module relates variants to noncoding regions of the genome. Transcript-level analysis allows identification of affected isoforms. VAT outputs VCF files as well as visualization summarizing the biological impact of annotated variants.

6.10. VARIANT. VARIANT (VARIant ANalysis Tool) (http://variant.bioinfo.cipf.es/) provides annotation of variants from next generation sequencing based on several different databases and repositories including dbSNP, 1000 Genomes Project, the GWAS catalog, OMIM, and COSMIC [36]. The provided annotations also include information on the regulatory or structural roles of the variants as well as the selective pressures on the affected genomic sites. Unlike other such tools, VARIANT utilizes a remote database and operates by interacting with this database through efficient RESTful Web Services. Currently VARIANT supports all human, mouse and rat genes. Analyzing variants generated by exome sequencing of families in which rare Mendelian diseases are segregated can be a time-consuming process.

6.11. VAR-MD. VAR-MD is a software tool to analyze variants derived from exome or whole genome sequencing in human pedigrees with Mendelian inheritance [51]. This algorithm outputs a ranked list of potential disease-causing variants based on predicted pathogenicity, Mendelian inheritance models, genotype quality, and population variant frequency data. This tool is unique in that it uses family-based annotation of sequence data to enhance mutation identification. VAR-MD is a Unix-based tool and is implemented in

Python. Independent functions of the program are usually run sequentially. In order to facilitate parallel analysis of multiple data sets, VAR-MD utilizes Galaxy for distributed resource management.

The various variant annotation tools differ in the types of variants they process. All algorithms process SNPs and indels, but only a few, such as ANNOVAR and VAT, can handle SVs. These tools also differ in the computing environment in which they are implemented. Some rely on command-line operation while others operate using web-based interfaces or virtual machines in the cloud. Some tools utilize local databases while other use up-to-date remote databases. These various tools also differ in the genomic regions that they target. For example, SNPeffect focuses on the proteome while other tools focus on the less obvious, but still functionally relevant regions. From the long list of possible variants, through filtering and annotation, a smaller list of most probably causal variants is generated.

7. Future Outlook and Conclusion

While the current tools in all three stages of the bioinformatics analysis are adequate, more data will enable further significant improvements. New technology and algorithms may significantly shift the field in unforeseeable ways, but several future improvements are predictable as (1) sequencing reads increase in length, (2) more genomes are completed, and (3) annotation databases are better populated.

First, as sequencing technology increases the base pair read length, alignment will become more accurate. Shorter reads match with a greater number of genome sites. As reads grow in length, they can be mapped more precisely with fewer options and thus less room for error. This is especially true in regions with low complexity or a high number of repeats, classically very difficult regions to map. Longer reads will make alignment an easier problem.

Second, the process of variant calling will benefit from larger databases of completed genomes. A variant is derived from comparison to the reference genome, and our set of reference genomes continues to grow. This will enable variant calling based on ethnic background, or based on populations of genomes instead of a single reference genome or a small set of reference genomes.

Third, while filtering appears unlikely to change significantly, annotation and functional prediction will be improved by more data and more-populated databases. For filtering, since the genetic models and removal of normal variants from tumor variants are based only on the genetics and the samples under study, additional information from the databases will not change these aspects much. By contrast, the efficacy of annotation is directly related to what is present in known databases. Different dimensions of data, such as functional, pathway, biochemical, or genetic annotation can all be improved as more genomes are sequenced and annotated. Moreover, current predictive algorithms such as SIFT and Polyphen are dependent on current database annotation. If large numbers of human genomes are sequenced, analysis need not resort to merely predicting the effect of a single

position; one can simply query that position in the millions of people that are sequenced and infer the deleterious effect.

Besides the more predictable changes that will follow naturally from more data, there are also opportunities for larger paradigm shifts in bioinformatics tools. First, emerging tools may be able to analyze samples not as a homogenous whole, but in ways that allow for tumor heterogeneity with differing populations of cells. Furthermore, single-cell and single-molecule methods are maturing. It is now more appreciated that the tumors consists of populations of cells, and that being able to determine the quantity and identity of these cells will not only help understand tumor population dynamics, but may also inform treatment and prognosis.

Second, thus far relatively few tools have integrated other high throughput modalities such as proteomics into genomic interpretation. In order to understand whether the mutation has biological significance, it is critical to know whether a gene is expressed on a transcript or protein level. As more multidimensional data is produced through projects such as ENCODE, TCGA, or 1000 Genomes, and high-throughput sample profiling becomes easier on a genomic, transcriptomic, and proteomic level, methods that can incorporate all this data will add power to the analysis.

Third, in additional to multidimensional data, there are also opportunities for systems biology methods to be incorporated to software packages. Protein-protein interaction datasets continue to grow as the human interactome is mapped, and knowledge of these molecular pathways can and should be integrated into genomics analysis. Understanding genes not only as isolated constructs but also as part of a greater system would better model the biological process.

Fourth, as more and more datasets are available and sequencing becomes cheaper, genomics analysis need no longer be based on a single genome, a comparison between an isolated pair of cancer genome samples, or larger, but still isolated, pedigrees. Current tools analyze single samples at a time and compare what is found with databases. Instead, tools that are able to analyze large numbers of genomes at the same time to sizes similar to genome-wide association studies will prove to be powerful.

Undoubtedly, the datasets used in genomics analysis will continue to grow in depth per individual and in the number of samples. Bioinformatics, more than ever before, will be the crucial step in making sense of the data flood. The incremental progress afforded by this flood will be critical and valuable, but researchers can also look forward to the yet-unknown paradigm shifts that loom over the horizon.

References

[1] E. R. Mardis, "Next-generation DNA sequencing methods," *Annual Review of Genomics and Human Genetics*, vol. 9, pp. 387–402, 2008.

[2] H. Li, B. Handsaker, A. Wysoker et al., "The Sequence Alignment/Map format and SAMtools," *Bioinformatics*, vol. 25, no. 16, pp. 2078–2079, 2009.

[3] P. Danecek, A. Auton, G. Abecasis et al., "The variant call format and VCFtools," *Bioinformatics*, vol. 27, no. 15, Article ID btr330, pp. 2156–2158, 2011.

[4] A. G. Day-Williams and E. Zeggini, "The effect of next-generation sequencing technology on complex trait research," *European Journal of Clinical Investigation*, vol. 41, no. 5, pp. 561–567, 2011.

[5] M. Ruffalo, T. LaFramboise, and M. Koyuturk, "Comparative analysis of algorithms for next-generation sequencing read alignment," *Bioinformatics*, vol. 27, no. 20, pp. 2790–2796, 2011.

[6] N. Homer and S. F. Nelson, "Improved variant discovery through local re-alignment of short-read next-generation sequencing data using SRMA," *Genome Biology*, vol. 11, no. 10, article R99, 2010.

[7] B. Langmead, C. Trapnell, M. Pop, and S. L. Salzberg, "Ultrafast and memory-efficient alignment of short DNA sequences to the human genome," *Genome Biology*, vol. 10, no. 3, article R25, 2009.

[8] B. Langmead and S. L. Salzberg, "Fast gapped-read alignment with Bowtie 2," *Nature Methods*, vol. 9, no. 4, pp. 357–359, 2012.

[9] H. Li and R. Durbin, "Fast and accurate short read alignment with Burrows-Wheeler transform," *Bioinformatics*, vol. 25, no. 14, pp. 1754–1760, 2009.

[10] H. Li, J. Ruan, and R. Durbin, "Mapping short DNA sequencing reads and calling variants using mapping quality scores," *Genome Research*, vol. 18, no. 11, pp. 1851–1858, 2008.

[11] H. Li and R. Durbin, "Fast and accurate long-read alignment with Burrows-Wheeler transform," *Bioinformatics*, vol. 26, no. 5, Article ID btp698, pp. 589–595, 2010.

[12] C. Alkan, S. Sajjadian, and E. E. Eichler, "Limitations of next-generation genome sequence assembly," *Nature Methods*, vol. 8, no. 1, pp. 61–65, 2011.

[13] F. Hach, F. Hormozdiari, C. Alkan et al., "MrsFAST: a cache-oblivious algorithm for short-read mapping," *Nature Methods*, vol. 7, no. 8, pp. 576–577, 2010.

[14] I. D. Dinov, F. Torri, F. Macciardi et al., "Applications of the pipeline environment for visual informatics and genomics computations," *BMC Bioinformatics*, vol. 12, article 304, 2011.

[15] C. Alkan, J. M. Kidd, T. Marques-Bonet et al., "Personalized copy number and segmental duplication maps using next-generation sequencing," *Nature Genetics*, vol. 41, no. 10, pp. 1061–1067, 2009.

[16] S. M. Rumble, P. Lacroute, A. V. Dalca, M. Fiume, A. Sidow, and M. Brudno, "SHRiMP: accurate mapping of short color-space reads," *PLoS Computational Biology*, vol. 5, no. 5, Article ID e1000386, 2009.

[17] M. David, M. Dzamba, D. Lister, L. Ilie, and M. Brudno, "SHRiMP2: sensitive yet practical short read mapping," *Bioinformatics*, vol. 27, no. 7, Article ID btr046, pp. 1011–1012, 2011.

[18] R. Li, Y. Li, K. Kristiansen, and J. Wang, "SOAP: short oligonucleotide alignment program," *Bioinformatics*, vol. 24, no. 5, pp. 713–714, 2008.

[19] R. Li, C. Yu, Y. Li et al., "SOAP2: an improved ultrafast tool for short read alignment," *Bioinformatics*, vol. 25, no. 15, pp. 1966–1967, 2009.

[20] C. M. Liu, K. F. Wong, E. M. K. Wu et al., "SOAP3: ultra-fast GPU-based parallel alignment tool for short reads," *Bioinformatics*, vol. 28, no. 6, pp. 878–879, 2012.

[21] R. Nielsen, J. S. Paul, A. Albrechtsen, and Y. S. Song, "Genotype and SNP calling from next-generation sequencing data," *Nature Reviews Genetics*, vol. 12, no. 6, pp. 443–451, 2011.

[22] A. McKenna, M. Hanna, E. Banks et al., "The genome analysis toolkit: a MapReduce framework for analyzing next-generation DNA sequencing data," *Genome Research*, vol. 20, no. 9, pp. 1297–1303, 2010.

[23] Cancer Genome Atlas Network, "Comprehensive molecular portraits of human breast tumours," *Nature*, vol. 490, no. 7418, pp. 61–70, 2012.

[24] D. L. Altshuler, R. M. Durbin, G. R. Abecasis et al., "A map of human genome variation from population-scale sequencing," *Nature*, vol. 467, no. 7319, pp. 1061–1073, 2010.

[25] D. C. Koboldt, K. Chen, T. Wylie et al., "VarScan: variant detection in massively parallel sequencing of individual and pooled samples," *Bioinformatics*, vol. 25, no. 17, pp. 2283–2285, 2009.

[26] D. C. Koboldt, Q. Zhang, D. E. Larson et al., "VarScan 2: somatic mutation and copy number alteration discovery in cancer by exome sequencing," *Genome Research*, vol. 22, no. 3, pp. 568–576, 2012.

[27] D. Challis, J. Yu, U. S. Evani et al., "An integrative variant analysis suite for whole exome next-generation sequencing data," *BMC Bioinformatics*, vol. 13, article 8, 2012.

[28] J. Hillman-Jackson, D. Clements, D. Blankenberg, J. Taylor, and A. Nekrutenko, "Using Galaxy to perform large-scale interactive data analyses," in *Current Protocols in Bioinformatics*, chapter 10, unit 10.5, 2012.

[29] H. P. Ji, "Improving bioinformatic pipelines for exome variant calling," *Genome Medicine*, vol. 4, no. 1, article 7, 2012.

[30] R. R. Lemos, M. B. Souza, and J. R. Oliveira, "Exploring the implications of INDELs in neuropsychiatric genetics: challenges and perspectives," *Journal of Molecular Neuroscience*, vol. 47, no. 3, pp. 419–424, 2012.

[31] S. A. Lee, H. S. Mun, H. Kim et al., "Naturally occurring hepatitis B virus X deletions and insertions among Korean chronic patients," *Journal of Medical Virology*, vol. 83, no. 1, pp. 65–70, 2011.

[32] U. Väli, M. Brandström, M. Johansson, and H. Ellegren, "Insertion-deletion polymorphisms (indels) as genetic markers in natural populations," *BMC Genetics*, vol. 9, article 8, 2008.

[33] G. Lunter, "Probabilistic whole-genome alignments reveal high indel rates in the human and mouse genomes," *Bioinformatics*, vol. 23, no. 13, pp. i289–i296, 2007.

[34] P. Krawitz, C. Rödelsperger, M. Jäger, L. Jostins, S. Bauer, and P. N. Robinson, "Microindel detection in short-read sequence data," *Bioinformatics*, vol. 26, no. 6, Article ID btq027, pp. 722–729, 2010.

[35] K. Ye, M. H. Schulz, Q. Long, R. Apweiler, and Z. Ning, "Pindel: a pattern growth approach to detect break points of large deletions and medium sized insertions from paired-end short reads," *Bioinformatics*, vol. 25, no. 21, pp. 2865–2871, 2009.

[36] D. G. MacArthur, S. Balasubramanian, A. Frankish et al., "A systematic survey of loss-of-function variants in human protein-coding genes," *Science*, vol. 335, no. 6070, pp. 823–828, 2012.

[37] C. A. Albers, G. Lunter, D. G. MacArthur, G. McVean, W. H. Ouwehand, and R. Durbin, "Dindel: accurate indel calls from short-read data," *Genome Research*, vol. 21, no. 6, pp. 961–973, 2011.

[38] J. A. Neuman, O. Isakov, and N. Shomron, "Analysis of insertion-deletion from deep-sequencing data: software evaluation for optimal detection," *Briefings in Bioinformatics*. In press.

[39] G. M. Cooper and J. Shendure, "Needles in stacks of needles: finding disease-causal variants in a wealth of genomic data," *Nature Reviews Genetics*, vol. 12, no. 9, pp. 628–640, 2011.

[40] E. S. Lander, "Initial impact of the sequencing of the human genome," *Nature*, vol. 470, no. 7333, pp. 187–197, 2011.

[41] L. A. Hindorff, P. Sethupathy, H. A. Junkins et al., "Potential eti-
ologic and functional implications of genome-wide association
loci for human diseases and traits," *Proceedings of the National
Academy of Sciences of the United States of America*, vol. 106, no.
23, pp. 9362–9367, 2009.

[42] P. Kumar, S. Henikoff, and P. C. Ng, "Predicting the effects of
coding non-synonymous variants on protein function using the
SIFT algorithm," *Nature Protocols*, vol. 4, no. 7, pp. 1073–1081,
2009.

[43] I. A. Adzhubei, S. Schmidt, L. Peshkin et al., "A method and
server for predicting damaging missense mutations," *Nature
Methods*, vol. 7, no. 4, pp. 248–249, 2010.

[44] P. S. Nair and M. Vihinen, "VariBench: A benchmark database-
for variations," *Human Mutation*. In press.

[45] P. Cingolani, A. Platts, L. Wang le et al., "A program for
annotating and predicting the effects of single nucleotide
polymorphisms, SnpEff: SNPs in the genome of Drosophila
melanogaster strain w1118, iso-2, iso-3," *Fly*, vol. 6, no. 2, pp.
80–92, 2012.

[46] G. De Baets, J. Van Durme, J. Reumers et al., "SNPeffect
4.0: on-line prediction of molecular and structural effects of
protein-coding variants," *Nucleic Acids Research*, vol. 40, pp.
D935–D939, 2012.

[47] K. Wang, M. Li, and H. Hakonarson, "ANNOVAR: functional
annotation of genetic variants from high-throughput sequencing data," *Nucleic Acids Research*, vol. 38, no. 16, Article ID
gkq603, p. e164, 2010.

[48] M. Yandell, C. D. Huff, H. Hu et al., "A probabilistic disease-gene
finder for personal genomes," *Genome Research*, vol. 21, no. 9,
pp. 1529–1542, 2011.

[49] L. Habegger, S. Balasubramanian, D. Z. Chen et al., "VAT:
a computational framework to functionally annotate variants
in personal genomes within a cloud-computing environment,"
Bioinformatics, vol. 28, no. 17, pp. 2267–2269, 2012.

[50] D. G. MacArthur, S. Balasubramanian, A. Frankish et al.,
"A systematic survey of loss-of-function variants in human
protein-coding genes," *Science*, vol. 335, no. 6070, pp. 823–828,
2012.

[51] M. Sincan, D. R. Simeonov, D. Adams et al., "VAR-MD: a
tool to analyze whole exome-genome variants in small human
pedigrees with mendelian inheritance," *Human Mutation*, vol.
33, no. 4, pp. 593–598, 2012.

17

Gene Expression Network Reconstruction by LEP Method Using Microarray Data

Na You, Peng Mou, Ting Qiu, Qiang Kou, Huaijin Zhu, Yuexi Chen, and Xueqin Wang

School of Mathematics & Computational Science, Sun Yat-Sen University, Guangzhou, Guangdong 510275, China

Correspondence should be addressed to Xueqin Wang, wangxq88@mail.sysu.edu.cn

Academic Editors: R. Jiang, W. Tian, J. Wan, and X. Zhao

Gene expression network reconstruction using microarray data is widely studied aiming to investigate the behavior of a gene cluster simultaneously. Under the Gaussian assumption, the conditional dependence between genes in the network is fully described by the partial correlation coefficient matrix. Due to the high dimensionality and sparsity, we utilize the LEP method to estimate it in this paper. Compared to the existing methods, the LEP reaches the highest PPV with the sensitivity controlled at the satisfactory level. A set of gene expression data from the HapMap project is analyzed for illustration.

1. Introduction

Genes on the chromosomes behave interactively controlling the gene expression profiles of a cluster of genes, and their own expressions are in turn regulated by a bundle of genes. Exploring the gene expression regulatory network is essentially important to understand the progress of complex diseases, find the causal genes, and develop new drugs. In the past decades, the development of microarray technology allows us to measure the expression levels of tens of thousands of genes simultaneously, providing an opportunity to study the complex relationships among genes. In order to reconstruct the gene expression network, for any two particular genes, the conditional independence given all other genes needs to be investigated.

Because of the convenience of describing the interactions among variables, the graphical models become a common choice to study the relationships between variables, including but not limited to Boolean network [1], Bayesian network [2–4], autoregression model [5], and graphical Gaussian model [6]. However, the statistical inference on the independence is not easy. Under the Gaussian assumption, the independence is identical to being uncorrelated, and the conditional dependence between variables is able to be represented by the partial correlation coefficient matrix. When the number of observations n is equal or greater than the number of variables p, [7] mentioned two ways to estimate the partial correlation coefficient matrix in the graphical Gaussian model. If $n < p$, neither of these two ways is applicable due to the singular matrix.

As a typical high-dimensional data, there are usually not many available chips, while a great number of genes are included in the microarray data analysis. Fortunately, more and more studies [8–10] showed that the gene expression network is sparse, which means, for a particular gene, it only interacts with a few other genes. This fact implies that the majority entries of the partial correlation coefficient matrix are zero. To efficiently explore the sparsity and identify nonzero entries, the penalized linear regression is established where the sum of squared residuals (SSR) plus a penalty term is minimized, and has been widely used to estimate the sparse partial correlation coefficient matrix to reconstruct the gene expression network using microarray data [7, 11].

The most pioneering penalized linear regression method, the least absolute shrinkage and selection operator (LASSO) proposed by [12], utilizes the L_1 penalty to shrink the estimate which is close to zero from non-zero to zero, but it shrinks the estimates for parameters farther away from zero more severely, leading to a substantial bias. The authors in [13] indicated that LASSO may cause a bias even in a simple regression and suggested the smoothly clipped absolute deviation (SCAD) method, where a nonconcave penalty term with desirable statistical properties, such as unbiasedness, sparsity, and continuity, was introduced. However, the SCAD penalty is not smooth, resulting in the optimization problem being complicated. Upon this, [14] proposed the Laplace error penalty (LEP) method with a penalty which is unbiased, sparse, continuous, and almost smooth.

In this paper, we will apply the LEP method to reconstruct the gene expression network, and compare it to LASSO and SCAD in the performance of estimating the partial correlation coefficient matrix. The paper is structured as follows. In Section 2, the LASSO, SCAD, and LEP methods will be briefly described. In Section 3, we will report the results of simulations and a real data analysis. A short discussion is given in Section 4.

2. Methods

The graphical Gaussian model, or GGM for abbreviation, is an undirected graphical model. Let $\mathbf{X} = (X_1,\ldots,X_p)'$ indicate a p-dimensional random variable, subject to the multivariate normal distribution $N(\boldsymbol{\mu},\Sigma)$, where $\boldsymbol{\mu}$ is the mean vector and Σ is the variance-covariance matrix. Given n samples from $N(\boldsymbol{\mu},\Sigma)$, $(x_{ij})_{p\times n}$, the partial correlation coefficient matrix $(\rho_{ij})_{p\times p}$, which reflects the conditional dependence between different components of $\mathbf{X}$, could be estimated by $\hat{\rho}_{ij} = \text{sign}(\hat{\beta}_{ij})\sqrt{\hat{\beta}_{ij}\hat{\beta}_{ji}}$, where $\hat{\beta}_{ij}$ is the estimator for β_{ij} in the linear regression model

$$X_{ij} = \sum_{1\le k\ne i\le p} \beta_{kj}X_{kj} + \epsilon_{ij}, \quad i = 1,2,\ldots,p; \; j = 1,2,\ldots,n, \tag{1}$$

ϵ_{ij}, $i = 1,2,\ldots,p$ and $j = 1,2,\ldots,n$, are independent and identically distributed, and independent of $\mathbf{X}$, and $\text{sign}(x)$ is an indicator function, being -1, 0, or 1 when x is smaller, equal, or greater than 0, respectively. For the "small N large P" problem, instead of the classical least square optimization, the objective function

$$\sum_{i=1}^{p}\sum_{j=1}^{n}\left(X_{ij} - \sum_{k\ne i}\beta_{kj}X_{kj}\right)^2 + \sum_{i=1}^{p}\sum_{1\le j\ne i\le N}p_\lambda\left(\beta_{ij}\right) \tag{2}$$

is minimized to get the estimator for β_{ij}, $\hat{\beta}_{ij}$, where $p_\lambda(\cdot)$ indicates a penalty function on the parameters. The formula $p_\lambda(\cdot)$ is essentially important. It not only determines the way to shrink the estimators, but also directly affects the complexity of the optimization algorithm. A good penalty function should have several desirable statistical properties, unbiasedness, sparsity, continuity [13], and smoothness [14].

The LASSO, proposed by [12], has the penalty $p_\lambda(\beta) = \lambda|\beta|$. Although it succeeded in many applications of variable selection, it shrinks the estimates of larger parameters more significantly than that of the smaller parameters, causing a substantial bias. The SCAD penalty function, suggested by [13], has the derivative $p_\lambda'(\beta) = \lambda\{I(|\beta| \le \lambda) + (\lambda\alpha - |\beta|)_+I(|\beta| > \lambda)/(\lambda(\alpha - 1))\}$. Beside the sparsity and continuity, it gains the unbiasedness but loses the smoothness. The SCAD penalty is made of piecewise quadratic

splines, making the optimization of (2) complicated. To overcome this problem, Wen et al. [14] proposed the LEP with penalty term

$$p_\lambda(\beta) = \lambda\left(1 - \exp\left(-\frac{|\beta|}{\kappa}\right)\right), \tag{3}$$

where λ and $\kappa > 0$ are two tuning parameters.

The LEP penalty not only satisfies the unbiasedness, sparsity, and continuity, but also is an almost smooth function. It emphasizes the smoothness and complexity, since the smooth function is more stable, and the complexity of optimization algorithm highly depends on the complexity of $p_\lambda(\cdot)$, which determines whether the proposed method could be widely applied, especially in the high-dimensional data situations. In order to solve the optimization problem, [14] extended the block coordinate gradient descent (BCGD) algorithm [15] and provided a faster computing algorithm, as will be shown in the simulation studies. For the details of the LEP method and the optimization algorithm, please refer to [14].

3. Results

3.1. Simulations. Suppose there are n microarray chips and p genes, then $n \times p$ equations with $p \times (p - 1)$ parameters are involved in (1). When p is fixed, increasing/decreasing n would increase/decrease the number of equations but the number of parameters would remain the same. In this case, the penalized linear regression, including LEP, LASSO and SCAD, performed as expected that is, their estimates became more or less accurate as n became larger or smaller (results not shown here). Therefore, in the following simulations, we fixed $n = 120$ and only varied $p = 10$ or 20.

In order to fully evaluate the performances of LEP, LASSO, and SCAD in different situations, four scenarios were set up. In each scenario, a covariance matrix Σ of size $p \times p$ was generated, and n random vectors of dimension p were sampled from the multivariate normal distribution $N(0,\Sigma)$ independently. The partial correlation coefficient matrix was then estimated from the sampled data. We fixed Σ and made 100 repetitions in each scenario to get the average of the estimates for fair comparison. In the first two scenarios $p = 10$, and $p = 20$ in scenario 3 and 4. Two data generating procedures used in [11] were employed to generate the covariance matrix Σ. In scenario 1 and 3, the (i, j)-element of Σ, $\sigma_{ij} = \exp(-a|s_i - s_j|)$, where $a = 2$ and $s_1 < s_2 < \cdots < s_p$ were generated by setting $s_i - s_{i-1}$, following a uniform distribution $U(0.5, 1)$. In scenario 2 and 4, a sparse precision matrix Ω was generated as proposed in [16], and $\Sigma = \Omega^{-1}$.

The partial correlation coefficient matrix was estimated by LEP, LASSO or SCAD, respectively, in each scenario. To evaluate the performances of different methods, the sensitivity which is the fraction of "true non-zero and also estimated non-zero parameters" to "true non-zero parameters" and PPV which is the fraction of "true non-zero and also estimated non-zero parameters" to "estimated non-zero parameters" were calculated. Furthermore,

TABLE 1: The sensitivity, PPV, and F_1 values in four scenarios of the simulation studies.

	PPV	Sensitivity	F_1	SSE	Time (s)
Scenario 1: $P = 10$					
LEP	0.934	0.708	0.805	1075.313	0.121
LASSO	0.602	0.908	0.724	1053.937	2.184
SCAD	0.891	0.727	0.801	1070.202	0.594
Scenario 2: $P = 10$					
LEP	0.926	0.826	0.873	1185.403	0.259
LASSO	0.833	0.916	0.873	1215.098	2.507
SCAD	0.932	0.828	0.877	1191.352	0.933
Scenario 3: $P = 20$					
LEP	0.778	0.707	0.741	2112.376	2.431
LASSO	0.467	0.868	0.607	2100.014	16.976
SCAD	0.693	0.741	0.716	2089.248	6.247
Scenario 4: $P = 20$					
LEP	0.831	0.834	0.832	2351.997	2.763
LASSO	0.667	0.910	0.770	2380.255	23.792
SCAD	0.735	0.852	0.789	2298.897	7.193

the F_1 score $= 2 \cdot$ sensitivity $\cdot$ PPV/(sensitivity + PPV) was also presented. The results in four scenarios were listed in Table 1.

As the number of genes p increases, the number of parameters to be estimated increases rapidly. Due to the sparsity of partial correlation coefficient matrix, the number of true zero parameters increases much more than that of true non-zero parameters, causing the chance of estimating a zero parameter to be non-zero increases more than that of estimating a non-zero parameter to be zero. As presented in Table 1, although the sensitivity of LEP did not change significantly as p increasing from 10 to 20, its PPV reduced obviously from ~90% in scenario 1 and 2 to ~80% in scenario 3 and 4. The LASSO and SCAD showed similarly. Note that beside the penalty term, the performances of different methods also depend on the true value of covariance matrix Σ, which was generated at the beginning of each scenario.

Across all the scenarios, although LASSO reached the highest sensitivity, its PPV was far lower than that of SCAD and LEP, which means that LASSO could identify more gene regulatory relationships, but there might be many false positives. Among these three methods, LEP achieved the highest PPV with its sensitivity controlled at similar level to that of SCAD. Its F_1 score also reached the highest value in scenario 1, 3, and 4. More importantly, using the algorithm proposed by [14], LEP was the fastest, whose computation time was almost 1/18, 1/10, 1/7 and 1/9 of LASSO and 1/5, 1/4, 1/3, and 1/3 of SCAD in four scenarios, respectively.

For intuitive illustration, we also plotted the relative frequency matrix for each method in each scenario, where the (i, j)-element indicates the relative frequency of non-zero estimates among 100 repetitions. The darker the color is, the higher the frequency of non-zero estimates is. The true partial correlation coefficient matrix was shown in the first panel of each row in Figure 1. From Figure 1, we can see

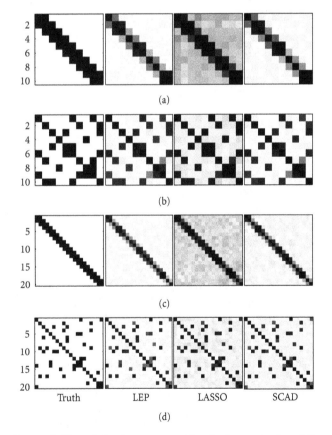

FIGURE 1: The relative frequency matrices in four scenarios of the simulation studies. The first, second, third and forth rows correspond to scenario 1, 2, 3 and 4, respectively.

that the color of LASSO is significantly darker than others, especially the truth, which means that LASSO estimated many true zero parameters to be non-zero, resulting in

TABLE 2: The number of edges connected with each gene in GSE6536 data example.

No.	Gene	LEP	LASSO	SCAD	Gene functions
1	ABCF1	0	9	1	ATP-binding cassette
2	EIF3D	0	8	1	Eukaryotic translation initiation factor 3
3	SRP14	0	8	1	Signal recognition particle 14 kDa (homologous Alu RNA-binding protein)
4	RPL28	0	8	0	Ribosomal protein L28
5	EIF3F	0	8	0	Eukaryotic translation initiation factor 3
6	CYP2A6	3	7	3	Cytochrome P450
7	RPL35	0	7	2	Ribosomal protein L35
8	GDI2	0	7	1	GDP dissociation inhibitor 2
9	RPL11	0	7	1	Ribosomal protein L11
10	GAS6	3	6	3	Growth arrest-specific 6
11	DAD1	1	6	2	Defender against cell death 1
12	RPL21	0	6	1	Ribosomal protein L21
13	EPHB3	3	5	3	EPH receptor B3
14	MMP14	2	5	4	Matrix metallopeptidase 14 (membrane inserted)
15	ESRRA	2	5	3	Estrogen-related receptor alpha
16	PRPF8*	2	5	0	PRP8 pre-mRNA processing factor 8 homolog (*S. cerevisiae*)
17	HSPA6	1	5	2	Heat shock 70 kDa protein 6 (HSP70B′)
18	PARK7	1	5	2	Parkinson protein 7
19	TARDBP	0	5	4	TAR DNA-binding protein
20	SEPT2	0	5	0	Septin 2
21	DDR1*	3	4	0	Discoidin domain receptor tyrosine kinase 1
22	TRADD	1	4	2	TNFRSF1A-associated via death domain
23	EIF4G2	0	4	1	Eukaryotic translation initiation factor 4 gamma
24	CAPNS1	0	4	0	Calpain, small subunit
25	PLD1	1	3	2	Phospholipase D1
26	UBA7*	2	2	0	Ubiquitin-like modifier activating enzyme 7
27	CYP2E1	0	2	1	Cytochrome P450
28	FNTB	1	1	1	Farnesyltransferase
29	GUCA1A	0	1	1	Guanylate cyclase activator 1A (retina)
30	CCL5	0	0	0	Chemokine (C-C motif) ligand 5

*Indicates LEP exclusive genes.

many false positives. Comparing to LASSO, the SCAD plot became much closer to the truth and LEP made a further improvement upon the SCAD plot.

3.2. A Real Data Example. In this section, the publicly available gene expression dataset GSE6536 (http://www.ncbi .nlm.nih.gov/geo/query/acc.cgi?acc=GSE6536) was investigated. There are gene expression values of 47,294 human transcripts from 270 HapMap individual samples [17], including 30 Caucasian trios of northern and western European background (CEU), 30 Yoruba trios from Ibadan, Nigeria (YRI), 45 unrelated individuals from Beijing, China (CHB), and 45 unrelated individuals from Tokyo, Japan (JPT). After the microarray data were log2-transformed and background corrected, within and across the population normalized, the gene expression values were saved in a matrix for further analysis, which also could be downloaded from the website mentioned above.

Frommlet et al. [18] listed 44 genes which are significantly differentially expressed across individual samples. Since the platform Sentrix Human-6 Expression BeadChip used in this experiment was publicly available in 2005, so far the gene annotation database has been updated a lot. Of those 44 genes, 14 either were found to be pseudogenes or have been removed as a result of standard genome annotation processing and therefore were excluded from our following analysis. The partial correlation coefficient matrix of the rest 30 genes were estimated using 270 samples data. In the graphical model, one non-zero estimate off diagonal in the partial correlation coefficient matrix corresponds to one edge connecting different genes on the graph. The number of edges connected with each gene was listed in Table 2.

As shown in Table 2, LASSO identified 76 edges between 30 genes, SCAD found 21 and LEP reported 13. The LASSO recognized that almost all of the genes interacted with others and identified much more edges than SCAD or LEP. To compare the performances of different methods, we only focus on the important genes which carry the most or secondly most number of edges. For LASSO, there is 1 such important gene with 9 edges and 4 with 8 edges each. The SCAD found 2 important genes with 4 edges each and 4 with 3 edges each. The LEP identified 4 with 3 edges each and 4 with 2 edges each.

For the important genes recognized by LASSO, none of them were taken to be important by SCAD or LEP. According to the gene functions described in Table 2, although these genes have very important functions, they usually accomplish these functions together with many others genes, and once they could not be normally expressed, these functions could be completed by other genes, then this would not significantly affect the gene expression in the network. On the contrary, the genes identified by SCAD or LEP usually have unique gene function, which could not be recovered by other genes once they are expressed abnormally, resulting in the irregular expression in the network.

Beside those 5 common genes identified by both of LEP and SCAD, LEP found 3 more exclusive genes and SCAD found 1 more exclusive gene. Those 3 LEP exclusive genes not only play a key role in the cellular mechanism, but also have very close relationships with other genes. Among them, PRPF8 (gene 16) is a component of both U2- and U12-dependent spliceosomes, which removes the vast majority of introns (more than 99%) in mammals [19, 20]. DDR1 (gene 21), one of the receptor tyrosine kinases, is important in the communication between the cells and their microenvironments and gets involved in many cellular activities, like growth, differentiation, and metabolism [21]. UBA7 (gene 26), widely expressed in a variety of cell types, belongs to the ubiquitin conjugation pathway, which is of fundamental and central importance [22]. However, the SCAD exclusive gene, TARDBP (gene 19), although plays an important role in modulating HIV-1 gene expression; it only represses transcription from the HIV-1 long terminal repeat, no other transcription from other promoters [23]. Due to this fact, it should not interact heavily with other genes, as the LEP concluded.

4. Discussion

In this paper, we applied the LEP method to estimate the partial correlation coefficient matrix to reconstruct the gene expression network. Comparing to the existing methods, for example, LASSO and SCAD, LEP reached the highest PPV, and its sensitivity was controlled at the similar level as SCAD. As seen from the relative frequency matrix plot in the simulation studies, LEP showed the superiority in exploring the sparsity of the partial correlation coefficient matrix.

There are two tuning parameters in the LEP penalty function. We used the EBIC criteria [24] to select the approximate values for parameters. But as seen from the simulation results (not shown here), any combination of κ and λ which satisfy some certain function relation would return very close estimation results. Therefore, we only need to vary one of κ and λ and keep the other a constant for parameter choosing. As in the real data analysis, we set $\kappa = 0.01$ and vary λ.

Acknowledgments

This work is partially supported by the Major State Basic Research Development Program (2012CB517900), NSFC (11001280), NDFGP (10151027501000066), RFDP (20090171110017), and the Fundamental Research Funds for the Central Universities.

References

[1] P. D'Haeseleer, S. Liang, and R. Somogyi, "Genetic network inference: from co-expression clustering to reverse engineering," *Bioinformatics*, vol. 16, no. 8, pp. 707–726, 2000.

[2] N. Friedman, M. Linial, I. Nachman, and D. Pe'er, "Using bayesian networks to analyze expression data," *Journal of Computational Biology*, vol. 7, no. 3-4, pp. 601–620, 2000.

[3] E. Segal, M. Shapira, A. Regev et al., "Module networks: identifying regulatory modules and their condition-specific regulators from gene expression data," *Nature Genetics*, vol. 34, no. 2, pp. 166–176, 2003.

[4] N. Friedman, "Inferring cellular networks using probabilistic graphical models," *Science*, vol. 303, no. 5659, pp. 799–805, 2004.

[5] R. Opgen-Rhein and K. Strimmer, "Learning causal networks from systems biology time course data: an effective model selection procedure for the vector autoregressive process," *BMC Bioinformatics*, vol. 8, supplement 2, article S3, 2007.

[6] J. Schäfer and K. Strimmer, "An empirical Bayes approach to inferring large-scale gene association networks," *Bioinformatics*, vol. 21, no. 6, pp. 754–764, 2005.

[7] N. Krämer, J. Schäfer, and A. L. Boulesteix, "Regularized estimation of large-scale gene association networks using graphical Gaussian models," *BMC Bioinformatics*, vol. 10, no. 1, article 384, 2009.

[8] T. I. Lee, N. J. Rinaldi, F. Robert et al., "Transcriptional regulatory networks in Saccharomyces cerevisiae," *Science*, vol. 298, no. 5594, pp. 799–804, 2002.

[9] S. Ma, Q. Gong, and H. J. Bohnert, "An Arabidopsis gene network based on the graphical Gaussian model," *Genome Research*, vol. 17, no. 11, pp. 1614–1625, 2007.

[10] R. D. Leclerc, "Survival of the sparsest: robust gene networks are parsimonious," *Molecular Systems Biology*, vol. 4, article 213, 2008.

[11] J. Fan, Y. Feng, and Y. Wu, "Network exploration via the adaptive lasso and scad penalties," *The Annals of Applied Statistics*, vol. 3, no. 2, pp. 521–541, 2009.

[12] R. Tibshirani, "Regression shrinkage and selection via the lasso," *Journal of the Royal Statistical Society B*, vol. 85, no. 1, pp. 267–288, 1996.

[13] J. Fan and R. Li, "Variable Selection via Nonconcave Penalized Likelihood and its Oracle Properties," *Journal of the American Statistical Association*, vol. 96, no. 456, pp. 1348–1360, 2001.

[14] C. Wen, S. Wang, and X. Wang, "Ultra-high dimensional variable selection based on global minimizers of penalized least squares," Tech. Rep., Sun Yat-Sen University, 2012.

[15] P. Tseng and S. Yun, "A coordinate gradient descent method for nonsmooth separable minimization," *Mathematical Programming*, vol. 117, no. 1-2, pp. 387–423, 2009.

[16] H. Li and J. Gui, "Gradient directed regularization for sparse Gaussian concentration graphs, with applications to inference of genetic networks," *Biostatistics*, vol. 7, no. 2, pp. 302–317, 2006.

[17] The International HapMap Consortium, "A haplotype map of the human genome," *Nature*, vol. 437, no. 7063, pp. 1299–1320, 2005.

[18] F. Frommlet, F. Ruhaltinger, P. Twarog, and M. Bogdan, "A model selection approach to genome wide association studies," 2010, http://arxiv.org/abs/1010.0124.

[19] H. R. Luo, G. A. Moreau, N. Levin, and M. J. Moore, "The human Prp8 protein is a component of both U2- and U12-dependent spliceosomes," *RNA*, vol. 5, no. 7, pp. 893–908, 1999.

[20] P. A. Sharp and C. B. Burge, "Classification of introns: U2-type or U12-type," *Cell*, vol. 91, no. 7, pp. 875–879, 1997.

[21] A. N. Shelling, R. Butler, T. Jones, S. H. Laval, J. M. Boyle, and T. S. Ganesan, "Localization of an epithelial-specific receptor kinase (EDDR1) to chromosome 6q16," *Genomics*, vol. 25, no. 2, pp. 584–587, 1995.

[22] K. Kok, R. Hofstra, A. Pilz et al., "A gene in the chromosomal region 3p21 with greatly reduced expression in lung cancer is similar to the gene for ubiquitin-activating enzyme," *Proceedings of the National Academy of Sciences of the United States of America*, vol. 90, no. 13, pp. 6071–6075, 1993.

[23] S. H. Ignatius Ou, W. U. Foon, D. Harrich, L. F. García-Martínez, and R. B. Gaynor, "Cloning and characterization of a novel cellular protein, tdp-43, that binds to human immunodeficiency virus type 1 tar dna sequence motifs," *Journal of Virology*, vol. 69, no. 6, pp. 3584–3596, 1995.

[24] J. Chen and Z. Chen, "Extended Bayesian information criteria for model selection with large model spaces," *Biometrika*, vol. 95, no. 3, pp. 759–771, 2008.

18

From Ontology to Semantic Similarity: Calculation of Ontology-Based Semantic Similarity

Mingxin Gan,[1] **Xue Dou,**[1] **and Rui Jiang**[2]

[1] *Dongling School of Economics and Management, University of Science and Technology Beijing, Beijing 100083, China*
[2] *Department of Automation, Tsinghua University, Beijing 100084, China*

Correspondence should be addressed to Mingxin Gan; ganmx@ustb.edu.cn and Rui Jiang; ruijiang@tsinghua.edu.cn

Academic Editors: Y. Cai, S. Mohan, C. Proctor, K. Spiegel, and J. Wang

Advances in high-throughput experimental techniques in the past decade have enabled the explosive increase of omics data, while effective organization, interpretation, and exchange of these data require standard and controlled vocabularies in the domain of biological and biomedical studies. Ontologies, as abstract description systems for domain-specific knowledge composition, hence receive more and more attention in computational biology and bioinformatics. Particularly, many applications relying on domain ontologies require quantitative measures of relationships between terms in the ontologies, making it indispensable to develop computational methods for the derivation of ontology-based semantic similarity between terms. Nevertheless, with a variety of methods available, how to choose a suitable method for a specific application becomes a problem. With this understanding, we review a majority of existing methods that rely on ontologies to calculate semantic similarity between terms. We classify existing methods into five categories: methods based on semantic distance, methods based on information content, methods based on properties of terms, methods based on ontology hierarchy, and hybrid methods. We summarize characteristics of each category, with emphasis on basic notions, advantages and disadvantages of these methods. Further, we extend our review to software tools implementing these methods and applications using these methods.

1. Introduction

Recent technical innovation in high-throughput experiments has been successfully bringing about a revolution in modern biological and biomedical studies. With microarrays, expression levels of thousands of genes can be simultaneously measured [1]. With yeast two-hybrid assays, pairwise interactions between thousands of proteins can be systematically detected [2, 3]. With tandem mass spectrometry, a large number of proteins can be sequenced and characterized rapidly [4]. Indeed, high-throughput experimental techniques have enabled the collection of a vast volume of omics data, while how to organize, interpret, and use these data has now become a serious issue [5]. Each type of data explains the biological system under investigation from a specific point of view. In order to get full understanding of the system, however, one needs to integrate multiple types of data— typically coming from different laboratories and obtained using different experimental techniques. Consequently, the data should be organized in such a way that is standard across different techniques and interpretable across different laboratories. In other words, information and knowledge included in the data should be described using a set of controlled vocabulary that is standardized. Fortunately, an ontology provides us with such a standard means of organizing information [5].

An ontology is an abstract description system for knowledge composition in a certain domain [6]. By organizing concepts (terms) in a domain in a hierarchical way and describing relationships between terms using a small number of relational descriptors, an ontology supplies a standardized vocabulary for representing entities in the domain [7]. Particularly, in biological and biomedical domains, there have been quite a few ontologies available [5]. For example, the gene ontology (GO), including three separate domains (biological process, molecular function, and cellular component), has been widely used as a standard vocabulary for annotating functions of genes and their products across different species [8]. The human phenotype ontology (HPO) has been explored to facilitate the description of human disease phenotypes with a set of standard terms [9]. The plant ontology (PO) has been utilized to describe plant structures and growth stages [10]. Particularly, in order to achieve the goal of providing standard annotations of multiple heterogeneous data sources using common controlled vocabularies, The open biological and biomedical ontologies (OBO) Foundry has been proposed to coordinate the development of ontologies in different biological and biomedical domains [5]. Up to October 20, 2012, there have been 8 mature ontologies and 107 candidate ontologies included in the OBO Foundry, covering 25 domains, including anatomy, health, phenotype, environment, and many others [5].

Many applications using domain ontologies need to quantify the relationship between two terms [11, 12]. A suitable measure of such relationship is the semantic similarity between the terms, given the underlying domain ontology [13]. Considering the hierarchical structure of an ontology [6], the semantic similarity between two terms is in general defined as a function of distance between the terms in a graph corresponding to the hierarchical structure of the underlying ontology. However, the concrete form of the function may be refined with further knowledge about the ontology or even entities that are already annotated by using the ontology, yielding a wide variety of approaches for calculating semantic similarities of terms [14–19]. More specifically, we classify these approaches into five categories: (1) methods based on semantic distance between terms, (2) methods based on information contents of terms, (3) methods based on features of terms, (4) methods based on the hierarchical structure of an ontology, and (5) hybrid methods. Since each category of methods has its own traits, it is indispensable to know which method is suitable for the application of interest. Motivated by this consideration, we summarize characteristics of each category of methods in this paper, provide a brief review of available software implementation of these methods, and introduce typical biological and biomedical applications that rely on ontologies.

2. Biological and Biomedical Ontologies

The rapid development of high-throughput biological experimental techniques has enabled the explosive increase of a wide variety of omics data, while the integrated use of these data appeals for the standard annotation of multiple heterogeneous data sources using common controlled vocabularies. To achieve this goal and coordinate the development of ontologies in different domains, the open biological and biomedical ontologies (OBO) Foundry has been proposed [5]. The OBO Foundry is a collaborative experiment that aims at creating controlled vocabularies for shared use across different biological and medical domains. Participants of the OBO Foundry have agreed in advance on the adoption of a set of principles that specify the best practices for the development of ontologies, for the purpose of developing a set of interoperable humanly validated reference ontologies for all major domains of biomedical research. As shown in Table 1,

TABLE 1: Domains in the OBO Foundry.

Index	Domain	Number
1	Adverse events, health	1
2	Algorithms	1
3	Anatomy	39 (3)
4	Anatomy and development	1
5	Anatomy, immunology	1
6	Behavior	1
7	Biochemistry	3 (1)
8	Biological function	1 (1)
9	Biological process	3 (1)
10	Biological sequence	1
11	Environment	3
12	Experiments	8
13	Genomic	1
14	Health	12
15	Information	1
16	Lipids	1
17	Medicine	2
18	Molecular structure	1
19	Neuroscience	3
20	Phenotype	8 (1)
21	Proteins	6 (1)
22	Provenance	1
23	Resources	1
24	Taxonomy	4
25	Other	11
	Total	115 (8)

up to October 20, 2012, there have been 8 mature ontologies and 107 candidate ontologies included in the OBO Foundry. These ontologies can further be classified into 25 domains, including anatomy, health, phenotype, and environment.

The 8 mature ontologies are listed in Table 2. Biological process, cellular component, and molecular function belong to the gene ontology (GO), which aims at standardizing representation of characteristics of genes and gene products across species via providing a controlled vocabulary of terms for describing annotations of gene products [20]. Specifically, biological process describes operations or sets of molecular events with a defined beginning and end. Molecular function describes elemental activities of gene products at the molecular level. The cellular component describes parts of a cell or its extracellular environment. The chemical entities of biological interest (ChEBI) provide a controlled vocabulary mainly for describing small chemical compounds, which are either products of nature or synthetic products used to intervene in the processes of living organisms [21]. The phenotypic quality (PATO) can be used in conjunction with phenotype annotations provided by other ontologies to describe qualities (such as red, ectopic, high temperature, fused, small, and edematous) for phenotypes [5, 22]. The protein ontology (PRO) is used to describe protein-related entities such as specific modified

TABLE 2: Mature ontologies in OBO.

Title	Domain	Prefix
Biological process	Biological process	GO
Cellular component	Anatomy	GO
Chemical entities of biological interest	Biochemistry	CHEBI
Molecular function	Biological function	GO
Phenotypic quality	Phenotype	PATO
Protein ontology	Proteins	PR
Xenopus anatomy and development	Anatomy	XAO
Zebrafish anatomy and development	Anatomy	ZFA

forms, orthologous isoforms, and protein complexes [23]. This ontology is separated into three domains: proteins based on evolutionary relatedness, protein forms produced from a given gene locus, and protein-containing complexes. The Xenopus anatomy and development (XAO) is designed to describe annotations of the model organism African clawed frog (*Xenopus laevis*) [24]. In this ontology, the lineage of tissues and the timing of their development are organized in a graphical view, hence facilitating the annotation of gene expression patterns, mutants, and morphant phenotypes of Xenopus. Similarly, the Zebrafish anatomy and development (XAO) provides a controlled vocabulary for annotating the anatomy of the model organism Zebrafish (*Danio rerio*) [25].

Many of the candidate ontologies have also been widely used in a variety of research areas. For example, in medical research, the human phenotype ontology (HPO) provides a means of describing phenotypic abnormalities encountered in human diseases [9]. This ontology is developed based on the Online Mendelian Inheritance in Man (OMIM) database [26] and medical literature, currently containing more than 10 thousand terms and over 50 thousand annotations to human-inherited diseases. In environmental science, the environment ontology (EnvO) is designed to support annotations of organisms or biological samples with environment descriptions [5].

3. Derivation of Semantic Similarity between Terms in an Ontology

3.1. Hierarchical Structure of an Ontology. Typically, an ontology is represented as a directed acyclic graph (DAG), in which nodes correspond to terms and edges represent relationships between the terms. In some ontologies, there is only one relationship between nodes, while in more general case, there exist more than one relationship between nodes. For example, the gene ontology defines 5 relationships between nodes: is_a, part_of, regulates, negatively_regulates, and positively_regulates [8], while the OBO relational ontology defines 13 relationships between nodes: is_a, part_of, integral_part_of, proper_part_of, located_in, contained_in, adjacent_to, transformation_of, derives_from, preceded_by, has_participant, has_agent, and instance_of [5].

In the DAG corresponding to an ontology, there is a node specified as the root. For every node in the ontology, there exists at least one path pointing from the root to the node. Every node in such a path is called an ancestor of the node, and the ancestor that immediately precedes the node in the path is called the parent of the node. Inversely, if a node is a parent of another node, the node is called a child of the parent. There might be more than one path from the root to a node. Consequently, a node may have several parent nodes, and vice versa. Given two nodes in an ontology, they must share a set of common ancestor nodes, and the one represents the most concrete concept is typically referred to as the lowest common ancestor of the two nodes. Discarding the direction of the edges in an ontology, there exists at least one path between every pair of two nodes.

3.2. Methods Based on Semantic Distance between Terms. Given a pair of two terms, c_1 and c_2, a well-known method with intuitive explicitness for assessing their similarity is to calculate the distance between the nodes corresponding to these terms in an ontology hierarchy; the shorter the distance, the higher the similarity. In the case that multiple paths between the nodes exist, the shortest or the average distance of all paths may be used. This approach is commonly referred to as the semantic distance method, since it typically yields a measure of the distance between two terms. The distance can then be easily converted into a similarity measure. Four main factors are normally considered in distance-based methods as follows

(1) density in the ontology graph: the higher the density, the nearer the distance between nodes;

(2) depths of nodes: the deeper the nodes located in, the more obvious the difference between the nodes;

(3) types of links: the normal type is is-a relation, and other relations such as part-of and substance-of are associated with the weight for edges;

(4) weights of links: edges connecting a certain node with all its child nodes can vary among different semantic weights.

In the last two decades, many efforts have been devoted to building various models to measure such distance in calculating similarities. Some representative algorithms include shortest path [27], connection weight [28], and Wu and Palmer [29].

Rada et al. proposed the shortest path method to calculate semantic similarity based on the ontology hierarchy, suggesting that the shortest path between two nodes was the simplest approach for measuring distance between two terms [27]. In mathematics, the formula for the distance between two nodes by the shortest path was denoted by $Sim(c_1, c_2) = 2MAX - L$, where c_1 and c_2 were the compared nodes, MAX the maximum path on the hierarchy, and L the shortest path. The main advantage of this method was its low complexity in calculation. Rada et al. hypothesized that when only the *is-a* relationship existed in a semantic network, semantic relatedness and semantic distance were equivalent. However, this method was short of consideration for different kinds of edges as well as the semantic relatedness representing these edges.

Sussna proposed an edge weight determination scheme, which considered the first three factors: the density of the graph, depths of nodes, and types of connections [28]. In their method, the distance or weight of the edge between adjacent nodes c_1 and c_2 was defined as

$$wt\left(c_1, c_2\right) = \frac{wt\left(c_1 \longrightarrow_r c_2\right) + wt\left(c_2 \longrightarrow_{r'} c_1\right)}{2d},$$

$$\text{given } wt\left(x \longrightarrow_r y\right) = \max_r - \frac{\max_r - \min_r}{n_r\left(x\right)}, \quad (1)$$

where $\longrightarrow_r$ was a relation of type r, $\longrightarrow_{r'}$ its inverse, d the depth of the deeper node, $\max_r$ and $\min_r$ the maximum and minimum weights for a relation of type r, respectively, and $n_r(x)$ the number of relations of type r leaving node x. This method exhibited an improvement in reducing the ambiguousness of multiple sense words by discovering the combination of senses from a set of common terms that minimizes total pairwise distance between senses. However, depth factor scaling and restricting the type of a link to a strictly hierarchical relation apparently impaired the performance of the method.

Alternatively, the common path technique calculated the similarity directly by the length of the path from the lowest common ancestor of the two terms to the root node [29]. In detail, Wu and Palmer [29] took into account the position relation of c_1, c_2 to their nearest common ancestor c to calculate similarity. Here, c was the node with fewest *is-a* relationship as their ancestor node which appeared at the lowest position on the ontology hierarchy. In mathematics, the formula calculating similarity between c_1 and c_2 was denoted as

$$\text{Sim}\left(c_1, c_2\right) = \frac{2H}{D_1 + D_2 + 2H}, \quad (2)$$

where D_1 and D_2 were, respectively, the shortest paths from c_1 and c_2 to c, and H the shortest path from c to the root. However, the calculation of similarity only cumulated shortest paths together with the consideration that all the edges were of the same weight. Hence, it might also potentially lose information of semantics represented by various types of edges existing in the ontology hierarchy.

However, in practical application, terms at the same depth do not necessarily have the same specificity, and edges at the same level do not necessarily represent the same semantic distance, and thus the issues caused by the aforementioned assumptions are not solved by those strategies [13]. Moreover, although distance is used to identify the semantic neighborhood of entity classes within their own ontologies, the similarity measure between neighborhoods is not defined based on such a distance measure.

3.3. Methods Based on Information Contents of Terms. A method based on information content typically determines the semantic similarity between two terms based on the

information content (IC) of their lowest common ancestor (LCA) node. The information content (IC) gives a measure of how specific and informative a term is. The IC of a term c can be quantified as the negative log likelihood $\text{IC}(c) = -\log P(c)$, where $P(c)$ is the probability of occurrence of c in a specific corpus (such as the UniProt Knowledgebase). Alternatively, the IC can be also computed from the number of children a term has in the ontology hierarchical structure [30], although this approach is less commonly used. On the ontology hierarchy, the occurrence probability of a node decreases when the layer of the node goes deeper, and hence the IC of the node increases. Therefore, the lower a node in the hierarchy, the greater its IC. There have been quite a few methods belonging to this category. For instance, Resnik put forward a first method that is based on information content and tested the method on WordNet [18]. Lin proposed a theoretic definition of semantic similarity using information content [15]. Jiang and Conrath improved the method of Resnik by introducing weights to edges [14]. Schlicker et al. proposed a method that is applicable to the gene ontology [31]. As mentioned by Wang et al. [32], methods based on information content may be inaccurate due to shallow annotations. Lee et al. also pointed out this drawback [33].

Resnik [18] used a taxonomy with multiple inheritance as the representational model and proposed a semantic similarity measure of terms based on the notion of information content. By analogy to information theory, this method defined the information content of a term as the negative algorithm of the probability of its occurrence and the similarity between two terms c_1 and c_2 as the maximal information content of all terms subsuming both c_1 and c_2, calculated by

$$\text{Sim}\left(c_1, c_2\right) = \max_{c \in S(c_1, c_2)} \left[-\log P\left(c\right)\right], \quad (3)$$

where $S(c_1, c_2)$ was the set of all the parents for both c_1 and c_2. Since the lowest common ancestor (LCA) had the maximum value of information content, recognizing the LCA of both c_1 and c_2 can be supported by this measure. The information content-based similarity measure was symmetric and transitive. Obvious advantages of this method were its simple calculation and easy formulation. However, in contrast to distance by Rada et al., the minimality axiom did not hold for Resnik's similarity measure. The similarity between a term and itself was the negative logarithm of its information content. Only the single term on top of the hierarchy reached the self-similarity of one. In addition, this method was only suitable for the ontology hierarchy with single relations; for example, all edges connecting terms represent only the same relationship, so it cannot be applied to the terms with either part-of relations or inferior relations.

Lin [15] proposed an alternative information theoretic approach. This method took into account not only the parent commonality of two query terms, but also the information content associated with the query terms. Three basic assumptions were normally given by Lin [15] in calculating the similarity between two terms as follows.

(1) The similarity between two terms was associated with their common properties: the more the common properties, the higher their similarity.

(2) The similarity between two terms was associated with their difference: the more the difference, the lower their similarity.

(3) The similarity between two terms reached the maximum value when they were totally the same.

Based on the above assumptions, given terms, c_i and c_j, their similarity was defined as

$$\text{Sim}\left(c_i, c_j\right) = \frac{2 \log P\left(c_0\right)}{\log P\left(c_i\right) + \log P\left(c_j\right)}, \quad (4)$$

where c_0 was the lowest common ancestor (LCA) of c_i and c_j, and $P(c_i)$ and $P(c_j)$ were the probabilities of occurrence. Not only the information content of LCA was considered in the calculation, but also their information content was taken into account in Lin's method. This measure could be seen as a normalized version of the Resniks method. Lin's values also increased in relation to the degree of similarity shown by two terms and decreased with their difference. However, the consideration of information content of two terms themselves caused a strong dependence on the high precision of the annotation information. Consequently, exact result can be generated only when mapping relationships between compared terms and other terms in the ontology hierarchy were precisely described, while the result would be near to 0 when annotations were abstract, yielding the problem of shallow semantic annotations. In fact, the difference between two terms with abstract annotations could be large, so it might be misleading to produce similarity values according to Lin's method.

Jiang and Conrath [14] proposed a combined approach that inherited the edge-based approach of the edge counting scheme, which was then enhanced by the node-based approach of the information content calculation. The factors of depths of nodes, the density around nodes, and the type of connections were taken into account in this measure. The simplified version of the measure was given as

$$\text{Dist}\left(w_1, w_2\right) = \text{IC}\left(c_1\right) + \text{IC}\left(c_2\right) - 2 \times \text{IC}\left(\text{LCA}\left(c_1, c_2\right)\right). \quad (5)$$

However, being relative measures, both the method of Lin and that of Jiang and Conrath were proportional to the IC differences between the terms and their common ancestor, independently of the absolute IC of the ancestor. To overcome this limitation, Schlicker et al. [31] proposed the relevance similarity measure. This method was based on Lin's measure but used the probability of annotation of the most informative common ancestor (MICA) as a weighting factor to provide graph placement as follows:

$$\text{Sim}\left(c_1, c_2\right) = \max_{c \in S(c_1, c_2)} \left(\frac{2 \times \log p\left(c\right)}{\log p\left(c_1\right) + \log p\left(c_2\right)} \times \left(1 - p\left(c\right)\right) \right). \quad (6)$$

All these measures overlooked the fact that a term can have several disjoint common ancestors (DCAs). To overcome this limitation, Couto et al. [34] proposed the

GraSM method, in which the IC of the MICA was replaced by the average IC of all DCA. Bodenreider et al. [35] developed a node-based measure that also used annotation data but did not rely on information theory. Focusing on the gene ontology, their method represented each term as a vector of all gene products annotated with the term and measured similarity between two terms by calculating the scalar product of their vectors. Riensche et al. used coannotation data to map terms between different GO categories and calculated a weighting factor, which could then be applied to a standard node-based semantic similarity measure [36].

3.4. Methods Based on Features of Terms. In feature-matching methods, terms are represented as collections of features, and elementary set operations are applied to estimate semantic similarities between terms. A feature-matching model in general consists of three components: distinct features of term A to term B, distinct features of term B to term A, and common features of terms A and B.

Using set theory, Tversky [37] defined a similarity measure according to a matching process, which generated a similarity value based on not only common but also distinct features of terms. This approach was in agreement with an information-theoretic definition of similarity [15]. Unlike the above-mentioned models based on semantic distance [27–29], this feature-matching model was not forced to satisfy metric properties. A similarity measure based on the normalization of Tversky's model and the set-theory functions of intersection ($D_1 \cap D_2$) and difference (D_1/D_2) was given as

$$\text{Sim}\left(c_1, c_2\right) = \frac{\left|D_1 + D_2\right|}{\left|D_1 \cap D_2\right| + \mu \left|D_1/D_2\right| + (\mu - 1)\left|D_2/D_1\right|},$$
$$\text{for } 0 \leq \mu \leq 1, \quad (7)$$

where D_1 and D_2 corresponded to description sets of c_1 and c_2, $|\ |$ the cardinality of a set, and μ a function that defines the relative importance of the noncommon features. The first term of a comparison (i.e., c_1) was referred to as the target, while the second term (i.e., c_2) was defined as the base. Particularly, intersections or subtractions of feature sets were based only on entire feature matches. This feature model allowed for representing ordinal and cardinal features, but the similarity measure did not account for their ordering.

In addition, the Matching-Distance Similarity Measure (MDSM) by Rodríguez et al. [38] and Rodríquez and Egenhofer [7, 39] was another feature model developed for similarity measurement of geospatial terms. This category of models was based on the ratio model that extends the original feature model by introducing different types of features and applying them to terms.

3.5. Methods Based on Hierarchical Structure of an Ontology. Typically, an ontology is represented as a directed acyclic graph (DAG), in which nodes correspond to terms, and edges represent relationships between the terms. A parent node may have several child nodes while a child node may have several parent nodes. Some nodes have high density around them while some have low density in the hierarchy. A method based on the structure of an ontology typically uses a distance measure to quantify the similarity between two nodes in the corresponding DAG of the ontology and then uses this measure to assess the relatedness between the corresponding terms in the ontology.

There have been quite a few methods that belong to this category. For example, Rada et al. converted the shortest path length between two terms into their semantic similarity [27]. Wu and Palmer calculated the distance from the root to the lowest common ancestor (LCA) node of two terms as their semantic similarity [29]. Leacock and Chodorow calculated the number of nodes in the shortest path between two terms and then used the number with the maximum depth of an ontology to quantify the relatedness of the terms [40]. Al-Mubaid and Nguyen quantified the commonality of two terms as their similarity [41]. Wang et al. proposed to aggregate contributions of common ancestor terms to semantic values of two terms in the calculation of their semantic similarity [19]. Zhang et al. improved the method of Wang et al. and proposed the combined use of the shortest path length and the depth of the LCA node [42]. The strategies that these methods employed included lengths of shortest paths, depths of nodes, commonalities between terms, semantic contributions of ancestor terms, and many others. Although the use of these strategies has enabled the successful application of these methods to a variety of problems, the existence of a drawback in these methods is also obvious. It is common that a term in an ontology has more than one parent node in the corresponding DAG, and thus two terms may have two or more LCA nodes. However, none of the above methods take such a situation of multiple LCA nodes into consideration in their calculation of semantic similarity.

Wang et al. evaluated measures proposed by Jiang and Conrath, Lin, and Resnik and tested these measures against gene coexpression data using linear correlation [19]. They pointed out that the distance from a term to the closest common ancestor might fail in accurately representing the semantic difference between two GO terms, since two terms near to the root of the ontology and sharing the same parent should have larger semantic difference than those far away from the root and having the same parent. In addition, considering that a GO term may have multiple parent terms with different semantic relationships, they also suggested that measuring the semantic similarity between two GO terms based only on the number of common ancestor terms might fail in recognizing semantic contributions of the ancestor terms to the two specific terms. In addition, from human perspectives, an ancestor term far away from a descendant term in the GO graph should contribute less to the semantics of the descendant term, while an ancestor term closer to a descendant term in the GO graph should contribute more.

According to the above understanding, Wang et al. presented GO as directed acyclic graphs (DAGs) in which terms form nodes and two kinds of semantic relations is-a and part-of form edges. They further defined the contribution of a GO term t to the semantics of GO term A as the S-value

of GO term t related to term A. Formally, a GO term A was defined as a graph $\text{DAG}_A = (A, T_A, E_A)$, where T_A was the set of GO terms in DAG_A, including A and all of its ancestors in the GO graph, and E_A was the set of edges connecting GO terms in DAG_A. For any term t in $\text{DAG}_A = (A, T_A, E_A)$, the S-value related to term A, $S_A(t)$ was then defined as

$$S_A(A) = 1,$$

$$S_A(t) = \max\left\{w_e \times S_A(t') \,|\, t' \in \text{children of }(t)\right\} \quad (t \neq A),$$
(8)

where w_e was the semantic contribution factor for edge $e \in E_A$ that links term t and its child term t'. Given $\text{DAG}_A = (A, T_A, E_A)$ and $\text{DAG}_B = (A, T_B, E_B)$, for terms A and B, respectively, the semantic similarity between these two terms, $S_{\text{GO}}(A, B)$, was defined as

$$S_{\text{GO}}(A, B) = \frac{\sum_{t \in T_A \cap T_B}(S_A(t) + S_B(t))}{\text{SV}(A) + \text{SV}(B)},$$
(9)

where $S_A(t)$ and $S_B(t)$ are S-values of term t related to terms A and B, respectively, and $\text{SV}(A)$ and $\text{SV}(B)$, defined as $\text{SV}(A) = \sum_{t \in T_A} S_A(t)$ and $\text{SV}(B) = \sum_{t \in T_B} S_B(t)$, were semantic values of terms A and B, respectively. Wang et al. further compared their measure against Resnik's method by clustering gene pairs according to their semantic similarity and showed that their measure produced more reasonable results. However, in Wang's method, the weights of the is-a and the part-of relations were empirically determined as 0.8 and 0.6, respectively, without theoretical analysis. Moreover, this method did not take into account the factor of the amount of nodes. In a subsequent study, Zhang et al. [42] pointed out that Wang's method overlooked the depth of the GO terms and proposed a measure to overcome this limitation.

Schickel-Zuber and Faltings [43] defined a similarity measure for hierarchical ontologies called Ontology-Structure-based Similarity (OSS). They pointed out that a quantitative measure of similarity should represent the ratio of numerical scores that may be assigned to each term, and thus the score of a term should be defined as a real-valued function normalized to the range of [0, 1] and should satisfy three assumptions. First, similarity scores depended on features of the terms. Second, each feature contributed independently to a score. Third, unknown and disliked features made no contribution to a score. In detail, the OSS measure first inferred the score of the term b from a, $S(b \mid a)$, by assigning terms in the ontology an a-priori score (APS) and computing relationships between scores assigned to different terms. Then, this method computed how much had been transferred between the two terms, $T(a, b)$. Finally, this method transformed the score into a distance value $D(a, b)$. Mathematically, the a-priori score of a term c with n descendants was calculated as

$$\text{APS}(c) = \frac{1}{n + 2},$$
(10)

implying that leaves of an ontology have an APS equal to 1/2, the mean of a uniform distribution in [0, 1]. Conversely, the lowest value was found at the root. It also implied that the difference in score between terms decreased when one traveled up towards the root of the ontology, due to the increasing number of descendants. Given two terms x and z in an ontology and their lowest common ancestor y, the distance value was calculated as

$$D(x, z) = \frac{\log(1 + 2\beta(z, y)) - \log(\alpha(x, y))}{\max D}, \quad (11)$$

where $\alpha(x, y)$ was a coefficient calculated as $\alpha(x, y) = \text{APS}(y)/\text{APS}(x)$, $\beta(z, y)$ a coefficient estimated by $\beta(z, y) = \text{APS}(z) - \text{APS}(y)$, and $\max D$ the longest distance between any two terms in the ontology.

Al-Mubaid and Nguyen [41] proposed a measure with common specificity and local granularity features that were combined nonlinearly in the semantic similarity measure. Compared with other measures, this method produces the highest overall correlation with human judgments in two ontologies. In mathematics, the semantic similarity between two terms was calculated as:

$$\text{Sem}(C_1, C_2)$$
$$= \log\left((\text{Path} - 1)^\alpha \times (D - \text{depth}((\text{LCS}(C_1, C_2))))^\beta + k\right), \quad (12)$$

where $\alpha > 0$ and $\beta > 0$ were contribution factors of two features, Path the length of the shortest path between the two terms, D the maximum depth, LCS the closest common ancestor of the two terms, and k a constant. Compared with other measures, this measure produced the highest overall correlation results with human judgments in two ontologies.

3.6. Hybrid Methods. Hybrid methods usually consider several features such as attribute similarity, ontology hierarchy, information content, and the depth of the LCA node simultaneously. One of the representative methods was OSS in which a priori score was used to calculate the distance between two terms, and then the distance was transformed into semantic similarity [43]. Another example was the method proposed by Yin and Sheng [44], which combined term similarity and description similarity.

4. Derivation of Semantic Similarity of Entities Annotated with an Ontology

With the semantic similarity scores between terms in an ontology calculated using either of the above methods, the derivation of semantic similarity of entities annotated with the ontology was typically conducted using either the average rule [15] or the mean-max rule [19].

Given two sets of terms T and S, the average rule calculated the semantic similarity between the two sets as the average of semantic similarity of the terms cross the sets as

$$\text{Sim}(T, S) = \frac{1}{|T| \times |S|} \sum_{t \in T} \sum_{s \in S} \text{Sim}(s, t). \quad (13)$$

Since an entity can be treated as a set of terms, the semantic similarity between two entities annotated with the ontology was defined as the semantic similarity between the two sets of annotations corresponding to the entities.

The mean-max rule defined the semantic similarity between a term t and a set of terms T in the ontology as the maximum similarity between the term and every term in the set as

$$\text{Sim}(t, T) = \max_{t' \in T} \text{Sim}(t, t'). \quad (14)$$

Then, the semantic similarity between two sets of terms T and S was calculated as

$$\text{Sim}(S, T) = \frac{1}{|S| + |T|} \left(\sum_{s \in S} \text{Sim}(s, T) + \sum_{t \in T} \text{Sim}(t, S) \right). \quad (15)$$

Finally, the semantic similarity between two entities annotated with the ontology was calculated as the semantic similarity between the two sets of annotations corresponding to the entities.

5. Software for Deriving Semantic Similarity Profiles

With the above methods for calculating semantic similarity of terms in an ontology and that of entities annotated with an ontology available, a natural demand in research is the development of user-friendly software tools that implement these methods. So far, there have been quite a few such software tools available, with examples including GOSemSim [45], seGOsa [46], DOSim [47], and many others.

Yu et al. developed GOSemSim [45] for calculating semantic similarity between GO terms, sets of GO terms, gene products, and sets of gene products. This tool was developed as a package for the statistical computing environment R and released under the GNU General Public License (GPL) within the Bioconductor project [48]. Consequently, GOSemSim was easy to install and simple to use. However, GOSemSim heavily depended on a number of packages provided by Bioconductor. For example, package GO.db was used by GOSemSim to obtain GO terms and relationships; packages org.Hs.eg.db, org.Rn.eg.db, org.Mm.eg.db, org.Dm.eg.db, and org.Sc.sgd.db were required in order to obtain annotations of gene products for human, rat, mouse, fly, and yeast, respectively. Although such a design scheme greatly alleviated the requirement of understanding specific formats of these annotations, the frequent access of annotation databases was typically the bottleneck of large-scale calculation of semantic similarity profiles for thousands of gene products.

Zheng et al. proposed seGOsa [46], a user-friendly cross-platform system to support large-scale assessment of gene ontology- (GO-) driven similarity among gene products. Using information-theoretic approaches, the system exploited both topological features of the GO and statistical features of the model organism databases annotated to the GO to assess semantic similarity among gene products. Meanwhile, seGOsa offered two approaches to assessing the similarity between gene products based on the aggregation of between-term similarities. This package has been successfully applied to assess gene expression correlation patterns and to support the integration of GO-driven similarity knowledge into data clustering algorithms. This package has also assessed relationships between GO-driven similarity and other functional properties, such as gene coregulation and protein-protein interactions in *Saccharomyces cerevisiae* and *Caenorhabditis elegans*. A database consisting of semantic similarity between gene products in both *Saccharomyces cerevisiae* and *Homo sapiens* has been successfully established using seGOsa and applied to the prediction of protein interaction networks.

Li et al. developed an R-based software package (DOSim) to compute the similarity between diseases and to measure the similarity between human genes in terms of diseases [47]. DOSim incorporated an enrichment analysis function based on the disease ontology (DO) and used this function to explore the disease feature of an independent gene set. A multilayered enrichment analysis using GO and KEGG [49] annotations that helped users to explore the biological meaning implied in a newly detected gene module was also included in the DOSim package. This package has been applied to calculate relationships between 128 cancer terms, and hierarchical clustering results of these cancers have shown modular characteristics. This package has also been used to analyse relationships of 361 obesity-associated genes, and results have shown the complex pathogenesis of obesity.

6. Applications of Semantic Similarity Profiles

Biological entities can be described using an ontology as a common schema as well as compared by means of semantic similarity to assess the degree of relatedness via the similarity in meaning of their annotations. In recent years, there has been a growing trend towards the adoption of ontologies to support comprehensive, large-scale functional genomics research. For example, it has been shown that incorporating knowledge represented in the gene ontology may facilitate large-scale predictive applications in functional genomics [7, 32, 50] and disease studies [12]. It has also been shown that phenotype ontologies benefit the understanding of relationship between human phenotypes [9, 11].

6.1. Inference of Disease Genes Based on Gene Semantic Similarity Networks. Uncovering relationships between phenotypes and genotypes is a fundamental problem in genetics. In the context of human-inherited diseases, pinpointing causative genes that are responsible for a specific type of disease will greatly benefit the prevention, diagnosis, and treatment of the disease [51]. Traditional statistical methods in this field, including family-based linkage analysis and population-based association studies, can typically locate the genetic risk to a chromosomal region that is 10–30 Mb long, containing dozens of candidate genes [52]. The inference of causative genes from these candidates hence receives more and more attention.

The inference of causative genes is typically modeled as a one-class novelty detection problem [51]. With annotations of a set of seed genes that are known to be responsible for a query disease of interest, candidate genes can be scored according to their functional similarity to the seeds and further prioritized according to their scores. To facilitate the discovery of causative genes for diseases that have no seed genes available, phenotypic similarity between diseases is incorporated. For example, [53] proposed to measure functional similarity between two genes using their proximity in a protein-protein interaction network and further designed a regression model to explain phenotypic similarity between two diseases using functional similarity between genes that were associated with the diseases. However, a protein-protein interaction network can typically cover less than half of known human genes, and thus greatly restricts the scope of application of their method.

To overcome this limitation, Jiang et al. calculated pairwise semantic similarity scores for more than 15,000 human genes based on the biological process domain of the gene ontology [12]. They demonstrated the positive correlation between semantic similarity scores and network proximity scores for pairs of proteins. Moreover, through a comprehensive analysis, they concluded that pairwise semantic similarity scores for genes responsible for the same disease were significantly higher than random selected genes. With these observations, they constructed a semantic similarity network for human genes according to a nearest neighbor rule, and they proposed a random walk model to infer causative genes for a query disease by integrating the phenotype similarity network of diseases and the semantic similarity network of human genes. They compared their methods with a number of the state-of-the-art methods and demonstrated the superior performance of their approach.

6.2. Inference of Drug Indications Based on Disease Semantic Similarity Profiles. The inference of potential drug indications is a key step in drug development [11]. This problem can be defined as follows: given a query disease, a set of small chemical compounds (potential drugs) and known associations between drugs and diseases rank small molecules such that drugs more likely to be associated with the query disease appear higher in the final ranking list. Bearing an analogy to the above problem of inferring causative genes for diseases, the inference of drug indications can greatly benefit from phenotypic similarity profiles of diseases.

A typical method for the derivation of phenotypic similarity profiles of diseases is text mining. For example, van Driel et al. [54] used the anatomy (A) and the disease (C) sections of the medical subject headings vocabulary (MeSH) to extract terms from the OMIM database and further represented the OMIM record (disease) as a vector of the corresponding phenotype features. Then, they defined the similarity score between two disease phenotypes as the cosine of angle between the two corresponding feature vectors. It has been shown that such similarities are positively correlated with a number of measures of functions of genes that are known to be associated with the diseases, suggesting the effectiveness of this approach.

Recently, the availability of the human phenotype ontology (HPO) [9] provides another means of deriving the phenotypic similarity profile of diseases. Given the ontology and annotations of diseases, Gottlieb et al. [11] proposed to first calculate semantic similarity between terms in the ontology using the method of Resnik [18]. Then, treating a disease as a set of terms in the ontology, they calculated pairwise similarity between OMIM diseases. Further analysis has shown the consistent clustering of diseases according to the semantic similarity profile derived this way (Hamosh et al., 2002). With the semantic similarity profile of diseases ready, Gottlieb et al. [11] further proposed a logistic regression model to predict drug indications for diseases and showed the effectiveness of this profile.

7. Conclusions and Discussion

The explosive increasing of a wide variety of omics data raises the demand of standard annotations of these data using common controlled vocabularies across different experimental platforms and different laboratories. Biological and biomedical ontologies [5], as abstract description systems for knowledge composition in the domain of life sciences, provide structured and controlled representations of terms in this field and, thus, reasonably meet this end. Targeting on the problem of quantifying the relationships between terms in an ontology, and relationships of entities annotated with an ontology, we have summarized a number of existing methods that calculate either semantic similarity between terms using structures of an ontology, annotations of entities, or both. We have further extended the review to the calculation of semantic similarity between entities annotated with an ontology and summarized typical applications that made use of biological and biomedical ontologies.

Although there have been quite a few methods for calculating semantic similarity between terms in biological and biomedical ontologies, the correctness of these methods largely depends on two factors: the quality of the annotation data and the correct interpretation of the hierarchical structure of an ontology. Particularly, for methods that depend on information contents of terms, noise existing in annotation data can adversely affect the correct estimation of the information contents and further bring noise into the resulting semantic similarity. For example, in gene ontology, a large proportion of annotations is inferred electronically by sequence similarity of gene products or other annotation databases. Whether such inferred annotations should be used in the calculation of information contents or not is still an open question. Furthermore, some gene products have been studied in more detail, while knowledge about some gene products is very limited. As a result, available annotations are biased towards heavily studied gene products, and quality of annotations is also biased. Such biased in annotations will also adversely affect the correctness of the derived information contents.

On the other hand, many biological and biomedical ontologies have multiple types of relationships between terms (e.g., is_a, part_of, etc.), and thus methods rely on structure of an ontology need to properly weigh different types of relationships between terms. How to determine such weight values, however, is an open question. For example, although Wang et al. [19] have suggested the weights of 0.6 and 0.8 for is_a and part_of relationships in gene ontology, respectively, whether these values are suitable for other ontologies is not systematically evaluated. Furthermore, for ontologies that have even more types of relationships, the determination of the weight values becomes a more serious problem.

As for applications that make use of ontologies, the problem needs to be cared about is the circularity. For example, information contents are calculated by using annotations, and thus using similarity in annotations to evaluate the goodness of semantic similarity derived from information contents is not appropriate. A direct consequence of overlooking such circularity will be the overestimation of the performance of an application—good in validation but poor in real situation.

Acknowledgments

This work was partly supported by the National Natural Science Foundation of China under Grants nos. 71101010 and 61175002, the Fundamental Research Funds for the Central Universities under Grant nos. FRF-BR-11-019A, and the Open Research Fund of State Key Laboratory of Bioelectronics, Southeast University.

References

[1] A. Schulze and J. Downward, "Navigating gene expression using microarrays—a technology review," *Nature Cell Biology*, vol. 3, no. 8, pp. E190–E195, 2001.

[2] T. Ito, T. Chiba, R. Ozawa, M. Yoshida, M. Hattori, and Y. Sakaki, "A comprehensive two-hybrid analysis to explore the yeast protein interactome," *Proceedings of the National Academy of Sciences of the United States of America*, vol. 98, no. 8, pp. 4569–4574, 2001.

[3] P. Uetz, L. Giot, G. Cagney et al., "A comprehensive analysis of protein′protein interactions in Saccharomyces cerevisiae," *Nature*, vol. 403, pp. 623–627, 2000.

[4] R. Aebersold and M. Mann, "Mass spectrometry-based proteomics," *Nature*, vol. 422, no. 6928, pp. 198–207, 2003.

[5] B. Smith, M. Ashburner, C. Rosse et al., "The OBO Foundry: coordinated evolution of ontologies to support biomedical data integration," *Nature Biotechnology*, vol. 25, no. 11, pp. 1251–1255, 2007.

[6] T. R. Gruber, "A translation approach to portable ontology specifications," *Knowledge Acquisition*, vol. 5, no. 2, pp. 199–220, 1993.

[7] M. A. Rodríguez and M. J. Egenhofer, "Determining semantic similarity among entity classes from different ontologies," *IEEE Transactions on Knowledge and Data Engineering*, vol. 15, no. 2, pp. 442–456, 2003.

[8] The Gene Ontology Consortium, "The Gene Ontology project in 2008," *Nucleic Acids Research*, vol. 36, pp. D440–D444, 2008.

[9] P. N. Robinson, S. Köhler, S. Bauer, D. Seelow, D. Horn, and S. Mundlos, "The human phenotype ontology: a tool for

annotating and analyzing human hereditary disease," *American Journal of Human Genetics*, vol. 83, no. 5, pp. 610–615, 2008.

[10] P. Jaiswal, S. Avraham, K. Ilic et al., "Plant Ontology (PO): a controlled vocabulary of plant structures and growth stages," *Comparative and Functional Genomics*, vol. 6, no. 7-8, pp. 388–397, 2005.

[11] A. Gottlieb, G. Y. Stein, E. Ruppin, and R. Sharan, "PREDICT: a method for inferring novel drug indications with application to personalized medicine," *Molecular Systems Biology*, vol. 7, article 496, 2011.

[12] R. Jiang, M. Gan, and P. He, "Constructing a gene semantic similarity network for the inference of disease genes," *BMC Systems Biology*, vol. 5, supplement 2, article S2, 2011.

[13] C. Pesquita, D. Faria, A. O. Falcão, P. Lord, and F. M. Couto, "Semantic similarity in biomedical ontologies," *PLoS Computational Biology*, vol. 5, no. 7, Article ID e1000443, 2009.

[14] J. J. Jiang and D. W. Conrath, "Semantic similarity based on corpus statistics and lexical taxonomy," in *Proceedings of the IInternational Conference on Research in Computational Linguistics*, pp. 19–33, 1997.

[15] D. Lin, "An information-theoretic definition of similarity," in *Proceedings of the 15th International Conference on Machine Learning*, pp. 296–304, Morgan Kaufmann, 1998.

[16] A. Maedche and S. Staab, "Measuring similarity between ontologies," in *Knowledge Engineering and Knowledge Management: Ontologies and the Semantic Web*, pp. 15–21, 2002.

[17] T. Pedersen, S. V. S. Pakhomov, S. Patwardhan, and C. G. Chute, "Measures of semantic similarity and relatedness in the biomedical domain," *Journal of Biomedical Informatics*, vol. 40, no. 3, pp. 288–299, 2007.

[18] P. Resnik, "Semantic similarity in a taxonomy: an information-based measure and its application to problems of ambiguity in natural language," *Journal of Artificial Intelligence Research*, vol. 11, pp. 95–130, 1999.

[19] J. Z. Wang, Z. Du, R. Payattakool, P. S. Yu, and C. F. Chen, "A new method to measure the semantic similarity of GO terms," *Bioinformatics*, vol. 23, no. 10, pp. 1274–1281, 2007.

[20] M. Ashburner, C. A. Ball, J. A. Blake et al., "Gene ontology: tool for the unification of biology," *Nature Genetics*, vol. 25, no. 1, pp. 25–29, 2000.

[21] K. Degtyarenko, P. de matos, M. Ennis et al., "ChEBI: a database and ontology for chemical entities of biological interest," *Nucleic Acids Research*, vol. 36, no. 1, pp. D344–D350, 2008.

[22] G. A. Thorisson, J. Muilu, and A. J. Brookes, "Genotype-phenotype databases: challenges and solutions for the post-genomic era," *Nature Reviews Genetics*, vol. 10, no. 1, pp. 9–18, 2009.

[23] A. S. Sidhu, T. S. Dillon, E. Chang, and B. S. Sidhu, "Protein ontology: vocabulary for protein data," in *Proceedings of the 3rd International Conference on Information Technology and Applications (ICITA '05)*, pp. 465–469, IEEE, July 2005.

[24] E. Segerdell, J. B. Bowes, N. Pollet, and P. D. Vize, "An ontology for Xenopus anatomy and development," *BMC Developmental Biology*, vol. 8, article 92, 2008.

[25] R. J. Bryson-Richardson, S. Berger, T. F. Schilling et al., "FishNet: an online database of zebrafish anatomy," *BMC Biology*, vol. 5, article 34, 2007.

[26] V. A. McKusick, "Mendelian inheritance in man and its online version, OMIM," *American Journal of Human Genetics*, vol. 80, no. 4, pp. 588–604, 2007.

[27] R. Rada, H. Mili, E. Bicknell, and M. Blettner, "Development and application of a metric on semantic nets," *IEEE Transactions on Systems, Man and Cybernetics*, vol. 19, pp. 17–30, 1989.

[28] M. Sussna, "Word sense disambiguation for free-text indexing using a massive semantic network," in *Proceedings of the 2nd International Conference on Information and Knowledge Management*, pp. 67–74, ACM, Washington, DC, USA, November 1993.

[29] Z. Wu and M. Palmer, "Verbs semantics and lexical selection," in *Proceedings of the 32nd Annual Meeting on Association for Computational Linguistics*, pp. 133–138, Association for Computational Linguistics, Las Cruces, NM, USA, 1994.

[30] N. Seco, T. Veale, and J. Hayes, "An intrinsic information content metric for semantic similarity in WordNet," *ECAI*. Citeseer, p. 1089, 2004.

[31] A. Schlicker, F. S. Domingues, J. Rahnenführer, and T. Lengauer, "A new measure for functional similarity of gene products based on gene ontology," *BMC Bioinformatics*, vol. 7, article 302, 2006.

[32] H. Wang, F. Azuaje, O. Bodenreider, and J. Dopazo, "Gene expression correlation and gene ontology-based similarity: an assessment of quantitative relationships," in *Proceedings of the IEEE Symposium on Computational Intelligence in Bioinformatics and Computational Biology (CIBCB '04)*, pp. 25–31, IEEE, October 2004.

[33] W. N. Lee, N. Shah, K. Sundlass, and M. Musen, "Comparison of ontology-based semantic-similarity measures," in *Proceedings of the American Medical Informatics Association Annual Symposium Proceedings*, pp. 384–388, American Medical Informatics Association, 2008.

[34] F. M. Couto, M. J. Silva, and P. M. Coutinho, "Semantic similarity over the gene ontology: family correlation and selecting disjunctive ancestors," in *Proceedings of the 14th ACM International Conference on Information and Knowledge Management*, pp. 343–344, ACM, November 2005.

[35] O. Bodenreider, M. Aubry, and A. Burgun, "Non-lexical approaches to identifying associative relations in the gene ontology," in *Proceedings of the Pacific Symposium on Biocomputing*, pp. 91–102, NIH, 2005.

[36] R. M. Riensche, B. L. Baddeley, A. P. Sanfilippo, C. Posse, and B. Gopalan, "XOA: web-enabled cross-ontological analytics," in *Proceedings of the IEEE Congress on Services*, pp. 99–105, July 2007.

[37] A. Tversky, "Features of similarity," *Psychological Review*, vol. 84, no. 4, pp. 327–352, 1977.

[38] M. A. Rodríguez, M. Egenhofer, and R. Rugg, "Assessing semantic similarities among geospatial feature class definitions," in *Interoperating Geographic Information Systems*, pp. 189–202, 1999.

[39] M. A. Rodríguez and M. J. Egenhofer, "Comparing geospatial entity classes: an asymmetric and context-dependent similarity measure," *International Journal of Geographical Information Science*, vol. 18, no. 3, pp. 229–256, 2004.

[40] C. Leacock and M. Chodorow, "Combining local context and WordNet similarity for word sense and WordNet similarity for word sense identification," in *WordNet: An Electronic Lexical Database*, C. Fellbaum, Ed., The MIT Press, Cambridge, Mass, USA, 1998.

[41] H. Al-Mubaid and H. A. Nguyen, "A cluster-based approach for semantic similarity in the biomedical domain," in *Proceedings of the 28th Annual International Conference of the IEEE Engineering in Medicine and Biology Society (EMBS '06)*, pp. 2713–2717, IEEE, September 2006.

[42] S. Zhang, X. Shang, M. Wang, and J. Diao, "A new measure based on gene ontology for semantic similarity of genes," in *Proceedings of the WASE International Conference on Information Engineering (ICIE '10)*, pp. 85–88, IEEE, August 2010.

[43] V. Schickel-Zuber and B. Faltings, "OSS: a semantic similarity function based on hierarchical ontologies," in *Proceedings of the 20th International Joint Conference on Artifical Intelligence*, pp. 551–556, Morgan Kaufmann, 2007.

[44] Y. Guisheng and S. Qiuyan, "Research on ontology-based measuring semantic similarity," in *Proceedings of the International Conference on Internet Computing in Science and Engineering (ICICSE '08)*, pp. 250–253, IEEE, January 2008.

[45] G. Yu, F. Li, Y. Qin, X. Bo, Y. Wu, and S. Wang, "GOSemSim: an R package for measuring semantic similarity among GO terms and gene products," *Bioinformatics*, vol. 26, no. 7, pp. 976–978, 2010.

[46] H. Zheng, F. Azuaje, and H. Wang, "seGOsa: software environment for Gene Ontology-driven similarity assessment," in *Proceedings of the IEEE International Conference on Bioinformatics and Biomedicine (BIBM '10)*, pp. 539–542, December 2010.

[47] J. Li, B. Gong, X. Chen et al., "DOSim: an R package for similarity between diseases based on disease ontology," *BMC Bioinformatics*, vol. 12, article 266, 2011.

[48] R. C. Gentleman, V. J. Carey, D. M. Bates et al., "Bioconductor: open software development for computational biology and bioinformatics," *Genome Biology*, vol. 5, no. 10, p. R80, 2004.

[49] H. Ogata, S. Goto, K. Sato, W. Fujibuchi, H. Bono, and M. Kanehisa, "KEGG: kyoto encyclopedia of genes and genomes," *Nucleic Acids Research*, vol. 27, no. 1, pp. 29–34, 1999.

[50] J. L. Sevilla, V. Segura, A. Podhorski et al., "Correlation between gene expression and GO semantic similarity," *IEEE/ACM Transactions on Computational Biology and Bioinformatics*, vol. 2, no. 4, pp. 330–338, 2005.

[51] Y. Moreau and L. C. Tranchevent, "Computational tools for prioritizing candidate genes: boosting disease gene discovery," *Nature Reviews Genetics*, vol. 13, no. 8, pp. 523–536, 2012.

[52] A. M. Glazier, J. H. Nadeau, and T. J. Aitman, "Genetics: finding genes that underline complex traits," *Science*, vol. 298, no. 5602, pp. 2345–2349, 2002.

[53] X. Wu, R. Jiang, M. Q. Zhang, and S. Li, "Network-based global inference of human disease genes," *Molecular Systems Biology*, vol. 4, article 189, 2008.

[54] M. A. van Driel, J. Bruggeman, G. Vriend, H. G. Brunner, and J. A. M. Leunissen, "A text-mining analysis of the human phenome," *European Journal of Human Genetics*, vol. 14, no. 5, pp. 535–542, 2006.

19

Hyperpolarization-Activated Current, I_f, in Mathematical Models of Rabbit Sinoatrial Node Pacemaker Cells

Arie O. Verkerk and Ronald Wilders

Department of Anatomy, Embryology and Physiology, Academic Medical Center, University of Amsterdam, P.O. Box 22700, 1100 DE Amsterdam, The Netherlands

Correspondence should be addressed to Ronald Wilders; r.wilders@amc.uva.nl

Academic Editor: Mohamed Boutjdir

A typical feature of sinoatrial (SA) node pacemaker cells is the presence of an ionic current that activates upon hyperpolarization. The role of this hyperpolarization-activated current, I_f, which is also known as the "funny current" or "pacemaker current," in the spontaneous pacemaker activity of SA nodal cells remains a matter of intense debate. Whereas some conclude that I_f plays a fundamental role in the generation of pacemaker activity and its rate control, others conclude that the role of I_f is limited to a modest contribution to rate control. The ongoing debate is often accompanied with arguments from computer simulations, either to support one's personal view or to invalidate that of the antagonist. In the present paper, we review the various mathematical descriptions of I_f that have been used in computer simulations and compare their strikingly different characteristics with our experimental data. We identify caveats and propose a novel model for I_f based on our experimental data.

1. A Funny Current

The sinoatrial node (SA node) is the normal pacemaker of the mammalian heart and generates the electrical impulse for the regular, rhythmic contraction of the heart. The intrinsic pacemaker activity, or spontaneous electrical activity, of an SA nodal pacemaker cell is based on the spontaneous diastolic depolarization that depolarizes the cell towards the action potential threshold. During this diastolic depolarization phase, there is a tiny net inward current across the cell membrane of no more than a few picoamps in amplitude. Animal studies, almost exclusively carried out on cells isolated from rabbit heart, have learned that this net inward current is the result of a complex interaction of multiple inward and outward ion currents, including a hyperpolarization-activated current of mixed ionic nature, known as "funny current," I_f, as reviewed elsewhere [1–9]. In line with its activation at hyperpolarized membrane potentials [10], thus generating an inward current during diastole, its enhancement by direct binding of cyclic AMP (cAMP) [11], and its principal presence in primary [12] and secondary pacemakers [13, 14], I_f is traditionally also named "pacemaker current." Of note, the pore-forming subunits of

the I_f channel are encoded by members of the HCN gene family, with members HCN1-4 (see [8] and primary references cited therein). HCN channels are not only expressed in the heart but also in the brain. In neuroscience, the HCN current is usually designated I_h.

In recent years, I_f has regained interest in several fields. First, I_f has become a target for pharmacological reduction of heart rate, which may be beneficial for heart failure patients. This reduction is achieved through the specific I_f blocker ivabradine, which has become available for clinical use, and represents a new approach in selective heart rate reduction [15]. Second, mutations in the HCN4 gene, encoding the major HCN isoform of the human SA node [16], have been associated with hereditary SA nodal dysfunction in several families [17–23]. Third, HCN channels are used in engineering a biological pacemaker, as summarized in numerous review papers, for example, [24–29]. In all of these fields, an appropriate quantitative model of the electrical activity of I_f is a desirable tool.

It should be noted that I_f depends on intracellular calcium levels, and conversely, through the mutual interactions between I_f amplitude, spontaneous firing frequency and intracellular Ca^{2+} cycling [30, 31]. Thus, a blockade of I_f by Cs^+ [30] or ivabradine [31] does not only affect firing frequency, but also intracellular Ca^{2+} cycling. In the interactions between the "membrane clock" (composed of voltage-dependent sarcolemmal currents and also designated "M clock," "voltage clock," or "ion channel clock") and the "calcium clock" or "Ca^{2+} clock" (composed of tightly coupled sarcoplasmic reticulum Ca^{2+} cycling molecules together with the electrogenic sodium-calcium exchanger), cAMP plays an important role [9]. It is, therefore, important to make measurements on I_f with the amphotericin-perforated patch configuration of the patch-clamp technique to avoid the dialyzing effects of the common whole-cell configuration. Instead of rupturing the membrane as in the whole-cell patch clamp configuration, amphotericin B is used to gain electrical access to the cell [32]. This substance makes minute holes in the membrane that allow the passage of small monovalent ions, thus leaving the cytosolic composition intact. In particular, the intracellular Ca^{2+} and cAMP levels are preserved.

Differences in recording conditions like the aforementioned patch clamp configurations may readily explain part of the variability in experimental data on I_f between laboratories. A further source of variability is observed in measurements on HCN channels in heterologous expression systems like HEK-293 cells [8]. Here, part of the variability can be attributed to differences in the expression level of members of the MinK family of single transmembrane spanning proteins, which are encoded by the *KCNE* gene family and can act as β-subunits for the HCN family of pore-forming α-subunits [33–35]. In particular, the MinK-related peptide 1 (MiRP1, encoded by *KCNE2*), with high mRNA levels in the rabbit SA node [33], may associate with HCN1, HCN2, and HCN4 and modulate the HCN channel expression and kinetics.

Originally, I_f was termed "funny current" because of its atypical characteristics, including its slow activation upon hyperpolarization rather than depolarization [10], its direct activation by cAMP [11], and its highly selective permeability to both Na^+ and K^+ ions [36] with a $P_{Na} : P_K$ permeability ratio of approximately $1 : 4$ under physiological conditions [37]. As a result of its mixed ionic nature, I_f exhibits a reversal potential of ≈ -30 mV if corrected for the liquid junction potential [38–40]. Thus, I_f is an inward current carried by sodium ions at diastolic membrane potentials. However, this Na^+ current is critically dependent on the presence of extracellular K^+ ions. It increases with increasing extracellular K^+ concentration, as does the $P_{Na} : P_K$ ratio, which saturates near the physiological extracellular K^+ concentration of ≈ 5 mM [41]. More recently, it was shown that I_f channels are also permeable, albeit to it small extent, to Ca^{2+} ions [42, 43], with the Ca^{2+} flux contributing to $\approx 0.5\%$ of the current produced by I_f [42]. However, the functional relevance of this permeability to Ca^{2+} remains unclear [44].

Another characteristic feature of HCN channels, and thus possibly of I_f, is their ability to undergo a "mode shift" in their voltage gating. This mode shift or "voltage hysteresis" has been studied for HCN1, HCN2, and HCN4 channels that were heterologously expressed in *Xenopus* oocytes or mammalian COS-7 or HEK-293 cells [45–49]. The voltage hysteresis is clearly present in HCN1 channels [45, 46, 48] but less pronounced in HNC2 channels [46, 47]. Whereas both Azene et al. [46] and Elinder et al. [47] concluded that voltage hysteresis is absent or almost absent in HNC4 channels, Xiao et al. [49] reported a clear hysteresis. Given that in most species, including rabbit, HCN4 is by far the most abundant HCN isoform in the SA node [8], it remains to be elucidated whether voltage hysteresis of I_f plays a functional role in cardiac pacemaker activity. However, voltage hysteresis may prove important in fine-tuning the firing frequency of gene- and cell-based biological pacemakers, in particular if these make use of HCN1 or HCN2 [46].

Despite the numerous experimental studies, the contribution of I_f to SA nodal pacemaker activity has been and still is a matter of, often intense, debate, particularly in relation to the calcium clock [50–64]. A complicating factor in this ongoing debate is created by the slow activation kinetics and negative activation profile of I_f relative to the time scale and voltage range of SA nodal diastolic depolarization, which makes only a small number of I_f channels activated during diastolic depolarization. In a total of 12 mathematical models of the pacemaker activity of rabbit SA nodal cells published between 1982 and 2003 quantitatively widely different mechanisms underlie spontaneous diastolic depolarization, as demonstrated by the 0.9–30% increase in cycle length upon block of I_f [65]. It is, therefore, not surprising that computer simulations, albeit with "updated" models, have not only been used to support a limited role for I_f [66] but also to underscore that I_f is "the major inward diastolic ionic current" [67].

2. Experimental Data

Figure 1 shows experimental data on I_f in isolated rabbit SA nodal myocytes obtained at physiological temperature using the amphotericin-perforated patch-clamp technique under voltage clamp conditions. To minimize contamination by K^+ and Ca^{2+} currents, data were recorded in the presence of 1 mM $BaCl_2$, 5 μM E4031, 5 μM chromanol 293b, 0.5 mM 4-aminopyridine, 5 μM nifedipine, and 40 μM $NiCl_2$ in the bath solution. The concentrations of K^+ and Na^+ in the bath solution were 5.4 and 140 mM, respectively, whereas those in the pipette solution were 145 and 10 mM, respectively. Of note, the data of Figure 1 are consistent with the data that we collected in previous studies under similar conditions [40, 68].

As an example of a voltage clamp trace, Figure 1(a) shows the membrane current in response to a voltage clamp step to -130 mV from a holding potential of -40 mV. In this example, the recorded current was not corrected for the capacitive transient that accompanies a voltage clamp step (Figure 1(a), arrows). At the end of the 2-s step to -130 mV, I_f is fully activated. From the "tail current" that is observed upon stepping back from -130 mV to potentials ranging between -110 and 0 mV (-40 mV in case of Figure 1(a)), one can derive the fully activated current-voltage relationship of Figure 1(b), in which the recorded current is normalized to membrane capacitance and thus expressed in pA/pF. From the linear fit

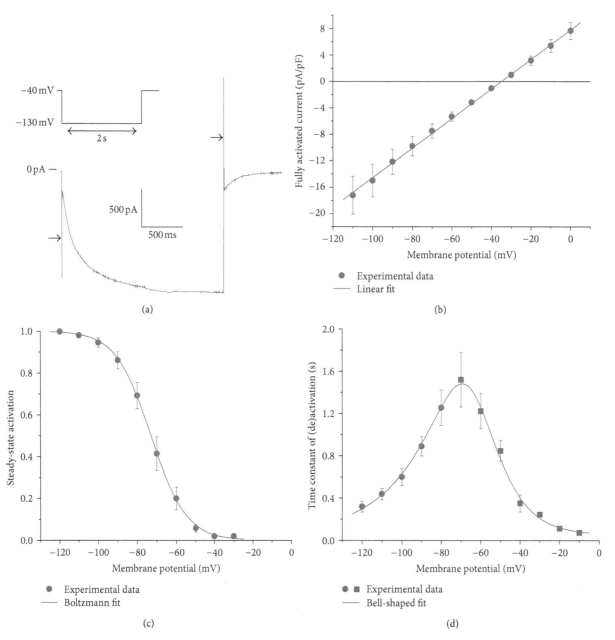

FIGURE 1: Characteristics of the hyperpolarization-activated current (I_f) in single pacemaker cells isolated from the rabbit sinoatrial node. (a) Current trace (blue) in response to a voltage clamp step from a holding potential of −40 mV to a test potential of −130 mV (inset). I_f activates during the 2-s step (step current) and deactivates during the subsequent step to −40 mV (tail current). Horizontal arrows indicate the capacitive transient. (b) Fully activated current, normalized to membrane capacitance, as derived from the tail current amplitude at potentials ranging between −110 and 0 mV. The red line is the linear fit to the experimental data. (c) Normalized steady-state activation derived from the tail current amplitude observed upon test potentials between −120 and −30 mV. The red curve is the Boltzmann fit to the experimental data. (d) Time constant of I_f activation (filled circles) and deactivation (filled squares). The red curve is a bell-shaped fit to the experimental data (see text). All membrane potential values are corrected for the estimated liquid junction potential.

to the data of Figure 1(b), assuming an ohmic current-voltage relationship, one obtains a fully activated I_f conductance of 0.224 nS/pF and an I_f reversal potential of −34.8 mV. Together with the sodium and potassium concentrations in the pipette and the bath, this reversal potential yields a $g_{f,\mathrm{Na}} : g_{f,\mathrm{K}}$ ratio of 0.491 and a $P_{\mathrm{Na}} : P_{\mathrm{K}}$ permeability ratio, according to the Goldman equation, of 1 : 4.3, in line with

aforementioned permeability ratio of 1 : 4 under physiological conditions [37].

If the tail current associated with test potentials between −120 and −30 mV is normalized to the tail current associated with the step to −130 mV, at which I_f is fully activated, one determines the voltage dependence of activation, that is, the steady-state activation of I_f at a series of membrane potentials

(Figure 1(c)). The red curve in Figure 1(c) results from the Boltzmann equation:

$$y_\infty = \frac{1}{\{1 + \exp\left[(V_m - V_{0.5})/k\right]\}}, \tag{1}$$

in which y_∞ is the degree of steady-state activation, V_m is the membrane potential, $V_{0.5}$ is the half-activation voltage, and k is the slope factor. The fitting procedure yielded $V_{0.5}$ and k values of −73.0 and 9.0 mV, respectively.

Ignoring the variable initial delay in I_f (de)activation, the I_f current traces closely resemble a monoexponential process, both during activation and deactivation (cf. Figure 1(a)), which at a given membrane potential can be well fitted using a single time constant τ. The resulting time constant data are shown in Figure 1(d). The red bell-shaped curve in Figure 1(d) represents

$$\tau = 0.05 + [75.8 \times \exp(0.083 \times V_m) \\ + 0.0233 \times \exp(-0.043 \times V_m)]^{-1}, \tag{2}$$

in which τ is the time constant of (de)activation in s and V_m is the membrane potential in mV. It is important to note that the fitted curve levels off at 50 ms for membrane potentials > −10 mV, in accordance with the experimental observation that I_f deactivation is fast but certainly not instantaneous at depolarized potentials [39, 69–71]. It should be noted that widely different values have been reported for the rate of deactivation near 0 mV, approximately ranging from 10–50 s^{-1} [39, 69–71], which translates into a time constant of deactivation of 20–100 ms. Thus, our value of 50 ms is in line with these experimental data but somewhat uncertain.

3. State Diagrams of the I_f Channel

Several kinetic schemes have been proposed to describe the behavior of the I_f channel, varying from a simple two-state scheme as diagrammed in Figure 2(a) to a complex scheme with as many as five open and three closed configurations [72]. In mathematical models of I_f in rabbit SA nodal pacemaker cells—either as a model of I_f per se or as part of a model of the pacemaker activity of SA nodal myocytes—two-, three-, and five-state kinetic schemes have been used in relation to I_f.

3.1. Two-State Model. In the two-state model (Figure 2(a)), the I_f channel flips between its open (conducting) state O and its closed (nonconducting) state C, controlled by a Hodgkin and Huxley [73] type y gate with voltage-dependent rate constants α and β. Accordingly, I_f is given by

$$I_f = y \times g_f \times (V_m - E_f), \tag{3}$$

in which g_f is the fully activated I_f conductance, E_f is the I_f reversal potential, and the gating variable y, with $0 \le y \le 1$, obeys the first-order differential equation:

$$\frac{dy}{dt} = \alpha \times (1 - y) - \beta \times y \tag{4}$$

or, equivalently,

$$\frac{dy}{dt} = \frac{(y_\infty - y)}{\tau}, \tag{5}$$

with

$$y_\infty = \frac{\alpha}{(\alpha + \beta)}, \\ \tau = \frac{1}{(\alpha + \beta)}. \tag{6}$$

In case of a voltage clamp step at time zero, the analytical solution to (4) becomes

$$y(t) = y_\infty - (y_\infty - y_0) \times \exp\left(-\frac{t}{\tau}\right). \tag{7}$$

The gating variable y thus attains a new steady-state value y_∞ in a monoexponential fashion with time constant τ.

The advantage of the two-state model is that it allows a direct translation of experimental data on I_f, which are commonly acquired under voltage clamp conditions and presented in terms of a Boltzmann equation like that of Figure 1(c) and time constants of (de)activation, into a mathematical description through

$$\alpha = \frac{y_\infty}{\tau}, \tag{8}$$

$$\beta = \frac{(1 - y_\infty)}{\tau}. \tag{9}$$

The two-state model has been used by DiFrancesco and Noble [70], Dokos et al. [74], and Zhang et al. [75].

3.2. Three-State Model. Experimentally, an initial delay or sigmoidal onset may be observed in both activation and deactivation of I_f under voltage clamp conditions. Following the approach by Hodgkin and Huxley [73] to describe the sigmoid course of activation of the potassium current in their nerve fibers, van Ginneken and Giles [39] introduced a second y gate in their mathematical description of I_f to account for the observed delay "semiquantitatively." Accordingly, I_f is now given by

$$I_f = y^2 \times g_f \times (V_m - E_f). \tag{10}$$

The experimentally determined Boltzmann curve then corresponds with y_∞^2 rather than y_∞, while determination of the rate constants α and β requires detailed analysis of the voltage clamp traces, as carried out by van Ginneken and Giles [39]. Unfortunately, they erroneously doubled their experimentally observed I_f decay rate to obtain the decay rate of y, whereas they should have halved it, as set out in detail by Dokos et al. [74].

With two independent gates, there are four different states of the channel (Figure 2(b)). However, because the two gates are kinetically identical, the four-state scheme of Figure 2(b) can be simplified to the three-state scheme of

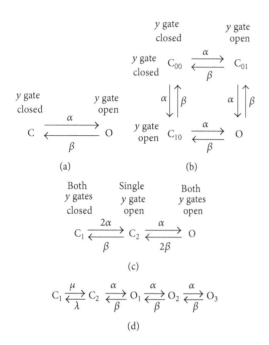

FIGURE 2: State diagrams of the I_f channel used in mathematical models of the hyperpolarization-activated current in rabbit sinoatrial node pacemaker cells. (a) Two-state model with a first-order Hodgkin and Huxley type y gate. The channel flips between its open state O and closed state C at rates α and β. (b) Hodgkin and Huxley type model with two identical y gates. (c) Three-state equivalent of the state diagram of (b). (d) Five-state model, with two closed states (C_1 and C_2) and three open states (O_1, O_2, and O_3), as used in the mathematical model of a rabbit sinoatrial node pacemaker cell by Sarai et al. [78].

Figure 2(c), in which the essentially identical states C_{01} and C_{10} of Figure 2(b) have been combined into a single state C_2. The three-state model of Figure 2(c), with two independent, kinetically identical y gates, has been employed by Demir et al. [76], Kurata et al. [77], Maltsev and Lakatta [66], and Severi et al. [67].

Unlike the two-state model of Figure 2(a), the three-state model accounts for the sigmoidal onset of I_f activation that may be observed in voltage clamp traces. It should, however, be realized that this delay in activation shows a remarkable variability and may even be absent [38, 39]. The three-state model accounts for the initial delay in I_f activation, but not for any delay in deactivation, but such delay in deactivation is not observed in case of moderate and short hyperpolarizations as take place during normal SA nodal pacemaker activity [39].

3.3. Five-State Model. In many mathematical models of I_f in rabbit SA nodal pacemaker cells, a two- or three-state kinetic scheme is used [39, 66, 67, 70, 74–77]. In the mathematical model of an SA nodal pacemaker cell by Sarai et al. [78], however, a five-state scheme is used with two closed states (C_1 and C_2) and three open states (O_1, O_2, and O_3), as diagrammed in Figure 2(d). This five-state scheme was introduced by Maruoka et al. [71] to describe I_f under

voltage clamp conditions and included in the "Kyoto model," which provides a common set of equations for ventricular myocytes and SA nodal pacemaker cells, by Matsuoka et al. [79] to account for the "sigmoidal onset of activation on hyperpolarization, and delayed removal of activation on depolarization beyond the reversal potential".

4. Mathematical Models of I_f

Apart from differences in the kinetic schemes, the aforementioned models of I_f in rabbit SA nodal pacemaker cells differ in the associated rate constants as well as the conductance and reversal potential of I_f, which together determine the course of I_f during an action potential, that is, under current clamp conditions. In this section, we present and discuss, in chronological order, the various models of I_f that we mentioned in the previous sections. Figures 3 and 4 and Table 1 summarize the main characteristics of the various models. At this point, the reader may want to consult Figures 3 and 4 and Table 1 and then move on to Section 5.

In several cases, the fully activated conductance and/or reversal potential of I_f were not explicitly stated in the model description and had to be determined from the relative sodium and potassium conductance of I_f, in combination with the intracellular and extracellular sodium and potassium concentrations of the model cell through

$$g_f \times \left(V_m - E_f\right) = g_{f,\mathrm{K}} \times \left(V_m - E_\mathrm{K}\right) + g_{f,\mathrm{Na}} \times \left(V_m - E_\mathrm{Na}\right), \tag{11}$$

where $g_{f,\mathrm{K}}$ and $g_{f,\mathrm{Na}}$ are the sodium and potassium conductance of I_f, respectively, and E_K and E_Na are the Nernst potentials for sodium and potassium, respectively. Conversely, (11) can be used to estimate the $g_{f,\mathrm{Na}} : g_{f,\mathrm{K}}$ ratio if E_f and the ion concentrations are known.

4.1. Model of DiFrancesco and Noble. The aim of DiFrancesco and Noble [70] was to provide a simple description of I_f "relevant to the reconstruction of the diastolic phase of the spontaneous action potential." They noted that, for reconstruction purposes, it would be sufficient to describe the kinetics of I_f with a simple first-order Hodgkin and Huxley [73] type model and that, in this context, a more complex model was not justified. Thus, they adopted the two-state model of Figure 2(a) and (3)–(6) to describe I_f. From their experimental data on I_f in SA nodal pacemaker cells they derived

$$y_\infty = \frac{1}{\left\{1 + \exp\left[0.10811 \times \left(V_m + 64\right)\right]\right\}}, \tag{12}$$

$$\tau = \frac{1}{\left[\exp\left(-2.00084 - 0.03584 \times V_m\right) + \exp\left(2.4 + 0.08 \times V_m\right)\right]} \tag{13}$$

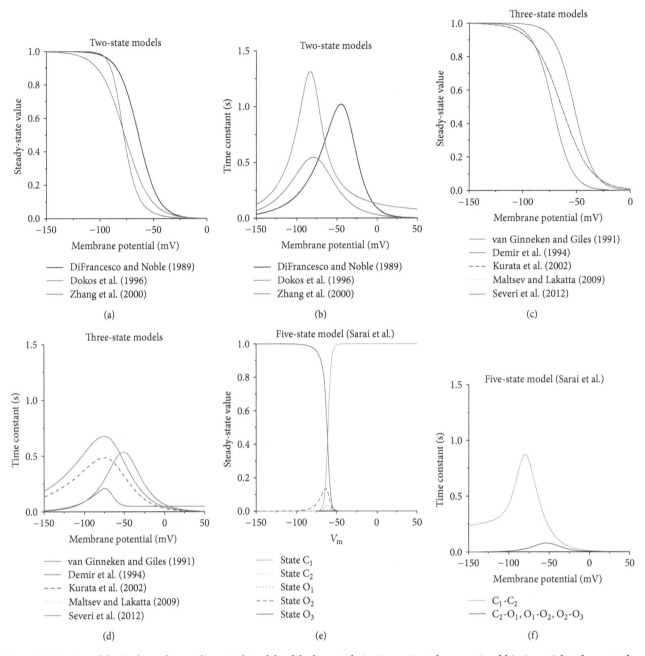

FIGURE 3: Kinetics of the I_f channel in mathematical models of the hyperpolarization-activated current in rabbit sinoatrial node pacemaker cells. ((a), (b)) Steady-state value (a) and time constant (b) of the gating variable y in the single-gate models by DiFrancesco and Noble [70], Dokos et al. [74], and Zhang et al. [75], as indicated. ((c), (d)) Steady-state value (c) and time constant (d) of the gating variable y in the two-gate models by van Ginneken and Giles [39], Demir et al. [76], Kurata et al. [77], Maltsev and Lakatta [66], and Severi et al. [67], as indicated. ((e), (f)) Steady-state values for each of the five states (e) and time constants for each of the four transitions (f) in the five-state model by Sarai et al. [78].

as equations for y_∞ and τ (in s), respectively, from which α and β can be derived through (8) and (9). The black curves in Figures 3(a) and 3(b), are constructed from (12) and (13), respectively. Figure 3(a) shows the steady-state value of y, that is, y_∞, for each of the two-state models discussed in Section 3, whereas Figure 3(b) shows the associated time constant for each of the models.

Figure 4(a) and, on expanded current and membrane potential scales, Figure 4(c) show the steady-state activation curve of I_f for each of the models discussed in Section 3. In addition, the curve that we determined experimentally (Figure 1(c)) is shown as a dark gray dashed curve. In case of the simple two-state model of DiFrancesco and Noble [70], the black curve of Figure 4(a) is identical to that of

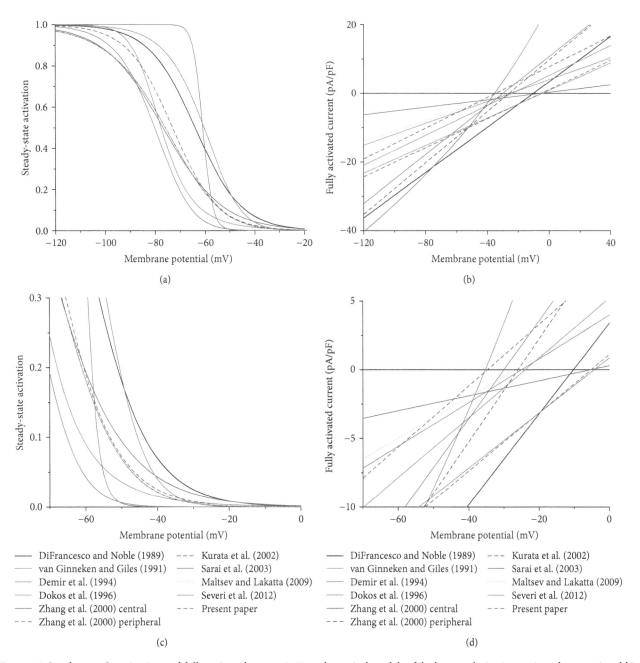

FIGURE 4: Steady-state I_f activation and fully activated current in 11 mathematical models of the hyperpolarization-activated current in rabbit sinoatrial node pacemaker cells. (a) Steady-state I_f activation. (b) Fully activated current. (c) Steady-state I_f activation on expanded activation and membrane potential scales. (d) Fully activated current on expanded current and membrane potential scales.

Figure 3(a). Figure 4(a) illustrates that the steady-state activation curve of DiFrancesco and Noble [70] is similar in shape to the curve that we presented in Section 2—Boltzmann curves with slope factors of 9.2 and 9.0, respectively—but that the half-activation voltage is more positive (−64 versus −73 mV, as listed in Table 1).

In their description of I_f, DiFrancesco and Noble [70] used a reversal potential of −10.3 mV and a fully activated conductance of 9909 pS, that is, 0.3303 nS/pF when normalized to their membrane capacitance of 30 pF. Thus, (3) reads

$$I_f = y \times 0.3303 \times \left(V_m + 10.3\right), \qquad (14)$$

with V_m expressed in mV and I_f in pA/pF. This yields the fully activated current that appears as a black line in Figure 4(b) and, on expanded current and membrane potential scales, in Figure 4(d). As can be appreciated from Figures 4(b) and 4(d), the fully activated conductance of 0.3303 nS/pF is ≈50% larger and the reversal potential of −10.3 mV is ≈25 mV more positive than in our experimental data.

4.2. Model of van Ginneken and Giles. van Ginneken and Giles [39] carried out a comprehensive study on I_f in isolated rabbit SA nodal pacemaker cells. They analyzed their

TABLE 1: Characteristics of the hyperpolarization-activated current (I_f).

	g_f (nS/pF)	E_f (mV)	$g_{f,\text{Na}} : g_{f,\text{K}}$ (ratio)	$V_{0.5}$ (mV)	τ_{-10} (ms)	τ_{+20} (ms)
Experimental data						
DiFrancesco and Noble [70]	≈0.33	−10 to −20	—	≈ −64	≈87	≈33
Van Ginneken and Giles [39]	0.22 ± 0.02	−24 ± 2	—	≈ −76	≈180	—
Present paper	0.22	−35	0.491	−73	71 ± 6	—
Mathematical models						
DiFrancesco and Noble [70]	0.3303	−10.3	—	−64	195	18
Van Ginneken and Giles [39]	0.2182	−24	—	−76	38	8
Demir et al. [76]	0.3569	−30	0.524	−80	25	25
Dokos et al. [74]	0.1595	−25	0.600	−78	151	104
Zhang et al. [75] central	0.0548	−5	1.000	−77	47	11
Zhang et al. [75] peripheral	0.2123	−5	1.000	−77	47	11
Kurata et al. [77]	0.3750	−26	0.622	−76	27	6
Sarai et al. [78]	0.5–0.6	−35	0.65–0.91	−61	10	3
Maltsev and Lakatta [66]	0.1500	−27	0.622	−76	27	6
Severi et al. [67]	0.2009	−4	1.000	−60	57	11
Present paper	0.2240	−35	0.491	−73	80	53

g_f: fully activated conductance; E_f: reversal potential; $g_{f,\text{Na}} : g_{f,\text{K}}$: ratio of sodium and potassium conductance; $V_{0.5}$: half-activation voltage; τ_{-10} and τ_{+20}: time constant of deactivation at −10 and +20 mV, respectively.
Experimental data are mean ± SEM. Data of DiFrancesco and Noble [70] and van Ginneken and Giles [39] are not corrected for liquid junction potential.

experimental data in terms of the three-state kinetic scheme of Figure 2(c) and arrived at

$$y_\infty = \frac{1}{\{1 + \exp\left[(V_m + 64)/13.5\right]\}} \tag{15}$$

for the steady-state value of y, with V_m expressed in mV, and at

$$\alpha = \exp\left[-0.0220741 \times (V_m + 386.9)\right],$$
$$\beta = \exp\left[0.052 \times (V_m - 73.08)\right] \tag{16}$$

for the associated rate constants, both expressed in ms^{-1}, which can be turned into y_∞ and τ for display in Figures 3(c) and 3(d) (green curves), through (6). The steady-state activation curve of I_f can be obtained by squaring y_∞ and is shown in Figures 4(a) and 4(c). In the physiological membrane potential range, it is highly similar to our Boltzmann fit of Figure 1(c), which appears in Figures 4(a) and 4(c) as a dark gray dashed curve.

In their experiments, van Ginneken and Giles [39] observed mean values of −24 mV and 12.0 nS for the reversal potential and fully activated conductance of I_f, respectively. When normalized to their mean membrane capacitance of 55 pF, the fully activated conductance becomes 0.2182 nS/pF, which is remarkably similar to the value of 0.224 nS/pF that we determined from our experiments (Figure 1). With these values, (10) reads

$$I_f = y^2 \times 0.2182 \times (V_m + 24), \tag{17}$$

with V_m expressed in mV and I_f in pA/pF. This yields the fully activated current that appears as a green line in Figures 4(b) and 4(d). The reversal potential of −24 mV is more positive

than we observed, but this may reflect differences in the bath and pipette solutions and the extent to which the data were corrected for the liquid junction potential.

Unfortunately, as already mentioned in Section 3.2, van Ginneken and Giles [39] erroneously doubled their experimentally observed decay rate in their analysis instead of halving it. This affects β and τ, but not y_∞. Furthermore, it should be noted that all experiments were carried out at a fixed temperature between 30 and 33°C (±1°C), which may have led to an underestimation of the rates of activation and deactivation.

4.3. Model of Demir et al. In their mathematical model of an SA nodal pacemaker cell, Demir et al. [76] based their equations for I_f on the data by van Ginneken and Giles [39]. They also used the three-state model of Figure 2(c), but reanalyzed the raw data of van Ginneken and Giles [39], validating their equations in a comparison of model-generated voltage clamp traces with those reported by van Ginneken and Giles [39]. Furthermore, they converted the thus obtained time constant values to a temperature of 37°C, assuming a Q_{10} of 2.3. This reanalysis led to

$$y_\infty = \frac{1}{\{1 + \exp\left[(V_m + 72.2)/9\right]\}}, \tag{18}$$

$$\tau = \left\{1.6483 \times \exp\left[-\frac{(V_m + 54.06)}{24.33}\right]\right.$$

$$\left. + \frac{14.01055}{\{0.7 + \exp\left[-(V_m + 60)/5.5\right]\}}\right\}^{-1} \tag{19}$$

as equations for y_∞ and τ (in s), respectively. The thus defined curves are shown in Figures 3(c) and 3(d) and are remarkably different from those based on the equations by van Ginneken and Giles [39]. This also holds for the steady-state activation curve of I_f obtained by squaring y_∞, which is shown in Figures 4(a) and 4(c).

In their model, Demir et al. [76] selected an I_f reversal potential of −30 mV. For the fully activated conductance, they chose of value of 19.63 nS, which turns into a value of 0.3569 nS/pF when normalized to the model's membrane capacitance of 55 pF, which Demir et al. [76] based on the mean value reported by van Ginneken and Giles [39]. With these values, (10) reads

$$I_f = y^2 \times 0.3569 \times (V_m + 30),\qquad(20)$$

with V_m expressed in mV and I_f in pA/pF. The associated fully activated current is shown in Figures 4(b) and 4(d).

4.4. Model of Dokos et al.

In 1996, two years after Demir et al. [76], Dokos et al. [74] also published a mathematical model of an SA nodal pacemaker cell. However, they used the simpler first-order Hodgkin and Huxley type model of Figure 2(a). As Demir et al. [76], Dokos et al. [74] also based their equations for the kinetics of I_f on the raw data by van Ginneken and Giles [39], arriving at

$$\alpha = \frac{0.36 \times (V_m + 137.8)}{\{\exp[0.066 \times (V_m + 137.8)] - 1\}},$$
$$\beta = \frac{0.1 \times (V_m + 76.3)}{\{1 - \exp[-0.21 \times (V_m + 76.3)]\}}\qquad(21)$$

for the rate constants α and β, both expressed in s^{-1}, which have been turned into y_∞ and τ for display in Figures 3(a) and 3(b) (blue curves), using (6). The steady-state activation curve is shown in Figures 4(a) and 4(c) and differs not only from that of van Ginneken and Giles [39] but also from that of Demir et al. [76].

Dokos et al. [74] selected values of the sodium and potassium conductance of I_f "to produce a reversal potential of −25 mV and a cycle length prolongation of ≈27% in the free-running model when I_f was abolished." The resulting reversal potential is −24.97 mV, and the resulting fully activated conductance is 5.102 nS, which turns into a value of 0.1595 nS/pF when normalized to the model's membrane capacitance of 32 pF, which Dokos et al. [74] adopted from the early model by Wilders et al. [80]. With these values, (3) reads

$$I_f = y \times 0.1595 \times (V_m + 24.97),\qquad(22)$$

with V_m expressed in mV and I_f in pA/pF. The associated fully activated current is shown in Figures 4(b) and 4(d).

4.5. Model of Zhang et al.

Zhang et al. [75] also used a single-gate description of I_f, as in Figure 2(a), in the mathematical model of an SA nodal pacemaker cell that they published in 2000. They created two versions, one for a small cell, with a

membrane capacitance of 20 pF, presumably originating from the center of the SA node, and one for a large cell, with a membrane capacitance of 65 pF, presumably originating from the periphery of the SA node. They introduced rate constants α and β, both in s^{-1}, given by

$$\alpha = \exp\left[-\frac{V_m + 78.91}{26.62}\right],$$
$$\beta = \exp\left[\frac{V_m + 75.13}{21.25}\right],\qquad(23)$$

which they validated in a comparison with the experimental data for y_∞ and τ of van Ginneken and Giles [39] and Liu et al. [81]. The associated y_∞ and τ are shown in Figures 3(a) and 3(b) (red curves) and the steady-state activation curve in Figures 4(a) and 4(c). These hold for both versions of the model.

Zhang et al. [75] assumed identical sodium and potassium conductance values for I_f. This results in a reversal potential of −5.25 mV, which differs from our experimentally observed value (Figure 1(b)) by 30 mV. The fully activated conductance of I_f was validated against the current-voltage relationships reported by Honjo et al. [82], who found that the fully activated current density of I_f (in pA/pF) of SA nodal cells increases with the membrane capacitance of the cells. Zhang et al. [75] selected a fully activated I_f conductance of 1.096 nS for their central cell model and 13.8 nS for their peripheral cell model. Normalized to the membrane capacitance of 20 and 65 pF, these values are 0.0548 and 0.2123 nS/pF, respectively. With these values, (3) reads

$$I_f = y \times 0.0548 \times (V_m + 5.25),\qquad(24)$$

for the central cell model and

$$I_f = y \times 0.2123 \times (V_m + 5.25),\qquad(25)$$

for the peripheral cell model, both with V_m expressed in mV and I_f in pA/pF. The associated fully activated current is shown as a red solid line for the central cell model and a dashed line for the peripheral cell model in Figures 4(b) and 4(d).

4.6. Model of Kurata et al.

In 2002, Kurata et al. [77] published "an improved mathematical model for a single pacemaker cell of the rabbit SA node." This primary cell model has a membrane capacitance of 32 pF, in line with the earlier models by Wilders et al. [80] and Dokos et al. [74]. The formulation for I_f was adopted from the model of Wilders et al. [80], who had in turn used the equations and parameters of van Ginneken and Giles [39] and arrived on potassium and sodium conductances of 7.4 and 4.6 nS, respectively, for I_f, based on the observed reversal potential of −24 mV. Thus, y_∞ is given by (15), which explains that the y_∞ curve in Figure 3(c) and the steady-state activation curve in Figures 4(a) and 4(c), of Kurata et al. [77] and van Ginneken and Giles [39], coincide.

The equation for the time constant τ was derived from the rate constants of (16) but corrected for 37°C by the use of a Q_{10} factor of 2.3 following Demir et al. [76], thus arriving at

$$\tau = \frac{0.71665}{\{\exp\left[-(V_m + 386.9)/45.3\right] + \exp\left[(V_m - 73.08)/19.23\right]\}}, \tag{26}$$

in which τ is in ms and 0.71665 is the correction factor for the temperature of 30–33°C in the experiments of van Ginneken and Giles [39]. Thus, the Kurata et al. [77] curve in Figure 3(d) is similar in shape but smaller in magnitude than the van Ginneken and Giles [39] curve.

For the fully activated conductance of I_f, Kurata et al. [77] used the value of 12 nS of van Ginneken and Giles [39], which, with their membrane capacitance of 32 pF, results in a normalized value of 0.375 nS/pF in the equation for I_f:

$$I_f = y^2 \times 0.375 \times (V_m + 26.02), \tag{27}$$

in which I_f is again expressed in pA/pF and V_m in mV. The reversal potential of −26.02 mV deviates from the value of −24 mV of the Wilders et al. [80] model, because there are some minor differences in sodium and potassium concentrations between the models. The fully activated current is shown in Figures 4(b) and 4(d).

4.7. Model of Sarai et al.

The SA nodal cell model of Sarai et al. [78] is part of the "Kyoto model" that was introduced by Matsuoka et al. [79] in 2003. As detailed in Section 3.3 and diagrammed in Figure 2(d), the I_f channel has two closed states (C_1 and C_2) and three open states (O_1, O_2, and O_3). The rate constants μ and λ that determine the rate of transitions between the two closed states C_1 and C_2 are given by

$$\mu = \frac{1}{[4.5 \times 10^7 \times \exp(V_m/8) + 500 \times \exp(V_m/200)]},$$
$$\lambda = \frac{1}{[10.5 \times \exp(-V_m/16.4) + 0.4 \times \exp(-V_m/400)]}, \tag{28}$$

where μ and λ are both in ms^{-1} and V_m in mV. The remaining three transitions (see Figure 2(d)) are all controlled by rate constants α and β given by

$$\alpha = \frac{1}{[3500 \times \exp(V_m/16.8) + 0.3 \times \exp(V_m/400)]},$$
$$\beta = \exp\left[\frac{V_m + 75.13}{21.25}\right], \tag{29}$$

where α and β are both in ms^{-1} and V_m in mV. Under steady-state conditions, most of the I_f channels are either in the closed state C_1 or in the open state O_3, as illustrated in Figure 3(e). The time constants associated with μ and λ and with α and β are both shown in Figure 3(f), which demonstrates that the transition between C_1 and C_2 is relatively slow and that the other transitions are relatively

fast. The steady-state activation of I_f can be computed from the fraction of I_f channels in each of the open states O_1, O_2, and O_3 as shown in Figure 3(e). This yields the curve shown in Figures 4(a) and 4(c), which is strikingly steep when compared to each of the other curves.

Unlike the other models, the fully activated current $I_{f,\text{full}}$ is not ohmic and thus linearly dependent on the membrane potential but determined by

$$I_{f,\text{full}} = 1.821 \times CF_{Na} + 7.7286 \times CF_K, \tag{30}$$

in which 1.821 and 7.7286 are the permeabilities for Na$^+$ and K$^+$ in pA/mM, and CF_{Na} and CF_K are given by the "constant-field equations"

$$CF_{Na} = \frac{\{V_m/(RT/F)\} \times \{[Na^+]_i - [Na^+]_e \times \exp(-V_m/(RT/F))\}}{\{1 - \exp(-V_m/(RT/F))\}},$$

$$CF_K = \frac{\{V_m/(RT/F)\} \times \{[K^+]_i - [K^+]_e \times \exp(-V_m/(RT/F))\}}{\{1 - \exp(-V_m/(RT/F))\}}, \tag{31}$$

in which $[Na^+]_i$, $[Na^+]_e$, $[K^+]_i$, and $[K^+]_e$ are the intracellular and extracellular concentrations of Na$^+$ and K$^+$ in mM, and the fraction RT/F is determined by the universal gas constant R, the absolute temperature T, and the Faraday constant F and amounts to 26.7 mV. Using (30)-(31) and the model concentrations of 140 mM for $[Na^+]_e$, 5.4 mM for $[K^+]_e$, ≈4.6 mM for $[Na^+]_i$, and ≈143 mM for $[K^+]_i$, one obtains the fully activated current as shown in Figures 4(b) and 4(d), with a reversal potential of −35.3 mV. In the membrane potential range from −65 to −40 mV, the curve is almost linear with a conductance of 0.5–0.6 nS/pF.

4.8. Model of Maltsev and Lakatta.

In 2009, Maltsev and Lakatta [66] published a mathematical model of an SA nodal pacemaker cell that is based on the model by Kurata et al. [77] but incorporates a submembrane "calcium clock" that interacts with the "membrane clock" in producing the pacemaker activity of the model cell [6, 9]. Maltsev and Lakatta [66] adopted the I_f kinetics of Kurata et al. [77]. This explains why the Maltsev and Lakatta [66] and Kurata et al. [77] curves in Figures 3(c) and 3(d) and Figures 4(a) and 4(c) coincide.

Maltsev and Lakatta [66] reduced the fully activated I_f conductance of Kurata et al. [77] by 60%, from 0.375 to 0.15 nS/pF. Furthermore, their (fixed) ion concentrations of 10, 140, 140, and 5.4 mM for $[Na^+]_i$, $[Na^+]_e$, $[K^+]_i$, and $[K^+]_e$, respectively, are slightly different from the concentrations in the model by Kurata et al. [77], resulting in an I_f reversal potential of −26.62 mV. Thus, the line representing the fully activated current of Maltsev and Lakatta [66] in Figures 4(b) and 4(d) is less steep and shifted by 0.6 mV compared to the line obtained from the Kurata et al. [77] model.

4.9. Model of Severi et al. The most recent mathematical model of a rabbit SA nodal pacemaker cell is that of Severi et al. [67], which they presented as "an updated computational model of rabbit sinoatrial action potential to investigate the mechanisms of heart rate modulation." In this model, the kinetic and conductive properties of I_f are largely based on the work of DiFrancesco and Noble from the 1980s. The kinetics are adopted from the early SA nodal cell model by Noble et al. [83], who used a Hodgkin and Huxley type model with two identical y gates, as in Figures 2(b) and 2(c). However, Severi et al. [67] shifted the associated y_∞ and τ curves to more depolarized potentials by ≈ 11 mV, based on experimental data from Altomare et al. [84] and Barbuti et al. [85], producing

$$y_\infty = \frac{1}{\{1 + \exp\left[(V_m + 52.5)/9\right]\}},$$

$$\tau =$$

$$\frac{0.7}{\{0.0708 \times \exp\left[-(V_m + 5.0)/20.28\right] + 10.6 \times \exp\left[V_m/18\right]\}}, \tag{32}$$

where V_m is in mV and τ in s. The y_∞ and τ curves are shown in Figures 3(c) and 3(d) and the steady-state activation curve in Figures 4(a) and 4(c).

According to the original description by DiFrancesco and Noble [86] and in line with Noble et al. [83], Severi et al. [67] assumed identical conductance values for the sodium and potassium components of I_f, with a total conductance of 6.429 nS. Because, as in the models by Wilders et al. [80], Dokos et al. [74], and Maltsev and Lakatta [66], the model cell has a membrane capacitance of 32 pF, the normalized I_f conductance amounts to 0.2009 nS/pF (Table 1). With the model concentrations for sodium and potassium ions, the I_f reversal potential amounts to -4.39 mV, which is 7.9 mV more positive than in the model by Noble et al. [83], due to differences in ion concentrations between the two models. Thus, I_f is given by

$$I_f = y^2 \times 0.2009 \times (V_m + 4.39), \tag{33}$$

in which I_f is expressed in pA/pF and V_m in mV and which yields the fully activated current shown in Figures 4(b) and 4(d).

4.10. Novel Model. Apart from the ten I_f models detailed in Sections 4.1–4.9, Figures 3 and 4 show curves labeled "present paper." These curves represent a novel model for I_f based on the experimental data that we presented in Section 2. We use the kinetic scheme of Figure 2(a) and describe I_f by

$$I_f = y \times 0.224 \times (V_m + 34.8), \tag{34}$$

with y_∞ and τ given by

$$y_\infty = \frac{1}{\{1 + \exp\left[(V_m + 73)/9\right]\}},$$

$$\tau = 0.05 + [75.8 \times \exp\left(0.083 \times V_m\right)$$

$$+ 0.0233 \times \exp\left(-0.043 \times V_m\right)]^{-1}, \tag{35}$$

where I_f is in pA/pF, V_m is in mV, and τ in s.

As can be appreciated from Figure 4(c), the steady-state activation curve of our model closely matches with that of van Ginneken and Giles [39], Kurata et al. [77], and Maltsev and Lakatta [66] in the physiological membrane potential range, whereas there are significant discrepancies with those of other models, in particular the models by DiFrancesco and Noble [70], Sarai et al. [78], and Severi et al. [67]. The I_f conductance of 0.224 nS/pF, on the other hand, closely matches the values of 0.2182, 0.2123, and 0.2009 nS/pF of the models by van Ginneken and Giles [39], Zhang et al. [75] (peripheral cell), and Severi et al. [67], respectively, as can be appreciated from the slope of the lines in Figure 4(d). However, Figure 4(d) also illustrates that the I_f reversal potential of the latter two models differs from that of our model by as much as 30 mV, which creates an almost twofold difference in I_f driving force near the maximum diastolic potential of an SA nodal action potential.

Our model does not have an explicit cAMP dependence. However, autonomic modulation of I_f can be incorporated through a shift of the steady-state activation curve along the voltage axis, by up to ≈ 10 mV in the positive direction for adrenergic modulation and up to ≈ 10 mV in the negative direction for cholinergic modulation. Such shift has been observed experimentally [11, 87] and has been incorporated in several models, for example, [88–92], to reflect the autonomic modulation of I_f through acetylcholine and (nor) adrenalin. In addition, a similar voltage shift should be applied to the time constant curve to account for the experimentally observed cAMP dependence of this curve [93]. The latter shift has been ignored in most models, but not in the recent model of Severi et al. [67].

5. Reconstruction of I_f

In the previous section, we have identified models of I_f in terms of characteristics derived from and related to voltage clamp experiments, including rate constants, steady-state activation, fully activated conductance, and reversal potential. In the present section, we show how these characteristics determine the course of I_f during an action potential, that is, under current clamp conditions.

5.1. Steady-State Current. Before reconstructing I_f during an action potential in Section 5.2, we use the data of Figure 4 to compute the steady-state current at -60 mV to get an impression of the amplitude of I_f that one might expect for each of the models. Figure 5(a) shows the steady-state activation at -60 mV in each of the 11 models. This steady-state activation ranges from 0.042 in the Demir et al. [76]

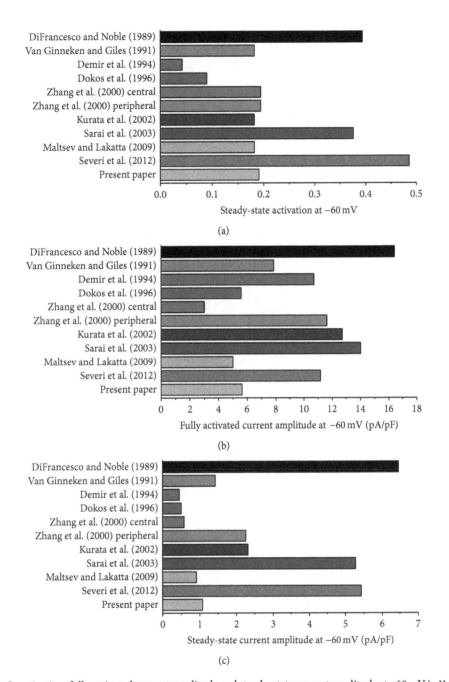

FIGURE 5: Steady-state I_f activation, fully activated current amplitude and steady-state current amplitude at −60 mV in 11 mathematical models of the hyperpolarization-activated current in rabbit sinoatrial node pacemaker cells. (a) Steady-state I_f activation. (b) Fully activated current amplitude. (c) Steady-state current amplitude.

model to 0.486, that is, almost 50% activation of I_f at −60 mV, in the Severi et al. [67] model, which constitutes an almost 12-fold difference. Most models, including the one based on our experimental data, predict a value near 19% for the steady-state activation at −60 mV (Figure 5(a)).

As for the steady-state activation, there is a wide difference in the fully activated current amplitude at −60 mV, which is not only determined by the I_f conductance but also by the I_f reversal potential as a determinant of the driving force. With a value of 16.4 pA/pF, the model by DiFrancesco and Noble [70] has the largest amplitude, whereas the central cell

model by Zhang et al. [75] shows the smallest amplitude with a value of 3.0 pA/pF, a 5.5-fold difference.

In combination, the steady-state activation of Figure 5(a) and the fully activated current amplitude of Figure 5(b) determine the amplitude of I_f that can be activated at −60 mV. We multiplied the fully activated current amplitude of Figure 5(b) by the steady-state activation of Figure 5(a) to arrive at the steady-state current amplitude of Figure 5(c). With values of 6.5, 5.3, and 5.4 pA/pF, respectively, the models by DiFrancesco and Noble [70], Sarai et al. [78], and Severi et al. [67] show a remarkably large amplitude. The smallest

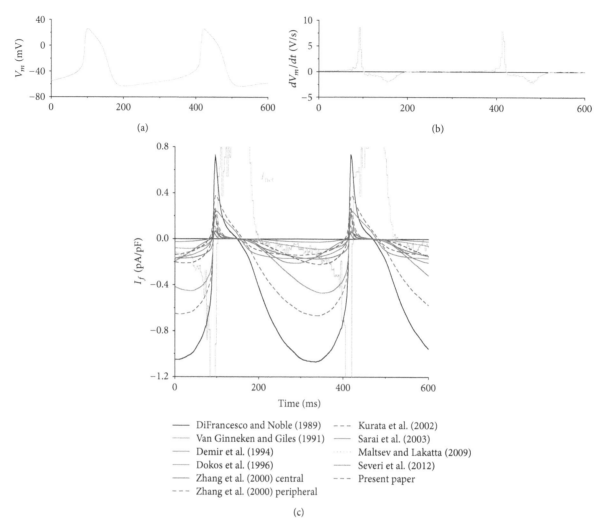

FIGURE 6: Numerical reconstruction of the time course of I_f during pacemaker activity of rabbit sinoatrial node cells. (a) Experimentally recorded action potentials of a single rabbit SA nodal pacemaker cell. (b) Associated time derivative (dV_m/dt). (c) Associated time course of I_f as reconstructed using the membrane potential values of the recorded action potentials and mathematical models of this current in rabbit sinoatrial node pacemaker cells. Also shown is the net membrane current (I_{net}), as derived from $I_{net} = -C_m \times dV_m/dt$, where C_m and V_m denote membrane capacitance and membrane potential, respectively.

amplitude is obtained with the models of Demir et al. [76], Dokos et al. [74], and Zhang et al. [75] (central cell), with values of 0.45, 0.50, and 0.58 pA/pF, respectively. Overall, there is a >14-fold range in I_f that can be activated at −60 mV according to the models of Figure 5(c). With values of 0.91 and 1.08 pA/pF, respectively, the model by Maltsev and Lakatta [66] and the model based on our experimental data show similar values.

5.2. Dynamics of I_f. Figure 5 shows that the amount of I_f that can be activated at −60 mV varies widely between the models, but this does not imply that this is also the case during the course of action potential. In the latter case, the rate at which I_f activates and deactivates plays an important role. Therefore, we subjected each of the models to an "action potential clamp": we reconstructed I_f during the experimentally recorded action potentials of Figure 6(a). These action potentials were applied as part of a sufficiently

long train, and I_f was computed according to the equations listed in Section 4. The resulting I_f traces are shown in Figure 6(c), together with the net membrane current, I_{net}, which was computed from the time derivative (dV_m/dt) of the membrane potential trace of Figure 6(a), as shown in Figure 6(b). From the current traces shown in Figure 6(c), we computed the diastolic I_f current amplitude at −60 mV (Figure 7(a)) as well as the maximum I_f current amplitude during diastole (Figure 7(b)). Also, we computed the charge carried by I_f during the 200 ms, 25 mV diastolic depolarization from the maximum diastolic potential of −63 mV to −38 mV (Figure 7(c)). Both Figure 6(c) and Figure 7(a) demonstrate that only a fraction of the steady-state current of Figure 5(c) is activated during an action potential. This fraction varies from 0.3% for the Sarai et al. model [78] to 42% for the Demir et al. model [76].

Figure 7(c) shows that, in the absence of other inward or outward membrane currents, the charge carried by I_f during

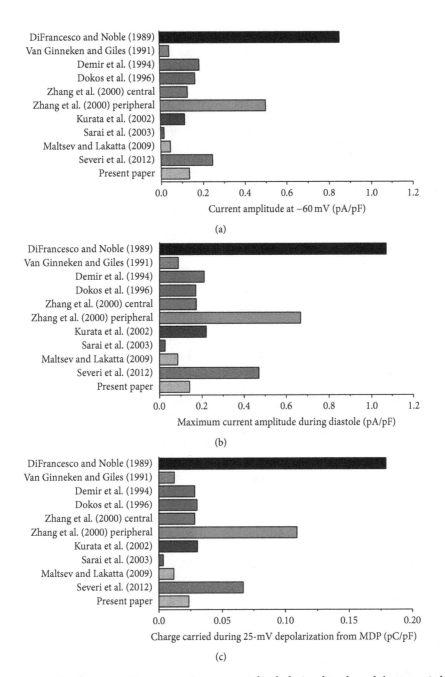

FIGURE 7: Diastolic I_f current amplitude at −60 mV, maximum I_f current amplitude during diastole, and charge carried by I_f during diastolic depolarization for each of the 11 reconstructed I_f current traces of Figure 6(c). (a) Diastolic I_f current amplitude at −60 mV. (b) Maximum I_f current amplitude during diastole. (c) Charge carried by I_f during the 25-mV, 200-ms diastolic depolarization from the maximum diastolic potential of −63 mV to −38 mV.

the 200 ms depolarization would be sufficient or almost sufficient to depolarize the membrane by the observed 25 mV. For example, our model based on the experimental data of Section 2 predicts a charge carried by I_f of 0.024 pC/pF, which is equivalent to a depolarization of 24 mV. Notably, the models of Maltsev and Lakatta [66] and Severi et al. [67] predict depolarizations of 12 and 67 mV, respectively.

With a peak inward current of only 0.027 pA/pF (Figures 6(c) and 7(b)), the smallest I_f is obtained with the Sarai et al. model [78], although a relatively large I_f can be

activated under steady-state conditions (Figure 5(c)). This emphasizes the important role of the rate at which I_f activates and deactivates, but in this particular case the exceptional steepness of the steady-activation curve (Figures 4(a) and 4(c)) also plays an important role. The importance of the rate of (de)activation is perhaps better illustrated with the Zhang et al. [75] peripheral and Kurata et al. [77] models that show a similar amplitude in Figure 5(c) but clearly different peak inward currents of 0.68 pA/pF for the Zhang et al. [75] peripheral cell model and threefold less, 0.23 pA/pF, for the Kurata et al. [77] model (Figures 6(c) and 7(b)). Of note, this cannot be explained by the use of a single-gate kinetic scheme by Zhang et al. [75] versus a double-gate scheme by Kurata et al. [77], as the effects of the selection of a single or double y gate on the reconstructed I_f are minimal [58, 83]. Rather, it may reflect the erroneously overestimated deactivation rate of I_f (see Sections 3.2 and 4.2) in the Kurata et al. [77] model, which also affects the traces obtained with the related models by van Ginneken and Giles [39] and Maltsev and Lakatta [66]. The latter two traces almost coincide despite the smaller I_f conductance in the Maltsev and Lakatta [66] model. Here, the faster kinetics of the Maltsev and Lakatta [66] I_f compensate for this smaller conductance.

In most models, I_f deactivates almost instantaneously at depolarized potentials, resulting in almost complete deactivation of I_f near the overshoot of the action potential and a slowly developing I_f during the subsequent diastolic phase. However, as set out in Section 2, I_f deactivation is fast but certainly not instantaneous at depolarized potentials. If this is taken into account, as in our novel model, I_f is available early in diastole and of relatively constant amplitude during diastolic depolarization. Interestingly, Zaza et al. [94] already noted that the presence of measurable inward 2 mM Cs^+ sensitive current almost immediately after repolarization in their action potential clamp experiments on rabbit SA nodal cells is apparently at odds with the slow kinetics of I_f activation at diastolic potentials, that this suggests that I_f may not deactivate completely during repetitive activity, and that this would also increase the amount of I_f available during diastolic depolarization.

6. Conclusion

The various mathematical descriptions of I_f that have been used in computer simulations show strikingly different characteristics when reconstructing the course of I_f during an action potential. This explains—at least to some extent—that some successfully use computer simulations to support their view that I_f plays a fundamental role in the generation of pacemaker activity and its rate control, while others provide computer simulation results in favor of their view that the role of I_f is limited to a modest contribution to rate control. We have identified some important caveats regarding the reconstruction of the course of I_f during an action potential through computer simulations. An obvious one is the use of appropriate activation kinetics and an appropriate value for the I_f conductance. The half-activation voltage and fully activated conductance of most models, with values of −80 to −60 mV and ≈0.2 nS/pF, respectively, are in line with the experimental data. However, the steep steady-state activation curve of the complex five-state model of Sarai et al. [78] is clearly at odds with the experimental data. A somewhat less obvious caveat is the selection of an I_f reversal potential that is in line with the experimental data. This reversal potential should be around −30 mV, but this is definitely not the case for the models of DiFrancesco and Noble [70], Zhang et al. [75], and Severi et al. [67]. The final and most important caveat

to be taken into account is that I_f deactivation is not almost instantaneous at depolarized potentials. In most models, including the recent models by Maltsev and Lakatta [66] and Severi et al. [67], this deactivation is much faster than can be deduced from the scarce experimental data, which likely results in an underestimation of I_f during diastolic depolarization. Our novel model for the reconstruction of I_f in mathematical models of SA nodal pacemaker cells is simple and straightforward but takes care of all of these caveats.

References

[1] H. Irisawa, H. F. Brown, and W. Giles, "Cardiac pacemaking in the sinoatrial node," *Physiological Reviews*, vol. 73, no. 1, pp. 197–227, 1993.

[2] M. R. Boyett, H. Honjo, and I. Kodama, "The sinoatrial node, a heterogeneous pacemaker structure," *Cardiovascular Research*, vol. 47, no. 4, pp. 658–687, 2000.

[3] H. Satoh, "Sino-atrial nodal cells of mammalian hearts: ionic currents and gene expression of pacemaker ionic channels," *Journal of Smooth Muscle Research*, vol. 39, no. 5, pp. 175–193, 2003.

[4] B. Couette, L. Marger, J. Nargeot, and M. E. Mangoni, "Physiological and pharmacological insights into the role of ionic channels in cardiac pacemaker activity," *Cardiovascular & Hematological Disorders*, vol. 6, no. 3, pp. 169–190, 2006.

[5] H. Dobrzynski, M. R. Boyett, and R. H. Anderson, "New insights into pacemaker activity: promoting understanding of sick sinus syndrome," *Circulation*, vol. 115, no. 14, pp. 1921–1932, 2007.

[6] V. A. Maltsev and E. G. Lakatta, "Normal heart rhythm is initiated and regulated by an intracellular calcium clock within pacemaker cells," *Heart Lung & Circulation*, vol. 16, no. 5, pp. 335–348, 2007.

[7] M. E. Mangoni and J. Nargeot, "Genesis and regulation of the heart automaticity," *Physiological Reviews*, vol. 88, no. 3, pp. 919–982, 2008.

[8] A. O. Verkerk, A. C. G. van Ginneken, and R. Wilders, "Pacemaker activity of the human sinoatrial node: role of the hyperpolarization-activated current, I_f," *International Journal of Cardiology*, vol. 132, no. 3, pp. 318–336, 2009.

[9] E. G. Lakatta, V. A. Maltsev, and T. M. Vinogradova, "A coupled SYSTEM of intracellular Ca^{2+} clocks and surface membrane voltage clocks controls the timekeeping mechanism of the heart's pacemaker," *Circulation Research*, vol. 106, no. 4, pp. 659–673, 2010.

[10] H. Brown and D. DiFrancesco, "Voltage-clamp investigations of membrane currents underlying pace-maker activity in rabbit sino-atrial node," *Journal of Physiology*, vol. 308, pp. 331–351, 1980.

[11] D. DiFrancesco and P. Tortora, "Direct activation of cardiac pacemaker channels by intracellular cyclic AMP," *Nature*, vol. 351, no. 6322, pp. 145–147, 1991.

[12] H. F. Brown, D. DiFrancesco, and S. J. Noble, "How does adrenaline accelerate the heart?" *Nature*, vol. 280, no. 5719, pp. 235–236, 1979.

[13] A. Noma, H. Irisawa, and S. Kokobun, "Slow current systems in the A-V node of the rabbit heart," *Nature*, vol. 285, no. 5762, pp. 228–229, 1980.

[14] D. DiFrancesco, "A study of the ionic nature of the pace-maker current in calf Purkinje fibres," *Journal of Physiology*, vol. 314, pp. 377–393, 1981.

[15] F. Roubille and J. C. Tardif, "New therapeutic targets in cardiology: heart failure and arrhythmia: HCN channels," *Circulation*, vol. 127, no. 19, pp. 1986–1996, 2013.

[16] N. J. Chandler, I. D. Greener, J. O. Tellez et al., "Molecular architecture of the human sinus node insights into the function of the cardiac pacemaker," *Circulation*, vol. 119, no. 12, pp. 1562–1575, 2009.

[17] E. Schulze-Bahr, A. Neu, P. Friederich et al., "Pacemaker channel dysfunction in a patient with sinus node disease," *Journal of Clinical Investigation*, vol. 111, no. 10, pp. 1537–1545, 2003.

[18] K. Ueda, K. Nakamura, T. Hayashi et al., "Functional characterization of a trafficking-defective *HCN4* mutation, D553N, associated with cardiac arrhythmia," *Journal of Biological Chemistry*, vol. 279, no. 26, pp. 27194–27198, 2004.

[19] R. Milanesi, M. Baruscotti, T. Gnecchi-Ruscone, and D. DiFrancesco, "Familial sinus bradycardia associated with a mutation in the cardiac pacemaker channel," *The New England Journal of Medicine*, vol. 354, no. 2, pp. 151–157, 2006.

[20] E. Nof, D. Luria, D. Brass et al., "Point mutation in the HCN4 cardiac ion channel pore affecting synthesis, trafficking, and functional expression is associated with familial asymptomatic sinus bradycardia," *Circulation*, vol. 116, no. 5, pp. 463–470, 2007.

[21] A. Laish-Farkash, M. Glikson, D. Brass et al., "A novel mutation in the HCN4 gene causes symptomatic sinus bradycardia in Moroccan Jews," *Journal of Cardiovascular Electrophysiology*, vol. 21, no. 12, pp. 1365–1372, 2010.

[22] P. A. Schweizer, N. Duhme, D. Thomas et al., "cAMP sensitivity of HCN pacemaker channels determines basal heart rate but is not critical for autonomic rate control," *Circulation: Arrhythmia and Electrophysiology*, vol. 3, no. 5, pp. 542–552, 2010.

[23] N. Duhme, P. A. Schweizer, D. Thomas et al., "Altered HCN4 channel C-linker interaction is associated with familial tachycardia-bradycardia syndrome and atrial fibrillation," *European Heart Journal*, 2013.

[24] R. B. Robinson, P. R. Brink, I. S. Cohen, and M. R. Rosen, "I_f and the biological pacemaker," *Pharmacological Research*, vol. 53, no. 5, pp. 407–415, 2006.

[25] C.-W. Siu, D. K. Lieu, and R. A. Li, "HCN-encoded pacemaker channels: from physiology and biophysics to bioengineering," *Journal of Membrane Biology*, vol. 214, no. 3, pp. 115–122, 2006.

[26] M. R. Rosen, P. R. Brink, I. S. Cohen, and R. B. Robinson, "Biological pacemakers based on I_f," *Medical & Biological Engineering & Computing*, vol. 45, no. 2, pp. 157–166, 2007.

[27] H. C. Cho and E. Marbán, "Biological therapies for cardiac arrhythmias: can genes and cells replace drugs and devices?" *Circulation Research*, vol. 106, no. 4, pp. 674–685, 2010.

[28] M. R. Rosen, R. B. Robinson, P. R. Brink, and I. S. Cohen, "The road to biological pacing," *Nature Reviews Cardiology*, vol. 8, no. 11, pp. 656–666, 2011.

[29] R. Li, "Gene- and cell-based bio-artificial pacemaker: what basic and translational lessons have we learned?" *Gene Therapy*, vol. 19, no. 6, pp. 588–595, 2012.

[30] M. M. G. J. van Borren, A. O. Verkerk, R. Wilders et al., "Effects of muscarinic receptor stimulation on Ca^{2+} transient, cAMP production and pacemaker frequency of rabbit sinoatrial node cells," *Basic Research in Cardiology*, vol. 105, no. 1, pp. 73–87, 2010.

[31] Y. Yaniv, S. Sirenko, B. D. Ziman, H. A. Spurgeon, V. A. Maltsev, and E. G. Lakatta, "New evidence for coupled clock regulation of the normal automaticity of sinoatrial nodal pacemaker cells: bradycardic effects of ivabradine are linked to suppression of intracellular Ca^{2+} cycling," *Journal of Molecular and Cellular Cardiology*, 2013.

[32] J. D. Lippiat, "Whole-cell recording using the perforated patch clamp technique," *Methods in Molecular Biology*, vol. 491, pp. 141–149, 2008.

[33] H. Yu, J. Wu, I. Potapova et al., "MinK-related peptide 1: a β subunit for the HCN ion channel subunit family enhances expression and speeds activation," *Circulation Research*, vol. 88, no. 12, pp. E84–E87, 2001.

[34] N. Decher, B. Bundis, R. Vajna, and K. Steinmeyer, "KCNE2 modulates current amplitudes and activation kinetics of HCN4: influence of KCNE family members on HCN4 currents," *Pflügers Archiv European Journal of Physiology*, vol. 446, no. 6, pp. 633–640, 2003.

[35] J. Qu, Y. Kryukova, I. A. Potapova et al., "MiRP1 modulates HCN2 channel expression and gating in cardiac myocytes," *Journal of Biological Chemistry*, vol. 279, no. 42, pp. 43497–43502, 2004.

[36] W.-K. Ho, H. F. Brown, and D. Noble, "High selectivity of the i_f channel to Na^+ and K^+ in rabbit isolated sinoatrial node cells," *Pflügers Archiv European Journal of Physiology*, vol. 426, no. 1-2, pp. 68–74, 1994.

[37] A. M. Frace, F. Maruoka, and A. Noma, "Control of the hyperpolarization-activated cation current by external anions in rabbit sino-atrial node cells," *Journal of Physiology*, vol. 453, pp. 307–318, 1992.

[38] D. DiFrancesco, A. Ferroni, M. Mazzanti, and C. Tromba, "Properties of the hyperpolarizing-activated current (i_f) in cells isolated from the rabbit sino-atrial node," *Journal of Physiology*, vol. 377, pp. 61–88, 1986.

[39] A. C. G. van Ginneken and W. Giles, "Voltage clamp measurements of the hyperpolarization-activated inward current I_f in single cells from rabbit sino-atrial node," *Journal of Physiology*, vol. 434, pp. 57–83, 1991.

[40] A. O. Verkerk, H. M. den Ruijter, J. Bourier et al., "Dietary fish oil reduces pacemaker current and heart rate in rabbit," *Heart Rhythm*, vol. 6, no. 10, pp. 1485–1492, 2009.

[41] A. M. Frace, F. Maruoka, and A. Noma, "External K^+ increases Na^+ conductance of the hyperpolarization-activated current in rabbit cardiac pacemaker cells," *Pflügers Archiv European Journal of Physiology*, vol. 421, no. 2-3, pp. 97–99, 1992.

[42] X. Yu, X.-W. Chen, P. Zhou et al., "Calcium influx through I_f channels in rat ventricular myocytes," *American Journal of Physiology Cell Physiology*, vol. 292, no. 3, pp. C1147–C1155, 2007.

[43] G. Michels, M. C. Brandt, N. Zagidullin et al., "Direct evidence for calcium conductance of hyperpolarization-activated cyclic nucleotide-gated channels and human native I_f at physiological calcium concentrations," *Cardiovascular Research*, vol. 78, no. 3, pp. 466–475, 2008.

[44] M. Biel, C. Wahl-Schott, S. Michalakis, and X. Zong, "Hyperpolarization-activated cation channels: from genes to function," *Physiological Reviews*, vol. 89, no. 3, pp. 847–885, 2009.

[45] R. Männikkö, S. Pandey, H. P. Larsson, and F. Elinder, "Hysteresis in the voltage dependence of HCN channels: conversion between two modes affects pacemaker properties," *Journal of General Physiology*, vol. 125, no. 3, pp. 305–326, 2005.

[46] E. M. Azene, T. Xue, E. Marbán, G. F. Tomaselli, and R. A. Li, "Non-equilibrium behavior of HCN channels: insights into the role of HCN channels in native and engineered pacemakers," *Cardiovascular Research*, vol. 67, no. 2, pp. 263–273, 2005.

[47] F. Elinder, R. Männikkö, S. Pandey, and H. P. Larsson, "Mode shifts in the voltage gating of the mouse and human HCN2 and HCN4 channels," *Journal of Physiology*, vol. 575, no. 2, pp. 417–431, 2006.

[48] A. Bruening-Wright and H. P. Larsson, "Slow conformational changes of the voltage sensor during the mode shift in hyperpolarization-activated cyclic-nucleotide-gated channels," *Journal of Neuroscience*, vol. 27, no. 2, pp. 270–278, 2007.

[49] Y. F. Xiao, N. Chandler, H. Dobrzynski et al., "Hysteresis in human HCN4 channels: a crucial feature potentially affecting sinoatrial node pacemaking," *Acta Physiologica Sinica*, vol. 62, no. 1, pp. 1–13, 2010.

[50] A. Noma, M. Morad, and H. Irisawa, "Does the "pacemaker current" generate the diastolic depolarization in the rabbit SA node cells?" *Pflügers Archiv European Journal of Physiology*, vol. 397, no. 3, pp. 190–194, 1983.

[51] D. DiFrancesco, "The contribution of the "pacemaker" current (i_f) to generation of spontaneous activity in rabbit sino-atrial node myocytes," *Journal of Physiology*, vol. 434, pp. 23–40, 1991.

[52] M. Vassalle, "The pacemaker current (I_f) does not play an important role in regulating SA node pacemaker activity," *Cardiovascular Research*, vol. 30, no. 2, p. 310, 1995.

[53] S. L. Lipsius, J. Hüser, and L. A. Blatter, "Intracellular Ca^{2+} release sparks atrial pacemaker activity," *News in Physiological Sciences*, vol. 16, no. 3, pp. 101–106, 2001.

[54] D. DiFrancesco, "Serious workings of the funny current," *Progress in Biophysics and Molecular Biology*, vol. 90, no. 1–3, pp. 13–25, 2006.

[55] S. Herrmann, J. Stieber, G. Stöckl, F. Hofmann, and A. Ludwig, "HCN4 provides a "depolarization reserve" and is not required for heart rate acceleration in mice," *The EMBO Journal*, vol. 26, no. 21, pp. 4423–4432, 2007.

[56] D. Harzheim, K. H. Pfeiffer, L. Fabritz et al., "Cardiac pacemaker function of HCN4 channels in mice is confined to embryonic development and requires cyclic AMP," *The EMBO Journal*, vol. 27, no. 4, pp. 692–703, 2008.

[57] E. G. Lakatta and D. DiFrancesco, "What keeps us ticking: a funny current, a calcium clock, or both?" *Journal of Molecular and Cellular Cardiology*, vol. 47, no. 2, pp. 157–170, 2009.

[58] A. O. Verkerk and R. Wilders, "Relative importance of funny current in human versus rabbit sinoatrial node," *Journal of Molecular and Cellular Cardiology*, vol. 48, no. 4, pp. 799–801, 2010.

[59] D. DiFrancesco, "Considerations on the size of currents required for pacemaking," *Journal of Molecular and Cellular Cardiology*, vol. 48, no. 4, pp. 802–803, 2010.

[60] V. A. Maltsev and E. G. Lakatta, "Funny current provides a relatively modest contribution to spontaneous beating rate regulation of human and rabbit sinoatrial node cells," *Journal of Molecular and Cellular Cardiology*, vol. 48, no. 4, pp. 804–806, 2010.

[61] D. DiFrancesco and D. Noble, "The funny current has a major pacemaking role in the sinus node," *Heart Rhythm*, vol. 9, no. 2, pp. 299–301, 2012.

[62] V. A. Maltsev and E. G. Lakatta, "The funny current in the context of the coupled-clock pacemaker cell system," *Heart Rhythm*, vol. 9, no. 2, pp. 302–307, 2012.

[63] D. DiFrancesco and D. Noble, "Rebuttal: "The funny current in the context of the coupled clock pacemaker cell system"," *Heart Rhythm*, vol. 9, no. 3, pp. 457–458, 2012.

[64] E. G. Lakatta and V. A. Maltsev, "Rebuttal: what I_f the shoe doesn't fit? "the funny current has a major pacemaking role in the sinus node"," *Heart Rhythm*, vol. 9, no. 3, pp. 459–460, 2012.

[65] R. Wilders, "Computer modelling of the sinoatrial node," *Medical & Biological Engineering & Computing*, vol. 45, no. 2, pp. 189–207, 2007.

[66] V. A. Maltsev and E. G. Lakatta, "Synergism of coupled subsarcolemmal Ca^{2+} clocks and sarcolemmal voltage clocks confers robust and flexible pacemaker function in a novel pacemaker cell model," *American Journal of Physiology Heart and Circulatory Physiology*, vol. 296, no. 3, pp. H594–H615, 2009.

[67] S. Severi, M. Fantini, L. A. Charawi, and D. DiFrancesco, "An updated computational model of rabbit sinoatrial action potential to investigate the mechanisms of heart rate modulation," *Journal of Physiology*, vol. 590, part 18, pp. 4483–4499, 2012.

[68] A. O. Verkerk, R. Wilders, R. Coronel, J. H. Ravesloot, and E. E. Verheijck, "Ionic remodeling of sinoatrial node cells by heart failure," *Circulation*, vol. 108, no. 6, pp. 760–766, 2003.

[69] K. Yanagihara and H. Irisawa, "Inward current activated during hyperpolarization in the rabbit sinoatrial node cell," *Pflügers Archiv European Journal of Physiology*, vol. 385, no. 1, pp. 11–19, 1980.

[70] D. DiFrancesco and D. Noble, "Current I_f and its contribution to cardiac pacemaking," in *Neuronal and Cellular Oscillators*, J. W. Jacklet, Ed., pp. 31–57, Marcel Dekker, New York, NY, USA, 1989.

[71] F. Maruoka, Y. Nakashima, M. Takano, K. Ono, and A. Noma, "Cation-dependent gating of the hyperpolarization-activated cation current in the rabbit sino-atrial node cells," *Journal of Physiology*, vol. 477, no. 3, pp. 423–435, 1994.

[72] D. DiFrancesco, "Characterization of the pace-maker current kinetics in calf Purkinje fibres," *Journal of Physiology*, vol. 348, pp. 341–367, 1984.

[73] A. L. Hodgkin and A. F. Huxley, "A quantitative description of membrane current and its application to conduction and excitation in nerve," *The Journal of Physiology*, vol. 117, no. 4, pp. 500–544, 1952.

[74] S. Dokos, B. Celler, and N. Lovell, "Ion currents underlying sinoatrial node pacemaker activity: a new single cell mathematical model," *Journal of Theoretical Biology*, vol. 181, no. 3, pp. 245–272, 1996.

[75] H. Zhang, A. V. Holden, I. Kodama et al., "Mathematical models of action potentials in the periphery and center of the rabbit sinoatrial node," *American Journal of Physiology Heart and Circulatory Physiology*, vol. 279, no. 1, pp. H397–H421, 2000.

[76] S. S. Demir, J. W. Clark, C. R. Murphey, and W. R. Giles, "A mathematical model of a rabbit sinoatrial node cell," *American Journal of Physiology*, vol. 266, no. 3, pp. C832–C852, 1994.

[77] Y. Kurata, I. Hisatome, S. Imanishi, and T. Shibamoto, "Dynamical description of sinoatrial node pacemaking: improved mathematical model for primary pacemaker cell," *American Journal of Physiology Heart and Circulatory Physiology*, vol. 283, no. 5, pp. H2074–H2101, 2002.

[78] N. Sarai, S. Matsuoka, S. Kuratomi, K. Ono, and A. Noma, "Role of individual ionic current systems in the SA node hypothesized by a model study," *Japanese Journal of Physiology*, vol. 53, no. 2, pp. 125–134, 2003.

[79] S. Matsuoka, N. Sarai, S. Kuratomi, K. Ono, and A. Noma, "Role of individual ionic current systems in ventricular cells hypothesized by a model study," *Japanese Journal of Physiology*, vol. 53, no. 2, pp. 105–123, 2003.

[80] R. Wilders, H. J. Jongsma, and A. C. G. van Ginneken, "Pacemaker activity of the rabbit sinoatrial node. A comparison of mathematical models," *Biophysical Journal*, vol. 60, no. 5, pp. 1202–1216, 1991.

[81] Z.-W. Liu, A.-R. Zou, S. S. Demir, J. W. Clark, and R. D. Nathan, "Characterization of a hyperpolarization-activated inward current in cultured pacemaker cells from the sinoatrial node," *Journal of Molecular and Cellular Cardiology*, vol. 28, no. 12, pp. 2523–2535, 1996.

[82] H. Honjo, M. R. Boyett, I. Kodama, and J. Toyama, "Correlation between electrical activity and the size of rabbit sino-atrial node cells," *Journal of Physiology*, vol. 496, no. 3, pp. 795–808, 1996.

[83] D. Noble, D. DiFrancesco, and J. C. Denyer, "Ionic mechanisms in normal and abnormal cardiac pacemaker activity," in *Neuronal and Cellular Oscillators*, J. W. Jacklet, Ed., pp. 59–85, Marcel Dekker, New York, NY, USA, 1989.

[84] C. Altomare, B. Terragni, C. Brioschi et al., "Heteromeric HCN1-HCN4 channels: a comparison with native pacemaker channels from the rabbit sinoatrial node," *Journal of Physiology*, vol. 549, no. 2, pp. 347–359, 2003.

[85] A. Barbuti, M. Baruscotti, and D. DiFrancesco, "The pacemaker current: from basics to the clinics," *Journal of Cardiovascular Electrophysiology*, vol. 18, no. 3, pp. 342–347, 2007.

[86] D. DiFrancesco and D. Noble, "Implications of the reinterpretation of iK2 for the modelling of the electrical activity of the pacemaker tissues in the heart," in *Cardiac Rate and Rhythm: Physiological, Morphological and Developmental Aspects*, L. N. Boumann and H. J. Jongsma, Eds., pp. 93–128, Martinus Nijhoff, The Hague, The Netherlands, 1982.

[87] A. Zaza, R. B. Robinson, and D. DiFrancesco, "Basal responses of the L-type Ca^{2+} and hyperpolarization-activated currents to autonomie agonists in the rabbit sino-atrial node," *Journal of Physiology*, vol. 491, no. 2, pp. 347–355, 1996.

[88] S. Dokos, B. G. Celler, and N. H. Lovell, "Vagal control of sinoatrial rhythm: a mathematical model," *Journal of Theoretical Biology*, vol. 182, no. 1, pp. 21–44, 1996.

[89] S. S. Demir, J. W. Clark, and W. R. Giles, "Parasympathetic modulation of sinoatrial node pacemaker activity in rabbit heart: a unifying model," *American Journal of Physiology*, vol. 276, no. 6, pp. H2221–H2244, 1999.

[90] H. Zhang, A. V. Holden, D. Noble, and M. R. Boyett, "Analysis of the chronotropic effect of acetylcholine on sinoatrial node cells," *Journal of Cardiovascular Electrophysiology*, vol. 13, no. 5, pp. 465–474, 2002.

[91] V. A. Maltsev and E. G. Lakatta, "A novel quantitative explanation for the autonomic modulation of cardiac pacemaker cell automaticity via a dynamic system of sarcolemmal and intracellular proteins," *American Journal of Physiology Heart and Circulatory Physiology*, vol. 298, no. 6, pp. H2010–H2023, 2010.

[92] H. Zhang, T. Butters, I. Adeniran et al., "Modeling the chronotropic effect of isoprenaline on rabbit sinoatrial node," *Frontiers in Physiology*, vol. 3, p. 241, 2012.

[93] D. DiFrancesco, "Dual allosteric modulation of pacemaker (f) channels by cAMP and voltage in rabbit SA node," *Journal of Physiology*, vol. 515, no. 2, pp. 367–376, 1999.

[94] A. Zaza, M. Micheletti, A. Brioschi, and M. Rocchetti, "Ionic currents during sustained pacemaker activity in rabbit sino-atrial myocytes," *Journal of Physiology*, vol. 505, no. 3, pp. 677–688, 1997.

20

Large Scale Association Analysis for Drug Addiction: Results from SNP to Gene

Xiaobo Guo,[1,2] Zhifa Liu,[1] Xueqin Wang,[2,3] and Heping Zhang[1]

[1] *Department of Biostatistics, Yale University School of Public Health, New Haven, CT 06520, USA*
[2] *Department of Statistical Science, School of Mathematics and Computational Science, Sun Yat-sen University, Guangzhou, Guangdong, China*
[3] *Zhongshan School of Medicine, Sun Yat-sen University, Guangzhou, Guangdong, China*

Correspondence should be addressed to Heping Zhang, heping.zhang@yale.edu

Academic Editors: R. Jiang, W. Tian, J. Wan, and X. Zhao

Many genetic association studies used single nucleotide polymorphisms (SNPs) data to identify genetic variants for complex diseases. Although SNP-based associations are most common in genome-wide association studies (GWAS), gene-based association analysis has received increasing attention in understanding genetic etiologies for complex diseases. While both methods have been used to analyze the same data, few genome-wide association studies compare the results or observe the connection between them. We performed a comprehensive analysis of the data from the Study of Addiction: Genetics and Environment (SAGE) and compared the results from the SNP-based and gene-based analyses. Our results suggest that the gene-based method complements the individual SNP-based analysis, and conceptually they are closely related. In terms of gene findings, our results validate many genes that were either reported from the analysis of the same dataset or based on animal studies for substance dependence.

1. Introduction

Genome-wide association studies (GWAS) have become a powerful tool in the identification of susceptible loci for numerous diseases [1]. A typical strategy in GWAS is to analyze single nucleotide polymorphisms (SNPs) individually and select the top SNPs by setting a stringent threshold for the P value. Then the top SNPs were mapped into functional regions such as a gene or pathway to facilitate further investigation of the corresponding gene and disease. Based on SNP-based association analysis, many genetic variants underlying complex diseases or traits were detected [2, 3]. Due to the large number of SNPs with each of which entails an association test, it is essential to control the type I error or false discovery rate [4]. A predefined P value $< 5 \times 10^{-8}$ is usually used as the threshold to declare a genome-wide significance SNP, which also limits the discoveries of the genes that are important to the disease. Also importantly, susceptible SNPs generally explain a small fraction of the risk—a phenomenon commonly referred to as the "missing heritability" [5, 6]. To alleviate this

problem, alternative methods have emerged to complement the simple SNP-based methods. Among those methods, gene-based analysis [7–9], which jointly analyzes the SNPs within genes, is a promising solution to improve the power of GWAS. Compared with the SNP-based approach, gene-based association analysis has certain advantages. First, gene is a unit of heredity and function, and hence the gene-based association approaches can provide direct insights into the heredity and functional mechanisms of complex traits [10]. Second, from the statistical perspective, the gene-based association approaches reduce the number of association tests in the order of millions to about 20,000 gene-based tests, which dramatically reduces the chance of false discovery. In addition, the gene-based methods are not affected by the heterogeneity of a single locus. Hence, the results are highly consistent across populations [11], which enhances the likelihood of replication.

Gene-based methods have been successfully applied to GWAS of complex diseases, including Crohn's disease [7], type 1 diabetes [12], and melanoma [8]. Despite the above-noted features of the gene-based association approach, there are few comparisons of genetic association analyses between SNP and gene-based methods. Here, we compare and relate these two approaches using the data from the Study of Addition: Genetics and Environment (SAGE) [13].

Recent studies show that there are many candidate genes associated with substance dependence. For example, GABRA2, CHRM2, ADH4, PKNOX2, GABRG3, TAS2R16, SNCA, OPRK1, and PDYN are well studied for alcohol addiction and have been replicated in many samples [13–28]. However, other candidate genes, such as KIAA0040, ALDH1A1, DKK2, and MANBA [25, 27, 29, 30], remain illusive. For addiction to nicotine, CHRNA5, CHRNA3, CHRNB4, and CSMD1 have been replicated in many studies [31–39].

Based on the analysis of the SAGE data, we report a number of susceptible loci at the SNP and/or gene levels, which validate many susceptibility loci that have been reported to be associated with substance dependence [13, 14, 25, 27, 29, 37, 38, 40–44]. Meanwhile, both SNP- and gene-based analyses reveal three novel risk genes: NCK2, DSG3, and PUSL1.

2. Materials and Methods

2.1. Dataset and Study Design. The dataset included 4,121 subjects in SAGE with six categories of substance dependence data: alcohol, cocaine, marijuana, nicotine, opiates, and other dependencies on drugs. The data were downloaded from dbGaP (study accession phs000092.v1.p1) [13]. SAGE [13] is a large case-control study which aims to detect susceptible genetic variants for addition. The subjects were recruited from eight study sites in seven states and the District of Columbia in the United States. All subjects' life time dependencies on these six dependencies are diagnosed by using the Diagnostic and Statistical Manual of Mental Disorders, Fourth Edition (DSM-IV). All samples were genotyped on ILLUMINA Human 1 M platform at the Center for Inherited Disease Research in Johns Hopkins University. In this paper, we strictly followed the quality control/quality assurance as we did in our previous analysis [14]. Genome-wide SNP data were filtered by setting thresholds: MAF > 5% and call rate > 90%. In addition, 60 duplicate genotype samples and 9 individuals with ethnic backgrounds other than African origin or European origin were excluded in our analysis. Finally, 3,627 unrelated samples with 859,185 autosomal SNPs passed the quality control procedures. To avoid population stratification, the dataset was stratified into four subsamples: 1,393 white women, 1,131 white men, 568 black women, and 535 black men. To capture most of the gene coding and regulatory variants, SNPs are considered being mapped to a gene if their physical locations are within 20 kilobases (kb) 5′ upstream and 10 kilobases (kb) 3′ downstream of gene coding regions [26]. In addition, SNPs are also assigned to a gene if they are in strong LD ($r^2 > 0.9$) with the initially assigned SNPs within the gene [10]. Together, around 533,639 SNPs were assigned to 18,699 protein coding genes (28.6 ± 47.7 (mean $\pm$ SD) SNPs per gene).

Following the conventional standards, we used $5.0E - 8$ and $2.5E - 6$ as the genome-wide significant thresholds for SNP-based and gene-based methods, respectively [4]. To increase the power of detecting potentially important SNPs that do not meet the stringent thresholds, we also considered relaxed thresholds. Specifically, SNPs with $P < 1.0E - 5$ and genes $P < 5.0E - 4$ were considered further. These P values are referred to as relaxed significance thresholds below. The selected SNPs were then mapped into the corresponding genes by the mapping rule proposed above.

2.2. Genetic Association Test at SNP and Gene Levels. We took several steps in testing the associations between genetic variants (SNP or gene) and substance dependenice. First, the P value of each SNP was evaluated by the logistic regression, and then the correlation coefficients (r^2) of all SNP pairs were calculated. The computation was performed in PLINK software (version 1.07) [45]. In the second step, we implemented the gene-based analysis in the open-source tool: Knowledge-Based Mining System for Genome-Wide Genetic Studies (KGG, version 2.0) [46] based on the association test results and LD files obtained from PLINK. Simes procedure (GATES) was employed in the gene-based association test [7]. Specifically, assume that m SNPs are assigned to a gene; an association test such as through the traditional logistic regression or linear regression is used to examine the association between the phenotype and each single SNP. This step yields m P values for m SNPs. GATES combines the available m P values within a gene by using a modified Simes test to give a gene-based P value. The summary P value is defined as

$$P_G = \text{Min} \left(\frac{m_e p_{(j)}}{m_{e(j)}} \right), \tag{1}$$

where $p_{(j)}$ is the jth smallest P value among the m SNPs; m_e is the effective number of independent P values among m SNPs within the gene, and $m_{e(j)}$ is the effective number of independent P values among the top j SNPs. The effective number of independent P values was derived by accounting for the LD structure among the specified SNPs; we refer to [7] on the calculation.

In order to compare the performance of the SNP-based and gene-based methods, in the SNP-based method, we selected those SNPs whose P values were less than $1.0E - 5$ and then mapped them into the corresponding genes. This allows us to compare the susceptible genes identified by both methods discussed above.

3. Results

3.1. Detecting Susceptibility Loci at the Relaxed Significance Level. Table 1 summarizes the susceptible genes identified by the SNP-based association test and gene-based association test at the relaxed significance level. In total, 207 genes passed the relaxed gene-based threshold, whereas only 64 genes with SNPs passed the relaxed SNP-based threshold.

Next, we performed a literature search on the genetic regions which contain the identified genes and filtered the

TABLE 1: Summary statistics for susceptibility loci identified by gene-based method and SNP-based method.

	Alcohol		Cocaine		Marijuana		Nicotine		Opiates		Other	
	G	S	G	S	G	S	G	S	G	S	G	S
Black men	4	3	4	1	6	2	5	2	8	2	9	5
Black women	4	3	8	5	9	3	7	3	3	1	6	3
White men	16	3	9	2	10	3	4	1	11	3	3	1
White women	20	5	12	2	10	2	11	1	4	5	24	3

G refers to gene-based method. S refers to SNP-based method.

TABLE 2: Summary of the candidate genes identified by the gene-based and SNP-based methods.

Chr	Gene	Source	P value (gene-based)[a]	Min P value (SNP-based)[b]	Detected SD[c]	Reported SD	Reference
1	KIAA0040	White women	$3.75E - 05$	$2.60E - 06$	Alcohol	Alcohol	[27, 44]
2	HAAO	White women	$4.40E - 04$	$3.02E - 05$	Cocaine	Alcohol	[41]
2	NCK2	Black men	$2.70E - 06$	$1.10E - 07$	Opiates	NA	NA
3	SH3BP5	White men	$1.20E - 04$	$4.24E - 06$	Cocaine	Alcohol	[13]
4	MANBA	White men	$4.63E - 04$	$3.47E - 05$	Alcohol	Alcohol	[29]
7	RELN	White men	$8.53E - 04$	$5.32E - 06$	Cocaine	Smoking	[37]
8	CSMD1	Black women	$1.23E - 02$	$8.50E - 06$	Nicotine	Smoking	[37, 38]
11	LRP5	White men	$4.01E - 05$	$1.58E - 06$	Opiates	Smoking	[42]
11	PKNOX2	White women	$1.84E - 04$	$2.20E - 06$	Alcohol	Alcohol	[13, 27, 41]
12	IFNG	White women	$1.16E - 04$	$1.57E - 05$	Opiates	Smoking	[37]
18	FAM38B	Black women	$9.24E - 04$	$5.61E - 06$	Cocaine	Smoking	[40]
18	PTPRM	Black women	$2.21E - 3$	$9.50E - 06$	Marijuana	Alcohol	[43]
22	MAPK1	Black women	$2.79E - 04$	$3.52E - 05$	Marijuana	Alcohol	[25]

[a]P value (gene-based): the P value obtained by the gene-based association test;
[b]min P value (SNP-based): the minimal P value of the SNPs within the corresponding gene;
[c]SD: substance dependence.

susceptible genetic regions which have been reported to associate with substance dependence for further investigation. In Table 2, we listed the filtered genes, their associated substance dependence type, the P values for the gene-based method, the minimal P value of SNPs within a gene, and their literature references and reported substance dependence.

In Figure 1, we plot the filtered genes obtained from the SNP-based and gene-based analyses by the position on the chromosomes against their log-transformed P values, $-\log_{10}(P)$. Each point for the SNP-based analysis in Figure 1 corresponds to the smallest SNP-based P value within the gene.

Overall, five genes, NCK2 (opiates dependence in black men), SH3BP5 (cocaine dependence in white men), LRP5 (opiates dependence in white men), KIAA0040 (alcohol dependence in white women), and PKNOX2 (alcohol dependence in white women), were identified by both the SNP-based and gene-based methods as meeting either of the relaxed significance levels for a specific dependence and within a gender-racial group. Four genes, MAPK1 (marijuana dependence in black women), MANBA (alcohol dependence in white men), HAAO (cocaine dependence in white women), and IFNG (opiates dependence in white women), met the threshold by the gene-based method only. We found that the significant signal of gene MAPK1 was mainly driven by SNPs: rs7290469 ($P = 3.25E-5$), rs9610271 ($P = 4.19E-5$), rs9610417 ($P = 5.38E-5$), and rs2876981

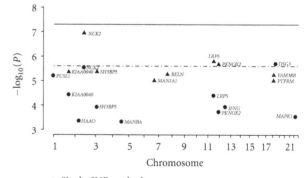

FIGURE 1: Comparison of candidate genes associated with substance dependence by the SNP- and gene-based analyses. A triangle represents the $-\log10$ transformed P value of the marked gene from the gene-based analysis, and a dot represents the $-\log10$ transformed the minimal P value of the SNPs within the marked gene. The solid and dashed ones are the genome-wide thresholds of SNP- and gene-based significance, respectively.

($P = 7.51E - 5$). The P values for these SNPs are slightly greater than the relaxed SNP-based threshold ($P < 1.0E - 5$), and hence the SNP-based method failed to detect them.

TABLE 3: Summary of genome-wide significant genes at the gene level (P value $< 1.0E - 5$) and their top SNPs with P value $< 1.0E - 3$.

Population	Substance dependence	Gene	Gene's P value	Top SNPs	SNP's P value
Black men	Opiates	NCK2	$2.70E - 06$	rs2377339	$1.10E - 07$
				rs7589342	$1.45E - 04$
				rs12995333	$1.89E - 04$
				rs12053259	$2.31E - 04$
				rs6747023	$3.90E - 04$
				rs879900	$7.72E - 04$
White men	Nicotine	DSG3	$1.99E - 06$	rs6701037	$1.20E - 07$
				rs1057302	$3.93E - 07$
				rs6425323	$2.94E - 04$
				rs1057239	$3.35E - 04$

Furthermore, four other genes, FAM38B (cocaine dependence in black women), PTPRM (marijuana dependence in black women), CSMD1 (nicotine dependence in black women), and RELN (cocaine dependence in white men), contain at least one SNP that met the SNP-based relaxed threshold of significance. The gene-based P values for FAM38B, PTPRM, and RELN are $9.27E - 4$, $2.21E - 3$, and $8.53E - 4$, respectively, which are greater than yet at the same order as the relaxed threshold (P value $< 5.0E - 4$). For CSMD1, 1,934 SNPs were mapped into it. Its signal was mainly determined by only five SNPs: rs2624087 (P value $= 8.50E - 6$), rs4875371 (P value $= 4.0E - 4$), rs2623607 (P value $= 6.89E - 4$), rs10503267 (P value $= 7.22E - 4$), and rs4875372 (P value $= 8.18E - 4$). Because there were only 5.3% of the SNPs (103 SNPs) with P value less than 0.05, the overall association from the gene became less significant.

3.2. Genome-Wide Significant Loci. Since none of the SNPs attained the genome-wide significance for any dependence by the SNP-based method, in this section we will only focus on the results from the gene-based method.

Table 3 presents the genes with gene-based P value $< 1.0E - 5$. This method identified one genome-wide significant gene, DSG3 (P value $= 1.99E - 6$) for nicotine dependence in white men. The P value of gene NCK2: $2.70E - 6$ is very close to the genome-wide significant threshold, which provided very strong evidence for the association of opiates in black men. As shown in Table 3, both NCK2 and DSG3 contained SNPs with strong signals; they are rs2377339 (P value $= 1.09E - 7$) for NCK2 gene and rs6701037 (P value $= 1.20E - 7$) and rs1057302 (P value $= 3.93E - 7$) for DSG3 gene. However, none of these SNPs reached genome-wide significance.

4. Discussion

In this paper, we thoroughly analyzed the SAGE data from the SNP-based and gene-based methods, and compared the results obtained from these two methods. Specifically, for each sex-racial group, we performed association analysis for the six categories of substance dependence separately. The gene-based method appears to be more powerful in detecting susceptibility loci.

Most of the genes identified in our study are supported by various reports in the literature related to the genetics of substance dependence [47, 48]. Based on some of the genes that we identified, here common genetic variants among different substance dependencies may exist [49].

Overall, we did not detect any genome-wide significant SNP when using the SNPs-based method. However, one gene, DSG3, is genome-wide significantly ($P = 2.70E - 6$) associated with nicotine dependence in the white men, according to the gene-based method. Another gene, NCK2, is nearly genome-wide significant ($P = 2.7E - 6$) in its association with substance dependence.

The SNP-based method and gene-based method are closely related. In fact, the SNP-based method can be viewed as a gene-based method using the extreme function, namely, the minimal P value of the SNPs within a gene, whereas the typical gene-based method uses a weighted approach. The advantages and limitations of these two approaches are similar to those between the extreme function and a weighted average.

We should point out that both the SNP-based and gene-based methods have their own advantages and disadvantages. The SNP-based method has its unique strength in identifying genes with only a small number of significant SNPs. However, since the SNP-based method focuses on a single SNP at a time, it is less powerful to detect a gene whose SNPs have weak marginal effects, but a strong joint effect. In our analysis, 207 genes passed the relaxed gene-based threshold, whereas only 64 genes passed the relaxed SNP-based threshold.

Both the SNP-based and gene-based methods can be conducted conveniently in commonly available software, such as PLINK [45] for the SNP-based method and KGG [46] for the gene-based method. For the SNP-based analysis, PLINK is the most convenient platform. For the SAGE GWAS data, it took about 25 minutes to do a genome-wide SNP scan on a regular desktop computer (Intel Core 2, 4 GB Memory). In our gene-based analysis, we used the SNP-based association results and the linkage disequilibrium (LD) files from PLINK as the input to the KGG software. After this preparation, it took about 30 minutes to perform the gene-based association scan with the same desktop as mentioned above.

Authors' Contributions

X. Guo and Z. Liu are contributed equally to this work.

Acknowledgments

This work was supported by Grant R01 DA016750-09 from the National Institute on Drug Abuse. Funding support for the Study of Addiction: Genetics and Environment (SAGE) was provided through the NIH Genes, Environment and Health Initiative (GEI) (U01 HG004422). SAGE is one of the genome-wide association studies funded as part of the Gene Environment Association Studies (GENEVA) under GEI. Assistance with phenotype harmonization and genotype cleaning, as well as with general study coordination, was provided by the GENEVA Coordinating Center (U01 HG004446). Assistance with data cleaning was provided by the National Center for Biotechnology Information. Support for the collection of datasets and samples was provided by the Collaborative Study on the Genetics of Alcoholism (COGA; U10 AA008401), the Collaborative Genetic Study of Nicotine Dependence (COGEND; P01 CA089392), and the Family Study of Cocaine Dependence (FSCD; R01 DA013423). Funding support for genotyping, which was performed at the Johns Hopkins University Center for Inherited Disease Research, was provided by the NIH GEI (U01HG004438), the National Institute on Alcohol Abuse and Alcoholism, the National Institute on Drug Abuse, and the NIH contract "High throughput genotyping for studying the genetic contributions to human disease" (HHSN268200782096C). The datasets used for the analyses described in this paper were obtained from dbGaP at http://www.ncbi.nlm.nih.gov/projects/gap/cgi-bin/study.cgi?study_id=phs000092.v1.p1 through dbGaP accession number phs000092.v1.p. The authors have no conflict of interests.

References

[1] M. I. McCarthy, G. R. Abecasis, L. R. Cardon et al., "Genome-wide association studies for complex traits: consensus, uncertainty and challenges," *Nature Reviews Genetics*, vol. 9, no. 5, pp. 356–369, 2008.

[2] P. R. Burton, D. G. Clayton, L. R. Cardon et al., "Genome-wide association study of 14,000 cases of seven common diseases and 3,000 shared controls," *Nature*, vol. 447, no. 7145, pp. 661–678, 2007.

[3] D. J. Hunter, P. Kraft, K. B. Jacobs et al., "A genome-wide association study identifies alleles in FGFR2 associated with risk of sporadic postmenopausal breast cancer," *Nature Genetics*, vol. 39, no. 7, pp. 870–874, 2007.

[4] F. Dudbridge and A. Gusnanto, "Estimation of significance thresholds for genomewide association scans," *Genetic Epidemiology*, vol. 32, no. 3, pp. 227–234, 2008.

[5] E. E. Eichler, J. Flint, G. Gibson et al., "Missing heritability and strategies for finding the underlying causes of complex disease," *Nature Reviews Genetics*, vol. 11, no. 6, pp. 446–450, 2010.

[6] T. A. Manolio, F. S. Collins, N. J. Cox et al., "Finding the missing heritability of complex diseases," *Nature*, vol. 461, no. 7265, pp. 747–753, 2009.

[7] M. X. Li, H. S. Gui, J. S. H. Kwan, and P. C. Sham, "GATES: a rapid and powerful gene-based association test using extended Simes procedure," *American Journal of Human Genetics*, vol. 88, no. 3, pp. 283–293, 2011.

[8] J. Z. Liu, A. F. McRae, D. R. Nyholt et al., "A versatile gene-based test for genome-wide association studies," *American Journal of Human Genetics*, vol. 87, no. 1, pp. 139–145, 2010.

[9] X. Guo, Z. Liu, X. Wang, and H. Zhang, "Genetic association test for multiple traits at gene level," *Genetic Epidemiology*. In press.

[10] K. Wang, M. Li, and H. Hakonarson, "Analysing biological pathways in genome-wide association studies," *Nature Reviews Genetics*, vol. 11, no. 12, pp. 843–854, 2010.

[11] B. M. Neale and P. C. Sham, "The future of association studies: gene-based analysis and replication," *American Journal of Human Genetics*, vol. 75, no. 3, pp. 353–362, 2004.

[12] B. Lehne, C. M. Lewis, and T. Schlitt, "From SNPs to genes: disease association at the gene level," *PLoS ONE*, vol. 6, no. 6, Article ID e20133, 2011.

[13] L. J. Bierut, A. Agrawal, K. K. Bucholz et al., "A genome-wide association study of alcohol dependence," *Proceedings of the National Academy of Sciences of the United States of America*, vol. 107, no. 11, pp. 5082–5087, 2010.

[14] X. Chen, K. Cho, B. H. Singer, and H. Zhang, "The nuclear transcription factor PKNOX2 is a candidate gene for substance dependence in European-origin Women," *PLoS ONE*, vol. 6, no. 1, Article ID e16002, 2011.

[15] J. Clarimon, R. R. Gray, L. N. Williams et al., "Linkage disequilibrium and association analysis of α-synuclein and alcohol and drug dependence in two American Indian populations," *Alcoholism: Clinical and Experimental Research*, vol. 31, no. 4, pp. 546–554, 2007.

[16] D. M. Dick, H. J. Edenberg, X. Xuei et al., "Association of GABRG3 with alcohol dependence," *Alcoholism: Clinical and Experimental Research*, vol. 28, no. 1, pp. 4–9, 2004.

[17] H. J. Edenberg, D. M. Dick, X. Xuei et al., "Variations in GABRA2, encoding the α2 subunit of the GABA a receptor, are associated with alcohol dependence and with brain oscillations," *American Journal of Human Genetics*, vol. 74, no. 4, pp. 705–714, 2004.

[18] H. J. Edenberg and T. Foroud, "The genetics of alcoholism: identifying specific genes through family studies," *Addiction Biology*, vol. 11, no. 3-4, pp. 386–396, 2006.

[19] H. J. Edenberg, J. Wang, H. Tian et al., "A regulatory variation in OPRK1, the gene encoding the κ-opioid receptor, is associated with alcohol dependence," *Human Molecular Genetics*, vol. 17, no. 12, pp. 1783–1789, 2008.

[20] T. Foroud, L. F. Wetherill, T. Liang et al., "Association of alcohol craving with α-synuclein (SNCA)," *Alcoholism: Clinical and Experimental Research*, vol. 31, no. 4, pp. 537–545, 2007.

[21] J. Gelernter, R. Gueorguieva, H. R. Kranzler et al., "Opioid receptor gene (OPRM1, OPRK1, and OPRD1) variants and response to naltrexone treatment for alcohol dependence: results from the VA Cooperative Study," *Alcoholism: Clinical and Experimental Research*, vol. 31, no. 4, pp. 555–563, 2007.

[22] T. Reich, "A genomic survey of alcohol dependence and related phenotypes: results from the Collaborative Study on the Genetics of Alcoholism (COGA)," *Alcoholism: Clinical and Experimental Research*, vol. 20, supplement 8, pp. 133A–137A, 1996.

[23] T. Reich, H. J. Edenberg, A. Goate et al. et al., "Genome-wide search for genes affecting the risk for alcohol dependence,"

American Journal of Medical Genetics, vol. 81, no. 3, pp. 207–215, 1998.

[24] J. Song, D. L. Koller, T. Foroud et al., "Association of GABAA receptors and alcohol dependence and the effects of genetic imprinting," *American Journal of Medical Genetics*, vol. 117, no. 1, pp. 39–45, 2003.

[25] B. Tabakoff, L. Saba, M. Printz et al. et al., "Genetical genomic determinants of alcohol consumption in rats and humans," *BMC Biology*, vol. 7, article 70, 2009.

[26] J. C. Wang, A. L. Hinrichs, S. Bertelsen et al., "Functional variants in TAS2R38 and TAS2R16 influence alcohol consumption in high-risk families of African-American origin," *Alcoholism: Clinical and Experimental Research*, vol. 31, no. 2, pp. 209–215, 2007.

[27] K. S. Wang, X. F. Liu, Q. Y. Zhang, Y. Pan, N. Aragam, and M. Zeng :, "A meta-analysis of two genome-wide association studies identifies 3 new loci for alcohol dependence," *Journal of Psychiatric Research*, vol. 45, no. 11, pp. 1419–1425, 2011.

[28] H. Zhang, H. R. Kranzler, B. Z. Yang, X. Luo, and J. Gelernter, "The OPRD1 and OPRK1 loci in alcohol or drug dependence: OPRD1 variation modulates substance dependence risk," *Molecular Psychiatry*, vol. 13, no. 5, pp. 531–543, 2008.

[29] G. Kalsi, P. H. Kuo, F. Aliev et al., "A systematic gene-based screen of chr4q22-q32 identifies association of a novel susceptibility gene, DKK2, with the quantitative trait of alcohol dependence symptom counts," *Human Molecular Genetics*, vol. 19, no. 20, Article ID ddq326, p. 4121, 2010.

[30] P. H. Kuo, G. Kalsi, C. A. Prescott et al., "Association of ADH and ALDH genes with alcohol dependence in the Irish Affected Sib Pair Study of alcohol dependence (IASPSAD) Sample," *Alcoholism: Clinical and Experimental Research*, vol. 32, no. 5, pp. 785–795, 2008.

[31] L. J. Bierut, "Genetic variation that contributes to nicotine dependence," *Pharmacogenomics*, vol. 8, no. 8, pp. 881–883, 2007.

[32] L. J. Bierut, P. A. F. Madden, N. Breslau et al., "Novel genes identified in a high-density genome wide association study for nicotine dependence," *Human Molecular Genetics*, vol. 16, no. 1, pp. 24–35, 2007.

[33] N. Caporaso, F. Gu, N. Chatterjee et al., "Genome-wide and candidate gene association study of cigarette smoking behaviors," *PLoS ONE*, vol. 4, no. 2, Article ID e4653, 2009.

[34] L. S. Chen, E. O. Johnson, N. Breslau et al., "Interplay of genetic risk factors and parent monitoring in risk for nicotine dependence," *Addiction*, vol. 104, no. 10, pp. 1731–1740, 2009.

[35] N. L. Saccone, S. F. Saccone, A. L. Hinrichs et al., "Multiple distinct risk loci for nicotine dependence identified by dense coverage of the complete family of nicotinic receptor subunit (CHRN) genes," *American Journal of Medical Genetics, Part B*, vol. 150, no. 4, pp. 453–466, 2009.

[36] S. F. Saccone, A. L. Hinrichs, N. L. Saccone et al., "Cholinergic nicotinic receptor genes implicated in a nicotine dependence association study targeting 348 candidate genes with 3713 SNPs," *Human Molecular Genetics*, vol. 16, no. 1, pp. 36–49, 2007.

[37] G. R. Uhl, T. Drgon, C. Johnson et al., "Genome-wide association for smoking cessation success: participants in the Patch in Practice trial of nicotine replacement," *Pharmacogenomics*, vol. 11, no. 3, pp. 357–367, 2010.

[38] G. R. Uhl, Q. R. Liu, T. Drgon et al., "Molecular genetics of successful smoking cessation: convergent genome-wide association study results," *Archives of General Psychiatry*, vol. 65, no. 6, pp. 683–693, 2008.

[39] R. B. Weiss, T. B. Baker, D. S. Cannon et al., "A candidate gene approach identifies the CHRNA5-A3-B4 region as a risk factor for age-dependent nicotine addiction," *PLoS Genetics*, vol. 4, no. 7, Article ID e1000125, 2008.

[40] M. J. Ahn, H. H. Won, J. Lee et al. et al., "The 18p11. 22 locus is associated with never smoker non-small cell lung cancer susceptibility in Korean populations," *Human Genetics*, vol. 131, no. 3, pp. 365–372, 2012.

[41] D. M. Dick, J. Meyers, F. Aliev et al., "Evidence for genes on chromosome 2 contributing to alcohol dependence with conduct disorder and suicide attempts," *American Journal of Medical Genetics, Part B*, vol. 153, no. 6, pp. 1179–1188, 2010.

[42] P. F. Giampietro, C. McCarty, B. Mukesh et al., "The role of cigarette smoking and statins in the development of postmenopausal osteoporosis: a pilot study utilizing the marshfield clinic personalized medicine cohort," *Osteoporosis International*, vol. 21, no. 3, pp. 467–477, 2010.

[43] G. Joslyn, A. Ravindranathan, G. Brush, M. Schuckit, and R. L. White, "Human variation in alcohol response is influenced by variation in neuronal signaling genes," *Alcoholism: Clinical and Experimental Research*, vol. 34, no. 5, pp. 800–812, 2010.

[44] L. J. Zuo, J. Gelernter, C. K. Zhang et al. et al., "Genome-wide association study of alcohol dependence implicates KIAA0040 on chromosome 1q," *Neuropsychopharmacology*, vol. 37, no. 2, pp. 557–566, 2012.

[45] S. Purcell, B. Neale, K. Todd-Brown et al., "PLINK: a tool set for whole-genome association and population-based linkage analyses," *American Journal of Human Genetics*, vol. 81, no. 3, pp. 559–575, 2007.

[46] http://bioinfo1.hku.hk:13080/kggweb//.

[47] K. R. Merikangas, M. Stolar, D. E. Stevens et al., "Familial transmission of substance use disorders," *Archives of General Psychiatry*, vol. 55, no. 11, pp. 973–979, 1998.

[48] W. R. True, A. C. Heath, J. F. Scherrer et al., "Interrelationship of genetic and environmental influences on conduct disorder and alcohol and marijuana dependence symptoms," *American Journal of Medical Genetics*, vol. 88, no. 4, pp. 391–397, 1999.

[49] M. D. Li and M. Burmeister, "New insights into the genetics of addiction," *Nature Reviews Genetics*, vol. 10, no. 4, pp. 225–231, 2009.

21

Network Completion Using Dynamic Programming and Least-Squares Fitting

Natsu Nakajima,[1] Takeyuki Tamura,[1] Yoshihiro Yamanishi,[2] Katsuhisa Horimoto,[3] and Tatsuya Akutsu[1]

[1] Bioinformatics Center, Institute for Chemical Research, Kyoto University Gokasho, Uji, Kyoto 611-0011, Japan
[2] Division of System Cohort, Multi-scale Research Center for Medical Science, Medical Institute of Bioregulation, Kyushu University, 3-1-1 Maidashi, Higashi-ku, Fukuoka, Fukuoka 812-8582, Japan
[3] Computational Biology Research Center, National Institute of Advanced Industrial Science and Technology, 2-4-7 Aomi, Koto-ku, Tokyo 135-0064, Japan

Correspondence should be addressed to Tatsuya Akutsu, takutsu@kuicr.kyoto-u.ac.jp

Academic Editors: W. Tian and X.-M. Zhao

We consider the problem of network completion, which is to make the minimum amount of modifications to a given network so that the resulting network is most consistent with the observed data. We employ here a certain type of differential equations as gene regulation rules in a genetic network, gene expression time series data as observed data, and deletions and additions of edges as basic modification operations. In addition, we assume that the numbers of deleted and added edges are specified. For this problem, we present a novel method using dynamic programming and least-squares fitting and show that it outputs a network with the minimum sum squared error in polynomial time if the maximum indegree of the network is bounded by a constant. We also perform computational experiments using both artificially generated and real gene expression time series data.

1. Introduction

Analysis of biological networks is one of the central research topics in computational systems biology. In particular, extensive studies have been done on inference of genetic networks using gene expression time series data, and a number of computational methods have been proposed, which include methods based on Boolean networks [1, 2], Bayesian networks [3, 4], time-delayed Bayesian networks [5], graphical Gaussian models [6–8], differential equations [9, 10], mutual information [11, 12], and linear classification [13]. However, there is not yet an established or standard method for inference of genetic networks, and thus it still remains a challenging problem.

One of the possible reasons for the difficulty of inference is that the amount of available high-quality gene expression time series data is still not enough, and thus it is intrinsically difficult to infer the correct or nearly correct network from such a small amount of data. Therefore, it is reasonable to try to develop another approach. For that purpose, we proposed an approach called network completion [14] by following Occam's razor, which is a well-known principle in scientific discovery. Network completion is, given an initial network and an observed dataset, to modify the network by the minimum amount of modifications so that the resulting network is (most) consistent with the observed data. Since we were interested in inference of signaling networks in our previous study [14], we assumed that activity levels or quantities of one or a few kinds of proteins can only be observed. Furthermore, since measurement errors were considered to be large and we were interested in theoretical analysis of computational complexity and sample complexity, we adopted the Boolean network [15] as a model of signaling networks. We proved that network completion is computationally intractable (NP-hard) even for tree-structured networks. In order to cope with this computational difficulty, we developed an integer linear programming-based method for completion of signaling pathways [16]. However, this method could not handle addition of edges because of its high computational cost.

In this paper, we propose a novel method, DPLSQ, for completing genetic networks using gene expression time series data. Different from our previous studies [14, 16], we employ a model based on differential equations and assume that expression values of all nodes can be observed. DPLSQ is a combination of least-squares fitting and dynamic programming, where least-squares fitting is used for estimating parameters in differential equations and dynamic programming is used for minimizing the sum of least-squares errors by integrating partial fitting results on individual genes under the constraint that the numbers of added and deleted edges must be equal to the specified ones. One of the important features of DPLSQ is that it can output an optimal solution (i.e., minimum squared sum) in polynomial time if the maximum indegree (i.e., the maximum number of input genes to a gene) is bounded by a constant. Although DPLSQ does not automatically find the minimum modification, it can be found by examining varying numbers of added/deleted edges, where the total number of such combinations is polynomially bounded. If a null network (i.e., a network having no edges) is given as an initial network, DPLSQ can work as an inference method for genetic networks.

In order to examine the effectiveness of DPLSQ, we perform computational experiments using artificially generated data. We also make computational comparison of DPLSQ as an inference method with other existing tools using artificial data. Furthermore, we perform computational experiments on DPLSQ using real cell cycle expression data of *Saccharomyces cerevisiae*.

2. Method

The purpose of network completion is to modify a given network with the minimum number of modifications so that the resulting network is most consistent with the observed data. In this paper, we consider additions and deletions of edges as modification operations (see Figure 1). If we begin with a network with an empty set of edges, it corresponds to network inference. Therefore, network completion includes network inference although it may not necessarily work better than the existing methods if applied to network inference.

In the following, $G(V, E)$ denotes a given network where V and E are the sets of nodes and directed edges respectively, where each node corresponds to a gene and each edge represents some direct regulation between two genes. Self loops are not allowed in E although it is possible to modify the method so that self-loops are allowed. In this paper, n denotes the number of genes (i.e., the number of nodes) and we let $V = \{v_1, \ldots, v_n\}$. For each node v_i, $e^-(v_i)$ and $\deg^-(v_i)$, respectively, denote the set of incoming edges to v_i and the number of incoming edges to v_i as defined follows:

$$e^-(v_i) = \left\{ v_j \mid \left(v_j, v_i \right) \in E \right\},$$

$$\deg^-(v_i) = \left| e^-(v_i) \right|.$$

(1)

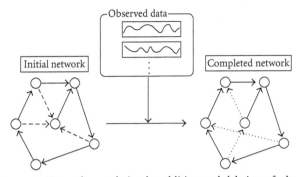

FIGURE 1: Network completion by addition and deletion of edges. Dashed edges and dotted edges denote deleted edges and added edges, respectively.

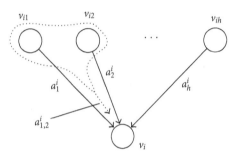

FIGURE 2: Dynamics model for a node.

DPLSQ consists of two parts: (i) parameter estimation and (ii) network structure inference. We employ least-squares fitting for the former part and dynamic programming for the latter part. Furthermore, there are three variants on the latter parts: (a) completion by addition of edges, (b) completion by deletion of edges, and (c) completion by addition and deletion of edges. Although the last case includes the first and second cases, we explain all of these for the sake of simplicity of explanation.

2.1. Model of Differential Equation and Estimation of Parameters. We assume that dynamics of each node v_i is determined by a differential equation:

$$\frac{dx_i}{dt} = a_0^i + \sum_{j=1}^h a_j^i x_{i_j} + \sum_{j<k} a_{j,k}^i x_{i_j} x_{i_k} + b^i \omega, \quad (2)$$

where $v_{i_1}, \ldots, v_{i_h}$ are incoming nodes to v_i, x_i corresponds to the expression value of the ith gene, and ω denotes a random noise. The second and third terms of the right-hand side of the equation represent linear and nonlinear effects to node v_i, respectively (see Figure 2), where positive a_j^i or $a_{j,k}^i$ corresponds to an activation effect and negative a_j^i or $a_{j,k}^i$ corresponds to an inhibition effect.

In practice, we replace derivative by difference and ignore the noise term as follows:

$$x_i(t+1) = x_i(t) + \Delta t \left(a_0^i + \sum_{j=1}^h a_j^i x_{i_j}(t) + \sum_{j<k} a_{j,k}^i x_{i_j}(t) x_{i_k}(t) \right),$$

(3)

where Δt denotes the time step.

We assume that time series data $y_i(t)$s, which correspond to $x_i(t)$s, are given for $t = 0, 1, \ldots, m$. Then, we can use the standard least-squares fitting method to estimate the parameters a_j^is and $a_{j,k}^i$s.

In applying the least-squares fitting method, we minimize the following objective function:

$$S_{i_1, i_2, \ldots, i_h}^i$$

$$= \sum_{t=1}^{m} \left| y_i(t+1) \right.$$

$$\left. - \left[y_i(t) + \Delta t \left(a_0^i + \sum_{j=1}^{h} a_j^i y_{i_j}(t) + \sum_{j<k} a_{j,k}^i y_{i_j}(t) y_{i_k}(t) \right) \right] \right|^2. \tag{4}$$

2.2. Completion by Addition of Edges. In this subsection, we consider the problem of adding k edges in total so that the sum of least-squares errors is minimized.

Let $\sigma_{k_j, j}^+$ denote the minimum least-squares error when adding k_j edges to the jth node, which is formally defined by

$$\sigma_{k_j, j}^+ = \min_{j_1, j_2, \ldots, j_{k_j}} S_{j_1, j_2, \ldots, j_{k_j}}^j, \tag{5}$$

where each v_{j_l} must be selected from $V - v_j - e^-(v_j)$. In order to avoid combinatorial explosion, we constrain the maximum k to be a small constant K and let $\sigma_{k_j, j}^+ = +\infty$ for $k_j > K$ or $k_j + \deg^-(v_j) \geq n$. Then, the problem is stated as

$$\min_{k_1 + k_2 + \cdots + k_n = k} \sum_{j=1}^{n} \sigma_{k_j, j}^+. \tag{6}$$

Here, we define $D^+[k, i]$ by

$$D^+[k, i] = \min_{k_1 + k_2 + \cdots + k_i = k} \sum_{j=1}^{i} \sigma_{k_j, j}^+. \tag{7}$$

Then, $D^+[k, n]$ is the objective value (i.e., the minimum of the sum of least-squares errors when adding k edges).

The entries of $D^+[k, j]$ can be computed by the following dynamic programming algorithm:

$$D^+[k, 1] = \sigma_{k, 1}^+,$$

$$D^+[k, j+1] = \min_{k'+k''=k} \left\{ D^+[k', j] + \sigma_{k'', j+1}^+ \right\}. \tag{8}$$

It is to be noted that $D^+[k, n]$ is determined uniquely regardless of the ordering of nodes in the network. The correctness of this dynamic programming algorithm can be seen by

$$\min_{k_1 + k_2 + \cdots + k_n = k} \sum_{j=1}^{n} \sigma_{k_j, j}^+ = \min_{k'+k''=k} \left\{ \min_{k_1 + k_2 + \cdots + k_{n-1} = k'} \sum_{j=1}^{n-1} \sigma_{k_j, j}^+ + \sigma_{k'', n}^+ \right\}$$

$$= \min_{k'+k''=k} D^+[k', n-1] + \sigma_{k'', n}^+. \tag{9}$$

2.3. Completion by Deletion of Edges. In the above, we considered network completion by addition of edges. Here, we consider the problem of deleting h edges in total so that the sum of least-squares errors is minimized.

Let $\sigma_{h_j, j}^-$ denote the minimum least-squares error when deleting h_j edges from the set $e^-(v)$ of incoming edges to v_j. As in Section 2.2, we constrain the maximum h_j to be a small constant H and let $\sigma_{h_j, j}^- = +\infty$ if $h_j > H$ or $\deg^-(v_j) - h_j < 0$. Then, the problem is stated as

$$\min_{h_1 + h_2 + \cdots + h_n = h} \sum_{j=1}^{n} \sigma_{k_j, j}^-. \tag{10}$$

Here, we define $D^-[k, i]$ by

$$D^-[k, i] = \min_{k_1 + k_2 + \cdots + k_i = k} \sum_{j=1}^{i} \sigma_{k_j, j}^-. \tag{11}$$

Then, we can solve network completion by deletion of edges using the following dynamic programming algorithm:

$$D^-[k, 1] = \sigma_{k, 1}^-,$$

$$D^-[k, j+1] = \min_{k'+k''=k} \left\{ D^-[k', j] + \sigma_{k'', j+1}^- \right\}. \tag{12}$$

2.4. Completion by Addition and Deletion of Edges. We can combine the above two methods into network completion by addition and deletion of edges.

Let $\sigma_{h_j, k_j, j}$ denote the minimum least-squares error when deleting h_j edges from $e^-(v_j)$ and adding k_j edges to $e^-(v_j)$ where deleted and added edges must be disjoint. We constrain the maximum h_j and k_j to be small constants H and K. We let $\sigma_{h_j, k_j, j} = +\infty$ if $h_j > H$, $k_j > K$, $k_j - h_j + \deg^-(v_j) \geq n$, or $k_j - h_j + \deg^-(v_j) < 0$ holds. Then, the problem is stated as

$$\min_{\substack{h_1 + h_2 + \cdots + h_n = h \\ k_1 + k_2 + \cdots + k_n = k}} \sum_{j=1}^{n} \sigma_{h_j, k_j, j}. \tag{13}$$

Here, we define $D[h, k, i]$ by

$$D[h, k, i] \min_{\substack{h_1 + h_2 + \cdots + h_i = h \\ k_1 + k_2 + \cdots + k_i = k}} \sum_{j=1}^{i} \sigma_{h_j, k_j, j}. \tag{14}$$

Then, we can solve network completion by addition and deletion of edges using the following dynamic programming algorithm:

$$D[h, k, 1] = \sigma_{h, k, 1},$$

$$D[h, k, j+1] = \min_{\substack{h'+h''=h \\ k'+k''=k}} \left\{ D[h', k', j] + \sigma_{h'', k'', j+1} \right\}. \tag{15}$$

2.5. Time Complexity Analysis. In this subsection, we analyze the time complexity of DPLSQ. Since completion by addition of edges and completion by deletion of edges are special cases of completion by addition and deletion of edges, we focus on completion by addition and deletion of edges.

First, we analyze the time complexity required per least-squares fitting. It is known that least-squares fitting for linear systems can be done in $O(mp^2 + p^3)$ time where m is the number of data points and p is the number of parameters. Since our model has $O(n^2)$ parameters, the time complexity is $O(mn^4 + n^6)$. However, if we can assume that the maximum indegree in a given network is bounded by a constant, the number of parameters is bounded by a constant, where we have already assumed that H and K are constants. In this case, the time complexity for least-squares fitting can be estimated as $O(m)$.

Next, we analyze the time complexity required for computing $\sigma_{h_j,k_j,j}$. In this computation, we need to examine combinations of deletions of h_j edges and additions of k_j edges. Since h_j and k_j are, respectively, bounded by constants H and K, the number of combinations is $O(n^{H+K})$. Therefore, the computation time required per $\sigma_{h_j,k_j,j}$ is $O(n^{H+K}(mn^4 + n^6))$ including the time for least-squares fitting. Since we need to compute $\sigma_{h_j,k_j,j}$ for $H \times K \times n$ combinations, the total time required for computation of $\sigma_{h_j,k_j,j}$s is $O(n^{H+K+1}(mn^4 + n^6))$.

Finally, we analyze the time complexity required for computing $D[h,k,i]$s. We note that the size of table $D[h,k,i]$ is $O(n^3)$, where we are assuming that h and k are $O(n)$. In order to compute the minimum value for each entry in the dynamic programming procedure, we need to examine $(H + 1)(K + 1)$ combinations, which is $O(1)$. Therefore, the computation time required for computing $D[h,k,i]$s is $O(n^3)$. Since this value is clearly smaller than the one for $\sigma_{h_j,k_j,j}$s, the total time complexity is

$$O\left(n^{H+K+1} \cdot (mn^4 + n^6)\right). \qquad (16)$$

Although this value is too high, it can be significantly reduced if we can assume that the maximum degree of an input network is bounded by a constant. In this case, the least-squares fitting can be done in $O(m)$ time per execution. Furthermore, the number of combinations of deleting at most h_j edges is bounded by a constant. Therefore, the time complexity required for computing $\sigma_{h_j,k_j,j}$s is reduced to $O(mn^{K+1})$. Since the time complexity for computing $D[h,k,i]$s remains $O(n^3)$, the total time complexity is

$$O\left(mn^{K+1} + n^3\right). \qquad (17)$$

This number is allowable in practice if $K \leq 2$ and n is not too large (e.g., $n \leq 100$).

3. Results

We performed computational experiments using both artificial data and real data. All experiments on DPLSQ were performed on a PC with Intel Core i7-2630QM CPU (2.00 GHz) with 8 GB RAM running under the Cygwin on Windows 7. We employed the liblsq library (http://www2.nict.go.jp/aeri/sts/stmg/K5/VSSP/install_lsq.html) for a least-squares fitting method.

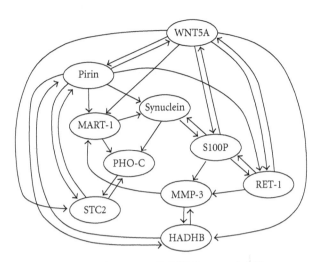

FIGURE 3: Structure of WNT5A network [17].

3.1. Completion Using Artificial Data. In order to evaluate the potential effectiveness of DPLSQ, we began with network completion using artificial data. To our knowledge, there is no available tool that performs the same task. Although some of the existing inference methods employ incremental modifications of networks, the number of added/deleted edges cannot be specified. Therefore, we did not compare DPLSQ for network completion with other methods (but we compared it with the existing tools for network inference).

We employed the structure of the real biological network named WNT5A (see Figure 3) [17]. For each node v_i with h input nodes, we considered the following model:

$$x_i(t+1) = x_i(t) + \Delta t \left(a_0^i + \sum_{j=1}^{h} a_j^i x_{i_j} + \sum_{j<k} a_{j,k}^i x_{i_j}(t) x_{i_k}(t) + b_i \omega \right), \qquad (18)$$

where a_j^is and $a_{j,k}^i$s are constants selected uniformly at random from $[-1, 1]$ and $[-0.5, 0.5]$, respectively. The reason why the domain of $a_{j,k}^i$s is smaller than that for a_j^is is that non-linear terms are not considered as strong as linear terms. It should also be noted that $b_i \omega$ is a stochastic term, where b_i is a constant (we used $b_i = 0.2$ in all computational experiments) and ω is a random noise taken uniformly at random from $[-1, 1]$.

For artificial generation of observed data $y_i(t)$, we used

$$y_i(t) = x_i(t) + o^i \epsilon, \qquad (19)$$

where o^i is a constant denoting the level of observation errors and ϵ is a random noise taken uniformly at random from $[1, -1]$. Since the use of time series data beginning from only one set of initial values easily resulted in overfitting, we generated time series data beginning from 20 sets of initial values taken uniformly at random from $[1, -1]$, where the number of time points for each set was set to 10 and $\Delta t = 0.2$ was used as the period between the consecutive two time points. Therefore, 20 sets of time series data, each of which consisted of 10 time points, were used per trial (200 time points were used in total per trial). It is to be noted that in our preliminary experiments, the use of too small Δt resulted in too small changes of expression values whereas the use of large Δt resulted in divergence of time series data. Therefore, after some trials, $\Delta t = 0.2$ was selected and used throughout the paper.

Under the above model, we examined several o^is as shown in Table 1. In order to examine network completion, WNT5A was modified by randomly adding h edges and deleting k edges and the resulting network was given as an initial network.

We evaluated the performance of the method in terms of the accuracy of the modified edges and the success rate. The accuracy is defined here by

$$\frac{h + k + \left| E_{\mathrm{orig}} \right| - \left| E_{\mathrm{orig}} \cap E_{\mathrm{cmpl}} \right|}{h + k}, \qquad (20)$$

where E_{orig} and E_{cmpl} are the sets of edges in the original network and the completed network, respectively. This value takes 1 if all deleted and added edges are correct and 0 if none of the deleted and added edges is correct. For each (h, k), we took the average accuracy over a combination of 10 parameters (a_j^is and $a_{j,k}^i$s) and 10 random modifications (i.e., addition of h edges and deletion of k edges to construct an initial network). The success rate is the frequency of the trials (among 10×10 trials) in which the original network was correctly obtained by network completion. The result is shown in Table 1. It is seen from this table that DPLSQ works well if the observation error level is small. It is also seen that the accuracies are high in the case of $h = 0$. However, no clear trend can be observed on a relationship between h, k values and the accuracies. It is reasonable because we evaluated the result in terms of the accuracy per deleted/added edge. On the other hand, it is seen that the success rate decreases considerably as h and k increase or the observation error level increases. This dependence on h and k is reasonable because the probability of having at least one wrong edge increases as the number of edges to be deleted and added increases. As for the computation time, the CPU time for each trial was within a few seconds, where we used the default values of $H = K = 3$. Although these default values were larger than h, k here, it did not cause any effects on the accuracy or the success rate. How to choose H and K is not a trivial problem. As discussed in Section 2.5, we cannot choose large H or K because of the time complexity issue. Therefore, it might be better in practice to examine several combinations of small values H and K and select the best result although how to determine the best result is left as another issue.

3.2. Inference Using Artificial Data. We also examined DPLSQ for network inference, using artificially generated time series data. In this case, we used the same network and dynamics model as previously mentioned but we let $E = \varnothing$ in the initial network. Since the method was applied to inference, we let $H = 0$, $K = 3$, and $k = 30$. It is to be noted that $\deg^{-}(v_i) = 3$ holds for all nodes v_i in the WNT5A network. Furthermore, in order to examine how CPU time changes as the size of the network grows, we made networks

with 30 genes and 50 genes (with $k = 90$ and $k = 150$) by making 3 and 5 copies of the original networks, respectively.

Since the number of added edges was always equal to the number of edges in the original network, we evaluated the results by the average accuracy, which was defined as the ratio of the number of correctly inferred edges to the number of edges in the correct network (i.e., the number of added edges). We examined observation error levels of 0.1, 0.3, 0.5, and 0.7, for each of which we took the average over 10 trials using randomly generated different parameter values (i.e., a_j^is and $a_{j,k}^i$s), where time series data were generated as in Section 3.1. The result is shown in Table 2, where the accuracy and the average CPU time (user time + sys time) per trial are shown for each case. It is seen from the table that the accuracy is high even for large networks if the error level is not high. It is also seen that although the CPU time grows rapidly as the size of a network increases, it is still allowable for networks with 50 genes.

We also compared DPLSQ with two well-known existing tools for inference of genetic networks, ARACNE [11, 12] and GeneNet [7, 8]. The former is based on mutual information and the latter is based on graphical Gaussian models and partial correlations. Computational experiments on ARACNE were performed under the same environment as that for DPLSQ, whereas those on GeneNet were performed on a PC with Intel Core i7-2600 CPU (3.40 GHz) with 16 GB RAM running under the Cygwin on Windows 7 because of the availability of the R platform on which GeneNet works. We employed datasets that were generated in the same way as for DPLSQ and default parameter settings for both tools.

Since both tools output undirected edges along with their significance values (or their probabilities), we selected the top M edges in the output where M was the number of edges in the original network and regarded $\{v_i, v_j\}$ as a correct edge if either (v_i, v_j) or (v_j, v_i) was included in the edge set of the original network. As in Table 2, we evaluated the results by the average accuracy, that is, the ratio of the number of correctly inferred edges to the number of edges in the original network.

The result is shown in Table 3. Interestingly, both tools have similar performances. It is also interesting that the performance does not change much in each method even if the level of observation error changes. Readers may think that the accuracies shown in Table 3 are close to those by random prediction. However, these accuracies were much higher than those obtained by assigning random probabilities to edges, and thus we can mention that these tools outputted meaningful results.

It is seen from Tables 2 and 3 that the accuracies by DPLSQ are much higher than those by ARACNE and GeneNet even though both directions of edges are taken into account for ARACNE and GeneNet. However, it should be noted that time series data were generated according to the differential equation model on which DPLSQ relies. Therefore, we can only mention that DPLSQ works well if time series data are generated according to appropriate differential equation models. It is to be noted that we can use

TABLE 1: Result on completion of WNT5A network, where the average accuracy is shown for each case.

No. deleted edges	No. added edges		Observation error level			
			0.1	0.3	0.5	0.7
$h = 0$	$k = 1$	Accuracy	0.990	0.910	0.730	0.410
		Success rate	0.99	0.91	0.73	0.41
$h = 0$	$k = 2$	Accuracy	1.000	0.955	0.670	0.395
		Success rate	1.00	0.91	0.42	0.17
$h = 1$	$k = 0$	Accuracy	0.990	0.850	0.470	0.240
		Success rate	0.99	0.85	0.47	0.24
$h = 1$	$k = 1$	Accuracy	0.995	0.845	0.405	0.210
		Success rate	0.99	0.71	0.11	0.02
$h = 1$	$k = 2$	Accuracy	0.983	0.843	0.470	0.190
		Success rate	0.95	0.58	0.11	0.00
$h = 2$	$k = 0$	Accuracy	1.000	0.795	0.440	0.215
		Success rate	1.00	0.67	0.18	0.01
$h = 2$	$k = 1$	Accuracy	0.996	0.833	0.453	0.223
		Success rate	0.99	0.53	0.05	0.01
$h = 2$	$k = 2$	Accuracy	1.000	0.862	0.517	0.285
		Success rate	1.00	0.56	0.03	0.01

TABLE 2: Result on inference of WNT5A network by DPLSQ.

		Observation error level			
		0.1	0.3	0.5	0.7
$n = 10$	Accuracy	1.000	0.966	0.803	0.620
	CPU time (sec.)	0.685	0.682	0.682	0.685
$n = 30$	Accuracy	0.995	0.914	0.663	0.443
	CPU time (sec.)	66.2	66.2	66.1	65.9
$n = 50$	Accuracy	0.999	0.913	0.613	0.392
	CPU time (sec.)	534.0	534.2	533.6	533.5

TABLE 3: Result on inference of WNT5A network using ARACNE and GeneNet, where the accuracy is shown for each case.

	Method	Observation error level			
		0.1	0.3	0.5	0.7
$n = 10$	ARACNE	0.523	0.523	0.523	0.526
	GeneNet	0.526	0.526	0.533	0.533
$n = 30$	ARACNE	0.332	0.328	0.326	0.326
	GeneNet	0.368	0.380	0.383	0.384
$n = 50$	ARACNE	0.308	0.312	0.310	0.391
	GeneNet	0.313	0.316	0.314	0.316

other differential equation models as long as parameters can be estimated by least-squares fitting.

As for computation time, both methods were much faster than DPLSQ. Even for the case of $N = 50$, each of ARACNE and GeneNet worked in less than a few seconds per trial. Therefore, DPLSQ does not have merits on practical computation time.

3.3. Inference Using Real Data. We also examined DPLSQ for inference of genetic networks using real gene expression data. Since there is no gold standard on genetic networks and thus we cannot know the correct answers, we did not compare it with the existing methods.

We employed a part of the cell cycle network of *Saccharomyces cerevisiae* extracted from the KEGG database [18], which is shown in Figure 4. Although the detailed mechanism of the cell cycle network is still unclear, we used this network as the correct answer, which may not be true. Although each of (MCM1, YOX1, YHP1), (SWI4, SWI6), (CLN3, CDC28), (MBP1, SWI6) constitutes a protein complex, we treated them separately and ignored the interactions

inside a complex because making a protein complex does not necessarily mean a regulation relationship between the corresponding genes.

As for time series data of gene expression, we employed four sets of times series data (alpha, cdc15, cdc28, elu) in [19] that were obtained by four different experiments. Since there were several missing values in the time series data, these values were filled by linear interpolation and data on some endpoint time points were discarded because of too many missing values. As a result, alpha, cdc15, cdc28, and elu datasets consist of gene expression data of 18, 24, 11, and 14 time points, respectively. In order to examine a relationship between the number of time points, and accuracy, we examined four combinations of datasets as shown in Table 4. We evaluated the performance of DPLSQ by means of the accuracy (i.e., the ratio of the number of correctly inferred edges to the number of added edges), where $K = 3$ and $k = 25$ were used. The result is shown in Table 4.

Since the total number of edges in both the original network and the inferred networks is 25 and there exist

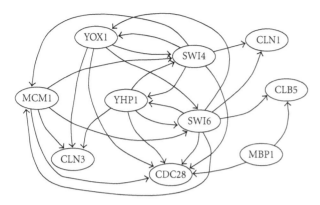

FIGURE 4: Structure of part of yeast cell cycle network.

$9 \times 10 = 90$ possible edges (excluding self loops), the expected number of corrected edges is roughly estimated as

$$\frac{25}{90} \times 25 = 6.944\ldots, \tag{21}$$

if 25 edges are randomly selected and added. Therefore, the result shown in Table 4 suggests that DPLSQ can do much better than random inference when appropriate datasets are provided (e.g., cdc15 only or cdc15+cdc28+alpha+elu). It is a bit strange that the accuracies for the first and last datasets are better than those for the second and third datasets because it is usually expected that adding more evidences results in more accurate networks. The reason may be that time series of cdc28 and alpha may contain larger measurement errors than those of cdc15 and elu, or some regulation rules that are hidden in Figure 4 may be activated under the conditions of cdc28 and/or alpha.

4. Conclusion

In this paper, we have proposed a network completion method, DPLSQ, using dynamic programming and least-squares fitting based on our previously proposed methodology of network completion [14]. As mentioned in Section 1, network completion is to make the minimum amount of modifications to a given network so that the resulting network is (most) consistent with the observed data. In our previous model [14], we employed the Boolean network as a model of networks and assumed that only expression or other values of one or a few nodes are observed. However, in this paper, we assumed that expression values of all nodes are observed, which correspond to gene microarray data, and regulation rules are given in the form of differential equations. The most important theoretical difference between this model and our previous model is that network completion can be done in polynomial time if the maximum indegree is bounded by a constant in this model whereas it is NP-hard in our previous model even if the maximum indegree is bounded by a constant. This difference arises not from the introduction of a least-squares fitting method but from the assumption that expression values of all nodes are observed.

It should also be noted that the optimality of the solution is not guaranteed in most of the existing methods for

TABLE 4: Result on inference of a yeast cell cycle network.

Experimental conditions	Accuracy
cdc15	11/25
cdc15 + cdc28	8/25
cdc15 + cdc28 + alpha	8/25
cdc15 + cdc28 + alpha + elu	11/25

inference of genetic networks, whereas it is guaranteed in DPLSQ if it is applied to inference of a genetic network with a bounded maximum indegree. Of course, the objective function (i.e., minimizing the sum of squared errors) is different from existing ones, and thus this property does not necessarily mean that DPLSQ is superior to existing methods in real applications. Indeed, the result using real gene expression data in Section 3.3 does not seem to be very good. However, DPLSQ has much room for extensions. For example, least-squares fitting can be replaced by another fitting/regression method (with some regularization term) and the objective function can be replaced by another function as long as it can be computed by sum or product of some error terms. Studies on such extensions might lead to development of better network completion and/or inference methods.

Acknowledgments

T. Akutsu was partially supported by JSPS, Japan (Grants-in-Aid 22240009 and 22650045). T. Tamura was partially supported by JSPS, Japan (Grant-in-Aid for Young Scientists (B) 23700017). K. Horimoto was partially supported by the Chinese Academy of Sciences Visiting Professorship for Senior International Scientists Grant no. 2012T1S0012.

References

[1] S. Liang, S. Fuhrman, and R. Somogyi, "REVEAL, a general reverse engineering algorithm for inference of genetic network architectures," in *Proceedings of the Pacific Symposium on Biocomputing*, vol. 3, pp. 18–29, 1998.

[2] T. Akutsu, S. Miyano, and S. Kuhara, "Inferring qualitative relations in genetic networks and metabolic pathways," *Bioinformatics*, vol. 16, no. 8, pp. 727–734, 2000.

[3] N. Friedman, M. Linial, I. Nachman, and D. Pe'er, "Using Bayesian networks to analyze expression data," *Journal of Computational Biology*, vol. 7, no. 3-4, pp. 601–620, 2000.

[4] S. Imoto, S. Kim, T. Goto et al., "Bayesian network and nonparametric heteroscedastic regression for nonlinear modeling of genetic network," *Journal of Bioinformatics and Computational Biology*, vol. 1, no. 2, pp. 231–252, 2003.

[5] T. F. Liu, W. K. Sung, and A. Mittal, "Learning gene network using time-delayed Bayesian network," *International Journal on Artificial Intelligence Tools*, vol. 15, no. 3, pp. 353–370, 2006.

[6] H. Toh and K. Horimoto, "Inference of a genetic network by a combined approach of cluster analysis and graphical Gaussian modeling," *Bioinformatics*, vol. 18, no. 2, pp. 287–297, 2002.

[7] R. Opgen-Rhein and K. Strimmer, "Inferring gene dependency networks from genomic longitudinal data: a functional data approach," *RevStat*, vol. 4, no. 1, pp. 53–65, 2006.

[8] R. Opgen-Rhein and K. Strimmer, "From correlation to causation networks: a simple approximate learning algorithm and its application to high-dimensional plant gene expression data," *BMC Systems Biology*, vol. 1, article 37, 2007.

[9] P. D'Haeseleer, S. Liang, and R. Somogyi, "Genetic network inference: from co-expression clustering to reverse engineering," *Bioinformatics*, vol. 16, no. 8, pp. 707–726, 2000.

[10] Y. Wang, T. Joshi, X. S. Zhang, D. Xu, and L. Chen, "Inferring gene regulatory networks from multiple microarray datasets," *Bioinformatics*, vol. 22, no. 19, pp. 2413–2420, 2006.

[11] A. A. Margolin, K. Wang, W. K. Lim, M. Kustagi, I. Nemenman, and A. Califano, "Reverse engineering cellular networks," *Nature Protocols*, vol. 1, no. 2, pp. 662–671, 2006.

[12] A. A. Margolin, I. Nemenman, K. Basso et al., "ARACNE: an algorithm for the reconstruction of gene regulatory networks in a mammalian cellular context," *BMC Bioinformatics*, vol. 8, supplement 1, no. 1, article S7, 2006.

[13] S. Kimura, S. Nakayama, and M. Hatakeyama, "Genetic network inference as a series of discrimination tasks," *Bioinformatics*, vol. 25, no. 7, pp. 918–925, 2009.

[14] T. Akutsu, T. Tamura, and K. Horimoto, "Completing networks using observed data," *Lecture Notes in Artificial Intelligence*, vol. 5809, pp. 126–140, 2009.

[15] S. A. Kauffman, *The Origins of Order: Self-Organization and Selection in Evolution*, Oxford University Press, New York, NY, USA, 1993.

[16] T. Tamura, Y. Yamanishi, M. Tanabe et al., "Integer programming-based method for completing signaling pathways and its application to analysis of colorectal cancer," *Genome Informatics*, vol. 24, pp. 193–203, 2010.

[17] S. Kim, H. Li, E. R. Dougherty et al., "Can Markov chain models mimic biological regulation?" *Journal of Biological Systems*, vol. 10, no. 4, pp. 337–357, 2002.

[18] M. Kanehisa, S. Goto, M. Furumichi, M. Tanabe, and M. Hirakawa, "KEGG for representation and analysis of molecular networks involving diseases and drugs," *Nucleic Acids Research*, vol. 38, no. 1, Article ID gkp896, pp. D355–D360, 2009.

[19] P. T. Spellman, G. Sherlock, M. Q. Zhang et al., "Comprehensive identification of cell cycle-regulated genes of the yeast Saccharomyces cerevisiae by microarray hybridization," *Molecular Biology of the Cell*, vol. 9, no. 12, pp. 3273–3297, 1998.

Permissions

The contributors of this book come from diverse backgrounds, making this book a truly international effort. This book will bring forth new frontiers with its revolutionizing research information and detailed analysis of the nascent developments around the world.

We would like to thank all the contributing authors for lending their expertise to make the book truly unique. They have played a crucial role in the development of this book. Without their invaluable contributions this book wouldn't have been possible. They have made vital efforts to compile up to date information on the varied aspects of this subject to make this book a valuable addition to the collection of many professionals and students.

This book was conceptualized with the vision of imparting up-to-date information and advanced data in this field. To ensure the same, a matchless editorial board was set up. Every individual on the board went through rigorous rounds of assessment to prove their worth. After which they invested a large part of their time researching and compiling the most relevant data for our readers. Conferences and sessions were held from time to time between the editorial board and the contributing authors to present the data in the most comprehensible form. The editorial team has worked tirelessly to provide valuable and valid information to help people across the globe.

Every chapter published in this book has been scrutinized by our experts. Their significance has been extensively debated. The topics covered herein carry significant findings which will fuel the growth of the discipline. They may even be implemented as practical applications or may be referred to as a beginning point for another development. Chapters in this book were first published by Hindawi Publishing Corporation; hereby published with permission under the Creative Commons Attribution License or equivalent.

The editorial board has been involved in producing this book since its inception. They have spent rigorous hours researching and exploring the diverse topics which have resulted in the successful publishing of this book. They have passed on their knowledge of decades through this book. To expedite this challenging task, the publisher supported the team at every step. A small team of assistant editors was also appointed to further simplify the editing procedure and attain best results for the readers.

Our editorial team has been hand-picked from every corner of the world. Their multi-ethnicity adds dynamic inputs to the discussions which result in innovative outcomes. These outcomes are then further discussed with the researchers and contributors who give their valuable feedback and opinion regarding the same. The feedback is then collaborated with the researches and they are edited in a comprehensive manner to aid the understanding of the subject.

Apart from the editorial board, the designing team has also invested a significant amount of their time in understanding the subject and creating the most relevant covers. They scrutinized every image to scout for the most suitable representation of the subject and create an appropriate cover for the book.

The publishing team has been involved in this book since its early stages. They were actively engaged in every process, be it collecting the data, connecting with the contributors or procuring relevant information. The team has been an ardent support to the editorial, designing and production team. Their endless efforts to recruit the best for this project, has resulted in the accomplishment of this book. They are a veteran in the field of academics and their pool of knowledge is as vast as their experience in printing. Their expertise and guidance has proved useful at every step. Their uncompromising quality standards have made this book an exceptional effort. Their encouragement from time to time has been an inspiration for everyone.

The publisher and the editorial board hope that this book will prove to be a valuable piece of knowledge for researchers, students, practitioners and scholars across the globe.

List of Contributors

Xingqin Qi
School of Mathematics and Statistics, Shandong University at Weihai, Weihai 264209, China

Edgar Fuller and Cun-Quan Zhang
Department of Mathematics, West Virginia University, Morgantown, WV 26506, USA

Qin Wu
School of IOT Engineering, Jiangnan University, Wuxi 214122, China

Muhammad Altaf Khan, Saeed Islam and Muhammad Arif
Department of Mathematics, Abdul Wali Khan University, Mardan, Khyber Pakhtunkhwa, Pakistan

Zahoor ul Haq
Department of Management Sciences, Abdul Wali Khan University, Mardan, Khyber Pakhtunkhwa, Pakistan

Daniel Baumgartner
Institute for Biomechanics, ETH Zurich, Zurich, Switzerland
School of Engineering, Winterthur, Switzerland

Jaroslav Naxera
Rontgeninstitut Zurich-Altstetten, Zurich, Switzerland

Jean Pierre Elsig
Spine Surgery, 8700 Kusnacht, Switzerland

Roland Zemp, Renate List, Mirjam Stoop and Silvio Lorenzetti
Institute for Biomechanics, ETH Zurich, Zurich, Switzerland

Bikash Ranjan Sahoo, Madhubanti Basu, Banikalyan Swain, Pallipuram Jayasankar and Mrinal Samanta
Fish Health Management Division, Central Institute of Freshwater Aquaculture (CIFA), Kausalyaganga, Bhubaneswar, Odisha 751002, India

Manas Ranjan Dikhit
Biomedical Informatics Centre, Rajendra Memorial Research Institute of Medical Sciences, Agamkuan, Patna, Bihar 800007, India

Wenbo Mu, Damian Roqueiro and Yang Dai
Department of Bioengineering, University of Illinois at Chicago, Chicago, IL 60607, USA

Cheng-Yu Yeh, Hsiang-Yuan Yeh, Carlos Roberto Arias and Von-Wun Soo
Department of Computer Science, National Tsing Hua University, Hsinchu 300, Taiwan
Institute of Information Systems and Applications, National Tsing Hua University, Hsinchu 300, Taiwan

Li Li and Luying Peng
Division of Medical Genetics, Tongji University School of Medicine, Shanghai 200092, China
Key Lab for Basic Research in Cardiology, Ministry of Education, Tongji University, Shanghai 200092, China

Hongmei Chen, Chang Liu, Fang Wang and Fangfang Zhang
Division of Medical Genetics, Tongji University School of Medicine, Shanghai 200092, China

Lihua Bai and Yihan Chen
Key Lab for Basic Research in Cardiology, Ministry of Education, Tongji University, Shanghai 200092, China

Hailin Chen and Vincent Van Buren
Department of Medical Physiology, Texas A&M HSC College of Medicine, Temple, TX 76504, USA

Shuqin Zhang
Center for Computational Systems Biology, School of Mathematical Sciences, Fudan University, Shanghai 200433, China

Ming-guo Qiu, Jing-na Zhang and Ye Zhang
Department of Medical Informatics and Medical Image, College of Biomedical Engineering and Medical Imaging, Third Military Medical University, Chongqing 400038, China

Qi-yu Li
Department of Anatomy, Third Military Medical University, Chongqing 400038, China

Bing Xie and Jian Wang
Department of Radiology, Southwest Hospital, Third Military Medical University, Chongqing 400038, China

Handong Ma, Yun Hao, Xinran Dong, Qingtian Gong, Jingqi Chen, Jifeng Zhang and Weidong Tian
Institute of Biostatistics, School of Life Science, Fudan University, 220 Handan Road, Shanghai 2004333, China

Amrita Roy Choudhury and Marjana Novič
Laboratory of Chemometrics, National Institute of Chemistry, Hajdrihova 19, 1001 Ljubljana, Slovenia

Nikolay Zhukov
Faculty of Mathematics, Informatics and Mechanics, University of Warsaw, Banacha 2, 02097Warszawa, Poland

Bikash R. Sahoo, Ganesh C. Sahoo and Manas R. Dikhit
Biomedical Informatics Centre, Rajendra Memorial Research Institute of Medical Science, Patna 800007, India

Rajiv K. Kar, Md. Yousuf Ansari, Priyanka Suryadevara and Pradeep Das
Biomedical Informatics Centre, Rajendra Memorial Research Institute of Medical Science, Patna 800007, India
Department of Pharmaco informatics, National Institute of Pharmaceutical Education and Research (NIPER), Hajipur 844102, India

Jiaxin Wu and Rui Jiang
MOE Key Laboratory of Bioinformatics and Bioinformatics Division, TNLIST/Department of Automation, Tsinghua University, Beijing 100084, China

Sher Afzal Khan
Department of Computer Sciences, Abdul Wali Khan University, Mardan, Khyber Pakhtunkhwa, Pakistan

Gul Zaman
Department of Mathematics, University of Malakand, Dir, Pakistan

Marisa P. Dolled-Filhart, Michael Lee Jr., Chih-wen Ou-yang, Rajini Rani Haraksingh and Jimmy Cheng-Ho Lin
Rare Genomics Institute, 4100 Forest Park Avenue, Suite 204, St. Louis, MO 63108, USA

Na You, Peng Mou, Ting Qiu, Qiang Kou, Huaijin Zhu, Yuexi Chen and Xueqin Wang
School of Mathematics & Computational Science, Sun Yat-Sen University, Guangzhou, Guangdong 510275, China

Mingxin Gan and Xue Dou
Dongling School of Economics and Management, University of Science and Technology Beijing, Beijing 100083, China

Rui Jiang
Department of Automation, Tsinghua University, Beijing 100084, China

Arie O. Verkerk and Ronald Wilders
Department of Anatomy, Embryology and Physiology, Academic Medical Center, University of Amsterdam, P.O. Box 22700, 1100 DE Amsterdam, The Netherlands

Zhifa Liu and Heping Zhan
Department of Biostatistics, Yale University School of Public Health, New Haven, CT 06520, USA

Xiaobo Guo
Department of Biostatistics, Yale University School of Public Health, New Haven, CT 06520, USA
Department of Statistical Science, School of Mathematics and Computational Science, Sun Yat-sen University, Guangzhou, Guangdong, China

Xueqin Wang
Department of Statistical Science, School of Mathematics and Computational Science, Sun Yat-sen University, Guangzhou, Guangdong, China
Zhongshan School of Medicine, Sun Yat-sen University, Guangzhou, Guangdong, China

Natsu Nakajima, Takeyuki Tamura and Tatsuya Akutsu
Bioinformatics Center, Institute for Chemical Research, Kyoto University Gokasho, Uji, Kyoto 611-0011, Japan

Yoshihiro Yamanishi
Division of System Cohort, Multi-scale Research Center for Medical Science, Medical Institute of Bioregulation, Kyushu University, 3-1-1 Maidashi, Higashi-ku, Fukuoka, Fukuoka 812-8582, Japan

Katsuhisa Horimoto
Computational Biology Research Center, National Institute of Advanced Industrial Science and Technology, 2-4-7 Aomi, Koto-ku, Tokyo 135-0064, Japan

Printed in the USA
CPSIA information can be obtained
at www.ICGtesting.com
JSHW051439221024
72173JS00006B/1519

9 781632 391186